REPRISE

A Complete Review Workbook for Grammar, Communication, and Culture

Printed on recyclable paper

National Textbook Company
a division of NTC/Contemporary Publishing Company
Lincolnwood, Illinois USA

Cover Photographs
Top: Thierry, French Government Tourist Office
Bottom and spine: Mark R. Pattis

Interior Map
Mountain High Maps ® Copyright © 1993 Digital Wisdom, Inc.

Acknowledgments
The publisher wishes to thank the following for permission to reproduce their material:

page 14: "Tout sur la Carte Kiwi" (SNCF, Paris, France); page 43: "C'est ma planète" (Paris pour l'environnement, Mairie de Paris, Paris, France); page 61: "Orlybus" (RATP, Paris, France); pages 74–75: "Paris mode d'emploi" (Mairie de Paris, Paris, France); page 89: "Fugain, Big Story" (*France Soir,* mardi 4 avril 1995); page 107: "Points forts" (*Le Figaro,* mercredi 1er mars 1995); page 121: "Nouvel An à New York en Concorde" (TMR, Marseille, France); page 221: "Nokia" (Agences France Télécom); page 242: "A temps, tout le temps" (UPS); page 273: "Résidence de l'Hôtel de Ville" (Guénier & Communication, Marignan Immobilier, Clichy, France); page 287: "Si vous n'allez pas souvent . . ." (Banque Directe, Paris, France); page 370: "Itineris" (France Telecom Mobiles); page 382: "L'école est fière" (EBS, Paris, France).

Thanks are owed as well to Cynthia Fostle, Roland Dubosq, and Myrna Bell Rochester for their invaluable editorial assistance.

Published by National Textbook Company, a division of NTC/Contemporary Publishing Company.

Manufactured in the United States of America.

7 8 9 VL 9 8 7 6 5 4 3 2

PREFACE

Reprise—A Complete Review Workbook for Grammar, Communication, and Culture is a powerful tool for review and progress in French. *Reprise* offers intermediate through advanced learners of French clear, concise, and well-organized **grammar explanations** with examples derived from **everyday usage,** most often in the format of conversational exchanges. These presentations of structure are easy to read and encourage students to see grammar as a **stepping stone to communication.** Student progress is enhanced by the straightforward and highly accessible format of the *Reprise* workbook, including the ample space provided to write answers and the side-of-page referencing of chapter topics.

The exercises in *Reprise* provide practice of all the grammar topics that learners of French at this level should know. Most of the engaging **exercises are contextualized,** with **instructions in French** that help set the scene and prepare students for the task at hand.

Vocabulary boxes provide a review of the vocabulary common to most first- and second-year French textbooks and present additional vocabulary that empowers learners to express themselves on a broad range of topics. Vocabulary items and expressions are **grouped thematically** and **integrated with the exercises.** Self-expression exercises encourage learners to use the target grammar and vocabulary to express their own ideas. A **final examination** of grammar topics is included so students can assess their progress and prepare for comprehensive examinations and competitions. And for easy reference, *Reprise* supplies easy-to read **verb charts** and an **end glossary** that contains all the words used in the exercises and the culture chapters.

Toward the end of most chapters of *Reprise* is an **Exercice oral** that encourages spoken expression. This oral exercise is often followed by a section called **Grammaire en action,** a reading comprehension exercise based on **authentic documents** that contain examples of the chapter's grammar topics. Users of *Reprise* will measurably increase their oral and written mastery of structure and vocabulary as they work through these informative and interesting materials selected from French-language newspapers, periodicals, and advertisements.

Chapter 28, **"Idioms, Expressions, and Proverbs,"** is an especially useful compendium of frequently used language, and the **Notes culturelles** found in every chapter enhance the grammar exercises by situating practice in authentic French contexts. The high interest level of this material further motivates students to work toward mastery of French.

Reprise is organized into twenty-eight grammar chapters and four culture chapters. The **culture chapters** address the history of the French language, the history of France, the literature of France and the French-speaking world, and French art, music, science, and technology. Following each culture chapter is a **short self-test** of the material covered.

Reprise bridges grammar practice and communication by emphasizing authentic language use and providing a cultural context for its structural exercises. It is practical, inviting, and easy to use. It will help learners acquire knowledge that will increase their confidence in using French to express their own thoughts, to comprehend those of French speakers, and to communicate in both speech and writing in a wide variety of settings.

CONTENTS

Part One: Verbs—Basic Forms and Uses

Part Two: Nouns and Their Modifiers; Pronouns

Part Three: Other Elements of the Sentence

22. Prepositions; prepositions with geographical names 288

Part Four: Verbs in Two-Clause Sentences

23. Relative clauses 315

24. The present subjunctive 331

25. The past subjunctive; literary subjunctives 349

26. The subjunctive (continued) 356

Part Five: Idiomatic Usage

Part Six: French and Francophone Culture

PART ONE

Verbs—Basic Forms and Uses

PRESENT TENSE

A verb is a word that expresses an action, occurrence, or state of being. In French, most verbs are divided into three classes, or conjugations, according to the ending of the infinitive:

first conjugation: **-er** verbs like **parler**
second conjugation: **-ir** verbs like **finir**
third conjugation: **-re** verbs like **rendre**

Verbs that fall into those three categories are called *regular* verbs.

The present tense of regular **-er, -ir,** *and* **-re** *verbs*

The present tense of a regular verb is formed by dropping the infinitive ending (**-er, -ir,** or **-re**) and adding the appropriate present tense ending.

- Verbs of the first conjugation (**-er** verbs) are conjugated like **parler** (*to speak*).

	singular	*plural*
first person	je parle	nous parl**ons**
second person	tu parle**s**	vous parl**ez**
third person	il/elle parle on parle	ils/elles parl**ent**

Some common **-er** verbs:

accepter *to accept*
accompagner *to accompany*
adorer *to adore, love*
aider *to help*
aimer *to like, love*
apporter *to bring*
apprécier *to appreciate (value, rate highly)*
arriver *to arrive*
bavarder *to chat*
cesser *to stop*
chanter *to sing*
chercher *to look for*
continuer *to continue*
danser *to dance*
décider *to decide*
déjeuner *to have lunch*
demander *to ask*
dépenser *to spend (money)*
dessiner *to draw*
détester *to hate*
dîner *to have dinner*
donner *to give*
écouter *to listen to*
emporter *to carry/take away, carry off*
emprunter *to borrow*
enseigner *to teach*
entrer *to enter, come/go in*
étudier *to study*
fermer *to close*
gagner *to earn, win*
garder *to keep*
habiter *to live (reside)*
hésiter *to hesitate*
inviter *to invite*
jouer *to play*
laisser *to let, leave behind*
laver *to wash*
marcher *to walk*
monter *to go up(stairs)*
montrer *to show*
organiser *to organize*
oublier *to forget*
parler *to speak*
passer *to pass; spend (time)*
penser *to think*
porter *to carry*
pratiquer *to practice*
préparer *to prepare*
présenter *to present*
prêter *to lend*
raconter *to tell, tell about, relate*

Continued.

refuser *to refuse*
regarder *to look at*
remercier *to thank*
rencontrer *to meet (by chance)*
rentrer *to return, go back*
retourner *to return, come/go back*
retrouver *to meet (by appointment)*
saluer *to greet*
supporter *to bear, stand*
téléphoner *to phone*
travailler *to work*
traverser *to cross*
trouver *to find*

- Verbs of the second conjugation (**-ir** verbs) are conjugated like **finir** (*to finish*).

	singular	*plural*
first person	je fin**is**	nous fin**issons**
second person	tu fin**is**	vous fin**issez**
third person	il/elle fin**it** on fin**it**	ils/elles fin**issent**

Some common **-ir** verbs:

applaudir *to applaud*
avertir *to warn*
bâtir *to build*
choisir *to choose*
désobéir *to disobey*
établir *to establish*
finir *to finish*
grossir *to get fat*
guérir *to cure, make better*
maigrir *to get thin*
mincir *to get thin*
obéir *to obey*
réfléchir *to think, reflect*
remplir *to fill*
réussir *to succeed*
rougir *to blush*

- Verbs of the third conjugation (**-re** verbs) are conjugated like **rendre** (*to give back*).

	singular	*plural*
first person	je rends	nous rend**ons**
second person	tu rends	vous rend**ez**
third person	il/elle rend on rend	ils/elles rend**ent**

Some common **-re** verbs:

attendre *to wait for*
confondre *to confuse*
défendre *to forbid*
descendre *to go down(stairs)*
entendre *to hear*
interrompre *to interrupt*
perdre *to lose*
prétendre *to claim*
rendre *to give back*
répondre *to answer*
rompre *to break, break off (especially figuratively)*
vendre *to sell*

Notes:

1. If the verb begins with a vowel or a mute **h,** then **je** becomes **j'**.

   j'arrive **j'**entends **j'**habite

2. The subject pronoun **on** refers to people in general or to a nonspecific subject. It is often equivalent to the passive voice in English.

Ici **on parle** français.	*French **is spoken** here.*
On cherche un secrétaire.	*Secretary **wanted.***

   In colloquial language, **on** + the third person singular verb means *we*.

Aujourd'hui **on dîne** au restaurant.	*Today **we're having dinner** at a restaurant.*
On habite à Paris maintenant.	***We live** in Paris now.*

3. Most verbs of the third conjugation (**-re** verbs) have a stem ending in **d** like **vendre.** Those few whose stems don't end in **d,** such as **rompre** (*to break*) and **interrompre** (*to interrupt*), add a **t** in the third person singular.

   il/elle rompt **il/elle** interrompt

A. Une soirée en famille. Hélène Poiret décrit une soirée passée en famille. Formez des phrases pour savoir ce qu'elle dit.

Modèle aujourd'hui/nous/passer la soirée/à la maison
➔ Aujourd'hui nous passons la soirée à la maison.

1. maman / préparer / un bon dîner

   ____

2. papa / finir / son livre

   ____

3. ma sœur Lise / attendre / un coup de téléphone

   ____

4. moi, je / écouter / une nouvelle cassette

   ____

5. maman / inviter nos cousins / à prendre le dessert avec nous

   ____

6. ils / accepter

   ____

7. mon cousin Philippe / jouer de la guitare

   ____

8. nous / chantons / ensemble

   ____

9. nous / applaudir

   ____

10. après, nous / bavarder / jusqu'à une heure du matin

    ____

B. **Des invités.** Les Trichard ont invité l'oncle Charles à dîner. Complétez les phrases de Robert Trichard avec les verbes entre parenthèses pour savoir ce qui s'est passé.

1. (attendre) Nous ________________ l'arrivée de l'oncle Charles et sa famille.
2. (dîner) Ils ________________ chez nous.
3. (arriver) Ils ________________ à sept heures.
4. (saluer) Je ________________ nos invités.
5. (apporter) L'oncle Charles ________________ des fleurs et des bonbons.
6. (remercier) Ma mère ________________ son frère.
7. (passer) Tout le monde ________________ à la salle à manger.
8. (remplir) Mon père ________________ les verres.

C. **À l'école.** C'est comment la classe de littérature de Raoul? Pour savoir, complétez les phrases avec les verbes entre parenthèses.

1. (entrer) Le professeur ________________ dans la salle de classe.
2. (choisir) Nous ________________ un poème pour analyser.
3. (regarder) Les étudiants ________________ leurs livres.
4. (chercher) Moi, je ________________ mon cahier.
5. (écouter) Tout le monde ________________ l'explication du professeur.
6. (réussir) Je demande à mon amie Gisèle, «Tu ________________ à comprendre ce poème?»
7. (répondre) Elle ________________ que oui.
8. (finir) La classe ________________ à dix heures et quart.
9. (fermer) Nous ________________ nos livres.
10. (descendre) Les étudiants ________________ au cours suivant.

Note culturelle

Dans les écoles françaises on donne beaucoup d'importance à l'étude de la littérature française et étrangère, et les étudiants au collège et au lycée lisent beaucoup. Il y a d'autres matières, comme la philosophie et la géographie (appelées **la philo** et **la géo** par les étudiants), qui sont très importantes dans le programme d'études français, mais qui n'existent presque pas au *high school* américain.

B Spelling changes in the present tense of regular *-er verbs*

First conjugation verbs whose stems end in **c, g,** or **y** have spelling changes in the present tense. These changes are required by the rules of French spelling.

- Verbs whose stems end in **c,** such as **commencer** (*to begin*), add a cedilla under the **c (ç)** in the **nous** form.

	singular	*plural*
first person	je commence	nous commen**ç**ons
second person	tu commences	vous commencez
third person	il/elle commence on commence	ils/elles commencent

Some common verbs like **commencer:**

annoncer *to announce*
avancer *to advance*
divorcer *to divorce*
effacer *to erase*
lancer *to launch*
menacer *to threaten*
placer *to place, invest*
prononcer *to pronounce*
remplacer *to replace*
renoncer *to resign, quit*

- Verbs whose stems end in **g,** such as **manger** (*to eat*), add an **e** after the **g** in the **nous** form.

	singular	*plural*
first person	je mange	nous mang**e**ons
second person	tu manges	vous mangez
third person	il/elle mange on mange	ils/elles mangent

Some common verbs like **manger:**

aménager *to fix up, convert (a room, etc.)*
arranger *to arrange*
changer *to change*
corriger *to correct*
décourager *to discourage*
déménager *to move (change residence)*
déranger *to bother*
diriger *to direct*
encourager *to encourage*
nager *to swim*
partager *to share*
plonger *to dive*
ranger *to put away*
rédiger *to draft, write*
voyager *to travel*

- Verbs whose stems end in **y**, such as **nettoyer** (*to clean*), change the **y** to **i** before a silent **e** (all the singular forms and the third person plural).

	singular	*plural*
first person	je nettoie	nous nettoyons
second person	tu nettoies	vous nettoyez
third person	il/elle nettoie on nettoie	ils/elles nettoient

Note: Verbs ending in **-ayer** may either make the above change or keep the **y** in all forms: **je paie** or **je paye**. Verbs in **-oyer** and **-uyer** must change **y** to **i** before a silent **e**.

Some common verbs like **nettoyer:**

balayer *to sweep*
effrayer *to frighten*
employer *to use*
ennuyer *to bore*
envoyer *to send*

essayer *to try, try on*
essuyer *to wipe*
payer *to pay*
renvoyer *to send back, dismiss*

tutoyer *to use the* **tu** *form to address someone*
vouvoyer *to use the* **vous** *form to address someone*

D. On fait le ménage. Complétez les phrases suivantes avec les verbes entre parenthèses pour savoir ce que Claudette Legrand et sa famille font pour mettre la maison en ordre pour la visite de leurs cousins.

1. (ranger) Ma sœur et moi, nous ______________________ nos affaires.
2. (balayer) Ma mère ______________________ le salon.
3. (nettoyer) Mon père ______________________ la cuisine.
4. (commencer) Mon frère et moi, nous ______________________ à travailler dans le jardin.
5. (essuyer) Mes grands-parents ______________________ les assiettes.
6. (essayer) J'______________________ d'aider tout le monde.

E. Est-ce que c'est comme ça dans votre classe de français? Répondez à ces questions sur votre classe de français. Utilisez **nous** comme sujet dans chaque réponse.

1. Est-ce que vous commencez à lire des livres en français?

____

2. Est-ce que vous corrigez vos copies en classe?

____

3. Est-ce que vous effacez les mots mal écrits?

____

4. Est-ce que vous employez le français dans vos conversations?

____

5. Est-ce que vous dérangez les autres étudiants?

____

6. Est-ce que vous tutoyez le professeur?

____

7. Est-ce que vous prononcez correctement?

____

8. Est-ce que vous rédigez des lettres en français?

____

C *First conjugation (-**er**) verbs with mute **e** as the stem vowel*

First conjugation verbs that have mute **e** as their stem vowel, such as **acheter** (*to buy*), change the mute **e** to **è** in those forms where the ending has a mute **e.**

	singular	*plural*
first person	j' achète	nous achetons
second person	tu achètes	vous achetez
third person	il/elle achète on achète	ils/elles achètent

Other verbs like **acheter:**

amener *to bring (someone)*
emmener *to take (someone)*
enlever *to remove, take off*
geler *to freeze*
lever *to pick up, raise*
mener *to lead*
peser *to weigh*
promener *to walk*

Note: Verbs like **appeler** (*to call*) double the consonant after the mute **e** instead of changing **e** to **è**.

	singular	*plural*
first person	j' appelle	nous appelons
second person	tu appelles	vous appelez
third person	il/elle appelle on appelle	ils/elles appellent

Other verbs like **appeler:**

épeler *to spell*
feuilleter *to leaf through*
jeter *to throw*
projeter *to plan*
rappeler *to call back*
rejeter *to reject*
renouveler *to renew*

D First conjugation (-er) verbs with é as the stem vowel

Verbs that have **é** as the stem vowel, such as **espérer** (*to hope*), change **é** to **è** when the ending has a mute **e.**

	singular	*plural*
first person	j' espère	nous espérons
second person	tu espères	vous espérez
third person	il/elle espère on espère	ils/elles espèrent

Note: In verbs such as **préférer** (*to prefer*), only the **é** before the infinitive ending changes to **è.**

	singular	*plural*
first person	je préfère	nous préférons
second person	tu préfères	vous préférez
third person	il/elle préfère on préfère	ils/elles préfèrent

Other verbs like **espérer** and **préférer:**

céder *to yield*
célébrer *to celebrate*
compléter *to complete*
protéger *to protect*
refléter *to reflect*
répéter *to repeat*
révéler to reveal

F. Entre amis. Refaites les questions suivantes en remplaçant le pronom **vous** par le pronom familier **tu.**

1. Est-ce que vous préférez travailler en été?

____

2. Qu'est-ce que vous espérez faire après l'université?

____

3. Combien est-ce que vous pesez?

____

4. Comment est-ce que vous épelez votre nom?

____

5. Est-ce que vous rejetez les idées extrémistes?

____

6. Où est-ce que vous achetez les livres pour les cours?

____

G. Portrait de Jean-Claude. Jean-Claude est un jeune homme dynamique. Formez les phrases indiquées pour savoir quels sont ses projets.

1. Jean-Claude / espérer devenir interprète

____

2. il / préférer les langues

____

3. il / projeter un voyage aux États-Unis

____

4. il / feuilleter des brochures de l'agence de voyages

____

5. il / renouveler son passeport

____

6. il / compléter un cours intensif d'anglais

____

7. ses idées / refléter l'influence de sa mère

____

8. elle / lui répéter toujours l'importance d'une orientation internationale

____

E *Uses of the present tense*

1. The French present tense has several meanings in English.

En général **nous nageons** dans une piscine, mais aujourd'hui **nous nageons** dans la mer.	*We generally **swim** in a pool, but today **we are swimming** in the ocean.*

2. The French present tense can express the future, especially if an expression in the sentence refers to future time.

—**Je t'emmène** en ville demain.	***I'll take you** downtown tomorrow.*
—Merci, tu es gentil. Mais demain **je travaille**.	*Thanks, that's nice of you. But **I'm working** tomorrow.*

3. The present tense + **depuis, il y a,** or **voilà** + a time expression is used to express an action that began in the past but continues into the present.

—**Depuis combien de temps (Depuis quand) attends-tu** l'autobus?	***How long have you been waiting for** the bus?*
—**J'attends depuis vingt minutes.**	***I've been waiting for twenty minutes.***
—**Il y a combien de temps que tu achètes** tes livres dans cette librairie?	***How long have you been buying** your books in this bookstore?*
—**Il y a deux ans (Voilà deux ans) que j'achète** mes livres ici.	***I've been buying** my books here **for two years**.*

H. Problèmes de bureau. Françoise n'aime pas son travail. Pour savoir ce qui se passe dans son bureau, complétez les phrases avec les verbes entre parenthèses et traduisez les phrases en anglais.

1. (changer) Demain je ____________ de travail.

   ____

2. (travailler) Il y a deux ans que je ____________ dans le même bureau.

   ____

3. (gagner) Je ____________ le même salaire depuis dix-huit mois.

   ____

4. (demander) Il y a dix mois que je ____________ une augmentation.

   ____

5. (répéter) Et il y a dix mois que mon chef ____________ la même réponse: Non.

   ____

6. (chercher) Tous mes collègues ____________ de nouveaux emplois.

   ____

7. (désirer) Il y a longtemps qu'ils ____________ renoncer à leur travail ici.

   ____

8. (annoncer) La semaine prochaine ils ____________ leur décision au chef.

   ____

I. Un professeur dynamique. Formez des phrases pour connaître les efforts de Madame Ferron, professeur de langues, pour envoyer ses étudiants faire des études à l'étranger. Employez **il y a, voilà,** ou **depuis** et variez les constructions.

MODÈLE Madame Ferron / huit ans / envoyer des étudiants à l'étranger
➔ Il y a (Voilà) huit ans que Madame Ferron envoie des étudiants à l'étranger.
ou
➔ Madame Ferron envoie des étudiants à l'étranger depuis huit ans.

1. Madame Ferron / dix ans / enseigner dans notre lycée

   ____

2. elle / huit ans / encourager les étudiants à étudier à l'étranger

   ____

3. elle / sept ans / organiser des voyages pour les étudiants

4. trois étudiants / quatre ans / passer un semestre au Québec chaque année

5. mon ami Charles / trois ans / étudier l'allemand

6. il / deux mois / projeter un voyage d'études en Allemagne

7. Charles / six semaines / feuilleter des brochures

8. Madame Ferron / un mois / chercher le programme idéal pour Charles

J. Comment est-ce que ça se dit? Traduisez les phrases suivantes en français. Faites attention aux formes verbales.

1. He takes off his shoes and puts on his slippers (**pantoufles**).

2. At the office, we draft and correct articles.

3. I'm cleaning the kitchen. I wipe the table and sweep the floor.

4. He leafs through the magazine but he buys the newspaper.

5. Are you (*familiar*) completing the work today? Or do you prefer to finish tomorrow?

K. Activité orale. Find out from a friend three things that he or she likes to do and how long he or she has been doing them. Report what you learn to another classmate.

L. La grammaire en action. Voici une publicité de la SNCF (Société Nationale des Chemins de Fer Français) qui annonce les réductions sur les billets de train offertes par la «carte Kiwi». Lisez l'annonce. Ensuite, refaites ces phrases tirées de l'annonce avec les sujets proposés.

Tout sur la carte Kiwi

Un enfant, une carte Kiwi et on voyage à moitié prix.

ÉCONOMIES RÉALISÉES AVEC LA CARTE KIWI PAR LA FAMILLE DE FRÉDÉRIC

▲ ***Fréderic a 13 ans. Il habite Orléans. Il a la carte KIWI. Avec sa sœur Fanny (10 ans), ses parents et sa tante Laure, il part à La Rochelle (360 km).***

▲ ***Fréderic et sa maman doivent se rendre à Strasbourg (625 km) pour une communion. La tante de Frédéric et sa cousine Lucie (8 ans) les accompagnent. Pour l'occasion, ils voyagent en 1re classe.***

▲ ***Le Grand-Père de Frédéric l'emmène avec 2 copains de lycée (13 ans chacun) à Paris (121 km) faire une promenade en bateau sur la Seine.***

1. On voyage à moitié prix. (nous)

   ____

2. Frédéric habite Orléans. (je)

   ____

3. Sa tante et sa cousine l'accompagnent. (sa mère)

   ____

4. Ils voyagent en première classe. (vous)

   ____

5. Son grand-père emmène Frédéric à Paris. (nous)

   ____

CHAPTER 2

PRESENT TENSE OF IRREGULAR VERBS

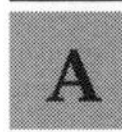

A Common irregular verbs

- French verbs not conjugated like **parler, finir,** or **rendre** are called irregular verbs. The two most important and most frequent irregular verbs are **avoir** (*to have*) and **être** (*to be*).

	avoir	
	singular	*plural*
first person	j' **ai**	nous **avons**
second person	tu **as**	vous **avez**
third person	il/elle **a**	ils/elles **ont**

	être	
	singular	*plural*
first person	je **suis**	nous **sommes**
second person	tu **es**	vous **êtes**
third person	il/elle **est**	ils/elles **sont**

- Also irregular are the verbs **aller** (*to go*) and **faire** (*to make, do*).

	aller	
	singular	*plural*
first person	je **vais**	nous **allons**
second person	tu **vas**	vous **allez**
third person	il/elle **va**	ils/elles **vont**

	faire	
	singular	*plural*
first person	je **fais**	nous **faisons**
second person	tu **fais**	vous **faites**
third person	il/elle **fait**	ils/elles **font**

Compounds of irregular verbs, such as **refaire** (*to redo*) and **défaire** (*to undo*), are conjugated like the simple verb.

- The irregular verb **prendre** (*to take*) and its compounds are frequently used.

	singular	*plural*
first person	je **prends**	nous **prenons**
second person	tu **prends**	vous **prenez**
third person	il/elle **prend**	ils/elles **prennent**

Conjugated like **prendre: apprendre** (*to learn*), **comprendre** (*to understand*), **reprendre** (*to start again*), **surprendre** (*to surprise*).

- Verbs like **venir** (*to come*) have the following forms:

	singular	*plural*
first person	je **viens**	nous **venons**
second person	tu **viens**	vous **venez**
third person	il/elle **vient**	ils/elles **viennent**

Conjugated like **venir: devenir** (*to become*), **revenir** (*to return*), **tenir** (*to hold*), **appartenir** (*to belong*), **maintenir** (*to maintain, support [financially]*), **obtenir** (*to obtain*), **retenir** (*to retain, hold back*), **soutenir** (*to support, hold up*).

- The irregular verbs **devoir** (*to owe, should, ought, must*), **pouvoir** (*to be able to*), and **vouloir** (*to want*) often occur before an infinitive.

devoir		
	singular	*plural*
first person	je **dois**	nous **devons**
second person	tu **dois**	vous **devez**
third person	il/elle **doit**	ils/elles **doivent**

pouvoir		
	singular	*plural*
first person	je **peux**	nous **pouvons**
second person	tu **peux**	vous **pouvez**
third person	il/elle **peut**	ils/elles **peuvent**

vouloir		
	singular	*plural*
first person	je **veux**	nous **voulons**
second person	tu **veux**	vous **voulez**
third person	il/elle **veut**	ils/elles **veulent**

A. ***Devoir* n'est pas toujours *vouloir.*** Ces gens doivent faire certaines choses, mais ils ne veulent pas. Répondez aux questions selon le modèle avec **devoir** et **vouloir**.

MODÈLE Martine travaille?
➔ Elle doit travailler, mais elle ne veut pas.

1. Tu passes la journée à la bibliothèque?

____

2. Catherine reste à la maison aujourd'hui?

____

3. Jean-Claude et Philippe vont chez le médecin?

____

4. Tes amis et toi, vous rentrez tôt?

____

5. Moi, je prépare le dîner?

____

6. Solange et moi, nous prenons un taxi?

____

B. **Qui fait quoi chez Hélène?** Hélène parle de sa famille, qui est assez grande. Chacun fait une partie des travaux du ménage. Utilisez les éléments proposés pour savoir ce qu'elle dit.

Vocabulaire utile

faire du bricolage *to do odd jobs, putter around*
faire les carreaux *to do the windows*
faire les courses *to do the shopping, marketing*
faire la cuisine *to do the cooking*
faire le jardin *to do the gardening*
faire le linge, faire la lessive *to do the laundry*
faire le(s) lit(s) *to make the bed(s)*
faire le ménage *to do the housework*
faire la vaisselle *to do the dishes*

1. moi / la vaisselle

____

2. mon grand-père / du bricolage

____

3. mes frères / le jardin

____

4. ma sœur et moi / les courses

____

5. ma grand-mère / la lessive

____

6. mon père / les carreaux

____

7. moi / les lits

____

8. ma mère, ma grand-mère et moi / la cuisine

____

B *Expressions with **avoir, être, faire,** and **prendre***

- Expressions with **avoir**

Physical sensations

avoir faim, soif, sommeil, chaud, froid *to be hungry, thirsty, sleepy, warm, cold*
avoir mal à la tête, aux yeux, à l'estomac *to have a headache, sore eyes, a stomach ache*
avoir mal au cœur *to be sick to one's stomach*

Other expressions

avoir de la chance *to be lucky*
avoir besoin de qqch *to need something*
avoir envie de qqch *to feel like (having) something*
avoir envie de faire qqch *to feel like doing something*
avoir l'intention de faire qqch *to intend to do something*
avoir raison *to be right*
avoir tort *to be wrong*

avoir ________ ans *to be ________ years old:*

—Quel âge avez-vous?	*How old are you?*
—J'ai dix-huit ans.	*I'm eighteen years old.*

avoir l'air + ***adjective*** *to look:*

Il a l'air triste, intelligent, distrait.	*He looks sad, intelligent, absent-minded.*

avoir l'air de + ***noun*** *to look like a:*

Elle a l'air d'une artiste, d'un professeur.	*She looks like an artist, a teacher.*

- Expressions with **être**

être au régime *to be on a diet*
être en vacances *to be on vacation*
être en colère *to be angry*
être bien to *be nice looking; be comfortable*
être de bonne/mauvaise humeur *to be in a good/bad mood*
être sur le point de faire qqch *to be about to do something*
être à l'heure *to be on time*
être en avance *to be early*
être en retard *to be late*
être de retour *to be back*
être d'accord avec qqn *to agree with someone*
être en train de faire qqch *to be busy doing something*

être à qqn *to belong to someone:*

À qui est ce stylo? — ***Who(m) does this pen belong to?***
C'est (Il est) à Yvette. — ***It's Yvette's. It belongs to Yvette.***

être à qqn de faire qqch *to be someone's turn (or responsibility) to do something:*

C'est à qui de jouer? — ***Whose turn is it to play?***
C'est à vous d'en parler au professeur. — ***It's up to you to talk to the teacher about it.***

- Expressions with **faire**

Weather expressions

Il fait beau/mauvais. *The weather's good/bad.*
Il fait chaud/froid. *It's hot/cold (outside).*
Il fait du soleil/vent. *It's sunny/windy.*
Il fait jour/nuit. *It's daytime/dark.*
Il fait un sale temps. *The weather is lousy.*
Il fait 30 degrés. *It's 30 degrees.*
Quel temps fait-il? *What's the weather?*
Quelle température fait-il? *What's the temperature?*

Other expressions

faire attention *to pay attention*
faire un voyage *to take a trip*
faire des projets *to make plans*
faire une promenade à pied, en voiture *to go for a walk, for a ride*
faire du sport, du jogging, du vélo *to play sports, to jog, to bike ride*
faire 10 kilomètres *to travel, cover 10 kilometers*
faire sa toilette *to wash up and get dressed (especially in the morning)*

- Expressions with **prendre**

prendre *to have (meals, food, drink)*
prendre le petit déjeuner *to have breakfast*
prendre un café, un thé, un Coca *to have coffee, tea, a Coke*
prendre un sandwich *to have a sandwich*
prendre une glace *to have an ice cream*

Other expressions

prendre froid, prendre un rhume *to catch cold*
prendre de l'essence *to get (buy) gasoline*
prendre du poids *to put on weight*
prendre qqn pour un autre *to mistake someone for somebody else*
passer prendre qqn *to go by to pick someone up*

Note culturelle

La France est un pays très varié. Sur une superficie un peu plus petite que celle du Texas se trouvent quatre types de climat très différents:

1. **Le climat continental:** Ce climat se trouve dans le centre et dans l'est du pays. C'est le climat de Paris et aussi de Nancy, de Metz et de Strasbourg. Dans cette région de la France, l'été est chaud, mais moins chaud que dans la plupart des États-Unis. L'hiver est froid et pluvieux, mais Paris ne connaît pas en général les températures basses et les neiges de l'est des États-Unis, par exemple.

2. **Le climat atlantique:** Ce climat est caractéristique de l'ouest de la France et de la côte nord qui se trouve face à l'Angleterre. Ce climat est plus modéré que le climat continental. L'hiver est assez doux et en été il ne fait pas très chaud. Mais il pleut beaucoup pendant toute l'année. Les spécialistes calculent que dans la région du climat atlantique il y a 240 jours de pluie par an.

3. **Le climat montagnard:** Comme l'indique son nom, c'est le climat des régions de montagne—les Alpes, les Pyrénées, le Massif central. À cause de l'élévation, l'été est court et l'hiver est long et il neige beaucoup.

4. **Le climat méditerranéen:** C'est le climat typique du Midi. Il se trouve sur la côte de la Méditerranée. Avec un hiver court et très doux (il ne gèle que rarement) et un été long, chaud et presque sans pluie, cette région est un grand centre touristique.

C. Synonymes. Écrivez sous chaque phrase une autre phrase formée avec une des expressions avec le verbe **avoir** qui a le même sens ou qui explique pourquoi le sujet a réalisé l'action.

1. Il veut dormir.

____

2. Je veux manger.

____

3. Nous voulons boire.

____

4. Elles ouvrent la climatisation.

____

5. Tu mets un pull-over.

____

6. Il entend des pas dans son appartement.

____

7. Vous donnez la réponse correcte.

____

8. On rougit.

____

9. Tu dis quelque chose qui n'est pas correct.

____

10. Elle a gagné deux fois à la loterie.

____

D. **Après l'accident.** Un groupe d'amis a eu un accident de route. L'un d'eux raconte où chacun a mal.

MODÈLE Marthe / tête ➔ Marthe a mal à la tête.

1. Pierre et Michèle / jambes

____

2. Frédéric / bras

____

3. Rachelle / dos

____

4. toi / épaule droite

____

5. moi / genoux

____

6. Alfred et moi / pieds

____

E. **Un voyage dans le Midi.** Complétez les phrases suivantes avec la forme correcte de **faire, avoir, être** ou **prendre** pour savoir comment les Duverger et leurs enfants passent leurs vacances.

1. Les Duverger et leurs deux enfants __________________ en vacances.
2. Ils __________________ envie de connaître Marseille.
3. «On __________________ un voyage dans le Midi!» disent les enfants.
4. Ils voyagent en TGV. Le train __________________ 800 kilomètres en moins de cinq heures.
5. Les Duverger __________________ soif quand ils arrivent à Marseille.
6. Ils __________________ une limonade dans le café de la gare.
7. Ils cherchent un guide. Le guide __________________ des projets.
8. Les Duverger __________________ attention quand le guide parle.
9. Le guide propose, «Aujourd'hui on __________________ une promenade en voiture pour connaître la ville.»
10. Les Duverger trouvent que c'est une excellente idée. Ils __________________ de l'essence et ils partent à la découverte de Marseille.

Note culturelle

Le Midi est le nom donné au sud de la France. La région la plus connue du Midi est sans doute la Provence. Douée d'un climat très doux, la Provence est un grand centre touristique. Les plages de la Côte d'Azur attirent des milliers de Français et d'étrangers. Ici on trouve Marseille, le premier port français; Grasse, centre de l'industrie du parfum; Aix-en-Provence, ville universitaire; Cannes, site du festival de cinéma le plus prestigieux du monde; Nice, connu pour ses plages et son carnaval et Monte-Carlo, lieu fréquenté pour ses casinos de renommée internationale.

Cette région était une province très appréciée de l'Empire romain et offre au visiteur des ruines romaines assez spectaculaires. En fait, le nom *Provence* dérive du mot latin *Provincia*. Les arènes d'Arles sont un amphithéâtre très bien conservé où ont lieu même de nos jours des courses aux taureaux. La Maison carrée de Nîmes est un petit temple romain presque intact qui se trouve au centre de la ville.

F. **Et toi?** Demandez à des camarades s'ils font les mêmes choses que vous.

Modèle Moi, j'ai envie de sortir.
➔ Toi aussi, tu as envie de sortir?

1. Moi, je prends un café.

____

2. Moi, j'ai faim.

____

3. Moi, je fais les courses maintenant.

____

4. Moi, j'ai vingt ans.

____

5. Moi, je suis en vacances.

____

6. Moi, j'ai mal à la tête.

____

7. Moi, je comprends l'italien.

____

8. Moi, je suis sur le point de sortir.

____

G. **Où ça?** Utilisez le verbe **être** pour décrire où se trouvent les personnes ou les établissements par rapport aux endroits indiqués dans chaque cas.

MODÈLE le magasin/à côté de/cinéma
➔ Le magasin est à côté du cinéma.

Les prépositions

à *to, at*
dans *in*
sur *on*
sous *under*
devant *in front of*
derrière *in back of*
près de *near*
loin de *far from*
à côté de *next to*
en face de *across from*
entre *between*
parmi *among*

Note the following contractions:

à + le ➔ au
à + les ➔ aux
de + le ➔ du
de + les ➔ des

1. le journal / sous / le banc

____

2. moi / à côté de / banc

____

3. mes amis / assis sur le banc

____

4. les arbres / derrière / le banc

____

5. toi et moi / près de / le lac

____

6. nous / en face de / le café

____

7. le lac / entre / la forêt et le pré (*meadow*)

____

8. vous / devant / le café

____

H. **C'est une belle journée qui commence!** Chantal ne travaille pas aujourd'hui. Elle est très contente. Complétez ces phrases avec la forme correcte de **faire, avoir, être** ou **prendre** pour savoir comment elle se prépare pour sortir.

1. Il est 7 heures. Il ________________ très beau aujourd'hui.
2. Il ________________ chaud.
3. Je ne travaille pas aujourd'hui et je ________________ de très bonne humeur.
4. J'________________ envie de sortir.

5. Je ________________ ma toilette.
6. Je ________________ le petit déjeuner.
7. Je ________________ des projets pour la journée.
8. Mon ami François va passer la journée avec moi. Le matin, nous ________________ du jogging.
9. L'après-midi nous ________________ une promenade en voiture.
10. Le soir nous ________________ une glace ensemble dans un café.

C *Irregular verbs resembling regular verbs*

- A small number of **-ir** verbs have the endings of **-er** verbs in the present tense. Study the conjugation of **ouvrir** (*to open*).

j' ouvre	nous ouvr**ons**
tu ouvr**es**	vous ouvr**ez**
il/elle ouvre	ils/elles ouvr**ent**

Conjugated like **ouvrir**: **accueillir** (*to welcome*), **couvrir** (*to cover*), **cueillir** (*to gather, pick [flowers]*), **découvrir** (*to discover*), **rouvrir** (*to reopen*), **souffrir** (*to suffer*).

- Another group of **-ir** verbs is conjugated like **-re** verbs. Study the conjugation of **partir** (*to leave, set out*).

je pars	nous part**ons**
tu pars	vous part**ez**
il/elle par**t**	ils/elles part**ent**

Conjugated like **partir: dormir** (*to sleep*), **mentir** (*to lie*), **repartir** (*to leave again*), **sentir** (*to feel*), **servir** (*to serve*), **sortir** (*to go out*).

- The verb **mettre** (*to put*) is conjugated like an **-re** verb, but it has only one **t** in the singular.

je mets	nous mett**ons**
tu mets	vous mett**ez**
il/elle met	ils/elles mett**ent**

Conjugated like **mettre: battre** (*to beat*), **combattre** (*to fight, combat*), **débattre** (*to debate*), **omettre** (*to omit*), **permettre** (*to permit*), **promettre** (*to promise*).

- The verbs **convaincre** (*to convince*) and **vaincre** (*to conquer*) have two stems. The singular stem ends in **-c,** and the plural stem ends in **-qu.**

je convaincs	nous convain**quons**
tu convaincs	vous convain**quez**
il/elle convainc	ils/elles convain**quent**

- Infinitives ending in **-aindre, -eindre,** and **-oindre** have two stems. The singular stem ends in **-n,** and the plural stem ends in **-gn.** They follow the pattern of the verb **craindre** (*to fear*).

je crain**s**	nous crai**gnons**
tu crain**s**	vous crai**gnez**
il/elle crain**t**	ils/elles crai**gnent**

Conjugated like **craindre: atteindre** (*to reach, attain*), **éteindre** (*to put out, extinguish*), **joindre** (*to join*), **peindre** (*to paint*), **plaindre** (*to pity*), **rejoindre** (*to rejoin*).

- Verbs like **connaître** (*to know*) have a singular stem ending in **-ai.** In the third person singular form, the **-i** changes to **-î.** The plural stem ends in **-ss.**

je connai**s**	nous connai**ssons**
tu connai**s**	vous connai**ssez**
il/elle conna**ît**	ils/elles connai**ssent**

Conjugated like **connaître: apparaître** (*to appear*), **disparaître** (*to disappear*), **paraître** (*to seem, appear*), **reconnaître** (*to recognize*).

- Verbs with infinitives ending in **-uire** like **construire** (*to build*) have two stems. The singular stem ends in **-i** and the plural stem ends in **-s.**

je construi**s**	nous construi**sons**
tu construi**s**	vous construi**sez**
il/elle construi**t**	ils/elles construi**sent**

Conjugated like **construire: conduire** (*to drive*), **détruire** (*to destroy*), **introduire** (*to introduce*), **produire** (*to produce*), **traduire** (*to translate*).

- The verb **recevoir** (*to receive*) is conjugated similarly to **devoir**. Note the change of **c** to **ç** before **o**.

je re**çois**	nous rece**vons**
tu re**çois**	vous rece**vez**
il/elle re**çoit**	ils/elles re**çoivent**

Conjugated like **recevoir: décevoir** (*to disappoint*), **apercevoir** (*to notice*).

I. Rien! Jean-Baptiste a une attitude très négative aujourd'hui, comme vous pouvez le voir par ses réponses. Suivez le modèle.

Modèle Vous servez quelque chose?
→ Non, je ne sers rien.

1. Vous craignez quelque chose?
2. Vous recevez quelque chose?
3. Vous devez quelque chose?
4. Vous construisez quelque chose?
5. Vous reconnaissez quelque chose?
6. Vous peignez quelque chose?
7. Vous traduisez quelque chose?
8. Vous découvrez quelque chose?

J. Un peintre qui réussit. L'art de Nicole évolue avec beaucoup de succès. Formez les phrases indiquées pour savoir comment.

1. Nicole / peindre / tous les jours
2. la nature / apparaître / dans ses tableaux
3. nous / apercevoir / son talent
4. nous / découvrir / de nouveaux thèmes
5. maintenant / Nicole / introduire / la vie de la ville dans son art
6. ses nouveaux tableaux / ne pas décevoir
7. le public / accueillir / son art avec enthousiasme

K. Nous aussi. Dans une conversation avec Lise Dulac, Monsieur et Madame Sauvignon découvrent qu'ils ont beaucoup en commun avec elle. Suivez le modèle.

MODÈLE Madame Dulac: Je sors le week-end.
➔ Monsieur et Madame Sauvignon: Nous aussi, nous sortons le week-end.

1. En été j'ouvre toutes les fenêtres.

____

2. J'accueille souvent des étudiants étrangers à la maison.

____

3. Je reçois beaucoup de lettres des étudiants étrangers.

____

4. Je conduis avec prudence.

____

5. Je connais beaucoup de monde dans le quartier.

____

6. Je pars en vacances au mois de juillet.

____

7. Je cueille des fleurs dans mon jardin.

____

8. Je peins en été.

____

L. Des vacances dans le désert. Refaites cette petite histoire pour qu'elle raconte les aventures (et mésaventures!) de Josette.

MODÈLE Alain et Marc ne travaillent pas cette semaine.
➔ Josette ne travaille pas cette semaine.

1. Alain et Marc partent en vacances.

   Josette ______________________________

2. Ils rejoignent des amis.

   Elle ______________________________

3. Ils conduisent une vieille voiture.

   Elle ______________________________

4. Ils dorment dans des hôtels très modestes.

   Elle ______________________________

5. Ils arrivent dans le désert.

   Elle ______________________________

6. Ils sentent la chaleur.
   Elle ______________________________

7. Ils souffrent d'allergies.
   Elle ______________________________

8. Ils repartent à la maison.
   Elle ______________________________

D *Other irregular verbs*

- **Écrire, savoir, vivre, boire, suivre**

écrire *to write*	
j' **écris**	nous **écrivons**
tu **écris**	vous **écrivez**
il/elle **écrit**	ils/elles **écrivent**

savoir *to know*	
je **sais**	nous **savons**
tu **sais**	vous **savez**
il/elle **sait**	ils/elles **savent**

vivre *to live*	
je **vis**	nous **vivons**
tu **vis**	vous **vivez**
il/elle **vit**	ils/elles **vivent**

boire *to drink*	
je **bois**	nous **buvons**
tu **bois**	vous **buvez**
il/elle **boit**	ils/elles **boivent**

suivre *to follow*	
je **suis**	nous **suivons**
tu **suis**	vous **suivez**
il/elle **suit**	ils/elles **suivent**

Expressions with **suivre: suivre un cours** (*to take a course*), **suivre un régime** (*to be on a diet*), **suivre l'actualité** (*to keep up with the news*).

- **Dire, lire, courir, mourir**

dire *to say, tell*	
je **dis**	nous **disons**
tu **dis**	vous **dites**
il/elle **dit**	ils/elles **disent**

lire *to read*	
je **lis**	nous **lisons**
tu **lis**	vous **lisez**
il/elle **lit**	ils/elles **lisent**

courir *to run*	
je **cours**	nous **courons**
tu **cours**	vous **courez**
il/elle **court**	ils/elles **courent**

mourir *to die*	
je **meurs**	nous **mourons**
tu **meurs**	vous **mourez**
il/elle **meurt**	ils/elles **meurent**

Expressions with **mourir: mourir de faim** (*to starve, be very hungry*), **mourir de soif** (*to be very thirsty*), **mourir d'ennui** (*to be bored to death*).

• **Voir** and **croire**

voir *to see*	
je **vois**	nous **voyons**
tu **vois**	vous **voyez**
il/elle **voit**	ils/elles **voient**

croire *to believe*	
je **crois**	nous **croyons**
tu **crois**	vous **croyez**
il/elle **croit**	ils/elles **croient**

M. Maintenant il s'agit de vacances à la plage. Raconte l'expérience de Josette.

1. Les cousins de Josette veulent aller au bord de la mer.
   Josette ____________________
2. Ils croient que ça va être amusant.
   Elle ____________________
3. Ils écrivent aux copains pour les inviter.
   Elle ____________________
4. Ils savent arriver à la plage.
   Elle ____________________
5. Ils boivent de l'eau parce qu'il fait chaud.
   Elle ____________________
6. Ils meurent de soif.
   Elle ____________________
7. Ils courent sur la plage pour faire de l'exercice.
   Elle ____________________
8. Ils voient le coucher du soleil (*sunset*) sur la mer.
   Elle ____________________
9. Ils disent que c'est très joli.
   Elle ____________________
10. Le soir, ils lisent des romans.
    Le soir, elle ____________________
11. Ils suivent l'actualité en écoutant la radio.
    Elle ____________________
12. Ils vivent des jours heureux au bord de la mer.
    Elle ____________________

E Verbal constructions

- The verbs **vouloir** and **pouvoir** are followed directly by an infinitive:

—Tu **veux jouer** au football avec nous? *Do you **want to play** soccer with us?*
—Je **ne peux pas sortir** aujourd'hui. *I **can't go out** today.*

- When **aller** is followed by an infinitive it expresses future time, like English *to be going to:*

—À quelle heure est-ce que vous **allez prendre** un café avec nos amis? *What time **are you going to have** a cup of coffee with our friends?*
—Aujourd'hui je **vais étudier.** Pas de café jusqu'à demain! *Today **I'm going to study.** No coffee till tomorrow!*

- Verbs of motion, such as **venir, sortir, monter,** and **descendre,** can also be followed directly by an infinitive:

—Je **descends faire** les courses. *I'**m going down to do** the shopping.*
—Et moi, je **sors prendre** les billets pour le concert de demain soir. *And I'**m going out to buy** the tickets for tomorrow night's concert.*

—Marc **vient chercher** son livre. *Marc **is coming to get** his book.*
—Il est dans ma chambre. Il **peut monter le chercher,** s'il veut. *It's in my room. He **can go upstairs to get it**, if he wants to.*

- The present tense of **venir** + **de** + an infinitive expresses an action that has just taken place.

—Je **viens de voir** Élise. *I **just saw** Élise.*
—Elle **vient de recevoir** une lettre de son frère. *She **just received** a letter from her brother.*

- When **savoir** is followed by an infinitive, it means *to know how to do something.*

—Tu **sais nager?** *Do you **know how to swim?***
—Oui, mais je **ne sais pas plonger.** *Yes, but I **don't know how to dive.***

—Elle **ne sait pas monter** à bicyclette. *She **doesn't know how to ride** a bike.*
—Mais elle **sait conduire** sa Ferrari. *But she **knows how to drive** her Ferrari.*

- **Apprendre** is followed by **à** before an infinitive.

—Tu **apprends à jouer** de la flûte? ***Are** you **learning to play** the flute?*
—Non, je joue déjà de la flûte. **J'apprends à jouer** du piano. *No, I already play the flute. I'**m learning to play** the piano.*

N. Moi aussi. Dites dans chaque cas que vous voulez faire la chose que votre camarade apprend à faire.

MODÈLE parler russe
→ —J'apprends à parler russe.
—Moi aussi, je veux parler russe.

1. danser

____

____

2. jouer aux échecs

3. chanter

4. conduire

5. faire la cuisine

6. programmer l'ordinateur

O. C'est déjà fait. Formez des échanges avec **aller** et **venir de** selon le modèle.

MODÈLE Baudouin / prendre un café
➔ —Est-ce que Baudouin va prendre un café?
—Mais il vient de prendre un café.

1. toi / faire le linge

2. les étudiants / déjeuner

3. vous deux / faire les courses

4. Christine / téléphoner à ses parents

5. nous / visiter les monuments

6. moi / voir un film

P. **Même pas pour la santé.** Ces gens savent ce qu'ils doivent faire pour être en forme, mais ils ne le font pas. Exprimez leur refus en suivant le modèle.

MODÈLE Jean-Pierre doit courir tous les jours.
➔ Il sait qu'il doit courir, mais il dit qu'il ne peut pas et qu'il ne veut pas.

1. Mes parents doivent marcher tous les jours.

____

____

2. Mes amis, vous devez faire de l'exercice.

____

____

3. Je dois nager une heure tous les jours.

____

____

4. Tu dois faire du sport.

____

____

5. Catherine doit suivre un régime pour maigrir.

____

____

6. Ma sœur et moi, nous devons faire du vélo.

____

Q. **Comment est-ce que ça se dit?** Traduisez les phrases suivantes en français.

1. When are you (**vous**) leaving?

____

2. We're leaving tomorrow.

____

3. And when are you coming back (**revenir**)?

____

4. I'm coming back on Friday. My wife and the children are coming back next week.

____

5. What are you (**tu**) doing today?

____

6. My wife and I are painting the house.

____

7. You (**vous**) know how to paint the house?

____

8. My brother is going to help us. *He* knows how to paint.

____

9. I'm coming to watch (**regarder**).

____

10. If you're coming, you're going to paint.

____

R. Ma journée. Avec un(e) camarade, parlez de votre journée—quand vous avez faim et soif, ce que vous prenez, quand vous sortez et quand vous êtes de retour, combien d'heures vous dormez, etc.

CHAPTER 3

NEGATIVE SENTENCES

A Basic negative structures

- Verbs are made negative by placing **ne** before the verb and **pas** after it.

—Je **ne** dîne **pas** au restaurant ce soir. Et toi?	*I'm* ***not*** *having dinner out this evening. How about you?*
—Moi, je **ne** travaille **pas**. Donc, je sors.	*I'm* ***not*** *working. So, I'm going out.*

- **Ne** becomes **n'** before a vowel.

Je **n'**aime pas écouter cette musique.	*I* ***don't*** *like listening to this music.*

- Note the similar negative constructions **ne** + verb + **jamais** meaning *never* and **ne** + verb + **plus** meaning *not anymore, no more.*

—Tu **n'**invites **plus** Jeanine.	*You* ***don't*** *ask Jeanine out* ***anymore.***
—Ce n'est pas la peine. Elle **n'**accepte **jamais.**	*It doesn't pay to. She* ***never*** *accepts.*

- **Ne** + verb + **personne** means *no one,* and **ne** + verb + **rien** means *nothing.*

—Vous cherchez quelqu'un, monsieur?	*Are you looking for someone, Sir?*
—Non, madame. Je **ne** cherche **personne**.	*No, ma'am. I'm* ***not*** *looking for* ***anyone****.*
—J'entends un bruit.	*I hear a noise.*
—Moi, je **n'**entends **rien**.	*I* ***don't*** *hear* ***anything****.*

- **Personne** and **rien** may be used as subjects. Then they precede the verb and are followed by **ne**.

—**Rien ne** change ici.	***Nothing*** *changes here.*
—C'est vrai. **Personne ne** déménage. Tout reste comme avant.	*It's true.* ***No one*** *moves out. Everything remains just as it was before.*

Positive and Corresponding Negative Words

Positive		Negative	
encore, toujours	*still*	**plus**	*no more*
encore, davantage	*more*	**plus**	*no more, not anymore*
quelquefois	*sometimes*	**jamais**	*never*
toujours	*always*	**jamais**	*never*
souvent	*often*	**jamais**	*never*
quelqu'un	*someone, somebody*	**personne**	*no one, nobody*
quelque chose	*something*	**rien**	*nothing*
quelque part	*somewhere*	**nulle part**	*nowhere*

A. Comme c'est triste. Pierrot n'est pas tout à fait content pendant ses premiers jours à l'université. Écrivez ses réponses négatives aux questions, en employant le mot négatif correspondant.

Modèle Est-ce que tu connais beaucoup de monde?
→ Non, je ne connais personne.

1. Est-ce que ta petite amie téléphone tous les jours?
2. Est-ce que tu manges avec quelqu'un?
3. Est-ce que tu regardes souvent la télé?
4. Est-ce que tu travailles encore?
5. Est-ce que quelqu'un organise des activités pour les nouveaux étudiants?
6. Est-ce que tu aimes quelque chose ici?

B. Ça va mieux. Pierrot est content à l'université maintenant. Écrivez ses réponses négatives aux questions, en employant le mot négatif correspondant.

1. Est-ce que tu es encore seul?
2. Est-ce que tu es triste quelquefois?
3. Est-ce que tu désires encore rentrer chez toi?
4. Est-ce que quelqu'un dérange les étudiants quand ils travaillent?
5. Est-ce que tu trouves quelque chose à critiquer?
6. Est-ce que quelque chose t'effraie maintenant?

Note culturelle

L'enseignement supérieur en France offre plusieurs filières aux étudiants. La plupart des étudiants assistent aux universités, dont on compte plus de 80 en France. Il y a des universités techniques, des études universitaires générales et des études universitaires qui préparent les étudiants pour les professions de santé. L'admission à l'université est ouverte à tout étudiant ayant son baccalauréat (diplôme donné à la fin des études secondaires à ceux qui réussissent à l'examen du bac).

Les universités sont organisées en U.F.R., c'est-à-dire, unités de formation et de recherche. L'U.F.R. est à peu près l'équivalent du département universitaire américain.

Les grandes écoles sont des institutions d'élite. L'entrée est par un concours très difficile. Parmi les grandes écoles les plus connues sont l'École nationale d'administration, l'École polytechnique, le Conservatoire national de musique, l'École des ponts et chaussées, et les Écoles normales supérieures spécialisées dans différentes matières.

La première université française est l'université de Paris, fondée en 1200 par le roi Philippe-Auguste. L'université de Paris attirait des étudiants de toute l' Europe et la langue qu'ils parlaient entre eux et la langue d'enseignement était le latin. D'où le nom du Quartier latin à Paris.

C. **Jamais!** Les étudiants racontent ce qu'ils ne font jamais à l'école. Écrivez ce qu'ils disent avec **jamais.**

Modèle fumer en classe
→ Nous ne fumons jamais en classe.

1. arriver en retard

____

2. interrompre le professeur

____

3. oublier nos devoirs

____

4. perdre nos livres

____

5. applaudir après la classe

____

6. jeter nos stylos en l'air

____

7. confondre les rois de France dans la classe d'histoire

____

8. jouer aux cartes en classe

____

D. Tout change. Josette retourne à son quartier après plusieurs années d'absence. Son amie Valérie lui raconte comment les choses ont changé. Écrivez ce qu'elle dit à Josette en employant **ne . . . plus.**

MODÈLE mon frère / travailler à la bibliothèque
→ Mon frère ne travaille plus à la bibliothèque.

1. les Dulac / habiter l'immeuble en face
2. M. Beauchamp / vendre sa poterie aux voisins
3. nous / acheter le journal au kiosque du coin
4. ma mère / descendre faire les courses tous les jours
5. moi / jouer du piano
6. Mme Duverger / enseigner au lycée du quartier
7. nos amis / passer beaucoup de temps dans le quartier

E. Quelle école! Dans cette école on ne s'occupe pas des étudiants. Écrivez des phrases avec le mot **personne** comme sujet pour expliquer tout ce qu'on ne fait pas.

MODÈLE aider les étudiants → Personne n'aide les étudiants.

1. avertir les étudiants
2. parler avec les étudiants
3. écouter les étudiants
4. saluer les étudiants
5. encourager les étudiants
6. donner des conseils aux étudiants

F. **Et vous?** Écrivez si vous faites ces activités souvent, quelquefois, jamais, ou si vous ne les faites plus.

1. jouer au volley-ball

____

2. étudier toute la nuit

____

3. parler au téléphone

____

4. regarder la télé

____

5. assister aux concerts de musique classique

____

6. dîner au restaurant avec tes amis

____

7. descendre à la rue en pyjama à 4 heures du matin

____

8. arriver en retard à l'école

____

B *Other negative structures*

- **Aucun(e)** with the meaning *no, not any* precedes a noun. **Ne** precedes the verb.

—Tu crois qu'il va rentrer?	*Do you think he's coming back?*
—Je **n'**ai **aucune idée.**	*I have **no idea**.*
—Ce cours est très difficile.	*This course is very difficult.*
—C'est que le professeur **ne** nous donne **aucun exemple.**	*That's because the teacher **doesn't** give us **any examples**.*

Note that **aucun(e)** is always used in the singular.

- **Aucun(e)** + noun or **aucun(e) des** + plural noun may function as the subject of a sentence. **Ne** precedes the verb.

Aucun ami n'accepte son invitation.	***No friend** accepts his invitation.*
Aucun de ses amis n'accepte son invitation.	***None of his friends** accepts his invitation.*

- **Ni . . . ni . . .** means *neither . . . nor. . . .* Like **aucun(e), personne,** and **rien,** it may either follow or precede the verb. **Ne** precedes the verb in both cases. When **ni . . . ni . . .** refers to the subject of the sentence, a plural verb is used.

—Je **ne** vois **ni Charles ni Hélène.**	*I don't see **either Charles or Hélène**.*
—**Ni Charles ni Hélène ne** sont là.	***Neither Charles nor Hélène** is here.*

- **(Ni) . . . non plus** is used to mean *neither* or *not either* in a sentence where the French equivalent of *nor* does not appear.

—Charles n'est pas là.	*Charles isn't here.*
—(Ni) Hélène non plus.	***Neither is Hélène. (Hélène either.)***
—Je n'aime pas le professeur d'informatique.	*I don't like the computer science teacher.*
—Moi non plus.	***Neither do I.***

- **Ne** + verb + **guère** means *hardly.*

Il **n'**est **guère** content.	*He's **hardly** happy.*

G. Un étudiant en difficulté. Jean-Marc a beaucoup de problèmes au lycée. Décrivez-les en employant **ni . . . ni . . .** dans chaque cas, selon le modèle.

Modèle arriver / en avance / à l'heure
➔ Il n'arrive ni en avance ni à l'heure.

1. aimer / la physique / la littérature

____

2. finir / ses devoirs / ses compositions

____

3. étudier / à la bibliothèque / à la maison

____

4. réfléchir / à son travail / à son avenir

____

5. demander des conseils / à ses amis / à ses professeurs

____

6. écouter / les conférences / les discussions

____

H. Un professeur paresseux. Utilisez le mot **aucun** pour savoir pourquoi les étudiants ne sont pas contents dans la classe du professeur Malherbe.

Modèle donner / devoir ➔ Il ne donne aucun devoir.

1. expliquer / texte

____

2. corriger / composition

____

3. recommander / livre

____

4. proposer / thème de discussion

____

5. présenter / idée

____

6. analyser / problème

____

C *Ne . . . que*

Ne . . . que means *only.* **Ne** precedes the verb and **que** precedes the word or words emphasized.

—Paulette aime la musique classique?	*Does Paulette like classical music?*
—Non, elle **n'**écoute **que** des chansons populaires.	*No, she listens **only** to popular songs.*
—Tu veux aller à Avignon par le train?	*Do you want to go by train to Avignon?*
—Je **ne** voyage **qu'**en voiture.	*I travel **only** by car.*

Ne . . . pas que means *not only.*

Il **n'**y a **pas que** le travail. Il faut vivre aussi.	*Work **isn't all there is**. You have to live too.*
Il **n'**aime **pas que** la physique. Il adore la géographie aussi.	*He **doesn't only** like physics. He loves geography too.*

I. Il n'y en a pas d'autre. Refaites les phrases suivantes avec **ne . . . que,** selon le modèle.

Modèle La chimie est la seule classe que j'aime.
➔ Je n'aime que la chimie.

1. Philippe est la seule personne que je respecte ici.

____

2. Ma chambre est la seule que je nettoie.

____

3. Alice est la seule personne que j'invite.

____

4. La littérature française est la seule qu'elle apprécie.

____

5. L'avenir est la seule chose à laquelle ils réfléchissent.

____

6. Odile est la seule personne à qui je téléphone.

____

7. Le football est le seul sport auquel je joue.

____

8. Le dîner est le seul repas qu'elle prépare à la maison.

____

J. Comment est-ce que ça se dit? Traduisez en français.

1. We're not making any (**de**) plans because we're not taking a (**de**) trip.

____

2. No one feels like leaving on vacation.

____

3. So (**donc**), we're not going anywhere.

____

4. We're not going either to the beach or to the mountains. Or to Paris either.

____

5. And we don't want to go abroad anymore.

____

K. Activité orale. Avec un(e) camarade de classe, discutez des choses que vous ne faites pas chez vous. Comparez les règles. Présentez à la classe les choses à ne pas faire que votre camarade et vous partagez.

L. La grammaire en action. Comment protège-t-on l'environnement? Voici des idées puisées dans un petit livre, *C'est ma planète—20 gestes simples pour l'environnement*, publié par la Mairie de Paris. Lisez les suggestions et ensuite écrivez sous chacune en employant le négatif ce que fait Albert, un garçon qui ne se soucie pas du tout de l'environnement. Par exemple, si vous lisez *J'économise l'eau*, vous écrivez *Albert n'économise pas l'eau*.

Vocabulaire utile

le bruit *noise*
l'essence *(fem.)* *gas(oline)*
éviter de faire qqch *to avoid doing something*
la pile *battery*
le plomb *lead*
rapporter *to bring back*
usagé *used*
le verre *glass*

1. «J'utilise les transports en commun, chaque fois que c'est possible.»

2. «J'utilise de l'essence sans plomb.»

3. «Je conduis tranquillement.»

4. «J'évite de faire du bruit.»

5. «Je jette le verre dans les conteneurs spéciaux.»

6. «Je rapporte les piles usagées à mon vendeur.»

CHAPTER 4

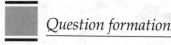

INTERROGATIVE SENTENCES

Question formation

There are three ways to change a statement into a question:

- In spoken French, statements are turned into questions by raising the pitch of the voice at the end of the sentence. The word order is the same as that of a statement.

—Tu descends avec moi?	*Are you coming downstairs with me?*
—Non, je reste ici. Tu retournes avant le dîner?	*No, I'm staying here. Are you coming back before dinner?*
—Non. Je dîne en ville.	*No, I'm having dinner in town.*

- In both spoken and formal French, **est-ce que** may be placed at the beginning of a statement to turn it into a question.

—**Est-ce que** vous écoutez souvent les concerts à la radio?	*Do you often listen to the concerts on the radio?*
—Oui, toujours. Et vous? **Est-ce que** vous aimez la musique classique aussi?	*Yes, all the time. And what about you? Do you like classical music too?*

- In formal French, especially in writing, statements are turned into questions by placing the subject pronoun after the verb and joining the two with a hyphen. This is called *inversion* of the subject and verb.

—**Travaillez-vous** ici, madame?	***Do you work** here, Ma'am?*
—Oui, monsieur. **Cherchez-vous** un emploi?	*Yes, Sir. **Are you looking** for a job?*

Note: The pronoun **je** is not used in inverted questions.

- If the third person singular form of a verb ends in a vowel, **-t-** is added between the verb form and the inverted subject pronoun **il, elle,** or **on**.

Parle-**t**-il français?	*Does he speak French?*
A-**t**-elle envie de sortir?	*Does she feel like going out?*
Salue-**t**-on le professeur en anglais?	*Does one greet the teacher in English?*

- In an inverted question, a noun subject remains before the verb and the corresponding pronoun is added after the verb.

—**Les étudiants** tutoient-**ils** leur professeur?	*Do the students use the **tu** form to their teacher?*
—Jamais. Ils vouvoient le professeur.	*Never. They use the **vous** form to the teacher.*
—**Le professeur** tutoie-**t-il** les étudiants?	*Does the teacher use the **tu** form to the students?*
—Quelquefois.	*Sometimes.*

- Negative questions with inversion are used only in formal style. The **ne** and **pas** surround the inverted pronoun and verb. These questions imply that the speaker expects the answer *yes.*

—**N'**appuie**-t-il pas** notre candidat?	*Doesn't he support our candidate?*
—Si, bien sûr. **Ne** partage**-t-il pas** nos idées?	*Yes, of course he does. Doesn't he share our ideas?*

- If the subject of a negative question is a noun, it remains in its position before **ne** and the corresponding pronoun is added after the verb.

—**Les musiciens** de cet orchestre **ne** jouent**-ils pas** merveilleusement?	*Don't the musicians in this orchestra play wonderfully?*
—Si. Et regardez. **Le public n'**écoute**-t-il pas** avec beaucoup de plaisir?	*Yes. And look. Isn't the public listening with great delight?*

Note: **Si**, not **oui**, is used to answer *yes* to a negative question.

- **N'est-ce pas** can be added to the end of any statement to ask a question to which the speaker expects the answer *yes*. The meaning is similar to that of negative questions.

Les musiciens jouent bien, **n'est-ce pas?**	*The musicians play well,* ***don't they?***

  Negative questions formed with rising intonation and without inversion expect the answer *no*.

—Tu ne regardes pas la télé?	*You're not watching TV?*
—Non, je téléphone.	*No, I'm making a phone call.*

A. Pour faire connaissance. Vous faites la connaissance d'un vieux monsieur. Vous lui posez des questions en employant l'inversion. Après, vous posez les mêmes questions à une nouvelle étudiante. Formez-les avec **est-ce que.**

Modèle parler français
➔ a. Parlez-vous français?
b. Est-ce que vous parlez français?

1. inviter souvent vos amis à dîner

   a. ________________________________

   b. ________________________________

2. apprécier la musique classique

   a. ________________________________

   b. ________________________________

3. habiter un beau quartier

   a. ________________________________

   b. ________________________________

4. chercher une maison à la campagne

   a. ________________________________

   b. ________________________________

5. travailler près de votre appartement
   a. ______________________________
   b. ______________________________
6. dîner généralement au restaurant
   a. ______________________________
   b. ______________________________

B. **L'amoureux.** Robert s'est entiché de (*has fallen for*) Chantal. Il se pose toutes sortes de questions à son sujet. Formez ses questions en employant l'inversion.

MODÈLE jouer au tennis ➔ Joue-t-elle au tennis?

1. aimer les maths comme moi
____
2. étudier les mêmes matières que moi
____
3. habiter près du lycée
____
4. penser à moi de temps en temps
____
5. travailler à la bibliothèque
____
6. déjeuner à la cantine du lycée
____

C. **L'ami de l'amoureux.** Robert confie son amour à son ami Philippe. Philippe lui pose des questions sur Chantal. Formez ses questions avec **est-ce que.**

MODÈLE tu / penser constamment à Chantal
➔ Est-ce que tu penses constamment à Chantal?

1. Chantal / habiter près de chez toi
____
2. tu / arriver au lycée à la même heure que Chantal
____
3. tu / saluer Chantal
____
4. Chantal / aimer les mêmes activités que toi
____
5. tu / déjeuner avec elle
____
6. Chantal / bavarder avec toi de temps en temps
____

D. La section française. Marie-Claire pose des questions à son conseiller sur la section française de son lycée. Elle emploie l'inversion. Que dit-elle?

MODÈLE M. Leclerc / apprécier la littérature française
➔ M. Leclerc apprécie-t-il la littérature française?

1. Mme Savignac / prononcer parfaitement l'anglais

2. M. Paul / enseigner l'espagnol aussi

3. Mlle Moreau / répondre toujours aux questions des étudiants

4. M. Michelet / arriver au lycée à 7 heures du matin

5. M. et Mme Lamoureux / enseigner dans le même lycée

6. Mme Leboucher / choisir des textes intéressants pour sa classe

7. les professeurs / organiser des activités pour les étudiants

8. les étudiants / aimer les cours de français

E. Des explications. Le conseiller du lycée explique à ses collègues ses idées sur les difficultés scolaires de certains étudiants en employant des questions négatives, formées avec inversion du sujet. Suivez le modèle pour écrire ses paroles.

MODÈLE regarder trop la télé
➔ Ne regardent-ils pas trop la télé?

1. déranger tout le monde

2. désobéir au professeur

3. perdre souvent leurs cahiers

4. bavarder trop en classe

5. confondre les dates

6. travailler sans intérêt

F. Un succès sûr. Dans une réunion d'affaires M. Bertin explique à ses collègues pourquoi il croit que leur nouvelle affaire va réussir. Écrivez ce qu'il leur dit en employant des questions négatives formées avec inversion du sujet. Le sujet est **nous** dans chaque cas. Suivez le modèle.

MODÈLE placer notre argent dans une excellente affaire
➔ Ne plaçons-nous pas notre argent dans une excellente affaire?

1. lancer une bonne affaire

____

2. diriger la compagnie d'une façon intelligente

____

3. engager de bons travailleurs

____

4. aménager les bureaux

____

5. changer nos stratégies selon chaque situation

____

6. commencer à gagner de l'argent

____

G. Après la réunion. Nous retrouvons M. Bertin avec un ami. Il lui explique les raisons pour lesquelles il croit que sa nouvelle affaire va réussir. Il utilise des questions négatives avec **on** au lieu de **nous.** Écrivez les questions deux fois, avec et sans inversion. Suivez le modèle.

MODÈLE placer notre argent dans une excellente affaire
➔ a. Ne place-t-on pas notre argent dans une excellente affaire?
b. On ne place pas notre argent dans une excellente affaire?

1. lancer une bonne affaire
   a. _______________
   b. _______________
2. diriger la compagnie d'une façon intelligente
   a. _______________
   b. _______________
3. engager de bons travailleurs
   a. _______________
   b. _______________

4. aménager les bureaux
   a. ______________________________
   b. ______________________________
5. changer nos stratégies selon chaque situation
   a. ______________________________
   b. ______________________________
6. commencer à gagner de l'argent
   a. ______________________________
   b. ______________________________

Note culturelle

La France se classe au quatrième rang mondial pour la valeur de ses marchandises exportées (après les États-Unis, le Japon et l'Allemagne). Cela signifie que la France est une des premières puissances industrielles du monde.

La France est un grand producteur d'acier et d'aluminium. Dans la production de l'automobile la France se trouve au quatrième rang mondial. Les différentes industries chimiques sont aussi très importantes et les noms des entreprises Rhône-Poulenc et Michelin sont connus dans le monde entier.

Les industries de pointe qui exploitent les nouvelles technologies sont importantes dans l'économie française. L'industrie nucléaire française joue un rôle important dans la production d'électricité. La France est un grand exportateur d'armements (on pense tout de suite aux avions Mirage) et est très avancée sur le plan de l'aérospatiale (l'Airbus et l'avion supersonique Concorde). La technologie française a produit le T.G.V. (train à grande vitesse) qui a transformé le réseau ferroviaire en France et en Europe. Dans le domaine de l'informatique, la société Honeywell-Bull, qui fabrique des ordinateurs, et la diffusion du Minitel, le micro-ordinateur possédé par 6 000 000 de Français, sont des exemples importants du progrès de la technologie.

Les industries de luxe restent importantes: le cristal de Baccarat, la porcelaine de Limoges, les parfums de Grasse sont appréciés dans tous les pays du monde. Il ne faut pas oublier l'industrie agro-alimentaire. La France se classe au premier rang parmi les pays de l'Union européenne pour sa production agricole. Les étrangers pensent toujours aux vins et aux fromages, mais la campagne française produit aussi de la viande et cultive une grande variété de fruits et de légumes. La pêche et l'exploitation des forêts sont aussi importantes.

H. Au contraire. Quelle confusion! Alain pose des questions, mais dans chaque cas, c'est le contraire qui est vrai. Écrivez des échanges composés d'une question négative et de la réponse qui indique l'inverse. Suivez le modèle.

MODÈLE les élèves / être en retard / être en avance
➔ —Les élèves ne sont pas en retard?
—Non, ils sont en avance.

1. Claire / arriver ce matin / arriver ce soir

2. Marc et Geneviève / être en classe / être malades

3. toi / avoir sommeil / avoir envie de sortir

4. moi / avoir raison / avoir tort

5. ton frère et toi / prendre le petit déjeuner à la maison / prendre un café à l'université

6. Lise / suivre un régime / prendre du poids

7. vos parents et vous / être en colère / être de bonne humeur

8. toi / sortir / rester à la maison

I. Et en plus. Écrivez des petits échanges composés d'une question négative et d'une réponse affirmative. Ajoutez à la réponse l'élément proposé entre parenthèses. Suivez le modèle.

MODÈLE toi / avoir faim / avoir soif
➔ —Tu n'as pas faim?
—Si, et j'ai soif aussi.

1. il / avoir mal au dos / avoir mal aux jambes

2. faire du vent / faire froid

3. toi / faire les lits chez toi / faire le linge

4. Marianne / jouer du violon / chanter

5. ta sœur et toi / apprendre à parler chinois / apprendre à écrire

6. moi / assister à la conférence / pouvoir aller au concert

J. **Comment est-ce que ça se dit?** Traduisez les questions suivantes en français. Employez l'inversion.

1. Is ecology important?

2. Do animals play an important role in our lives (*singular in French*)?

3. Do people (**les gens**) suffer because of pollution?

4. Are vegetables good for one's health?

5. Are cigarettes harmful (**faire mal**)?

K. **Activité orale.** Quelles questions poseriez-vous à un(e) nouvel(le) étudiant(e) pour parvenir à (*get to*) le (la) connaître? Avec un(e) camarade de classe jouez cette conversation entre deux jeunes qui font connaissance.

L. **La grammaire en action: Des grands titres en forme de questions.** Voici de grands titres à l'interrogatif relevés dans des journaux et des revues français. Remarquez qu'ils emploient tous l'inversion caractéristique du français littéraire. Refaites chaque question avec **est-ce que.**

1. L'ORDINATEUR VA-T-IL ÉCRIRE À NOTRE PLACE?

____

2. **LES LIONS SONT-ILS MALADES DE LA PESTE?**

____

3. **MOREAU A-T-IL DES AMBITIONS PRÉSIDENTIELLES?**

____

4. **LA RUSSIE PEUT-ELLE DEVENIR UNE VRAIE DÉMOCRATIE?**

____

5. **LES NOUVELLES MÉTHODES SCOLAIRES SONT-ELLES VRAIMENT BONNES?**

____

CHAPTER 5

IMPERATIVE

- The imperative is used to give a command or make a request. For most verbs, the imperative is formed by using the **tu, vous,** or **nous** form of the present tense without the subject pronoun. This is true of both positive and negative commands.

Finis tes devoirs. **Ne perds pas** ton temps.	***Finish*** *your homework.* ***Don't waste*** *your time.*
Attendez un moment. **Ne partez pas.**	***Wait*** *a moment.* ***Don't leave.***
Rentrons maintenant. **Ne passons plus** de temps ici.	***Let's go back home*** *now.* ***Let's not spend*** *any more time here.*

- In the imperative **tu** form of regular **-er** verbs, the final **-s** of the present tense form is dropped. The **-s** is also dropped in the imperative **tu** forms of **aller** and **-ir** verbs conjugated like **-er** verbs, such as **ouvrir** and **souffrir.**

Téléphone à tes parents. **N'oublie pas.**	***Call*** *your parents.* ***Don't forget.***
On sonne. **Va. Ouvre** la porte.	*The doorbell is ringing.* ***Go open*** *the door.*

- Some verbs have irregular imperative forms.

être: **sois, soyons, soyez**
avoir: **aie, ayons, ayez**
savoir: **sache, sachons, sachez**

A. Comment être un bon élève. Écrivez les conseils d'un professeur à ses élèves. Employez le négatif de l'impératif.

MODÈLE perdre / vos devoirs → Ne perdez pas vos devoirs.

Vocabulaire utile

Verbes

déchirer *to tear*
laisser *to leave*
mâcher *to chew*
salir *to dirty*

Substantifs

les bandes dessinées *comics*
la calculette *calculator*
la copie *composition, exercises*
le pupitre *student's desk at school*

1. déchirer / vos copies

____

2. laisser / vos crayons sur la table

____

3. manger / dans la salle de classe

4. mâcher / de chewing-gum en classe

5. salir / la salle de classe

6. faire / de bruit

7. jeter / de papiers par terre

8. interrompre / le professeur

9. lire / de bandes dessinées en classe

10. oublier / vos calculettes

B. Projets de vacances. Jean-Claude et Arlette parlent de leurs vacances. À chaque idée de Jean-Claude, Arlette propose une autre possibilité. Employez l'impératif de la première personne du pluriel pour reproduire leur conversation. Suivez le modèle.

MODÈLE —On reste à Paris? (aller en Italie)
→ —Non, ne restons pas à Paris. Allons en Italie.

1. On part la semaine prochaine? (attendre la fin du mois)

2. On prend l'avion? (prendre le train)

3. On descend dans un hôtel de luxe? (choisir une auberge)

4. On visite les monuments en taxi? (louer une voiture)

5. On assiste aux concerts? (aller voir les pièces de théâtre)

6. On mange dans le restaurant de l'hôtel? (dîner dans les restaurants de la ville)

C. Des conseils à une amie qui part. Michèle dit à son amie Ghislaine ce qu'il faut faire pour passer une semaine dans les Alpes. Refaites les phrases suivantes à l'impératif familier. Suivez le modèle.

MODÈLE Il faut faire des projets précis.
➔ Fais des projets précis.

1. D'abord, il faut descendre dans la rue.

____

2. Ensuite, il faut chercher une librairie.

____

3. Là-bas, il faut demander un livre sur les Alpes.

____

4. Il faut rentrer tout de suite à ton appartement.

____

5. Après, il faut lire le livre.

____

6. Il faut choisir ton itinéraire.

____

7. Après, il faut téléphoner à l'agent de voyages.

____

8. Finalement, il faut faire les valises.

____

Note culturelle

Le relief français présente beaucoup de variété. Les plaines du centre-nord et du sud-ouest contrastent avec le terrain plus montagneux du sud et de l'est.

Les massifs, le Massif central, le Massif armoricain (Bretagne), les Ardennes (à la frontière belge) et les Vosges (Alsace), sont de hauts plateaux coupés par des vallées. Ce sont des formations géologiques très anciennes et l'érosion millénaire a réduit la hauteur des montagnes. Les montagnes les plus élevées en France sont les Pyrénées qui séparent la France et l'Espagne, les Alpes sur la frontière italienne et suisse, et le Jura, situé sur la frontière suisse. Ces montagnes sont des formations plus jeunes que les massifs. Le mont Blanc (altitude: 4 807 mètres), un pic alpin, est la montagne la plus élevée de France.

D. De mère en fille. Mme Élouard explique à sa fille ce qu'il faut faire pour acheter une nouvelle robe. Écrivez ses conseils en employant l'impératif familier des verbes indiqués.

MODÈLE prendre le journal ➔ Prends le journal.

1. lire les annonces
2. regarder les rabais
3. aller aux grands magasins
4. essayer les vêtements qui te plaisent
5. choisir une robe
6. payer avec la carte de crédit
7. revenir à la maison
8. mettre ta nouvelle robe

E. On fait des projets. Richard et Zoë vont passer la journée ensemble. Ils expriment leurs idées en employant l'impératif.

MODÈLE passer la journée ensemble
➔ Passons la journée ensemble.

1. aller en ville
2. prendre le train de 9 heures
3. descendre à la gare centrale
4. faire une promenade
5. regarder les vitrines des magasins
6. déjeuner dans un bon restaurant

7. chercher un bon film

8. après le film, flâner dans le jardin public

9. acheter des livres dans une librairie

10. rentrer par le train de 5 heures

F. Ce qu'on doit faire. Véronique donne des conseils à son amie Geneviève. À chaque question de son amie elle répond par un impératif négatif suivi de l'impératif affirmatif du verbe entre parenthèses. Écrivez les réponses en suivant le modèle.

MODÈLE Je dois attendre? (partir tout de suite)
➔ Non, n'attends pas. Pars tout de suite.

1. Je dois mentir? (dire la vérité)

2. Je dois descendre? (rester en haut)

3. Je dois lire le texte? (écrire la composition)

4. Je dois suivre ce régime? (faire du sport)

5. Je dois mincir? (prendre du corps)

6. Je dois préparer le déjeuner? (faire la vaisselle)

7. Je dois nettoyer la cuisine? (balayer l'escalier)

8. Je dois jeter cette robe? (offrir les vieux vêtements aux voisins)

G. Quel enfant! Le fils de Mme Bouvier est toujours en train de faire quelque chose de catastrophique. Employez le négatif de l'impératif familier pour écrire ce qu'elle lui défend de faire. Suivez le modèle.

Vocabulaire utile

Verbes		*Substantifs*	
cacher	*to hide*	**le frigo**	*refrigerator*
débrancher	*to unplug*	**l'ordinateur** *(masc.)*	*computer*
grimper	*to climb*	**le portefeuille**	*wallet*
renverser	*to knock over*	**la poubelle**	*trash can*

MODÈLE jouer avec les allumettes
➔ Ne joue pas avec les allumettes!

1. renverser la bouteille
2. écrire sur les murs
3. débrancher l'ordinateur
4. jeter mon portefeuille à la poubelle
5. dessiner sur mon cahier
6. grimper sur la table
7. laisser le frigo ouvert
8. cacher les clés de la voiture

H. On a des invités ce soir. Les Lary ont invité leurs amis à dîner ce soir. Employez la deuxième personne du pluriel de l'impératif pour écrire ce que Mme Lary demande à ses fils de faire. Suivez le modèle.

MODÈLE être prêts de bonne heure
➔ Soyez prêts de bonne heure.

1. descendre à 7 heures et demie
2. aller à la boulangerie

3. acheter du pain

____

4. traverser la rue

____

5. entrer chez le marchand de légumes

____

6. prendre un kilo d'asperges et de la salade

____

7. passer à la boucherie

____

8. chercher le poulet que j'ai commandé hier

____

9. rentrer tout de suite

____

10. commencer à préparer le dîner

____

I. Comment est-ce que ça se dit? Quels conseils donneriez-vous à un camarade ou à deux camarades pour réussir dans la classe de français? Employez l'impératif.

1. Arrive on time.

   À un camarade: _______________

   À deux camarades: _______________

2. Listen to the teacher.

   À un camarade: _______________

   À deux camarades: _______________

3. Don't sleep in class.

   À un camarade: _______________

   À deux camarades: _______________

4. Never forget the book.

   À un camarade: _______________

   À deux camarades: _______________

5. Answer the questions.

   À un camarade: _______________

   À deux camarades: _______________

6. Repeat after the teacher.

   À un camarade: _______________

   À deux camarades: _______________

7. Try to understand the teacher.

   À un camarade: ______

   À deux camarades: ______

8. Don't bother the other students.

   À un camarade: ______

   À deux camarades: ______

J. Exercice oral. Avec un(e) camarade, jouez une des scènes suivantes:

1. Une mère donne des conseils à son fils quand il commence ses études au collège.
2. Un professeur en colère dit à ses élèves ce qu'ils doivent faire pour avoir une bonne note.
3. Un épicier dit à son commis (*clerk*) ce qu'il doit faire avant l'ouverture du magasin.
4. Deux amis se proposent des activités pour la semaine de vacances en décembre.

K. La grammaire en action. Voici une annonce pour l'Orlybus, un service d'autobus entre Paris et l'aéroport. Elle consiste en quatre impératifs. Lisez-les et refaites-les à la deuxième personne du singulier et à la première personne du pluriel.

Vocabulaire utile

décoller: se dit de l'avion qui quitte la terre
descendre: Les passagers **descendent** de l'autobus à la fin du voyage.
embarquer: monter dans un bateau ou dans un avion; partir en voyage
monter: Les passagers **montent** dans l'autobus.

2ème personne du singulier	1ère personne du pluriel
1. ______	5. ______
2. ______	6. ______
3. ______	7. ______
4. ______	8. ______

Orlybus

ORLY N'A JAMAIS ÉTÉ AUSSI PROCHE

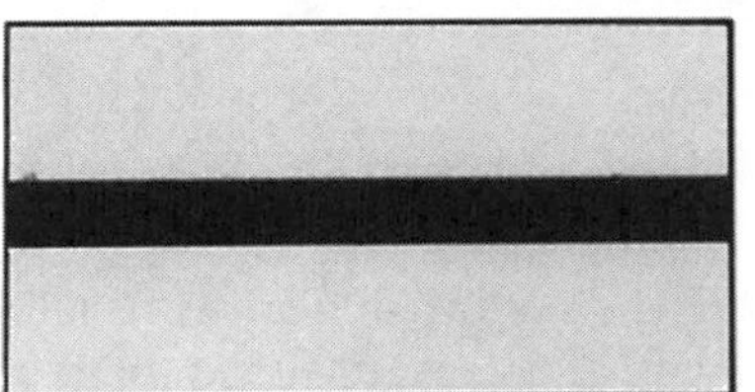

1 - MONTEZ

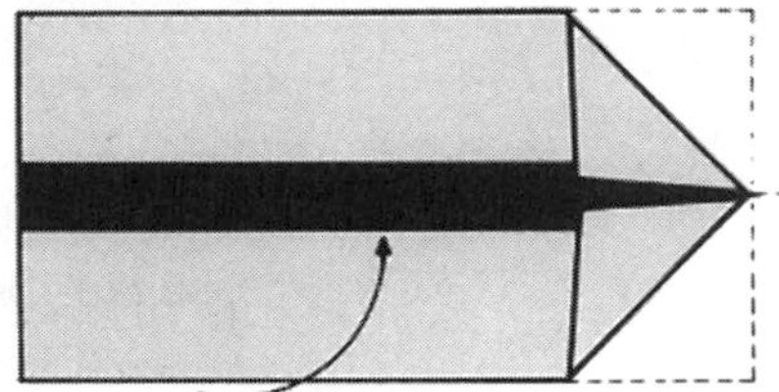

2 - DESCENDEZ

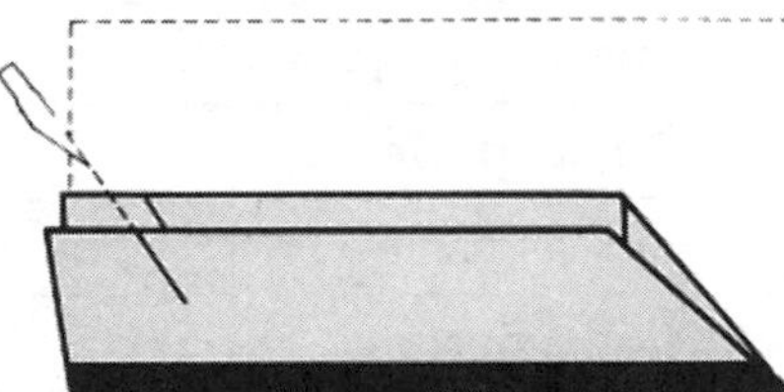

3 - EMBARQUEZ

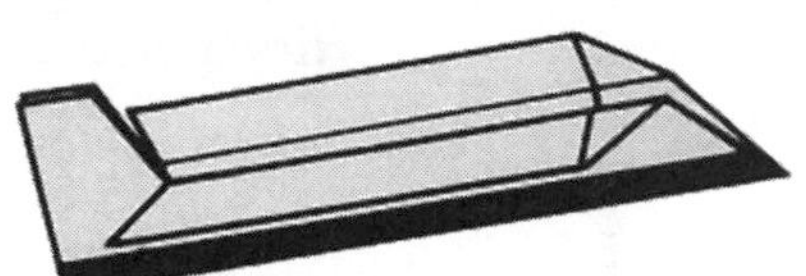

4 - DÉCOLLEZ

CHAPTER 6

PASSÉ COMPOSÉ

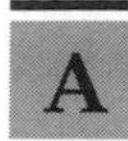

A *Passé composé with **avoir***

- The passé composé is used to express an action completed in the past. The passé composé of most verbs consists of a present tense form of the auxiliary verb **avoir** followed by a past participle. Here is the conjugation of **parler** in the passé composé.

parler *to speak*		
first person	j' **ai parlé**	nous **avons parlé**
second person	tu **as parlé**	vous **avez parlé**
third person	il/elle **a parlé**	ils/elles **ont parlé**

- The past participle of a regular verb is formed by replacing the infinitive ending by the appropriate participle ending: **-é** for **-er** verbs, **-i** for **-ir** verbs, and **-u** for **-re** verbs.

  parl**er** ➔ parl**é**   fin**ir** ➔ fin**i**   vend**re** ➔ vend**u**

  Many common verbs have irregular past participles:

  apprendre ➔ appris
  atteindre ➔ atteint
  avoir ➔ eu
  boire ➔ bu
  comprendre ➔ compris
  conduire ➔ conduit
  connaître ➔ connu
  construire ➔ construit
  courir ➔ couru
  couvrir ➔ couvert
  craindre ➔ craint
  croire ➔ cru
  découvrir ➔ découvert
  devoir ➔ dû
  dire ➔ dit
  écrire ➔ écrit
  être ➔ été
  faire ➔ fait
  instruire ➔ instruit
  joindre ➔ joint
  lire ➔ lu
  mettre ➔ mis
  ouvrir ➔ ouvert
  paraître ➔ paru
  peindre ➔ peint
  pouvoir ➔ pu
  prendre ➔ pris
  produire ➔ produit
  recevoir ➔ reçu
  savoir ➔ su
  souffrir ➔ souffert
  suivre ➔ suivi
  tenir ➔ tenu
  venir ➔ venu
  vivre ➔ vécu
  voir ➔ vu
  vouloir ➔ voulu

- The negative of the passé composé is formed by placing **ne** before the conjugated form of **avoir** and **pas** (or most other negative words) after it.

  —Tu **n'**as **pas** encore fait tes devoirs? — *Have**n't** you done your homework yet?*
  —Non, je **n'**ai **rien** écrit. Je **n'**ai **jamais** eu tant de difficulté. — *No, I have**n't** written anything. I've **never** had so much trouble.*

  Personne and **nulle part,** however, follow the past participle.

  —Tu **n'**as vu **personne** hier soir? — *Did**n't** you see **anyone** last night?*
  —Non. J'ai cherché mes amis partout, mais je **n'**ai rencontré **personne** **nulle part.** — *No. I looked for my friends everywhere, but I did**n't** run into **anyone** **anywhere.***

- When inversion is used to ask a question in the passé composé, the subject pronoun and the auxiliary verb are inverted. In negative questions, the **ne** and **pas** (or most other negative words) are placed around the inverted auxiliary verb and pronoun. Negative questions with inversion in the passé composé are limited to formal language.

—**Les Durand ont-ils décidé** de vendre leur appartement?	***Have the Durands decided*** *to sell their apartment?*
—Oui. **N'avez-vous pas vu** l'annonce dans le journal?	*Yes.* ***Didn't you see*** *the advertisement in the newspaper?*

A. C'était hier. Vous faites la même réponse à toutes les questions de votre ami(e). Employez le passé composé pour lui dire que tout s'est passé hier. Suivez le modèle.

MODÈLE —Vous travaillez aujourd'hui?
➔ —Non. Mais j'ai travaillé hier.

1. Jean nage aujourd'hui?
____
2. Christine et toi, vous déjeunez en ville aujourd'hui?
____
3. Marc prend de l'essence aujourd'hui?
____
4. Toi et moi, nous nettoyons notre chambre aujourd'hui?
____
5. Les étudiants rédigent un thème aujourd'hui?
____
6. Tu apprends le vocabulaire aujourd'hui?
____
7. Jacquot fait le linge aujourd'hui?
____
8. Vous finissez aujourd'hui, vous deux?
____
9. Tu attends tes amis aujourd'hui?
____
10. Alice répond en classe aujourd'hui?
____
11. Les étudiants obtiennent les résultats de l'examen aujourd'hui?
____
12. Le film reprend aujourd'hui?
____

13. Tu as mal à l'estomac aujourd'hui?

____

14. Je suis en avance aujourd'hui?

____

15. Il fait beau aujourd'hui?

____

B. **Une aventure routière.** Jean-Pierre a pris la voiture hier, mais il a eu des difficultés. Refaites son histoire au passé composé pour savoir ce qui lui est arrivé.

L'automobile

au bord de la rue *at the side of the street*
avoir un pneu crevé *to have a flat tire*
faire le plein *to fill up with gas*
faire une promenade en voiture *to go for a ride*
garer la voiture *to park the car*
le pneu *tire*
pousser la voiture *to push the car*
la station-service *gas station*

1. J'invite mon copain Serge à faire une promenade en voiture avec moi.

____

2. Nous décidons d'aller à la campagne.

____

3. Nous faisons le plein avant de partir.

____

4. Tout d'un coup, nous entendons un bruit.

____

5. Nous avons un pneu crevé.

____

6. Nous poussons la voiture au bord du boulevard.

____

7. Nous achetons un nouveau pneu à la station-service.

____

8. Nous dépensons tout notre argent.

____

9. Nous ne pouvons pas aller à la campagne.

____

10. Je remonte le boulevard.

____

11. Je gare la voiture devant mon immeuble.

____

12. Serge et moi, nous passons la journée devant la télé.

____

C. Un nouvel ordinateur. Colette raconte comment elle a acheté un nouvel ordinateur. Refaites son histoire au passé composé.

1. Je décide d'acheter un nouvel ordinateur.

____

2. Mon père et moi, nous lisons une brochure ensemble.

____

3. Nous demandons d'autres brochures.

____

4. Mon père trouve un revendeur (*dealer*) bien informé.

____

5. Nous posons beaucoup de questions au revendeur.

____

6. Il répond patiemment à nos questions.

____

7. Nous choisissons un ordinateur multimédia.

____

8. J'achète des logiciels (*software packages*).

____

9. Mon père trouve des CD-ROM intéressants.

____

10. Je mets mon nouvel ordinateur dans ma chambre.

____

D. Une lettre de son cousin. Marie reçoit une lettre de son cousin François. Pour savoir de quoi il s'agit, formez des phrases au passé composé avec les éléments proposés.

1. Marie / recevoir une lettre

____

2. elle / ouvrir l'enveloppe

____

3. elle / lire la lettre

____

4. son cousin François / écrire la lettre

5. il / être malade

6. il / passer deux semaines à l'hôpital

7. Marie / montrer la lettre à ses parents

8. ils / dire à Marie de téléphoner à François

9. elle / inviter François à passer les vacances chez elle

10. François / accepter

11. il / être très content

12. il / promettre d'arriver au début du mois de juillet

B *Passé composé with* ***être***

- A small number of French verbs form the passé composé with **être** rather than **avoir.** Most of these verbs express motion or describe a change in state. When the passé composé is formed with **être,** the past participle agrees in gender and number with the subject. Study the passé composé of **aller** (*to go*).

je **suis allé(e)**	nous **sommes allé(e)s**
tu **es allé(e)**	vous **êtes allé(e)(s)**
il **est allé** elle **est allée**	ils **sont allés** elles **sont allées**

The following verbs are conjugated with **être** as the auxiliary in the passé composé:

arriver ➔ je **suis arrivé(e)**
descendre ➔ je **suis descendu(e)**
devenir ➔ je **suis devenu(e)**
entrer ➔ je **suis entré(e)**
monter ➔ je **suis monté(e)**
mourir ➔ il (elle) **est mort(e)**
naître ➔ je **suis né(e)**
partir ➔ je **suis parti(e)**
rentrer ➔ je **suis rentré(e)**
rester ➔ je **suis resté(e)**
retourner ➔ je **suis retourné(e)**
sortir ➔ je **suis sorti(e)**
tomber ➔ je **suis tombé(e)**
venir ➔ je **suis venu(e)**

Such verbs are also conjugated with **être** when a prefix is added:

redescendre ➔ je **suis redescendu(e)** *I went back down*
remonter ➔ je **suis remonté(e)** *I went back up*
repartir ➔ je **suis reparti(e)** *I left again*
revenir ➔ je **suis revenu(e)** *I came back*

E. Ma soirée. Marguerite raconte ce qu'elle a fait hier soir. Pour savoir ce qu'elle dit, formez des phrases au passé composé avec les éléments proposés.

1. je / arriver chez moi vers 5 heures et demie

____

2. je / poser mes affaires sur le lit

____

3. je / redescendre

____

4. je / aller au supermarché pour acheter quelque chose à manger

____

5. je / rentrer tout de suite

____

6. je / préparer mon dîner

____

7. Lise et Solange / passer vers 7 heures

____

8. elles / rester une heure

____

9. elles / partir à 8 heures

____

10. je / faire mes devoirs

____

11. je / regarder les informations à la télé

____

12. je / fermer le poste vers 11 heures pour me coucher

____

F. Pas cette fois. Hélène est sortie avec Robert et Richard, les jumeaux. Elle explique à son amie Elvire que cette fois tout a été différent. Utilisez le passé composé pour écrire ses réponses à Elvire. Suivez le modèle.

MODÈLE —Robert et Richard mangent rarement au restaurant.
➔ —Cette fois ils ont mangé au restaurant.

1. Robert et Richard arrivent toujours en retard.

____

2. Robert et Richard parlent toujours du football.

____

3. Ils commandent toujours un sandwich.

____

4. Ils boivent beaucoup de Coca avec le repas.

___

5. Ils sortent toujours la calculette pour vérifier l'addition.

___

6. Ils ne paient jamais.

___

7. Ils ne laissent jamais de pourboire.

___

8. Ils rentrent tout de suite après le repas.

___

G. Dormir à la belle étoile. Nicolas et ses amis sont allés faire du camping. Ils ont eu une surprise pas très agréable dans le bois à côté de la Seine, en amont (*upstream*) de Paris. Pour savoir ce qui s'est passé, formez des phrases au passé composé avec les éléments proposés.

À la campagne

affreux *horrible*
coucher, dormir à la belle étoile *to sleep outdoors*
dresser la tente *to set up the tent*
épuisé *exhausted*
être pris de panique *to be overcome by panic*
ne pas fermer l'œil de la nuit *not to sleep a wink all night*
hurler *to scream, shriek*
plier la tente *to fold up the tent*
ramper *to creep*
le sac de couchage *sleeping bag*

1. trois de mes amis et moi, nous / vouloir coucher à la belle étoile

___

2. nous / aller à la campagne

___

3. nous / camper à côté du fleuve

___

4. Claude et moi, nous / faire un feu

___

5. Marc et Philippe / dresser les tentes

___

6. nous / manger autour du feu

___

7. vers 9 heures, nous / entrer sous nos tentes

8. chacun / entrer dans son sac de couchage

9. soudain, je / entendre un cri affreux

10. Marc / remarquer un serpent sous la tente

11. Philippe et lui / sortir de la tente en courant

12. nous / être pris de panique

13. le serpent / partir en rampant

14. je crois que le pauvre serpent / avoir peur

15. nous / arrêter de hurler

16. chacun / rentrer sous sa tente

17. personne / fermer l'œil de la nuit

18. le matin nous / plier les tentes

19. nous / retourner chez nous

20. tout le monde / être épuisé

Note culturelle

La France est traversée par un réseau de cinq fleuves principaux:

1. La Seine, le fleuve qui traverse Paris, est très navigable. La Seine naît en Bourgogne et se jette dans la Manche, près du port qui s'appelle Le Havre.
2. La Loire est le plus long fleuve de France, mais est peu navigable. Elle n'est pas très profonde, mais ses eaux montent en hiver et produisent des crues violentes. La navigation est possible seulement à partir de la ville de Nantes, dans l'estuaire où la Loire se jette dans l'Atlantique.
3. Le Rhin prend sa source en Suisse et se jette dans la mer du Nord. Il forme la frontière entre la France et l'Allemagne et est navigable pour les péniches. Le Rhin est une source importante d'énergie électrique.
4. Le Rhône naît en Suisse et traverse le lac Léman à la frontière suisse. Il continue vers le sud pour se jeter dans la Méditerranée près de Marseille. Comme celles du Rhin, les eaux du Rhône produisent beaucoup d'électricité.
5. La Garonne prend sa source dans les Pyrénées et se jette dans l'Atlantique à Bordeaux où ses eaux forment un estuaire qui s'appelle la Gironde. Peu navigable à cause de ses eaux violentes, la Garonne fournit beaucoup d'électricité, ses crues servant à faire marcher les turbines des centrales hydroélectriques.

C *Special situations*

- Several verbs usually conjugated with **être** in the passé composé are conjugated with **avoir** when they have direct objects.

monter, descendre

Le chasseur **a monté nos bagages.**	*The bellhop **took up our luggage.***
Mais nous **avons descendu nos valises** tout seuls.	*But we **brought our suitcases down** by ourselves.*

entrer, rentrer, sortir

Je **n'ai pas encore entré les données.**	***I haven't yet entered the data.***
Qui **a rentré le lait**?	*Who **brought in the milk**?*
Elle **a sorti son mouchoir.**	*She **took out her handkerchief.***

- The verb **passer** is conjugated with **être** in the passé composé when it means *to come by, to stop by to see, to visit, to be over.*

Le facteur **est** déjà **passé**.	*The mail carrier **has already come by**.*
Hier ma cousine **est passée** me voir.	*My cousin **stopped by** to see me yesterday.*
Le pire **est passé**.	*The worst **is over**.*

- In most other cases, **passer** is conjugated with **avoir.**

Elle **a passé** son permis de conduire.	*She **took** her driving test.*
Ils **ont passé** une année en Suisse.	*They **spent** a year in Switzerland.*

H. **Quelle journée!** Les Vaillancourt ont eu une journée très compliquée hier. Complétez les phrases suivantes avec le passé composé des verbes entre parenthèses pour savoir tout ce qui s'est passé.

Vocabulaire utile

l'aîné(e) *the older child*
le (la) cadet(te) *the younger child*
étendre le linge sur le fil *to hang the clothes on the line*

1. (sortir) M. Vaillancourt _______________ la voiture du garage à 5 heures du matin.
2. (partir) Il _______________ au travail.
3. (monter) Il _______________ la rue de la République, comme toujours.
4. (voir) Mais aujourd'hui il _______________ qu'il y avait des travaux.
5. (devoir) Il _______________ changer de route.
6. (arriver) Il _______________ en retard.
7. (demander) Mme Vaillancourt _______________ à ses filles de l'aider.
8. (sortir) Elle _______________ au bureau.
9. (faire) L'aînée _______________ le linge.
10. (étendre) La cadette _______________ le linge sur le fil.
11. (descendre) Ensuite, les deux sœurs _______________ faire les courses.
12. (descendre) Elles _______________ l'escalier de l'immeuble.
13. (rentrer) Elles _______________ dans une demi-heure.
14. (monter) Elles _______________ les paquets.
15. (entrer) Quand elles _______________ dans l'appartement,
16. (commencer) il _______________ à pleuvoir.
17. (dire) «Le linge!» _______________ l'aînée.
18. (rentrer) Les deux _______________ le linge à toute vitesse.

D Agreement of the past participle

- The past participle of a verb conjugated with **avoir** agrees in gender and number with a preceding direct object. The preceding direct object may be a noun, an object pronoun, or a relative pronoun.

Quelle **pièce** avez-vous vue?	*Which **play** did you see?*
Combien de **sandwichs** a-t-il mangés?	*How many **sandwiches** did he eat?*
Elle a acheté une nouvelle robe. Elle **l'a mise** aujourd'hui.	*She bought a new dress. She wore **it** today.*
Les fenêtres sont fermées. Personne ne **les** a ouvertes aujourd'hui.	*The windows are closed. No one opened **them** today.*
Il m'a montré **les articles qu'**il a lus.	*He showed me **the articles that** he read.*
On va publier **les histoires qu'**elle a **écrites.**	*They're going to publish **the stories that** she wrote.*

- The past participle does not agree with a preceding indirect object.

Marthe? Je **lui** ai téléphoné.	*Marthe? I called **her** up.*
Et tes parents? Tu **leur** as écrit?	*What about your parents? Did you write **to them**?*

I. Élisabeth s'installe à Paris. Complétez l'histoire suivante avec le participe passé des verbes entre parenthèses. Faites les accords nécessaires.

Élisabeth a __________________ (1. quitter) le Québec pour la France. On lui a __________________ (2. offrir) un bon emploi et elle l'a __________________ (3. accepter). Elle a __________________ (4. faire) ses valises et elle a __________________ (5. prendre) l'avion. Elle est __________________ (6. arriver) à Paris il y a un mois. Elle a tout de suite __________________ (7. commencer) à chercher un appartement. Les annonces qu'elle a __________________ (8. lire) sur le journal promettaient beaucoup, mais les appartements qu'elle a __________________ (9. voir) n'étaient pas très jolis et étaient très chers. Quelqu'un lui a __________________ (10. donner) l'adresse d'une agence immobilière. Elle l'a __________________ (11. chercher). Elle est __________________ (12. entrer) et a __________________ (13. demander) à l'employé de l'aider. Les appartements qu'on lui a __________________ (14. montrer) n'étaient pas mal. L'appartement qu'elle a __________________ (15. choisir) n'était pas loin de son travail. Il se trouvait dans une petite rue qu'elle a __________________ (16. trouver) très agréable. Après, elle a __________________ (17. commencer) à travailler. Au bureau, on l'a __________________ (18. présenter) à tout le monde, et on l'a __________________ (19. accueillir) très amicalement. Elle est très contente à Paris maintenant.

Note culturelle

L'importance de la région parisienne en France est un exemple d'une des caractéristiques de la culture française: la centralisation. À travers l'Ancien Régime, l'Empire de Napoléon et les Républiques, Paris a toujours joué un rôle dominant qu'aucune ville américaine n'a jamais joué dans la vie des USA.

La région parisienne comprend huit départements, 2,2% du territoire national, mais elle a une population de plus de dix millions d'habitants, presque le cinquième de la population française. Paris et sa région sont le centre culturel, économique et politique du pays. Les grands musées, les salles de concerts, l'opéra n'ont pas d'égal en province. 75% des entreprises ont leur siège à Paris ou dans la région. Paris est aussi le centre financier du pays. Comme capitale de la France, Paris regroupe tous les ministères du gouvernement et tous les bureaux officiels. Toutes les ambassades étrangères et beaucoup d'organismes internationaux y sont logés aussi.

J. Lequel? Votre ami(e) s'intéresse à plusieurs de vos affaires. Dans chaque cas demandez-lui s'il s'agit de la chose que vous aviez hier. Employez le verbe entre parenthèses dans votre réponse et faites attention à l'accord du participe passé.

MODÈLE —Fais voir ta calculatrice. (acheter)
➔ —La calculatrice que j'ai achetée hier?

1. Montre-moi tes devoirs. (faire)

____

2. Je peux lire la lettre de Michèle? (recevoir)

____

3. Où est ta composition? (rédiger)

____

4. Tu as un nouveau sac à dos? (acheter)

____

5. Fais voir ton appareil photo. (employer)

____

6. Montre-moi ta nouvelle cassette vidéo. (regarder)

____

7. Je peux écouter tes nouveaux disques compacts? (écouter)

____

8. Fais voir tes nouvelles chaussures. (mettre)

____

9. Je veux voir tes lunettes de soleil. (porter)

____

10. Tu me prêtes les revues? (lire)

____

K. Au cinéma. Racontez en français cette histoire de Sébastien et Berthe.

1. Yesterday I called Berthe.
2. I asked her, "Do you want to go the movies?"
3. She answered, "Yes."
4. I went by to pick her up at seven o'clock.
5. She came downstairs and we took the bus.
6. We got to (= *arrived at*) the movie theater at 7:30.
7. I bought the tickets right away.
8. Berthe and I looked for a café.
9. We had a cup of coffee and a pastry.
10. I looked at my watch.
11. I said, "It's 7:55."
12. We quickly went back to the movie theater and went in.

L. Exercice oral. Avec un(e) camarade parlez des choses que vous avez faites hier. Après, racontez à un(e) autre camarade les choses que vous avez faites tous les deux. Employez le passé composé dans votre conversation.

M. La grammaire en action. Lisez ces annonces placées dans un guide touristique par des restaurants parisiens. Après, reliez les descriptions de la colonne de gauche au nom de l'établissement auquel elles font allusion.

LE PETIT BEDON
38, rue Pergolèse - 75016 Paris
- Monsieur Marchesseau a confié la direction du «Petit Bedon» au directeur le plus connu de Paris, Claude Guibert.

- Verbs whose stem ends in **i** have two **i**'s in the **nous** and **vous** forms of the imperfect.

  nous étud**ii**ons   vous étud**ii**ez

- All verbs are regular in the imperfect except **être.**

être	
j' ét**ais**	nous ét**ions**
tu ét**ais**	vous ét**iez**
il/elle ét**ait**	ils/elles ét**aient**

A. Avant c'était différent. Avec le présent et l'imparfait construisez des phrases qui expliquent que tout a changé. Suivez le modèle.

MODÈLE je / travailler tous les jours
➔ Je ne travaille plus tous les jours. Avant je travaillais tous les jours.

1. vous / croire à cette histoire

   ____

2. il / lire en allemand

   ____

3. elles / faire les carreaux

   ____

4. tu / habiter en ville

   ____

5. ils / vivre bien

   ____

6. mon chien / obéir

   ____

7. elle / rougir

   ____

8. je / répondre en classe

   ____

9. tu / voyager

   ____

10. elle / prononcer correctement

    ____

11. vous / apprécier la musique classique

    ____

12. ils / ranger leurs affaires

    ____

B. Ma jeunesse. Caroline parle de son enfance. Formez des phrases à l'imparfait pour savoir comment elle vivait à l'époque.

1. nous / avoir une maison dans un quartier tranquille
2. elle / être grande
3. la maison / avoir dix pièces
4. mes parents / travailler en ville
5. ils / aller au bureau en autobus
6. l'arrêt / être au coin de la rue
7. beaucoup d'autres jeunes filles / habiter dans notre rue
8. je / jouer avec elles
9. nous / aller à l'école ensemble
10. je / garder souvent ma petite sœur Marguerite
11. je / l'emmener au parc
12. nous / être tous très contents

C. Grand-mère évoque son enfance. La grand-mère de Nicolas raconte ses souvenirs. Formez des phrases à l'imparfait pour savoir ce qu'elle dit.

1. nous / vivre à la campagne
2. je / partager une chambre avec ma sœur
3. nous / ne pas avoir beaucoup d'argent
4. mais on / être heureux

5. je / nager dans le lac

6. les enfants / courir dans les champs

7. mes parents / élever des vaches

8. nous / vendre le lait

9. ton grand-père / commencer à venir me voir

10. je / avoir 18 ans

D. Nos vacances à l'époque. Un groupe d'amis évoque les souvenirs de leurs vacances quand ils étaient jeunes. Formez des phrases à l'imparfait pour savoir comment ils ont passé leurs vacances. Faites attention aux adverbes de temps utilisés dans les phrases.

MODÈLE Alfred: tous les ans / nous / aller / à la campagne
➔ Nous allions tous les ans à la campagne.

1. Lise: souvent / je / passer les vacances / chez ma tante

2. Michel: toujours / je / vouloir / aller au bord de la mer

3. Christine: chaque été / ma famille et moi, nous / visiter / une région de France

4. Paul: tous les ans / mes cousins / m'inviter / chez eux

5. Marianne: le plus souvent / nous, on / prendre les vacances en hiver

6. Robert: en général / ma cousine Élisabeth / venir / chez nous à Paris

7. Françoise: d'habitude / nous / partir / en Suisse

8. Guy: tous les étés / mon père / louer / un appartement à Nice

B *Uses of the imperfect tense: The imperfect contrasted with the passé composé*

- The imperfect tense focuses on past actions or conditions as processes rather than as completed events. It emphasizes the action or condition itself rather than its beginning or end. One use of the imperfect is to express repeated or ongoing actions in the past.

—Qu'est-ce que tu **faisais** quand tu **habitais** à Cannes?	*What **did** you **use to do** when you **lived** in Cannes?*
—J'**allais** tous les jours à la plage.	*I **would go** to the beach every day.*
—Est-ce que tu **avais** des cours l'après-midi?	***Did** you **use to have** classes in the afternoon?*
—Non, j'**étais** à la faculté le matin. L'après-midi j'**allais** au travail.	*No, I **used to be** at the university in the morning. In the afternoon I **used to go** to work.*

- The imperfect is also used to describe things and people in the past.

Mes amis **étaient** tous diligents. Ils **étudiaient** sérieusement et **s'intéressaient** à leur travail. Mais ils **savaient** s'amuser aussi. Ils **étaient** tous très gentils et les professeurs du lycée les **trouvaient** sympathiques et intelligents.	*My friends **were** all diligent. They **studied** seriously and **took an interest** in their work. But they **knew how** to have a good time too. They **were** all very nice and the high school teachers **found** them pleasant and intelligent.*

- The passé composé, in contrast to the imperfect, expresses specific actions and events that were started and completed at a specific time in the past.

J'**ai pris** le petit déjeuner, j'**ai mis** mon manteau et je **suis sorti.**	*I **had** breakfast, **put on** my coat, and **left** the house.*

- The imperfect and the passé composé may appear in the same sentence. The imperfect provides the background for the event stated in the passé composé. In such instances, the imperfect may describe time, weather, or an action that was going on when another event happened.

Il **était** 7 heures et demie quand elle **est rentrée.**	*It **was** 7:30 when she **returned home.***
Quand on **est sortis** du restaurant, il **pleuvait.**	*When we **left** the restaurant it **was raining**.*
Je **lisais** quand Jacques **a frappé** à la porte.	*I **was reading** when Jacques **knocked** at the door.*

E. Un temps trop variable. Jeanine a vu pas mal de changements atmosphériques pendant sa journée. Formez des phrases avec les éléments proposés en employant un imparfait et un passé composé pour savoir ce qui lui est arrivé.

Modèle faire du soleil / je / descendre prendre l'autobus
→ Il faisait du soleil quand je suis descendue prendre l'autobus.

1. faire du vent / je / arriver à l'arrêt

____

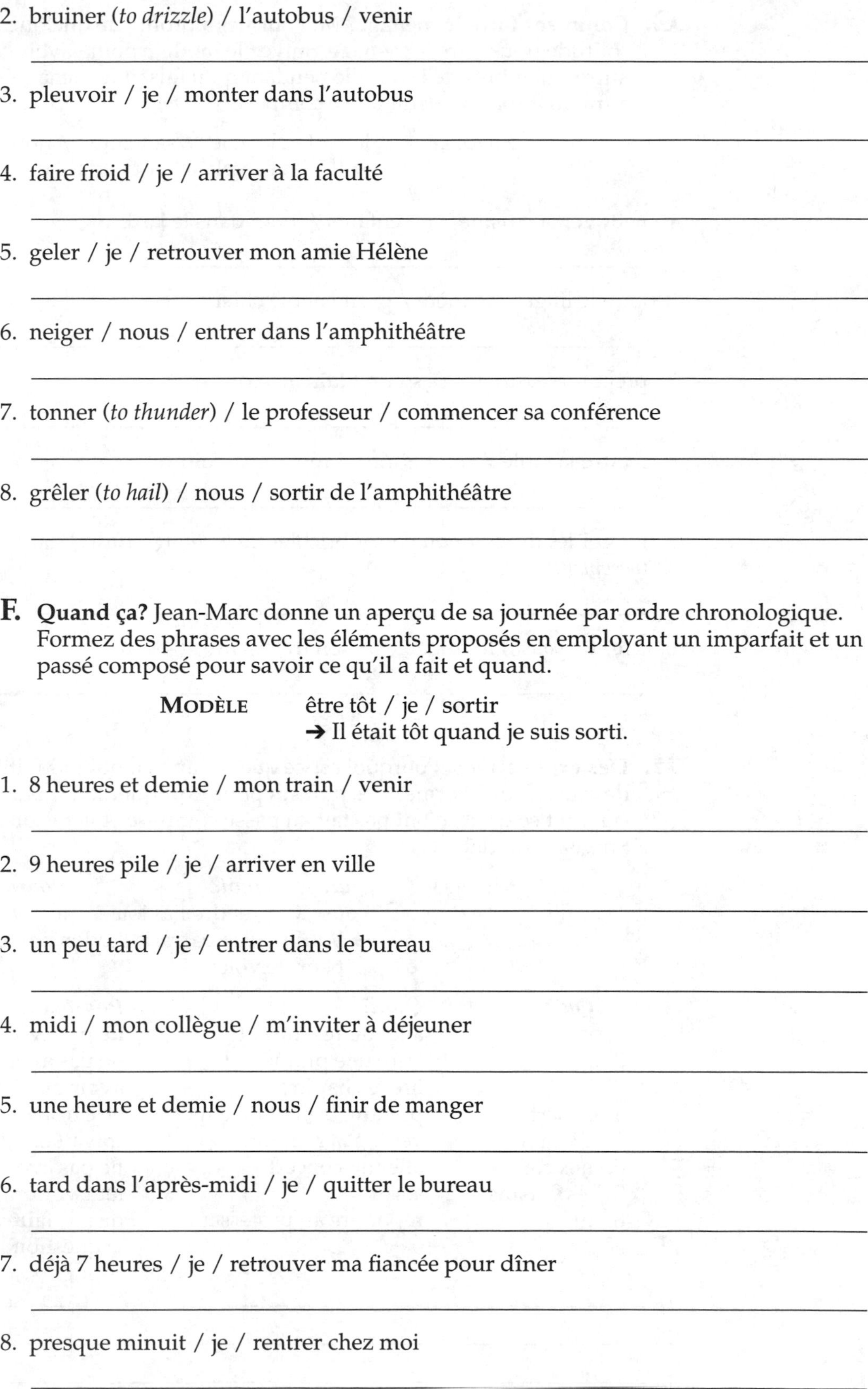

2. bruiner (*to drizzle*) / l'autobus / venir

____

3. pleuvoir / je / monter dans l'autobus

____

4. faire froid / je / arriver à la faculté

____

5. geler / je / retrouver mon amie Hélène

____

6. neiger / nous / entrer dans l'amphithéâtre

____

7. tonner (*to thunder*) / le professeur / commencer sa conférence

____

8. grêler (*to hail*) / nous / sortir de l'amphithéâtre

____

F. Quand ça? Jean-Marc donne un aperçu de sa journée par ordre chronologique. Formez des phrases avec les éléments proposés en employant un imparfait et un passé composé pour savoir ce qu'il a fait et quand.

MODÈLE être tôt / je / sortir
→ Il était tôt quand je suis sorti.

1. 8 heures et demie / mon train / venir

____

2. 9 heures pile / je / arriver en ville

____

3. un peu tard / je / entrer dans le bureau

____

4. midi / mon collègue / m'inviter à déjeuner

____

5. une heure et demie / nous / finir de manger

____

6. tard dans l'après-midi / je / quitter le bureau

____

7. déjà 7 heures / je / retrouver ma fiancée pour dîner

____

8. presque minuit / je / rentrer chez moi

____

G. Comment faire le ménage? M. Fournier a profité de quelques moments de solitude pour faire le ménage. Suivez le modèle pour savoir ce que faisaient les autres membres de la famille pendant qu'il faisait le ménage. Chaque phrase aura un imparfait et un passé composé.

MODÈLE laver le plancher / sa femme / dormir
➔ Il a lavé le plancher pendant que sa femme dormait.

1. nettoyer la cuisine / les enfants / jouer dans le jardin

____

2. faire le linge / sa mère / promener le chien

____

3. préparer le dîner / sa sœur / faire les courses

____

4. mettre la table / son fils aîné / réparer la voiture

____

5. ranger les livres / son père / bricoler (*to fix things, tinker*) dans le sous-sol (*basement*)

____

6. cirer (*to polish*) les meubles / son frère / lire le journal

____

H. Des explications. Pourquoi est-ce que ces amis n'ont pas fait les choses qu'ils devaient faire? Formez des phrases pour expliquer leur manque d'action en écrivant ce qu'ils n'ont pas fait au passé composé et la raison à l'imparfait. Suivez le modèle.

MODÈLE

Qui?	*Quoi?*	*Pourquoi?*
vous	prendre l'avion	avoir peur de voler

➔ Vous n'avez pas pris l'avion parce que vous aviez peur de voler.

	Qui?	*Quoi?*	*Pourquoi?*
1.	je	aller au restaurant	ne pas avoir envie de sortir
2.	nous	faire une promenade	ne pas avoir le temps
3.	je	lire le chapitre	avoir mal à la tête
4.	Albert	prendre le petit déjeuner	être trop occupé
5.	Chantal	venir à la réunion	travailler
6.	nos copains	aller au concert	ne pas avoir d'argent
7.	les voisins	sortir	leur voiture être en panne
8.	tu	répondre au professeur	ne pas faire attention à sa question

1. ______________________________
2. ______________________________
3. ______________________________
4. ______________________________
5. ______________________________

6. ____________________
7. ____________________
8. ____________________

I. On se souvient de Josette. Un groupe d'amis parle du moment où chacun a fait la connaissance de Josette. Écrivez ce qu'ils disent en suivant le modèle.

MODÈLE avoir dix-huit ans
➔ Quand j'ai connu Josette, elle avait dix-huit ans.

1. être étudiante
____
2. travailler déjà
____
3. être institutrice
____
4. sortir avec Frédéric
____
5. être mariée
____
6. avoir deux enfants
____

J. Dormir (mal) à la campagne. Alain et Guy ont passé une mauvaise nuit sous leur tente à cause du sale temps qu'il faisait. Formez des phrases pour raconter leur mésaventure. Les deux propositions seront à l'imparfait.

MODÈLE faire du soleil / ils / voyager en voiture
➔ Il faisait du soleil pendant qu'ils voyageaient en voiture.

1. le ciel / être couvert / ils / chercher un endroit pour camper
____
2. bruiner / les deux garçons / dresser leur tente
____
3. pleuvoir / Guy / faire un feu
____
4. faire du vent / Alain / cuisiner
____
5. la température / baisser / ils / manger
____

6. des éclairs / illuminer le ciel / ils / ouvrir les sacs de couchage

7. tonner / les deux garçons / essayer de dormir

8. mais le matin / faire beau / ils / plier leur tente

C *Other uses of the imperfect tense*

- The imperfect is used with time expressions to describe an action that started in the past and was still going on when another action occurred.

—Depuis combien de temps y avait-il que **vous habitiez** à Paris quand on vous a offert le poste à Perpignan?	*For how long **had you been living** in Paris when they offered you the job in Perpignan?*
—Il y avait dix ans que **j'étais** à Paris quand je suis parti pour le Languedoc.	***I had been** in Paris for ten years when I left for Languedoc.*

Note that the phrases used before the time expressions are also in the imperfect: **combien de temps y avait-il que, il y avait dix ans que.**

- **Si** plus the imperfect tense makes a suggestion, similar to English *How about . . . ?* or *What if . . . ?* It is especially common with either **nous** or **on** as the subject. With **tu** or **vous** it can express impatience or irritation.

Si nous **sortions**?	***How about going out?***
Si on **partait** déjà?	***What if** we **leave** now?*
—**Si** nous nous **dépêchions** un peu? —Et **si** tu te **taisais**?	***How about if** we **hurry up**?* *And **how about if** you **keep quiet**?*

K. L'imprévu. Dites combien de temps ces gens faisaient ce qu'ils faisaient quand quelque chose d'imprévu est arrivé. Traduisez les phrases en anglais.

MODÈLE je / regarder la télé / une heure / Mon cousin a frappé à la porte.
→ Je regardais la télé depuis une heure quand mon cousin a frappé à la porte. *ou*
Il y avait (Ça faisait) une heure que je regardais la télé quand mon cousin a frappé à la porte.
I had been watching TV for an hour when my cousin knocked at the door.

1. vous / attendre le bus / vingt minutes / Jean-Claude est venu vous prendre avec sa voiture.

2. nous / étudier à la bibliothèque / six heures / Christine nous a invités à dîner chez elle.

3. Odile / dormir / dix minutes / Le téléphone a sonné.

____

____

4. Sylvain / entrer des données / deux heures / Il y a eu une panne d'électricité (*power failure*).

____

____

5. Brigitte / faire du jogging / une heure / Il a commencé à pleuvoir.

____

____

6. Alain / ranger ses affaires / dix minutes / Ses amis l'ont appelé pour jouer au football.

____

____

L. J'ai une idée! Marcelle s'ennuie. Son amie Claire lui propose des activités. Écrivez deux fois ses idées, une fois avec **nous,** la seconde avec **on.** Suivez le modèle.

MODÈLE aller au cinéma ➔ a. Si nous allions au cinéma?
b. Si on allait au cinéma?

1. jouer aux cartes
   a. ______________________________
   b. ______________________________
2. acheter le journal
   a. ______________________________
   b. ______________________________
3. passer chez Françoise
   a. ______________________________
   b. ______________________________
4. regarder un film à la télé
   a. ______________________________
   b. ______________________________
5. manger au restaurant
   a. ______________________________
   b. ______________________________
6. commencer nos devoirs
   a. ______________________________
   b. ______________________________

D Special meanings of certain verbs

- Some common verbs have different meanings in the imperfect and the passé composé.

savoir
Il **savait** l'adresse. — *He **knew** the address.*
Il **a su** l'adresse. — *He **found out** the address.*

connaître
Tu **connaissais** mon voisin? — ***Did** you **know** my neighbor?*
Tu **as connu** mon voisin? — ***Did** you **meet** my neighbor?*

pouvoir
Il **ne pouvait pas** sortir. — *He **couldn't** go out. (It was hard for him.)*
Il **n'a pas pu** sortir. — *He **couldn't** (and didn't) go out.*

vouloir
Je **voulais** partir. — *I **wanted** to leave.*
J'ai **voulu** partir. — *I **tried** to leave.*
Je **ne voulais pas** partir. — *I **didn't want** to leave.*
Je **n'ai pas voulu** partir. — *I **refused** to leave.*

avoir
Elle **avait** faim. — *She **was** hungry.*
Elle **a eu** faim. — *She **got** hungry.*

The imperfect forms of **pouvoir** and **vouloir** don't indicate whether the action of the infinitive took place or not.

M. Comment dit-on cela en français? Donnez l'équivalent français de ces phrases en anglais. Faites attention aux exemples ci-dessus.

1. Did you (**vous**) know the name of the street where she lives?
No, but I found it out this morning.

____

____

2. Did they want to spend the day in town?
Yes, but they couldn't.

____

____

3. I was able to work yesterday, but I refused to leave the house.

____

4. Did you (**tu**) get the letter yesterday?
No, I'd had the letter for a week.

____

____

5. Did you (**vous**) meet the professor?
   I knew him already.

   ____

   ____

N. Une visite au musée. Racontez cette histoire au passé en choisissant pour chaque verbe soit l'imparfait, soit le passé composé selon le cas.

Je/J' ___*suis allé(e)___ (aller) au musée. Je/J' ________________

(1. vouloir) voir les peintures de la Renaissance. Je/J' ________________

(2. entrer) d'abord dans les salles italiennes qui ________________ (3. être) à

côté des salles françaises. Il y ________________ (4. avoir) beaucoup de

tableaux très intéressants. Je/J' ________________ (5. voir) des peintures

fabuleuses. Après, je/j' ________________ (6. passer) aux salles françaises.

Ensuite, je/j' ________________ (7. monter) voir l'art du 20ème siècle. J'y

________________ (8. trouver) des œuvres fantastiques. Après une heure,

je/j' ________________ (9. descendre) à la librairie parce que

je/j' ________________ (10. vouloir) acheter des cartes postales.

J'y ________________ (11. remarquer) deux livres sur l'art qui

me/m' ________________ (12. intéresser) beaucoup, mais je

ne/n' ________________ (13. avoir) pas assez d'argent pour les acheter.

Je ne/n'________________ (14. acheter) que deux cartes postales.

Je/J' ________________ 15. (décider) de rentrer demain pour acheter les

deux livres.

O. Fernand cherche du travail. Racontez cette histoire au passé en choisissant pour chaque verbe soit l'imparfait, soit le passé composé selon le cas.

Fernand Bercot ___*voulait*___ (vouloir) travailler à Paris. Donc, il

________________ (1. quitter) son petit village dans la Gironde et

il ________________ (2. prendre) le train pour Paris.

Il ________________ (3. arriver) dans la capitale il y a trois ans. Il

n'________________ (4. avoir) même pas une chambre et il n'y

________________ (5. connaître) personne. Mais dans une semaine il ________________ (6. trouver) un poste de garçon de café. Il ________________ (7. falloir) travailler beaucoup, mais il ________________ (8. recevoir) pas mal de pourboires. Il ________________ (9. vivre) dans une chambre d'hôtel très modeste pour faire des économies. Après un an et demi il ________________ (10. renoncer) à son travail. Il ________________ (11. inviter) son frère Joseph à le rejoindre à Paris. Fernand ________________ (12. mettre) assez d'argent de côté pour monter un café. Son frère et lui ________________ (13. ouvrir) un petit bistrot dans le quinzième arrondissement. Ils ________________ (14. être) ouvriers, mais maintenant ils ________________ (15. devenir) propriétaires d'un café!

Notes culturelles

- La Gironde est un département de l'ouest de la France dont le chef-lieu est le grand port atlantique de Bordeaux. Ce département est situé dans une grande région viticole qui produit des vins français très connus: Médoc, Saint-Émilion, Sauternes.
- Paris est divisé en vingt arrondissements, chacun possédant une mairie où se trouvent les bureaux administratifs. Il existe aussi un maire de la ville de Paris. Jacques Chirac, élu président de la France en 1995, avait été élu maire de Paris à trois reprises: en 1977, en 1983 et en 1989.

P. Hier, nous avons . . . Causez avec un(e) camarade au sujet de la journée que vous (et vos copains) avez passée hier. Pour chaque (ou pour presque chaque) action que vous mentionnez, décrivez aussi les circonstances: l'heure, le temps qu'il faisait, les actions des autres, etc. Comparez votre journée avec celle de votre camarade.

Q. Michel Fugain, chanteur. Lisez l'article suivant adapté de *France-Soir,* un quotidien parisien, et répondez aux questions ci-dessous.

FUGAIN

BIG STORY

Avec son nouvel album «Plus ça va», Michel est devenu son propre producteur et a quitté son personnage «d'enfant attardé». Il trouve que même sa voix a changé!

Le nouvel album de Michel Fugain «Plus ça va» vient de sortir (EMI) et le rend un soupçon fébrile. Il a aussi prévu le Casino de Paris pour octobre avec une tournée avant et après.

J'ai hâte de me retrouver sur scène. La dernière fois, en 1993, on a tellement turbiné qu'on est arrivés sur les genoux. Mais quand même, c'est le bonheur.

Fugain a cultivé une voix à «caractère». Ce nouvel album, tramé d'histoires d'amour, a été enregistré à Léon, dans les Landes, avec la complicité d'auteurs inspirés comme Claude Lemesle, Kent et Brice Homs.

«Ma voix a changé, dit-il, je me suis aperçu que j'avais enfin mon âge. J'ai essayé de passer un mot simple et fort. Avant j'étais un adolescent attardé. Je dois cette progression à l'arrivée au monde de mon dernier fils, 2 ans.»

Ce garçon, toujours bouillant, est enfin devenu un homme. Il est donc trois fois papa et même «jeune papa», précise-t-il. Et il s'annonce producteur de son propre album. Une façon pour lui de prendre son destin en main.

La vague hippie avait laissé des pétales de fleur autour des campus. L'ambiance était baignée d'une fraîcheur naïve. C'était l'époque bénie, où l'on refaisait le monde tous les matins. «On a vécu, après 68, une explosion totale, les enfants comme le succès. Tout allait bien, mais vite. Nous n'avions pas le temps de réaliser.»

Michel Fugain s'accorde, après le tourbillon, cinq années de pause.

«J'ai glandé. Voilà! Mais vraiment glandé. Je me demandais si vraiment je devais reprendre. Il faut préciser que plus personne ne me voulait.» Michel Fugain estime qu'il revient de loin.

Vocabulaire

s'apercevoir *to notice*
attardé *slow*
avoir hâte de *to be eager to*
béni *blessed*
bouillant *fiery*
enregistrer *to record*
fébrile *feverish, excited*
glander (*slang*) *to do nothing, loll around*
passer un mot *to send a message*
prévoir *to plan*
un soupçon *a small amount*
le tourbillon *whirlwind*
la tournée *tour*
tramé de *woven with*
turbiner (*slang*) *to work*

Notes culturelles

- Tous les grands chanteurs passent par Le Casino, une grande salle de variétés au centre de Paris.
- Les Landes est une région de l'ouest de la France, sur la côte atlantique. L'intérieur est une grande plaine sableuse plantée d'une vaste forêt de pins.
- L'année 1968 a été caractérisée par une révolte des étudiants de Paris qui a mené a des émeutes (*riots*) dans la capitale et à l'introduction des styles hippie en France.

Indiquez si ces phrases sont vraies ou fausses d'après l'article que vous avez lu.

_____ 1. «Plus ça va» est le nom du nouvel album de Michel Fugain.

_____ 2. Il ne fait pas de tournées cette année parce qu'il va chanter au Casino de Paris.

_____ 3. Il n'a pas beaucoup envie de chanter au Casino.

_____ 4. La naissance de son troisième enfant l'a rendu plus adolescent que jamais.

_____ 5. Fugain a été le producteur de son dernier album.

_____ 6. Après 1968, il a eu très peu de succès.

_____ 7. Il a abandonné sa carrière pendant cinq ans.

_____ 8. Michel ne savait pas s'il devait recommencer sa carrière de chanteur.

CHAPTER 8

REFLEXIVE VERBS

A Conjugation and use of reflexive verbs

- Reflexive verbs are called *pronominal verbs* in French because they always appear with an object pronoun that refers to the same person or thing as the subject.

se réveiller (*to wake up*)	
je **me** réveille	nous **nous** réveillons
tu **te** réveilles	vous **vous** réveillez
il/elle **se** réveille on **se** réveille	ils/elles **se** réveillent

- The reflexive pronoun usually precedes the conjugated verb.

—Je **me lève** toujours de bonne heure.	*I always* ***get up*** *early.*
—Et est-ce que tu **te couches** aussi de bonne heure?	*And do you also* ***go to bed*** *early?*
—Non, je ne **m'endors** pas avant minuit.	*No, I don't* ***fall asleep*** *before midnight.*

Note that in a negative sentence, **ne** precedes the reflexive pronoun and **pas** follows the conjugated verb.

- Reflexive verbs are used to express many routine actions.

se brosser les cheveux *to brush one's hair*
se brosser les dents *to brush one's teeth*
se coucher *to go to bed*
se couper les cheveux *to cut one's hair*
se couper/se limer les ongles *to cut/file one's nails*
se déshabiller *to get undressed*
s'endormir *to fall asleep*
s'habiller *to get dressed*
se laver *to wash up*
se laver la tête *to wash one's hair*
se laver les mains, la figure *to wash one's hands, one's face*
se lever *to get up*
se maquiller *to put on makeup*
se peigner *to comb one's hair*
se raser *to shave*
se reposer *to rest*
se sécher les cheveux *to dry one's hair*

Note that when a body part receives the action of a reflexive verb, the definite article is used to express possession.

A. **Jumeaux (*Twins*).** Jérôme et Paul sont des jumeaux. Paul décrit leur journée. Suivez le modèle.

Modèle se réveiller à 7 heures
→ Je me réveille à 7 heures.
Jérôme se réveille à 7 heures aussi.

Le matin

1. se lever tout de suite

2. se brosser les dents

3. se peigner

4. se raser

5. s'habiller

Le soir

6. se laver les mains

7. se laver la figure

8. se reposer

9. se coucher à 11 heures

10. s'endormir tout de suite

B. C'est la mère des jumeaux qui parle. Maintenant c'est la mère de Jérôme et de Paul qui décrit leur journée typique. Suivez le modèle.

MODÈLE se réveiller à 7 heures
➔ Ils se réveillent à 7 heures.

Le matin

1. se lever tout de suite
____
2. se brosser les dents
____
3. se peigner
____
4. se raser
____
5. s'habiller
____

Le soir

6. se laver les mains
____
7. se laver la figure
____
8. se reposer
____
9. se coucher à 11 heures
____
10. s'endormir tout de suite
____

C. Notre journée. Marthe et Vivienne décrivent une matinée typique. Employez dans chaque cas la première personne du pluriel pour savoir ce qu'elles font.

MODÈLE se réveiller de bonne heure
➔ Nous nous réveillons de bonne heure.

1. se lever immédiatement
____
2. se laver les mains et la figure
____
3. se brosser les dents
____

4. se laver la tête

___

5. se sécher les cheveux

___

6. se maquiller

___

7. se peigner

___

8. se brosser les cheveux

___

9. se limer les ongles

___

10. s'habiller avec soin

___

D. Au cinéma. Jacques raconte sa sortie au cinéma avec ses copains. Formez des phrases avec les éléments donnés pour voir ce qui s'est passé.

Vocabulaire utile

s'approcher de *to approach*
s'arrêter *to stop*
s'asseoir *to sit down*
se dépêcher *to hurry up*
se diriger vers *to head towards*
s'éloigner de *to move away from*
s'installer *to move in, settle in*
se promener *to take a walk*
se réunir *to get together*
se trouver *to be located*

1. je /se réunir / avec mes copains

___

2. ils / se trouver / dans un café du centre

___

3. je / s'approcher / du café

___

4. mes copains / se lever

___

5. nous / s'éloigner du café

___

6. nous / se diriger / vers le cinéma

___

7. nous / se dépêcher

8. nous / s'arrêter au guichet pour prendre les billets

9. nous entrons dans le cinéma et nous / s'asseoir

B *The infinitive of reflexive verbs*

- When the infinitive of a reflexive verb is used with another verb, such as **aller, pouvoir,** or **vouloir,** the reflexive pronoun precedes the infinitive and agrees with the subject.

—**Tu** vas **te** promener?	*Are **you** going to take a walk?*
—**Je** veux **me** promener, mais je ne peux pas.	***I** want to take a walk, but I can't.*
—**Vous** devez **vous** dépêcher un peu.	***You** must hurry up.*
—**Nous** allons **nous** fâcher si vous ne vous taisez pas.	***We**'re going to get angry if you don't keep still.*

- Such constructions are negated by putting **ne . . . pas** around the conjugated verb.

Je **ne** vais **pas** me promener.	*I'm **not** going to take a walk.*
Nous **ne** voulons **pas** nous dépêcher.	*We do**n't** want to hurry.*

E. Sentiments. Exprimez les sentiments et les réactions des gens indiqués en utilisant un verbe à l'infinitif.

MODÈLE Jean / aller / s'amuser → Jean va s'amuser.

Les émotions

s'amuser *to have a good time*
s'animer *to feel more lively*
se calmer *to calm down*
s'embêter *to be/get bored*
s'énerver *to get nervous, upset*
s'ennuyer *to be/get bored*
s'enthousiasmer *to get enthusiastic*
se fâcher *to get angry*
s'impatienter *to get impatient*
s'inquiéter *to worry*
se mettre en colère *to get angry*
s'offenser *to get insulted, offended*
se passionner (pour) *to get excited (about)*
se préoccuper *to worry*
se sentir *to feel*

1. je / ne pas vouloir / s'inquiéter

2. vous / devoir / se calmer

3. il / ne pas pouvoir / se sentir triste

4. elles / ne pas vouloir / s'ennuyer

____

5. tu / ne pas devoir / se mettre en colère

____

6. nous / ne pas aller / s'offenser

____

7. le professeur / aller / s'impatienter

____

8. tu / devoir / s'animer

____

F. **Cette fois ça va être différent.** Employez **aller** suivi d'un infinitif pour exprimer que cette fois les sentiments vont changer. Suivez le modèle.

MODÈLE il / s'amuser
➔ En général, il ne s'amuse pas, mais cette fois il va s'amuser.

1. je / se fâcher

____

2. elles / s'énerver

____

3. tu / s'impatienter

____

4. il / s'offenser

____

5. nous / s'inquiéter

____

6. vous / s'embêter

____

7. je / se sentir de trop (*in the way*)

____

8. tu / se passionner

____

G. **Conseils psychologiques.** Employez le verbe **devoir** suivi d'un infinitif pour donner des conseils pour maîtriser les émotions. Suivez le modèle.

MODÈLE tu / ne pas devoir / s'énerver
➔ Tu ne dois pas t'énerver.

1. vous / devoir / se calmer

____

2. elle / devoir / s'amuser un peu

____

3. je / devoir / se sentir heureux (heureuse)

____

4. nous / ne pas devoir / se mettre en colère

____

5. ils / devoir / s'enthousiasmer

____

6. tu / ne pas devoir / s'impatienter

____

7. je / devoir / s'animer un peu

____

8. vous / ne pas devoir / s'offenser

____

The passé composé of reflexive verbs

- All reflexive verbs are conjugated with **être** in the passé composé. The reflexive pronoun is placed immediately before the conjugated form of **être,** and the past participle agrees in gender and number with the reflexive pronoun if that pronoun is a direct object.

se laver (*to wash up*)	
je **me suis lavé(e)**	nous **nous sommes lavé(e)s**
tu **t'es lavé(e)**	vous **vous êtes lavé(e)s**
il **s'est lavé** elle **s'est lavée**	ils **se sont lavés** elles **se sont lavées**

- When a direct object follows a reflexive verb (as in **se laver les mains**), the reflexive pronoun is an indirect object. In such cases the past participle does not agree with the reflexive pronoun.

se laver les mains (*to wash one's hands*)	
je **me suis lavé les mains**	nous **nous sommes lavé les mains**
tu **t'es lavé les mains**	vous **vous êtes lavé les mains**
il **s'est lavé les mains** elle **s'est lavé les mains**	ils **se sont lavé les mains** elles **se sont lavé les mains**

- In the negative, **ne** precedes the reflexive pronoun and **pas** follows the conjugated form of **être.**

Nicole **ne** s'est **pas** réveillée de bonne heure parce qu'elle **ne** s'est **pas** couchée de bonne heure.

*Nicole did**n't** wake up early because she did**n't** go to bed early.*

H. Ne t'impatiente pas! Formez de petites conversations entre deux copines. La première veut savoir quand les choses vont se faire. La seconde lui répond qu'on les a déjà faites. Suivez le modèle.

MODÈLE les enfants / se laver
→ Solange: Quand est-ce que les enfants vont se laver?
Annick: Ils se sont déjà lavés.

Vocabulaire utile

se charger de qqch *to take charge of something, be responsible for something*
se détendre *to relax*
se fatiguer *to get tired*
s'intéresser à qqun/à qqch *to be interested in someone/something*
se mettre à faire qqch *to begin to do something*
se mettre en route *to get going*
s'occuper de qqch *to take care of something*
se soigner *to take care of oneself*

1. tu / se mettre à préparer le dîner

___

___

2. les enfants / se coucher

___

___

3. Josette et toi / s'occuper du linge

___

___

4. tu / se reposer

___

___

5. Elvire / se laver la tête

___

___

6. tu / se limer les ongles

___

___

7. Carole et Paulette / se calmer

___

___

8. je / se brosser les cheveux

I. **Pas encore.** Madame Goulet est pressée parce que sa famille doit partir en vacances. Mais personne n'est prêt. Utilisez le passé composé avec **pas encore** pour exprimer les réponses à ses questions.

MODÈLE —Marc, tu viens de te laver, n'est-ce pas?
→ —Non, je ne me suis pas encore lavé.

1. Christine, tu viens de te lever, n'est-ce pas?
2. Chéri, tu viens de te raser, n'est-ce pas?
3. Marc et Christine, vous venez de vous brosser les dents, n'est-ce pas?
4. Christine, tu viens de te laver la tête, n'est-ce pas?
5. Chéri, tu viens de t'habiller, n'est-ce pas?
6. Marc et Christine, vous venez de vous peigner, n'est-ce pas?

J. **Une excursion du collège.** Le collège a organisé une excursion à Versailles pour les étudiants. Décrivez leur départ en formant des phrases au passé composé à partir des éléments donnés.

1. Olivier et Jean / se réveiller de bonne heure
2. Christine / se laver la tête
3. Monique et Véronique / se préparer pour le départ
4. Mireille / se dépêcher comme une folle
5. Christian et Pierre / se charger de la nourriture
6. tous les étudiants / se réunir devant le collège

7. ils / s'asseoir dans les autocars

___

8. les autocars / s'éloigner de l'établissement

___

Notes culturelles

- Le collège est l'école où on réalise le premier cycle de l'enseignement secondaire. On va au collège après l'école primaire et on y reste quatre ans. Les étudiants au collège suivent tous le même programme: français, maths, sciences, langue étrangère, histoire et géographie. La scolarité française est obligatoire jusqu'à seize ans. À peu près 50 pour cent des élèves continuent leurs études au lycée et préparent leur «bac» (diplôme donnant accès à l'université).
- En 1661 Louis XIV, appelé aussi «le Roi Soleil», décide de construire son palais dans ce petit village à 14 kilomètres au sud-ouest de Paris. Une équipe de plus de 30 000 ouvriers dirigés par le roi y édifient, au cours de 50 ans, un palais magnifique entouré de jardins à la française. Versailles a eu son importance dans l'histoire américaine aussi. En 1783 on y signe le traité qui mettait fin à la guerre de l'Indépendance et qui reconnaissait l'indépendance de la république fédérée des États-Unis.

K. **Zéro de conduite.** Grand-mère se plaint de la conduite de ses petits-enfants hier, quand toute la famille est venue lui rendre visite. Formez des phrases au passé composé pour voir ce qui est arrivé.

La mauvaise conduite

se cacher *to hide*
s'échapper de *to run away from, escape from*
se mettre en panique *to fly into a panic*
se moquer de qqn/de qqch *to make fun of someone/something*
se mouiller *to get wet*
se plaindre de qqn/de qqch *to complain about someone/something*
se salir *to get dirty*

1. le petit Claude / se mouiller la chemise en buvant un Coca

___

2. Marlise / se salir dans le garage

___

3. les jumeaux / se moquer du voisin

___

4. les parents de Philippe / se mettre en panique

___

5. leur fils / s'échapper de la maison

6. Caroline / se plaindre de tout

7. le petit Baudoin / se cacher au sous-sol

8. Odile / se couper au doigt avec un couteau

9. moi / se fatiguer

10. je / se coucher de bonne heure

D *Reciprocal reflexive verbs*

- A plural reflexive pronoun may be used with a verb to express reciprocity (English *each other*).

—Vous **vous parlez** souvent?	*Do you **speak to each other** often?*
—Oui, nous **nous téléphonons** tous les jours.	*Yes, we **phone each other** every day.*
—Marc et Constance **se voient** souvent?	*Do Marc and Constance **see each other** often?*
—Oui, ils **se donnent rendez-vous** après leur cours.	*Yes, they **make an appointment to see each other** after their class.*

- The passé composé of a reciprocal verb is formed like the passé composé of any other reflexive verb. To determine whether agreement of the past participle is necessary, consider whether the corresponding nonreflexive verb takes a direct object.

Ils **se sont vus.**	*They **saw each other.***
Ils **se sont parlé.**	*They **spoke to each other.***

Des verbes réciproques

***s'acheter des cadeaux** *to buy gifts for each other*
s'aider, s'entraider *to help each other*
s'aimer *to love each other*
se comprendre *to understand each other*
se connaître *to know each other*
se détester *to hate each other*
***se donner rendez-vous** *to make an appointment to see each other*
***s'écrire** *to write to each other*
***se mentir** *to lie to each other*
***se parler** *to speak to each other*
***se poser des questions** *to ask each other questions*
se regarder *to look at each other*
se rencontrer *to meet, run into each other*
***se ressembler** *to look alike*
***se téléphoner** *to phone each other*
se voir *to see each other*

*Reflexive pronoun is an *indirect object.*

L. Pas hier. Répondez à l'affirmatif aux questions qu'on vous pose, mais dites que hier c'était différent. Utilisez le passé composé et faites attention à l'accord du participe.

MODÈLE Vous vous rencontrez souvent?
→ Oui, mais hier nous ne nous sommes pas rencontrés.

1. Vous vous voyez souvent?

____

2. Vous vous écrivez souvent?

____

3. Vous vous parlez souvent?

____

4. Vous vous téléphonez souvent?

____

5. Vous vous donnez souvent rendez-vous?

____

6. Vous vous aidez souvent?

____

7. Vous vous accompagnez souvent?

____

8. Vous vous invitez souvent?

____

M. Histoire d'amour. Racontez le triste amour de Félix et Geneviève. Utilisez le pronom **ils** et le passé composé dans chaque phrase. Remarquez qu'il y a des verbes qui ne sont pas pronominaux.

Les rapports humains

se disputer *to argue*
s'entendre bien/mal avec qqn *to get along/not get along with someone*
se fiancer (avec qqn) *to get engaged (to someone)*
se marier (avec qqn) *to get married (to someone)*
rompre (avec qqn) *to break off (with someone)*
tomber amoureux (amoureuse) de qqn *to fall in love with someone*

1. se voir

____

2. se connaître

____

3. se parler

____

4. se comprendre

____

5. tomber amoureux

____

6. s'acheter des petits cadeaux

____

7. se fiancer

____

8. après un temps/se disputer

____

9. se mentir

____

10. rompre

____

11. ne pas se marier

____

E *The imperative of reflexive verbs*

- In negative commands, the reflexive pronoun precedes the verb.

Ne **t'**énerve pas!	*Don't get upset!*
Ne **vous** levez pas.	*Don't get up.*
Ne **nous** approchons pas.	*Let's not get closer.*

- In affirmative commands, the reflexive pronoun is placed after the verb and connected to it by a hyphen. **Te** changes to **toi** when placed after the verb.

Asseyez-**vous.**	*Sit down.*
Dépêchons-**nous.**	*Let's hurry up.*
Habille-**toi** et mets-**toi** à étudier.	*Get dressed and start studying.*

N. Quelle lenteur! Employez l'impératif des verbes réfléchis pour dire à un ami (et à deux amis) ce qu'ils doivent faire pour ne pas être en retard.

MODÈLE se réveiller → *À un ami:* Réveille-toi.
À deux amis: Réveillez-vous.

	À un ami	*À deux amis*
1. se lever	________	________
2. s'habiller	________	________
3. se dépêcher	________	________
4. se laver les mains	________	________
5. ne pas s'énerver	________	________
6. ne plus se reposer	________	________
7. ne pas se disputer	________	________
8. ne pas se recoucher	________	________
9. se diriger vers la porte	________	________
10. se préparer pour partir	________	________

O. On s'encourage. Employez l'impératif de la première personne du pluriel pour dire à un ami ce qu'il faut faire pour ne pas être en retard.

MODÈLE se lever → Levons-nous.

1. se raser ________
2. s'habiller ________
3. se dépêcher ________
4. se laver les mains ________
5. ne pas s'énerver ________
6. ne plus se reposer ________
7. ne pas se disputer ________
8. s'aider ________
9. se diriger vers la porte ________
10. se préparer pour partir ________

F *Other reflexive constructions and reflexive verbs*

- When inversion is used to form questions with reflexive verbs, the subject pronoun is placed after the verb; the reflexive pronoun remains before the verb. The use of inversion to form questions with reflexive verbs is limited to formal written style and very formal speech.

Vous intéressez-vous à l'art moderne?	***Are you interested*** *in modern art?*
Les prisonniers **se sont-ils** échappés?	***Did*** *the prisoners* ***escape****?*
Ne vous efforcez-vous pas de progresser?	***Aren't you striving*** *to progress?*

Ne se sont-elles pas vues dans le Midi?	***Didn't they see each other*** *in the south of France?*

- A reflexive verb in the third person singular can sometimes be the equivalent of the English passive voice.

Ça ne **se fait** pas.	*That's not* ***done****.*
C'est un livre qui **se lit** beaucoup.	*It's a book that* ***is read*** *a lot.*
Cette ville **s'appelle** Valence.	*This city* ***is called*** *Valence.*

- Here are some other useful reflexive verbs:

s'adresser à qqn *to address, speak to, be aimed at*
s'en aller *to go away*
s'apercevoir de qqch *to notice something*
s'attendre à qqch *to expect something*
se débarrasser de qqn/de qqch *to get rid of someone, something*
se demander *to wonder*
se donner la peine de faire qqch *to take the trouble to do something*
se fier à qqn/qqch *to trust someone/something*
s'habituer à qqch *to get used to, accustomed to something*
se méfier de qqn/qqch *to distrust/be wary of someone/something*
se passer de qqch *to do without something*
se perdre *to get lost*
se priver de qqch *to deprive oneself of something*
se rappeler qqch *to recall, remember something*
se servir de qqch *to use something*
se soucier de qqn/qqch *to worry, be concerned about someone/something*
se souvenir de qqn/qqch *to remember someone/something*
se tromper de qqch *to go to/select the wrong thing*

P. Posez vos questions! Refaites ces questions dans la langue soignée (*formal*) en employant l'inversion.

1. Est-ce que ce produit se vend bien?

____

2. Est-ce que les étudiants s'amusent au bal?

____

3. Est-ce que vous ne vous dirigez pas vers la sortie?

____

4. Est-ce qu'ils se sont approchés du guichet?

____

5. Est-ce que nous ne nous éloignons pas du centre de la ville?

____

6. Pourquoi est-ce que vos amis ne se sont plus réunis?

____

7. Pourquoi est-ce que tu ne t'intéresses plus au cinéma?

____

8. À quelle heure est-ce qu'elles se sont mises en route?

9. Est-ce qu'ils ne se sont pas offensés?

10. Est-ce qu'elle s'est souvenue de moi?

11. Pourquoi est-ce qu'elle ne s'est pas habituée à la vie française?

12. Est-ce que vous vous attendez à le voir?

Q. **Comment est-ce que ça se dit?** Employez des verbes pronominaux pour exprimer ces phrases en français.

1. They have gone away. I plan (**compter**) to go away too.

2. We took the wrong train.

3. This park is called **le jardin du Luxembourg.**

4. That is not said.

5. I am wary of dogs that I don't know.

6. He never used to worry about his work.

7. We trusted our friends.

8. Do you remember Professor Gauthier?

9. They didn't take the trouble to look for a good hotel.

10. I wonder if they got lost.

R. **Exercice oral.** Avec un(e) camarade décrivez votre journée—ce que vous faites le matin, comment vous arrivez à l'école, les gens que vous y voyez et vos sentiments, ce que vous faites en rentrant chez vous, etc. Votre camarade décrira la sienne. Comparez les deux journées et présentez les différences et les similarités à une troisième personne.

S. La grammaire en action. Lisez les avis suivants qui relèvent tous du domaine de l'éducation. Faites attention aux verbes pronominaux employés dans le texte et répondez aux questions. Avant de lire, essayez de deviner le sens des mots suivants.

1. l'autoapprentissage
   a. on apprend avec un professeur
   b. on apprend seul
2. agrémenté
   a. accompagné par quelque chose de beau ou d'utile
   b. ennuyeux et inutile
3. polyvalent
   a. qui ne vaut pas grand-chose
   b. compréhensif, varié
4. les scolaires
   a. les bâtiments de l'école
   b. les élèves
5. les métiers
   a. les professions
   b. les maladies

Langues étrangères
❑ Destiné à l'autoapprentissage de langues, Assimil vient de publier «Le vietnamien sans peine». Ce livre offre de courtes leçons quotidiennes, agrémentées d'un dessin. À cela s'ajoute aussi un coffret de cassettes. Le niveau atteint au bout des 63 leçons est celui de la conversation courante de base.

L'Europe à l'école
❑ L'Association Jean-Monnet et Sources d'Europe se sont associées pour une expérience unique au service des scolaires. Chaque jeudi, «une journée européenne à Paris» est proposée aux écoles afin de faire découvrir la construction européenne et l'Europe d'aujourd'hui.

Guitare
❑ Atla, la première grande école de guitare polystyle, vient d'ouvrir ses portes au cœur du quartier de la musique entre Pigalle et les Abbesses. Cet établissement propose la découverte et l'enseignement polyvalent de la guitare: rock, jazz, brésilien, etc. Ouverte à tous, l'école s'adresse à la fois aux professionnels et aux amateurs.

Guide informatique des métiers
❑ L'Onisep et la Direction des lycées et collèges du ministère de l'Éducation nationale proposent le premier CD-ROM sur les métiers. Conçu pour un public de collégiens, ce produit multimédia, lisible sur Mac et PC, regroupe une trentaine de métiers, en fonction d'une clé d'intérêt: s'occuper des enfants, d'animaux, travailler au contact avec la nature . . .

Notes

- **Assimil** maison d'édition française connue pour ses cours de langues étrangères
- **Jean Monnet** économiste français, un des grands promoteurs de l'unité européenne
- **Onisep** Office National d'Information sur les Enseignements et les Professions
- **Pigalle et Abbesses** deux stations de métro dans la partie nord de Paris

Après la lecture, indiquez si ces phrases sont vraies ou fausses.

Langues étrangères

_____ 1. Le cours de vietnamien se réalise avec un professeur.

_____ 2. Le livre est accompagné de cassettes.

_____ 3. Il n'y a pas de dessins dans le livre.

Guitare

_____ 4. À Atla on enseigne à jouer de la guitare.

_____ 5. L'enseignement à Atla est limité à la guitare classique.

_____ 6. Les cours de guitare sont pour les débutants uniquement.

L'Europe à l'école

_____ 7. La journée européenne est destinée aux élèves dans les écoles.

_____ 8. On veut enseigner aux élèves ce que c'est que l'idée de l'union des pays européens.

_____ 9. On présente la journée européenne tous les jours.

Guide informatique des métiers

_____ 10. Le CD-ROM sur les métiers est pour les étudiants universitaires.

_____ 11. Le CD-ROM explique à peu près 30 métiers.

_____ 12. Les métiers présentés sont classés par domaine d'intérêt.

CHAPTER 9 FUTURE AND CONDITIONAL; CONDITIONAL SENTENCES (1)

A The future tense

- The future tense expresses an action that will take place in the future (English: *I will speak, we will finish*). The future tense of regular verbs is formed by adding the following endings to the infinitive: **-ai, -as, -a, -ons, -ez, -ont.**

parler	
je parler**ai**	nous parler**ons**
tu parler**as**	vous parler**ez**
il/elle parler**a**	ils/elles parler**ont**

finir	
je finir**ai**	nous finir**ons**
tu finir**as**	vous finir**ez**
il/elle finir**a**	ils/elles finir**ont**

- Verbs whose infinitive ends in **-re** drop their final **-e** before the future tense endings.

rendre	
je rendr**ai**	nous rendr**ons**
tu rendr**as**	vous rendr**ez**
il/elle rendr**a**	ils/elles rendr**ont**

- Some verbs have an irregular stem in the future tense. The endings are *regular* in all cases.

être	je **ser**ai	**venir**	je **viendr**ai	**pouvoir**	je **pourr**ai
faire	je **fer**ai	**vouloir**	je **voudr**ai	**voir**	je **verr**ai
aller	j'**ir**ai	**acquérir**	j'**acquérr**ai	**devoir**	je **devr**ai
avoir	j'**aur**ai	**courir**	je **courr**ai	**recevoir**	je **recevr**ai
savoir	je **saur**ai	**envoyer**	j'**enverr**ai	**décevoir**	je **décevr**ai
tenir	je **tiendr**ai	**mourir**	je **mourr**ai	**pleuvoir**	il **pleuvr**a

- Related verbs have the same irregularities in their stems.

devenir je **deviendr**ai   **revenir** je **reviendr**ai

- The future of **il faut** is **il faudra.** The future of **il y a** is **il y aura.**

- Verbs that change a mute **e** to **è** before a mute **e** in the present tense (such as **acheter**) also change **e** to **è** in all forms of the future tense. Verbs that double their final consonant before a mute **e** in the present tense (such as **appeler**) have the same change in all persons of the future tense.

acheter	j'**achèter**ai	**appeler**	j'**appeller**ai
amener	**j'amèner**ai	**jeter**	je **jetter**ai

- However, verbs such as **espérer** and **préférer** retain **é** in future tense.

espérer	j'**espérer**ai	**préférer**	je **préférer**ai

- The future of **s'asseoir** is either **je m'assiérai** or **je m'assoirai** (without the **e** of the infinitive).

A. C'est pour demain. Tout ce qu'on allait faire aujourd'hui, on a remis (*postponed*) pour demain. Répondez à ces questions en suivant le modèle.

MODÈLE Jean ne fait pas les courses aujourd'hui?
➔ Non, il fera les courses demain.

1. Mademoiselle, vous ne faites pas le ménage aujourd'hui?

____

2. Tes parents ne reviennent pas aujourd'hui?

____

3. Ton ami ne va pas au lycée aujourd'hui?

____

4. Je ne travaille pas aujourd'hui, monsieur?

____

5. Je ne réponds pas aujourd'hui?

____

6. Tu ne sais pas la réponse aujourd'hui?

____

7. Papa, je n'envoie pas la lettre aujourd'hui?

____

8. Nous n'emmenons pas les enfants au zoo aujourd'hui?

____

9. Les autres professeurs et vous, vous ne projetez pas le film aujourd'hui?

____

10. Les étudiants ne complètent pas leur travail aujourd'hui?

____

B. Je crois. Serge, optimiste, parle avec un copain impatient. Serge croit que tout se réalisera. Écrivez ses réponses en suivant le modèle.

MODÈLE Un copain: Le prof vient ou ne vient pas?
Serge: Je crois qu'il viendra.

1. Je réussis ou je ne réussis pas?

2. Nos copains descendent ou ne descendent pas?

3. Théo va ou ne va pas?

4. Il neige ou il ne neige pas?

5. Tu sors ou tu ne sors pas?

6. Marie et moi, nous arrivons à l'heure ou nous n'arrivons pas à l'heure?

7. Tes parents nous prêtent la voiture ou ne nous prêtent pas la voiture?

8. Tu complètes tes devoirs ou tu ne complètes pas tes devoirs?

C. **Je ne sais pas.** Dites dans chaque cas que vous ne savez pas si l'action arrivera. Suivez le modèle.

MODÈLE Est-ce qu'il vient demain?
➔ Je ne sais pas s'il viendra.

1. Est-ce qu'ils partent demain?

2. Est-ce que vous travaillez demain?

3. Est-ce que je passe l'examen demain?

4. Est-ce que le professeur revient demain?

5. Est-ce que les enfants vont à l'école demain?

6. Est-ce que tu conduis demain?

7. Est-ce que les étudiants lisent demain?

8. Est-ce qu'on projette un film demain?

9. Est-ce que tu veux venir demain?

10. Est-ce que ton copain peut rentrer demain?

D. Des projets pour l'été. La famille Ramonet est très nombreuse. Le départ en Languedoc pour passer l'été n'est donc pas facile. Formez des phrases au futur à partir des éléments donnés pour dire ce que chaque membre de la famille fera pour faciliter ce départ.

1. maman / faire les valises
2. la fille aînée / s'occuper des petits
3. papa / se charger de la voiture
4. tout le monde / se réveiller à 7 heures du matin
5. tous les membres de la famille / se dépêcher
6. personne / se mettre en colère
7. les enfants / s'entraider
8. les grands-parents / préparer le petit déjeuner
9. la tante Marie / fermer les fenêtres
10. les Ramonet / se mettre en route vers 10 heures du matin

Note culturelle

- Le Languedoc-Roussillon est une région du Midi située entre la Provence et la frontière espagnole. La ville la plus importante du Roussillon est Perpignan.
- Le Languedoc est connu pour son vignoble qui est responsable de 12% de la production mondiale du vin. Pour les touristes, le Languedoc offre la ville de Carcassonne, une forteresse médiévale très bien conservée et le fameux aqueduc romain, le pont du Gard.
- Le chef-lieu du Languedoc-Roussillon est Montpellier, ville universitaire et site d'une industrie électronique importante. D'autres villes importantes de la région sont Narbonne, Béziers et Sète.

B Use of the future after **quand** and other conjunctions

- The future tense is used after **quand** (*when*), **lorsque** (*when*), **dès que** (*as soon as*), **aussitôt que** (*as soon as*), and **après que** (*after*) when a future event is implied.

Téléphone-moi **quand tu seras** prêt.	*Phone me* ***when you're*** *ready.*
Je passerai te prendre **dès que tu m'appelleras.**	*I'll come by and pick you up* ***as soon as you call me.***
Quand tu verras ma voiture, descends.	***When you see*** *my car, come downstairs to the street.*
Je te ramènerai **aussitôt que la réunion finira.**	*I'll bring you back* ***as soon as the meeting is over.***

Note that English uses the present tense, not the future, in such clauses.

E. On se met en route. Odile Dulac explique quand sa famille fera les choses nécessaires pour partir à la montagne. Cette année les Dulac vont dans la région Midi-Pyrénées. Formez des phrases à partir des éléments donnés pour voir ce qu'elle dit. Mettez les propositions principales au futur.

1. je / faire ma valise / dès que / le linge / être sec

   ___

2. les enfants / s'habiller / quand / ils / rentrer de l'école

   ___

3. nous / manger / quand / maman / revenir du marché

   ___

4. mon frère / mettre les valises dans la voiture / aussitôt que / papa / revenir de la station-service

   ___

5. nous / choisir la route / quand / je / trouver la carte

   ___

6. nous / partir / quand / faire beau

   ___

7. nous / chercher un hôtel / lorsque / nous / arriver à Aurillac

   ___

8. je / se coucher / aussitôt que / nous / être dans l'hôtel

   ___

Note culturelle

- La région Midi-Pyrénées se situe entre les pays aquitains et le Languedoc, dans les Pyrénées centrales. Luchon est une station thermale très connue, très fréquentée par les touristes.
- La ville la plus importante et le chef-lieu de la région est Toulouse. Centre de la civilisation provençale au moyen âge et gouvernée par les comtes de Toulouse, la ville a souffert à l'époque de la croisade albigeoise.
- Aujourd'hui Toulouse est un grand centre industriel et scientifique, spécialisé dans l'aéronautique. On y construit les avions Airbus et les fusées spatiales Ariane.

F. Conseils et ordres. Employez l'impératif et le futur pour donner des conseils et des ordres. Suivez le modèle.

Modèle	**Conseil/ordre**	**Quand**
	(à ton ami Pierre) s'asseoir	quand / le professeur / entrer
	➔ Assieds-toi quand le professeur entrera.	

	Conseil /ordre	**Quand**
1.	(à tes amis) sortir	dès que/la cloche/sonner
2.	(à ton amie Lise) téléphoner	aussitôt que/Albert/arriver
3.	(à tes camarades) se mettre à prendre des notes	quand/le professeur/commencer sa conférence
4.	(à ton petit frère) descendre à la cuisine	quand/je/t'appeler
5.	(à Jean-Luc et Ghislaine) venir me voir	quand/vous/pouvoir
6.	(à ta sœur) fermer la porte à clé	quand/tu/s'en aller
7.	(à Mme Chiclet) dire bonjour de ma part à votre fils	quand/vous/le voir
8.	(à tes parents) lire ma lettre	dès que/vous/la recevoir

1. ______________________________
2. ______________________________
3. ______________________________
4. ______________________________
5. ______________________________
6. ______________________________
7. ______________________________
8. ______________________________

C The conditional

- The conditional expresses what might happen or what would happen if certain conditions existed. It is formed by adding the endings of the imperfect tense to the infinitive or to the irregular future tense stem.

parler	
je parler**ais**	nous parler**ions**
tu parler**ais**	vous parler**iez**
il/elle parler**ait**	ils/elles parler**aient**

finir	
je finir**ais**	nous finir**ions**
tu finir**ais**	vous finir**iez**
il/elle finir**ait**	ils/elles finir**aient**

rendre	
je rendr**ais**	nous rendr**ions**
tu rendr**ais**	vous rendr**iez**
il/elle rendr**ait**	ils/elles rendr**aient**

être	
je ser**ais**	nous ser**ions**
tu ser**ais**	vous ser**iez**
il/elle ser**ait**	ils/elles ser**aient**

- The same spelling changes that appear in the future appear in the conditional.

  acheter j'**achèter**ais appeler j'**appeller**ais préférer je **préférer**ais

- The conditional of **il faut** is **il faudrait.** The conditional of **il y a** is **il y aurait.**
- The conditional tense is the equivalent of English *would* + verb. It should not be confused with the use of *would* to describe a repeated action in the past (imperfect tense).

Si tu voulais te baigner, on **irait** à la plage.	*If you wanted to go swimming, we **would go** to the beach.*
On **allait** à la plage tous les jours quand on était petits.	*We **would go** to the beach every day when we were children.*

G. **Si on pouvait.** On ferait les choses dont on a envie si on pouvait. Employez le conditionnel du verbe principal et l'imparfait de **pouvoir** pour exprimer cette idée en suivant le modèle.

MODÈLE —Jean a envie de partir.
→ —Oui, il partirait s'il pouvait.

1. J'ai envie de rentrer.

___

2. Monique et Danielle ont envie de faire du ski.

___

3. Tu as envie de devenir poète.

___

4. Odile et moi, nous avons envie de nous voir tous les jours.

___

5. J'ai envie de me mettre en route.

___

6. Richard a envie de se promener.

___

7. Sylvie et toi, vous avez envie d'acheter du pain.

___

8. Mon copain et moi, nous avons envie d'être de retour.

___

H. **Moi non plus.** Quand on vous dit ce que vos amis n'ont pas fait, dites dans chaque cas que vous ne feriez pas ces choses non plus. Employez le conditionnel dans vos réponses.

MODÈLE —Je ne me suis pas baigné dans ce lac.
→ —Moi non plus, je ne me baignerais pas dans ce lac.

1. Charles n'a pas pris la voiture.

___

2. Martine n'a pas fait la vaisselle.

___

3. Olivier et Chantal ne se sont pas assis dans le jardin.

___

4. Je n'ai pas regardé la télé aujourd'hui.

___

5. Les enfants n'ont pas enlevé leur pull.

___

6. Le collège n'a pas projeté ce film.

7. Les étudiants n'ont pas répété ces slogans.

8. Solange n'a pas couru.

I. Impossible! Employez le conditionnel pour dire dans chaque cas que la nouvelle qu'on vient de vous annoncer est sûrement fausse.

MODÈLE —On dit que Pierre est parti.
➔ —Impossible! Il ne partirait pas.

1. On dit que vous avez renoncé à votre travail.
2. On dit que Catherine a rejeté notre offre.
3. On dit que Philippe s'est levé pendant la classe.
4. On dit que les professeurs ont fait grève.
5. On dit que tu exagères.
6. On dit que j'ai perdu les billets.
7. On dit que Laurent est tombé en skiant.
8. On dit que le petit Baudoin a jeté son dîner à la poubelle.

D *Conditional sentences (1)*

A conditional sentence consists of two clauses: an "if" (or **si**) clause and a result clause.

- If an event is likely to happen, the present is used in the **si** clause and the present, future, or imperative is used in the result clause.

S'il **pleut,** nous **restons** chez nous.	*If it **rains,** we **stay** home.*
Viens me voir si tu **as** le temps.	***Come** see me if you **have** time.*
Si tu **t'en vas,** tes parents **se fâcheront.**	*If you **leave**, your parents **will get angry**.*

- If an event is unlikely to happen or is contrary to fact, the imperfect is used in the **si** clause and the conditional is used in the result clause.

Je t'**aiderais** si je **pouvais.** — *I'**d help** you if I **could**. (Fact: I can't help you. But if I could, I would.)*

S'il **parlait** espagnol, il **s'habituerait** à la vie mexicaine. — *If he **spoke** Spanish, he **would get used** to Mexican life. (Fact: He doesn't speak Spanish. But if he did, he would get used to Mexican life.)*

Conditional Sentences: Summary of Tenses	
***Si* Clause**	**Result Clause**
Present	Present, future, or imperative
Imperfect	Conditional

J. Des progrès personnels pour Jean-Pierre. Jean-Pierre doit se transformer pour être un jeune homme à la page. Employez des phrases composées d'une supposition (**si**) à l'imparfait et d'une proposition principale au conditionnel pour exprimer ce que Jean-Pierre doit faire.

Modèle Jean-Pierre ne lit jamais le journal. Il ne sait pas ce qui se passe dans le monde.
➔ Si Jean-Pierre lisait le journal, il saurait ce qui se passe dans le monde.

1. Jean-Pierre ne s'habille pas bien. Les autres étudiants se moquent de lui.

____

2. Jean-Pierre ne fait pas de sport. Il ne connaît pas beaucoup de monde.

____

3. Jean-Pierre ne s'intéresse pas à ses études. Il n'est pas préparé en classe.

____

4. Jean-Pierre s'absente souvent. Les professeurs se fâchent contre lui.

____

5. Jean-Pierre lit des bandes dessinées (*comics*) en classe. Les profs sont furieux.

____

6. Jean-Pierre mange toujours seul. Il ne parle pas avec les autres étudiants.

____

K. Déménagement. Les Fantin essaient de décider où placer leurs meubles dans leur nouvelle maison. Exprimez leurs idées avec une phrase composée d'une supposition au présent et d'une proposition principale au futur. Suivez le modèle.

Modèle on/mettre la chaîne stéréo dans le séjour / on/pouvoir écouter des disques ensemble
➔ Si on met la chaîne stéréo dans le séjour, on pourra écouter des disques ensemble.

1. maman / installer la machine à laver au sous-sol / nous / avoir plus de place dans la cuisine

____

2. je / mettre la lampe à côté du fauteuil / je / pouvoir lire

____

3. nous / nettoyer le tapis / nous / le mettre dans le salon

____

4. tu / trouver la table en plastique / tu / pouvoir la mettre sur la terrasse

____

5. on / laisser l'ordinateur dans ma chambre / je / faire mes devoirs sans embêter les autres

____

6. les déménageurs / monter une étagère dans ma chambre / je / ranger tous mes livres

____

L. **Il y a toujours des problèmes quand on déménage.** Refaites chaque phrase en supposition avec **si** à l'imparfait + proposition principale au conditionnel pour exprimer tout ce qui manque dans la nouvelle maison des Didier.

MODÈLE On n'a pas de lave-vaisselle. On fait la vaisselle à la main.
➔ Si on avait un lave-vaisselle, on ne ferait pas la vaisselle à la main.

1. On n'a pas deux postes de télé. On ne peut pas regarder la télé dans le séjour.

____

2. Cette maison n'a pas de grenier (*attic*). Il n'y a pas de place pour les boîtes.

____

3. La cheminée ne fonctionne pas. Nous ne pouvons pas faire un feu.

____

4. On n'a pas de tableaux dans le salon. Le salon n'est pas accueillant (*cozy*).

____

5. Je n'ai pas de chaîne stéréo dans ma chambre. J'écoute mes disques dans le séjour.

____

6. Le frigo est tellement petit. Maman fait les courses plusieurs fois par semaine.

____

7. Tu ne décroches (*take down*) pas les rideaux. Je ne peux pas les laver.

____

8. Cette fenêtre ne se ferme pas bien. Il fait froid dans ma chambre.

____

M. Problèmes de santé. Quelles seraient les réactions de ces amis à des problèmes de santé hypothétiques? Composez des phrases avec une supposition avec **si** à l'imparfait et une proposition principale au conditionnel à partir des éléments donnés. Suivez le modèle.

MODÈLE

Si	*Proposition principale*
Marie/se couper au doigt	elle/mettre un pansement

→ Si Marie se coupait au doigt, elle mettrait un pansement.

Comment est-ce qu'on se soignerait?

aller pieds nus *to go barefoot*
attraper un rhume *to catch a cold*
avoir mal à la tête *to have a headache*
le comprimé d'aspirine *aspirin tablet*
se couper au doigt *to cut one's finger*
être en forme *to be in shape*
se faire mal (au pied) *to hurt oneself (one's foot)*
maigrir *to lose weight*
mettre un pansement *to put on a bandage*
ordonner *to prescribe*
tomber malade *to get sick*

	Si	*Proposition principale*
1.	je/se sentir mal	je/aller chez le médecin
2.	il me faut/maigrir	je/ne manger que des légumes et des fruits
3.	il/sortir sous la pluie	il/attraper un rhume
4.	elle/tomber malade	elle/se reposer
5.	nous/aller pieds nus	nous/se faire mal au pied
6.	tu/avoir mal à la tête	tu/prendre des comprimés d'aspirine
7.	le médecin/m'ordonner des antibiotiques	je/ne pas les prendre
8.	je/être en forme	je/ne pas se fatiguer tellement

1. ______________________________
2. ______________________________
3. ______________________________
4. ______________________________
5. ______________________________
6. ______________________________
7. ______________________________
8. ______________________________

N. Activité orale. Discutez avec un(e) camarade de vos projets pour l'avenir. Employez le futur pour les choses que vous comptez faire et des phrases avec **si** pour exprimer les circonstances nécessaires pour réaliser vos projets.

MODÈLES Quand j'aurai dix-huit ans, j'irai à l'université.
Si j'ai de la chance, on me donnera une bourse d'études.
Si j'étais riche, je n'aurais pas besoin d'une bourse d'études.

O. La grammaire en action. Lisez cette annonce pour un voyage à New York en Concorde, l'avion supersonique franco-britannique, et choisissez la réponse correcte aux questions.

Vocabulaire utile

le grand cru *vin de première qualité*
le réveillon *grand dîner célébré à Noël et la veille du 1er janvier*

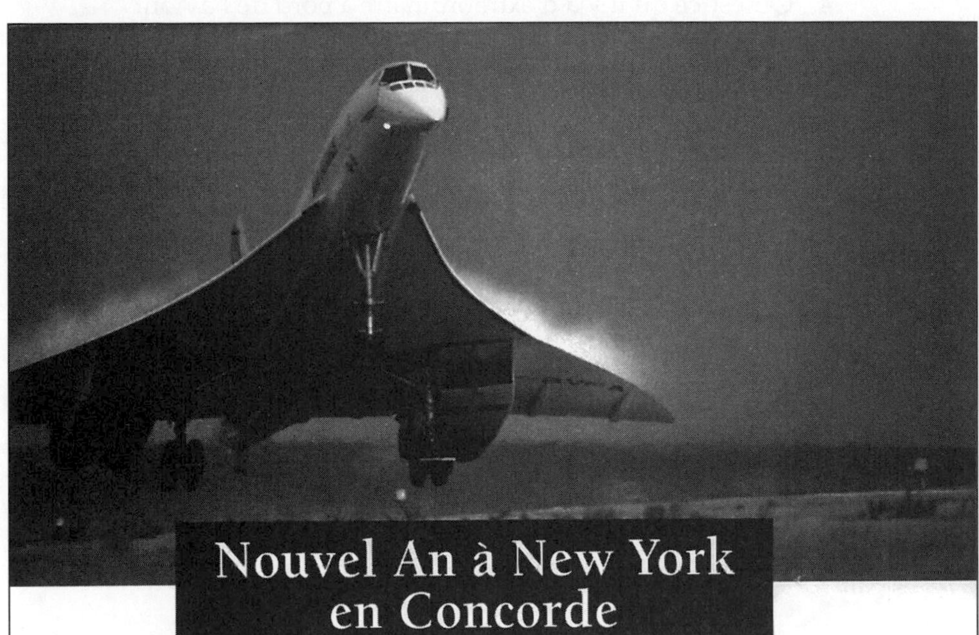

Nouvel An à New York en Concorde

__Premier bonheur :__ le trajet Paris-New- York en Concorde, l'avion le plus rapide du monde. Il vous emmène à 2200 km/h, effaçant ainsi la fatigue des longs trajets. Dès que vous monterez à bord, vous apprécierez l'incomparable prestige français. Vous découvrirez de vous-même le service sublime : déjeuner princier dans la grande tradition culinaire française, grands crus de vins et de champagne, hôtesses merveilleuses de distinction et de gentillesse, qui savent se mettre à votre service personnel. Un tel confort à une telle vitesse, il faut l'avoir goûté au moins une fois dans votre vie.

__Deuxième bonheur :__ le séjour à l'hôtel Plazza, l'un des plus beaux et des plus luxueux palaces du monde. Remarquablement situé, il vous permet de vous plonger aussitôt dans la vie New-Yorkaise : en quelques minutes à pied, vous êtes à Central Park ou sur la 5e Avenue, ou encore à Rockfeller Center ou à l'Empire State Building. Au cours de ces trois jours de fête, vous pourrez survoler Manhattan en hélicoptère, visiter Ellis Island et la Statue de la Liberté, effectuer une croisière dans la baie de New York, sans compter bien sûr au réveillon inoubliable.

PRIX AVION ET SÉJOUR, 38900 F.

TMR France,
349, avenue du Prado, 13417 MARSEILLE CEDEX 08
Tél : (16) 91 71 92 10 - 91 77 88 99 - Fax : (16) 91 71 92 12

1. Le chiffre 2200 km/h. exprime . . .
   a. le prix du voyage.
   b. la vitesse de l'avion.
2. Quand est-ce que le touriste commence à apprécier le prestige français?
   a. En montant dans l'avion.
   b. En arrivant à New York.
3. Combien de temps dure l'excursion?
   a. Trois jours.
   b. De Noël au nouvel an.
4. Qu'est-ce qu'il y a d'extraordinaire à bord de l'avion?
   a. Un long trajet.
   b. Un repas magnifique.
5. Quels sont les avantages de l'hôtel Plaza?
   a. Le confort et la vitesse.
   b. Sa situation et son luxe.
6. Comment est-ce qu'on fête le nouvel an pendant le voyage?
   a. On effectue une croisière dans la baie de New York.
   b. On organise un réveillon.

CHAPTER 10 PLUPERFECT, FUTURE PERFECT, AND PAST CONDITIONAL; CONDITIONAL SENTENCES (2)

A *The pluperfect (le plus-que-parfait)*

- The pluperfect tense (English: *had done something*) consists of the imperfect of the auxiliary verb (either **avoir** or **être**) plus the past participle.

chercher	
j' **avais cherché**	nous **avions cherché**
tu **avais cherché**	vous **aviez cherché**
il/elle **avait cherché**	ils/elles **avaient cherché**

arriver	
j' **étais arrivé(e)**	nous **étions arrivé(e)s**
tu **étais arrivé(e)**	vous **étiez arrivé(e)(s)**
il **était arrivé** elle **était arrivée**	ils **étaient arrivés** elles **étaient arrivées**

- Reflexive verbs are conjugated with **être** in the pluperfect, just as they are in the passé composé.

se réveiller	
je **m'étais réveillé(e)**	nous **nous étions réveillé(e)s**
tu **t'étais réveillé(e)**	vous **vous étiez réveillé(e)(s)**
il **s'était réveillé** elle **s'était réveillée**	ils **s'étaient réveillés** elles **s'étaient réveillées**

- The rules for agreement of the past participle in all the compound tenses are the same as in the passé composé.
- The pluperfect expresses a past action that occurred before another past action that is either mentioned in the same sentence or understood from context.

—Jean n'a pas mangé avec vous? —Non. Quand Jean est arrivé, nous **avions** déjà **mangé**.	*Jean didn't eat with you?* *No. When Jean arrived, we **had** already **eaten.***
—Pourquoi est-ce que tu n'as pas répondu au téléphone? Tu ne t'**étais** pas encore **réveillé**?	*Why didn't you answer the telephone? **Hadn't** you **awakened** yet?*
—Si, je **m'étais** déjà **levé.**	*Yes, I **had** already **gotten up**.*
Je lui ai demandé s'il **avait lu** le livre. Il m'a répondu qu'il ne l'**avait** pas encore **acheté.**	*I asked him if he **had read** the book. He answered me that he **hadn't** yet **bought** it.*

A. Jacques était absent. Lisez l'histoire de la classe du professeur Jourdain ce matin. Refaites chaque phrase au passé. Les verbes au présent passeront au passé composé; les verbes au passé composé passeront au plus-que-parfait.

1. Les étudiants ont pris leur place quand le professeur Jourdain entre.

____

2. Le professeur a déjà commencé à parler quand Marc sort son cahier.

____

3. Rachelle s'est endormie quand le professeur commence à poser des questions.

____

4. Le professeur a fini sa conférence quand la cloche sonne.

____

5. Nous nous sommes assis dans la cantine quand Jacques arrive.

____

6. Il nous demande si nous avons assisté à la classe du professeur Jourdain.

____

7. Hélène lui répond que nous avons tous été présents.

____

8. Je lui prête les notes que j'ai prises.

____

B. Explications. On n'a pas fait ces choses hier parce qu'on les avait déjà faites avant-hier. Employez le plus-que-parfait dans vos explications. Suivez le modèle.

MODÈLE Pourquoi est-ce que Claude n'a pas apporté les fleurs hier?
➔ C'est qu'il avait déjà apporté les fleurs avant-hier.

1. Pourquoi est-ce que Joëlle ne t'a pas téléphoné hier?

____

2. Pourquoi est-ce que Renée n'est pas venue te voir hier?

____

3. Pourquoi est-ce que les garçons n'ont pas demandé le nom du médecin hier?

____

4. Pourquoi est-ce que tu n'as pas passé ton permis de conduire hier?

____

5. Pourquoi est-ce que Jeanne et Martine n'ont pas fait leur travail hier?

____

6. Pourquoi est-ce que tu n'as pas posté la lettre hier?

____

7. Pourquoi est-ce que Charles n'a pas fait le plein hier?

____

8. Pourquoi est-ce que ta mère n'a pas balayé la cuisine hier?

____

C. Déjà fait à 8 heures et demie du matin. Employez le plus-que-parfait pour exprimer tout ce qu'on avait déjà fait à 8 heures et demie quand les amis ont sonné à la porte.

MODÈLE (je / se réveiller)
➔ Quand mes amis ont sonné à 8 h 30, je m'étais réveillé(e).

1. ma sœur / prendre une douche

____

2. ma mère / préparer le petit déjeuner

____

3. je / se lever

____

4. mon amie Ghislaine / téléphoner deux fois

____

5. mon père / ne pas partir pour le bureau

____

6. je / relire mes notes de biologie

____

7. mes frères / mettre leurs livres dans leurs serviettes (*briefcases*)

____

8. je / ne pas s'habiller

____

D. C'est ce qu'elle a demandé. On peut supposer que Gilberte veut savoir toutes ces choses parce qu'elle a posé des questions au sujet de chacune. Exprimez cette idée en utilisant le plus-que-parfait, comme dans le modèle.

MODÈLE Tu crois que Gilberte veut savoir si nous avons réservé une table?
➔ Elle m'a demandé si nous avions réservé une table.

1. Tu crois que Gilberte veut savoir si nous avons invité Suzanne?

____

2. Tu crois que Gilberte veut savoir si Marc a fini ses devoirs?

____

3. Tu crois que Gilberte veut savoir si j'ai trouvé un emploi?

____

4. Tu crois que Gilberte veut savoir si Marie et Claire ont choisi une spécialisation?

____

5. Tu crois que Gilberte veut savoir si nos amis se sont réunis hier?

____

6. Tu crois que Gilberte veut savoir si M. Jourdain s'est fâché?

____

7. Tu crois que Gilberte veut savoir si Paul et Christine se sont fiancés?

____

8. Tu crois que Gilberte veut savoir si nous nous sommes trompés de train?

____

B *The future perfect (**le futur antérieur**)*

- The future perfect tense (English: *will have done something*) consists of the future of the auxiliary verb (**avoir** or **être**) plus the past participle.

chercher	
j' **aurai cherché**	nous **aurons cherché**
tu **auras cherché**	vous **aurez cherché**
il/elle **aura cherché**	ils/elles **auront cherché**

arriver	
je **serai arrivé(e)**	nous **serons arrivé(e)s**
tu **seras arrivé(e)**	vous **serez arrivé(e)(s)**
il **sera arrivé** elle **sera arrivée**	ils **seront arrivés** elles **seront arrivées**

se réveiller	
je **me serai réveillé(e)**	nous **nous serons réveillé(e)s**
tu **te seras réveillé(e)**	vous **vous serez réveillé(e)(s)**
il **se sera réveillé** elle **se sera réveillée**	ils **se seront réveillés** elles **se seront réveillées**

- The future perfect expresses a future action that will have been completed before another future action takes place or before an implied or specified time in the future.

J'**aurai fini** vers 5 heures du soir. — *I **will have finished** around 5:00 P.M.*

Elle **sera arrivée** avant nous. — *She **will have arrived** before us.*

Ils **se seront installés** avant le mois de septembre. — *They **will have moved in** before the month of September.*

- The future perfect is used after the conjunctions **quand, lorsque, dès que, aussitôt que,** and **après que** when the verb in the main clause is in the future tense.

Je te téléphonerai **quand la lettre sera arrivée.**	*I'll phone you* ***when the letter arrives.***
Nous partirons **aussitôt que Chantal aura fini** son travail.	*We'll leave* ***as soon as Chantal has finished*** *her work.*

E. Qui aura fait quoi? Votre ami et vous, vous vous dirigez vers la grande fête de fin d'année. Vous expliquez à votre ami que tout doit marcher comme sur des roulettes (*come off beautifully*) parce que tout a été très bien organisé. Employez le futur antérieur pour lui dire qui se sera chargé de chaque tache essentielle.

1. Marie-France / préparer les hors-d'œuvre

   ____

2. Claude et Alain / aller chercher les boissons

   ____

3. Sylvie / mettre les couverts

   ____

4. Jean-Paul / choisir les cassettes

   ____

5. Sophie et Odile / inviter tout le monde

   ____

6. Hervé et Nathalie / décorer la salle

   ____

7. Marguerite / acheter les gobelets (*paper cups*)

   ____

8. Robert / organiser les attractions (*entertainment*)

   ____

F. Trop tard. Utilisez le futur antérieur après **quand** pour dire que dans chaque cas il sera trop tard. Employez le futur dans la proposition principale.

Modèle tu / arriver / je / sortir
➔ Tu arriveras quand je serai sorti.

1. il / m'offrir un coup de main / je / finir

   ____

2. elle / sonner à la porte / nous / se coucher

   ____

3. tu / venir / tout le monde / partir

   ____

4. ils / trouver la carte / nous / se perdre

5. nous / arriver / ils / fermer le restaurant

6. il /nous renseigner / nous / trouver la solution

7. elle / apporter le pain / nous / finir de manger

8. vous / venir nous prendre en voiture / nous / partir en autocar

G. **Récompensé ou puni?** Expliquez pourquoi ces gens seront récompensés ou punis à partir des éléments proposés. Employez le futur dans la proposition principale et le futur antérieur dans la proposition introduite par **parce que.** Suivez le modèle.

MODÈLE tu / être grondé *parce que* tu / ne rien faire
→ Tu seras grondé parce que tu n'auras rien fait.

Récompenses et punitions

agir *to act*
comme il faut *properly*
se conduire *to behave*
donner un prix *to give a prize*
gronder *to scold*
louer *to praise*
récompenser *to reward*
sécher un cours *to cut class*

1. tu / recevoir une bonne note *parce que* tu / étudier sérieusement

2. on / donner un prix à Marc *parce qu'*il /rédiger la meilleure composition

3. on / récompenser les étudiants *parce qu'*ils / se conduire comme il faut

4. les journaux / louer cet agent de police *parce qu'*il / agir héroïquement

5. le petit Pierrot / être grondé / ne pas ranger ses affaires

6. ses parents / gronder Michèle *parce qu'*elle / sécher ses cours

____

7. je / répondre à toutes les questions de l'examen *parce que* je / comprendre la matière

____

8. tout le monde / être déçu *parce que* nos cousins / ne pas arriver

____

H. En famille. Laurent Duval raconte une soirée que sa famille passera ensemble. Formez des phrases à partir des éléments proposés pour savoir ce qu'il dit. Employez le futur dans la proposition principale et le futur antérieur dans la proposition relative. Faites attention à l'accord du participe passé.

MODÈLE nous / prendrons des hors-d'œuvre que ma sœur et moi / préparer
→ Nous prendrons des hors-d'œuvre que ma sœur et moi, nous aurons préparés.

1. nous / manger un dîner magnifique *que* nous / cuisiner

____

2. je / écouter le disque compact *que* je / acheter

____

3. maman / servir un dessert formidable avec la pâtisserie / *qu'*elle / acheter

____

4. ma sœur / nous raconter l'histoire du roman *qu'*elle / lire

____

5. mon père / lire des articles dans la revue *qu'*il / acheter

____

6. nous / tous regarder le film / *que* nous / louer

____

7. mon père et moi, nous / parler des articles *qu'*il / lire

____

8. ma sœur / chanter les nouvelles chansons *qu'*elle / apprendre à l'école

____

C *The conditional perfect* (**le conditionnel passé**)

- The conditional perfect (English: *would have done something*) consists of the conditional of the auxiliary verb (**avoir** or **être**) plus the past participle.

chercher	
j' **aurais cherché**	nous **aurions cherché**
tu **aurais cherché**	vous **auriez cherché**
il/elle **aurait cherché**	ils/elles **auraient cherché**

arriver	
je **serais arrivé(e)**	nous **serions arrivé(e)s**
tu **serais arrivé(e)**	vous **seriez arrivé(e)(s)**
il **serait arrivé** elle **serait arrivée**	ils **seraient arrivés** elles **seraient arrivées**

se réveiller	
je **me serais réveillé(e)**	nous **nous serions réveillé(e)s**
tu **te serais réveillé(e)**	vous **vous seriez réveillé(e)(s)**
il **se serait réveillé** elle **se serait réveillée**	ils **se seraient réveillés** elles **se seraient réveillées**

- The conditional perfect usually labels an event that *did not take place* in the past.

—Tu **m'aurais aidé**? — ***Would** you **have helped** me?*
—J'**aurais** tout **fait** pour t'aider. — *I **would have done** everything to help you.*

—Vous **vous seriez souvenu** de lui? — ***Would** you **have remembered** him?*
—Non, je **ne** l'**aurais pas reconnu.** — *No, I **wouldn't have recognized** him.*

I. Je n'aurais pas fait une chose pareille. Vous n'auriez pas fait tout ce que vos copains ont fait. Dites-le en employant le conditionnel passé.

Modèle: Je me suis baigné dans le fleuve.
➔ Moi, je ne me serais pas baigné(e) dans le fleuve.

1. Philippe s'est couché à 5 heures du matin.

____

2. Claudette a pris rendez-vous avec le professeur Bouvard.

____

3. Mireille et Louis se sont mis en route sous la pluie.

____

4. Alain a fait dix kilomètres à pied.

____

5. Christine a cueilli des fleurs dans le jardin public.

6. Serge et Frédéric ont cru à l'histoire que Marc a racontée.

7. Lise et Blanche ont dépensé tout leur argent.

8. Chantal a oublié la date de la réception.

J. **Eux, ils l'auraient fait.** Marcel avait peur de faire ce qu'il fallait faire. Les autres copains n'auraient pas eu peur. Exprimez cette idée en employant le conditionnel passé.

Modèle J'avais peur de parler avec le professeur. (Cécile)
➔ Vraiment? Cécile aurait parlé avec le professeur.

1. J'avais peur de conduire la voiture d'André. (Guillaume)

2. J'avais peur de descendre. (Jacqueline et Martin)

3. J'avais peur d'interrompre. (Vincent et moi)

4. J'avais peur de répondre. (moi)

5. J'avais peur d'employer ce mot. (Albert)

6. J'avais peur de plonger. (Simone et moi)

7. J'avais peur de déranger Georges. (Ségolène)

8. J'avais peur de me disputer avec lui. (Solange et Marie)

D *Conditional sentences (2)*

- To express a hypothetical situation that is contrary to a past fact, French uses the pluperfect in the **si** clause and the past conditional in the result clause.

—Jean-Claude n'est pas arrivé.	*Jean-Claude hasn't arrived.*
—S'il **était arrivé,** nous **aurions dîné** ensemble.	*If he **had arrived**, we **would have had dinner** together.*
—Je n'ai pas étudié.	*I didn't study.*
—Si tu **avais étudié,** tu **aurais réussi** les examens.	*If you **had studied**, you **would have passed** the exams.*

—Alice ne nous a pas vus.	*Alice didn't see us.*
—C'est vrai. Si elle nous **avait vus,** elle **se serait approchée** de notre table.	*That's true. If she* ***had seen*** *us, she* ***would have come over*** *to our table.*

K. Moi, je l'aurais fait aussi. Dites que vous auriez fait toutes ces choses si Berthe les avait faites. Suivez le modèle.

> **MODÈLE** Berthe n'est pas sortie hier.
> → Mais si elle était sortie hier, moi aussi, je serais sorti(e).

1. Berthe n'est pas allée en ville hier.
2. Berthe n'a pas acheté de livres hier.
3. Berthe ne s'est pas promenée hier.
4. Berthe n'a pas envoyé ses paquets hier.
5. Berthe n'a pas pris son billet hier.
6. Berthe ne s'est pas préparée pour partir hier.
7. Berthe n'a pas écouté le disque hier.
8. Berthe n'a pas travaillé hier.

L. Si on avait fini notre travail! Qu'est-ce que les copains auraient fait s'ils avaient fini leurs devoirs? Employez une phrase avec une proposition subordonnée au plus-que-parfait commençant par **si** et une proposition indépendante au conditionnel passé. Suivez le modèle.

> **MODÈLE** Marc n'a pas appris le nouveau vocabulaire. (aller au cinéma)
> → Si Marc avait appris le nouveau vocabulaire, il serait allé au cinéma.

1. Rachelle n'a pas rédigé sa composition. (se réunir avec ses amis)
2. Philippe n'a pas relu ses leçons de chimie. (pouvoir jouer au football)

3. Louise et Danielle n'ont pas préparé le compte rendu. (aller aux grands magasins)

____

4. Olivier et Jean-Luc ne sont pas allés au laboratoire de langues. (regarder la télé)

____

5. Françoise et Guy n'ont pas étudié l'histoire du dix-septième siècle. (aller danser)

____

6. Mireille n'a pas fait les problèmes de maths. (sortir avec Charles)

____

7. Monique et Édouard n'ont pas révisé leurs notes de littérature française. (dîner en ville)

____

8. Jean-François n'a pas appris le poème par cœur. (jouer aux jeux vidéo)

____

M. Résumés. Résumez chaque échange par une phrase composée d'une proposition subordonnée au plus-que-parfait commençant par **si** et une proposition indépendante au conditionnel passé. Suivez le modèle.

Modèle

Thierry: Pourquoi est-ce que tu n'as pas répondu à ma lettre?
Georges: Je ne l'ai pas reçue.
➔ Georges aurait répondu à la lettre de Thierry s'il l'avait reçue.

1. Yves: Pourquoi est-ce que tu ne m'as pas salué à la cantine?
Michèle: Je ne t'ai pas vu.

____

2. Roger: Pourquoi est-ce que tu ne m'as pas téléphoné?
Sylvie: J'ai passé toute la journée à la bibliothèque.

____

3. Judith: Pourquoi est-ce que tu ne m'as pas dit qu'il y avait un examen aujourd'hui?
Damien: Je ne m'en suis pas souvenu.

____

4. Julie: Pourquoi est-ce que tu n'as pas suivi ton régime?
Ariane: J'ai eu envie de manger du chocolat.

____

5. Sonia: Pourquoi est-ce que tu n'as pas fait le ménage?
Nicolas: Je n'ai pas eu le temps.

____

6. Roland: Pourquoi est-ce que tu n'as pas pris ta bicyclette?
Patrick: Je me suis foulé la cheville (*sprained my ankle*).

____

7. Grégoire: Pourquoi est-ce que Virginie et toi, vous n'êtes pas sortis?
   Paul: Nous avons dû étudier.

   ____

8. Hélène: Pourquoi est-ce que tu n'es pas venu à la faculté?
   Louis: Je suis allé chez le médecin.

   ____

N. Création. Les personnes indiquées ont fait des choses surprenantes. Expliquez pourquoi en employant une phrase composée d'une proposition subordonnée au plus-que-parfait commençant par **si** et une proposition indépendante au conditionnel passé.

MODÈLE Le professeur ne s'est pas fâché contre Pierrot.
➔ Il se serait fâché contre Pierrot s'il avait entendu les paroles de Pierrot (s'il avait vu les dessins de Pierrot, etc.).

1. Christine ne s'est pas amusée à la surboum.

   ____

2. Les touristes ne se sont pas mis en route hier.

   ____

3. M. Marsaud ne s'est pas chargé de la collecte.

   ____

4. Tu n'as pas assisté au concert.

   ____

5. Le médecin ne m'a pas ordonné des antibiotiques.

   ____

6. Émile n'a pas ses devoirs.

   ____

7. Charlotte n'est pas venue nous voir.

   ____

8. Bernard et Stéphane n'ont pas joué au basket aujourd'hui.

   ____

O. Exercice oral. Avec un groupe de deux ou trois camarades, parlez de comment votre vie aurait été différente si votre famille et vous, vous aviez fait les choses d'une façon différente. Employez des phrases avec **si** pour exprimer les possibilités.

CHAPTER 11

PASSÉ SIMPLE

A *Formation and use of the passé simple*

- The passé simple is a literary tense used only in formal speeches and writing. Like the passé composé, it expresses an action that was completed in the past. The passé simple of regular **-er** verbs is formed by dropping the **-er** from the infinitive and adding the endings **-ai, -as, -a, -âmes, -âtes, -èrent.**

parler	
je parl**ai**	nous parl**âmes**
tu parl**as**	vous parl**âtes**
il/elle parl**a**	ils/elles parl**èrent**

In the passé simple, **aller** is conjugated like a regular **-er** verb.

- Infinitives ending in **-cer** change **c** to **ç** and infinitives ending in **-ger** insert an **e** in all forms of the passé simple except the **ils** form.

lancer	
je lançai	nous lançâmes
tu lanças	vous lançâtes
il/elle lança	ils/elles lancèrent

manger	
je mang**eai**	nous mang**eâmes**
tu mang**eas**	vous mang**eâtes**
il/elle mang**ea**	ils/elles mang**èrent**

- The passé simple of regular **-ir** and **-re** verbs is formed by dropping the infinitive ending and adding **-is, -is, -it, -îmes, -îtes, -irent.**

finir	
je fin**is**	nous fin**îmes**
tu fin**is**	vous fin**îtes**
il/elle fin**it**	ils/elles fin**irent**

rendre	
je rend**is**	nous rend**îmes**
tu rend**is**	vous rend**îtes**
il/elle rend**it**	ils/elles rend**irent**

- Irregular **-ir** verbs like **dormir** and **partir** form the passé simple like **finir: je dormis, je partis.** Irregular **-re** verbs like **battre** and **suivre** form the passé simple like **rendre: je battis, je suivis.**

A. Au passé simple! Transformez ces formes verbales du passé composé au passé simple.

1. j'ai gagné ________________
2. tu as commencé ________________
3. elle a choisi ________________
4. elles t'ont attendu ________________
5. vous avez espéré ________________
6. tu as nagé ________________
7. il m'a encouragé ________________
8. nous avons déménagé ________________
9. je suis descendu ________________
10. tu as annoncé ________________
11. ils ont rangé ________________
12. elles ont défendu ________________
13. vous avez obéi ________________
14. nous avons entendu ________________
15. j'ai remplacé ________________
16. on a rédigé ________________
17. nous avons réfléchi ________________
18. vous avez essayé ________________
19. tu es allé ________________
20. nous avons partagé ________________

B *The passé simple of irregular verbs*

- Some irregular verbs form the passé simple using the same endings as regular **-ir** and **-re** verbs.

Infinitive	**Stem**	**Passé simple**
s'asseoir	**ass-**	je **m'assis**
conduire	**conduis-**	je **conduisis**
dire	**d-**	je **dis**
écrire	**écriv-**	j'**écrivis**
faire	**f-**	je **fis**
joindre	**joign-**	je **joignis**
mettre	**m-**	je **mis**
naître	**naqu-**	je **naquis**
peindre	**peign-**	je **peignis**
prendre	**pr-**	je **pris**
rire	**r-**	je **ris**
voir	**v-**	je **vis**

- Most irregular verbs that have a past participle ending in **-u** have a stem that resembles their past participle. The endings for such verbs are **-s, -s, -t, -ˆmes, -ˆtes, -rent.** They follow the pattern of **avoir.**

avoir	
j' **eus**	nous **eûmes**
tu **eus**	vous **eûtes**
il/elle **eut**	ils/elles **eurent**

Infinitive	Stem	Passé simple
boire	**bu-**	je **bus**
connaître	**connu-**	je **connus**
courir	**couru-**	je **courus**
croire	**cru-**	je **crus**
devoir	**du-**	je **dus**
falloir	**fallu-**	il **fallut**
lire	**lu-**	je **lus**
pleuvoir	**plu-**	il **plut**
pouvoir	**pu-**	je **pus**
recevoir	**reçu-**	je **reçus**
savoir	**su-**	je **sus**
valoir	**valu-**	il **valut**
vivre	**vécu-**	je **vécus**
vouloir	**voulu-**	je **voulus**

- Some verbs have special forms in the passé simple.

être: **je fus, tu fus, il/elle fut; nous fûmes, vous fûtes, ils/elles furent**

mourir: **je mourus, tu mourus, il/elle mourut, nous mourûmes, vous mourûtes, ils/elles moururent**

verbs like **venir:** **je vins, tu vins, il/elle vint; nous vînmes, vous vîntes, ils/elles vinrent**

B. Transformation. Refaites cette petite histoire au passé simple.

1. La nuit est tombée.

____

2. La ville est devenue silencieuse.

____

3. Les habitants sont rentrés chez eux.

____

4. On a fermé les magasins.

____

5. Je suis entré dans un bistrot.

____

6. Je me suis assis à une petite table.

____

7. J'ai attendu Michèle.

____

8. Elle a voulu me voir.

____

9. Elle m'a rejoint à 7 heures.

____

10. Nous avons pris un café ensemble.

____

11. Nous sommes sortis.

____

12. Nous nous sommes promenés dans la ville endormie.

____

13. Michèle m'a dit:

____

14. «J'ai décidé de te quitter.»

____

15. Elle a rompu avec moi.

____

16. Je n'ai rien pu faire.

____

17. Je suis rentré chez moi.

____

18. J'ai pleuré.

____

C. Transformation. Refaites cette petite histoire au passé simple.

1. Marthe est sortie de sa maison.

____

2. Elle a marché à travers champ.

____

3. Elle s'est approchée du fleuve.

____

4. Elle y a vu trois amis.

____

5. Ils l'ont saluée.

____

6. Ils l'ont invitée à manger avec eux.

____

7. Elle a accepté.

____

8. Elle s'est assise avec eux.

____

9. Ils ont partagé leur déjeuner avec elle.

____

10. Soudain, le temps a changé.

____

11. Il a commencé à pleuvoir.

____

12. Les quatre amis sont revenus en ville.

____

13. Ils se sont mouillés un peu.

____

14. Ils ont cherché un café.

____

15. Ils ont commandé un chocolat.

____

16. Ils ont bu leur chocolat ensemble.

____

CHAPTER 12 PRESENT PARTICIPLES; USES OF THE INFINITIVE

A *The present participle*

- The French present participle corresponds to the English *-ing* form of a verb (*going, seeing, doing*).
- The present participle of most verbs is formed by dropping **-ons** from the present tense **nous** form and adding **-ant.**

parler ➔ nous parl~~ons~~ ➔ **parlant**	lire ➔ nous lis~~ons~~ ➔ **lisant**
finir ➔ nous finiss~~ons~~ ➔ **finissant**	prendre ➔ nous pren~~ons~~ ➔ **prenant**
rendre ➔ nous rend~~ons~~ ➔ **rendant**	écrire ➔ nous écriv~~ons~~ ➔ **écrivant**

- Only three verbs have irregular present participles:

avoir ➔ **ayant** être ➔ **étant** savoir ➔ **sachant**

- A present participle may be used as an adjective or a verb. When used as an adjective, a present participle usually follows the noun or pronoun it modifies and agrees with it in gender and number.

de l'eau **courante** (<courir)	***running*** *water*
les numéros **gagnants** (<gagner)	*the* ***winning*** *numbers*
des histoires **touchantes** (<toucher)	***touching*** *stories*

- When used as a verb, the present participle often follows the preposition **en.**

1. **En** + present participle may express an action that is happening at the same time as the action of the main verb.

Ici on ne parle pas **en travaillant.**	*Here people don't talk* ***while working.***
En entrant dans le café, nous avons vu notre amie Diane.	***Upon entering*** *the café, we saw our friend Diane.*

2. It may also express how or why something is done.

On ne maigrit pas **en mangeant** des glaces.	*You don't get thinner* ***by eating*** *ice cream.*
J'ai fait des progrès en français **en lisant** beaucoup.	*I made progress in French* ***through reading*** *a lot.*

- The present participle may also be used without **en.**

Ayant peur d'arriver en retard, nous sommes partis de très bonne heure.	***Being afraid*** *to arrive late, we left very early.*

- The present participle may be used instead of a relative clause. In this case it is invariable. This construction is typical of formal speech and writing.

les trains **venant** de l'étranger (**venant** = qui viennent)	*trains* ***coming*** *from abroad*

des employés **parlant** français (**parlant** = qui parlent)	*employees **speaking** French*
un autobus **montant** le boulevard (**montant** = qui monte)	*a bus **going up** the boulevard*

A. **Des conseils.** Marie-Josette donne des conseils à son petit frère qui entre au collège. Refaites chacune de ses phrases en changeant la proposition commençant par **si** au gérondif.

Modèle Tu apprendras beaucoup si tu fais attention.
➔ Tu apprendras beaucoup en faisant attention.

1. Tu auras une bonne note si tu fais tes devoirs de maths tous les jours.

2. Tu arriveras à l'heure si tu quittes la maison à 7 heures et demie.

3. Si on apprend toutes les dates par cœur, on évite les problèmes dans le cours d'histoire.

4. Si tu écoutes des programmes en anglais à la radio, tu te prépareras pour l'examen oral.

5. On évite la fatigue si on organise son travail.

6. Si on regarde très peu la télé, on peut toujours finir son travail.

B. **La langue administrative.** Pour écrire des phrases typiques des avis officiels, remplacez la proposition subordonnée par le participe présent correspondant. Puisque ce participe est une forme verbale, il ne s'accorde pas avec le substantif.

Modèle Les visiteurs qui désirent visiter le musée sont priés d'attendre à gauche.
➔ Les visiteurs désirant visiter le musée sont priés d'attendre à gauche.

1. Les voyageurs qui partent pour le Nord sont priés de passer au quai numéro 3.

2. Nous annonçons un retard pour tous les avions qui proviennent d'Afrique.

3. Le docteur Gobert verra les malades qui souffrent d'un problème gastrique.

4. Les étudiants qui passent leurs examens demain doivent arriver au lycée à 8 heures.

5. C'est un manuel d'anglais qui contient tout le vocabulaire essentiel.

____

6. Voici une carte qui montre le site des centrales nucléaires.

____

B *Uses of infinitives*

- In French, the infinitive can serve as the subject of a sentence. English usually uses the *-ing* form of the verb in this case.

Voir, c'est **croire**.	***Seeing** is **believing**.*
Apprendre le français en six mois n'est pas facile!	***Learning** French in six months is not easy!*
Vivre à Paris, c'est mon rêve.	***Living** in Paris is my dream.*

- The infinitive can also follow another verb. Depending on which verb it follows, it may or may not be preceded by a preposition. The following verbs are followed directly by an infinitive.

aimer *to like*	**espérer** *to hope*
aimer mieux *to prefer*	**oser** *to dare*
aller *to be going to*	**penser** *to intend*
avoir beau *to do (something) in vain*	**pouvoir** *to be able*
compter *to intend*	**préférer** *to prefer*
désirer *to want*	**savoir** *to know how*
détester *to hate*	**vouloir** *to want*
devoir *should, must, ought*	

—**Tu comptes partir** en vacances en février?	***Do you intend to leave** for vacation in February?*
—Non, **je déteste voyager** en hiver.	*No, **I hate traveling** in the winter.*
—**Tu préfères y aller** en été?	***Do you prefer to go** in the summer?*
—**J'aime mieux prendre** mes vacances au printemps.	***I prefer to take** my vacation in the springtime.*

- Verbs of motion are followed directly by an infinitive.

—**Je descends faire les courses.** Tu as besoin de quelque chose?	***I'm going down to do the shopping.** Do you need anything?*
—**Tu peux aller** me **chercher** un journal français?	***Can you go get** me a French newspaper?*

- The expressions **il faut** (*one must, you have to*) and **il vaut mieux** (*it's better to*) are also followed directly by the infinitive. These expressions are not conjugated for person: impersonal **il** is the only possible subject. They are conjugated for tense, however.

imperfect:	**il fallait, il valait mieux**
passé composé:	**il a fallu, il a mieux valu**
future:	**il faudra, il vaudra mieux**
conditional:	**il faudrait, il vaudrait mieux**

C. Les fêtes et les célébrations. Exercez-vous à employer la construction *verbe + infinitif* en ajoutant les verbes entre parenthèses aux phrases. Vous verrez comment les Maurois et leurs amis passent l'année.

MODÈLE Les Maurois restent chez eux le jour de Noël. (préférer)
→ Les Maurois préfèrent rester chez eux le jour de Noël.

L'année des Français

le 1er janvier: le jour de l'An. On s'offre de petits cadeaux appelés «étrennes».
le 6 janvier: la fête des Rois. Célébration de l'arrivée des Mages au berceau (*cradle*) de Jésus-Christ. On fête cette journée en mangeant un gâteau plat appelé «la galette des Rois» qui a une fève (*bean*) cachée. La personne qui trouve la fève dans son morceau est nommée le roi ou la reine de la fête.
le 8 mai: on commémore la victoire des Alliés et la fin de la Deuxième Guerre mondiale en Europe. On commémore la fin de la Première Guerre mondiale le 11 novembre, anniversaire de l'Armistice de 1918.
l'Ascension: fête religieuse célébrée le sixième jeudi après Pâques.
la Pentecôte: fête religieuse célébrée dix jours après l'Ascension, toujours un lundi. Pour beaucoup de Parisiens, c'est l'occasion de passer une fin de semaine de trois jours à la campagne.
le 14 juillet: la fête nationale française. Il y a un défilé militaire aux Champs-Elysées à Paris et on danse dans les rues. On commémore la prise de la Bastille, événement qui a marqué le début de la Révolution française.
le 15 août: l'Assomption. On célèbre la fête de la Sainte Vierge.
le 1er novembre: le Toussaint, ou la Fête de tous les saints. Le 2 novembre est le jour des Morts. On va dans les cimetières fleurir les tombes (*put flowers on the graves*).
le 24 décembre: la veillée de Noël. Célébrée en famille avec un grand repas (le réveillon). On va aussi à l'église pour la messe de minuit.
le 25 décembre: Noël. Dans les familles, on se réunit autour du sapin (*fir tree*) où on a placé des cadeaux.
le 31 décembre: la Saint-Sylvestre. On célèbre avec un réveillon et on se souhaite une bonne année.

1. Les Maurois font un grand réveillon pour la Saint-Sylvestre. (aimer)

   ____

2. Ils s'offrent des étrennes le jour de l'An. (aller)

   ____

3. Le 6 janvier ils invitent des amis pour manger la galette des Rois. (espérer)

   ____

4. La grand-mère passe le dimanche de Pâques avec eux. (vouloir)

   ____

5. Le 8 mai ils vont en Normandie pour commémorer la victoire des Alliés en 1945. (compter)

6. Leurs amis les Dufau les invitent pour la Pentecôte. (devoir)

7. Eux, ils invitent les Dufau à Paris pour le 14 juillet. (penser)

8. Pour l'Assomption ils sont dans leur maison à la campagne. (désirer)

9. Ils vont fleurir les tombes de leurs parents décédés (*deceased*) le 2 novembre. (devoir)

10. Ils vont à la messe de minuit le 24 décembre. (aller)

D. **Au bord de la mer.** Ajoutez les verbes entre parenthèses à ces phrases pour voir comment un groupe d'amis a passé ses vacances au bord de la mer. Employez le même temps verbal que celui de la phrase donnée.

1. Philippe nageait tous les jours. (vouloir)

2. Alice et Géraldine ont fait du tourisme. (pouvoir)

3. Georges ne nageait pas très bien. (savoir)

4. Il s'éloignait de la plage. (ne pas oser)

5. Claudette et Brigitte jouaient au tennis. (préférer)

6. Louis visitait les petits villages des alentours. (aimer)

7. Solange a acheté des souvenirs. (ne pas pouvoir)

8. Richard a écrit beaucoup de lettres. (devoir)

C Verb + *à* + *infinitive*

- Some verbs require the preposition **à** before a following infinitive.

s'amuser à *to enjoy oneself (by doing)*
apprendre à *to learn how to*
arriver à *to manage to*
s'attendre à *to expect to*
avoir à *to have to*
chercher à *to try to*
commencer à *to begin to*
se consacrer à *to devote oneself to*
consentir à *to consent to*
continuer à *to continue*
se décider à *to make up one's mind to*
s'ennuyer à *to get/be bored (doing something)*
s'exercer à *to practice*
s'habituer à *to get used to*
hésiter à *to hesitate to*
s'intéresser à *to be interested in*
se mettre à *to begin to*
s'obstiner à *to persist stubbornly in*
parvenir à *to manage to, succeed in*
passer son temps à *to spend one's time doing*
penser à *to be thinking of (doing something)*
se préparer à *to get ready to*
se résigner à *to resign oneself to*
réussir à *to succeed in*
songer à *to be thinking of (doing something)*
tendre à *to tend to*
tenir à *to insist on*

—Henri **s'obstine à causer** avec tous les touristes allemands.	*Henri **persists in chatting** with all the German tourists.*
—Il **s'exerce à parler** allemand.	*He's **practicing speaking** German.*
—Il **parviendra à chasser** tous les touristes de Paris.	*He'**ll succeed in chasing** all the tourists away from Paris.*
—Tu exagères. Les touristes **s'amusent à converser** avec lui.	*You're exaggerating. The tourists **enjoy conversing** with him.*

- Some verbs require a direct object before **à** + infinitive.

aider qqn à faire qqch *to help someone do something*
autoriser qqn à faire qqch *to authorize someone to do something*
encourager qqn à faire qqch *to encourage someone to do something*
engager qqn à faire qqch *to urge someone to do something*
forcer qqn à faire qqch *to force someone to do something*
inviter qqn à faire qqch *to invite someone to do something*
obliger qqn à faire qqch *to oblige someone to do something*

—**J'ai invité les Deschênes à passer** la Pentecôte avec nous.	***I invited the Deschênes to spend** Pentecost with us.*
—**Ils vous aideront à préparer** les repas. Ils adorent faire la cuisine.	***They'll help you prepare** meals. They love to cook.*

- With **apprendre** when it means *to teach* and with **enseigner,** an indirect object is required before **à** + infinitive.

apprendre/enseigner à qqn à faire qqch *to teach someone to do something*

E. La boum de Ghislaine. Ghislaine veut donner une surprise-party chez elle. Complétez le récit de ses préparatifs en ajoutant la préposition **à** aux phrases où elle manque. Si on n'a pas besoin de mettre la préposition **à** devant l'infinitif, marquez le blanc d'un **X.**

1. Nous pensons __________ organiser une boum.
2. Je tiens __________ donner une boum formidable.

3. Michèle va __________ préparer des sandwichs.
4. Alfred et Robert doivent __________ s'occuper des boissons.
5. Ils tendent __________ oublier tout ce qu'ils ont à acheter.
6. Olivier invitera ses amis __________ venir.
7. Moi, je me consacrerai __________ mettre de l'ordre dans notre appartement.
8. Ma mère sait __________ faire une délicieuse tarte au citron.
9. Je l'aiderai __________ en faire deux ou trois.

F. On modifie un peu le message. Refaites chacune des phrases avec les éléments proposés entre parenthèses pour connaître les occupations et préoccupations d'un groupe d'étudiants.

MODÈLES Vous sortez. (pouvoir) ➔ Vous pouvez sortir.
Vous sortez. (on/obliger) ➔ On vous oblige à sortir.

1. Nous lisons un livre par semaine. (le professeur/encourager)

____

2. Je rédige mes dissertations à l'ordinateur. (aimer mieux)

____

3. Jacques finira son compte rendu demain. (réussir)

____

4. Philomène fait de l'allemand. (son chef/engager)

____

5. Vous cherchez du travail. (l'administration de l'école/autoriser)

____

6. Henri et Jules reçoivent une mauvaise note en maths. (se résigner)

____

7. Chantal révise ses notes d'histoire. (continuer)

____

8. Odile recopie ses notes. (passer son temps)

____

D *Verb + **de** + infinitive*

- Some verbs and expressions are joined to a following infinitive by the preposition **de.**

s'abstenir de *to refrain from*
accepter de *to agree to*
s'arrêter de *to stop*
avoir l'intention de *to intend to*
avoir peur de *to be afraid of*
avoir raison de *to be right to*
avoir tort de *to be wrong to*
brûler de *to be burning to, dying to*
se charger de *to make sure to, to see to it that something is done*
choisir de *to choose to*
craindre de *to fear*
décider de *to decide to*
se dépêcher de *to hurry to*

s'empêcher de *to refrain from*
s'empresser de *to hurry, rush to*
entreprendre de *to undertake to*
essayer de *to try to*
s'étonner de *to marvel at*
éviter de *to avoid*
s'excuser de *to apologize for*
finir de *to finish*
se flatter de *to claim to (be able to)*
mériter de *to deserve to*
oublier de *to forget to*
parler de *to talk about*
promettre de *to promise to*
se proposer de *to set out, mean, intend to*
refuser de *to refuse to*
regretter de *to regret*
résoudre de *to resolve to*
risquer de *to risk, run the risk of*

- **Venir de** means *to have just done something.*

Je **viens de voir** Jacquot.	*I **have just seen** Jacquot.*

- Note the following uses of prepositions other than **à** or **de** before an infinitive:

finir par faire qqch *to end up, wind up doing something*
commencer par faire qqch *to begin by doing something*

Study the following pairs of contrasting examples.

Il **commence à chercher** du travail.	*He's **beginning to look for** work.*
Il **commence par chercher** du travail.	*He's **beginning by looking for** work.*
Il **a fini de** nous **aider.**	*He **finished helping** us.*
Il **a fini par** nous **aider**.	*He **wound up helping** us.*

G. **Élections au lycée.** Nous essayons d'organiser les élections aux comités des délégués de classe (*student council*), mais ce n'est pas facile. Complétez les phrases suivantes avec les prépositions qui manquent pour savoir ce qui se passe. Si la phrase est complète telle qu'elle est, marquez le blanc d'un **X.**

1. Les étudiants se proposent __________ organiser les élections aux comités des délégués de classe.
2. Ils se mettent __________ chercher des candidats.
3. Ils comptent __________ procéder aux élections (*hold the election*) au mois de novembre.
4. Antoinette Dubois veut __________ se porter candidate.
5. Elle ne mérite pas __________ être élue.
6. Nous encourageons d'autres étudiants __________ se présenter.
7. Mais ils ne s'empressent pas __________ se porter candidats.
8. Je viens __________ parler avec Lise Léotard.
9. Elle s'intéresse un peu __________ participer aux comités.
10. Si elle se décide __________ se présenter,
11. il faudra __________ organiser sa campagne.
12. Mais en ce moment, nous craignons __________ ne pas avoir assez de candidats.

H. Dix jours à Paris. La classe de français de Mme Richard passe dix jours à Paris. Les élèves sont pressés de tout voir et de tout faire, et chacun s'intéresse à quelque chose de différent. Formez des phrases avec les éléments donnés pour voir comment ils profitent de leur séjour.

1. Loïc et Charles / tenir / voir un match de football

 ____

2. Marie-Noëlle / s'empresser / s'acheter des livres

 ____

3. Mme Richard / descendre tous les jours / acheter des journaux

 ____

4. Albert / se flatter / connaître parfaitement toutes les lignes de métro

 ____

5. Berthe et Christine / entreprendre / organiser un pique-nique au Bois de Boulogne

 ____

6. Philippe / compter / visiter le marché aux timbres

 ____

7. Chantal / passer son temps / regarder les robes aux grands magasins

 ____

8. tous les étudiants / brûler / visiter le Louvre

 ____

9. Martin / essayer / organiser une journée à la campagne

 ____

10. Paulette et Mireille / espérer / avoir le temps de voir Montmartre

 ____

I. Changement d'habitudes. Jean-Pierre a eu des difficultés au lycée cette année. Son oncle raconte une conversation qu'il a eue avec son neveu. Exprimez la narration de l'oncle en français en faisant attention à l'enlacement du verbe et de l'infinitif.

1. I have just spoken with Jean-Pierre.

 ____

2. I explained to him that he risks wasting the school year (**l'année scolaire**).

 ____

3. I encouraged him to begin studying seriously.

 ____

4. He must refrain from going out every day.

 ____

5. He promised to pay attention in class.

6. He apologized for getting (**avoir eu**) bad grades.

7. He's not going to waste any more time watching TV.

8. He has made up his mind to be a good student.

9. I intend to speak with Jean-Pierre next week.

10. We will try to talk every week until the end of the school year.

E *Verb + direct object + **de** + infinitive*

- A group of verbs that take **de** before the following infinitive take a direct object as well.

accuser qqn de faire qqch *to accuse someone of doing something*
convaincre qqn de faire qqch *to convince someone to do something*
décourager qqn de faire qqch *to discourage someone from doing something*
empêcher qqn de faire qqch *to prevent someone from doing something*
féliciter qqn d'avoir fait qqch *to congratulate someone for having done something*
persuader qqn de faire qqch *to persuade someone to do something*
prier qqn de faire qqch *to beg someone to do something*
remercier qqn de faire qqch *to thank someone for doing something*

- Another group of verbs that take **de** before the following infinitive take an indirect object.

commander/ordonner à qqn de faire qqch *to order someone to do something*
conseiller à qqn de faire qqch *to advise someone to do something*
déconseiller à qqn de faire qqch *to advise someone not to do something*
défendre/interdire à qqn de faire qqch *to forbid someone to do something*
demander à qqn de faire qqch *to ask someone to do something*
dire à qqn de faire qqch *to tell someone to do something*
pardonner à qqn de faire qqch *to forgive someone for doing something*
permettre à qqn de faire qqch *to allow someone to do something*
promettre à qqn de faire qqch *to promise someone to do something*
proposer/suggérer à qqn de faire qqch *to suggest to someone to do something*
reprocher à qqn de faire qqch *to reproach someone for doing something*

J. Comment aider nos amis? Il y a beaucoup de copains qui ont des difficultés au collège. Sophie et Daniel s'ingénient à trouver des idées pour les aider. Écrivez leurs solutions en utilisant **il faut** et les mots proposés entre parenthèses.

MODÈLE —Marc n'ouvre jamais le manuel d'histoire. (convaincre/le lire)
→ —Il faut le convaincre de le lire.

1. Régine ne révise jamais son vocabulaire anglais. (encourager/apprendre les mots)

____

2. Christophe s'endort en classe. (commander/faire attention)

____

3. Brigitte n'est jamais chez elle et elle n'étudie pas. (déconseiller/sortir tous les jours)

____

4. Olivier ne participe pas aux discussions. (persuader/répondre)

____

5. Chantal et Robert parlent tout le temps pendant la classe. (dire/se taire)

____

6. Gérard et Louis ne pensent qu'au football. (conseiller/se concentrer sur leurs études)

____

7. Philippe dit qu'il ne comprend rien à la géométrie. (aider/résoudre les problèmes)

____

8. Baudoin et Micheline pensent s'absenter le jour de l'examen. (dissuader/le faire)

____

K. En famille. Les membres de la famille Chéron s'aiment bien et essaient de s'entraider et de se conseiller. Utilisez le vocabulaire et les éléments proposés pour décrire leurs rapports familiaux. Employez le passé composé.

MODÈLE la tante Rosette/conseiller/son neveu Pierrot/se coucher tôt
→ La tante Rosette a conseillé à son neveu Pierrot de se coucher tôt.

La famille

la mère *mother*
le père *father*
le fils *son*
la fille *daughter*
le frère (aîné/cadet) *(older/younger) brother*
la sœur (aînée/cadette) *(older/younger) sister*
la grand-mère *grandmother*
le grand-père *grandfather*
le petit-fils *grandson*
la petite-fille *granddaughter*
la tante *aunt*
l'oncle *uncle*
le neveu *nephew*
la nièce *niece*
le cousin *male cousin*
la cousine *female cousin*
le beau-père *father-in-law, stepfather*
la belle-mère *mother-in-law, stepmother*
les beaux-parents *in-laws*
***le beau-fils, le gendre** *son-in-law*
***la belle-fille, la bru** *daughter-in-law*
le beau-frère *brother-in-law*
la belle-sœur *sister-in-law*
le demi-frère *stepbrother, half-brother*
la demi-sœur *stepsister, half-sister*

*__Beau-fils__ and __belle-fille__ can also mean *stepson* and *stepdaughter.*

1. le grand-père / convaincre / son gendre Guillaume / ne pas quitter son travail

2. les enfants de Guillaume et Sylvie / s'empresser / apporter des fleurs à la tante Émilie

3. le petit Bertrand / demander / sa mère / lui acheter une bicyclette

4. la grand-mère / pardonner / sa petite-fille Giselle / avoir oublié son anniversaire

5. Guillaume et Sylvie / féliciter leur fille Christine / avoir eu 18 à l'examen de philo

6. l'oncle François / enseigner / sa nièce / se servir de l'ordinateur

7. Anne-Marie / interdire / sa fille Mireille / sortir avec Frédéric

8. Nadine / prier / ses parents / l'emmener au bord de la mer

9. Sylvie / inviter ses beaux-parents / dîner

10. Guillaume / proposer / ses parents / passer leurs vacances avec sa famille

L. Et chez vous? Comment est-ce qu'on vit dans votre famille? Choisissez des mots des trois colonnes pour faire huit phrases qui décrivent les rapports familiaux chez vous. Faites attention aux objets directs et indirects et aux prépositions employées devant l'infinitif.

mon père/ma mère	aider	aider à faire le ménage
mes parents	conseiller	conduire prudemment
mon grand-père	déconseiller	faire les courses pour lui/elle/eux/elles
ma grand-mère	défendre	jouer aux jeux vidéo
mes grands-parents	demander	manger en famille le dimanche
mon frère (aîné/cadet)	empêcher	nettoyer ma chambre
ma sœur (aînée/cadette)	encourager	prendre mes études au sérieux
mon oncle/ma tante	ordonner	ranger mes affaires
mon cousin/ma cousine	permettre	se coucher tôt en semaine
	proposer	trop parler au téléphone

1. ______________________________
2. ______________________________
3. ______________________________
4. ______________________________
5. ______________________________
6. ______________________________
7. ______________________________
8. ______________________________

F *Adjective or noun + preposition + infinitive*

- Most adjectives and nouns take **de** before a following infinitive.

—Tu étais **surprise d'apprendre** que notre équipe a perdu le match? — *Were you **surprised to learn** that our team lost the game?*
—Oui. Mais ils sont **sûrs de gagner** le match de dimanche. — *Yes. But they're **sure to win** the game on Sunday.*
—Sans doute. Ils ont **un** grand **désir de gagner.** — *No doubt. They have **a** great **desire to win.***

- Some adjectives and nouns take **à,** however. For example:

être déterminé(e) à *to be determined to*
être prêt(e) à *to be ready to*
être le premier/le troisième/le seul/le dernier (la première/la troisième/la seule/la dernière) à *to be the first/third/only/last to*

Je suis **déterminée à être la première à avoir** 20 à l'examen de maths. — *I'm **determined to be the first to get** a 20 on the math test.*

- Adjectives modified by **trop** or **assez** take **pour** before a following infinitive.

—Pierrot est **trop petit pour comprendre.** — *Pierrot is **too little to understand.***
—Mais il **est assez intelligent pour se conduire** comme il faut. — *But he is **intelligent enough to behave** the way he ought to.*

M. À compléter. Complétez les phrases suivantes avec la préposition qui manque.

1. Marie n'est pas prête __________ passer son examen de chimie.
2. Elle dit qu'elle est sûre __________ ne pas y réussir.
3. Mais elle est déterminée __________ passer l'été à réviser la chimie.
4. Je serais enchanté __________ vous aider à faire le ménage.
5. Je serais le premier __________ vous aider si je pouvais.
6. Mais je suis trop maladroit (*clumsy*) __________ vous être utile.
7. Je ne suis pas heureux __________ voir le petit Albert jouer aux jeux vidéo.
8. C'est une mauvaise idée __________ laisser un enfant perdre son temps de cette façon.
9. Il est le seul élève de sa classe __________ passer tant de temps devant l'écran.
10. Il est assez intelligent __________ comprendre l'importance de ce que je lui dis.

G *Faire + infinitive*

- To express the idea that one person has, gets, or causes another person to do something, French uses the verb **faire** followed by an infinitive.

—Tu **as fait redécorer** ton appartement?	*Have you **had** your apartment **redecorated**?*
—J'**ai fait repeindre** le salon, c'est tout.	*I **had** the living room **repainted**, that's all.*
—La voiture est en panne. Je ne peux pas la **faire démarrer**.	*The car isn't working. I can't **get** it **to start**.*
—Il faut la **faire réparer**, alors.	*Then we have to **have** it **repaired**.*

- The person you have do the work or perform the action may appear at the end of the sentence if there is no other object.

Mme Ducros fait étudier **ses enfants**.	*Mrs. Ducros makes **her children** study.*
L'institutrice fait chanter **ses élèves**.	*The schoolteacher has **her pupils** sing.*

- When the sentence contains two objects, the object of the infinitive is direct and the object of **faire** is indirect. The indirect object may be preceded by **par** or **à.**

J'ai fait repeindre mon appartement **par M. Jollivet**. J'ai fait repeindre mon appartement **à M. Jollivet**.	*I had **Mr. Jollivet** repaint my apartment.*

- One or both of the objects in the above example can be replaced by an object pronoun. The object pronouns always precede **faire.**

Je **le lui** ai fait repeindre.	*I had **him** repaint **it**.*

The past participle of **faire** does not agree with a preceding direct object in this construction.

N. **Problèmes du logement.** Les Giraud viennent d'acheter une maison à Grenoble. La maison est charmante, mais les Giraud découvrent qu'il y a beaucoup de travail à faire avant qu'ils puissent emménager. Lisez la liste des problèmes et employez **il faut** et le causatif pour dire ce qu'il faut faire dans chaque cas pour rendre la maison habitable.

MODÈLE La peinture de la cuisine est vieille. (repeindre)
➔ Il faut la faire repeindre.

Pour aménager une maison

crevassé *cracked (ground)*
débarrasser *to clear out*
se décoller *to peel off*
installer *to install*
insuffisant *insufficient*
se lézarder *to crack (wall)*
la lumière *light*
marcher *to work (appliance)*
le papier (peint) *wallpaper*
remplacer *to replace*
retapisser *to repaper*

1. Le papier du salon se décolle. (retapisser)

   ____

2. La lumière dans la salle à manger ne marche pas. (réparer)

   ____

3. Le plancher des chambres à coucher est très sale. (nettoyer)

   ____

4. La fenêtre du balcon est cassée. (remplacer)

   ____

5. Le trottoir est crevassé. (paver)

   ____

6. Les murs se lézardent. (plâtrer)

   ____

7. Le garage est plein de vieux meubles. (débarrasser)

   ____

Note culturelle

La ville de Grenoble, située dans les Alpes, est une belle ville cosmopolite. Grenoble est une ville universitaire qui compte environ 40 000 étudiants. À Grenoble on trouve aussi le Centre de Recherches Nucléaires où travaillent ensemble des scientifiques français et étrangers. Pour les vacances d'hiver Grenoble est une destination préférée parce que les stations de ski aux alentours de la ville sont nombreuses et excellentes. Capitale de la région appelée le Dauphiné, Grenoble était le lieu des Jeux olympiques en 1968. La population de l'agglomération urbaine de Grenoble dépasse les 400 000 habitants.

O. Une institutrice de première (*first-rate*). Mlle Arnaud est une institutrice excellente qui sait faire progresser ses élèves. Employez le causatif pour exprimer sa façon de résoudre les problèmes de ses élèves et d'organiser sa classe.

MODÈLE Jérôme jette des papiers par terre. (balayer la salle de classe)
➔ Mlle Arnaud lui fait balayer la salle de classe.

1. Catherine n'aime pas parler en classe. (réciter des poèmes)

____

2. André a peur de parler devant tout le monde. (présenter son travail devant un petit groupe)

____

3. Monique et Suzanne bavardent en classe. (écrire une composition)

____

4. Samuel ne comprend pas les problèmes de maths. (relire l'explication dans son livre)

____

5. Les élèves sont fatigués après un examen. (regarder un film)

____

6. Quelques élèves apprennent plus vite que les autres. (aider leurs camarades)

____

7. Le directeur arrive à la porte de sa salle de classe. (observer une leçon de français)

____

8. Nous nous intéressons à la musique. (écouter la chanson que les élèves ont apprise)

____

P. Les causes. Votre ami fait des observations. Vous lui signalez la personne ou la chose qui est la cause des actions qu'il remarque.

MODÈLE Les étudiants travaillaient. (leur professeur)
➔ Leur professeur les a fait travailler.

Quelques actions

démarrer *to start (car)*
grelotter *to shiver*
pleurer *to cry*
pousser *to grow*
rager *to fume (with anger)*
rire *to laugh*
soupirer *to sigh*
sourire *to smile*
trembler *to shake, tremble*

1. Élise pleurait. (son petit ami)
____
2. Les fenêtres tremblaient. (le vent)
____
3. J'ai vu les belles roses qui poussaient chez ton voisin. (mon voisin)
____
4. Les élèves lisaient. (leur institutrice)
____
5. Les enfants riaient. (le clown)
____
6. La voiture démarrait. (le mécanicien)
____
7. La mère souriait. (ses enfants)
____
8. La vieille dame soupirait. (la chaleur)
____
9. Le chien grelottait. (le froid)
____
10. Le client rageait. (la vendeuse)
____

Q. Exercice oral. Posez des questions à un(e) camarade sur ce qu'on l'encourage à faire, sur ce qu'on lui permet de faire, sur ce qu'on lui demande de faire, sur ce qu'on lui fait faire, etc. Employez des tournures avec l'infinitif. Votre camarade vous répondra en employant ces structures et vous posera des questions pareilles à son tour.

PART TWO

Nouns and Their Modifiers; Pronouns

CHAPTER 13 NOUNS: GENDER, NUMBER, AND ARTICLES; USES OF ARTICLES

A *Gender and number of nouns; definite and indefinite articles*

A noun is a word that names a person, place, thing, idea, or quality. Articles, which are often used before nouns, are either definite or indefinite. A definite article identifies something or someone specific (*the* apple, *the* teacher). An indefinite article is more general (*an* apple, *a* teacher).

- French nouns are either masculine or feminine. Most nouns add **-s** to form the plural. There are four forms of the French definite article.

	masculine	*feminine*
singular	**le** crayon **l'**homme	**la** table **l'**école
plural	**les** crayons **les** hommes	**les** tables **les** écoles

Note that both masculine and feminine singular nouns beginning with a vowel or a mute **h** take the definite article **l'**.

- There are three forms of the French indefinite article.

	masculine	*feminine*
singular	**un** crayon **un** homme	**une** table **une** école
plural	**des** crayons **des** hommes	**des** tables **des** écoles

English has no plural indefinite article. French **des** is often equivalent to *some* or *any*.

A. À l'école. Ajoutez à chaque substantif l'article défini et écrivez le syntagme (*phrase*) au pluriel.

MODÈLE ___le___ garçon ___les garçons___

1. ________ cahier ________________
2. ________ calculette ________________
3. ________ étudiant ________________
4. ________ serviette ________________
5. ________ papier ________________
6. ________ stylo ________________

7. ________ leçon ____________________
8. ________ calendrier ____________________
9. ________ bibliothèque ____________________
10. ________ dictionnaire ____________________
11. ________ histoire ____________________
12. ________ cloche ____________________
13. ________ exposé ____________________
14. ________ cantine ____________________
15. ________ magnétoscope ____________________

B. **Au magasin de vêtements.** Ajoutez à chaque substantif l'article indéfini et écrivez le syntagme au pluriel.

MODÈLE ___un___ chapeau ___des chapeaux___

1. ________ pull ____________________
2. ________ chemise ____________________
3. ________ pantalon ____________________
4. ________ cravate ____________________
5. ________ rayon ____________________
6. ________ vendeur ____________________
7. ________ vendeuse ____________________
8. ________ robe ____________________
9. ________ maillot de bain ____________________
10. ________ veste ____________________
11. ________ costume ____________________
12. ________ chemisier ____________________
13. ________ solde ____________________
14. ________ blouson ____________________
15. ________ anorak ____________________

B *Plural nouns*

- Most French nouns form their plural by adding **-s.** There are some exceptions.
- Singular nouns ending in **-s, -x,** or **-z** do not change form in the plural.

le cour**s**	les cour**s**	un pri**x**	des pri**x**
une foi**s**	des foi**s**	la voi**x**	les voi**x**
le moi**s**	les moi**s**	le ne**z**	les ne**z**

- Most nouns ending in **-al** have a plural form ending in **-aux.**

l'anim**al**	les anim**aux**	l'hôpit**al**	les hôpit**aux**
le chev**al**	les chev**aux**	l'idé**al**	les idé**aux**
le génér**al**	les génér**aux**	le journ**al**	les journ**aux**

There are some exceptions: **le bal → les bals, le carnaval → les carnavals, le festival → les festivals, le récital → les récitals.**

- Nouns ending in **-au, -eau,** or **-eu** add **-x** to form the plural.

le bat**eau**	les bat**eaux**	le chev**eu**	les chev**eux**
le bur**eau**	les bur**eaux**	le **jeu**	les **jeux**

Exception: le pn**eu** (*tire*) → les pn**eus.**

- Most nouns ending in **-ou** add **-s** to form the plural, but some add **-x.**

le cl**ou** (*nail*)	les cl**ous**	le tr**ou** (*hole*)	les tr**ous**

But:

le ch**ou**	les ch**oux**	le bij**ou**	les bij**oux**
le gen**ou**	les gen**oux**		

- Some nouns have irregular plurals.

le ciel	les **cieux**	monsieur	**messieurs**
l'œil	les **yeux**	madame	**mesdames**
le travail	les **travaux**	mademoiselle	**mesdemoiselles**

- Family names in French do not change form in the plural.

—Vous connaissez **les Durand**?	*Do you know **the Durands**?*
—Non, mais je sais qu'ils sont les voisins **des Chevalier.**	*No, but I know that they are neighbors **of the Chevaliers**.*

- Some nouns are used mainly in the plural.

les ciseaux *scissors*
les frais *expenses, cost*
les mathématiques, les maths *math*
les mœurs *morals*
les vacances *vacation*

- Some nouns, especially abstract nouns, have no plural.

la foi *faith*
la paix *peace*
la patience *patience*

- Numbers and letters used as nouns also have no plural.

«Femme» s'écrit avec deux **m.**	*"Femme" is written with two **m's**.*
Il y a deux **cinq** dans mon numéro.	*There are two **fives** in my phone number.*

C. Pas un mais deux. Répondez dans chaque cas que vous cherchez/voulez/avez *deux,* pas *un* des substantifs mentionnés.

MODÈLE Vous cherchez un stylo?
→ Je cherche deux stylos.

1. Vous voulez un chapeau?

____

2. Vous assistez au festival?

____

3. Vous avez un neveu?

____

4. Votre nom s'écrit avec un **l**?

____

5. Vous cherchez un monsieur?

____

6. Vous étudiez un vitrail?

____

7. Vous prononcez un discours?

____

8. Vous cherchez un métal?

____

9. Vous prenez un morceau?

____

10. Vous visitez un pays?

____

11. Vous avez un choix?

____

12. Vous préparez un repas?

____

13. Vous lisez un journal?

____

14. Vous changez un pneu?

____

15. Vous avez un rival?

____

C *Determining the gender of nouns*

- Most nouns referring to males are masculine. Most nouns referring to females are feminine.

un homme	une femme
un garçon	une fille
un père	une mère
un oncle	une tante

- Many feminine nouns are formed by adding **-e** to the masculine form.

un saint ➔ une saint**e**	un marchand ➔ une marchand**e**
un rival ➔ une rival**e**	un employé ➔ une employé**e**
un cousin ➔ une cousin**e**	un ami ➔ une ami**e**

- In other cases, the masculine ending is changed to a feminine ending.

-ien ➔ **-ienne**	un Ital**ien** ➔ une Ital**ienne**
-on ➔ **-onne**	un patr**on** ➔ une patr**onne**
-eur ➔ **-euse**	un vend**eur** ➔ une vend**euse**
-teur ➔ **-trice**	un ac**teur** ➔ une ac**trice**
-er ➔ **-ère**	un bouch**er** ➔ une bouch**ère**
-ier ➔ **-ière**	un épic**ier** ➔ une épic**ière**

- The suffix **-esse** forms the feminine of some masculine nouns.

  un prince ➔ une princ**esse**
  un dieu ➔ une dé**esse**

- Many nouns have the same form for both masculine and feminine; only the article changes to indicate the gender of the person referred to.

un/une artiste	un/une camarade	un/une élève	un/une enfant

- Some nouns are masculine even when they refer to women.

un poète	un écrivain	un médecin	un professeur
un auteur	un ingénieur	un ministre	un sculpteur
un docteur	un juge	un peintre	un témoin (*witness*)

Ma femme est **un auteur** très connu.	*My wife is a very famous author.*
Ta sœur est **un** très bon **peintre**.	*Your sister is a very good painter.*

- Other nouns are grammatically feminine even when they refer to men.

une brute	une vedette (*film star*)
une personne	une victime

—Marc est **une personne** sympathique, n'est-ce pas?	*Mark is **a** nice **person**, isn't he?*
—Tu trouves? Tout le monde dit que c'est **une brute**.	*You think so? Everyone says that he's **a beast**.*

D. À compléter. Choisissez le mot qui complète ces phrases.

1. Dans mon quartier l'________________ et son mari sont très aimables. (épicier/épicière)
2. Élizabeth est devenue ________________. (pharmacien/pharmacienne)
3. Cette étudiante est ________ artiste formidable. (un/une)
4. Notre ami Frédéric est ________ des victimes de l'accident. (un/une)
5. Tu connais ________ violiniste? Il est italien, je crois. (le/la)
6. On dit que Joseph Mercier est ________ vedette de l'année. (le/la)
7. Leur fille est ________ enfant de sept ans. (un/une)
8. Ma mère est ________ seul ingénieur de l'équipe. (le/la)

E. Elle aussi. Écrivez que les femmes mentionnées ont les mêmes caractéristiques que les hommes.

Modèle Jacquot est clarinettiste. (sa sœur)
➔ Sa sœur est clarinettiste aussi.

1. Albert est musicien. (Marguerite)

____

2. Louis? Il est épicier. (Émilie)

____

3. Mon cousin est un élève de cette école primaire. (ma nièce)

____

4. Charles? C'est un Breton. (Éloïse)

____

5. Jean-Paul Sartre est un écrivain célèbre. (Simone de Beauvoir)

____

6. Pierre a été victime de son imprudence. (Hélène)

____

7. Maurice est un instituteur formidable. (Lise)

____

8. M. Chauvin est le propriétaire de l'établissement. (Mme Chauvin)

____

9. Son mari est l'avocat de la défense. (sa femme)

____

10. Olivier est un médecin respecté. (Chantal)

____

11. Cet homme est aviateur. (cette femme)

____

12. Roger est un nageur formidable. (Mireille)

____

13. Paul est notre champion. (Caroline)

____

14. Je connais M. Duval, le commerçant. (Mme Mercier)

____

D *Determining the gender of nouns (continued)*

- Although many French nouns give no clue to their gender (**le peuple, la foule**), some have endings that do indicate gender.

Masculine endings:

-age	un avantage, un orage, un voyage (*but* **la page, la plage**)
-eau	un bateau, un cadeau, un couteau (*but* **l'eau** (*fem.*), **la peau**)
-et	le jouet, le secret, le sujet
-ing	le camping, le dancing, le shopping
-isme	le socialisme, le communisme, le tourisme
-ment	un bâtiment, le commencement, un monument
-oir	un espoir, le mouchoir, le trottoir
-ou	le bijou, le clou, le genou

Feminine endings:

-ace la glace, la menace, la surface
-ance la brillance, la chance, l'importance
-ade une ambassade, une promenade, une salade (*but* **le stade**)
-ière la frontière, la lumière, la manière
-ine une aspirine, la cuisine, la piscine (*but* **le magazine**)
-ise une chemise, une surprise, une valise
-sion la décision, l'inversion, la télévision
-esse la jeunesse, la politesse, la promesse
-tion la nation, la production, la programmation
-ette une bicyclette, la calculette, la cassette
-té la liberté, la société, la spécialité
-tude une attitude, la gratitude, la solitude
-ure une aventure, la lecture, la voiture

• Some nouns can be either masculine or feminine, depending on their meaning.

le critique *critic*
la critique *criticism, review*

le livre *book*
la livre *pound*

le poste *job, radio or TV set*
la poste *mail, postal service*

le tour *tour, trip*
la tour *tower*

le voile *veil*
la voile *sail*

F. Masculin ou féminin? Choisissez l'article correct dans chaque cas.

1. François s'est acheté ________ mobylette. (un/une)
2. Ce que tu as dit est vraiment ________ compliment. (un/une)
3. La natation est ________ activité agréable. (un/une)
4. ________ côtelette d'agneau, s'il vous plaît. (Un/Une)
5. ________ cyclisme est un sport important en France. (Le/La)
6. ____________ émission comptez-vous regarder ce soir? (Quel/Quelle)
7. Je n'ai pas compris ________ message. (le/la)
8. Le pharmacien m'a donné ________ ordonnance. (un/une)
9. Elle aime ________ peinture. (le/la)
10. Est-ce que tu as vu ________ stade? (le/la)
11. Le petit Georges a mangé ________ tartine. (un/une)
12. J'ai perdu ________ rasoir. (mon/ma)
13. Il dit toujours ________ vérité. (le/la)
14. Vous avez lu ________ critique du film? (le/la)
15. Je veux voir les informations. Est-ce que je peux allumer ________ poste? (le/la)
16. Elle a acheté ________ livre de pommes. (un/une)
17. ________ voile couvrait le visage de la mariée (*bride*). (Un/Une)
18. Ce bateau a fait ________ tour du monde. (le/la)

E *C'est* versus *il/elle est*

- French has two constructions to identify a noun referring to a person (*he's a . . . , she's a . . .*).

  1. **Il est/Elle est** or **ils sont/elles sont** is used before an unmodified noun of profession, religion, or nationality. Note that no indefinite article is used in this construction.

—**Il est** médecin?	***Is he** a doctor?*
—Non, sa femme est médecin. Lui, **il est** scientifique.	*No, his wife is a doctor. **He's** a scientist.*
—**Ils sont** protestants, les Duvalier?	*Are the Duvaliers Protestants?*
—Lui, **il est** protestant. Elle, **elle est** catholique.	***He's** a Protestant. **She's** a Catholic.*

  2. If the noun is modified (even by just an article), **c'est** or **ce sont** must be used. **C'est un/une** is the most common construction to identify things.

—**C'est** un avocat?	***Is he** a lawyer?*
—Non, **ce n'est pas** un avocat. **C'est un** juge.	*No, **he's not** a lawyer. **He's** a judge.*
—**Ce sont** des soldats?	***Are they** soldiers?*
—Non, **ce sont** des pilotes.	*No, **they're** pilots.*

G. Identifications. Complétez ces phrases en indiquant le choix correct.

1. ______________ un journal français. (C'est/Il est)
2. ______________ vendeuse. (C'est/Elle est)
3. ______________ français. (Ce sont/Ils sont)
4. ______________ des commerçants. (Ce sont/Ils sont)
5. ______________ le propriétaire de la boutique. (C'est/Il est)
6. ______________ une salade délicieuse. (C'est/Elle est)
7. ______________ notre patronne. (C'est/Elle est)
8. ______________ vedette de cinéma. (C'est/Elle est)
9. ______________ architecte. (C'est/Il est)
10. ______________ professeurs. (Ce sont/Ils sont)

F *The partitive*

- The partitive article is an indefinite article used to express an indefinite quantity or part of something (English: *some, any*). The partitive article consists of **de** + **le, la,** or **l'. De** + **le** contracts to **du.** The plural of the partitive article is **des.**

du lait	**de la** patience	**de** l'eau	**des** sandwichs
du pain	**de la** crème	**de** l'or	**des** pommes

- After a negative, the partitive article is **de (d')** unless the verb is **être.** If the verb is **être,** the partitive article retains its full form. **De (D')** also replaces the indefinite article after a negative.

—Tu **n'**as **pas** encore acheté **de** pain! — *You haven't bought any bread yet!*
—Tu **n'**as vraiment **pas de** patience. — *You really don't have any patience, do you?*

—C'est du lait, ça? — *Is that milk?*
—Non, **ce n'est pas du** lait. C'est de la crème. — *No, it's not milk. It's cream.*

—Tu as **une** voiture? — *Do you have a car?*
—Non, je **n'**ai **pas de** voiture. — *No, I don't have a car.*

H. **Il ne reste rien à la charcuterie.** Jean-Claude est entré chez le charcutier du quartier pour acheter quelque chose à manger, mais il ne reste rien dans la boutique. Écrivez des échanges entre l'employé et Jean-Claude en suivant le modèle.

MODÈLE œufs durs
→ —Vous avez des œufs durs?
—Non, monsieur. Il n'y a plus d'œufs durs.

1. jambon
2. salade niçoise
3. fromage
4. carottes râpées
5. saucisson
6. saumon fumé
7. quiches
8. sandwichs

I. On a fait les courses à moitié. Tout le monde est sorti acheter à manger, mais personne n'a acheté tout ce qu'il fallait. Employez le partitif pour le dire, en suivant le modèle.

MODÈLE Marc/acheter/lait/eau minérale
→ Marc a acheté du lait, mais il n'a pas acheté d'eau minérale.

1. Suzanne / chercher / farine / œufs

___

2. moi / rapporter / pain / beurre

___

3. Laurent / trouver / champignons / salade

___

4. Élisabeth / prendre / pommes / oranges

___

5. toi et moi / acheter / petits pois / haricots verts

___

6. vous / rapporter / fromage / yaourt

___

7. toi / chercher / viande / poulet

___

8. les garçons / prendre / lait / Coca

___

J. C'est quoi, ça? Antoinette ne reconnaît pas tous les plats qu'on a préparés. Elle demande à son amie de lui expliquer ce qu'ils sont. Suivez le modèle.

MODÈLE crème/yaourt
→ —C'est de la crème, ça?
—Non, ce n'est pas de la crème. C'est du yaourt.

1. bœuf / porc

___

___

2. poulet / dindon

___

___

3. haricots verts / endives

___

___

4. riz / couscous

5. vin / champagne

6. thon / saumon

7. bouillabaisse / soupe à l'oignon

8. crème caramel / glace

Notes culturelles

- Le couscous est un plat nord-africain, diffusé en France par le contact avec l'Afrique du Nord et par les immigrés maghrébins en France. C'est une spécialité à base de semoule à laquelle on ajoute de la viande et des légumes. Souvent on y ajoute aussi des merghez, de petites saucisses nord-africaines d'un goût très relevé.
- La bouillabaisse est un plat typique de Marseille (et de toute la Provence). On la prépare à partir de poissons variés et de fruits de mer que l'on fait cuire dans de l'eau ou du vin blanc. On y ajoute de l'ail et des condiments pour relever la saveur du poisson et des fruits de mer.
- La crème caramel est un dessert qui ressemble au flan espagnol. Il est préparé à base de crème et de sucre fondu et roussi par l'action du feu.

G *Expressions of quantity*

- After expressions of quantity, **de** is used instead of the partitive.

assez de *enough*
autant de *as much, as many*
beaucoup de *much, many*
Combien de? *how much? how many?*
moins de *less*
peu de *few, little, not much*
plus de *more*
tant de *so much, so many*
trop de *too much, too many*
un peu de *a little (bit of)*

- **De** is also used in expressions of weights and measures such as the following:

  une boîte de *a box of*
  une bouteille de *a bottle of*
  un kilo de *a kilo of*
  une livre de *a pound of*

  —J'ai **deux bouteilles de** lait. — *I have **two bottles of** milk.*
  —Alors, j'ai **autant de** lait que toi. — *Then I have **as much** milk **as** you do.*
  —**Combien de** viande as-tu achetée? — ***How much** meat did you buy?*
  —J'ai pris **un kilo de** bœuf et **une livre de** jambon. — *I got **a kilo of** beef and **a pound of** ham.*

- However, if the noun following the preposition **de** is specific in any of the above cases, the definite article is used, and will contract with the preposition.

  Peu **des** étudiants ont compris. — *Few **of the** students understood.*
  Les enfants ont mangé beaucoup **du** chocolat que je leur ai donné. — *The children ate much **of the** chocolate that I gave them.*

- **La plupart** (*most*) and **bien** (*a lot*) are followed by **de** + article.

  —Il étudie **la plupart du** temps? — *Does he study **most of the** time?*
  —Oui, il a **bien des** livres à lire. — *Yes, he has **a lot of** books to read.*

- The phrase **ne** + verb + **que** (*only*) is not really a negative and is followed by the partitive.

  Tu **ne** dis **que des** sottises. — *You're saying **only** silly things.*

- Note the use of the partitive with school subjects after the verb **faire:**

  faire des maths, de la physique — *to study (major in) math, physics*

- In formal style, **de** replaces the partitive before an adjective that *precedes* the noun.

  Nous avons fait **de grands** efforts. — *We made **great** efforts.*

  However, this rule is increasingly disregarded in all styles.

  Elle a acheté **des belles** fleurs. — *She bought **some beautiful** flowers.*

  However, **d'autres** is used in all styles.

  Avez-vous **d'autres** projets? — *Do you have **other** plans?*
  Oui, on en a **d'autres.** — *Yes, we have **others**.*

K. À compléter. Indiquez lequel des articles proposés est le choix correct.

1. Il prend ________ thé. (du/de)
2. Tu as besoin ________ courage. (du/de)
3. Ils m'ont servi ________ côtelettes de veau. (des/de)
4. Moi, je ne mange pas ________ veau. (un/du/de)
5. Elle ne fait que ________ bêtises. (de/des)
6. Nous cherchons ________ crayons. (des/de)
7. Ce soir on prépare ________ poulet. (du/de)
8. Combien ________ cours suivez-vous? (des/de)
9. Nous avons autant ________ problèmes que vous. (des/de)
10. Achète une livre ________ poires. (des/de)

11. La plupart _________ étudiants sont sympathiques. (des/de)
12. Les professeurs donnent trop _____ travail. (du/de)
13. Il ne lit plus les mêmes livres. Il en lit _________ autres. (d'/des)
14. Bien _________ jounalistes ont écrit à ce sujet. (des/de)

L. Comment est-ce que ça se dit? Traduisez les échanges suivants en français.

1. We need coffee.
   I bought coffee.
   How much coffee did you buy?
   Enough coffee. And I bought three hundred grams of tea too.

____

____

____

____

2. Most of the books that I read were interesting.
   Too many of the books that I read were boring.

____

____

H *Uses of articles*

- The definite article designates a specific noun.

—Je vais te montrer **le dessert.**	*I'm going to show you* ***the dessert.***
—**Le dessert** que tu as préparé?	***The dessert*** *you prepared?*

- The French definite article labels nouns used in a general sense. English nouns are used without any article in this meaning.

La démocratie et **la liberté** sont des traits essentiels de la France.	***Democracy*** *and* ***freedom*** *are basic characteristics of France.*

  Contrast the general and specific uses of the definite article in the following example:

J'adore **la viande,** mais je n'aime pas **la viande** qu'on sert dans ce bistrot.	*I love* ***meat*** *(in general), but I don't like* ***the meat*** *they serve in that bistrot (specific).*

- In a restaurant the definite article is often used when ordering.

Pour moi, **le rosbif** et pour ma femme, **le canard à l'orange.**	*I'll have* ***roast beef*** *and my wife will have* ***duck in orange sauce.***

- The French indefinite article is used much the way its English equivalent is. However, it is not used after **il/elle est** when followed by an unmodified noun of profession, nationality, or religion.

Les Bois sont professionnels. Lui, **il est avocat** et elle, **elle est professeur.**	*The Bois are professionals.* ***He's a lawyer*** *and* ***she's a teacher.***

- In a restaurant the indefinite article is often used to designate a serving of something:

  Un café et **un** petit rouge, s'il vous plaît. — ***A cup of*** *coffee and* ***a glass of*** *red wine, please.*

- The partitive article before names of foods and beverages designates an indefinite quantity. English may or may not use the words *some* or *any* in these cases.

  —Tu veux boire **du** chocolat? — *Would you like to drink hot chocolate?*
  —Non, merci. Tu as **du** café? — *No, thanks. Do you have* ***any*** *coffee?*

- Compare the uses of the articles with the word **thé** in the following sentences.

  Le thé est une boisson d'origine orientale. — ***Tea*** *is a drink that comes from the Orient. (general)*

  J'aime **le thé** que vous avez acheté. — *I like* ***the tea*** *that you bought. (specific)*

  Un thé, s'il vous plaît. — ***A cup of tea****, please. (a standard serving, said to a waiter)*

  Après mon dîner, je bois **du thé**. — *After my dinner, I drink* ***tea****. (indefinite quantity)*

- After the prepositions **avec** and **sans** no article is used unless the noun is modified.

  —Il a écouté **avec** attention. — *He listened with attention (attentively).*
  —Et il a rédigé une composition **sans** fautes. — *And he wrote a composition without mistakes.*

  Il a agi **avec** courage. — *He acted courageously.*
  Il a agi **avec un** courage admirable. — *He acted with admirable courage.*

M. **Qu'est-ce qui manque?** Complétez les phrases suivantes avec l'article qui manque. Si aucun article ne manque, marquez le blanc d'un **X.**

1. Pour moi, _________ coq au vin et _________ pommes de terre à la lyonnaise.
2. Tu ne veux pas _________ bœuf?
3. Non, je mange très peu _________ viande. Je préfère _________ poulet.
4. Garçon! _________ limonade et _________ citron pressé, s'il vous plaît.
5. Je regrette, mais nous n'avons plus _________ citron pressé.
6. Alors, _________ jus d'orange.
7. Pour un étudiant en médecine, _________ diligence est très importante.
8. Il lui faut un peu de _________ repos aussi.
9. Mais, en général, _________ étudiants en médecine ont très peu de _________ temps pour se reposer.
10. Tu aimes _________ cinéma français?
11. Oui, il y a _________ films qui m'ont beaucoup plu. Mais je crois que je préfère _________ films italiens.
12. On passe _________ nouveaux films italiens au Pathé cette semaine. Tu veux aller les voir?

13. Oui, bien sûr. Mais j'ai tant ________ travail. On va voir. Si j'ai ________ temps libre, on ira au Pathé.
14. ________ ordinateur est essentiel dans ________ bureaux modernes.
15. C'est pour ça que beaucoup ________ étudiants font ________ informatique.
16. ________ informatique est une des matières les plus étudiées aujourd'hui.
17. La plupart ________ étudiants ont un ordinateur dans leur chambre.
18. ________ jeux électroniques sont aussi appréciés que ________ logiciels scientifiques.

N. **Comment?** Traduisez les phrases suivantes en français. Choisissez parmi les substantifs suivants pour traduire les adverbes anglais par une phrase prépositive commençant par **avec** ou **sans.**

attention	haine	joie	soin
courage	intelligence	peur	tendresse

1. He spoke intelligently.

____

2. She acted courageously.

____

3. We set out fearlessly.

____

4. He answered hatefully.

____

5. He played joylessly.

____

6. He wrote (**rédiger**) his composition carelessly.

____

7. She spoke to him tenderly.

____

8. He listened attentively.

____

O. **Exercice oral.** Avec trois ou quatre camarades, jouez une scène au restaurant. Posez des questions au garçon et commandez les plats et les boissons. Faites attention à l'emploi des articles.

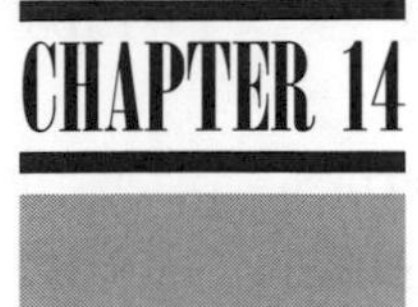

CHAPTER 14 STRESSED PRONOUNS; SUBJECT-VERB AGREEMENT

A *Stressed pronouns—forms and usage*

- Stressed pronouns are used to emphasize a noun or pronoun used as a subject or object, or to replace a noun used as a subject or object.

	singular	*plural*
first person	**moi**	**nous**
second person	**toi**	**vous**
third person	**lui/elle**	**eux/elles**

Moi, je fais du latin, mais **lui, il** fait du grec. — *I'm taking Latin, but* ***he****'s taking Greek.*

—**Nous, on** travaille aujourd'hui. Et **toi**? — ***We****'re working today. What about* ***you****?*

—Je vais à la plage, **moi.** — ***I****'m going to the beach.*

- A stressed pronoun may stand alone in answer to a question.

—Qui fait le ménage aujourd'hui? Toi? — *Who's doing the housework today? You?*

—Pas moi. **Eux.** — *Not me.* ***They are.***

- The stressed pronouns are used after **c'est** and **ce sont** to identify people.

C'est moi/C'est toi/C'est lui/C'est elle/C'est nous/C'est vous.
But: **Ce sont eux/Ce sont elles.**

Colloquially one says **C'est eux/C'est elles;** in the negative, **Ce n'est pas eux. Ce n'est pas elles.** Note also the questions **Qui est-ce?** (*formal*) and **C'est qui?** (*informal*).

- The stressed pronouns are used after prepositions.

—Tu pars **sans elle**? — *Are you leaving* ***without her****?*
—Pas du tout. Elle vient **chez moi** et nous partons ensemble. — *Not at all. She's coming* ***to my house*** *and we're leaving together.*

- The stressed pronouns are also used after **ne . . . que.**

Je **ne** connais **que toi** à Paris. — *You're the* ***only*** *one I know in Paris.*

Il **n'**aime **qu'eux.** — *He likes* ***only them****.*

- The stressed pronoun **soi** (*himself, herself, themselves*) is used with indefinite pronouns or to avoid ambiguity.

Chacun pour **soi**.	*Every man for **himself**.*
Il ne faut pas parler toujours de **lui**.	*One shouldn't talk about **him** all the time.*
Il ne faut pas parler toujours de **soi**.	*One shouldn't talk about **oneself** all the time.*

A. Vacances. Formez des phrases exprimant un contraste avec les éléments proposés. Employez des pronoms disjoints.

MODÈLE je/aller au bord de la mer / ils/aller à la montagne
➔ Moi, je vais au bord de la mer. Eux, ils vont à la montagne.

1. nous/partir en Italie / elles/partir en Grèce

____

____

2. je/prendre le train / ils/partir en voiture

____

____

3. tu/faire de l'alpinisme / il/faire de la natation

____

____

4. mes cousins/aller à la campagne / on (= nous)/aller leur rendre visite

____

____

5. je/avoir trois semaines de vacances / vous/avoir un mois

____

____

6. je/préférer voyager seul / tu/préférer voyager en groupe

____

____

7. on (= nous)/compter faire du cyclisme / il/vouloir faire du tourisme

____

____

8. elle/faire un stage linguistique en Allemagne / tu/te détendre

____

____

Note culturelle

- C'était la tradition française que presque tous les employés et ouvriers prenaient leurs vacances au mois d'août, ce qui créait des embouteillages monstres sur la route et des entassements de voyageurs dans les trains. De nos jours, l'idée d'étaler les vacances fait des progrès.
- Les vacances d'hiver sont très appréciées, surtout par les étudiants qui n'ont pas de cours entre Noël et le jour de l'An et qui peuvent profiter de cet intervalle pour faire du ski.
- Les destinations de prédilection en France pour les vacanciers sont les côtes de Bretagne et la Côte d'Azur en été. Ceux qui aiment faire du camping peuvent se diriger vers le centre du pays. Pour les vacances d'hiver, les Alpes autour de Grenoble attirent des milliers de skieurs.

B. **Tu as tort!** Un copain vous dit des choses erronées sur vos habitudes, vos allées et venues, etc. Corrigez ses impressions en formant une phrase négative. Mettez le pronom **moi** à la fin.

MODÈLE —Je sais que tu aimes les films d'horreur.
→ —Tu as tort! Je n'aime pas les films d'horreur, moi.

1. Je sais que tu sors avec Émilie.

____

2. Je sais que tu te lèves à 8 heures.

____

3. Je sais que tu dors en classe.

____

4. Je sais que tu joues de la clarinette.

____

5. Je sais que tu cherches du travail.

____

6. Je sais que tu vas chez Olivier après les cours.

____

C. **Mon ami Philippe? Jamais!** Un copain a des impressions fausses sur votre ami Philippe. Corrigez ses idées avec une phrase négative au passé composé contenant le mot **jamais.** Mettez le pronom **lui** à la fin.

MODÈLE —Ton ami Philippe sort avec Odile.
→ —Qu'est-ce que tu dis? Il n'est jamais sorti avec Odile, lui.

1. Ton ami Philippe dort en classe.

2. Ton ami Philippe est toujours en retard.

3. Ton ami Philippe interrompt le professeur.

4. Ton ami Philippe se dispute avec Serge.

5. Ton ami Philippe se moque des cours.

6. Ton ami Philippe dérange les autres étudiants.

D. **Réponses mystérieuses.** Un copain curieux vous pose beaucoup de questions. Répondez-lui au négatif, en remplaçant la personne en italique par le pronom disjoint convenable.

MODÈLE —Tu es arrivé avec *Richard*?
➔ —Non, je ne suis pas arrivé avec lui.

1. Ce cadeau est pour *moi*?

2. Tu comptes dîner avec *Janine et François*?

3. Tu as l'intention de passer chez *Paulette?*

4. Je peux compter sur *toi*?

5. Est-ce que Suzanne a été invitée par *Jacques*?

6. Est-ce que le professeur est fâché contre *Alice et toi*?

7. Est-ce que tu t'assieds derrière *Adrienne*?

8. Est-ce que tu as une attitude hostile envers *mes copains*?

E. **Qui est-ce?** Écrivez des échanges pour vérifier l'identité des gens que vous voyez. Employez **c'est/ce sont** et un pronom disjoint selon le modèle.

MODÈLE les Durand là-bas / les Devaux
—Ce sont les Durand là-bas?
➔ —Non, ce n'est pas eux. Ce sont les Devaux.

1. toi dans la photo / ma sœur Barbara

____

2. moi le suivant (*next*) / lui

____

3. M. Charpentier assis sur le banc / notre voisin M. Beauchamp

____

4. Adèle Malmaison dans la boutique / Mlle Lachaux

____

5. nos amis là, à l'entrée du lycée / d'autres étudiants

____

6. Gisèle et Marie-Claire à l'arrêt d'autobus / Christine et Yvette

____

F. **Il n'y a pas d'autres.** Répondez aux questions suivantes à l'affirmatif. Utilisez l'expression **ne . . . que** suivi d'un pronom disjoint pour indiquer que la personne (les personnes) mentionnée(s) est (sont) le seul objet du sentiment exprimé. Suivez le modèle.

MODÈLE —Elle invite M. Breuil?
➔ —Oui. Elle n'invite que lui.

1. Tu m'aimes?

____

2. On respecte cet agent de police?

____

3. Les étudiants admirent le professeur Triquet?

____

4. Les juges estiment cette avocate?

____

5. Vous nous aidez?

____

6. Il apprécie les musiciens de cet orchestre?

____

7. Ils encouragent leurs filles?

____

8. Il amène sa sœur?

____

G. **Joyeux anniversaire.** Complétez ce paragraphe avec les pronoms qui manquent (disjoints et conjoints) pour savoir ce qu'on a fait pour fêter l'anniversaire de Florence.

Demain, c'est l'anniversaire de Florence et moi, (1) __________ voulais organiser une surboum pour (2) __________. J'ai téléphoné à mon amie Hélène. (3) __________, elle adore les fêtes, et je savais qu'elle voudrait m'aider. «Qui est-ce que tu veux inviter?» m'a-t-elle demandé. «Aide-(4) __________ à faire la liste, lui ai-je répondu. On invite Serge?»

—Oui, (5) __________, il est très sympathique et il aime danser.

—On invite Philippe et Charles?

—Oui, (6) __________, ce sont de grands blagueurs et ils font rire tout le monde.

—Et le cadeau de Florence? Qu'est-ce qu'on doit acheter pour (7) __________? Je n'ai vraiment pas d'idées, (8) __________. Tu peux proposer quelque chose, (9) __________?

—On va demander à Janine et à Claire. Elles, (10) __________ ont toujours de bonnes idées quand il s'agit de cadeaux.

Nous nous sommes réunies avec Janine et Claire et nous sommes allées avec (11) __________ aux grands magasins. Tout était très cher, et (12) __________, on n'avait pas beaucoup d'argent. Tout d'un coup, Janine a dit: «Regarde! Des foulards de soie en solde. Allons les regarder.» Nous en avons choisi un pour Florence et la vendeuse a fait un joli paquet.

La fête de Florence a été un grand succès. Nous avions invité une vingtaine d'amis et ils sont tous venus. Florence a été vraiment très émue, et le foulard lui a beaucoup plu.

—Vous êtes vraiment de très bonnes amies, (13) __________. Vous m'avez rendue très heureuse.

—Non, c'est (14) __________ la bonne amie, Florence. C'est un plaisir de faire tout ça pour (15) __________.

B Subject-verb agreement with stressed pronouns and other special cases

- After the phrase **c'est** + stressed pronoun + **qui,** the verb agrees with the stressed pronoun.

—**C'est toi qui t'en vas?**	***Are you the one who's leaving?***
—Non. **C'est moi qui suis** de garde. **Ce sont eux qui partent.**	*No.* ***I'm the one who's*** *on duty.* ***They're the ones who are leaving.***
—**C'est vous qui faites** du japonais?	***Are you the ones who are studying*** *Japanese?*
—Non. **C'est nous qui étudions** le russe.	*No.* ***We're the ones who are studying*** *Russian.*

- Compound subjects linked by **et** or **ou** or **ni . . . ni . . .** are usually followed by a third person plural verb. When the subject is linked by **ni . . . ni . . . , ne** precedes the verb.

L'argent ou l'influence sont utiles.	***Money or influence are*** *useful.*
Ni l'un ni l'autre ne viendront nous voir.	***Neither one will come*** *to see us.*

However, the phrase **l'un ou l'autre** (*one or the other*) is followed by a singular verb.

L'un ou l'autre viendra nous voir.	***One or the other will come*** *to see us.*

- The third person plural is used after expressions of quantity, such as **beaucoup, la plupart, trop, combien, une foule, une multitude.** But the singular is used after **la foule de.**

Beaucoup (de touristes) **visitent** la ville.	***Many*** *(tourists)* ***visit*** *the city.*
Une foule d'étudiants sont allés voir le directeur.	***A crowd of students went*** *to see the director.*
La foule d'étudiants a été reçue par lui.	***The crowd of students was*** *received by him.*

- After approximate numbers ending in **-aine** and fractions, either the singular or the plural is used.

Une vingtaine d'ingénieurs travaille/travaillent ici.	***About twenty engineers work*** *here.*
La moitié arrive/arrivent à l'heure.	***Half arrive*** *on time.*

H. Quel verbe? Choisissez la forme du verbe qui complète les phrases.

Qualités et émotions

l'amitié (*fem.*) *friendship*
l'amour (*masc.*) *love*
les apparences (*fem.*) *appearances*
le bonheur *happiness*
le courage *courage*
l'exactitude (*fem.*) *punctuality, exactness*
la force *strength*
la générosité *generosity*
la haine *hatred*
le malheur *unhappiness, misfortune*
la paresse *laziness*
la peur *fear*
la politesse *politeness*
la prudence *caution*

1. L'amitié et l'amour __________ (est/sont) des sentiments importants.
2. Ni son courage ni sa force ne __________ (l'a/l'ont) sauvé.
3. La haine ou la peur __________ (est/sont) responsables de son malheur.
4. C'est toi qui __________ (fais/fait) la vaisselle aujourd'hui.
5. Beaucoup d'assiettes sales __________ (t'attend/t'attendent) à la cuisine.
6. Combien __________ (vit/vivent) dans la peur dans ce pauvre pays?
7. L'exactitude et la prudence __________ (est/sont) les traits principaux de son caractère.
8. Il y a beaucoup d'étudiants ici. Le quart __________ (vient/viennent) de l'étranger.
9. C'est vous qui __________ (peut/pouvez) m'aider.
10. Voilà Olivier et Baudoin. L'un ou l'autre __________ (viendra/viendront) ce soir.

I. En français! Traduisez ces phrases en français.

1. He's buying bread. We're buying wine.

____

2. We saw Julien and Colette. We went over to (**s'approcher de**) them.

____

3. Gérard thinks only about himself.

____

4. Are you the one who teaches history?

____

5. We came in after him but before you (*sing.*).

____

6. Many received our invitations but only half accepted.

____

7. And I thought you were inviting only me!

____

8. There are Marc and Serge. One or the other knows the answer.

____

J. Exercice oral. Apportez des photos de famille pour montrer à un(e) camarade de classe. Il (Elle) vous posera des questions au sujet des personnes photographiées: «C'est toi? C'est ta cousine Agnès?» Utilisez autant de pronoms disjoints que possible dans les questions et les réponses.

CHAPTER 15 POSSESSIVE AND DEMONSTRATIVE ADJECTIVES AND PRONOUNS

A Possession and possessive adjectives

- Possession in French is expressed by the preposition **de. De** is repeated before each owner.

la maison **de** mon oncle	*my uncle's house*
les cahiers **de** Janine et **d'**Alice	*Janine's and Alice's notebooks*

- French possessive adjectives agree in gender and number with the noun they modify.

before masculine singular nouns	
mon vélo	**notre** vélo
ton vélo	**votre** vélo
son vélo	**leur** vélo

before feminine singular nouns	
ma cassette	**notre** cassette
ta cassette	**votre** cassette
sa cassette	**leur** cassette

before all plural nouns	
mes vélos, **mes** cassettes	**nos** vélos, **nos** cassettes
tes vélos, **tes** cassettes	**vos** vélos, **vos** cassettes
ses vélos, **ses** cassettes	**leurs** vélos, **leurs** cassettes

- The possessive adjectives **son, sa, ses** may mean *his, her,* or *its,* depending on the owner. The form of the adjective agrees with the noun possessed.

Marie a **son** vélo et Pierre a **sa** moto.	*Marie has **her** bike and Pierre has **his** motorcycle.*

- Before a feminine noun beginning with a vowel or a mute **h, mon, ton, son** replace **ma, ta, sa.**

mon adresse   **ton** école   **son** histoire

- To emphasize or clarify a possessor, French uses the preposition **à** plus a stressed pronoun.

—Monique et Philippe ont pris sa voiture.	*Monique and Philippe took his/her car.*
—Sa voiture **à lui** ou sa voiture **à elle**?	***His** car or **her** car?*
Mon ordinateur **à moi** est plus rapide que leur ordinateur **à eux**.	***My** computer is faster than **their** computer.*

- The word **propre** (*own*) may also be used to add emphasis.

Je l'ai vu de mes **propres** yeux.	*I saw it with my **own** eyes.*

A. Voilà. Utilisez **voilà** suivi d'un adjectif possessif pour signaler à votre amie que les objets dont elle parle sont tout près.

MODÈLE —Tu as un livre?
→ —Oui. Voilà mon livre.

1. Edouard a une voiture?
2. Nous avons une calculatrice?
3. Nos copains ont des disques?
4. Tu as des cartes?
5. J'ai des lettres?
6. Odile a un chien?
7. Marc et Chantal ont des billets?
8. Les étudiants ont une salle de réunion?
9. Jean-Marc a un sac à dos?
10. Nathalie a un ordinateur?

B. C'est sûrement à quelqu'un d'autre. Dites dans chaque cas que le véhicule n'est pas à la personne proposée. Utilisez les adjectifs possessifs dans vos réponses.

MODÈLE —La jeep est à vous?
→ —Non. Ce n'est pas ma jeep.

Les véhicules

un autobus *bus*
un bateau *boat*
une bicyclette *bicycle*
un camion *truck*
une caravane *trailer camper*
une mobylette *moped*
une moto *motorcycle*
une voiture de sport *sports car*

1. La moto est à tes cousins?

2. Les voitures de sport sont à ton frère?

3. La caravane est à toi et à ta famille?

4. La mobylette est à Paul?

5. L'autobus est à la compagnie?

6. Le camion est à vous deux?

7. Le bateau est à toi?

8. La bicyclette est à Yves?

Note culturelle

L'industrie automobile est très importante en France. La France occupe le quatrième rang parmi les pays qui produisent des automobiles avec presque quatre millions de voitures par an. Elle occupe le cinquième rang mondial dans la production des camions, avec un demi-million de véhicules par an.

Les deux compagnies principales dans la production de l'automobile sont Renault et Peugeot-Citroën. Cette industrie est très importante dans le commerce international français: presque la moitié des voitures de fabrication française sont exportées.

C. À qui? Vous entendez une phrase dans laquelle l'identité du possesseur est ambigüe. Demandez des précisions au moyen de la préposition **à** et d'un pronom disjoint. Suivez le modèle.

Modèle —Christine et Maurice sont venus avec ses parents.
➔ —Ses parents à elle ou ses parents à lui?

1. Voilà Jacques et Madeleine avec sa mère.

2. Monsieur Lachaux et sa nouvelle épouse vivent avec ses enfants.

3. Les garçons et les filles sont arrivés dans leur voiture.

4. J'ai vu Olivier et Suzanne avec son cousin.

____

5. Quand je vous ai vus, Anne-Marie et toi, vous promeniez un chien.

____

6. Il veut revoir Paulette avant son départ.

____

D. Le bureau du club des étudiants en biologie. Les étudiants en biologie ont organisé un club et l'école leur a donné une petite salle pour installer leur bureau. Annette raconte ce que chaque étudiant a apporté au bureau. Employez des adjectifs possessifs pour savoir ce qu'elle dit.

MODÈLE Georges/enveloppes
➔ Georges a donné ses enveloppes.

Au bureau

une affiche *poster*
un annuaire *telephone book*
un calendrier *calendar*
un dictionnaire scientifique *science dictionary*
un feutre *felt-tipped pen*
une imprimante *printer*
du papier à lettres *stationery*
un répondeur *answering machine*

1. Roger / affiche

____

2. Louise et Simone / répondeur

____

3. Charles / feutres

____

4. Hélène / imprimante

____

5. le professeur de biologie / papier à lettres

____

6. Albert et vous / calendrier

____

7. moi / annuaire

____

8. toi / dictionnaire scientifique

____

B *Possessive pronouns*

- The English possessive pronouns are *mine, yours, his, hers, ours, theirs.* Those forms are used to replace a possessive adjective and noun. The French possessive pronouns consist of the definite article and a special possessive form. A possessive pronoun agrees in gender and number with the noun it replaces.

masculine singular	*feminine singular*	*masculine plural*	*feminine plural*
le mien	**la mienne**	**les miens**	**les miennes**
le tien	**la tienne**	**les tiens**	**les tiennes**
le sien	**la sienne**	**les siens**	**les siennes**
le nôtre	**la nôtre**	**les nôtres**	
le vôtre	**la vôtre**	**les vôtres**	
le leur	**la leur**	**les leurs**	

- **Le sien, la sienne, les siens, les siennes** may mean *his, hers,* or *its,* depending on the owner. The form of the pronoun agrees with the noun it replaces.

Moi, j'ai **ma calculatrice**, mais Pierre n'a pas **la sienne.**	*I have* ***my calculator****, but Pierre doesn't have* ***his.***
Nous aimons **notre quartier**, mais elle préfère **le sien.**	*We like* ***our neighborhood****, but she prefers* ***hers.***

- The articles **le** and **les** of the possessive pronouns contract with **à** and **de.**

—Tu penses à mon problème? —Non. Je pense **au mien.**	*Are you thinking about my problem?* *No. I'm thinking* ***about mine.***
—Elle se souvient de nos idées? —Non. Elle se souvient **des siennes.**	*Does she remember our ideas?* *No. She remembers* ***hers.***

E. On a tout laissé au lycée. Employez un pronom possessif dans chaque cas pour dire que tout le monde a laissé ses affaires au lycée.

MODÈLE toi/calculatrice/moi
→ Toi, tu as ta calculatrice, mais moi, j'ai laissé la mienne au lycée.

1. moi / cahier / Françoise

____

2. nous / stylos / nos copains

____

3. toi / carte / le professeur

____

4. David / sac à dos / Christine

____

5. Odile / bouquins / moi

____

6. vous / dictionnaire / nous

7. mes amis / agendas / vous

8. les enfants / crayons / toi

Note culturelle

Dans le système éducatif français, le lycée représente la deuxième étape de la formation secondaire, la première étant le collège. Au lycée, les étudiants préparent le baccalauréat en trois ans. À part le baccalauréat traditionnel, il existe depuis 1986 le baccalauréat professionnel donné aux étudiants spécialisés dans les études techniques.

Pendant la première année au lycée tous les étudiants étudient les mêmes matières, et l'étude de la langue française est considérée la plus importante. À la fin de cette première année au lycée (appelée «seconde» en France), les élèves choisissent (basées sur un examen) une des trois filières offertes: ES (économique et social), L (littéraire) ou S (scientifique). Dans les lycées techniques on offre aussi différentes sections de spécialisation.

Les deux dernières années du lycée s'appellent «première» et «terminale». En terminale les élèves consacrent leur temps à la préparation du baccalauréat.

F. **Ici et en bas.** La moitié des choses cherchées est ici, l'autre moitié est en bas. Employez des pronoms possessifs pour le dire, comme dans le modèle.

Modèle — Je cherche tes livres et les livres de Jean-Pierre.
→ Les miens sont ici, les siens sont en bas.

1. Je cherche mes copies et les copies des élèves.

2. Je cherche votre carte de crédit et la carte de crédit de Renée.

3. Je cherche notre carnet de chèques et le carnet de chèques de Rémi.

4. Je cherche tes photographies et les photographies du professeur.

5. Je cherche mes clés et les clés de nos amis.

6. Je cherche mon manteau et le manteau de Jacqueline.

G. C'est le mien. Répondez aux questions suivantes avec la préposition de la question et le pronom possessif correspondant. Suivez le modèle.

MODÈLE —Avec quel professeur parles-tu?
➔ —Avec le mien.

1. À quels amis téléphones-tu?
2. Dans quel laboratoire travaillent-ils?
3. De quelles clarinettes jouez-vous, vous deux?
4. À quelle tragédie pense-t-il?
5. De quelles affaires s'occupe-t-elle?
6. Contre quels étudiants le professeur est-il fâché?
7. De quel stylo vous servez-vous?

H. Contrastes. Un groupe de camarades de classe parle des différences qu'ils ont trouvées entre eux en faisant connaissance pendant la première semaine de l'année scolaire. Exprimez ce qu'ils disent en français.

1. Pierre and I use calculators. His is old, mine is new.
2. My English teacher is nice, yours is unpleasant.
3. Christine's backpack is red, mine is green.
4. My friends are better in math (**plus calés en maths**) than yours (are).
5. Your tests are hard. Ours are harder.
6. Solange's composition (**rédaction**) is long. Mine is longer.
7. My day (**journée**) is shorter than theirs.
8. The school's computers are more powerful (**puissants**) than his (are).

I. Exercice oral. Avec un(e) camarade, jouez l'exercice précédent. Trouvez les différences et les ressemblances entre vous deux. Après, présentez les résultats de votre discussion à un(e) troisième camarade en employant autant de possessifs que possible.

C *Demonstrative adjectives*

A demonstrative adjective points out a specific person or thing (*this* book, *that* story, *these* cassettes, *those* stores). The French demonstrative adjective by itself does not distinguish between *this* and *that.*

- The French demonstrative adjective has four forms. The form agrees with the noun it modifies.

	masculine	*feminine*
singular	**ce** crayon *this/that pencil* **cet** homme *this/that man*	**cette** table *this/that table*
plural	**ces** crayons *these/those pencils*	**ces** tables *these/those tables*

Note that before a masculine singular noun beginning with a vowel or mute **h,** the form **cet** is used.

- To distinguish between *this* and *that,* **-ci** is added to a noun to mean *this* or *these* and **-là** is added to mean *that* or *those.*

—Votre classe lit **ce** livre-**ci** ou **ce** livre-**là**? *Is your class reading **this** book or **that** book?*

—Nous lisons **ce** livre-**ci. Ces** romans-**là** sont pour l'année prochaine. *We're reading **this** book. **Those** novels are for next year.*

J. Dans le rayon d'informatique. Julie cherche un nouvel ordinateur et des accessoires. Elle demande au vendeur le prix de tout ce qu'elle voit. Écrivez ce qu'elle dit avec des adjectifs démonstratifs comme dans le modèle.

MODÈLE moniteur
➔ Vous pouvez me dire le prix de ce moniteur, s'il vous plaît?

L'ordinateur

le clavier *keyboard*
le disque dur *hard drive*
la disquette *diskette*
le lecteur de CD-ROM *CD-ROM drive*
le logiciel *software package*
la souris *mouse*
l'unité de disque (*fem.*) *disk drive*

1. ordinateur

____

2. unité de disque

____

3. disquettes

____

4. logiciel

____

5. lecteur de CD-ROM

____

6. disque dur

____

7. clavier

____

8. souris

____

K. Préférences. Utilisez l'adjectif démonstratif convenable avec le suffixe **-là** pour indiquer quel objet on préfère dans chaque cas.

MODÈLE —Tu aimes la cravate de Jacques?
➔ —Oui, mais je préfère cette cravate-là.

1. Les étudiants aiment les livres d'histoire?

____

2. Tu aimes l'anorak de Fabien?

____

3. Germaine aime le chapeau de Colette?

____

4. Ta copine et toi, vous aimez les bijoux de Mme Deschamps?

____

5. Les voisins aiment leur appartement?

____

6. Tu aimes les quartiers du centre?

____

7. Tu aimes l'immeuble où habite Jean-Claude?

____

L. Choisissez! Vous travaillez dans le rayon de vêtements d'un grand magasin. Utilisez les adjectifs démonstratifs suivis des suffixes **-ci** et **-là** pour demander des précisions aux clients quand ils veulent voir quelque chose. Suivez le modèle.

MODÈLE —Je voudrais voir ce foulard, s'il vous plaît.
➔ —Ce foulard-ci ou ce foulard-là?

1. Montrez-moi le pantalon, s'il vous plaît.

____

2. Je pourrais voir l'imperméable, s'il vous plaît?

____

3. Les chaussettes que vous avez derrière vous m'intéressent.

____

4. Voudriez-vous me montrer la robe bleue, s'il vous plaît?

____

5. Je voudrais essayer l'anorak, s'il vous plaît.

____

6. Ce tee-shirt ferait mon affaire.

____

7. Je voudrais voir les sandales, s'il vous plaît.

____

8. Vous me permettez d'essayer la veste jaune, s'il vous plaît?

____

D *Demonstrative pronouns*

- French demonstrative pronouns (English: *this one, that one, the one; these, those, the ones*) agree with the noun they refer to.

	masculine	*feminine*
singular	**celui**	**celle**
plural	**ceux**	**celles**

- As with demonstrative adjectives, **-ci** or **-là** can be added to the noun to distinguish between *this/that* and *these/those.*

—Quel logiciel recommandez-vous?	*Which software package do you recommend?*
—**Celui-ci** est plus utile que **celui-là**.	***This one** is more useful than **that one**.*
—Quelle est la différence entre les imprimantes?	*What is the difference between these printers?*
—**Celles-ci** sont plus chères que **celles-là**.	***These** are more expensive than **those**.*

- Demonstrative pronoun + **-ci** and demonstrative pronoun + **-là** are also used to mean *the latter* and *the former,* respectively. The pronouns agree with the nouns they refer to. In French, *the latter* (**-ci**) precedes *the former* (**-là**).

L'industrie et l'agriculture sont importantes en France. **Celle-ci** emploie moins d'ouvriers que **celle-là**.	*Industry and agriculture are important in France. **The latter** employs fewer workers than **the former**.*

- A demonstrative pronoun may be followed by the relative pronoun **qui** or **que** to mean *the one(s)*. The demonstrative pronoun may also be followed by **de** to signal possession.

—Quel livre a-t-il pris? **Celui qui** était sur la chaise?	*Which book did he take? **The one that** was on the chair?*
—Oui, c'était **celui qu'**il cherchait.	*Yes. That was **the one that** he was looking for.*
—Mais c'était **celui de mon frère**.	*But it was **my brother's**.*

—J'ai lu les revues françaises; **celles qui** étaient sur votre bureau. — *I read the French magazines;* ***the ones that*** *were on your desk.*
—**Celles de** la nouvelle étudiante française? — *The new* ***French student's****?*
—Oui. **Celles qu'**elle a apportées de France. — *Yes.* ***The ones that*** *she brought from France.*

- The pronouns **ceci** (*this*) and **cela** (*that*) refer to situations rather than to specific nouns. In modern French, **cela** (or **ça** in spoken language) tends to be used instead of **ceci.**

—Et avec **ceci**? — *Anything else?*
—**Cela** suffit, merci. — ***That's*** *enough, thank you.*
—Il a perdu son travail. C'est dur, **ça**. — *He lost his job. That's a very difficult situation.*
—Oui, mais c'est **ça**, la vie! — *Yes, but* ***that****'s life!*

M. **Un client difficile.** À la charcuterie, Jean-Marc n'aime rien de ce qu'on lui montre. Écrivez ce qu'il dit en utilisant les pronoms démonstratifs. Suivez le modèle.

MODÈLE Vous voulez un peu de ce fromage, monsieur?
➔ Non, pas celui-là.

1. Vous voulez un peu de cette salade niçoise, monsieur?
____
2. Vous voulez un peu de ce jambon, monsieur?
____
3. Vous voulez un peu de ce saucisson, monsieur?
____
4. Vous aimez ces biscuits, monsieur?
____
5. Vous voulez quelques tranches (*slices*) de cette quiche, monsieur?
____
6. Vous voulez un peu de cette choucroute, monsieur?
____
7. Vous aimez les crudités, monsieur?
____
8. Vous voulez un peu de ce rosbif, monsieur?
____

N. **Les affaires qui traînent.** Formez des échanges qui identifient les possesseurs des objets que les étudiants ont laissé traîner dans la salle de permanence (*study hall*). Suivez le modèle.

MODÈLE bonnet gris / Philippe / Stéphane
➔ —Qui a oublié ce bonnet gris? Philippe?
—Non, je crois que c'est celui de Stéphane.

1. Walkman / Gisèle / Josette

2. stylo / Colin / Luc

3. chaussures / Fabien / Martin

4. gants / Julie / Hélène

5. cahiers / Eugénie et Colette / Élisabeth et Monique

6. calculatrice / Gérard / Paul

7. lunettes / Loïc / Thomas

O. Quel bon goût. Gabrielle aime tout ce que son amie Thérèse achète, possède, emploie, etc. Utilisez les pronoms démonstratifs et les verbes entre parenthèses pour voir ce qu'elle dit. Suivez le modèle.

MODÈLE Tu aimes les pulls en coton? (porter)
➔ Pas tellement. Mais j'aime celui que tu portes.

1. Tu aimes les petits pois? (préparer)

2. Tu aimes la musique des années quarante? (jouer)

3. Tu aimes les voitures allemandes? (conduire)

4. Tu aimes la soupe à l'oignon? (servir)

5. Tu aimes les lunettes de soleil? (porter)

6. Tu aimes les spaghettis? (faire)

____

7. Tu aimes les sandales? (acheter)

____

P. En français! Écrivez l'équivalent français des phrases suivantes.

1. This exercise is not well done. This is unacceptable.

____

2. This book is more difficult than that one.

____

3. They always arrive late. I don't like that.

____

4. The port of Marseilles* and the port of Cherbourg are important. The former is bigger than the latter. (*Switch in French to:* ***The latter is less big than the former.***)

____

____

5. —Whose suitcases are these?
—That one belongs to me.

____

____

6. I didn't say that. I don't think like that.

____

Q. Exercice oral. Jouez une scène de départ. Un(e) ami(e) vous aide à faire les valises et vous demande s'il faut emporter les choses qu'il (elle) voit dans votre chambre. Vous précisez dans chaque cas que vous emportez quelque chose d'autre. Employez autant d'adjectifs et de pronoms démonstratifs et possessifs que possible. Par exemple: **Cette brosse-là n'est pas la mienne. Je vais emporter celle-ci.** Travaillez avec un(e) camarade de classe.

*NOTE:	*English*	*French*
	Marseilles	Marseille
	Lyons	Lyon

The names of these two cities have no final "s" in French.

CHAPTER 16 INTERROGATIVE ADJECTIVES AND PRONOUNS

A *Interrogative adjectives*

- The interrogative adjective **quel** (*which, what*) agrees in gender and number with the noun it modifies.

	masculine	*feminine*
singular	**Quel** train? *Which train?*	**Quelle** classe? *Which class?*
plural	**Quels** trains? *Which trains?*	**Quelles** classes? *Which classes?*

- **Quel(le)(s)** may be preceded by a preposition.

  De quel livre est-ce que vous parlez? — *What book are you talking **about**?*
  Pour quelle compagnie travaille-t-il? — *What company does he work **for**?*

- **Quel(le)(s)** is used before forms of **être** in sentences where English uses *what.*

  Quelle est la différence? — ***What**'s the difference?*
  Quelles sont vos idées? — ***What** are your ideas?*

- **Quel(le)(s)** may also be used in exclamations. The implication may be either positive or negative.

  Quelle catastrophe! — ***What a** catastrophe!*
  Quels restaurants! — ***What** restaurants!*

A. Pour préciser. Utilisez l'adjectif interrogatif **quel** pour demander des précisions sur les objets qu'on mentionne. Suivez le modèle.

MODÈLE —Jacqueline m'a montré les livres.
→ —Quels livres?

1. Philippe m'a prêté le vélo.

   ____

2. Jocelyne et Vivienne ont écouté les disques compacts.

   ____

3. Lucette a joué avec la raquette.

   ____

4. J'ai conduit la voiture.

   ____

5. Tu me donnes la carte, s'il te plaît.

   ____

6. Marc est sur la moto.

___

7. Montrez-moi la chambre.

___

8. J'ai perdu les jumelles.

___

9. Serge se sert de la caméra.

___

10. Moi, je me sers de l'appareil-photo.

___

B. Des précisions. Dans chaque cas, demandez qu'on précise de quel article il s'agit. Utilisez l'adjectif interrogatif **quel** et faites attention à l'accord du participe passé. Suivez le modèle.

MODÈLE —Jacqueline a acheté des livres.
➔ —Quels livres a-t-elle achetés?

1. Monique a pris des billets.

___

2. Alain et Crispin sont entrés dans un restaurant.

___

3. Gabrielle a besoin d'une revue.

___

4. Les étudiants ont parlé avec un de leurs professeurs.

___

5. Marguerite a fait un exercice difficile.

___

6. Yves a reçu une mauvaise note dans une de ses classes.

___

7. Mes parents ont acheté des médicaments.

___

8. Les enfants ont regardé des émissions à la télé.

___

C. Exclamations. Formez l'exclamation convenable dans chaque cas en écrivant la forme correcte de **quel** devant un des deux substantifs proposés.

1. Le cousin de Marie-Christine est mort dans un accident de la route.

a. ___ tragédie! b. ___ courage!

2. Eugène a gagné 40 000 francs à la loterie!

a. ________________ horreur! b. ________________ chance!

3. Le toit de leur maison s'est effondré *(caved in)*.

a. ________________ malheur! b. ________________ merveille!

4. Germaine a séché *(cut)* tous ses cours cette semaine.

a. ________________ bêtise! b. ________________ diligence!

5. Il y a eu un tremblement de terre en Italie.

a. ________________ plaisir! b. ________________ catastrophe!

6. Les grands-parents de François lui ont donné de l'argent pour acheter ses livres.

a. ________________ générosité! b. ________________ politesse!

7. Julien refuse de travailler.

a. ________________ paresse! b. ________________ talent!

D. Une touriste pleine d'admiration. Odile Jobert montre sa ville à Élisabeth, une étudiante américaine. Élisabeth aime tout ce qu'elle voit. Exprimez son admiration avec **quel** et l'adjectif proposé. Suivez le modèle.

Modèle la place de la République/très joli
→ —Voilà la place de la République.
—Quelle place! Elle est très jolie.

1. les rues piétonnes / très animé

____

____

2. les cafés / charmant

____

____

3. le stade / énorme

____

____

4. le jardin public / beau

____

____

5. la cathédrale / magnifique

____

____

6. les librairies / intéressant

____

____

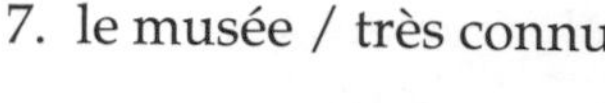

7. le musée / très connu

____

____

8. les grands magasins / élégant

____

____

Note culturelle

Le tourisme est la deuxième industrie de France (après l'industrie automobile). Plus de 60 000 000 de touristes étrangers arrivent aux frontières françaises tous les ans. Le séjour moyen de ces visiteurs est de neuf jours. Plus de 2 000 000 d'Américains visitent la France chaque année. Pour accueillir ces touristes, la France compte plus de 500 000 chambres d'hôtel.

B *Interrogative pronouns*

- French interrogative pronouns agree in gender and number with the noun they refer to.

	masculine	*feminine*
singular	**lequel** *which (one)*	**laquelle** *which (one)*
plural	**lesquels** *which (ones)*	**lesquelles** *which (ones)*

—Un de nos élèves est tombé malade. *One of our students got sick.*
—**Lequel**? ***Which one?***

—Mon frère travaille dans une banque. *My brother works in a bank.*
—Dans laquelle? ***In which one?***

—Il y a deux robes qui sont pour toi. *There are two dresses which are for you.*
—**Lesquelles?** ***Which ones?***

- The prepositions **à** and **de** contract with the interrogative pronoun.

—Nous allons à un pays étranger. *We're going to a foreign country.*
—**Auquel?** ***To which one?***

—J'ai besoin de ces journaux. *I need those newspapers.*
—**Desquels?** Il y en a tant. ***Which ones****? There are so many.*

- The following pronouns are used for *who, whom* in questions:

qui or **qui est-ce qui** *who (subject)*
qui *whom (object of verb, requires inversion of subject of verb)*

Qui sort? ***Who****'s going out?*

Qui cherchez-vous? ***Whom*** *are you looking for?*

Qui as object may be replaced by **Qui est-ce que** without inversion.

Qui est-ce que vous cherchez? ***Whom*** *are you looking for?*

- The interrogative pronoun *what* as object of the verb is rendered either **Que** (with inversion) or **Qu'est-ce que** (without inversion).

Que voulez-vous?	***What*** *do you want?*
Qu'est-ce que vous voulez?	***What*** *do you want?*

- *What* as subject of the sentence is rendered **Qu'est-ce qui** (without inversion).

Qu'est-ce qui te fait mal?	***What*** *hurts you?*

- Both **qui** and **qui est-ce que** can be used after prepositions. **Que** becomes **quoi** after prepositions, **qu'est-ce que** becomes **quoi est-ce que.**

À qui pensez-vous?	***About whom*** *are you thinking?*
À qui est-ce que vous pensez?	***About whom*** *are you thinking?*
De quoi avez vous besoin?	***What*** *do you need?*
De quoi est-ce que vous avez besoin?	***What*** *do you need?*

E. Ça m'intéresse. Demandez à votre ami(e) quel objet l'intéresse. Employez le pronom interrogatif dans vos réponses comme dans le modèle.

MODÈLE —Ce livre m'intéresse.
➔ —Lequel? Celui-là?

1. Ce film m'intéresse.

____

2. Ces revues m'intéressent.

____

3. Ce cours m'intéresse.

____

4. Ces émissions m'intéressent.

____

5. Cette photo m'intéresse.

____

6. Ces disques m'intéressent.

____

7. Cet itinéraire m'intéresse.

____

F. Exactement. Posez des questions avec le pronom interrogatif **lequel** pour savoir exactement de quel objet il s'agit. Suivez le modèle et faites attention aux contractions obligatoires.

MODÈLE —Il cherche les chaussures de sport.
➔ —Lesquelles cherche-t-il exactement?

1. Je veux l'anorak.

____

2. Elle met les bottes.

____

3. Nous lavons les pulls.

4. J'ai besoin des chaussettes de laine.

5. Elle cherche les collants.

6. Ils pensent aux vêtements.

7. Je prends le blue-jean.

G. En colonie de vacances. Les affaires des enfants qui font un séjour dans cette colonie de vacances sont en pagaïe. Les animateurs essaient de les restituer, ce qui n'est pas facile. Utilisez les pronoms interrogatifs, démonstratifs et possessifs pour écrire les réponses des enfants aux questions des animateurs. Suivez le modèle.

MODÈLE —Ce sont tes valises, Claudette?
➔ —Lesquelles? Ah, non. Celles-là ne sont pas les miennes.

On part en colonie

la colonie de vacances *summer camp*
le couteau de poche *pocket knife*
la couverture *blanket*
les jumelles *binoculars*
la lampe de poche *flashlight*
la raquette de tennis *tennis racket*
le sac à dos *backpack*
le sac de couchage *sleeping bag*
la tente *tent*

1. C'est ta raquette de tennis, Baudoin?

2. Ce sont tes pulls, Richard?

3. C'est le sac à dos d'Yvette?

4. Ce sont vos sacs de couchage, Marc et Paul?

5. Ce sont les lettres de Christine et Mireille?

6. C'est ta lampe de poche, Colin?

7. Ce sont vos couvertures, Ombeline et Josette?

____

8. Ce sont tes jumelles, Alice?

____

9. C'est ton couteau de poche, Serge?

____

10. C'est la tente de Michèle?

____

H. Des questions. Complétez les questions suivantes avec le pronom qui manque.

1. ________ (Who) travaille ici?
2. ________ (What) tu as fait hier?
3. ________ (What) vous avez acheté pour le déjeuner?
4. ________ (What) vous intéresse?
5. Avec ________ (whom) tu es sorti?
6. Sur ________ (what) avez-vous écrit?

Note culturelle

La colonie de vacances est une des possibilités qui permettent aux jeunes Français de passer une partie de l'été au contact de la nature. Le camping et le caravaning ont aussi connu un très grand essor en France. La France compte plus de 9 000 terrains de camping et 6 000 000 de campeurs par an.

I. Exercice oral. Jouez l'exercice G avec un(e) camarade en employant les objets qu'on trouve dans la salle de classe et vos affaires personnelles. Vous pouvez varier la structure des questions et des réponses pourvu que vous utilisiez tous les pronoms que vous avez appris.

CHAPTER 17 ADJECTIVES; COMPARATIVE AND SUPERLATIVE

A *Gender of adjectives*

Adjectives give information about nouns and pronouns (a *small* box, a *different* book).

- French adjectives agree in gender and number with the noun or pronoun they modify. Most masculine adjectives add **-e** to form the feminine.

  grand ➔ **grande** *big*
  espagnol ➔ **espagnole** *Spanish*
  prochain ➔ **prochaine** *next*
  noir ➔ **noire** *black*
  gris ➔ **grise** *gray*
  petit ➔ **petite** *little, small*
  compliqué ➔ **compliquée** *complicated*
  poli ➔ **polie** *polite*
  bleu ➔ **bleue** *blue*

- Adjectives with a masculine form ending in **-e** do not change form in the feminine.

  bizarre ➔ **bizarre** *strange, peculiar*
  difficile ➔ **difficile** *difficult*
  drôle ➔ **drôle** *funny*
  jaune ➔ **jaune** *yellow*
  logique ➔ **logique** *logical*
  rouge ➔ **rouge** *red*

- Most masculine adjectives ending in **-x** have feminine forms ending in **-se.**

  dangereux ➔ **dangereuse** *dangerous*
  généreux ➔ **généreuse** *generous*
  heureux ➔ **heureuse** *happy*
  merveilleux ➔ **merveilleuse** *marvelous*
  nerveux ➔ **nerveuse** *nervous*
  sérieux ➔ **sérieuse** *serious*

- Masculine adjectives ending in **-f** have feminine forms ending in **-ve.**

  actif ➔ **active** *active*
  naïf ➔ **naïve** *naïve*
  neuf ➔ **neuve** *new*
  sportif ➔ **sportive** *athletic*

- Adjectives ending in **-el, -en,** or **-on** double the final consonant before adding **-e.**

  actu**el** ➔ actu**elle** *present, present-day*
  cru**el** ➔ cru**elle** *cruel*
  canadi**en** ➔ canadi**enne** *Canadian*
  europé**en** ➔ europé**enne** *European*
  b**on** ➔ b**onne** *good*
  mign**on** ➔ mign**onne** *cute*

  Gentil (*nice, friendly*), **pareil** (*similar*), and **nul** (*none, not any*) also double the final **-l** before adding **-e: gentille, pareille, nulle.**

- Some masculine adjectives ending in **-s** have feminine forms ending in **-sse.**

  bas ➔ **basse** *low*
  épais ➔ **épaisse** *thick*
  gras ➔ **grasse** *fat, fatty*
  gros ➔ **grosse** *big, fat*

- Some masculine adjectives ending in **-et** have feminine forms ending in **-ète.**

  compl**et** ➔ compl**ète** *complete*
  discr**et** ➔ discr**ète** *discreet*
  inqui**et** ➔ inqui**ète** *restless, upset*
  secr**et** ➔ secr**ète** *secretive*

- Some masculine adjectives ending in **-et** or **-ot** double the final **-t** before adding **-e.**

  coqu**et** ➔ coqu**ette** *flirtatious*
  mu**et** ➔ mu**ette** *mute*
  s**ot** ➔ s**otte** *foolish*

- Masculine adjectives ending in **-er** have feminine forms ending in **-ère.**

  am**er** ➔ am**ère** *bitter*
  derni**er** ➔ derni**ère** *last*
  étrang**er** ➔ étrang**ère** *foreign*
  lég**er** ➔ lég**ère** *light*

- Masculine adjectives derived from verbs and ending in **-eur** have feminine forms ending in **-euse.**

  flatt**eur** ➔ flatt**euse** *flattering*
  tromp**eur** ➔ tromp**euse** *deceptive*

- Some adjectives have irregular feminine forms.

  beau ➔ **belle** *beautiful, handsome*
  blanc ➔ **blanche** *white*
  bref ➔ **brève** *brief*
  doux ➔ **douce** *sweet, gentle, soft*
  faux ➔ **fausse** *false*
  favori ➔ **favorite** *favorite*
  fou ➔ **folle** *mad, crazy*
  frais ➔ **fraîche** *fresh*
  franc ➔ **franche** *frank*
  grec ➔ **grecque** *Greek*
  long ➔ **longue** *long*
  nouveau ➔ **nouvelle** *new*
  public ➔ **publique** *public*
  roux ➔ **rousse** *redheaded*
  sec ➔ **sèche** *dry*
  vieux ➔ **vieille** *old*

- Some adjectives are invariable. They do not change form to reflect gender or number.

  un pantalon **chic** ***stylish*** *pants*
  une robe **chic** *a* ***stylish*** *dress*

  des chaussures **marron** ***brown*** *shoes*
  des chaussettes **marron** ***brown*** *socks*

A. Tous les deux. Répondez aux questions en disant que la deuxième chose ou personne mentionnée a la même caractéristique que la première. Suivez le modèle.

MODÈLE —Ce lycée est grand. Et cette école?
➔ —Elle est grande aussi.

1. Ce pain est très frais. Et cette tarte?

   ____

2. Ce café est amer. Et votre bière?

   ____

3. Mon voisin est très sot. Et votre voisine?

   ____

4. Ce compte rendu est complet. Et cette page?

   ____

5. Ce tableau est ancien. Et cette sculpture?

   ____

6. Le frère de Rosette est brun. Et sa sœur?

   ____

7. Le concert est merveilleux. Et la pièce de théâtre?

____

8. Le président est très discret. Et sa secrétaire?

____

9. Son père est roux. Et sa tante?

____

10. Le film est sensationnel. Et la musique?

____

11. Leur cousin est sportif. Et leur cousine?

____

12. Leur fils est mignon. Et leur fille?

____

B. Substitution. Refaites les locutions suivantes en faisant les substitutions indiquées.

MODÈLE un garçon intelligent (fille) ➔ une fille intelligente

1. le gouvernement actuel (administration)

____

2. une histoire drôle (récit)

____

3. un chapeau chic (écharpe)

____

4. une conclusion logique (résultat)

____

5. le théâtre grec (langue)

____

6. l'ordre public (opinion)

____

7. un enfant nerveux (mère)

____

8. une valise légère (paquet)

____

9. une chanson favorite (film)

____

10. un fromage exquis (viande)

____

11. un calme trompeur (tranquillité)

____

12. un goût délicat (nourriture)

____

B Plural of adjectives

- Most French adjectives are made plural by adding **-s** to the masculine or feminine singular form.

  noir ➔ noir**s** poli ➔ poli**s** heureuse ➔ heureuse**s**
  bon ➔ bon**s** drôle ➔ drôle**s** blanche ➔ blanche**s**

- Masculine singular adjectives ending in **-s** or **-x** do not change form in the plural.

  des gâteaux délicieu**x** *delicious cakes*
  des bâtiments ba**s** *low buildings*

- Adjectives ending in **-eau** such as **beau, nouveau** add **-x** to form the masculine plural.

  de beau**x** jardins *beautiful gardens*
  des mots nouveau**x** *new words*

- Most masculine singular adjectives ending in **-al** have plural forms ending in **-aux.**

  des plans géni**aux** *brilliant plans*
  des problèmes soci**aux** *social problems*

  But the adjectives **banal, fatal, final, natal,** and **naval** form the masculine plural by adding **-s.**

  les examens final**s** *final exams*
  leurs pays natal**s** *their native countries*

C. Pas un mais deux. Répondez dans chaque cas qu'il s'agit de deux choses, pas d'une seule.

Modèle —Tu as vu un beau monument?
➔ —J'ai vu deux beaux monuments.

1. Tu vas passer un examen oral?

____

2. Tu as vu un film affreux?

____

3. Il y a un gros immeuble dans cette rue?

____

4. Tu as l'examen final aujourd'hui?

____

5. Il a un cousin roux?

____

6. Il a écrit un livre banal?

7. Il étudie un cas spécial?

8. Ils ont fait un voyage dangereux?

9. Tu as appris un mot nouveau?

10. Il y a un œuf frais dans le frigo?

11. Nous allons visiter un monument national?

12. Tu as acheté un produit local?

D. On court les magasins. Vous demandez des choses dans différents magasins. Qu'est-ce le vendeur ou la vendeuse vous répond? Suivez le modèle.

MODÈLE —Je cherche une robe longue.
➔ —Voici les robes longues.

1. Je cherche un parfum français.

2. Je voudrais un légume frais.

3. J'ai besoin d'un journal espagnol.

4. Je veux acheter un fromage crémeux.

5. Montrez-moi, s'il vous plaît, un fromage gras.

6. J'ai besoin d'un pantalon gris.

7. Vous avez un foulard bleu?

8. Je voudrais lire un roman québécois.

E. La vie intellectuelle. Formez des phrases qui seraient utiles dans des discussions intellectuelles en ajoutant la forme correcte des adjectifs aux substantifs donnés.

1. **actuel**
   a. les élections ____________
   b. l'économie ____________
   c. les conflits ____________
2. **international**
   a. des efforts ____________
   b. des organisations ____________
   c. une entreprise ____________
3. **grec**
   a. la poésie ____________
   b. les régions ____________
   c. les dialectes (*masc.*) ____________
4. **classique**
   a. la musique ____________
   b. les philosophes ____________
   c. les chansons ____________
5. **religieux**
   a. une croyance ____________
   b. des sentiments ____________
   c. des conceptions ____________
6. **européen**
   a. l'union ____________
   b. les pays ____________
   c. les langues ____________
7. **concret**
   a. des exemples ____________
   b. une application ____________
   c. des actions ____________
8. **étranger**
   a. des influences ____________
   b. la littérature ____________
   c. les ambassadeurs ____________
9. **fictif** (*fictional*)
   a. des personnages ____________
   b. une situation ____________
   c. des histoires ____________
10. **naval**
   a. l'école ____________
   b. des combats ____________
   c. les bases ____________

C *Position of adjectives*

- Most French adjectives follow the noun they modify.

C'est un garçon **intelligent**.	*He's an **intelligent** boy.*
C'est une femme **cultivée**.	*She's a **cultured** woman.*

- Some common adjectives referring to beauty, age, goodness, and size usually precede the noun.

beau *beautiful, handsome*	**gros** *big, fat*	**mauvais** *bad*
bon *good*	**jeune** *young*	**nouveau** *new*
gentil *nice, friendly*	**joli** *pretty*	**petit** *small*
grand *big*	**long** *long*	**vieux** *old*

Nous sommes arrivés à ce **petit** hôtel après un **long** voyage.	*We arrived at this **small** hotel after a **long** trip.*

- Special forms of **beau, nouveau,** and **vieux** are used before masculine singular nouns beginning with a vowel.

un **beau** bâtiment	un **nouveau** bâtiment	un **vieux** bâtiment
un **bel** immeuble	un **nouvel** immeuble	un **vieil** immeuble

- Ordinal numbers and some other common adjectives usually precede the noun they modify.

autre *other*	**plusieurs** *several*	**quelques** (*pl.*) *a few*
chaque *each*	**premier** *first*	**tel** *such*

Prenez la **troisième** rue à gauche. — *Turn left at the* ***third*** *street.*
Chaque étudiant a **plusieurs** livres. — ***Each*** *student has* ***several*** *books.*

- When more than one adjective is used to describe a noun, each adjective is placed in its usual position. If two adjectives occupy the same position before or after the noun, they are joined by **et.**

un **bon** compte rendu **intéressant** — *a* ***good, interesting*** *report*
un compte rendu **intéressant et compréhensif** — *an* ***interesting, comprehensive*** *report*
un **long et mauvais** compte rendu — *a* ***long, bad*** *report*

- Some adjectives can either follow or precede a noun, but their meaning changes depending on their position. Usually, they have a literal meaning when they follow the noun and a figurative meaning when they precede it.

un **ancien** combattant *a* ***former*** *soldier (veteran)*
une ville **ancienne** *an* ***old, ancient*** *city*

un **brave** homme *a* ***decent*** *man*
un soldat **brave** *a* ***brave*** *soldier*

certains pays ***certain (some)*** *countries*
un échec **certain** *a* ***sure*** *failure*

mon **cher** ami *my* ***dear*** *friend*
une voiture **chère** *an* ***expensive*** *car*

la **dernière** fois *the* ***last (final)*** *time*
l'année **dernière** ***last (the preceding)*** *year*

la **même** idée *the* ***same*** *idea*
le jour **même** *the* ***very*** *day*

un **pauvre** homme *a* ***poor (unfortunate)*** *man*
un homme **pauvre** *a* ***poor (penniless)*** *man*

la **prochaine** fois *the* ***next (following)*** *time*
la semaine **prochaine** ***next*** *week*

ma **propre** chambre *my* ***own*** *room*
une chambre **propre** *a* ***clean*** *room*

un **sale** quartier *a* ***nasty (awful)*** *neighborhood*
un quartier **sale** *a* ***dirty*** *neighborhood*

la **seule** femme *the* ***only*** *woman*
une femme **seule** *a woman* ***alone***

un **simple** citoyen *an* ***ordinary*** *citizen*
un texte **simple** *a* ***simple*** *text*

un **vrai** ami *a* ***real*** *friend*
une histoire **vraie** *a* ***true*** *story*

F. Identifiez. Complétez les réponses de Micheline aux questions de son amie Solange en écrivant un des adjectifs de la liste ci-dessus dans le blanc convenable. Faites attention au placement de l'adjectif pour exprimer l'idée communiquée par chaque échange entre les deux amies.

Modèle Solange: Ta nouvelle jupe a coûté beaucoup d'argent?
➔ Micheline: Oui, c'est une ______ jupe chère.

1. Solange: Tu as déjà étudié avec M. Deschênes?
   Micheline: Oui, c'est mon ______________ professeur ______________.
2. Solange: Tu es allée en Bretagne il y a un mois?
   Micheline: Oui, j'y suis allée le ______________ mois ______________.
3. Solange: Tes voisins les Durand n'ont pas beaucoup d'argent, n'est-ce pas?
   Micheline: C'est vrai. C'est une ______________ famille ______________.
4. Solange: Tu n'as pas fait de fautes à l'examen de maths?
   Micheline: J'étais la ______________ étudiante/l'étudiante ______________ à résoudre tous les problèmes.
5. Solange: Hélène est toujours disposée à nous aider.
   Micheline: Oui, c'est une ______________ amie ______________.
6. Solange: Olivier ne nettoie jamais son appartement.
   Micheline: Tu as raison. C'est un ______________ appartement ______________.
7. Solange: Tous les détails de l'histoire sont exacts.
   Micheline: Oui, c'est une ______________ histoire ______________.
8. Solange: Tes parents t'ont offert une bicyclette pour ton anniversaire, n'est-ce pas?
   Micheline: Oui, j'a ma ______________ bicyclette ______________ maintenant.

G. Décrivons! Formez des descriptions en partant des éléments donnés. Faites attention au genre, au nombre et aux formes spéciales des adjectifs.

Modèle jeune/professeurs ➔ de jeunes professeurs

1. beau / terrasse ______________
2. vieux / églises ______________
3. vieux / objet ______________
4. nouveau / ordinateur ______________
5. nouveau / industrie ______________
6. vieux / instruments ______________
7. beau / îles ______________
8. beau / accent ______________
9. nouveau / usines ______________
10. beau /animaux ______________
11. vieux / assiette ______________
12. nouveau / avions ______________

H. À l'école avec Odile. Odile décrit ses compagnons, ses professeurs, ses classes et le lycée où elle étudie. Pour voir ce qu'elle dit, ajoutez les adjectifs entre parenthèses aux phrases pour modifier les substantifs en italique. Faites attention à l'accord et au placement des adjectifs.

MODÈLE Mon professeur de français est une *femme.* (intelligent, cultivé)
→ Mon professeur de français est une femme intelligente et cultivée.

1. Nous assistons aux conférences dans une *salle.* (grand, ancien)

____

2. Pour la classe d'anglais nous préparons des *exposés.* (petit, intéressant)

____

3. Dans la classe de maths nous subissons des *épreuves.* (long, difficile)

____

4. Derrière le lycée il y a un *jardin.* (petit, joli)

____

5. J'y vais souvent avec mon ami Philippe. C'est un *garçon.* (beau, gentil)

____

6. Nous parlons des *poèmes* qu'il faut préparer. (nouveau, français)

____

7. Il y a des *professeurs* au lycée. (plusieurs, excellent)

____

8. Ils font des *cours.* (passionnant, utile)

____

I. Et maintenant il s'agit de vous. Décrivez ces aspects de votre vie en ajoutant deux adjectifs à chaque phrase pour modifier les substantifs en italique.

1. Mon ami X est un *garçon.*

____

2. Mon amie X est une *fille.*

____

3. Mon professeur d'anglais est un *homme*/une *femme.*

____

4. J'habite dans une *maison*/un *appartement.*

____

5. J'habite dans un *quartier.*

____

6. J'aime les *chansons.*

____

7. Mes amis et moi, nous aimons les *films.*

____

8. Je préfère les *conversations.*

____

D *Comparison of adjectives, adverbs, nouns, and verbs*

One object or person may be seen as having more, less, or the same amount of a characteristic as another object or person. To express this, French and English use comparative constructions.

- To make comparisons of superiority, French uses the construction **plus** + adjective + **que.**

Le boulevard est **plus large que** notre rue. — *The boulevard is **wider than** our street.*

- To make comparisons of inferiority, French uses the construction **moins** + adjective + **que.**

Mais le boulevard est **moins large que** l'autoroute. — *But the boulevard is **less wide than** (**not as wide as**) the superhighway.*

- To make comparisons of equality, French uses the construction **aussi** + adjective + **que.**

Le boulevard est **aussi large que** l'avenue de la République. — *The boulevard is **as wide as** the Avenue of the Republic.*

- The adjectives **bon** and **mauvais** have irregular comparative forms.

bon(ne)(s) ➔ **meilleur(e)(s)**   mauvais(e)(s) ➔ **pire(s)**

Ce restaurant est **meilleur que** l'autre. — *This restaurant is **better than** the other one.*

Le bruit est **pire** ici **que** dans mon quartier. — *The noise is **worse** here **than** in my neighborhood.*

- Adverbs are compared in the same way as adjectives.

Elle répond **plus poliment que** lui. — *She answers **more politely than** he does.*

Elle répond **moins poliment que** lui. — *She answers **less politely than** he does.*

Elle répond **aussi poliment que** lui. — *She answers **as politely as** he does.*

- The adverbs **bien** and **mal** have irregular comparative forms: **mieux** (*better*) and **pire** (*worse*). **Pire** may be replaced by **plus mal.** The comparative of **beaucoup** is **plus,** and the comparative of **peu** is **moins.**

—On dit que M. Morot enseigne **mieux que** Mme Richard. — *They say that Mr. Morot teaches **better than** Mrs. Richard.*
—J'en doute. Ses étudiants écrivent **pire (plus mal) que** les étudiants de Mme Richard. — *I doubt it. His students write **worse than** Mrs. Richard's students do.*

- When verbs are compared, **autant** replaces **aussi** in comparisons of equality.

Je travaille **plus/moins que** toi. — *I work **more/less than** you do.*
Je travaille **autant que** toi. — *I work **as much as** you do.*

- The comparison of nouns resembles the comparison of verbs. **De** is used before the noun.

Il a **plus/moins de soucis que** nous.	*He has **more/fewer worries than** we do.*
Il a **autant de soucis que** nous.	*He has **as many worries as** we do.*

- In comparisons, **que** may be followed by a noun, a stressed pronoun, a demonstrative or possessive pronoun, a prepositional phrase, or an adjective. In the last case, the adjective functions as a noun.

Le chemisier jaune est plus chic que **le vert**.	*The yellow blouse is more stylish than **the green one.***
Les petits enfants étudient autant que **les grands**.	*The little children study as much as **the big ones.***
Ce roman est moins intéressant que **ceux de l'autre auteur**.	*This novel is not as interesting as **the ones by the other author**.*

J. Notre ville. Faites les comparaisons indiquées par le signe arithmétique.

MODÈLE le lycée/− vieux/l'école primaire
➔ Le lycée est moins vieux que l'école primaire.

1. le stade / + grand / salle de concert

____

2. les cinémas / + nombreux / les théâtres

____

3. la faculté de médecine / = importante / la faculté de droit

____

4. le jardin zoologique reçoit / = visiteurs / la bibliothèque municipale

____

5. le musée scientifique / − grand / le musée d'art

____

6. les restaurants ici / = chers / les restaurants parisiens

____

7. les rues de la vieille ville / + étroites / les rues des quartiers modernes

____

8. le quartier des affaires / − animé / le quartier des étudiants

____

9. la piscine municipale / + bonne / la plage au bord du fleuve

____

10. la maison de la culture offre / = activités / le centre communautaire (*community center*)

____

K. Un moment difficile au lycée. Ces lycéens sont très occupés. Exprimez ce qu'ils font en employant la comparaison des substantifs (**plus de, moins de, autant de**). Suivez le modèle.

MODÈLES Richard lit trois romans. Odile en lit deux.
➔ Richard lit plus de romans qu'Odile.
Richard lit trois romans. Odile en lit quatre.
➔ Richard lit moins de romans qu'Odile.
Richard lit trois romans. Odile en lit trois aussi.
➔ Richard lit autant de romans qu'Odile.

1. Frédéric suit cinq cours. Marc en suit quatre.

____

2. Sylvie écrit deux thèmes. Robert en écrit un.

____

3. Monique subit trois examens. Marcelle en subit quatre.

____

4. Maurice résout (*solves*) trois problèmes de maths. Philippe en résout trois aussi.

____

5. Marie-Laure étudie deux langues étrangères. Alfred en étudie deux aussi.

____

6. Claudine apprend trois poèmes. Chantal en apprend quatre.

____

7. Hervé analyse cinq œuvres. Charles en analyse quatre.

____

8. Julie fait six expériences de chimie. Serge en fait six aussi.

____

L. Les impressions. Un(e) ami(e) vous dit ses impressions. Vous les contradisez moyennant des comparaisons, selon les indications données. Faites attention aux signes arithméthiques et suivez le modèle.

MODÈLES —J'ai l'impression que Corinne ne travaille pas beaucoup. (+/les autres)
➔ —Ce n'est pas vrai. Elle travaille plus que les autres.
—J'ai l'impression que Corinne ne travaille pas beaucoup. (=/les autres)
➔ —Ce n'est pas vrai. Elle travaille autant que les autres.

1. J'ai l'impression que ton frère dort trop. (−/moi)

____

2. J'ai l'impression que Danielle n'étudie pas beaucoup. (+/Éliane)

____

3. J'ai l'impression que notre professeur parle trop. (– /le professeur de Justine)

____

4. J'ai l'impression que ton chien ne mange pas beaucoup. (= /les autres chiens)

____

5. J'ai l'impression que tu ne lis pas beaucoup. (+ /toi)

____

6. J'ai l'impression que Paul ne comprend pas beaucoup. (= /les autres étudiants)

____

M. Les professeurs parlent de leurs étudiants. Exprimez ces idées avec le comparatif des adverbes en refaisant les phrases selon les modèles.

MODÈLES Jacques travaille sérieusement. Laurent, pas tellement.
➔ Jacques travaille plus sérieusement que Laurent.
Jacques travaille sérieusement. Laurent, même plus.
➔ Jacques travaille moins sérieusement que Laurent.
Jacques travaille sérieusement. Laurent aussi.
➔ Jacques travaille aussi sérieusement que Laurent.

1. Monique répond intelligemment. Christine, même plus.

____

2. Édouard rédige soigneusement. Louis, pas tellement.

____

3. Nicole travaille rapidement. Lucien aussi.

____

4. Anne-Marie écoute attentivement. Guillaume, aussi.

____

5. Gérard oublie souvent. Paulette, même plus.

____

6. François se comporte bien. Georges, pas tellement.

____

N. Et vous? Faites des comparaisons entre cette année à l'école et l'année dernière quant aux choses indiquées. Utilisez des pronoms démonstratifs après **que** et faites attention à la forme des adjectifs.

MODÈLE mes classes/difficile
➔ Mes classes sont plus/moins/aussi difficiles que celles de l'année dernière.

1. nos manuels / intéressant

____

2. mes camarades de classe / sympathique

____

3. les professeurs / exigeant

____

4. les devoirs / facile

____

5. la nourriture qu'on sert à la cantine (*lunchroom*) / bon

____

6. mon horaire / commode

____

7. la classe de français / passionnant

____

8. les bals qu'on organise / amusant

____

O. Comparez. Choisissez des élements des trois colonnes pour exprimer des comparaisons basées sur votre expérience personnelle.

ma chambre	grand	la chambre de X
ma maison	petit	la maison de X
mon appartement	joli	l'appartement de X
mes disques compacts	beau	les disques compacts de X
mon école	laid	l'école de X
ma rue	moderne	la rue de X
mon quartier	intéressant	le quartier de X
mes amis	bon	les amis de X
mes professeurs	mauvais	les professeurs de l'année dernière
mes classes	tranquille	mes cousins
mes devoirs	bruyant	les classes de X
	sale	les devoirs de X
	propre	les devoirs donnés par X
	sympathique	
	gentil	
	intelligent	
	difficile	
	facile	
	passionnant	
	ennuyeux	

1. ____
2. ____
3. ____
4. ____
5. ____
6. ____
7. ____
8. ____

P. Ces vacances—meilleures ou pires? Les membres de la famille Grandet reviennent de leurs vacances en Auvergne. Ils les comparent avec les vacances en Bretagne l'année dernière. En partant des éléments donnés, écrivez les phrases qu'ils disent. L'élément après **que,** c'est-à-dire, le deuxième terme de la comparaison, doit être un pronom.

MODÈLE la piscine qu'on avait en Bretagne était / + grand / la piscine qu'on avait en Auvergne
→ La piscine qu'on avait en Bretagne était plus grande que celle qu'on avait en Auvergne.

1. le voyage en train était / + long / le voyage de l'année dernière

2. l'hôtel en Auvergne était / + luxueux / l'hôtel où on est descendu en Bretagne

3. le paysage auvergnat était / + montagneux / le paysage de Bretagne

4. le poisson en Bretagne était / + bon / le poisson qu'on a servi en Auvergne

5. les grandes randonnées qu'on a faites en Auvergne étaient / + intéressant / les grandes randonnées qu'on a faites en Bretagne

6. les restaurants en Auvergne étaient / − cher / les restaurants de Bretagne

7. les nuits en Auvergne étaient / + frais / les nuits de Bretagne

Note culturelle

La Bretagne est une région maritime de l'ouest de la France. C'est une région de langue celtique (le breton), peuplée au cinquième siècle par des réfugiés d'Angleterre. Le paysage contient des monuments de pierre (les menhirs et les dolmens) relevant des traditions celtiques et de la religion païenne. Depuis longtemps une région pauvre qui vivait de la pêche et de la forêt, la Bretagne subit maintenant une profonde transformation grâce à la technologie, aux entreprises et au tourisme.

L'Auvergne est une région montagneuse du Massif central. La ville la plus importante de la région est Clermont-Ferrand. Cette ville industrielle est le site des usines Michelin où l'on fabrique des pneus et le centre d'une industrie pharmaceutique. Les touristes sont attirés par le paysage auvergnat, un paysage de montagnes, de plaines et de lacs, et aussi par les nombreuses stations thermales. Parmi les stations thermales, la plus connue est Vichy dont les eaux sont réputées très bonnes pour les maladies du foie et les maladies digestives en général.

E Superlative of adjectives, adverbs, and nouns

- The superlative of an adjective is formed by placing the definite article before **plus** or **moins** and the adjective. When the adjective follows the noun, the definite article appears both before the noun and before **plus** or **moins.**

—Où se trouve **le restaurant le plus connu** ici?	*Where is **the most well-known restaurant** here?*
—**Les restaurants les plus célèbres** et **les plus chers** se trouvent dans ce quartier.	***The most famous** and **the most expensive restaurants** are found in this neighborhood.*

- The English preposition *in* after a superlative is translated by **de.**

—Quel est le magasin le plus élégant **de** cette ville?	*What is the most elegant store **in** this city?*
—On dit que «Chez Cartier» est un des magasins les plus élégants **du** pays.	*They say that «Chez Cartier» is one of the most elegant stores **in** the whole country.*

- If an adjective usually precedes the noun, its superlative form also precedes the noun. Only one definite article is required.

Chantal est **la meilleure élève** de la classe.	*Chantal is **the best student** in the class.*
Paris est **la plus grande ville** de France.	*Paris is **the biggest city** in France.*

- The superlative of an adverb is formed with **le plus** or **le moins.**

—Lise s'exprime **le plus clairement de** tous les élèves.	*Lise expresses herself **the most clearly of** all the pupils.*
—Et elle parle **le moins lentement** aussi.	*And she speaks **the least slowly** too.*

- The superlatives of **bien** and **mal** are irregular: **le mieux** (*the best*), **le pis** (*the worst*). In modern usage, **le plus mal** is used instead of **le pis.**

—On dit que ce professeur enseigne **le mieux.**	*They say that this teacher teaches **best.***
—J'en doute. Ses étudiants écrivent **le plus mal de** tous.	*I doubt it. His students write **the worst of** all.*

- The phrases **le plus** (*the most*) and **le moins** (*the least*) can be used after verbs. These are the superlatives of **beaucoup** and **peu,** respectively.

—C'est Alain qui travaille **le plus.**	*Alain is the one who works **the most.***
—Et qui gagne **le moins.**	*And who earns **the least.***

- The phrases **le plus de** (*the most*) and **le moins de** (*the least, the fewest*) are used before nouns.

—Toi, tu manges **le plus de** viande.	*You eat **the most** meat.*
—Et **le moins de** légumes.	*And **the fewest** vegetables.*

Q. Notre classe. Formez des superlatifs pour décrire les étudiants de la classe. Faites attention aux signes arithmétiques.

MODÈLE Charles / − attentif ➔ Charles est le moins attentif.

1. Marylène / + diligent
2. Jacques et Pierre / − obéissant
3. Solange / + sympathique
4. Irène et Marie / − travailleur
5. Olivier / + intelligent
6. Anne-Marie / + bavard
7. Jean-Paul / + charmant
8. Colette et Brigitte / − préparé

R. Visite de la ville. Rachelle fait visiter sa ville à ses amis. Elle leur explique tout en employant des superlatifs. Écrivez ce qu'elle leur dit.

MODÈLE c'est/bibliothèque/important/ville
➔ C'est la bibliothèque la plus importante de la ville.

1. voilà / place / imposant / ville
2. ici vous voyez / cathédrale / ancien / région
3. en face il y a / université / connu / pays
4. c'est / rue / long / ville
5. dans cette rue il y a / magasins / beau / région

6. voilà / charcuterie / apprécié / quartier

____

7. devant nous il y a / hôtel / international / pays

____

8. dans cette rue se trouvent / cafés / fréquenté / ville

____

9. ici vous voyez / maison / vieux / ville

____

10. voilà / stade / grand / région

____

S. La classe de littérature. Le professeur et les étudiants expliquent les aspects superlatifs des œuvres qu'ils lisent.

MODÈLE roman/émouvant/siècle
➔ C'est le roman le plus émouvant du siècle.

1. poème / connu / littérature européenne

____

2. pièce de théâtre / représenté / année

____

3. comédie / applaudi / théâtre national

____

4. roman / vendu / la littérature moderne

____

5. tragédie / estimé / notre théâtre

____

6. poète / merveilleux / son siècle

____

7. romancier / lu / monde

____

8. dramaturge / apprécié / notre époque

____

T. Les meilleurs et les pires. Dans ce groupe d'étudiants il y a des jeunes extraordinaires. Exprimez leurs distinctions (pas toutes sont positives) avec le superlatif des adverbes. Faites attention aux signes arithméthiques et suivez le modèle.

Modèle Jean/courir/vite (+)
➔ C'est Jean qui court le plus vite.

1. Lucie / parler / poliment (+)
____
2. Olivier / travaille / efficacement (−)
____
3. Albert / étudier / sérieusement (−)
____
4. Suzanne / chanter / bien (+)
____
5. Hélène / arriver en retard / souvent (+)
____
6. Roger / répondre / calmement (+)
____

U. Vos opinions. Écrivez des phrases en français pour identifier les choses ou les personnes spécifiées.

Modèle the most interesting class this year
➔ La classe la plus intéressante cette année est la classe de littérature américaine.

1. the hardest book you are reading
____
2. the worst song of the year
____
3. the student who studies most seriously
____
4. the member of your family who eats most quickly
____
5. the friendliest teacher in the school
____
6. the most expensive store in town
____
7. the best compact disk or tape you have
____
8. the restaurant you like the most
____

V. Exercice oral. Travaillez avec un(e) camarade de classe. Décrivez votre maison ou appartement, votre voiture, vos amis, votre école. Ne vous limitez pas à décrire—faites aussi des comparaisons entre les pièces de votre logement, entre votre voiture et celle des voisins, etc.

W. Le téléphone mobile. Lisez la publicité pour le téléphone mobile NOKIA 2110 et répondez aux questions suivantes.

1. Que veut dire le mot «puce»? Pourquoi est-ce qu'on a inventé le terme «télépuce» pour décrire le NOKIA 2110?
2. Quelle comparaison fait-on entre la taille de ce téléphone et sa puissance (un phénomène à double titre)?
3. Quelles précisions donne-t-on sur sa taille?
4. Où est-ce que ce petit téléphone rentre (*fits*)?
5. Quelle comparaison fait-on entre le NOKIA 2110 et les autres téléphones GSM?

CHAPTER 18

OBJECT PRONOUNS

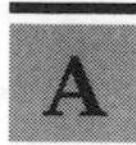

A Direct object pronouns

- A direct object is the person or thing that receives the action of a verb.

Je vois **Jean**.	*I see **John**.*
Nous ne voyons pas **le magasin**.	*We don't see **the store**.*
J'ouvre **mon livre**.	*I open **my book**.*
Elle porte **ses lunettes**.	*She's wearing **her glasses**.*

- To avoid repetition, direct object nouns are often replaced by direct object pronouns.

direct object pronouns		
	singular	*plural*
first person	**me, m'** *me*	**nous** *us*
second person	**te, t'** *you*	**vous** *you*
third person	**le, l'** *him, it* **la, l'** *her, it*	**les** *them*

- Direct object pronouns precede the conjugated verb. Note that before a verb beginning with a vowel or mute **h, me, te, le, la** become **m', t', l'.**

—Est-ce que tu achètes **ce livre**? —Non. Je **le** regarde tout simplement.	*Are you buying **that book**?* *No. I'm just looking at **it**.*
—**Me** retrouvez-vous en ville? —Oui. Nous **t'**attendons au café de la Gare.	*Will you meet **me** in town?* *Yes. We'll wait for **you** at the Café de la Gare.*
—Tu aimes **ces nouvelles chansons**? —Pas du tout. Je **les** déteste.	*Do you like **these new songs**?* *Not at all. I hate **them**.*

- Direct object pronouns precede the auxiliary verb in compound tenses. Remember that a past participle agrees in gender and number with a direct object noun or pronoun that precedes it.

—As-tu vu **Daniel**? —Je **l'**ai cherché, mais je ne **l'**ai pas trouvé.	*Have you seen **Daniel**?* *I looked for **him,** but I didn't find **him**.*
—Je **t'**ai appelé, mais tu ne **m'**as pas entendu.	*I called **you,** but you didn't hear **me**.*
—Si. Je **t'**ai salué, mais tu ne **m'**as pas vu.	*Yes I did. I waved hello to **you,** but you didn't see **me**.*

—Et **les lettres**? Où est-ce que vous **les** avez mises?	*What about* ***the letters****? Where did you put* ***them****?*
—Je **les** ai jetées à la poubelle. Je croyais que vous **les** aviez déjà lues.	*I threw* ***them*** *in the garbage. I thought that you had already read* ***them****.*

- When a verb is followed by an infinitive, the direct object pronoun comes before the verb of which it is the direct object—usually the infinitive.

—Vous pouvez **nous** déposer en ville?	*Can you drop* ***us*** *off downtown?*
—Je regrette, mais je ne peux pas **vous** prendre.	*I'm sorry, but I can't take* ***you*** *(give* ***you*** *a lift).*
—Je peux **t'**aider?	*Can I help* ***you****?*
—Oui, merci. Tu vois cette chaise? Tu peux **la** monter au deuxième étage.	*Yes, thank you. Do you see this chair? You can take* ***it*** *up to the third floor.*

- Several verbs that take indirect objects in English take direct objects in French.

attendre qqn/qqch *to wait for someone/something*
chercher qqn/qqch *to look for someone/something*
demander qqch *to ask for something*
écouter qqn/qqch *to listen to someone/something*
payer qqch *to pay for something*
regarder qqn/qqch *to look at someone/something*

A. Au magasin de vêtements. Ombeline est dans une boutique. Continuez le récit de ce qu'elle fait pour acheter les vêtements qu'il lui faut en utilisant les verbes entre parenthèses et les pronoms de complément direct. Suivez le modèle.

Modèle —Voilà la porte du magasin. (ouvrir)
➔ —Elle l'ouvre.

1. Voilà les robes. (regarder)

   ____

2. Voilà une robe dans sa taille. (essayer)

   ____

3. La robe ne lui plaît pas. (ne pas prendre)

   ____

4. Elle aime ce chemisier. (acheter)

   ____

5. Elle veut voir les foulards en soie. (chercher)

   ____

6. Elle trouve un foulard qui va bien avec son nouveau chemisier. (prendre)

   ____

7. Elle passe au rayon des chapeaux. (regarder)

   ____

8. Il y a deux chapeaux qui l'intéressent. (essayer)

   ____

9. Ils sont très chers. (ne pas acheter)

____

10. Mais elle va acheter le foulard. (payer)

____

Note culturelle

La mode féminine est une des industries de luxe qui a fait la réputation de la France à l'étranger. Le monde de la mode s'appelle «la Haute Couture» et les noms des couturiers français comme Coco Chanel, Christian Dior, Pierre Cardin et Yves Saint Laurent sont célèbres dans le monde entier, pas seulement pour les vêtements, mais pour les autres produits de luxe: parfums, eau de cologne, etc.

Il y a beaucoup de boutiques à Paris où on peut voir les créations de ces couturiers dans les vitrines. Elles se trouvent dans les beaux quartiers de la rive droite (entre l'Opéra et la place Charles de Gaulle) et à Saint-Germain-des-Prés (rive gauche).

Les défilés de mode à Paris, où les couturiers présentent leurs collections, sont de vrais événements mondains qui rassemblent une foule de gens élégants.

B. Emménagement. La famille Jonquières est en train d'emménager dans leur nouvelle maison. Mme Jonquières répond aux questions des déménageurs sur l'emplacement des meubles. Employez les mots entre parenthèses pour écrire ses réponses et remplacez les compléments directs par des pronoms. Suivez le modèle.

Modèle —Et le lave-vaisselle, madame? (installer/cuisine)
➔ —Vous pouvez l'installer dans la cuisine.

1. Et ce sofa, madame? (mettre/salon)

____

2. Et ce lit, madame? (monter/à la chambre de mon fils)

____

3. Et la machine à laver? (descendre/au sous-sol)

____

4. Et cette chaîne stéréo? (laisser/salon)

____

5. Et cette table? (placer/salle à manger)

____

6. Et ces vêtements? (mettre/penderie)

____

7. Et cet ordinateur? (monter/à la chambre de ma fille)

____

8. Et ces fauteuils? (laisser/salon)

____

C. Pas possible! Michel répond au négatif aux questions de son ami. Écrivez ce qu'il dit avec le pronom convenable.

MODÈLE —Tu m'aides?
➔ —Non, je ne peux pas t'aider.

1. Tu me déposes en ville?

____

2. Tu m'emmènes à la poste?

____

3. Tu me raccompagnes?

____

4. Tu m'attends?

____

5. Tu nous rejoins, Sara et moi?

____

6. Tu nous appelles?

____

7. Tu nous invites?

____

8. Tu nous présentes?

____

D. On s'organise. Les étudiants s'organisent pour nettoyer le foyer d'étudiants avant de partir pour l'été. Employez le(s) nom(s) entre parenthèses pour répondre aux questions. Remplacez les compléments directs des questions par des pronoms et employez la construction **aller** + ***infinitif.*** Suivez le modèle.

MODÈLE —Qui fait le linge? (Jean-Claude)
➔ —Jean-Claude va le faire.

Le nettoyage

balayer *to sweep*
la casserole *pot*
épousseter (j'époussette) *to dust*
faire le linge *to do the laundry*
faire le lit *to make the bed*
faire les carreaux *to wash the windows*
laver *to wash*
les meubles (masc.) *furniture*
nettoyer *to clean*
les ordures (fem.) *garbage*
le parquet *wooden floor*
passer l'aspirateur *to run the vacuum cleaner*
la poêle *frying pan*
récurer *to scour*
sortir *to take out*
les toilettes (fem.) *bathroom*

1. Qui balaie la cuisine? (Sabine)

____

2. Qui lave les verres? (Marc et David)

3. Qui nettoie les toilettes? (Élisabeth et Stéphanie)

4. Qui fait les lits? (moi)

5. Qui sort les ordures? (Édouard)

6. Qui passe l'aspirateur? (Barbara)

7. Qui époussette les meubles? (Charles et Michèle)

8. Qui fait les carreaux? (Odile et François)

9. Qui récure les casseroles et les poêles? (Louis et Denise)

10. Et qui lave tous les parquets? (toi!)

E. Tout est déjà fait. Répondez au passé composé aux questions de votre ami sur les devoirs. Remplacez les compléments directs des questions par des pronoms. Faites attention à l'accord du participe passé.

MODÈLE —Tu ne lis pas le chapitre 12?
➔ —Je l'ai déjà lu.

1. Tu n'écris pas la composition?

2. Marc et Paul ne rédigent pas le thème?

3. Catherine et toi, vous ne faites pas les problèmes de maths?

4. Lise n'apprend pas les poèmes par cœur?

5. Tu n'étudies pas la pièce de théâtre?

6. Christine ne fait pas l'expérience au laboratoire?

7. Olivier ne révise pas les leçons d'histoire?

8. Baudoin et Philippe ne regardent pas les œuvres d'art?

____

9. Tu n'écoutes pas les bandes magnétiques pour le cours d'espagnol?

____

10. Tu ne relis pas tes notes de philosophie?

____

B *Indirect object pronouns*

- An indirect object is the person to whom or for whom an action is done. It is connected to its verb by the preposition **à.**

J'écris **à Jean**.	*I write (**to**) **John**.*
Les élèves parlent **au professeur**.	*The students talk **to the teacher**.*
Nous donnons des cadeaux **à nos amis**.	*We give gifts **to our friends**.*

- The French indirect object pronouns refer only to people. **Lui** may mean either *to/for him* or *to/for her,* depending on its context.

indirect object pronouns		
	singular	*plural*
first person	**me**	**nous**
second person	**te**	**vous**
third person	**lui**	**leur**

The indirect object pronouns follow the same rules for position as the direct object pronouns.

—Les parents de cet enfant ont de la chance. Il **leur** obéit toujours.	*That child's parents are lucky. He always obeys **them.***
—C'est vrai. Il ne **leur** désobéit jamais.	*That's true. He never disobeys **them.***
—Ce chapeau **vous** va très bien.	*That hat looks very good **on you.***
—Il **vous** plaît?	*Do you like it?*
—Et Louis? Il a faim?	*What about Louis? Is he hungry?*
—Oui. Je **lui** prépare un sandwich.	*Yes. I'm making a sandwich **for him.***
—Je vais **leur** téléphoner ce soir.	*I'm going to phone **them** this evening.*
—S'ils ne sont pas là, tu peux **leur** laisser un message au répondeur.	*If they're not there, you can leave **them** a message on the answering machine.*

- Several verbs that take direct objects or have other constructions in English take indirect objects in French.

aller bien à qqn *to look nice on someone*
convenir à qqn *to suit someone, be convenient for someone*
désobéir à qqn *to disobey someone*
obéir à qqn *to obey someone*
plaire à qqn *to please someone*
répondre à qqn *to answer someone*
téléphoner à qqn *to call, phone someone*

- Many verbs take two objects: a direct object (a thing) and an indirect object (a person).

  apporter qqch à qqn *to bring something to someone*
  dire qqch à qqn *to tell/say something to someone*
  donner qqch à qqn *to give something to someone*
  demander qqch à qqn *to ask someone for something*
  envoyer qqch à qqn *to send something to someone*
  expliquer qqch à qqn *to explain something to someone*
  laisser qqch à qqn *to leave something for someone*
  montrer qqch à qqn *to show something to someone*
  offrir qqch à qqn *to give something to someone (as a gift)*
  prêter qqch à qqn *to lend something to someone*
  rendre qqch à qqn *to give something back to someone*
  vendre qqch à qqn *to sell something to someone*

  Note that in **présenter qqn à qqn** (*to introduce someone to someone*), both the direct and the indirect objects refer to people.

- With several French verbs, **à** is the equivalent of English *from.*

  acheter qqch à qqn *to buy something from someone*
  arracher qqch à qqn *to snatch something from someone*
  cacher qqch à qqn *to hide something from someone*
  emprunter qqch à qqn *to borrow something from someone*
  enlever qqch à qqn *to take something away from someone*
  louer qqch à qqn *to rent something from someone*
  prendre qqch à qqn *to take something from someone*
  voler qqch à qqn *to steal something from someone*

  Sentences such as **Je lui ai acheté la voiture** may mean either *I bought the car* ***from*** *him/her* or *I bought the car* ***for*** *him/her,* depending on the context.

F. Oui et non. Employez les mots entre parenthèses et un pronom complément d'objet indirect pour dire dans chaque cas ce qu'on **ne fait pas.** Suivez le modèle.

MODÈLE Je prête mon crayon à Luc. (mon stylo)
➔ Je ne lui prête pas mon stylo.

1. Nous donnons des conseils à nos voisins. (argent)

   ____

2. Annette me montre ses photos. (lettres)

   ____

3. J'ai écrit une carte postale à mes cousins. (lettre)

   ____

4. Les Dufau vendent leur maison aux Masson. (voiture)

   ____

5. Je vais offrir une montre à ma petite amie. (collier)

   ____

6. Vous envoyez des dessins à votre frère. (affiches)

   ____

7. Mon chien m'apporte le journal. (mes pantoufles)

____

8. Il a dit son adresse au médecin. (son numéro de téléphone)

____

9. Le professeur a expliqué les problèmes à ses étudiants. (la méthode)

____

10. Je vais demander la voiture à mon père. (argent pour l'essence)

____

G. Ce qu'il faut faire. Les employés d'un grand bureau demandent à leur chef ce qu'ils doivent faire aujourd'hui. Il leur répond avec l'expression **il faut** et un pronom complément d'objet indirect. Suivez le modèle pour savoir exactement ce qu'il dit.

MODÈLE —Et pour nos clients en Tunisie? (envoyer le rapport)
➔ —Il faut leur envoyer le rapport.

Les affaires

l'agence (fem.) *agency*
l'annonce (fem.) *ad*
le banquier/la banquière *banker*
la cargaison *shipment*
le fournisseur/la fournisseuse *supplier*
la gamme *range, line*
la note *bill*
le produit *product*
le rapport *report*
régler la note *to pay the bill, settle the account*
le représentant/la représentante *representative*
le vendeur/la vendeuse *salesperson*

1. Et pour M. Delavigne? (écrire une lettre)

____

2. Et pour nos fournisseurs en Allemagne? (payer la dernière cargaison de marchandises)

____

3. Les Régnier n'ont pas encore réglé la note. (envoyer la note encore une fois)

____

4. M. Sarda a déjà appelé deux fois ce matin. (prêter trois cent mille francs)

____

5. L'agence Autos-Jour a téléphoné. (louer trois voitures et un camion)

____

6. Votre banquier a téléphoné. (emprunter un million de francs)

____

7. La représentante du journal est arrivée. (montrer les nouvelles annonces)

____

8. Nos vendeurs vont arriver à 11 heures. (présenter la nouvelle gamme de produits)

____

H. Conseils et recommandations. Un groupe de copains parlent des camarades qui avaient besoin d'aide. Écrivez les solutions qu'ils ont trouvées en formant des phrases au passé composé avec des pronoms compléments d'objet indirect. Suivez le modèle.

MODÈLE —Émile aimait bien mon ordinateur.
tu donner / une heure au clavier (*keyboard*)
➔ —Tu lui as donné une heure au clavier.

1. Marguerite ne pouvait pas aller à pied au lycée.
son père / prêter la voiture

____

2. Albert a perdu sa montre.
nous / offrir une montre pour son anniversaire

____

3. Monique ne comprenait pas ce texte.
moi, je / expliquer les idées du livre

____

4. Richard et Serge voulaient jouer au football.
nous / demander de jouer avec nous

____

5. Nathalie est malade et ne peut pas sortir.
vous / apporter des revues et des journaux

____

6. Sylvie et Maude voulaient étudier pour l'examen d'histoire.
nous / rendre les livres que nous leur avions empruntés

____

7. Mathieu a été absent hier. Il a manqué tous ses cours.
nous / montrer nos notes

____

8. Hélène et Robert sont maintenant en Corse.
moi, je / envoyer une lettre

____

9. Solange nous a écrit il y a deux semaines.
nous / répondre

____

10. Alfred et Gilles ne savaient pas qu'il y une boum vendredi.
nous / téléphoner

____

C Pronoun *y*

- A preposition of location (**à, en, dans, sur, sous, devant, derrière,** etc.) plus a noun referring to a place or thing can be replaced by **y.**

—Vous allez tous **à Paris**? —Oui, nous **y** passons nos vacances.	*Are you all going* ***to Paris****?* *Yes, we're spending our vacation* ***there****.*
—As-tu répondu **à sa lettre**? —Oui. J'**y** ai déjà répondu.	*Have you answered* ***his letter****?* *Yes. I have already answered* ***it****.*
—Tu travailles **dans ce bureau**? —Non, je n'**y** travaille plus.	*Do you work* ***in this office****?* *No, I don't work* ***there*** *anymore.*
—Où est la monnaie? **Sur la table**? —Oui. J'**y** ai laissé l'argent.	*Where's the change?* ***On the table****?* *Yes. I left the money* ***there****.*

- **Y** may refer to an entire phrase, clause, or idea. Sometimes **y** has no direct English equivalent.

—Il est difficile de traverser la rue parce qu'il y a tant de voitures. —Tu as raison. Il faut **y** prendre garde. (**y** = **aux voitures**)	*It's hard to cross the street because there are so many cars.* *You're right. We have to be careful* ***(of them)****.* (**prendre garde à qqch**)
—Alice n'aime pas son travail. —Elle doit **y** renoncer. (**y** = **à son travail**)	*Alice doesn't like her work.* *She ought to quit.* (**renoncer à qqch**)
—Les idées de cet auteur sont difficiles. —J'**y** réfléchis beaucoup. (**y** = **aux idées**)	*This author's ideas are difficult.* *I think* ***about them*** *a lot.* (**réfléchir à qqch**)

- The pronoun **y** follows the same rules for position as direct and indirect object pronouns.

I. Jamais de la vie! Les gens ne font jamais ces activités. Dites-le en employant le pronom **y.**

MODÈLE —Tu vas souvent à Lille?
➔ —Non, je n'y vais jamais.

1. Lucie travaille au sous-sol?

 ____

2. Maurice et François étudient à la terrasse du café du coin?

 ____

3. Ton petit ami attend devant le cinéma?

 ____

4. Vos parents passent leurs vacances au bord de la mer?

 ____

5. Vous achetez à manger dans cette charcuterie?

 ____

6. Les enfants jouent derrière l'immeuble?

 ____

7. Les voisins se réunissent sur le toit?

8. Tu laisses tes livres sur l'escalier?

9. Tu manges parfois dans la voiture?

10. Les étudiants viennent souvent à ce restaurant?

J. Conseillez et rassurez. Votre amie exprime ses doutes. Employez l'expression **il faut,** le pronom **y** et le verbe ou l'expression entre parenthèses pour lui donner un conseil ou pour la rassurer. Suivez le modèle.

> **MODÈLE** —J'ai du mal à me concentrer sur le livre de philosophie. (faire attention)
> ➔ —Il faut y faire attention.

1. Je n'ai pas encore fait de projets de vacances. (penser)

2. Je suis inquiète au sujet de mon avenir. (réfléchir)

3. On dit que les rues de cette ville sont dangereuses la nuit. (prendre garde)

4. Notre plan ne pourra pas réussir. (renoncer)

5. Cette matière m'ennuie. C'est pour ça que mes notes sont mauvaises. (s'intéresser)

6. Je ne sais pas si je pourrai devenir médecin. (rêver)

7. J'ai des doutes sur ses explications. (croire)

8. On m'attend au bureau du professeur. (aller)

D Pronoun *en*

- An indefinite or a partitive article plus a noun can be replaced by the pronoun **en.** **En** often means *some* or *any* in this context.

—Tu veux **du jus**? —Non, je n'**en** veux pas.	*Do you want **any juice**?* *No, I don't want **any**.*
—Connaissez-vous **des professeurs** ici? —Oui, j'**en** connais.	*Do you know **any teachers** here?* *Yes, I know **some.***

- **En** may replace nouns used with expressions of quantity or numbers. In such cases, **en** may have no direct English equivalent.

—As-tu beaucoup **de travail**? —J'**en** ai trop. (**en** = **de travail**)	*Do you have a lot of **work**?* *I have too much.*
—Robert a des frères? —Oui, il **en** a trois.	*Does Robert have any brothers?* *Yes, he has three (**brothers**).*
—Tu n'as que trois cents francs? —J'**en** ai perdu deux cents.	*You have only three hundred francs?* *I lost two hundred (**francs**).*

- **En** may replace the construction **de** + noun or infinitive.

—Pauline est-elle revenue **de France**? —Elle **en** revient jeudi.	*Has Pauline come back **from France**?* *She's coming back (**from there**) Thursday.*
—Les étés passés en Bretagne étaient merveilleux, n'est-ce pas? —Oui. Je m'**en** souviens. (**en** = **des étés**)	*The summers spent in Brittany were wonderful, weren't they?* *Oh, yes. I remember **them**.*
—Ton fils a-t-il peur **de jouer avec mon chien**? —Oui. Il **en** a peur.	*Is your son afraid **to play with my dog**?* *Yes. He's afraid (**to do it**).*

- The pronoun **en** follows the same rules for position as direct and indirect object pronouns. In compound tenses, the past participle does not agree with **en.**

K. Votre ville. Répondez aux questions suivantes. Employez le pronom **en** dans vos réponses. Vos réponses peuvent être négatives ou affirmatives, selon le cas.

Vocabulaire urbain

bordé de *lined with*
de luxe *luxury (as adj.)*
encombré de *blocked by, congested with*
un espace vert *a green space, park*
manquer de *to lack, to be short of*
se méfier de *to be wary of, distrustful of*
le promeneur *stroller, walker*
regorger de *to be bursting with*
la sécurité personnelle *personal safety*
se soucier de *to worry about*
se vanter de *to boast of*

1. Est-ce que la ville se vante de ses musées?

   ____

2. Est-ce que les magasins regorgent de vêtements de luxe?

   ____

3. Est-ce que les rues sont pleines de promeneurs?

4. Est-ce qu'il faut se soucier de sa sécurité personnelle?

5. Est-ce que vous vous méfiez de la ville la nuit?

6. Est-ce que les trottoirs sont bordés d'arbres?

7. Est-ce que les rues sont encombrées de véhicules?

8. Est-ce que votre ville manque d'espaces verts?

L. **Rectification.** Votre ami(e) se trompe sur les quantités. Corrigez ce qu'il (elle) vous dit avec les chiffres donnés et le pronom **en.**

Modèle —Paulette a deux frères, n'est-ce pas? (4)
→ —Non, elle en a quatre.

1. Il y a vingt élèves dans cette classe, n'est-ce pas? (32)

2. Stéphane gagne mille cinq francs par semaine, n'est-ce pas? (2100)

3. Vous avez cent vingt pages à lire, n'est-ce pas? (250)

4. Nous avons parcouru (*covered, traveled*) quatre cents kilomètres, n'est-ce pas? (300)

5. Tu as eu soixante-dix dollars d'amende (*fine*), n'est-ce pas? (90)

6. Leur nouvelle maison a trois salles de bains, n'est-ce pas? (5)

7. Nous allons acheter dix biftecks, n'est-ce pas? (15)

8. Tu veux une douzaine d'œufs, n'est-ce pas? (deux douzaines)

M. C'est déjà fait. Répondez aux questions de votre ami(e) sur ce qui se passe à l'université en disant que tout s'est déjà accompli. Utilisez le pronom **en** dans chaque cas.

Modèle —Pierre va-t-il acheter des livres?
➔ —Il en a déjà acheté.

1. Chantal et Odile comptent-elles suivre des cours de chimie?
____
2. L'étudiant va-t-il se plaindre de ses classes?
____
3. Est-ce que Bernard va être accablé de travail?
____
4. M. Dumarier va-t-il se charger des inscriptions?
____
5. Est-ce que Mme Martel va jouer du piano?
____
6. François va-t-il se mêler des affaires des autres étudiants?
____
7. Est-ce que Michel compte faire du japonais?
____
8. Anne-Marie peut-elle demander des conseils sur son programme d'études?
____
9. Est-ce que Gilbert va revenir de la faculté?
____
10. Le professeur Froissard va-t-il donner des devoirs?
____

E *Double object pronouns*

- When a sentence contains two object pronouns, the pronouns take the following order:

me **te** **se** **nous** **vous**	*before*	**le, l'** **la, l'** **les**	*before*	**lui** **leur**	*before*	**y**	*before*	**en**

- Double object pronouns follow the same rules of position as single object pronouns.

—Est-ce que ton père te prête la voiture?	*Does your father lend you the car?*
—Non, il ne **me la** prête jamais.	*No, he never lends **it to me**.*
—Tu vas donner les cadeaux aux enfants?	*Are you going to give the gifts to the children?*
—Oui, je vais **les leur** donner.	*Yes, I'm going to give **them to them**.*
—Marcelle a sa calculatrice?	*Does Marcelle have her calculator?*
—Oui, je **la lui** ai rendue hier.	*Yes, I returned **it to her** yesterday.*
—Nos cousins ont besoin d'argent.	*Our cousins need money.*
—Nous pouvons **leur en** envoyer.	*We can send **them some**.*
—C'est une très belle avenue.	*This is a very beautiful avenue.*
—Oui, nous **nous y** promenons souvent.	*Yes, we often take a walk **here**.*

N. Ce qu'il faut faire. Employez les verbes entre parenthèses et deux pronoms compléments d'objet pour dire ce qu'il faut faire (ou ce qu'on va faire) dans chaque cas. Suivez le modèle.

MODÈLE —Odile ne sait pas l'adresse de Philippe. (je/aller/dire)
➔ —Je vais la lui dire.

1. Marie-France ne reçoit pas de lettres. (nous/devoir/écrire)

____

2. Serge veut voir tes notes de physique. (je/aller/prêter)

____

3. Ousmane a besoin de son manuel de chimie. (nous/devoir/rendre)

____

4. Rachelle prend le déjeuner au bistrot d'en face. (tu/pouvoir/retrouver)

____

5. Suzanne et Ghislaine veulent voir tes photos. (je/avoir l'intention de/montrer)

____

6. Yves et Marc cherchent des affiches. (il faut/donner)

____

7. Je ne comprends pas ces mots. (je/aller/expliquer)

____

8. Nous voudrions du parfum de France. (Marguerite/pouvoir/rapporter)

____

9. Les enfants adorent le jardin. (vous/pouvoir/amener)

____

10. La vie ici n'est pas facile. (nous/devoir/s'habituer)

____

O. Mais si! Votre ami se trompe. Les choses qui, selon lui, n'arrivent pas sont déjà arrivées. Dites-le-lui en employant le passé composé et deux pronoms compléments d'objet. Suivez le modèle.

MODÈLE —Sabine n'offre jamais de cadeaux à ses frères.
➔ —Mais si! Elle leur en a déjà offert.

1. Albert ne sert jamais de boissons à ses invités.
2. Tu ne donnes jamais de conseils à Philippe.
3. Serge et Robert ne s'opposent pas au programme politique de notre parti.
4. Marc et Justine ne se servent jamais de cet ordinateur.
5. Louise et toi, vous ne vous rendez pas compte du problème.
6. Olivier ne nous rend jamais les choses qu'il nous emprunte.
7. Cette femme ne lit jamais de livres à ses enfants.
8. Ces parents n'enseignent pas le français à leurs enfants.
9. Ce professeur ne propose jamais de thèmes intéressants à ses étudiants.
10. Toi, tu ne m'envoies jamais de cartes postales.

P. Proposons des solutions. Employez **si** suivi de l'imparfait, les mots entre parenthèses et deux pronoms compléments d'objet pour proposer des solutions aux problèmes posés par votre amie.

MODÈLE —Nathalie n'a pas de romans en français.
(envoyer deux ou trois)
➔ —Si on lui en envoyait deux ou trois?

1. Maurice et Frédéric admirent nos disques compacts. (prêter)
2. Monique est à la bibliothèque de Beaubourg. (retrouver)
3. Madeleine et Lise n'ont pas la voiture pour aller au travail aujourd'hui. (amener)

4. Jean-Paul aime les croissants que nous faisons. (apporter une demi-douzaine)

___

5. Agnès sort du bureau à 5 heures. (aller attendre)

___

6. Cette rue a l'air dangereux. (s'éloigner)

___

7. Nous avons une lettre à écrire et cet ordinateur est libre. (se servir pour la rédiger)

___

8. Philippe et son frère nous ont demandé le journal d'hier. (donner)

___

9. Eugénie a tous nos livres d'histoire. (demander)

___

10. Charles et sa femme s'intéressent à notre chaîne stéréo. (vendre)

___

Note culturelle

Le centre national d'art et de culture Georges Pompidou est un bâtiment très moderne situé dans un des vieux quartiers de Paris. À cause de son adresse rue Beaubourg, on l'appelle souvent «Beaubourg» tout court. Beaubourg abrite un musée d'art moderne et une grande bibliothèque publique avec plus de 550 000 titres. Il y a aussi une *médiathèque*, qui offre au public un laboratoire de langues spécialisé dans les méthodes audiovisuelles et des salles de musique.

On y organise souvent des débats et des expositions. Le Centre Pompidou est un vrai centre culturel et reçoit plus de 12 000 000 de visiteurs chaque année.

F *Restrictions on the use of object pronouns*

- The object pronouns **me, te, nous, vous, lui, leur** cannot follow a reflexive pronoun. The preposition **à** or **de** plus a stressed pronoun is used instead. **En** does not replace **de** plus animate noun when the **de** is part of a verbal expression, as in **s'approcher de** and **avoir peur de.** Compare:

  Je me fie **à ce dictionnaire.** → Je m'**y** fie.
  Je me fie **à ce médecin**. → Je me fie **à lui**.

  J'ai peur **des avions**. → J'**en** ai peur.
  J'ai peur **de nos professeurs**. → J'ai peur **d'eux**.

  Nous nous approchons **de la ville.** → Nous nous **en** approchons.
  Nous nous approchons **de notre père.** → Nous nous approchons **de lui**.

Q. Oui, bien sûr. Répondez aux questions de votre ami(e) à l'affirmatif. Remplacez les mots en caractères gras (**boldface**) par le pronom convenable.

MODÈLE —Est-ce que vous vous fiez **à votre mémoire**?
→ —Oui, nous nous y fions.

1. Est-ce que tu te fies **à tes amis**?
____
2. Est-ce que Paulette s'intéresse **à la géologie**?
____
3. Est-ce que Jean-Luc s'intéresse **à Paulette**?
____
4. Est-ce que le petit Victor a honte **de ce qu'il a fait**?
____
5. Est-ce que son père a honte **du petit Victor**?
____
6. Est-ce que tu te souviens **de ton séjour en Espagne**?
____
7. Est-ce que tu te souviens **des gens que tu y as connus**?
____
8. Est-ce que le détective doute **de l'explication de M. Arnaud**?
____
9. Est-ce que le détective se doute **de M. Arnaud**?
____
10. Est-ce que vous avez peur **des voyages en bateau**?
____

G *Object pronouns in affirmative commands*

- In affirmative commands, object pronouns follow the verb and are joined to it with a hyphen. **Me** and **te** become **moi** and **toi** after a command form.

Dites-**nous** ce qui est arrivé.	*Tell **us** what happened.*
Les journaux? Mettez-**les** sur la table.	*The newspapers? Put **them** on the table.*
Aide-**moi**!	*Help **me**!*

- Although the final **-s** of the **tu** form is usually dropped in the imperative of **-er** verbs, it is restored (and pronounced) before **y** and **en** in affirmative commands.

—J'ai envie de manger des pommes. —Achète**s-en**.	*I feel like eating apples.* *Buy **some**.*
—J'aime mes vacances en Bretagne. —Reste**s-y** plus longtemps.	*I love my vacation in Brittany.* *Stay **there** longer.*

- When an affirmative command contains two object pronouns, the pronouns take the order shown below. **Moi** + **en** becomes **m'en** and **toi** + **en** becomes **t'en** in affirmative commands.

le, l' **la, l'** **les**	*before*	**moi** **toi** **lui** **nous** **vous** **leur**	*before*	**y**	*before*	**en**

—Je viens de recevoir mes photos. —Montre-**les-moi**.	*I've just received my photos.* *Show **them to me**.*
—Regarde, j'ai du jus de fruits. —Donne-**m'en**. J'ai très soif.	*Look, I have some fruit juice.* *Give **me some**. I'm very thirsty.*
—Je peux me servir de ton stylo? —Volontiers. Sers-**t'en**.	*May I use your pen?* *Gladly. Use **it**.*

- In affirmative commands, **y** is replaced by **là** or **là-bas** after **me/moi, te/toi, le, la** if **y** refers to a place.

—Tu vas être à la bibliothèque? —Oui, attends-**moi là-bas**.	*Are you going to be at the library?* *Yes, wait for **me there**.*

R. On donne des ordres. Répondez aux questions par l'impératif des verbes entre parenthèses, si possible. Remplacez les substantifs des questions par des pronoms compléments d'objet.

Modèle —Ces bonbons ont l'air délicieux.
(tu/prendre/plusieurs)
➔ —Prends-en plusieurs.

1. Je ne veux plus rester ici. (tu/s'en aller)

____

2. Veux-tu que je te dépose devant la faculté? (tu/déposer)

____

3. J'ai de la salade. En veux-tu? (tu/donner)

____

4. Nous n'aimons pas le programme du nouveau directeur. (vous/s'opposer)

____

5. Ces gens me rendent nerveux. (tu/s'éloigner)

____

6. Je vais m'habiller dans la salle de bains. Ça va? (tu/s'habiller)

____

7. Devons-nous nous arrêter à côté du parc? (vous/s'arrêter)

____

8. Qui va s'occuper du dîner? (tu/se charger)

____

9. Je crois que j'ai votre disquette. (vous/rendre)

____

S. En français. Exprimez les idées suivantes en français.

1. I asked him for his literature book, but he didn't give it to me.

____

2. He doesn't have his car anymore because someone stole it from him.

____

3. These people are interested in your house. Sell it to them. (*formal*)

____

4. We asked the teacher questions about the lesson, but he didn't answer them.

____

5. I looked for French newspapers and found two. I'll show them to you. (*familiar*)

____

6. She's on the third floor. Go up (to there) and you'll see her. (*familiar*)

____

7. The children were playing on the roof, but they have come down (from there).

____

8. You've made soup. Bring me some and I'll taste (**essayer**) it.

____

T. Exercice oral. Parlez avec un(e) camarade de classe au sujet des choses et objets que vous avez et des plats que vous aimez manger. Formez les questions pour évoquer des réponses qui contiennent un ou deux pronoms compléments d'objet.

U. La grammaire en action. Lisez l'annonce suivante insérée par une compagnie américaine de livraisons (*deliveries*) active en Europe (et que vous reconnaîtrez sans aucune difficulté) et répondez aux questions ci-dessous. En lisant l'annonce, faites attention à l'emploi des pronoms compléments d'objet.

A TEMPS TOUT LE TEMPS. UPS LANCE LA GARANTIE MONDIALE VERS DES MILLIERS DE VILLES ET DE CENTRES D'AFFAIRES DANS LE MONDE.

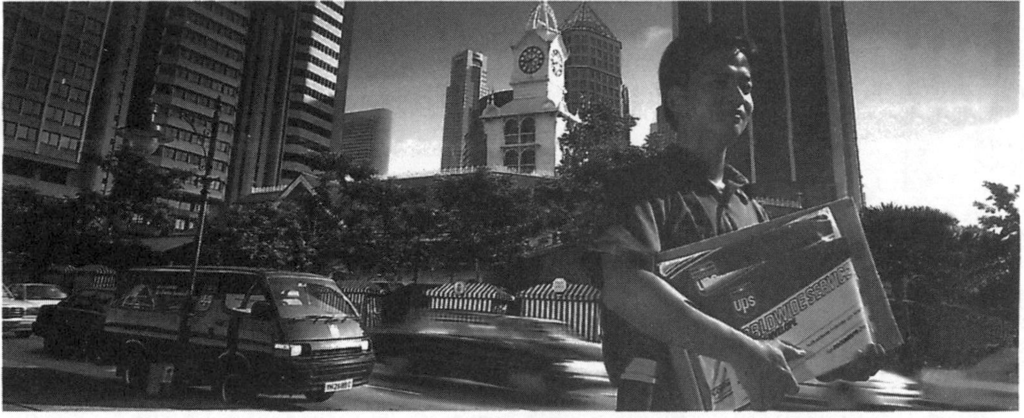

Nous pourrions vous demander une confiance aveugle.
Mais nous préférons vous ouvrir les yeux...
... sur la Garantie Worldwide Express d'UPS.
Notre réseau, nos équipes et notre logistique mondiale
sont d'une totale fiabilité.
Alors en toute confiance, nous garantissons contractuellement les délais
de livraison de vos colis et documents Express
vers des milliers de villes et centres d'affaires dans le monde.
A temps, tout le temps. Ou UPS vous rembourse.
Nous vous donnons notre parole pour qu'à votre tour,
vous puissiez donner la vôtre.

Partenaire Mondial des Jeux Olympiques

Aussi sûr que si vous vous en chargiez vous-même.

M.CANN Worldwide Express, marque déposée d'UPS

1. Comment l'annonce exprime-t-elle l'idée que voir, c'est croire?
2. Pourquoi le client peut-il se fier à UPS pour les délais (*time it takes*) de livraison?
3. Que fait la compagnie si le colis (*parcel*) ou document arrive en retard?
4. Expliquez la phrase «Nous vous donnons notre parole pour qu'à votre tour vous puissiez donner la vôtre».
5. Qui est la seule personne qui puisse occuper des colis et des documents du client avec la fiabilité (*reliability*) d'UPS?

PART THREE

Other Elements of the Sentence

CHAPTER 19

NUMBERS; TIME; DATES

Cardinal numbers to 99

- The cardinal numbers from 0 to 20 are:

0	zéro	7	sept	14	quatorze
1	un, une	8	huit	15	quinze
2	deux	9	neuf	16	seize
3	trois	10	dix	17	dix-sept
4	quatre	11	onze	18	dix-huit
5	cinq	12	douze	19	dix-neuf
6	six	13	treize	20	vingt

Un and **une** are the only numbers that agree in gender with a following noun. The forms for *one* are the same as the indefinite article.

- From 20 to 59 French counts by tens, as does English. Note that **un(e)** is joined to the multiples of ten by **et.** The other units (2 through 9) are joined by a hyphen.

21	vingt et un(e)	28	vingt-huit	41	quarante et un(e)
22	vingt-deux	29	vingt-neuf	42	quarante-deux
23	vingt-trois	30	trente	43	quarante-trois
24	vingt-quatre	31	trente et un(e)	50	cinquante
25	vingt-cinq	32	trente-deux	51	cinquante et un(e)
26	vingt-six	33	trente-trois	52	cinquante-deux
27	vingt-sept	40	quarante	53	cinquante-trois

Une is used instead of **un** before a feminine noun: **vingt et une pages, cinquante et une femmes.**

- From 60 to 99 French counts by twenties. The units 1 through 19 are added to the multiple of twenty. **Un(e)** is joined by a hyphen, not by **et,** to **quatre-vingts.** Note also that **quatre-vingts** loses its final **-s** before another number.

60	soixante	74	soixante-quatorze	88	quatre-vingt-huit
61	soixante et un(e)	75	soixante-quinze	89	quatre-vingt-neuf
62	soixante-deux	76	soixante-seize	90	quatre-vingt-dix
63	soixante-trois	77	soixante-dix-sept	91	quatre-vingt-onze
64	soixante-quatre	78	soixante-dix-huit	92	quatre-vingt-douze
65	soixante-cinq	79	soixante-dix-neuf	93	quatre-vingt-treize
66	soixante-six	80	quatre-vingts	94	quatre-vingt-quatorze
67	soixante-sept	81	quatre-vingt-un(e)	95	quatre-vingt-quinze
68	soixante-huit	82	quatre-vingt-deux	96	quatre-vingt-seize
69	soixante-neuf	83	quatre-vingt-trois	97	quatre-vingt-dix-sept
70	soixante-dix	84	quatre-vingt-quatre	98	quatre-vingt-dix-huit
71	soixante et onze	85	quatre-vingt-cinq	99	quatre-vingt-dix-neuf
72	soixante-douze	86	quatre-vingt-six		
73	soixante-treize	87	quatre-vingt-sept		

A. Dix de plus. Votre ami(e) se trompe. Chaque chiffre qu'il (elle) mentionne doit être majorée de dix. Corrigez ses calculs.

MODÈLE —Je crois qu'il y a vingt-deux étudiants dans cette classe.
➔ —Non. Il y a trente-deux étudiants.

1. Je crois que nous avons besoin de soixante et un livres.

2. Je crois que ça coûte soixante-neuf dollars.

3. Je crois que cette ville est à quarante-huit kilomètres d'ici.

4. Je crois que son oncle a cinquante-six ans.

5. Je crois qu'ils ont passé soixante-treize jours en Suisse.

6. Je crois que tu as reçu un chèque pour quatre-vingts francs.

7. Je crois que je dois téléphoner à quatre-vingt-une personnes.

8. Je crois que nos amis arrivent le seize avril.

B. Corrections. Corrigez les numéros selon les indications données entre parenthèses. Écrivez les numéros en lettres.

MODÈLE —Il habite 23, rue de la Paix. (33)
➔ —Non. Il habite trente-trois, rue de la Paix.

1. Son numéro de téléphone est le 03.87.34.44.56. (le 03.87.34.44.57)

2. Il a payé 77 francs. (99)

3. La grand-mère d'Yvette a 65 ans. (76)

4. Ils ont invité 60 personnes à la réception. (82)

5. Dans cette cité (*housing development*) il y a 82 appartements. (95)

6. Nous avons fait 68 kilomètres à vélo. (74)

7. La charcuterie a coûté 70 francs. (80)

____

8. Des représentants de 85 pays sont venus au congrès (*convention*) international. (98)

____

B *Cardinal numbers 100 and above*

- Round multiples of 100 are written with a final **-s.** However, the final **-s** of **cents** drops before another number.

100	cent	201	deux cent un
200	deux cents	326	trois cent vingt-six
300	trois cents	572	cinq cent soixante-douze

- The word for *thousand,* **mille,** is invariable. Note that neither **cent** (*100*) nor **mille** (*1000*) is preceded by **un.** (Compare English ***one** hundred,* ***one** thousand.*)

1.000	mille	100 000	cent mille
1.001	mille un	200 000	deux cent mille
1.200	mille deux cents, douze cents	582 478	cinq cent quatre-vingt-deux mille quatre cent soixante-dix-huit
2.000	deux mille		
3.500	trois mille cinq cents		
10.000	dix mille		

French uses a period or a space to separate thousands where English uses a comma. The comma is used in French numbers as a decimal point: **2,5** =**deux virgule cinq.**

- The French word **million** is a noun and is followed by **de** before another noun. However, if other numbers come between **million** and the noun, **de** is not used. Note that **cent** is pluralized directly before the word **million.**

un million de livres
deux millions d'habitants
trois millions trois cent mille étudiants
deux cents millions de Russes
deux cent soixante-cinq millions d'Américains

- The French word for *billion* is **un milliard. Milliard** is a noun like **million: cinq milliards d'êtres humains.** The French term **un billion** means *a trillion.*

C. Autour du monde. Voici les chiffres de la population de plusieurs pays. Écrivez ces chiffres en lettres.

MODÈLE La France: 57 000 000
➔ La France a cinquante sept millions d'habitants.

1. l'Espagne: 40 000 000

____

2. le Danemark: 5 200 000

____

3. le Japon: 124 800 000

____

4. la Chine: 1 200 000 000

5. l'Argentine: 33 500 000

6. la Suisse: 7 000 000

7. le Nigeria: 95 100 000

8. le Viêt-nam: 71 800 000

D. La population urbaine française. Employez les chiffres de 1990 pour comparer la population des villes avec celle de l'agglomération urbaine (*metropolitan area*). Écrivez les nombres en lettres.

MODÈLE

ville	*aggl. urb.*	*ville*
Reims	206 437	180 620

→ L'agglomération urbaine de Reims a deux cent six mille quatre cent trente-sept habitants dont cent quatre-vingt mille six cent vingt habitent dans la ville même.

	ville	*aggl. urb.*	*ville*
1.	Paris	9 318 821	2 152 423
2.	Lyon	1 262 223	415 487
3.	Marseille	1 230 936	800 550
4.	Lille	959 234	172 142
5.	Bordeaux	696 364	210 336
6.	Toulouse	650 336	358 688
7.	Nice	516 740	342 439
8.	Nantes	496 078	244 995

1.

2.

3.

4.

5.

6. ______________________________

7. ______________________________

8. ______________________________

E. Maintenant c'est à vous de faire des recherches démographiques. Trouvez la population de six villes américaines ou canadiennes, dont trois au-dessus d'un million d'habitants et trois au-dessous. Écrivez le nom de chaque ville et sa population en chiffres et en lettres.

1. ______________________________
2. ______________________________
3. ______________________________
4. ______________________________
5. ______________________________
6. ______________________________

C *Ordinal numbers*

- To form most ordinal numbers, the suffix **-ième** is added to the cardinal number. One exception is **un/une,** for which the ordinal number is **premier/première.** Numbers ending in **-e** drop the **-e** before adding **-ième.** The ordinal **second(e)** is synonymous with **deuxième.** Note the spellings of the words for *fifth* and *ninth.*

deuxième *second*	**dixième** *tenth*	**millième** *thousandth*
quatrième *fourth*	**quatorzième** *fourteenth*	**quatorze centième** *fourteen hundredth*
cinquième *fifth*	**dix-septième** *seventeenth*	**trois mille cinq centième** *thirty-five hundredth*
huitième *eighth*	**vingtième** *twentieth*	
neuvième *ninth*	**centième** *hundredth*	

- The word **premier/première** is only used to mean *first.* Ordinals such as *twenty-first* and *one hundred first* are formed regularly.

vingt et unième *twenty-first*	**quatre-vingt-unième** *eighty-first*
soixante et onzième *seventy-first*	**cent unième** *one hundred first*

- Ordinal numbers are abbreviated as follows: **1er, 1ère, 2e, 3e,** etc.

- Ordinal numbers are used to express fractions, except for **la moitié** (*half*), **le tiers** (*third*), and **le quart** (*fourth*).

le quart des élèves	***a quarter*** *of the students*
les cinq sixièmes des enseignants	***five sixths*** *of the teaching staff*

- French uses cardinal numbers, not ordinal numbers for dates and after the names of kings and queens (except for *first*, when **premier/première** is used).

le premier juin	Henri **IV** (= Quatre)
le vingt-cinq août	Charles **II** (= Deux)

- French uses the suffix **-aine** to create nouns designating approximate numbers.

une dixaine de lettres	***about ten*** *letters*
une vingtaine d'étudiants	***about twenty*** *students*
des centaines de gagnants	***hundreds*** *of winners*

F. Mon Dieu, que c'est haut! Un groupe de jeunes Français fait un stage à Chicago. Ils travaillent tous dans un énorme gratte-ciel. L'un d'eux, Gilbert, écrit à sa famille à Paris et donne des précisions «d'altitude» sur lui-même et sur ses amis. Attention: Dans les bâtiments français, **le premier étage** est l'équivalent du deuxième étage aux États-Unis. L'étage qui est au niveau du trottoir s'appelle **le rez-de-chaussée.** Albert emploie le système français.

MODÈLE Alberte/13 ➔ Alberte travaille au douzième étage.

1. moi/74

____

2. Gilles/22

____

3. Dorothée/96

____

4. Richard et Maurice/40

____

5. Paulette/19

____

6. Suzanne et Émilie/85

____

7. Marc/46

____

8. Josette/80

____

G. En français! Traduisez les phrases suivantes en français.

1. the forty-fifth day

____

2. a third of the children

____

3. the fifty-ninth lesson

____

4. the hundredth letter

____

5. three eighths of the students

____

6. about thirty books

____

7. the three thousandth issue (**le numéro**)

____

8. Louis the Ninth

____

Note culturelle

On emploie les nombres ordinaux en France pour les années d'éducation secondaire, mais à l'inverse de l'anglais. Au point de vue d'un Américain, on compte à rebours. Les étudiants commencent le collège en sixième et terminent en troisième. Le lycée va de la seconde à la première et la dernière année s'appelle «terminale».

D *Telling time*

- To ask the time in French the question **Quelle heure est-il?** (or more colloquially, **Il est quelle heure?**) is used. The response is the phrase **il est** followed by the hour.

Il est **une heure.**	*It's* ***one o'clock.***
Il est **onze heures.**	*It's* ***eleven o'clock.***

- Minutes past the hour until the half hour are added directly to the hour. The words **quart** and **demie** are joined by **et.**

Il est **quatre heures cinq.**	*It's* ***five past four.***
Il est **quatre heures et quart.**	*It's* ***a quarter past four.***
Il est **quatre heures vingt.**	*It's* ***twenty past four.***
Il est **quatre heures et demie.**	*It's* ***four thirty.***

- Minutes before the hour are expressed by the word **moins. Moins le quart** means *a quarter to the hour.*

Il est cinq heures **moins vingt.**	*It's* ***twenty to*** *five.*
Il est cinq heures **moins le quart.**	*It's* ***a quarter to*** *five.*

- For *twelve noon,* French uses **il est midi,** and for *twelve midnight,* **il est minuit.** Minutes past these hours are expressed as above.

Il est **midi moins le quart.**	*It's* ***a quarter to twelve*** *(A.M.).*
Il est **midi et demi.**	*It's* ***twelve thirty*** *(P.M.).*
Il est **minuit dix.**	*It's* ***ten past twelve*** *(A.M.).*
Il est **minuit et quart.**	*It's* ***a quarter past twelve*** *(A.M.).*

- The preposition **à** is used to indicate the time at which something happens.

—**À** quelle heure est-elle arrivée?	*What time did she arrive?*
—**À** huit heures moins le quart.	***At*** *a quarter to eight.*

- Some useful expressions relating to clock time:

Il est six heures **pile.**	*It's six o'clock* ***sharp.***
Il est **tard/tôt.**	*It's* ***late/early.***
Il se lève **tard.**	*He gets up* ***late.***
Il se couche **tôt/de bonne heure.**	*He goes to bed* ***early.***
Je suis **en retard/en avance.**	*I'm* ***late/early.***
Je suis **à l'heure.**	*I'm* ***on time.***
Ma montre **avance** (de cinq minutes).	*My watch* ***is*** *(five minutes)* ***fast.***
Ma montre **retarde** (de cinq minutes).	*My watch* ***is*** *(five minutes)* ***slow.***
être matinal(e)	*to be an early riser*
se coucher tôt	*to go to bed early*
faire la grasse matinée	*to sleep late, sleep in*

- French uses a 24-hour clock for official purposes, such as transportation and entertainment schedules. In this system of telling time, **douze heures** and **vingt-quatre heures** replace **midi** and **minuit,** respectively. Minutes after the hour are counted from one to fifty-nine. **Et, moins, quart,** and **demie** are not used. Phrases such as **du matin, de l'après-midi, du soir,** and **de la nuit,** which are French equivalents of A.M. and P.M., are also not used in the 24-hour system.

La première séance du film est à **18 h 14.**	*The first showing of the film is at* ***6:14 P.M.***
Le train pour Berlin part à **13 h 48**.	*The train for Berlin leaves at* ***1:48 P.M.***
Le départ est prévu pour **0 h 35**.	*Departure is scheduled for* ***12:35 A.M.***
Boutique fermée entre **12 h** et **14 h**.	*Shop closed between noon and* ***2 P.M.***

H. La famille Raynaud revient des vacances. Le jour du retour des Raynaud a été très mouvementé. Écrivez ce qui s'est passé et à quelle heure. Suivez le modèle.

MODÈLE 6 h/les enfants/se lever
➔ Il est six heures. Les enfants se lèvent.

1. 7 h / Mme Raynaud / mettre les dernières choses dans les valises

   ____

2. 7 h 30 / les Raynaud / prendre le petit déjeuner / à l'hôtel

   ____

3. 8 h 20 / le chasseur (*bellhop*) / descendre leurs bagages

   ____

4. 8 h 35 / M. Raynaud / appeler un taxi

   ____

5. 9 h 05 / les Raynaud / arriver à la gare

   ____

6. 9 h 15 / le petit Charles / tomber et se faire mal au genou

   ____

7. 9 h 30 / le pharmacien de la gare / mettre un pansement sur le genou de Charles

   ____

8. 9 h 45 / les Raynaud / prendre leurs places dans le train pour Paris

____

9. 9 h 55 / le train / partir

____

10. 3 h 20 / ils / arriver à Paris

____

I. La journée de M. Cavalli, épicier. M. Léon Cavalli est propriétaire d'une épicerie à Lille. Il décrit sa journée. Reconstruisez ces phrases en partant des éléments donnés pour savoir ce qui est arrivé et à quelle heure.

MODÈLE moi/se lever/5 h 30
➔ Je me suis levé à cinq heures et demie.

1. moi / arriver à la boutique / 6 h 15

____

2. la livraison (*delivery*) du lait et des œufs / venir / 6 h 35

____

3. mes commis (*clerks*) / arriver / 6 h 50

____

4. nous / ouvrir l'épicerie / 7 h pile

____

5. la première cliente / franchir le seuil (*cross the threshold*) / 7 h 10

____

6. ma sœur / passer me voir / 10 h 45

____

7. nous / fermer pour le déjeuner / 1 h 40

____

8. moi / rouvrir ma boutique / 3 h 30

____

Note culturelle

Lille est une importante ville française située dans le nord du pays tout près de la frontière belge. Avec les villes de Tourcoing et de Roubaix, Lille forme une grande agglomération de presque un million de personnes. Comme Lyon, Lille rêve d'un rôle européen. Sa situation lui offre cette possibilité. Pour s'équiper pour l'avenir, les Lillois construisent un nouveau métro et développent leurs universités. Lille a aussi un splendide musée des beaux-arts.

J. Des sports à la télé. Voici l'horaire des émissions de la chaîne Eurosport pris dans *Le Figaro* du 14 mars 1995. Lisez le programme et répondez aux questions en employant l'heure officielle.

EUROSPORT

8.30 Eurogolf. Au sommaire : l'Open du Maroc. A Agadir. **9.30** Athlétisme. Championnats du monde en salle. A Barcelone (Espagne). **11.30** Ski nordique. Championnats du monde. 9/19 mars. 15 km messieurs style libre. A Thunder Bay (Canada). **13.00** Eurogoals. **14.30** Speedworld. Indy, Formule 1, NASCAR, Formule 3000, rallye, moto. Tout sur le monde de la vitesse. **16.30** Ski nordique. Championnats du monde. 9/19 mars. 10 km dames style libre. A Thunder Bay (Canada). Commentaires : Marc Mingola. En direct. **17.30** Eurogoals. **18.30** Eurotennis. Le magazine du tennis ATP, WTA et ITF. Commentaires : Denis Brogniart et Frédéric Viard. **19.30** Eurosportnews. **20.00** Ski nordique. Championnats du monde. 9/19 mars. Saut à skis par équipes. K90. A Thunder Bay (Canada). Commentaires : Jean-Charles Sabattier. En direct. **22.00** Basket-ball. Championnat d'Europe. Quart de finale. Match retour. Limoges / Pesaro (Italie). A Limoges. 23.30 Euroski. Le magazine de tous les skis. **0.30** Football. Coupe d'Europe. Juventus (Italie)/ Eintracht Francfort (Allemagne), dans le cadre des quarts de finale de la coupe de l'UEFA et Chelsea (Angleterre)/ Bruges (Belgique), quarts de finale de la coupe des vainqueurs. **2.30** Fin.

1. Quel sport vient du Maroc? À quelle heure est-ce qu'on peut le voir?

____

2. À quelle heure est-ce qu'on peut voir les courses d'automobile?

____

3. À quelle heure est-ce qu'on peut écouter les commentaires de Marc Mingola? Quel sport est-ce qu'il explique?

____

4. À quelle heure est-ce qu'on peut voir un match entre une équipe italienne et une équipe allemande?

____

5. À quelle heure l'émission se termine-t-elle?

____

6. Écrivez l'heure officielle des émissions suivantes:

   a. Eurogoals _______________________

   b. Eurotennis _______________________

   c. Basket-ball _______________________

   d. Athlétisme _______________________

   e. Eurosportnews _______________________

K. À la gare de Genève. Voici une liste de départs des trains en gare de Genève. Lisez la liste et répondez aux questions en employant l'heure officielle.

Heure	Pour	Voie
5 58	Zurich	4
9 05	Genève-Aéroport	3
10 22	Lyon-Perrache	7
13 08	Dortmund (Allemagne)	6
14 06	La Plaine	5
15 35	Milan (Italie)	8
16 50	Paris	8
17 22	Lausanne	4
19 10	Paris	8
19 25	Zurich	4
20 25	Naples (Italie)	4
21 58	Bern	4
22 50	Barcelone (Espagne)	7
23 02	Zagreb (Croatie)	4
23 12	Nice	7
23 15	Genève-Aéroport	3

1. Quels trains y a-t-il pour Paris?

2. À quelle heure y a-t-il un train pour La Plaine?

3. À quelle heure part le train pour Zurich?

4. Quels trains y a-t-il pour l'Italie?

5. À quelle heure peut-on prendre le train pour Bern?

6. Quels trains y a-t-il pour des villes françaises à part Paris?

7. À quelle heure doit-on prendre le train s'il faut prendre l'avion à onze heures du matin?

8. Quel train y a-t-il pour l'Allemagne? pour l'Espagne?

9. Vous voulez arriver à Zurich le soir. Quel train prendrez-vous?

10. Quand y a-t-il un train pour Lausanne?

E Days, dates, and years

- Here are the words for the days of the week and the months and seasons of the year.

Les jours de la semaine

lundi *Monday*
mardi *Tuesday*
mercredi *Wednesday*
jeudi *Thursday*
vendredi *Friday*
samedi *Saturday*
dimanche *Sunday*

Les mois de l'année

janvier *January*
février *February*
mars *March*
avril *April*
mai *May*
juin *June*
juillet *July*
août *August*
septembre *September*
octobre *October*
novembre *November*
décembre *December*

Les saisons

le printemps *spring*
l'été *summer*
l'automne *fall, autumn*
l'hiver *winter*

- To specify *when* something happens, French uses several patterns.

1. No preposition is used before days of the week.

Il arrivera **lundi.** — *He'll arrive **on Monday**.*

Je l'ai vue **dimanche.** — *I saw her **on Sunday**.*

2. **Le** is used before the days of the week to indicate repeated or regular action.

—Je n'ai pas de cours **le mardi.** — *I don't have classes **on Tuesdays.***
—Et moi, je travaille **le vendredi**. — *And I work **on Fridays.***

3. The preposition **en** is used before months of the year and the names of the seasons, except for **au printemps.**

—Tu prends tes vacances **en juillet**? — *Are you taking your vacation **in July?***
—Non. Je n'aime pas partir **en été**. Je prends mes vacances **en mai**. — *No. I don't like to go on vacation **in the summer**. I take my vacation **in May**.*
—Tu as raison. C'est agréable, les vacances **au printemps**. — *You're right. Vacationing **in the spring** is very pleasant.*

- To express dates, French uses cardinal numbers, except for **le premier.** The definite article **le** precedes the date. Note that as with days of the week, no preposition is used for *on.*

—Je croyais que tes cousins arrivaient **le trente novembre.** — *I thought your cousins were arriving **on November thirtieth**.*
—Non, c'était prévu pour **le premier décembre.** — *No, it was scheduled **for the first of December**.*

When dates are written in figures, the day precedes the month.

4.3.98 — *March 4, 1998*

- Years are usually expressed in hundreds, although **mil** may also be used. **En** is used to express the year in which something happened.

en dix sept-cent quatre-vingt-neuf
en mil sept cent quatre-vingt-neuf } *in 1789*

Je suis né **en dix-neuf cent soixante-dix-neuf.** — *I was born **in 1979**.*

As in English, the last two numbers are often used in speech to express the years of the present century.

Elle est partie en **quatre-vingt-onze.** — *She left in '91.*

- Some useful expressions relating to the days and dates:

Quelle est la date (aujourd'hui)?	*What's today's date?*
Le combien sommes-nous?	*What's today's date?*
C'est le premier juin.	*It's June first.*
Nous sommes le premier juin.	*It's June first.*
Quel jour sommes-nous?	*What day is it?*
C'est mercredi.	*It's Wednesday.*
Nous sommes mercredi aujourd'hui.	*It's Wednesday today.*
au début de juin	*at the beginning of June*
à la mi-juin	*in the middle of June*
vers la fin de juin	*towards the end of June*
Il te rendra ton argent la semaine des quatre jeudis.	*You'll never get your money back from him. (English: in a month of Sundays)*
des gens endimanchés	*people dressed in their Sunday best*
un peintre du dimanche	*an amateur painter*
Poisson d'avril!	*April fool!*

L. **L'année de Francine.** Francine est une étudiante américaine qui écrit à Anne-Marie, son amie française. Dans sa lettre elle lui raconte tout ce qui s'est passé dans l'année. Avant d'écrire, elle fait une liste des dates importantes. Aidez-la en écrivant les dates en français.

1. January 2: retour des vacances ______________________
2. January 24: examens finals ______________________
3. February 14: la Saint-Valentin—dîner avec Jean-Claude

   ____
4. March 10: bal au centre communautaire ______________________
5. April 1: poisson d'avril (*April Fool's Day*) ______________________
6. May 28: parade pour le jour des Morts au Champ d'Honneur (*Memorial Day*)

   ____
7. June 24: dernier jour de classes ______________________
8. July 4: jour de l'Indépendance (fête nationale) ______________________
9. July 16: boulot (*job*) commence (au restaurant) ______________________
10. August 30: j'ai rompu avec Jean-Claude ______________________
11. September 6: premier jour de cours—j'ai connu Philippe

    ____
12. November 25: Thanksgiving ______________________

M. Histoire de France du dixième au dix-neuvième siècle. Écrivez ces dates importantes de l'histoire française.

MODÈLE Charlemagne couronné «empereur des Romains» par le pape Léon III: 25.12.800
➔ le vingt-cinq décembre huit cents

1. Hughes Capet élu roi à Noyon: 1.7.987
2. commencement de la première croisade: départ des croisés armés: 15.8.1096
3. bataille de Bouvines: Philippe Auguste bat Jean sans Terre et ses alliés: 27.7.1214
4. Jeanne d'Arc brûlée à Rouen: 30.5.1431
5. édit de Nantes: 15.4.1598
6. Louis XIV devient roi de France: 7.6.1654
7. prise de la Bastille: 14.7.1789
8. déclaration de l'Empire (Napoléon Empereur) par le Sénat: 18.5.1804
9. création de la Troisième République: 4.9.1870

N. Examen d'histoire. Françoise étudie pour l'examen d'histoire contemporaine. Aidez-la en choisissant l'année correcte pour chaque événement donné. Écrivez votre réponse en lettres.

1. début de la Première Guerre mondiale (1914 ou 1915)
2. fin de la Première Guerre mondiale (1918 ou 1919)
3. début de la crise économique mondiale (1927 ou 1929)
4. commencement de la Deuxième Guerre mondiale (1938 ou 1939)
5. chute (*fall*) de Paris (1940 ou 1941)

6. fin de la Seconde Guerre mondiale (1944 ou 1945)

____

7. De Gaulle devient Président de la Cinquième République (1957 ou 1958)

____

8. l'Algérie indépendante (1962 ou 1964)

____

Note culturelle

Le général Charles de Gaulle a dirigé les Forces de la France Libre (c'est-à-dire, l'armée française en exil) pendant la Deuxième Guerre mondiale. En 1958, en pleine crise économique et coloniale (soulèvement de l'Algérie), de Gaulle est élu Président de la Cinquième République. Il a participé à la rédaction de la constitution de la Cinquième République qui a donné à la France un régime présidentiel.

O. Et maintenant il s'agit de vous. Faites une liste des dates de naissance (jour, mois, année) de vos frères et sœurs, de vos parents, de vos meilleurs amis. Écrivez les dates en lettres.

1. ______________________________
2. ______________________________
3. ______________________________
4. ______________________________
5. ______________________________
6. ______________________________
7. ______________________________
8. ______________________________

P. En français! Exprimez ces idées en français.

1. —What's today's date?
   —It's March twenty-first.

   ____

   ____

2. He'll never come to see us (= He'll come to see us in a month of Sundays).

   ____

3. I'm only an amateur painter.

   ____

4. —What day is it?
   —It's Saturday.

   ____

   ____

5. You (*plural*) are all dressed up (*in your Sunday best*).

____

6. I'm going to Italy in the spring.

____

7. —What time is it?
—It's eight o'clock sharp.
—Good. I'm early.

____

____

____

8. —Has John gotten up already?
—No. He's not an early riser, you know.
—I know he likes to sleep in.

____

____

____

Q. **Exercice oral.** Travaillez avec un(e) camarade. Posez des questions sur les grands moments de sa vie: Quand a-t-il/elle emménagé ici, quand est-il/elle né(e), quand compte-t-il/elle commencer à travailler, etc. Votre camarade vous posera le même genre de questions.

CHAPTER 20

ADVERBS

A *Adverbs of manner*

Adverbs give information about verbs, adjectives, other adverbs, or an entire sentence. Adverbs of manner tell how something is done.

- Most adverbs of manner are formed by adding **-ment** to the feminine form of the adjective.

Masculine	*Feminine*	*Adverb*
actif	**active**	**activement** *actively*
amer	**amère**	**amèrement** *bitterly*
certain	**certaine**	**certainement** *certainly*
cruel	**cruelle**	**cruellement** *cruelly*
doux	**douce**	**doucement** *gently, softly*
franc	**franche**	**franchement** *frankly*
lent	**lente**	**lentement** *slowly*
public	**publique**	**publiquement** *publicly*
sérieux	**sérieuse**	**sérieusement** *seriously*

- If the masculine singular form of an adjective ends in a vowel, **-ment** is added directly to that form.

Masculine	*Adverb*
absolu	**absolument** *absolutely*
facile	**facilement** *easily*
poli	**poliment** *politely*
sincère	**sincèrement** *sincerely*
vrai	**vraiment** *really, truly*

- If the masculine singular form of an adjective ends in **-ant** or **-ent, -ant** is replaced by **-amment** and **-ent** is replaced by **-emment.**

Adjective	*Adverb*
constant	**constamment** *constantly*
courant	**couramment** *fluently*
prudent	**prudemment** *carefully*
récent	**récemment** *recently*

- Some adjectives form adverbs by adding **-ément.**

Adjective	*Adverb*
aveugle	**aveuglément** *blindly*
commun	**communément** *commonly*
confus	**confusément** *confusedly*
énorme	**énormément** *enormously*
intense	**intensément** *intensely*
obscur	**obscurément** *obscurely*
précis	**précisément** *precisely*
profond	**profondément** *profoundly, deeply*
uniforme	**uniformément** *uniformly*

- A number of adjectives can be used as adverbs, mostly in set phrases. The masculine singular form of the adjective is used.

  parler (tout) bas *to speak (very) softly*
  sentir bon *to smell good*
  acheter/vendre cher *to buy/sell at a high price*
  coûter cher *to cost a lot*
  payer cher *to pay a high price for*
  s'arrêter court *to stop short*
  aller tout droit *to go straight ahead*
  travailler dur *to work hard*
  parler/crier fort *to speak/yell, cry out loudly*
  lire tout haut *to read aloud*
  mettre la radio plus haut *to turn the radio up louder*
  sentir mauvais *to smell bad*

- Some adverbs are irregular.

Adjective	*Adverb*
gai	**gaiment** *gaily*
gentil	**gentiment** *gently*
bref	**brièvement** *briefly*
bon	**bien** *well*
mauvais	**mal** *badly*
meilleur	**mieux** *better*
pire	**pis** *worse*

- Some other common adverbs of manner do not end in **-ment.**

  ainsi *thus*
  debout *up, awake, standing up*
  exprès *on purpose*
  vite *quickly*
  volontiers *gladly*

A. Pour décrire des actions. Formez les adverbes qui correspondent aux adjectifs suivants. Après cet exercice, vous serez prêt(e) à décrire une vaste gamme d'actions.

Modèle personnel ➔ personnellement

1. affreux ______________
2. intelligent ______________
3. correct ______________
4. possible ______________
5. gentil ______________
6. triste ______________
7. massif ______________
8. gai ______________
9. confus ______________
10. fréquent ______________
11. moral ______________
12. pratique ______________
13. généreux ______________
14. actuel ______________
15. évident ______________
16. léger ______________
17. long ______________
18. précis ______________
19. exact ______________
20. complet ______________

B. Comment est-ce qu'ils ont parlé? Formez des adverbes pour décrire comment ces personnes s'adressent au professeur.

MODÈLE —Sarah est sincère quand elle parle avec le professeur?
➔ —Oui, elle lui parle sincèrement.

1. Frédéric est nerveux quand il parle avec le professeur?
____
2. Lise est confuse quand elle parle avec le professeur?
____
3. Paul est honnête quand il parle avec le professeur?
____
4. Anne et Barbara sont tristes quand elles parlent avec le professeur?
____
5. Luc et Jean-Claude sont furieux quand ils parlent avec le professeur?
____
6. Thérèse est patiente quand elle parle avec le professeur?
____
7. Odile et Marc sont polis quand ils parlent avec le professeur?
____
8. Fanny est discrète quand elle parle avec le professeur?
____
9. Éric et Jacques sont intenses quand ils parlent avec le professeur?
____
10. Serge est gentil quand il parle avec le professeur?
____

C. Décrivez les actions. Refaites les phrases suivantes en employant le verbe qui correspond au substantif et l'adverbe qui correspond à l'adjectif.

MODÈLE Est-ce que les réponses de Victor sont intelligentes?
➔ Oui, il répond intelligemment.

1. Est-ce que le travail de Paulette est diligent?
____
2. Est-ce que les réactions de son frère sont violentes?
____
3. Est-ce que les dessins de cette artiste sont bons?
____
4. Est-ce que les sorties de votre sœur sont fréquentes?
____

5. Est-ce que la prononciation des ces élèves est mauvaise?

____

6. Est-ce que son amour pour elle est aveugle?

____

7. Est-ce que les punitions de l'institutrice sont uniformes?

____

8. Est-ce que les réflexions de ce philosophe sont profondes?

____

B *The use and position of adverbs of manner*

- Adverbs of manner ending in **-ment** and the adverbs **bien, mal, mieux, pis,** and **vite** usually directly follow the verb they modify. In compound tenses, short adverbs usually follow the auxiliary verb, and longer adverbs usually follow the past participle.

—Julie et Bruno se disputent **constammant.**	*Julie and Bruno argue* ***constantly.***
—Après le dîner, ils se sont disputés **amèrement** et Julie a **vite** quitté le salon.	*After dinner, they argued* ***bitterly,*** *and Julie* ***quickly*** *left the living room.*

- When an adverb modifies an adjective or another adverb, it precedes the word it modifies.

Cette lettre est **très importante.**	*This letter is* ***very important.***
Les spectateurs étaient **profondément émus.**	*The audience was* ***deeply moved.***

- Adverbs of manner ending in **-ment** can be replaced by **avec** plus the corresponding noun.

joyeusement ➔ avec joie	**discrètement ➔ avec discrétion**
violemment ➔ avec violence	**amèrement ➔ avec amertume**

- **Sans** + noun is often the equivalent of English adverbs ending in *-lessly* or English adverbs formed from negative adjectives.

sans espoir	*hopelessly*	**sans hésitation**	*unhesitatingly*
sans honte	*shamelessly*	**sans succès**	*unsuccessfully*

- **D'une façon, d'une manière, d'un ton,** or **d'un air** plus an adjective may be used in place of an adverb or when no adverb exists.

d'une façon compétente	*competently*	**d'un ton moqueur**	*mockingly*
d'une manière compatible	*compatibly*	**d'un air indécis**	*indecisively*

D. Formez vos phrases! Mettez les éléments donnés en ordre pour former des phrases correctes. Faites attention à la position des adverbes.

MODÈLE expliqué/bien/problème/le/a/le professeur
➔ Le professeur a bien expliqué le problème.

1. mal / le vocabulaire / prononces / tu
2. nettoie / la cuisine / elle / soigneusement
3. ridicule / trouvons / ce projet / complètement / nous
4. étroitement / sont / les membres de cette famille / unis
5. sans / marche / il / empressement
6. d'une façon / les enfants / de / se sont conduits / déplaisante
7. dur / Marcelle / à / travaille / la bibliothèque
8. une / acceptée / c'est / largement / idée
9. le / ont / ils / texte / compris / vite
10. m' / elle / répondu / a / brusquement

E. Pour reconnaître les adverbes. Les locutions suivantes peuvent être traduites par des adverbes en anglais. Écrivez à côté de chacune d'elles une traduction convenable.

1. d'un ton insultant ____________
2. sans doute ____________
3. avec gentillesse ____________
4. avec indignation ____________
5. d'un ton sec ____________
6. d'une façon extravagante ____________
7. avec décision ____________
8. avec intelligence ____________

F. L'expression adverbiale. Consultez la liste des substantifs ci-dessous et employez-les avec les prépositions **avec** et **sans** pour traduire les adverbes anglais.

la cérémonie *ceremony*
la colère *anger*
l'effort *effort*
l'imagination *imagination*
l'indifférence *indifference*
la tolérance *tolerance*
le goût *taste*
le tact *tact*

1. effortlessly ______________________________
2. tastefully ______________________________
3. unimaginatively ______________________________
4. unconcernedly ______________________________
5. angrily ______________________________
6. tolerantly ______________________________
7. unceremoniously ______________________________
8. tactlessly ______________________________

C *Adverbs of time*

- Adverbs of time tell when or in what order something happens.

actuellement *at present*
alors *then*
après *after, afterwards*
après-demain *the day after tomorrow*
aujourd'hui *today*
auparavant *previously, beforehand*
aussitôt *immediately*
autrefois *formerly, in the past*
avant *before*
avant-hier *the day before yesterday*
bientôt *soon*
d'abord *at first*
de bonne heure *early*
déjà *already, ever*
demain *tomorrow*
dernièrement *lately*
désormais *from now on*
encore *still, yet, again*
encore une fois *again*
enfin *at last, finally*
ensuite *next, following that*
hier *yesterday*
jamais *never*
longtemps *for a long time*
maintenant *now*
n'importe quand *anytime*
parfois *sometimes*
précédemment *previously*
quelquefois *sometimes*
rarement *rarely, seldom*
récemment *recently*
souvent *often*
tard *late*
tôt *early*
toujours *always*
tout à l'heure *a short while ago; very soon*
tout de suite *immediately*

- Adverbs of time usually follow the verb, but they often occur at the beginning of sentences.

Je vais **quelquefois** au théâtre.
Quelquefois je vais au théâtre.

Il travaillait **auparavant** à Lille.
Auparavant il travaillait à Lille.

- Many phrases expressing points in time function as adverbial phrases.

le week-end
en semaine *during the week*
la semaine dernière/prochaine
le matin/l'après-midi
le soir/la nuit
tous les jours

toute la journée	**une fois, deux fois,** etc.
tous les ans	**une/deux fois par semaine/mois**
tous les mois	**mardi**
toutes les semaines	**le mardi**
le lendemain *the day after*	**mardi prochain**
la veille *the evening before*	**mardi dernier**

G. Trouvez dans la deuxième colonne des antonymes pour les adverbes de temps de la première colonne.

_____ 1. tard	a. autrefois
_____ 2. actuellement	b. avant
_____ 3. hier	c. jamais
_____ 4. souvent	d. demain
_____ 5. toujours	e. rarement
_____ 6. après	f. tôt

H. **Qu'est-ce vous faites et quand?** En choisissant des éléments des trois groupes (ou en ajoutant d'autres éléments), écrivez dix phrases qui parlent de vos activités et de celles des gens que vous connaissez.

moi, je	arriver	auparavant
nous	partir	tout de suite
mes parents	se lever	____ fois par semaine
mon frère/ma sœur	se coucher	tous les jours
mon meilleur ami _______	faire ses devoirs	le matin/soir
ma meilleure amie _______	rentrer	l'après-midi
mon petit ami _______	faire du jogging	tous les soirs/matins
ma petite amie _______	faire du sport	le samedi/dimanche
les autres étudiants	aller au cinéma	quelquefois
il y a des étudiants qui	nous faire passer un examen	dernièrement
le professeur	passer un examen	souvent
le directeur	sortir	hier/avant-hier
	travailler	demain/après-demain
		désormais

1. ____________________
2. ____________________
3. ____________________
4. ____________________
5. ____________________
6. ____________________
7. ____________________
8. ____________________
9. ____________________
10. ____________________

D *Adverbs of place*

- Adverbs of place tell where something happens.

ailleurs *elsewhere, somewhere else*
autour *around*
d'ailleurs *besides*
dedans *inside*
dehors *outside*
derrière *behind*
dessous *below*
dessus *above*
devant *in front*
en bas *down, downstairs*
en haut *up, upstairs*
ici *here*
là *there*
là-bas *over there*
loin *far away*
n'importe où *anywhere*
nulle part *nowhere*
nulle part ailleurs *nowhere else*
partout *everywhere*
partout ailleurs *everywhere else*
près *near*
quelque part *somewhere*

- In everyday language, both spoken and written, **ici** is often replaced by **là.**

Je regrette, mais Mme Poirier n'est pas **là.** — *I'm sorry, but Mrs. Poirier is not* ***here.***

- **Là-** can be added to some of the above adverbs of place.

là-dedans *in there*
là-dessous *underneath there*
là-dessus *on top of it, on it*
là-haut *up there*

I. Antonymes. Trouvez dans la deuxième colonne des antonymes pour les adverbes de lieu de la première colonne.

_____ 1. ici — a. dessus
_____ 2. dedans — b. nulle part
_____ 3. loin — c. derrière
_____ 4. dessous — d. dehors
_____ 5. partout — e. là
_____ 6. devant — f. en haut
_____ 7. en bas — g. près

J. Une belle maison. Rendez plus précise cette description d'une belle maison en ajoutant les adverbes de lieu donnés entre parenthèses aux phrases. On peut placer ces adverbes à la fin de la phrase, et parfois au début aussi.

MODÈLE Je remarque une maison. (là-bas)
➔ Je remarque une maison là-bas.

1. C'est une jolie maison. Il y a des arbres. (autour)

____

2. Il y a un jardin. (derrière)

____

3. Je regarde le salon. (en bas)

____

4. Je voudrais voir les chambres (en haut)

5. Je cherche les propriétaires. (partout)

6. Je ne les vois pas. (nulle part)

7. Travaillent-ils? (dehors)

8. Je les entends. (quelque part)

9. Il y a deux voix. (tout près)

10. Les voilà. (devant)

K. Du temps et du lieu. Traduisez les conversations suivantes en français en faisant attention aux adverbes de temps et de lieu.

1. —Yesterday I looked for my watch everywhere.
   —I saw it somewhere. Did you look (for it) upstairs?

2. —It rains here every week.
   —I know. I wish I lived elsewhere.

3. —I didn't go anywhere on Wednesday.
   —Neither did I. I seldom go out during the week.

4. —Formerly I used to do the shopping (**faire le marché**) every day.
   —At present you do the marketing once a week, right?

5. —I would go to see her anytime, anywhere.
   —You won't have to go far. There she is, over there.

E Adverbial phrases

- Prepositional phrases often function as adverbs of time, place, and manner. The preposition **dès** and the compound preposition **à partir de** combine with time words to tell when something happened.

  dès le matin *from the morning on*
  dès le début *from the beginning*
  dès mon retour *as soon as I get back*
  à partir d'aujourd'hui *from today on*
  à partir de demain *from tomorrow on*
  à partir d'hier *starting yesterday*

- Adverbial phrases of time with the prepositions **dans** and **en:**

  dans l'avenir/dans le passé *in the future/in the past*
  dans un mois *in a month*
  dans un moment *in a moment*
  en ce moment *at this time*
  dans cinq minutes *in five minutes (five minutes from now)*
  en cinq minutes *in five minutes (time it takes to do something)*
  d'aujourd'hui en huit *a week from today*
  en avance *early (relative to a point in time)*
  en retard *late (relative to a point in time)*

- Adverbial phrases beginning with the preposition **à:**

  Phrases of time

  à l'heure *on time*
  à temps *in time*
  à l'époque *at the time, at that time*
  à l'époque où nous sommes *in this day and age*
  à leur arrivée *when they arrived*
  à leur retour *when they returned*

  Phrases of place

  à trois kilomètres de la ville *three kilometers from the city*
  à trois heures de Paris *three hours from Paris*
  à droite/à gauche *to, on the right/to, on the left*

  Phrases of manner

  à merveille *wonderfully*
  à pied *on foot*
  à cheval *on horseback*
  à la hâte *hastily, in a rush*
  à peine *hardly*

- Adverbial phrases beginning with the preposition **de:**

  d'habitude, d'ordinaire *usually*
  de temps en temps *from time to time*
  du matin au soir *from morning to night*
  de bonne heure *early*
  de mois en mois/de jour en jour *from month to month/from day to day*
  marcher d'un bon pas *to walk at a good pace*

- Adverbial phrases with the preposition **en:**

  en avant *in front, ahead*
  en arrière *in back*
  en face *across the way*
  en tout cas *in any case*
  en plus *moreover*
  en train/autobus/avion/voiture *by train, bus, plane, car*
  en désordre, en pagaille *in a mess*
  en groupe *in a group*

- Adverbial phrases with the preposition **par:**

par hasard *by chance*
par la force *by force*
par écrit *in writing*
par terre *on the ground*
par ici/là *this way/that way*
par conséquent *consequently*
par intervalles *intermittently*
payer par chèque *to pay by check*
par la poste *through the mails, by mail*

- The preposition **sur** has idiomatic uses in phrases of time:

sur les 3 heures *at about 3 o'clock*
sur le moment *at first*
sur une année *over (over the period of) a year*
un jour sur deux *every other day*

- The following miscellaneous phrases with **sans** are often translated by English adverbs:

sans but *aimlessly*
sans chaussures *barefoot*
sans doute *doubtlessly*
sans faute *without fail*
sans mal *without any trouble, without difficulty*

L. Mon rendez-vous. M. Perrin explique les difficultés qu'il a eues pour ne pas manquer son rendez-vous. Ajoutez les prépositions qui manquent pour savoir ce qui lui est arrivé.

J'avais rendez-vous à 3 heures. Je ne voulais pas arriver (1) _________ retard. Je suis donc parti (2) _________ les 2 heures pour arriver un peu (3) _________ avance. Il pleuvait. Je ne pouvais pas aller (4) _________ pied (5) _________ un temps pareil. J'ai décidé d'aller (6) _________ autobus. Mais l'autobus n'est pas venu. (7) _________ conséquent, j'ai pris un taxi. Je m'étais (8) _________ peine assis quand le taxi a eu un pneu crevé. Je suis descendu du taxi et j'ai commencé à marcher (9) _________ un bon pas. Je me trouvais (10) _________ vingt minutes du bureau où on m'attendait. Tout à fait (11) _________ hasard mon ami Michel est passé dans sa voiture. Il a klaxonné pour attirer mon attention. Il m'a emmené (12) _________ voiture et on est arrivés (13) _________ cinq minutes. Je suis arrivé (14) _________ temps!

M. Les soucis d'un jeune professeur. Alfred Saint-Martin est un jeune professeur d'histoire dans un lycée de Tours. Il a une classe difficile. Pour savoir ce qu'il en pense et ce qu'il compte faire, refaites les phrases suivantes en y ajoutant la traduction française des phrases adverbiales données entre parenthèses.

1. J'ai fait un effort pour organiser la classe. (*right from the start*)

____

2. J'ai dit aux étudiants qu'il est défendu de venir en classe. (*barefoot*)

____

3. Je leur ai dit que je ne veux pas qu'ils laissent la salle de classe. (*in a mess*)

____

4. Ils ne doivent laisser ni leurs livres ni leurs papiers. (*on the ground*)

5. Jean-Claude Mercier vient au cours. (*every other day*)

6. Noëlle Chenu se promène dans les couloirs. (*aimlessly*)

7. Elle travaille un peu. (*intermittently*)

8. Elle prépare ses devoirs. (*hurriedly*)

9. Lise Monnet est la meilleure étudiante de la classe. (*doubtlessly*)

10. Elle travaille. (*wonderfully*)

11. Les autres étudiants l'admirent. (*usually*)

12. Nous avons une semaine de congé. (*starting tomorrow*)

13. Je vais faire un effort pour améliorer cette classe. (*as soon as we get back*)

14. Nous allons faire des excursions. (*from time to time*)

15. Nous irons à Chambord. (*in a group*)

16. Les vieilles méthodes ne sont pas toujours bonnes. (*in this day and age*)

17. Je jugerai cette expérience. (*over four months*)

Note culturelle

Chambord est un des châteaux de la Loire les plus connus. Il a été construit par François Ier et est un magnifique exemple du style de la Renaissance. François Ier a eu beaucoup d'importance dans l'évolution de la civilisation française. Il a remplacé le latin par le français dans les jugements et dans les autres documents officiels. Il a réuni à la cour des écrivains et des artistes. Il a fondé le Collège de France, un établissement d'enseignement consacré à la recherche, indépendant de l'Université, et l'Imprimerie nationale pour imprimer les actes officiels du royaume.

N. **La grammaire en action.** Lisez l'annonce suivante pour un immeuble de luxe en faisant attention aux adverbes et aux phrases prépositionnelles qui fonctionnent comme des adverbes. Ensuite, répondez aux questions.

PARIS - LES LILAS

Nouvelles mesures
gouvernementales.
Parlons-en ensemble.

Guénier & Communication

"Résidence de l'Hôtel de Ville", Passage de La Mairie

A 50 m. DU METRO...

Faites le bon choix !

A 300 m. de Paris et 50 m. du métro, en plein cœur des Lilas où cohabitent harmonieusement passé historique et rénovation dynamique du centre ville, c'est avec la même exigence que Marignan Immobilier réalise la Résidence de l'Hôtel de Ville.

Achetez juste et bien !

Une résidence d'exception de 45 appartements, **du studio au 5 pièces duplex.** Architecture et prestations de grande qualité, **avec balcons et grandes terrasses** pour quelques privilégiés.

Venez découvrir dès maintenant cette résidence et le prêt à taux zéro.

Bureau de vente sur place : 6 à 10, Passage de La Mairie, Les Lilas.

Ouvert : Lundi, jeudi et vendredi de 14h à 19h samedi et dimanche de 10h à 13h et de 14h30 à 19h.

48 97 91 33
MARIGNAN IMMOBILIER
3 RUE DU 8 MAI 1945 - 92110 CLICHY - TEL.: 41 27 15 50

FONCIER HABITAT

Écrivez l'adverbe ou la phrase prépositionnelle qui exprime les idées suivantes:

1. la distance de l'immeuble du métro

____

2. la distance de l'immeuble de Paris

____

3. comment coexistent aux Lilas le passé historique et la rénovation du centre ville

____

4. l'appartement peut être acquis à un très bon prix

____

5. à partir de quand on peut venir voir l'appartement

____

6. jours d'ouverture du bureau de vente

____

7. heures d'ouverture du bureau de vente pendant le week-end

____

CHAPTER 21

NEGATIVES AND INDEFINITES

A Negative words

- In Chapter 3 we reviewed the following positive and corresponding negative words:

encore, toujours *still*	**plus** *no more*
encore, davantage *more*	**plus** *no more, not anymore*
quelquefois *sometimes*	**jamais** *never*
toujours *always*	**jamais** *never*
souvent *often*	**jamais** *never*
quelqu'un *someone, somebody*	**personne** *no one, nobody*
quelque chose *something*	**rien** *nothing*
quelque part *somewhere*	**nulle part** *nowhere*

- Here are some additional pairs of corresponding positive and negative expressions:

déjà *ever*	**jamais** *never*
déjà *already*	**pas encore** *not yet*
soit . . . soit/soit . . . ou *either . . . or*	**ni . . . ni** *neither . . . nor*
ou *or*	**ni** *neither, nor*

- In both simple and compound tenses, **ne** precedes the conjugated verb and the negative word usually follows the conjugated verb.

—Est-ce que tu as déjà été en Belgique?	*Have you ever been to Belgium?*
—Non, je **n'**y suis **jamais** allé.	*No, I've* ***never*** *gone there.*
—Nous passerons l'été soit à Nice, soit en Espagne. Et vous?	*We'll spend the summer* ***either*** *in Nice* ***or*** *in Spain. How about you?*
—Nous **ne** partons **ni** dans le Midi, **ni** à l'étranger. Nous travaillons cet été.	*We won't be going* ***either*** *to the south of France* ***or*** *abroad. We're working this summer.*

- More than one negative word can be used in a sentence: **ne . . . plus jamais** *or* **ne . . . jamais plus** (*never again*), **ne . . . plus rien** (*nothing else, nothing more*), **ne . . . plus personne** (*nobody else, no one any more*), etc.

—Il **n'**y a **jamais personne** ici.	*There's* ***never anyone*** *here.*
—C'est qu'il **n'**y a **plus rien** à faire.	*That's because there's* ***nothing more*** *to do.*

- Negative words can stand by themselves.

—Connais-tu beaucoup de monde ici?	*Do you know a lot of people here?*
—**Personne**.	***No one.***
—Qu'est-ce que vous cherchez?	*What are you looking for?*
—**Rien**.	***Nothing.***

- Both **ne** and the negative words **pas, rien, jamais,** and **plus** precede an infinitive. **Personne,** however, follows an infinitive.

Je vous conseille de **ne pas** y **aller**.	*I advise you* ***not to go*** *there.*
Il m'a dit de **ne jamais revenir**.	*He told me* ***never to come back.***
On passe la journée à **ne rien faire**.	*We spend the day* ***doing nothing.***
Je préfère **ne voir personne**.	*I prefer* ***not to see anyone.***

- After the word **que** in comparisons, French uses negative words.

—J'ai l'impression que Vincent est **plus paresseux que jamais**.	*I have the impression that Vincent is* ***lazier than ever.***
—Vous vous trompez. Il travaille **mieux que personne.**	*You're mistaken. He works* ***better than anyone.***

- Before adjectives, nouns, pronouns, or adverbs, **non** or **pas** is usually used. **Non** is more formal, **pas** is more colloquial.

—Tu es éreinté?	*Are you exhausted?*
—**Pas éreinté (Non éreinté).** Un peu fatigué.	***Not exhausted.*** *A little tired.*
Il travaille mardi, **pas jeudi (non jeudi).**	*He's working Tuesday,* ***not Thursday.***

A. Hubert le rêveur. Hubert passe son temps à rêver. Essayez de le ramener à la réalité en employant les mots négatifs nécessaires.

Modèle Je gagne toujours à la loterie.
➔ Ne dis pas d'idioties! Tu ne gagnes jamais à la loterie.

1. Quelqu'un me donnera un million de francs.

____

2. Quelques filles me croient le plus beau garçon du lycée.

____

3. J'ai souvent vingt à l'examen de philo.

____

4. La femme du Président de la République m'a envoyé quelque chose.

____

5. Mon père va m'offrir soit une Ferrari ou une Jaguar.

____

6. Il me reste toujours quelque chose de l'argent que j'ai reçu pour mon anniversaire.

____

7. Je connais quelqu'un à Istamboul.

____

8. Je connais quelqu'un à Singapour aussi.

____

9. J'irai quelque part avec Solange.

10. Si je n'aime pas mes cadeaux, on m'offrira quelque chose d'autre.

Note culturelle

Le premier tirage de la Loterie nationale a eu lieu à Paris en 1933. Avant son remplacement par le Loto national en 1990, les Français achetaient environ 7 millions de billets par semaine. Le Loto national vend en moyenne 13 millions de bulletins par semaine. Et qui gagne? En 1992, 73 Français ont gagné plus de 10 millions de francs au Loto. Il y a quatre tirages de Loto par semaine, et on peut jouer par Minitel.

B. Marceline la trouble-fête (*party-pooper*). Marcelline est tellement pessimiste au sujet de la surboum qu'on a organisée qu'elle donne le cafard (*depresses*) à tout le monde. Écrivez les réactions de Marcelline aux idées de ses copains en employant les mots négatifs convenables.

Modèle Tout le monde viendra à notre surboum.
➔ Personne ne viendra à notre surboum.

1. Chacun apportera quelque chose à manger.

2. Nous boirons quelque chose.

3. Nous écouterons soit des cassettes soit des disques compacts.

4. Jeanine a déjà acheté du jus de fruits.

5. Olivier a une nouvelle cassette.

6. Odile amène toujours quelqu'un d'intéressant.

7. Ces boums sont toujours amusantes.

8. Après la boum, nous irons nous promener quelque part.

C. Comment est-ce que cela se dit? Traduisez les échanges suivants en français en faisant attention à l'emploi des mots négatifs.

1. —Don't you have any more packages?
   —No. I don't have anything more.

   ____

   ____

2. —That pastry cook makes cakes better than anyone.
   —Yes. That's why he has more clients than ever.

   ____

   ____

3. —He never brings anything when we invite him to dinner.
   — Don't invite him ever again.

   ____

   ____

4. —Have you ever spoken with Alfred?
   —No. He doesn't understand either English or French. I prefer not to speak to him.

   ____

   ____

D. Tout change. Quels changements y a-t-il eu à l'école depuis que vous y allez? Faites une liste de cinq choses **qu'on n'y fait plus.** Par exemple, **On ne sert plus de bonbons à la cantine.**

1. ____
2. ____
3. ____
4. ____
5. ____

E. Jamais de la vie! Quelles choses sont interdites à l'école? Chez vous en famille? Au travail, si vous travaillez? Faites une liste de cinq choses **qu'on n'y fait jamais.** Par exemple, **On ne fume jamais en classe.**

1. ____
2. ____
3. ____
4. ____
5. ____

F. Les coutumes. Il y a des choses qu'on ne fait pas, non pas parce qu'elles sont interdites, mais parce que nos coutumes nous empêchent de les faire. Faites une liste de cinq choses **que personne ne ferait.** Par exemple, **Personne ne viendrait à l'école en pyjama.** Le ridicule n'est pas exclu, bien sûr.

1. ____________________
2. ____________________
3. ____________________
4. ____________________
5. ____________________

B *Indefinite words and expressions*

- Many English indefinite expressions begin with the word *some.* They are often the positive counterparts of negative words.

quelquefois	*sometimes*	**quelque chose**	*something*
quelqu'un	*someone, somebody*	**quelque part**	*somewhere*

- The word *some* before a noun is expressed in French either by the partitive article or by **quelques,** which is more emphatic.

Je n'ai que **quelques** mots à vous dire.	*I have only* ***a few*** *words to say to you.*
Vous trouverez **quelques** idées intéressantes dans cet article.	*You'll find* ***some*** *interesting ideas in this article.*

- The pronoun *some* when used emphatically is rendered by **quelques-uns, quelques-unes.** The pronoun **en** usually appears in the sentence.

—As-tu acheté des journaux français? —J'**en** ai acheté **quelques-uns**.	*Did you buy any French newspapers?* *I bought* ***some*** *(=* ***a few****).*
—As-tu acheté des revues françaises? —J'**en** ai acheté **quelques-unes**.	*Did you buy any French magazines?* *I bought* ***some*** *(=* ***a few****).*

- When *some* is the subject of the sentence and means *some people,* its French equivalent is **certains.** It often occurs in conjunction with **d'autres** (*others*).

Certains appuient cette nouvelle loi, **d'autres** sont contre.	***Some*** *support this new law,* ***others*** *are against (it).*

In everyday French, **certains** and **d'autres** as subjects are often replaced by **il y en a qui** and **il y en a d'autres qui,** respectively: **Il y en a qui** appuient cette nouvelle loi, **il y en a d'autres qui** sont contre.

- To express *someone or other, somewhere or other, something or other,* etc., French uses **je ne sais** plus the appropriate interrogative word.

je ne sais qui *someone or other*
je ne sais quoi *something or other*
je ne sais où *somewhere or other*
je ne sais comment *somehow*
je ne sais quel + ***noun*** *some + (noun) or other*
je ne sais quand *sometime or other*
je ne sais pourquoi *for some reason or other*
je ne sais combien *I'm not sure how much/many*

—Jacqueline est allée **je ne sais où** aujourd'hui.	*Jacqueline went **somewhere or other** today.*
—Oui. Le dimanche elle va rendre visite à **je ne sais qui** à Fontainebleau.	*Yes. On Sundays she goes to visit **someone** in Fontainebleau.*
—Il s'est sauvé de l'accident **je ne sais comment**.	***Somehow or other** he saved himself from the crash.*
—Quelle chance! Cette tragédie a fait **je ne sais combien** de victimes.	*What luck! That tragedy caused **I don't know how many** deaths.*

- *Any* in the sense of *it doesn't matter which one* is expressed in French by **n'importe** followed by the appropriate interrogative word.

n'importe qui *anyone*
n'importe quoi, quoi que ce soit *anything*
n'importe où *anywhere*
n'importe comment *anyhow*
n'importe quel + ***noun*** *any + noun*
n'importe lequel, laquelle, lesquels, lesquelles *whichever one(s), any one(s)*
n'importe quand *at any time*
n'importe combien *any amount, no matter how much, how many*

—Qu'est-ce que tu veux manger?	*What do you want to eat?*
—**N'importe quoi**.	***Anything.***
—Et où est-ce que tu veux aller après?	*And where do you want to go afterwards?*
—**N'importe où**.	***Anywhere.***

- Remember that the English word *any* and the words it appears in (*anyone, anything, anywhere*) are translated by negative words in French if the sentence is negative, and by indefinite words and expressions if the sentence is positive. Contrast the following pairs of sentences.

—Est-ce qu'il en sait **quelque chose**?	*Does he know **anything** about it?*
—Non. Il **n'**en sait **rien**.	*No. He **doesn't** know **anything** about it.*
—Allez-vous **quelque part** cette semaine?	*Are you going **anywhere** this week?*
—Non, nous **n'**allons **nulle part**.	*No, we're **not** going **anywhere**.*

- Sometimes when English *any* is used in a negative sentence, its French equivalent is one of the expressions with **n'importe.** The word *just* often appears before *any* in the English sentence in this case.

Je ne vais pas offrir **n'importe quoi**.	*I'm not going to give **just anything** as a gift.*
Nous ne voulons pas passer le temps avec **n'importe qui**.	*We don't want to spend time with **just anyone**.*

G. Exprimez votre indifférence. Répondez aux questions suivantes en employant une des expressions avec **n'importe.** Par vos réponses vous montrez que le choix entre les possibilités vous est égal.

Modèle —Avec qui est-ce que je dois parler?
➔ —Avec n'importe qui.

1. Qu'est-ce que tu veux boire?
2. Où est-ce que tu veux manger?
3. Quel journal est-ce que je dois acheter?
4. Quand est-ce que tu veux partir?
5. À quel cinéma veux-tu aller?
6. Combien d'argent vas-tu payer?
7. Comment est-ce que tu comptes le convaincre?
8. À qui est-ce que nous pouvons demander le chemin?

H. On n'est pas au courant. Refaites les phrases suivantes en employant une des expressions avec **je ne sais.** Les deux phrases doivent signifier plus ou moins la même chose.

Modèle Elle va nous offrir quelque chose. Je n'ai pas la moindre idée de ce que c'est.
➔ Elle va nous offrir je ne sais quoi.

1. Marc ne se souvient pas de la personne à qui il a donné le message.
2. On ignore avec quel professeur elle va parler.
3. Personne ne comprend pourquoi elles se sont mises en colère.
4. Personne ne savait combien de pilules le malade avait prises.
5. Je ne vois pas comment il a réussi aux examens.
6. On ne nous a pas dit quand nos cousins arriveraient.

I. En français, s'il vous plaît. Exprimez les idées suivantes en français. Faites attention aux particularités des mots indéfinis et négatifs.

1. a. You can find that bread in any bakery.

   ____

   b. There isn't any bakery around here.

   ____

   c. He works in some bakery.

   ____

   d. There are *some* bakeries in this neighborhood. Some are very good.

   ____

2. a. They're buying something.

   ____

   b. Are they buying anything?

   ____

   c. They're not buying anything.

   ____

   d. They're buying something (or other).

   ____

   e. They're not buying just anything.

   ____

3. a. We love these songs and are learning some of them.

   ____

   b. We're learning *some* songs.

   ____

   c. We can learn any songs.

   ____

   d. We can learn any one.

   ____

   e. We didn't learn any song (at all).

   ____

4. a. We can leave anytime.

   ____

   b. They're going to leave at sometime or other.

   ____

5. a. Anyone can do that.

____

b. No one can do that.

____

c. Some can do that, others can't.

____

C *Indefinite words and expressions (continued)*

- When an indefinite or negative word or expression is followed by an adjective, the preposition **de** is placed between them. The adjective is always masculine singular.

  quelqu'un/personne d'intelligent *someone/no one intelligent*
  quelque chose/rien de délicieux *something/nothing delicious*
  Quoi de neuf? *What's new?*
  un je ne sais quoi de fascinant *something fascinating*

- The phrase **d'autre** translates *else* with **quelqu'un, quelque chose, personne, rien,** and **quoi: quelqu'un/quelque chose/rien d'autre** (*someone/something/nothing else*), **Quoi d'autre?** (*What else?*). Note also **ailleurs** (*elsewhere*) and **nulle part ailleurs** (*nowhere else*).

  De followed by a masculine singular adjective is also used after **qu'est-ce qu'il y a** and **ce qu'il y a.**

  Qu'est-ce qu'il y a de plus amusant pour les enfants que le guignol? — ***What is more fun*** *for children than a puppet show?*

- The word **chaque** means *each.* The corresponding pronoun (*each one*) is **chacun, chacune.**

  —Avez-vous apporté quelque chose pour **chaque** enfant? — *Have you brought something for* ***each*** *child?*
  —Oui, j'ai un cadeau pour **chacun.** — *Yes, I have a gift for* ***each (one).***

- The word **tout** has several uses in French. As an adjective it has four forms: **tout, toute, tous, toutes.**

  1. When it directly precedes a singular noun, it means *every.*

     Tout enfant doit aller à l'école. — ***Every child*** *must go to school.*

     This is similar in meaning to **tous/toutes** + definite article + plural noun.

     Tous les enfants doivent aller à l'école. — ***All children*** *must go to school.*

  2. **Tout/toute** + definite article + singular noun means *all the, the whole.* Compare **toute la ville** (*the whole city*) with **toute ville** (*every city*).

  3. Study the meanings of **tous/toutes les** + number.

     Il vient **tous les trois mois.** — *He comes* ***every three months (every third month).***

     Prenez. C'est pour **tous les deux.** — *Take it. It's for* ***both of you.***

     Nous sommes sortis **tous les quatre.** — ***All four of us*** *went out.*

- **Tout** as a pronoun means *everything.*

J'espère que **tout** va bien.	*I hope **everything** is all right.*
Tout est en règle.	***Everything** is in order.*

- **Tous** as a pronoun (final **s** pronounced) means *everyone.* It is followed by a plural verb when it is the subject of the sentence.

Ils sont **tous** revenus.	*They **all** came back.*
Tous ont demandé de vous voir.	***Everyone** has asked to see you.*

Tout le monde + singular verb is the most common way to express *everyone.* To express *the whole world,* French uses **le monde entier.**

Tout le monde a demandé de te voir.	***Everyone** has asked to see you.*

Note culturelle

Le guignol est le théâtre de marionnettes classique de France. «Guignol» est le nom du personnage principal dans ce théâtre. Guignol et son ami Gnafron jouent le rôle de rebelles contre les agents de l'autorité. Le guignol français est d'origine lyonnaise et les personnages actuels remontent au dix-huitième siècle.

J. À compléter. Choisissez parmi les possibilités proposées celle qui complète correctement la phrase.

1. Le médecin m'a dit de ne rien manger ____________________ sucré. (quelque chose/de/*no word required*)
2. Si Jean-Marc ne peut pas le faire, on va demander à quelqu'un ____________. (d'autre/autre/ailleurs)
3. ________________ étudiante doit rédiger une composition. (Chacune/Toutes les/Chaque/Chacun)
4. Je ne veux aller nulle part ________________. (d'autre/autrement/ailleurs/autre)
5. Il y a trois belles églises dans la ville et nous les avons visitées ____________. (tous/toutes/tout/chacune/chaque)

K. En français, s'il vous plaît! Exprimez les phrases suivantes en français.

1. Everyone is happy now.

   ____

2. He takes a business trip every three weeks.

   ____

3. Give us something good to eat, mom!

   ____

4. You should contact someone else.

   ____

5. I have three little (female) cousins and I want to buy a doll for each.

____

6. Every café serves croissants.

____

7. There's something frightening (**effrayant**) about him. (= **Il a . . .**)

____

D *Idioms and expressions with negative and indefinite words*

Expressions with **jamais:**

Jamais deux sans trois. *Misfortunes always come in three's.*
à jamais *forever*
à tout jamais *forever and ever*
Jamais de la vie! *Not on your life!*
Il n'en manque jamais une! *He's always blundering. He always puts his foot in it.*

Expressions with **quelque(s):**

Il est trois heures et quelques. *It's a little past three.*
Je suis quelque peu déçu. *I'm a little disappointed.*

Expressions with **ni . . . ni:**

Cette histoire n'a ni queue ni tête. *This story doesn't make any sense at all.*
Cela ne me fait ni chaud ni froid. *It's all the same to me. I don't feel strongly about it.*

Expressions with **rien:**

De rien. *You're welcome.*
Ça ne fait rien. *It doesn't matter. That's OK. (Answer to* **Pardon**.*)*
Comme si de rien n'était. *As if nothing had happened.*
Si cela ne vous fait rien. *If you don't mind.*
Rien qu'à le voir, on sait qu'il est gentil. *Just by looking at him you know he's nice.*
Je veux te parler, rien que cinq minutes. *I want to talk to you, just five minutes.*
Tu dis ça rien que pour m'embêter. *You're saying that just to annoy me.*
Ce n'est pas pour rien qu'il t'a dit ça. *It's not without good reason that he told you that.*
Rien ne sert de pleurer. *It's no use crying.*
Cet article n'a rien à voir avec nos recherches. *This article has nothing to do with our research.*
Il a peur d'un rien. *He's afraid of every little thing.*
Un rien la fait rire. *She laughs at every little thing.*
Moi, j'y mettrais un rien de poivre. *I'd add a dash of pepper.*
C'est un/une rien du tout. *He/She is a nobody.* or *He/She is a worthless person.*

Expressions with **chacun:**

Chacun son goût/Chacun ses goûts. *Everyone to his own taste.*
Chacun pour soi! *Every man for himself!*
Chacun à son tour. *Each one in his turn.*

Expressions with **certain:**

d'un certain âge *middle-aged*
Elle a un certain charme. *She has a certain charm.*

Expressions with **ailleurs:**

Il est ailleurs/Il a l'esprit ailleurs. *He's miles away (not paying attention).*
d'ailleurs *moreover, besides*
partout ailleurs *everywhere else*

Expressions with **nul,** etc:

Il est nul/Elle est nulle en philosophie. *He/She's a very poor philosophy student.*
C'est une vraie nullité. *He's (She's) a real wash-out.*
un travail nul, une composition nulle *a worthless piece of work, a worthless composition*
faire match nul *to tie (sports)*

L. Comment l'exprimer? Choisissez la possibilité qui exprime l'idée indiquée.

1. You want to to tell a friend that he's not paying attention.
   a. Tu es une vraie nullité.
   b. Tu as l'esprit ailleurs.
2. You want to say that a certain place is not very selective in its admission policies.
   a. On admet tout un chacun.
   b. C'est un rien du tout.
3. You want to say that a friend is always making serious errors in judgment.
   a. Rien qu'à le voir, on s'en rend compte.
   b. Il n'en manque jamais une.
4. You react to a story that makes no sense to you.
   a. Cette histoire n'a ni queue ni tête.
   b. Cette histoire ne me fait ni chaud ni froid.
5. You reassure someone who said "excuse me" because he thought he stepped on your toe.
   a. Si cela ne vous fait rien.
   b. Cela ne fait rien.
6. You tell someone that you won't take much of her time.
   a. Rien que cinq minutes.
   b. Une heure et quelques.
7. You tell someone it's no use crying.
   a. Rien ne sert de pleurer.
   b. Tu pleures pour un rien.
8. You want to say that Mr. X is a nobody.
   a. C'est un rien du tout.
   b. C'est un travail nul.
9. You want to express a categorical refusal.
   a. Comme si de rien n'était.
   b. Jamais de la vie!
10. You want to deny any connection between something and yourself.
    a. Cela ne me fait rien du tout.
    b. Ça n'a rien à voir avec moi.

M. **Qu'est-ce que cela veut dire?** Choisissez la possibilité qui exprime la même idée que la première phrase.

1. Un rien l'effraie.
   a. Rien ne l'effraie.
   b. Tout l'effraie.
2. Mets un rien de sel dans la soupe.
   a. La soupe a besoin d'un peu de sel.
   b. Ne mets plus de sel dans la soupe.
3. C'est un homme d'un certain âge.
   a. Il a environ cinquante ans.
   b. Je sais exactement quel âge il a.
4. Il fait ça rien que pour nous faire peur.
   a. Il évite de faire des choses qui nous feraient peur.
   b. La seule raison pour laquelle il fait ça est pour nous faire peur.
5. Ils ont fait match nul.
   a. Les deux équipes n'ont pas joué.
   b. Les deux équipes ont eu le même nombre de points.
6. Rien qu'à l'entendre, on sait qu'elle a du talent.
   a. Si tu l'entendais seulement, tu te rendrais compte de son talent.
   b. En l'entendant, tu te rends compte qu'elle n'a pas de talent.
7. Il est trois heures et quelques.
   a. Il est presque quatre heures.
   b. Il est entre trois heures et trois heures dix.
8. Ce n'est pas pour rien que je t'ai dit ça.
   a. Je n'ai dit ça pour aucune raison.
   b. J'avais une très bonne raison pour te le dire.

N. **La grammaire en action.** Ne plus aller à la banque? Est-ce qu'on peut faire toutes les opérations bancaires par ordinateur et par téléphone? Réponse affirmative en France de la part de Banque Directe. Lisez l'annonce suivante, faites attention aux constructions négatives et répondez aux questions ci-dessous.

Vocabulaire utile

l'agence (fem.) *branch, branch office*
la contravention *fine*
se déplacer *to move, budge*
effectuer *to carry out, transact*
l'embouteillage (masc.) *traffic jam*
enregistrer *to record, enter*
l'épargne (fem.) *savings*
les espèces (fem.) *cash*
le jour de valeur *waiting period*
le numéro vert *toll-free number*
placer *to invest*
le prélèvement *deduction*
productif *interest-bearing*
le virement *transfer*

« Si vous n'allez pas souvent à votre banque, faites un effort : n'y allez plus du tout »

Pourquoi supporter les embouteillages, les contraventions, braver le mauvais temps pour passer à la banque alors que maintenant la Banque Directe existe ? **24 heures sur 24 et 6 jours sur 7, vous pouvez joindre vos Conseillers** afin qu'ils réalisent toutes vos opérations bancaires, effectuent un virement, vous donnent un accord pour un crédit, ou placent votre épargne. Et comme la Banque Directe n'a pas d'agences, elle peut **vous offrir un ensemble unique d'avantages financiers.** Par exemple : virements et prélèvements gratuits, compte-chèque productif, pas de jours de valeur ni sur les espèces ni sur les chèques (chèques enregistrés immédiatement). **Tout cela sans jamais vous déplacer.** Autant de raisons de rejoindre la Banque Directe, plus une : **la garantie du Groupe Paribas.**

N° VERT 05 103 104

"banque directe"

PAS BESOIN DE SE VOIR POUR S'ENTENDRE

Vrai ou faux? Après avoir lu attentivement le texte de l'annonce, indiquez si les phrases suivantes sont vraies ou fausses.

_____ 1. L'homme à gauche a reçu une contravention.

_____ 2. Pour aller à Banque Directe, il faut se déplacer.

_____ 3. Si on rejoint Banque Directe, on peut faire toutes les opérations bancaires sans aller à une agence.

_____ 4. Avec Banque Directe on sacrifie les intérêts donnés par les autres banques sur son compte-chèques.

_____ 5. Il faut payer les coups de téléphone Banque Directe.

_____ 6. Banque Directe est une banque sans agences.

_____ 7. «Pas besoin de se voir pour s'entendre» veut dire que le contact personnel est essentiel dans les opérations bancaires.

CHAPTER 22 PREPOSITIONS; PREPOSITIONS WITH GEOGRAPHICAL NAMES

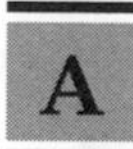

A The preposition *à*

A preposition is a word that links two elements of a sentence: **le livre *de* Janine, entrer *dans* la cuisine, parler *à* lui, finir *de* travailler.**

The preposition **à** has many uses in French. Remember its contractions: **à** + **le** → **au; à** + **les** → **aux. À** is also used before infinitives in many constructions (see Chapter 12). In addition, **à:**

- Expresses direction and location in space

  aller **à la banque** *to go* ***to the bank***
  être **à la banque** *to be* ***at the bank***

- Labels distance in time and space

  habiter **à quinze kilomètres de** Paris *to live* ***fifteen kilometers from*** *Paris*
  être **à trois heures de** Marseille *to be* ***three hours from*** *Marseilles*

- Expresses the point in time at which something happens (clock time, age)

  À quelle heure le train part-il? ***What time*** *does the train leave?*
  arriver **à 7 heures du soir** *to arrive* ***at seven in the evening***
  à dix-huit ans ***at (the age of) eighteen years***

- Expresses the manner or style in which something is done

  manger **à la française** *to eat* ***French style***
  coucher **à quatre dans une chambre** *to sleep* ***four to a room***

- Labels the principal ingredient in a dish or a characteristic feature

  un sandwich **au fromage** *a* ***cheese*** *sandwich*
  une glace **aux fraises** ***strawberry*** *ice cream*
  la femme **au chapeau** *the woman* ***in (wearing) the hat***
  une chemise **à manches longues** *a* ***long-sleeved*** *shirt*

- Expresses possession or belonging to someone

  Ce stylo est **au prof.** *This pen is* ***the teacher's.***
  C'est bien gentil **à toi.** *That's really nice* ***of you.***

- Expresses the means by which something is done

  fait **à la main** *made by hand*
  aller **à bicyclette, à pied** *to go* ***by bike, on foot***
  écrire **au crayon** *to write* ***in pencil***

- Is used in expressions of measurement

  faire du 70 **à l'heure** *to do 70 kilometers* ***an hour***
  vendre **au kilo, au mètre** *to sell* ***by the kilogram, by the meter***
  être payé **au mois** *to be paid* ***by the month***
  un à un, peu à peu ***one by one, little by little***

- Indicates the purpose for which an object is intended

  une tasse **à** thé *a teacup*
  sandwichs **à** emporter *sandwiches to take out*

The preposition **à** also:

- Is used with nouns derived from verbs or with infinitives as a replacement for a subordinate clause

  à mon arrivée *when I got there (upon my arrival)*
  à notre retour *when we got back (upon our return)*
  à l'entendre chanter *when I heard him/her sing (upon hearing him/her sing)*
  à la réflexion *if you think about it (upon second thought)*

- Translates as *at* and *to* with certain nouns

  à ma grande surprise, joie *to my great surprise, joy*
  à sa consternation *to his dismay*
  à la demande de tous *at everyone's request*

- Expresses a standard for judging or knowing (and means *by, according to, from*)

  reconnaître quelqu'un **à sa voix** *to recognize someone* ***by his/her voice***
  À ce que j'ai compris, il ne viendra pas. ***From what I understood,*** *he won't come.*
  juger quelque chose **aux résultats** *to judge something* ***by the results***

- Some idioms and useful expressions with the preposition **à**:

  Location (spatial and figurative)

  se couper au doigt *to cut one's finger*
  Qui est à l'appareil? *Who's calling?*
  à côté *next door, nearby*
  à côté de *next to*
  à deux pas de chez moi *right near my house*
  Je ne me sens pas à la hauteur. *I don't feel up to, equal to the task.*
  être à la page *to be up-to-date*
  à la une *on the front page*

  Time

  à la fois *at the same time, at once*
  à l'instant *a moment ago*
  à ses heures (libres) *in one's free time*
  à plusieurs reprises *several times*
  à tout moment *all the time*

  Manner

  à souhait *to perfection*
  aimer quelqu'un à la folie *to be mad, wild about someone*
  à juste titre *rightfully*
  à l'endroit *right side out (of clothing)*
  à l'envers *inside out (of clothing)*
  être à l'étroit *to be cramped for space*

étudier quelque chose à fond *to study something thoroughly*
lire à haute voix *to read aloud*
un vol à main armée *armed robbery*
à la perfection *perfectly, just right*
à titre confidentiel *off the record*
à titre de père *as a father, in my role as a father*
à tort *wrongfully*
à tour de rôle *in turn*

Price, purpose, and degree

avoir quelque chose à bon compte *to get something cheap*
faire les choses à moitié *to do things halfway*
à peine *hardly*
acheter quelque chose à prix d'or *to pay through the nose for something*
à tout prix *at all costs*
à la longue *in the long run*
tout au plus *at the very most*

Sentences, interjections, and exclamations

À votre santé! *To your health!*
À la poubelle! *Get rid of it! Throw it out!*
Au feu! *Fire!*
Au voleur! *Stop! Thief!*
au fait *by the way*
À la ligne. *New paragraph (in dictation).*
à propos *by the way*
À quoi bon? *What's the use?*
À suivre. *To be continued.*
Au suivant! *Next! Who's next?*

A. Expliquez les différences. Comprenez-vous la différence de sens qui existe entre les deux expressions de chaque paire? Expliquez-la en anglais.

1. à la une / à la page

____

2. à plusieurs reprises / à la fois

____

3. à l'étroit / à la hauteur

____

4. une bouteille à lait / une bouteille de lait

____

5. au suivant / à suivre

____

B. Synonymes ou antonymes? Indiquez si les expressions suivantes sont synonymes ou antonymes.

	synonymes	*antonymes*
1. à juste titre / à tort	_____	_____
2. à souhait / à la perfection	_____	_____
3. à l'appareil / au téléphone	_____	_____
4. à l'endroit / à l'envers	_____	_____
5. à propos / au fait	_____	_____
6. à bon compte / à prix d'or	_____	_____
7. à tour de rôle / tour à tour	_____	_____

C. Comment est-ce que cela se dit? Exprimez ces expressions en français.

1. chocolate ice cream ____________________
2. the man in the blue suit ____________________
3. to our great sadness ____________________
4. to sell by the pound ____________________
5. to recognize someone by his voice ____________________
6. off the record ____________________
7. in one's free time ____________________
8. to read aloud ____________________
9. two hundred meters from the movie theater ____________________
10. the girl with blond hair ____________________
11. to cut one's finger ____________________
12. at the very most ____________________

D. On cause. Complétez ces échanges avec les expressions qui manquent.

1. a. —Tu as le journal. Qu'est-ce qu'il y a ____________________ (on the front page)?

   b. —Un vol ____________________ (armed) dans le métro.

2. a. —Tu sais, papa, j'aime Philippe ____________________ (madly).

   b. —Babette, ma fille, ____________________ (as a father), je te dirai que tu es trop jeune.

3. a. —Tu as eu cette robe ____________________ (at a good price)?

   b. —Au contraire! Je l'ai payée ____________________ (through the nose)!

4. a. —Marie-Claude a appris son rôle ____________________ (perfectly).

   b. —Oui, elle ne fait pas les choses ____________________ (halfway).

B *The preposition* ***de***

Like **à,** the preposition **de** has many uses in French. Remember its two contractions: **de + le → du; de + les → des. De** is also used as the partitive article (see Chapter 13) and before infinitives in many constructions (see Chapter 12). It also:

- Expresses possession

  le livre **de l'étudiant** *the* ***student's*** *book*
  les rues **de Paris** *the streets* ***of Paris***
  le contenu **du livre** *the contents* ***of the book***

- Expresses starting point or origin

  partir **de Paris** *to leave* ***from Paris***
  sortir **de la boutique** *to go out* ***of the shop***
  Il est **du Sénégal.** *He's* ***from Senegal.***
  le train **de Lyon** *the train* ***from/to Lyons***

- Expresses the contents of something

  une tasse **de thé** *a cup* ***of tea***
  une collection **de poupées** *a* ***doll*** *collection*

- Labels the characteristic feature. The English equivalent is often a compound noun (noun + noun)

  la société **de consommation** *the* ***consumer*** *society*
  une classe **d'anglais** *an* ***English*** *class*

- Labels the cause

  mourir **de faim** *to die* ***of hunger***
  fatigué **du voyage** *tired* ***from the trip***

- Is used with **changer de** + singular noun to express *to change* + singular or plural noun

  changer **de train, d'avion** *to change* ***trains, planes***
  changer **de direction** *to change* ***direction***
  changer **d'avis, d'idée** *to change* ***one's mind***

- Labels the means

  écrire **de la main gauche** *to write* ***with one's left hand***
  faire quelque chose **de ses propres mains** *to do something* ***with one's own hands***

- Is used in many expressions of measurement

  un bifteck **de 500 grammes** ***a five-hundred-gram*** *steak*
  une route longue **de 30 kilomètres** ***a thirty-kilometer****-long road*
  augmenter son salaire **de 1000 francs** *to raise someone's salary* ***by 1000 francs***
  plus grand(e) **d'une tête** ***a head*** *taller*
  Ce fleuve a **850 mètres de large** et **100 mètres de profondeur**. *This river is* ***850 meters wide*** *and* ***100 meters deep.***

- Introduces phrases that express the manner in which something is done

  connaître quelqu'un **de vue** *to know someone* ***by sight***
  répéter **de mémoire** *to repeat* ***from memory***

- Introduces nouns in apposition

  la région **de Bourgogne** *the **Burgundy** region*
  le nom **de Maubrey** *the name **Maubrey***
  Quel temps **de chien!** *What **lousy** weather!*

- Is used in some expressions of place and time:

  de ce côté ***on this side***
  de l'autre côté ***on the other side***
  du côté de la bibliothèque ***in the direction of** the library*
  de côté et d'autre ***here and there; on both sides***
  du temps de Napoléon ***in** Napoleon's time*
  de nos jours ***in** our day*
  travailler **de** jour, **de** nuit *to work days, nights*
  Ils n'ont rien fait **de** toute l'année. *They've done nothing all year.*
  Je n'ai rien fait de pareil **de** toute ma vie. *I've done nothing like that **in** my entire life.*

- Some idioms and useful expressions with the preposition **de**:

Time

d'abord *first*
trois jours de suite *three days in a row*
de bonne heure early
de bon matin *early in the morning*

Appositions

C'est un drôle de numéro. *He/She is a strange character.*
C'est une drôle d'idée. *It's a strange idea.*
Espèce d'imbécile! *You idiot!*

Origin, manner, and other categories

C'est de la part de qui, s'il vous plaît? *Who's calling, please?*
du coup *as a result*
ne pas être d'attaque *not to feel up to it*
d'autre part *on the other hand*
poser une question de but en blanc *to ask a question just like that, point-blank, suddenly*
se heurter de face, de front *to collide head on*
un billet de faveur *complimentary ticket*
du reste *moreover*
Cette pièce sert d'étude. *This room is used as a study.*

Note culturelle

Le Sénégal est un des pays francophones situés sur la côte occidentale du continent africain. La colonisation française commence en 1638; le pays devient indépendant en 1960 sous le président Léopold Senghor, connu aussi comme poète. L'économie tourne autour de l'agriculture (cacahuètes, millet, canne à sucre) et de l'élevage (vaches, chèvres, cochons, moutons). La pêche et les mines sont aussi importantes. Le développement de l'industrie comprend le traitement des produits agricoles, la production du ciment et d'autres matériaux de construction. La population est de presque 10 millions; la capitale est Dakar.

E. Est-ce *à* ou *de*? Complétez ces phrases avec **à** ou **de.** Si aucune préposition n'est nécessaire, marquez l'espace d'un X. N'oubliez pas que dans certains cas il faudra employer les contractions **au, aux, du, des.**

1. Elle est contente ________ notre travail.
2. J'ai soif. Je vais acheter une bouteille ________ jus de pomme.
3. Tu prends ton thé dans un verre ________ vin? Comme c'est bizarre.
4. Si tu veux écrire à tes parents, je te donnerai du papier _____ lettres.
5. Je lui ai demandé s'il voulait m'accompagner. Il a fait «non» ________ la tête.
6. ________ l'aide! Je suis tombé et je ne peux pas me lever!
7. Nous n'avons rien fait ________ toute la semaine.
8. Nous allons ________ côté de la place. Tu viens avec nous?
9. Ma chambre est longue ________ quatre mètres et a trois mètres ________ large.

F. Expliquez les différences. Comprenez-vous la différence de sens qui existe entre les deux expressions de chaque paire? Expliquez-la en anglais.

1. de suite / à suivre

____

2. de hauteur / à la hauteur

____

3. à côté / de côté

____

4. Il est au Japon. / Il est du Japon.

____

5. une corbeille à papier / une corbeille de papier

____

6. travailler de jour / travailler à la journée

____

G. La vie en famille. Mme Gilbert écrit à son amie Vivienne Mauriac pour lui donner des nouvelles de sa famille. Pour savoir ce qu'elle dit, complétez sa lettre avec des prépositions ou des phrases commençant par **à** ou **de.**

Ma chère Vivienne:

Tu me pardonneras de ne pas avoir écrit avant. Tout va très bien ici. Les enfants grandissent. Mon fils Paul est déjà plus grand que moi (1) ________________ (by a head). Il dit qu'il veut être pilote. C'est une (2) ________________ (strange idea), n'est-ce pas? J'espère qu'il va (3) ________________ (change his mind).

Brigitte étudie à la (4) ______________ (medical school). Elle se lève tous les jours

(5) ______________ (early in the morning) pour lire. Ses cours sont difficiles et il faut qu'elle

étudie tout (6) ______________ (thoroughly). Paul va au lycée qui est

(7) ______________ (right near) de chez nous.

Mon mari voyage beaucoup pour affaires. Demain il revient

(8) ______________ (from) New York et la semaine prochaine il prend le train

(9) ______________ (for) Genève où il va passer une semaine. Il n'a jamais autant

voyagé (10) ______________ (in his whole life).

Et toi, qu'est-ce que tu deviens? J'attends de tes nouvelles avec impatience. Écris-moi.

Toutes mes amitiés,

Sylvie

H. Comprenez-vous? Laquelle des deux possibilités signifie plus ou moins la même chose que l'expression donnée?

1. C'est un drôle de numéro.
   a. C'est une personne bizarre.
   b. Elle n'a pas de numéro de téléphone.
2. Je la connais de vue.
   a. Je la vois.
   b. Je sais qui c'est quand je la vois.
3. Jacquot est plus petit de trois centimètres.
   a. Jacquot mesure trois centimètres de moins que quelqu'un.
   b. Jacquot mesure moins de trois centimètres.
4. l'idiot de son mari
   a. Son mari est un idiot.
   b. Son mari a un idiot.
5. du côté de la gare
   a. tout près de la gare
   b. vers la gare
6. On a donné un billet de faveur à Marc.
   a. Marc n'a pas payé le billet.
   b. Marc n'a pas voulu le billet.
7. Il m'a posé la question de but en blanc.
   a. Il a hésité à me poser la question.
   b. Il m'a posé la question brusquement.
8. Mon oncle m'a servi de professeur de maths.
   a. Mon oncle a trouvé quelqu'un pour m'enseigner les maths.
   b. Mon oncle m'a enseigné les maths lui-même.

9. C'est une classe d'arabe.
   a. Les étudiants sont arabes.
   b. On y enseigne l'arabe.
10. C'est de la part de qui?
   a. Qui est à l'appareil?
   b. Qui est celui qui part?

C *The prepositions **avec** and **sans***

- The preposition **avec** expresses accompaniment, much like English *with*.

Attends, j'irai **avec toi**.	*Wait, I'll go **with you**.*
Je suis d'accord **avec vous**.	*I agree **with you**.*

- **Avec** labels the cause.

Avec l'inflation, tout le monde parle des prix.	***With inflation**, everyone is talking about prices.*
J'ai peur de conduire **avec toute cette neige.**	*I'm afraid to drive **with all this snow**.*

- **Avec** expresses *in addition to*.

Et **avec cela (ça)**, madame?	***Anything else**, Ma'am? (in a store)*
Il n'a pas étudié et **avec ça** il a séché le cours.	*He didn't study, and **on top of that** he cut class.*

- The preposition **sans** is the equivalent of English *without*.

Notre équipe a dû jouer **sans** notre meilleur joueur.	*Our team had to play **without** our best player.*
Sans argent on ne peut rien faire.	***Without** money you can't do anything.*
Je me suis couché **sans** avoir fini mon travail.	*I went to bed **without** having finished my work.*

- **Avec** + noun is often the equivalent of an English adverb, as reviewed in Chapter 20.

avec joie, **avec** colère *joyfully, angrily*

- **Sans** can mean *if it weren't for . . .*, or *but for. . . .*

Sans ce plan, on se serait perdus.	***If it weren't for this street map**, we would have gotten lost.*

- The preposition **sans** + noun is often the equivalent of an English adjective ending in *-less* or an adjective with a negative prefix such as *un-* or *in-*.

sans abri, sans domicile fixe (S.D.F.) ***homeless***
une situation **sans remède** *a **hopeless** situation*
un film **sans intérêt** *an **uninteresting** film*
une femme **sans préjugés** *an **unprejudiced, unbiased** woman*
sans doute, sans effort ***doubtless, effortless***

- The use of **sans** with negative words eliminates the need for **ne**. The partitive article often becomes **de** after **sans** because of the implied negative meaning of the preposition.

  sans parler à personne *__without__ speaking to anyone*
  sans rien faire *__without__ doing anything*
  sans jamais l'avoir vu *__without__ ever having seen him*
  sortir **sans** faire **de** bruit *to go out __without__ making __any__ noise*

- Some idioms and useful expressions with the prepositions **avec** and **sans**:

  se lever avec le jour *to get up at the crack of dawn*
  se fâcher avec quelqu'un *to get angry with someone*
  prendre des gants avec quelqu'un *to handle someone with kid gloves*
  se mettre en rapport/en relation avec *to get in touch with*

  être sans le sou *to be broke*
  être sans travail, sans emploi *to be out of work, unemployed*
  les sans-emploi *the unemployed*
  sans faute *without fail*
  sans plus *that's all, nothing more*
  sans aucun doute *without a doubt*
  Sans façons! *Sincerely!, Let's not stand on ceremony!, I really mean it!*
  sans ça *otherwise*
  être un sans-gêne *to be inconsiderate*
  sans oublier *last but not least*
  sans broncher *without flinching*

I. ***Sans* ou *avec*?** Complétez les phrases françaises avec la préposition **sans** ou **avec** pour qu'elles aient à peu près le même sens que leur traduction anglaise.

1. *He's an unimaginative man.* C'est un homme _________ imagination.
2. *She answered bitterly.* Elle a répondu _________ amertume.
3. *They write effortlessly.* Ils écrivent _________ effort.
4. *Come eat with us! I really mean it!* Viens manger avec nous! _________ façons!
5. *If it weren't for her, we wouldn't have finished the job.* _________ elle, nous n'aurions pas fini le travail.
6. *With the ice on the road, driving is difficult.* _________ le verglas, il est difficile de conduire.
7. *You have to handle him carefully.* Il faut le prendre _________ des gants.
8. *Don't go out barefoot.* Ne sors pas _________ chaussures.
9. *You have to speak sweetly to her.* Il faut lui parler _________ douceur.
10. *He threw himself into the fray unflinchingly.* Il s'est lancé au combat _________ broncher.

J. **En français, s'il vous plaît!** Donnez l'équivalent français de ces expressions. Utilisez **avec** ou **sans** dans chaque cas.

1. doubtless ____
2. otherwise ____

3. to get up at the crack of dawn ______
4. heartless ______
5. the unemployed ______
6. lovingly ______
7. kindly ______
8. broke, down and out ______
9. Anything else? ______
10. unhesitatingly ______

D *The prepositions* ***en*** *and* ***dans***

- The prepositions **en** and **dans** both mean *in*. **En** is used directly before a noun; **dans** must be followed by an article (definite, indefinite, or partitive) or by some other determiner, such as a possessive or demonstrative adjective.

aller **en ville** *to go* ***downtown***
dans la ville ***in the*** *city*

être **en prison** *to be* ***in jail***
dans cette prison ***in this*** *jail*

habiter **en banlieue** *to live* ***in the suburbs***
dans une banlieue éloignée ***in a*** *distant suburb*

- **En** is used to mean *as* or *like.*

Je te parle **en ami.** *I'm speaking to you* ***as a friend.***
Il agit **en prince.** *He's acting* ***like a prince.***

- **En** is used to express location within a period of time.

en automne, **en** juillet, **en** 1996 ***in*** *the fall,* ***in*** *July,* ***in*** *1996*
faire quelque chose **en** deux semaines *to do something* ***in*** *two weeks*
de jour **en** jour ***from*** *day* ***to*** *day, daily*

- **En** labels the means of transportation.

voyager **en** train, **en** avion *to travel* ***by*** *train,* ***by*** *plane*
rentrer **en** taxi, **en** car *to go back* ***by*** *cab,* ***by*** *intercity bus*

- **En** marks the condition or appearance.

être **en** nage *to be all sweated up*
être **en** bonne santé *to be in good health*
être **en** pyjama *to be in one's pajamas*
être **en** guerre *to be at war*
en hâte *in a hurry*
en désordre, **en** pagaille *in disorder, in a mess*

- **En** marks transformation into something else.

transformer la ferme **en** atelier *to transform the farm* ***into*** *a workshop*
se déguiser **en** prêtre *to disguise oneself* ***as*** *a priest*
casser quelque chose **en** morceaux *to break something* ***into*** *pieces*
traduire **en** italien *to translate* ***into*** *Italian*

- **En** marks the material of which something is made (as does **de**).

  un collier **en or** *a* ***gold*** *necklace*
  un couteau **en acier inoxydable** *a* ***stainless steel*** *knife*
  une jupe **en laine** *a* ***woolen*** *skirt*
  C'est **en quoi**? ***What's*** *it* ***made of?***

- **En** is used before **plein** to mean *in the middle of.*

  en pleine ville ***right in the middle of*** *the city*
  en plein hiver ***in the middle of*** *winter*
  être **en plein** travail *to be* ***in the middle of*** *one's work*

- **En** is used to form some common adverbial expressions.

  en haut, **en** bas *upstairs, downstairs*
  en avant, **en** arrière *forward, backward*
  en face *opposite*
  en tout cas *in any case*
  en plus *besides, in addition*

- Some idioms and useful expressions with **en**:

  être en garde *to be on guard*
  être en tournée *to be on tour (of a performer)*
  être en vacances, en voyage *to be on vacation, on a trip*
  en moyenne *on the average*
  croire en Dieu *to believe in God*
  avoir confiance en quelqu'un *to have confidence in someone*
  C'est sa mère en plus jeune. *She's a younger version of her mother.*
  Avez-vous cette serviette en cuir noir? *Do you have this briefcase in black leather?*
  en direct *live (TV, radio broadcast)*
  en différé *recorded (TV, radio broadcast)*
  en danger *in danger*
  en semaine *during the week*
  être en pleine forme *to be in good physical shape*

- Some expressions in which **en** is followed by an article or determiner:

  en l'honneur de *in honor of*
  en l'absence de *in the absence of*
  en mon nom *in my name*
  en sa faveur *in his favor*

- **Dans** is used to express location (English *in*).

  dans la boîte ***in*** *the box*
  dans la rue ***in*** *the street*
  dans le train ***in*** *the train*

- **Dans** is used to express location in time (English *in, in the course of, during*).

  dans la semaine ***during*** *the week (cf.* ***en semaine****)*
  dans la journée, la soirée ***during*** *the course of the day, the evening*
  dans la matinée, l'après-midi ***during*** *the morning, afternoon*
  Tout sera prêt **dans** cinq jours. *Everything will be ready* ***in*** *five days.*

- **Dans** is used to express figurative location.

  dans la situation actuelle ***in*** *the present situation*
  dans ces conditions ***given*** *these conditions*
  être **dans** les affaires *to be* ***in*** *business*

- **Dans** is used in contexts where English uses *from, on,* or *into.*

  boire **dans** une tasse *to drink* ***from*** *a cup*
  prendre quelque chose **dans** une boîte *to take something* ***from*** *a box*
  copier quelque chose **dans** un livre *to copy something* ***from*** *a book*
  dans l'avion ***on*** *the plane*
  mettre quelque chose **dans** le tiroir *to put something* ***into*** *the drawer*
  monter **dans** le train *to get* ***on*** *the train*
  On s'est croisés **dans** l'escalier. *We ran into each other* ***on*** *the stairs.*

- Some idioms and useful expressions with **dans**:

  Ce n'est pas dans mes projets. *I'm not planning to do that.*
  Qu'est-ce qui se passe dans sa tête? *What's gotten into him? What can he be thinking of?*
  partir/aller passer ses vacances dans les Alpes *to leave for/spend one's vacation in the Alps*
  errer dans les rues/dans la ville *to wander through the streets/through the city*
  dans les coulisses *behind the scenes*
  coûter dans les mille francs *to cost in the neighborhood of a thousand francs*
  dans le doute *when in doubt*
  être dans le pétrin *to be in a jam, in a fix*
  dans le sens de la longueur *lengthwise*

K. Est-ce *en* ou *dans*? Complétez les paragraphes suivants avec **en** ou **dans.**

Le nouvel appartement des Truffaut

Les Truffaut ont acheté un nouvel appartement. Je crois qu'il leur a coûté (1) ________ les 500.000 mille francs. L'appartement n'est pas (2) ________ la ville de Paris parce qu'ils préfèrent habiter (3) ________ banlieue. Mais leur bureau est (4) ________ ville. Ils y vont (5) ________ train.

Christine Urbain parle de ses vacances

J'ai envie de partir (6) ________ vacances. J'aime passer mes vacances (7) ________ les Alpes. J'adore partir (8) ________ été. Il fait beau et je mets un short (9) ________ coton tous les jours. Je commence à faire mes préparatifs. Tout sera prêt (10) ________ cinq jours et je pourrai partir!

Un collègue en difficulté

Je ne sais pas ce qui se passe avec Édouard. Son bureau est (11) ________ pagaille. Lui qui était toujours (12) ________ pleine forme ne fait plus d'exercice. Je me demande ce qui se passe (13) ________ sa tête. Le chef n'a plus confiance (14) ________ lui. J'ai l'impression que son poste est (15) ________ jeu et Édouard ne semble pas s'en rendre compte.

Une réception diplomatique

Dimanche il y aura une réception (16) ________ l'honneur de l'ambassadeur du Maroc. La réception aura lieu (17) ________ l'après-midi. On invite (18) ________ moyenne une quarantaine de personnes. (19) ________ la situation actuelle, ces réceptions sont importantes. L'ambassade se trouve (20) ________ une rue tranquille.

Note culturelle

Le Maroc est un pays situé au coin nord-ouest de l'Afrique. La population est d'origine berbère, nom de la langue et culture des premiers habitants. Cette population s'islamise à la suite des invasions arabes qui commencent en 683. Presque toute la population aujourd'hui est de religion musulmane, mais un tiers des marocains parlent encore le berbère. La colonisation française commence vers 1825 quand la France et le Maroc signent un traité qui accorde à la France la position de la nation la plus favorisée.

En 1912, le Maroc accepte le protectorat français, statut qui durera jusqu'à l'indépendance en 1956. La langue française reste importante au Maroc, et beaucoup de Marocains émigrent en France pour travailler.

La capitale de ce pays de presque 40 millions d'habitants est Rabat, située sur la côte atlantique. Les villes de Casablanca, de Tanger et d'Agadir sont très connues, comme l'est aussi le centre touristique de Marrakech. Le tourisme est une des industries les plus importantes du pays et le Maroc reçoit plus de 3 millions de visiteurs chaque année.

L. Comment est-ce que cela se dit? Exprimez les expressions suivantes en français.

1. on the stairs ________
2. to be bathed in sweat ________
3. a taller version of his father ________
4. behind the scenes ________
5. upstairs ________
6. in the middle of the night ________
7. lengthwise ________
8. to be in a fix ________
9. to be in business ________
10. to be in pajamas ________
11. at war ________
12. What's it made of? ________

E *Sur, sous, and related prepositions*

- **Sur** usually corresponds to English *on* and **sous** corresponds to English *under.* However, there are cases where the two French prepositions have unexpected English equivalents.
- **Sous** may correspond to English *at* or *in.*

  sous l'équateur *at the Equator*
  sous la tente *in the tent*
  sous la pluie *in the rain*
  sous le soleil *in the sunshine*
  avoir quelque chose **sous** les yeux *to have something* ***before*** *one's eyes*
  avoir quelque chose **sous** la main *to have something* ***at*** *hand*

- **Sous** may express location in time, usually within a period or historical event.

  sous la Révolution ***at the time of*** *the Revolution*
  sous le règne de Napoléon ***in*** *Napoleon's reign*
  sous peu ***shortly***

- **Sous** has idiomatic uses.

  présenter **sous** un jour favorable *to present* ***in*** *a favorable light*
  sous peine d'amende ***on*** *penalty of a fine*
  sous l'influence de ***under*** *the influence of*
  sous une identité d'emprunt ***under*** *an assumed identity*
  étudier la question **sous** tous les angles *to study the question* ***from*** *every angle*

- **Sur** may correspond to English *at* or *in* in an expression of position.

  sur le stade ***at*** *the stadium*
  sur la place (du marché) ***at*** *the market place*
  sur la chaussée ***in*** *the roadway*
  sur le journal (*colloquial*) ***in*** *the newspaper*
  acheter quelque chose **sur** le marché *to buy something* ***at*** *the market*
  Il pleut **sur** toute la France. *It's raining all* ***over*** *France.*

- **Sur** expresses approximate time.

  arriver **sur** les 3 heures *to arrive at* ***around*** *3 o'clock*
  Elle va **sur** ses dix-huit ans. *She's going* ***on*** *eighteen.*

- **Sur** expresses English *out of* in statements of proportion and measure.

  deux fois **sur** trois *two times* ***out of*** *three*
  une femme **sur** dix *one woman* ***in*** *ten*
  un jour **sur** trois *every third day*
  un lundi **sur** deux *every other Monday*

- **Sur** labels the subject of a piece of writing or conversation (English *about*).

  un article **sur** la santé *an article* ***about*** *health*
  interroger le soldat **sur** son régiment *to question the soldier* ***about*** *his regiment*

- **Sur** has many figurative and idiomatic uses.

  La clé est restée **sur** la porte. *The key was left* ***in*** *the door.*
  Je n'ai pas les documents **sur** moi. *I don't have the documents* ***on*** *me.*
  revenir **sur** ses pas *to retrace one's steps*
  être **sur** la bonne/mauvaise piste *to be* ***on*** *the right/wrong track*
  vivre les uns **sur** les autres *to live one* ***on top of*** *the other*

Cet enfant a eu grippe **sur** grippe. *This child has had **one** flu **after the other**.*

Il revient toujours **sur** la même question. *He keeps going back **to** the same matter.*
Elle est revenue **sur** son idée. *She thought better of it.*

- **Sur** and **sous** have corresponding adverbs: **dessus** (*over it, on top of it*) and **dessous** (*beneath it, underneath*).

La chaise boîte. Ne mets pas ta valise **dessus.** *The chair is uneven. Don't put your suitcase **on top of it.***

Tu vois tous ces papiers? La lettre est **dessous.** *Do you see all those papers? The letter is **underneath them.***

- The adverbs have the compound forms **au-dessus** and **au-dessous**.

habiter **au-dessus/au-dessous** *to live **upstairs/downstairs***

- A**u-dessus de** and **au-dessous de** are compound prepositions.

les enfants **au-dessus de** dix ans *children **over** ten years of age*
Il fait dix degrés **au-dessus de** zéro. *It's ten degrees **above** zero.*
rien **au-dessus de** 100 francs *nothing **over** 100 francs*
C'est **au-dessus de** mes forces. *It's **too much** for me.*
les jeunes **au-dessous de** dix-huit ans *young people **under** eighteen years old*
être **au-dessous de** sa tâche *to be not **up to** one's task*
Il croit que c'est **au-dessous de** lui de faire le ménage. *He thinks that it's **beneath** him to do the housework.*

- **Par-dessus de** and **en dessous de** also appear in some expressions.

J'en ai **par-dessus** la tête. *I'm fed up with it.*
par-dessus le marché *on top of everything, in addition to everything*
faire quelque chose en dessous *to do something underhanded*
être en dessous de la moyenne *to be below average*

- Some common expressions with **dessus** and **dessous**:

aller bras dessus, bras dessous *to walk arm in arm*
sens dessus-dessous *topsy-turvy, in complete disorder*

M. Exprimez en français! Écrivez les phrases suivantes en français.

1. I'm fed up with it.

____

2. Jacques and Marie walk arm in arm.

____

3. These students are below average.

____

4. The detective is on the right track.

____

5. We bought apples at the marketplace.

____

6. I like to take walks in the rain.

____

7. I'm free every other Saturday.

8. He works under an assumed identity.

9. She thinks work is beneath her.

10. Children below ten years of age don't pay.

11. It's too much for me.

12. He wrote an article about Tunisia.

Note culturelle

La Tunisie, avec l'Algérie et le Maroc, forme le Maghreb (*ouest* en arabe), trois anciennes colonies françaises dans le nord de l'Afrique qui sont des pays francophones importants. Bien que l'arabe soit la langue officielle des trois pays, le français reste un important véhicule d'éducation et de culture.

La Tunisie, comme ses pays voisins du Maghreb, était de langue et de culture berbères avant l'invasion des Arabes qui commence en 647 et qui finit par arabiser et islamiser le pays.

En 1881, le protectorat français est établi en Tunisie. Il dure jusqu'en 1956 quand la Tunisie gagne son indépendance. Le pays vit de l'agriculture, de l'élevage, du pétrole et du gaz, de plusieurs industries et du tourisme. Plus de trois millions de vacanciers étrangers visitent la Tunisie chaque année.

F *Entre, pour,* and *par*

- The preposition **entre** means *between*.

  Il y a un jardin **entre** les deux maisons. — *There is a garden* ***between*** *the two houses.*

- **Entre** has many figurative uses.

  entre parenthèses/guillemets — ***in*** *parentheses/quotation marks*
  entouré **entre** quatre murs — *shut* ***in***
  entre nous — ***just between*** *us*
  Il n'y a rien de commun **entre** eux. — *They have nothing* ***in*** *common.*
  J'ai cette revue **entre** les mains. — *I have that magazine* ***in*** *my hands.*

- **Entre** appears in some important idioms.

  entre chien et loup — *at twilight*
  entre la poire et le fromage — *at the end of a meal*
  parler **entre** ses dents — *to mumble*

- Note the use of **d'entre** to translate *of* before a disjunctive pronoun after expressions of quantity, numbers, negative words, and interrogatives.

  beaucoup **d'entre** nous *many **of** us*
  deux **d'entre** eux *two **of** them*
  personne **d'entre** nous *none **of** us*
  Qui **d'entre** vous? *Who **among** you?*

- The preposition **pour** usually translates into English as *for*.

  J'ai apporté quelque chose **pour** toi. *I've brought something **for** you.*

- The preposition **pour** means *for* with expressions of time. It usually indicates future time.

  Je pars **pour** trois jours. *I'm leaving **for** three days.*
  J'en ai **pour** cinq minutes. *I'll be done **in** five minutes.*

- **Pour** means *to* or *in order to* before an infinitive.

  Tu ne dis ça que **pour** me fâcher. *You're only saying that **to** make me angry.*

- **Pour** occurs in idiomatic expressions.

  Tant d'histoires **pour** si peu de chose! *So much fuss **over** such a small thing!*
  garder le meilleur **pour** la fin *to save the best **for** last*
  un sirop **pour** la toux *a cough syrup*
  être **pour** la peine de mort *to be **for (in favor of)** the death penalty*
  Et **pour** cause! *And **for** good reason!*
  Pour être fâché, je le suis! *Talk about being angry, I am angry!*

- **Par** usually translates into English as *through* or *by*, especially with the passive voice.

  Il est sortie **par** la porte de devant. *He went out **through** the front door.*
  jeter quelque chose **par** la fenêtre *to throw something **out of** the window*
  un tableau peint **par** Louis David *a picture painted **by** Louis David*
  obtenir quelque chose **par** la force *to get something **by** force*

- **Par** is used to denote position in certain expressions of place and time.

  Tu ne vas pas sortir **par** un temps pareil! *You're not going to go out **in** weather like this!*
  être/tomber **par** terre *to be/fall **on** the ground*
  deux fois **par** mois *twice a month*
  par les temps qui courent *these days*

- **Par** occurs in idiomatic expressions.

  par ici, par là *this way, that way*
  par conséquent *consequently*
  par mégarde ***by** accident*
  par intervalles *intermittently*
  par cœur ***by** heart*
  faire quelque chose **par** amitié, **par** amour *to do something **out of** friendship, **out of** love*
  Il a fini **par** ennuyer tout le monde. *He wound up annoying everyone.*

N. La vie est parfois compliquée. Complétez les narrations suivantes avec les prépositions **entre, pour** ou **par.**

La mère de Maurice est furieuse!

Ma mère est furieuse. (1) __________ être furieuse, elle l'est! Elle dit que c'est (2) __________ cause. Je vais vous dire ce qui s'est passé. J'étais avec mes amis. Il faisait très mauvais. Plusieurs (3) __________ nous sommes sortis (4) __________ la tempête. Moi, je me suis enrhumé. Maintenant je prends du sirop (5) __________ la toux et des pastilles (6) __________ la grippe. Et je garde le meilleur (7) __________ la fin. Ma mère a attrapé mon rhume. (8) __________ conséquent, elle prend le sirop et les pastilles avec moi.

Les problèmes de Philippe

(9) __________ nous, je crois que Philippe est déprimé. Il dit des bêtises (10) __________ mégarde et parle souvent (11) __________ ses dents. Il laisse ses papiers (12) __________ terre et il se fâche (13) __________ un rien. Il va finir (14) __________ ennuyer tout le monde.

G *Other prepositions*

- **Devant** (*in front of*) and **derrière** (*behind*) are used to express position and location.

  devant le lycée *__in front of__ the high school*
  derrière l'arbre *__behind__ the tree*

- **Avant** (*before*), like **après** (*after*), is used to talk about time.

  avant huit heures *__before__ eight o'clock*
  après l'examen *__after__ the test*

- **Avant** becomes **avant de** before an infinitive.

  avant de partir *__before__ leaving*

- **Après** is usually used with the perfect infinitive (**avoir** or **être** + past participle).

  après avoir fini le travail *__after finishing__ the work*
  après être sorti(e)(s) *__after going out__*

- **À travers** means *through, across.*

  partir **à travers** champs/bois *to set off __across__ country, __through__ the woods*
  voir le paysage **à travers** la vitre *to see the scenery __through__ the window*

- **Chez** means *at the house of, at the store of,* or, figuratively, *with, among.*

  passer le dimanche **chez mon oncle** *to spend Sunday __at my uncle's house__*
  acheter du poulet **chez le boucher** *to buy chicken __at the butcher's__*
  aller **chez le dentiste** *to go __to the dentist__*
  C'est une coutume **chez les Allemands**. *It's a custom __among the Germans__.*

- **Contre** means *against.*

  s'appuyer **contre** le mur *to lean __against__ the wall*

Contre has other English equivalents in certain contexts.

se fâcher/être en colère **contre** quelqu'un *to get/be angry* ***with*** *someone*
Nous sommes tout à fait **contre**. *We're totally* ***against (it)****.*
dix voix **contre** cinq *ten votes* ***to*** *five*
échanger/troquer un livre **contre** un logiciel *to exchange/swap a book* ***for*** *a software program*

- **Vers** means *toward* in space and time; **envers** means *toward* figuratively, in the sense of an attitude or gesture toward someone.

aller **vers** Lille *to go* ***toward*** *Lille*
vers cinq heures ***around*** *five o'clock*
votre gentillesse **envers** moi *your kindness* ***toward*** *me*

- **Hors de** and **en dehors de** mean *outside of* when referring to spatial position.

hors de/en dehors de l'appartement ***out of, outside of*** *the apartment*

Hors de and **hors** (in certain fixed expressions only) can be used figuratively.

hors d'haleine ***out of*** *breath*
hors de danger ***out of*** *danger*
hors jeu ***offside***

- Other prepositions:

à cause de *because of*
au sujet de *about (on the subject of)*
d'après *according to*
durant *during*
environ *about (approximately)*
loin de *far from*
malgré *in spite of*
parmi *among*
pendant *during*
près de *near*
quant à *as for*
selon *according to*
suivant *according to*

O. Comprenez-vous? Écrivez l'équivalent anglais de ces phrases.

1. On se verra vers 6 heures.

____

2. D'après le médecin, il n'est pas hors de danger.

____

3. On vit mieux en dehors de la ville.

____

4. Il a été très généreux envers ses enfants.

____

5. Elle regarde à travers la fenêtre.

____

6. Le professeur a parlé au sujet de l'examen.

____

7. Il me faut passer chez mon avocat.

____

8. Je te donne ces timbres contre cette pièce.

____

P. Et en français? Écrivez ces phrases en français.

1. according to the newspapers ______
2. during the class ______
3. in spite of the difficulty ______
4. near the station ______
5. as for me ______
6. three votes to two ______
7. about ten students ______
8. offside (out of play) ______
9. across country ______
10. with, among French people ______
11. before going downstairs ______
12. after going downstairs ______

H *Prepositions with geographical names*

- French uses the definite article before names of countries, provinces, regions, and continents.

la France	*France*	**le Midi**	*the south of France*
la Bretagne	*Brittany*	**l'Europe**	*Europe*

- French uses the preposition **en** to express motion toward or location in a country (or province or region) if the place name is feminine singular. The definite article is not used.

aller **en** Italie	*to go **to** Italy*
partir **en** Pologne	*to leave **for** Poland*
faire un voyage **en** Chine	*to take a trip **to** China*

- **En** is also used before masculine singular countries beginning with a vowel. The definite article is not used.

émigrer **en** Israël	*to emigrate **to** Israel*

Note: **Israël** is not usually accompanied by the definite article: **Israël est un pays du Moyen-Orient.**

- To express *from* with the above categories of place names, **de** or **d'** is substituted for **en**.

revenir **d'**Italie	*to return **from** Italy*
être **de** Pologne	*to be **from** Poland*
partir **d'**Israël	*to leave **from** Israel*
arriver **d'**Haïti	*to arrive **from** Haiti*

- For masculine singular place names that do not begin with a vowel, and masculine and feminine plural place names, *to* or *in* is expressed by **à** plus the definite article (**au** or **aux**).

aller/être **au** Portugal	*to go to/be **in** Portugal*
aller/être **au** Japon	*to go to/be **in** Japan*
aller/être **aux** États-Unis	*to go to/be **in** the United States*
aller/être **aux** Antilles	*to go to/be **in** the West Indies*

- To express *from* with the above place names, **de** plus the definite article (**du** or **des**) is used.

revenir **du** Danemark	*to come back* ***from*** *Denmark*
revenir **du** Canada	*to come back* ***from*** *Canada*
revenir **du** Viêt-nam	*to come back* ***from*** *Vietnam*
revenir **des** Pays-Bas	*to come back* ***from*** *the Netherlands*

- With the names of most islands, French uses **à** (sometimes **à la** for feminine names) to express *to* and **de** (sometimes **de la**) to express *from.*

à (l'île) Maurice, **de** (**l'**île) Maurice	***to/from*** *Mauritius*
à la Réunion, **de la** Réunion	***to/from*** *Reunion Island*
à Porto Rico, **de** Porto Rico	***to/from*** *Puerto Rico*
à la Guadeloupe, **de la** Guadeloupe	***to/from*** *Guadeloupe*
à la Martinique, **de la** Martinique	***to/from*** *Martinique*

Note: Some islands, however, take **en: en Sicile, en Corse, en Sardaigne**.

- Before names of cities, French uses **à** to express *to* or *in* and **de** to express *from.*

à Montréal, **de** Montréal	***to/in*** *Montreal,* ***from*** *Montreal*
à Genève, **de** Genève	***to/in*** *Geneva,* ***from*** *Geneva*
à New York, **de** New York	***to/in*** *New York,* ***from*** *New York*
à Saïgon, **de** Saïgon	***to/in*** *Saigon,* ***from*** *Saigon*

- Some cities have a definite article as part of their name: **Le Havre, La Rochelle, Le Caire** (*Cairo*), **La Havane** (*Havana*), **La Nouvelle-Orléans** (*New Orleans*). The article is kept when **à** or **de** is used with these names and the appropriate contractions are made.

Le Havre: **au, du** Havre	*Le Havre:* ***to/in, from*** *Le Havre*
La Rochelle: **à La, de La** Rochelle	*La Rochelle:* ***to/in, from*** *La Rochelle*

- All place names take the definite article when modified. **En** becomes **dans** when the article is used. The preposition **à** also changes to **dans** when the place name is modified.

dans l'Europe du vingtième siècle	***in*** *twentieth-century Europe*

- French uses **en** to express *in* or *to* and **de** to express *from* before the following states that are grammatically feminine: **Californie, Caroline du Nord/Sud, Géorgie, Floride, Louisiane, Pennsylvanie, Virginie, Virginie Occidentale.** The rest of the states are grammatically masculine, and either **dans le** or **au** may be used. Before states beginning with a vowel, **dans l'** or **en** may be used.

  dans le Texas, **au** Texas, **du** Texas
  dans l'Alabama, **en** Alabama, **de l'**Alabama, **d'**Alabama

- Notice the differences in the prepositions used with provinces or states and cities with the same name.

le Québec, Québec	*Quebec Province, Quebec City*
au Québec, **à** Québec	***to/in*** *Quebec Province,* ***to/in*** *Quebec City*
du Québec, **de** Québec	***from*** *Quebec Province,* ***from*** *Quebec City*

Note also **le New York** (*New York State*) and **New York** (*New York City*), and **le Mexique** (*Mexico*) and **Mexico** (*Mexico City*).

Note culturelle

La Guadeloupe et la Martinique sont deux départements d'outre-mer, c'est-à-dire, éloignés de la France continentale. Les habitants de ces deux îles des Antilles sont des citoyens français. Ces deux îles ont été colonisées par les Français en 1635. Les autres départements d'outre-mer sont la Réunion (île à l'est de Madagascar), la Guyane (sur la côte nord de l'Amérique du Sud) et Saint-Pierre-et-Miquelon (archipel voisin de Terre-Neuve). On emploie l'acronyme DOM-TOM pour parler des départements d'outre-mer et des territoires d'outre-mer.

Feminine countries

l'Europe

l'Allemagne *Germany*
l'Angleterre *England*
l'Autriche *Austria*
la Belgique *Belgium*
la Bosnie *Bosnia*
la Croatie *Croatia*
l'Écosse *Scotland*
l'Espagne *Spain*
la France *France*
la Grèce *Greece*
l'Irlande *Ireland*
l'Italie *Italy*
la Norvège *Norway*
la Pologne *Poland*
la République Tchèque *Czech Republic*
la Russie *Russia*
la Serbie *Serbia*
la Slovaquie *Slovakia*
la Suède *Sweden*
la Suisse *Switzerland*

l'Afrique

l'Afrique du Sud *South Africa*
l'Algérie *Algeria*
la Côte-d'Ivoire *Ivory Coast*
l'Égypte *Egypt*
la Libye *Libya*
la Mauritanie *Mauritania*
la Mozambique *Mozambique*
la Tunisie *Tunisia*

l'Asie et l'Océanie

l'Arabie Saoudite *Saudi Arabia*
l'Australie *Australia*
la Chine *China*
la Corée *Korea*
l'Inde *India*
la Jordanie *Jordan*
la Nouvelle-Zélande *New Zealand*
les Philippines *the Philippines*
la Syrie *Syria*
la Thaïlande *Thailand*
la Turquie *Turkey*

l'Amérique

les Antilles *West Indies*
l'Argentine *Argentina*
la Colombie *Colombia*
Haïti *Haiti*
la République Dominicaine *Dominican Republic*

Masculine countries

l'Europe

le Danemark *Denmark*
le Luxembourg *Luxemburg*
les Pays-Bas *Netherlands*
le Portugal *Portugal*

l'Afrique

le Congo *the Congo*
le Mali *Mali*
le Maroc *Morocco*
le Sénégal *Senegal*
le Soudan *Sudan*
le Zaïre *Zaire*

l'Asie et l'Océanie

le Cambodge *Cambodia*
l'Irak *Iraq*
l'Iran *Iran*
Israël *Israel*
le Japon *Japan*
le Koweït *Kuwait*
le Liban *Lebanon*
le Pakistan *Pakistan*
le Viêt-nam *Vietnam*

l'Amérique

le Brésil *Brazil*
le Canada *Canada*
le Chili *Chile*
les États-Unis *United States*
le Mexique *Mexico*
le Pérou *Peru*

Q. **Des étudiants à l'étranger.** Un groupe de jeunes Belges fait un stage d'un an dans différents pays. Dites en chaque cas le pays et la ville où ils se trouvent.

Modèle Willie/France/Paris
→ Willie travaille en France, à Paris.

1. Monique / Canada / Québec
____
2. Olivier / États-Unis / La Nouvelle-Orléans
____
3. Mariek / Japon / Tokyo
____
4. Fernand / Brésil / Sao Paolo
____
5. Gérard / Mexique / Mexico
____
6. Stella / Haïti / Port-au-Prince
____
7. Luc / Sénégal / Dakar
____
8. Brigitte / Pays-Bas / Amsterdam
____
9. Sylvie / Égypte / Le Caire
____
10. Béatrice / Portugal / Lisbonne
____
11. Jan / Viêt-nam / Saïgon
____
12. Raymond / Israël / Jérusalem
____

R. **D'où sont-ils?** Faites des phrases pour exprimer l'origine de ces étudiants internationaux.

Modèle Jacques/France
→ Jacques est de France.

1. Fatima / Irak
____
2. Lise / Bruxelles
____

3. Martin et Santos / Chili

4. Sven / Danemark

5. Rosa et Laura / Naples

6. Mei-Li / Chine

7. Amalia / Mexico

8. Fred et Jane / Californie

9. Kimberly / Vermont

10. Odile / Luxembourg

11. Corazon / Philippines

12. Mies / Pays-Bas

13. Hanako et Hiro / Japon

14. Bill / États-Unis

15. Olivier / Le Havre

PART FOUR

Verbs in Two-Clause Sentences

CHAPTER 23

RELATIVE CLAUSES

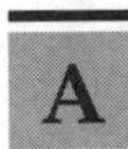

The relative pronouns **qui** and **que**

- A relative clause describes someone or something mentioned in the main clause. A relative clause begins with a relative pronoun, such as *who, whom, which,* or *that.* The noun that the relative pronoun refers to is called the antecedent. Relative clauses are in boldface italics in the examples below.

*the woman **who studies a lot***	*Who* is the relative pronoun, *woman* is the antecedent.
*the students **whom we helped***	*Whom* is the relative pronoun, *students* is the antecedent.
*the computer **that I use***	*That* is the relative pronoun, *computer* is the antecedent.

- The French relative pronouns **qui** and **que** are used for both people and things. **Qui** is used when the relative pronoun is the subject of its clause. **Que** is used when the relative pronoun is the direct object of the verb in its clause.

la femme **qui étudie beaucoup**	**Qui** is the relative pronoun, subject of the verb **étudier**.
un ordinateur **qui est facile à utiliser**	**Qui** is the relative pronoun, subject of the verb **être**.
les étudiants **que nous avons aidés**	**Que** is the relative pronoun, direct object of the verb **aider**.
l'ordinateur **que j'ai utilisé**	**Que** is the relative pronoun, direct object of the verb **utiliser**.

Note: In relative clauses introduced by **qui,** the verb agrees with **qui,** which has the same person and number as the antecedent.

- Relative pronouns can never be omitted in French the way they often are in English.

l'homme **que** je connais	*the man (**whom**) I know*
les articles **que** je lis	*the articles (**that**) I read*

- When the verb of the relative clause is in a compound tense conjugated with **avoir,** the past participle agrees with the relative pronoun **que,** which is a preceding direct object. The gender and number of **que** is determined by its antecedent.

les jeunes filles qu'il a invitées	***the girls whom** he invited*
la robe que tu as mise	***the dress** you put on*

Note: The relative pronoun **que** becomes **qu'** before a vowel or mute **h.**

- When the verb of the relative clause is in a compound tense conjugated with **être,** the past participle agrees with the relative pronoun **qui** because **qui** is the subject of the verb in the relative clause. The antecedent determines the gender and number of **qui.**

les étudiantes qui sont arriv**ées**	***the students who*** *arrived*
l'assiette qui est tomb**ée**	***the plate that*** *fell*

A. **Est-ce *qui* ou *que*?** Complétez les phrases suivantes avec **qui** ou **que.** Toutes les phrases ont quelque chose à voir avec le monde du lycée.

Le cours de philo

1. Voilà le professeur ________ enseigne le cours de philosophie.
2. C'est un cours ________ tout le monde aime bien.
3. Nous avons des lectures ________ sont très difficiles, mais passionnantes.
4. Les questions ________ le prof nous pose font penser.
5. Voilà Jean-Claude. C'est lui ________ reçoit les meilleures notes en philo.
6. Il dit que c'est une matière ________ le passionne.
7. Notre professeur est un homme ________ Jean-Claude admire beaucoup.

Le cours de chimie

8. Ma meilleure amie est une fille ________ s'appelle Géraldine.
9. C'est quelqu'un ________ je connais depuis longtemps.
10. C'est le cours de chimie ________ nous intéresse le plus.
11. Géraldine et moi, nous faisons tous les problèmes ________ le prof nous donne à résoudre.
12. Notre professeur est une femme ________ a écrit plusieurs livres de chimie.
13. Géraldine et moi, nous avons acheté un des bouquins ________ elle a écrit.
14. C'est un livre ________ est très utile pour l'étudiant.
15. C'est un livre ________ nous avons recommandé à tous nos amis.
16. Le prof de chimie est une femme ________ on respecte beaucoup.

B. **Des précisions.** Les propositions relatives, comme les adjectifs, servent à préciser, à identifier. Formez des propositions relatives pour mieux expliquer à votre ami(e) de qui ou de quoi il s'agit.

MODÈLES —Quel livre veux-tu? (Il y a un livre sur la table.)
➔ —Le livre qui est sur la table.

—Quels gants est-ce Paulette va mettre?
(Son petit ami lui a acheté des gants.)
➔ —Les gants que son petit ami lui a achetés.

La santé

agir *to work (of medicines)*
le cabinet *doctor's office*
le centre diététique *health food store*
le comprimé *tablet*
conseiller *to advise, recommend*
la crème *cream*
donner le vertige à *to make dizzy*
l'infirmière (fem.) *nurse*
ordonner *to prescribe*
la pilule *pill*
la piqûre *injection*
le régime *diet*
le sirop pour la toux *cough syrup*
suivre un régime *to follow a diet*
le vertige *dizziness*
la vitamine *vitamin*

1. Quel médecin est-ce que je dois aller voir? (Il a son cabinet dans ce bâtiment.)

 ____

2. Quels comprimés prends-tu? (Mon médecin m'a ordonné ces comprimés.)

 ____

3. Quel régime est-ce qu'il faut suivre? (J'ai trouvé un régime au centre diététique.)

 ____

4. Quel sirop pour la toux agit vite? (J'ai laissé un sirop sur la table.)

 ____

5. Quelle piqûre t'a fait mal? (L'infirmière m'a fait une piqûre hier.)

 ____

6. Quelles pilules t'ont donné le vertige? (J'ai pris les pilules hier.)

 ____

7. Quelle crème utilises-tu pour la peau? (Le pharmacien m'a conseillé une crème.)

 ____

8. Quelles vitamines prends-tu? (Les vitamines sont bonnes pour le cœur.)

 ____

C. **Encore des précisions.** La personne qui parle emploie des propositions relatives pour identifier la personne ou la chose à laquelle elle fait allusion. Suivez les modèles.

MODÈLES —Quel ordinateur?
a. Olivier l'utilise.
 ➔ —L'ordinateur qu'Olivier utilise.
b. Il a beaucoup de mémoire.
 ➔ —L'ordinateur qui a beaucoup de mémoire.

1. Quel professeur?
 a. Tous les étudiants l'adorent.

 ____

 b. Il enseigne le français et l'espagnol.

 ____

c. Il vient de se marier.

___

d. Mes parents le connaissent.

___

2. Quelle maison?

a. Jeanne et Richard l'ont achetée.

___

b. Elle a un jardin et une piscine.

___

c. On l'a construite en 1975.

___

d. Elle est en briques.

___

3. Quels cadeaux?

a. Mon frère et moi, nous les avons reçus il y a une semaine.

___

b. Mon oncle et ma tante nous les ont envoyés.

___

c. Je te les ai montrés hier.

___

d. Ils t'ont beaucoup plu.

___

4. Quel restaurant?

a. Nos amis l'ont ouvert l'année dernière.

___

b. Il a une ambiance alsacienne.

___

c. Il a des nappes rouges.

___

d. Beaucoup d'artistes le fréquentent.

___

5. Quel sénateur?

a. Le peuple l'a élu l'année dernière.

___

b. Il a promis de combattre l'inflation.

___

c. Il est marié avec une journaliste.

____

d. Les ouvriers l'appuient.

____

B *Preposition + **qui** and **lequel***

- The relative pronoun **qui** may serve as the object of a preposition. In such cases, it refers only to people. There is no agreement of the past participle in compound tenses when **qui** is preceded by a preposition.

l'homme **à qui** je donne le livre	*the man I'm giving the book **to***
la femme **à qui** nous pensons	*the woman **that** we're thinking **of***
les étudiants **à qui** j'ai parlé	*the students **whom** I spoke **to***

- **Lequel** is the relative pronoun that refers primarily to things after a preposition. It agrees in gender and number with its antecedent.

	masculine	*feminine*
singular	**lequel**	**laquelle**
plural	**lesquels**	**lesquelles**

The prepositions **à** and **de** combine with the forms of **lequel** as follows.

	masculine	*feminine*
singular	**auquel, duquel**	**à laquelle, de laquelle**
plural	**auxquels, desquels**	**auxquelles, desquelles**

l'examen **auquel** j'ai réussi	*the test I passed* (**réussir à**)
la matière **à laquelle** je m'intéresse	*the subject I'm interested **in*** (**s'intéresser à**)
les bureaux **auxquels** vous téléphonez	*the offices you telephone* (**téléphoner à**)
les études **auxquelles** il s'applique	*the studies he applies himself **to*** (**s'appliquer à**)

D. Continuons à préciser. Formez des phrases qui ont des propositions relatives commençant par **à.** N'oubliez pas la différence de construction qu'il faut respecter entre les antécédents animés et inanimés.

MODÈLE Quel cours est bon? (J'ai assisté à un cours.)
➔ Le cours auquel j'ai assisté.

1. Avec quelle fille Roland va-t-il sortir? (Il pense à une fille tout le temps.)

____

2. Quelle lettre vas-tu me montrer? (J'ai répondu à cette lettre.)

____

3. Quel débat as-tu écouté? (Nos copains ont pris part à ce débat.)

____

4. De quelles habitudes le médecin parle-t-il? (Il faut renoncer à ces habitudes.)

____

5. Avec quel homme est-ce qu'elle s'est mariée? (Elle se fiait à cet homme.)

____

6. Quels clients sont venus? (Nous avons téléphoné à ces clients.)

____

7. Quels détails aimez-vous? (Vous avez veillé à ces détails.)

____

8. Quelles méthodes as-tu recommandées? (Je crois à ces méthodes.)

____

E. Quel drame! Complétez les phrases suivantes avec le pronom relatif convenable. Toutes les phrases font allusion aux éléments d'une histoire d'amour entre Élisabeth et Antoine.

1. la lettre ______________ Élisabeth a répondu
2. les parents ______________ les deux jeunes gens n'ont pas obéi
3. le concert de rock ______________ ils ont assisté
4. Georges, l'ami ______________ Antoine se confiait
5. Odile, la fille ______________ Antoine a connue dans la classe d'éducation civique
6. les rapports entre les deux ______________ la jalousie d'Élisabeth a nui
7. les conversations avec Odile ______________ Antoine a dû renoncer
8. la querelle d'amour ______________ Georges s'est mêlé
9. la mauvaise situation ______________ l'intervention de Georges a remédié
10. le rapprochement ______________ a eu lieu entre Élisabeth et Antoine

C *Dont*

- The relative pronoun **dont** replaces the preposition **de** plus a relative pronoun. **Dont** immediately follows its antecedent and can refer to either people or things.

1. **Dont** is used when the verb or expression in the relative clause requires the preposition **de** before an object.

un professeur **dont** je me souviens	*a teacher (**whom**) I remember* (**se souvenir de**)
les affaires **dont** il s'occupe	*the matters **that** he's taking care of* (**s'occuper de**)
les employés **dont** j'ai besoin	*the employees **that** I need* (**avoir besoin de**)

2. **Dont** is used when **de** introduces a phrase that modifies another noun. (The English equivalent is usually *whose* or *of which.*)

un étudiant **dont** je connais les parents	*a student **whose** parents I know* **(les parents de l'étudiant)**
une idée **dont** on comprend l'importance	*an idea **whose** importance (the importance **of which**) we understand* **(l'importance de l'idée)**
un auteur **dont** j'ai lu tous les livres	*an author, all of **whose** books I have read* **(tous les livres de l'auteur)**

Notice the word order in the clause introduced by **dont.** Also notice that when **dont** is used to express possession, the definite article is used in place of a possessive adjective.

3. **Dont** is used with numbers and expressions of quantity.

des articles **dont** j'ai lu **quelques-uns**	*articles, **some of which** I've read* **(quelques-uns des articles)**
des étudiants **dont une dizaine** sont français	*some students, **about ten of whom** are French* **(une dizaine des étudiants)**
trois hommes **dont deux** médecins	*three men, **of whom two** are doctors* **(deux des trois hommes)**

- **De qui** or **de** + a form of **lequel** may also be used to refer to people and things, but **dont** is usually the preferred form.

F. De qui s'agit-il exactement? Précisez de qui il s'agit en employant une proposition relative qui commence par **dont.** Dans chaque cas, l'équivalent anglais commence par le mot *whose.*

Modèle —Quel journaliste? (Tout le monde lit ses articles.)
➔ —Le journaliste dont tout le monde lit les articles.

1. Quelle fille? (Sa mère est médecin.)
____
2. Quel ami? (Son oncle travaille au ministère.)
____
3. Quel sénateur? (Le pays entier a écouté son discours.)
____
4. Quels ouvriers? (Leur syndicat compte entreprendre une grève.)
____
5. Quels étudiants? (On a publié leur rapport.)
____
6. Quel professeur? (Son cours est toujours plein.)
____
7. Quelle infirmière? (Tout le monde admire son travail.)
____

8. Quelle programmeuse? (Ses logiciels se vendent très bien.)

____

9. Quels voisins? (Leurs enfants assistent à cette école.)

____

10. Quel groupe de rock? (Tous les jeunes écoutent ses chansons.)

____

G. En une seule phrase, s'il vous plaît! Faites de chaque paire de phrases une seule phrase en vous servant du pronom relatif convenable. Choisissez entre **qui, que, à qui, auquel** et **dont.**

Modèle La cordonnerie est le métier. Ils vivent de ce métier.
→ La cordonnerie est le métier dont ils vivent.

Un séjour dans une ville de province

1. Notre guide nous a montré un paysage. Nous nous sommes émerveillés de ce paysage.

____

2. Nous avons visité les murailles. La vieille ville est entourée de ces murailles.

____

3. Une amie nous a invités au festival de danse. Elle prenait part à ce festival.

____

4. Nous sommes allés voir une rue. On transformait cette rue en rue piétonne.

____

5. On est allés voir une comédie. On a beaucoup ri de cette comédie.

____

6. Nous avons essayé la cuisine régionale. La ville se vante de sa cuisine.

____

7. On nous a signalé l'absence d'une université. Nous nous sommes aperçus de cette absence.

____

8. C'est la vie universitaire. La ville manquait de vie universitaire.

____

9. Nous avions des amis dans la région. Nous avons téléphoné à ces amis.

____

10. Nous avons passé une belle journée avec eux. Nous nous souvenons encore de cette journée.

____

Une crise dans l'administration nationale

11. La crise est arrivée. Tout le monde avait peur de cette crise.

____

12. Un ministre faisait mal les fonctions. Il était responsable de ces fonctions.

____

13. C'était un homme respecté. Personne ne se doutait de lui.

____

14. Ce ministre est un homme bien en vue (*prominent*). La nation entière se fiait à lui.

____

15. On dit qu'il a donné des emplois à des gens non qualifiés. Plusieurs de ces gens étaient ses parents et amis.

____

16. Ils faisaient un travail. On commençait à se plaindre de ce travail.

____

17. Il y avait cent employés au ministère. On a congédié une trentaine de ces employés.

____

18. C'est la confiance de la nation. Le ministre a abusé de la confiance de la nation.

____

D *Other relatives*

- Relative pronouns may follow other prepositions besides **à** and **de.** The relative pronoun **qui** is used to refer to people after all prepositions except **entre** and **parmi. Lequel** can be used to refer to both people and things, although **qui** is usually preferred for people. After **entre** and **parmi,** a form of **lequel** must be used.

Animate antecedents

les amis sur qui je compte (*also:* **sur lesquels**)	***the friends** I rely **on***
l'employée dont je vous ai parlé (*also:* **de qui, de laquelle**)	***the employee whom** I spoke to you **about***
le cousin chez qui j'habite	***the cousin at whose house** I live*
les deux jeunes filles entre lesquelles il s'est assis	***the two girls** he sat **between***
les quatre garçons parmi lesquels Janine a choisi	***the four boys among whom** Janine chose*

Inanimate antecedents

la table sur laquelle j'ai posé mes affaires	***the table** I put my things **on***
l'immeuble dans lequel elle habite	***the apartment house that** she lives **in***
la tente sous laquelle j'ai dormi	***the tent that** I slept **in***

- Prepositions of location and direction plus a relative pronoun can be replaced by **où.**

  la table **où** j'ai posé mes affaires — ***the table where*** *I put my things*
  l'immeuble **où** elle habite — ***the apartment house where*** *she lives*

- **Où** can also be used as a relative pronoun after time words. **Que** is also possible.

  le jour où elle est partie / **le jour qu'**elle est partie — ***the day*** *she left*

- After a compound preposition ending in **de** (such as **à cause de**) or a noun phrase ending in **de** (such as **dans la classe de**), **dont** must be replaced by **qui** (for people) or a form of **de** + **lequel** (for both things and people).

  la gare près de laquelle je travaille — ***the station*** *I work* ***near***
  l'étudiante au sujet de qui je vous ai parlé — ***the student about whom*** *I spoke to you*
  les voisins à cause de qui nous avons dû déménager — ***the neighbors because of whom*** *we had to move*

H. Le style soutenu. Traduisez les phrases suivantes en anglais. Elles ont toutes des propositions subordonnées compliquées et sont typiques du style journalistique ou littéraire.

La conférence de presse

à la suite de *following*
au bout de *at the end of (space)*
au cours de *during, during the course of*
le chômage *unemployment*
la coutume *custom*
défavorisé *underprivileged*
la démarche *step, measure*
se démettre de *to resign from*
fonder *to found*
prédire *to predict*
routier *pertaining to roads*

1. Le gouvernement a fait une démarche dont les conséquences sont à regretter.

   ____

2. Les agents de police ont fait un effort dont notre équipe reconnaît l'importance.

   ____

3. C'est une crise économique en conséquence de laquelle le chômage a augmenté.

   ____

4. On attend une déclaration du général sous les ordres de qui l'armée combattait.

   ____

5. Notre pays participe à un effort international dont on prédit le succès.

____

6. Elle a eu une maladie à la suite de laquelle elle a dû se démettre de son poste.

____

7. Ils ont fait une étude des conditions dans lesquelles vivent les défavorisés de notre ville.

____

8. Nous assistions à la conférence de presse au cours de laquelle on a annoncé les nouveaux projets de construction routière.

____

I. **Gestion critiquée.** Ajoutez le pronom relatif convenable à ces phrases pour savoir pourquoi Philippe Duhamel et Micheline Arnaud ne sont pas d'accord avec les plans de leur entreprise. Dans plusieurs cas il faut ajouter aussi la préposition qui manque.

Vocabulaire utile

être d'accord avec *to be in agreement with*
se familiariser avec *to familiarize oneself with*
insister sur *to insist on*
se renseigner sur *to get information about*

1. Nous n'avons pas assisté à la réunion pendant ________________ on a pris la décision.
2. Ils commencent un programme d'action ________________ nous ne sommes pas d'accord.
3. Nous croyons qu'il produira des résultats ________________ on ne s'attend pas.
4. Ils ne peuvent pas assurer la qualité ________________ nous insistons.
5. Ils ne connaissent pas le marché ________________ nous nous sommes familiarisés.
6. Il y a trop de choses ________________ ils ne se sont pas renseignés.
7. C'est un projet contre ________________ nous allons protester.
8. On va exposer toutes les mauvaises conséquences ________________ nous nous méfions.

J. Au pays de mes ancêtres. Christine montre à son amie Julie le village où elle est née et où sa famille a toujours vécu. Ajoutez le pronom relatif convenable à la conversation entre les deux filles. Dans plusieurs cas il faut ajouter aussi la préposition qui manque.

À la campagne

le chêne *oak tree*	**grimper aux arbres** *to climb trees*
la clôture *fence*	**le jardin potager** *vegetable garden*
l'étang (masc.) *pond*	**le peuplier** *poplar tree*

Christine: Viens, je vais te montrer la maison dans (1) ____________________ on habitait. La voilà.

Julie: La maison à côté de (2) ____________________ il y a deux chênes?

Christine: Justement. Ce sont les arbres (3) ____________________ on grimpait, mes frères et moi, quand on était petits et entre (4) ____________________ il y avait avant un petit banc en bois.

Julie: Est-ce que je peux voir ta chambre?

Christine: Oui, montons. La voilà, la chambre dans (5) ____________________ je couchais. Et voilà la fenêtre par (6) ____________________ je regardais la neige en hiver.

Julie: Et cette clôture?

Christine: C'est la clôture derrière (7) ____________________ il y a un champ.

Julie: Je vois un chemin à gauche.

Christine: Oui, c'est un chemin le long (8) ____________________ il y a des peupliers.

Julie: Tu ne m'as pas dit qu'il y avait aussi un étang?

Christine: Ah, oui, l'étang sur (9) ____________________ on patinait en hiver. On peut y aller, ce n'est pas loin. Et chemin faisant, je te présenterai aux voisins chez (10) ____________________ je passais beaucoup de temps. Ils avaient un fils (11) ____________________ j'étais amoureuse.

Julie: Et qu'est-ce qu'il est devenu, ce fils?

Christine: Il était beaucoup plus âgé que moi. Il a passé plusieurs années à Lyon au cours (12) ____________________ il s'est marié.

E Relatives without antecedents

- When there is no antecedent in the main clause, French uses **ce qui** if the relative is the subject of its clause or **ce que** if it is the direct object.

—Je ne vois pas **ce qui** t'inquiète. — *I don't see **what**'s upsetting you.*
—**Ce qui** reste à faire me tracasse. — ***What** there is left to do is worrying me.*
—Dis-moi **ce que** tu veux. — *Tell me **what** you want.*
—**Ce que** je préfère, c'est de partir. — ***What** I prefer is to leave.*

- When the verb of the relative clause requires the preposition **de** before an object, **ce dont** is used.

—Je n'ai pas trouvé **ce dont** j'avais besoin. — *I haven't found **what** I needed. (**avoir besoin de**)*
—Tu veux que je te prête **ce dont** je me sers? — *Do you want me to lend you **what** I use? (**se servir de**)*

- **Ce qui, ce que,** and **ce dont** can also refer to a preceding clause.

Il arrive toujours à l'heure, **ce qui** me plaît. — *He always arrives on time, **which** I like.*
Il parle trois langues, **ce que** j'admire. — *He speaks three languages, **which** I admire.*
Il est très travailleur**, ce dont** on s'est aperçu. — *He's very hard-working, **which** people have noticed.*

Ce qui and **ce que** are used after **tout** to express *all that, everything that.*

Il m'a montré **tout ce qu'**il a écrit. — *He showed me **everything that** he wrote.*
Tout ce qui est sur la table est pour toi. — ***All that** is on the table is for you.*

- The demonstrative pronouns **celui, celle, ceux, celles** are common before the relative pronouns **qui** and **que,** and mean *he/she who, they who, the one(s) who, those who.*

Ceux qui le connaissent l'estiment. — ***Those who** know him admire him.*
Celui qui désobéit sera puni. — ***He who** disobeys will be punished.*
Il y a plusieurs étudiantes françaises, mais il faut parler avec **celles qui** connaissent Marseille. — *There are several (female) French students here, but you have to speak with **the ones who** are familiar with Marseilles.*

- Note that in proverbs **qui** is often used by itself to mean *he who.*

Rira bien **qui** rira le dernier. — ***He who** laughs last laughs best.*
Qui aime bien châtie bien. — *Spare the rod, spoil the child. (**He who** loves, punishes.)*

K. À compléter. Complétez les phrases suivantes avec les pronoms relatifs qui manquent. Parfois l'équivalent anglais sera donné pour vous aider.

1. —Avec qui comptes-tu parler? Avec Daniel ou Baudoin?
   —Peu importe. Avec ____________ (*the one who*) je trouverai à la fac.
2. Tu veux un peu de ____________ je mange?
3. ____________ s'est passé est merveilleux.
4. Je trouve bête ____________ (*everything that*) il dit.
5. Il s'est marié avec ____________ (*the one who*) il a connue l'été dernier.
6. Il faut cacher ____________ les enfants ont peur.
7. Nous n'avons pas accepté ____________ ils nous ont offert.
8. Il dit qu'il aura de bonnes notes, ____________ je doute.
9. Elle est très cultivée, ____________ nous plaît.
10. Je ne comprends pas ____________ vous allez étudier en Belgique.
11. On se demande ____________ a pu l'offenser.
12. Je te remercie de tout ____________ tu as fait pour moi.

L. Jacqueline est amoureuse. Jacqueline a un petit ami Luc, dont elle est amoureuse. Voici la lettre qu'elle écrit à son sujet à son amie Éliane. Complétez-la avec **ce qui, ce que** ou **ce dont.**

Ma chère Éliane:

Je te remercie de ta lettre. Luc et moi, on continue à sortir ensemble. Tu m'as demandé (1) ________ il fait. Il est étudiant en sciences. (2) ________ l'intéresse, c'est la chimie. Je comprends (3) ________ Luc étudie parce que je m'intéresse à la chimie aussi.

Je vais t'expliquer (4) ________ nous faisons quand nous sortons. Nous allons beaucoup au cinéma et au théâtre. (5) ________ nous attire, ce sont les films étrangers. Nous en voyons beaucoup. (6) ________ nous avons besoin est un bon magnétoscope pour pouvoir en regarder à la maison aussi. Tu comprends que Luc et moi, nous avons les mêmes goûts, (7) ________ est une bonne chose.

Je ne sais pas (8) ________ nous allons faire pendant l'été. Luc veut faire un stage dans une entreprise à Singapour, mais moi, je dois travailler ici. C'est-à-dire que nous ne nous verrons pas pendant deux mois, (9) ________ j'ai peur. Luc me rassure en disant que deux mois, ce n'est pas l'éternité, (10) ________ est vrai.

Bon, Éliane, écris-moi et dis-moi tout (11) ________ tu fais maintenant. Tu m'as écrit que tu penses changer de faculté, (12) ________ je me doutais. Je sais que tu trouves la médecine moins intéressante maintenant. Qu'est-ce que tu comptes faire, alors? Écris-moi dès que tu auras une petite minute de libre.

Je t'embrasse,

Jacqueline

M. Exercice d'ensemble. Joignez les deux phrases françaises en une seule au moyen d'un pronom relatif. Suivez le modèle.

MODÈLE J'ai écouté une cassette. Je vais te la prêter.
→ J'ai écouté une cassette que je vais te prêter.

À la recherche d'un nouvel emploi

1. Élisabeth a un poste. Elle veut en démissionner.
2. Il y a d'autres emplois. Elle essaie de se renseigner là-dessus.
3. Elle manque de qualifications. Nous ne pouvons pas nous en passer dans mon bureau.
4. Elle a téléphoné à d'autres entreprises. Je lui en ai donné le nom.
5. Il y a des cours d'orientation (*guidance*). Elle y assiste.
6. Il y a de nouveaux logiciels (*software*) pour le bureau. Élisabeth se familiarise avec eux.
7. Elle a déjà trouvé une entreprise. Elle voudrait travailler pour cette entreprise.

Mon petit déjeuner

8. Je vais te montrer les choses. J'ai besoin de ces choses pour préparer mon petit déjeuner.
9. Voilà le réchaud (*hot plate*). Je fais mon café sur ce réchaud.
10. Voici le bol. Je bois mon café du matin dans un bol.
11. Voilà la boulangerie. J'achète mes croissants et mon pain dans cette boulangerie.
12. Voilà la porte de la boutique. Il y a une enseigne (*sign*) au-dessus de la porte.

Note culturelle

- Le petit déjeuner typique des Français est très simple: du café et du pain avec du beurre ou de la confiture. Le café du matin ne se sert pas traditionnellement dans une tasse, mais dans un bol sans anse (*handle*). Le café du matin se boit en général sans lait, mais avec du sucre. Aujourd'hui, il y a beaucoup de Français (surtout les enfants) qui mangent des céréales le matin. L'influence américaine a fait de Kellogg's une marque assez connue en France.
- Le pain qu'on mange le matin est souvent le pain qui reste du jour antérieur et qu'on fait griller. Si on veut du pain frais, les boulangeries sont ouvertes très tôt, et on peut descendre acheter une baguette encore chaude pour prendre avec son café.
- Si l'on prend le petit déjeuner dans un café ou dans un hôtel, on trouvera pas seulement du pain mais aussi des croissants et des brioches avec le café du matin, et le café se boit le plus souvent dans une tasse.

N. Exercice d'ensemble. Exprimez les idées suivantes en français.

1. I understood everything that they said.

____

2. Those who came early found seats.

____

3. There's the station near which she works.

____

4. Here is the café in front of which I saw her.

____

5. This is a book without which I can't finish my work.

____

6. I don't see the park that we are going toward.

____

7. We went to the city where she works.

____

8. We met the teacher our friend had talked about.

____

9. What he remembers is a secret.

____

10. What he participates in is interesting.

____

CHAPTER 24

THE PRESENT SUBJUNCTIVE

A *Moods of verbs*

The mood of a verb indicates how the speaker views a statement. The indicative mood is used to express facts and describe reality. The imperative mood is used to express commands. And the subjunctive mood is used to express wishes, desires, necessities, emotions, opinions, doubts, suppositions, and other more subjective conditions.

Indicative mood

Nous faisons nos devoirs. — ***We do** our homework.*

Imperative mood

Faisons nos devoirs tout de suite! — ***Let's do** our homework right away!*

Subjunctive mood

Le professeur exige **que nous fassions** nos devoirs tous les soirs. — *The teacher demands **that we do** our homework every night.*

The subjunctive mood is used much more frequently in French than it is in English. It typically appears in dependent and relative clauses.

B *Forms of the present subjunctive*

- To form the present subjunctive of most verbs, drop the **-ons** ending from the present tense **nous** form and add the endings **-e, -es, -e, -ions, -iez, -ent.**

rentrer	finir	vendre
que je rentr**e**	que je finiss**e**	que je vend**e**
que tu rentr**es**	que tu finiss**es**	que tu vend**es**
qu'il/qu'elle rentr**e**	qu'il/qu'elle finiss**e**	qu'il/qu'elle vend**e**
que nous rentr**ions**	que nous finiss**ions**	que nous vend**ions**
que vous rentr**iez**	que vous finiss**iez**	que vous vend**iez**
qu'ils/qu'elles rentr**ent**	qu'ils/qu'elles finiss**ent**	qu'ils/qu'elles vend**ent**

- Regular **-er** verbs that have changes in the vowel in the present tense stem, such as **acheter** and **compléter,** have those changes in the subjunctive as well.

  que j'ach**è**te/que nous ach**e**tions
  que je compl**è**te/que nous compl**é**tions

- Most irregular verbs follow the same pattern as the regular verbs: the endings of the present subjunctive are added to the stem. Study the subjunctive of **lire, écrire,** and **joindre.**

lire	**écrire**	**joindre**
que je lis**e** que tu lis**es** qu'il/qu'elle lis**e**	que je écriv**e** que tu écriv**es** qu'il/qu'elle écriv**e**	que je joign**e** que tu joign**es** qu'il/qu'elle joign**e**
que nous lis**ions** que vous lis**iez** qu'ils/qu'elles lis**ent**	que nous écriv**ions** que vous écriv**iez** qu'ils/qu'elles écriv**ent**	que nous joign**ions** que vous joign**iez** qu'ils/qu'elles joign**ent**

- Irregular verbs such as **boire, venir,** and **prendre,** which have variations in the stem in the present indicative, show the same changes in the present subjunctive.

boire	**venir**	**prendre**
que je boiv**e** que tu boiv**es** qu'il/qu'elle boiv**e**	que je vienn**e** que tu vienn**es** qu'il/qu'elle vienn**e**	que je prenn**e** que tu prenn**es** qu'il/qu'elle prenn**e**
que nous buv**ions** que vous buv**iez** qu'ils/qu'elles boiv**ent**	que nous ven**ions** que vous ven**iez** qu'ils/qu'elles vienn**ent**	que nous pren**ions** que vous pren**iez** qu'ils/qu'elles prenn**ent**

- The verbs **aller, avoir, être, vouloir, faire, savoir,** and **pouvoir** are irregular in the subjunctive.

  Two stems:

aller	**avoir**
que j'**aille** que tu **ailles** qu'il/qu'elle **aille**	que j'**aie** que tu **aies** qu'il/qu'elle **ait**
que nous **allions** que vous **alliez** qu'ils/qu'elles **aillent**	que nous **ayons** que vous **ayez** qu'ils/qu'elles **aient**

être	**vouloir**
que je **sois** que tu **sois** qu'il/qu'elle **soit**	que je **veuille** que tu **veuilles** qu'il/qu'elle **veuille**
que nous **soyons** que vous **soyez** qu'ils/qu'elles **soient**	que nous **voulions** que vous **vouliez** qu'ils/qu'elles **veuillent**

One stem:

faire	**pouvoir**	**savoir**
que je **fasse** que tu **fasses** qu'il/qu'elle **fasse**	que je **puisse** que tu **puisses** qu'il/qu'elle **puisse**	que je **sache** que tu **saches** qu'il/qu'elle **sache**
que nous **fassions** que vous **fassiez** qu'ils/qu'elles **fassent**	que nous **puissions** que vous **puissiez** qu'ils/qu'elles **puissent**	que nous **sachions** que vous **sachiez** qu'ils/qu'elles **sachent**

The verb **valoir** is conjugated like **aller** in the present subjunctive: que **je vaille,** que **nous valions.**

C *Uses of the subjunctive: imposition of will, necessity, getting someone to do something*

- The subjunctive is used after verbs that express wanting, preferring, needing, making, or forcing someone to do something.

—**Je** ne **veux** pas **qu'il parte**.	*I don't **want him to leave**.*
—Alors **je vais empêcher qu'il s'en aille**.	*Then **I'll keep him from going away.***
—**J'exige que Baudoin soit** là.	***I demand that Baudoin be** here.*
—**Il faut que nous l'invitions**, alors.	***We must invite him** then.*
—**Je suggère que vous traduisiez** l'article.	***I suggest that you translate** the article.*
—**Il est nécessaire que vous** m'**aidiez**.	***It's necessary for you to help** me.*

- The following verbs are followed by the subjunctive:

aimer mieux que *to prefer*
attendre que *to wait until, wait for*
avoir besoin que *to need*
demander que *to request, ask*
désirer que *to desire, want, wish*
empêcher que *to prevent, keep*
exiger que *to demand*
ordonner que *to order*
permettre que *to allow*
préférer que *to prefer*
recommander que *to recommend*
souhaiter que *to wish*
suggérer que *to suggest*
vouloir que *to want*

- The following impersonal expressions signifying imposition of will are followed by the subjunctive.

il est nécessaire/urgent que *it is necessary/urgent*
il est essentiel/important que *it is essential/important*
il est indispensable/utile que *it is indispensable/useful*
il faut que *it is necessary, one has to*

- For the subjunctive to be used, the subjects of the main clause and the subordinate clause must be different. If the subjects of the two clauses are the same, the infinitive is used.

Je veux que **tu** reviennes.	***I** want **you** to come back.*
Je veux revenir.	***I** want to come back.*
Ils préfèrent que **nous** restions.	***They** prefer that **we** stay.*
Ils préfèrent rester.	***They** prefer to stay.*

A. Moi, je ne veux pas. Un ami vous dit ce que font les autres. Répondez-lui dans chaque cas que vous, vous ne voulez pas que les autres fassent ces choses. Employez le subjonctif dans la proposition subordonnée.

MODÈLE —Marie étudie huit heures par jour.
→ —Moi, je ne veux pas qu'elle étudie huit heures par jour.

1. Serge fait du japonais.
___
2. Élisabeth laisse les fenêtres ouvertes.
___
3. Richard sort avec Hélène.
___
4. Louis boit du vin.
___
5. Je vois un vieux film.
___
6. Michel sait ton adresse.
___
7. Chantal est triste.
___
8. Robert et Thérèse ont peur.
___
9. Daniel maigrit.
___
10. Moi, je grossis.
___

B. La surboum de samedi soir. C'est à vous d'organiser la surboum de samedi. Dites ce que chacun doit faire.

MODÈLE je veux/Marie/inviter ses cousins
→ Je veux que Marie invite ses cousins.

1. je préfère / Marc / choisir le gâteau
___
2. il est nécessaire / Lise et Rachelle / aller chercher les boissons
___
3. il est important / Roland et Jacqueline / pouvoir venir
___

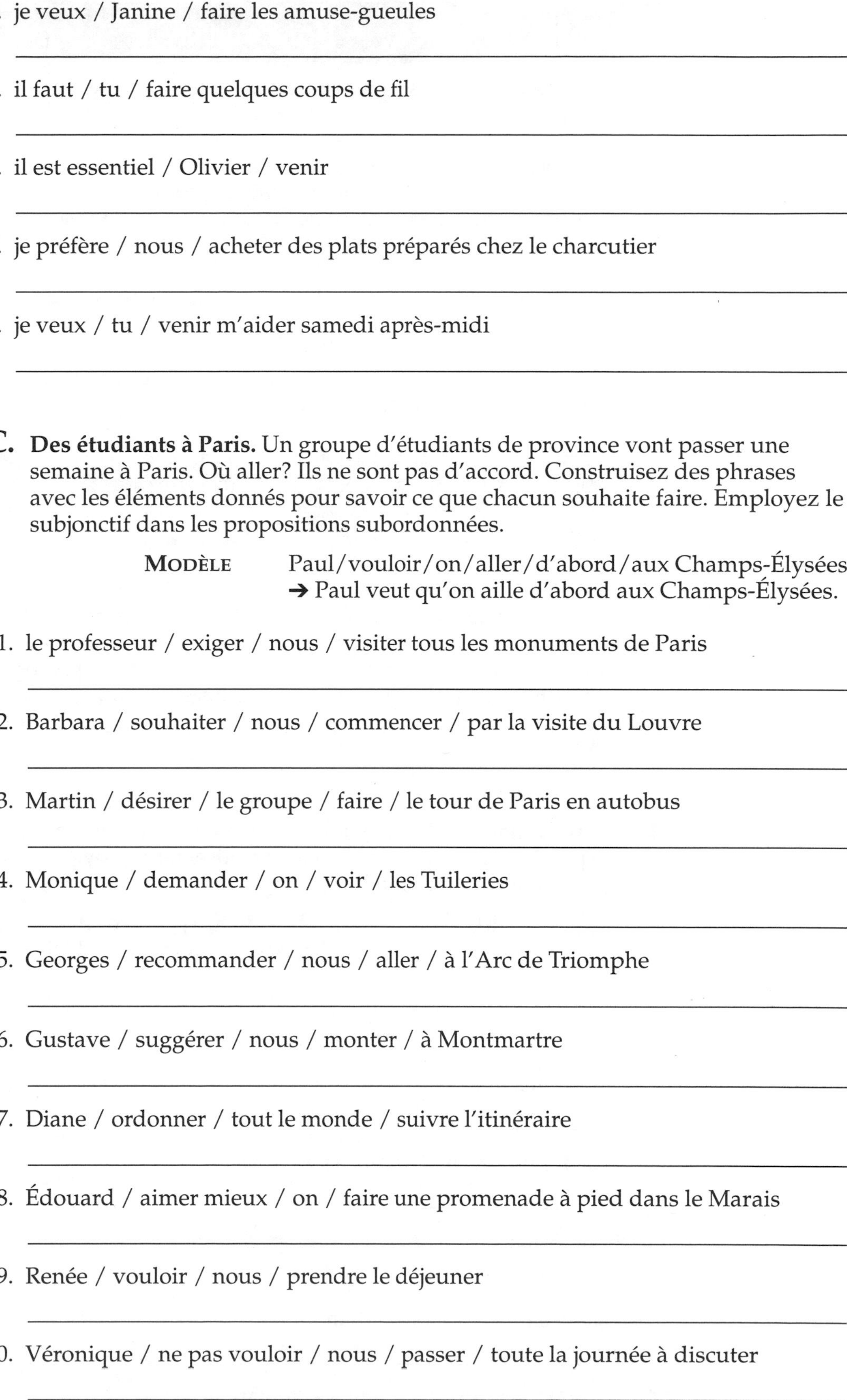

4. je veux / Janine / faire les amuse-gueules

____

5. il faut / tu / faire quelques coups de fil

____

6. il est essentiel / Olivier / venir

____

7. je préfère / nous / acheter des plats préparés chez le charcutier

____

8. je veux / tu / venir m'aider samedi après-midi

____

C. **Des étudiants à Paris.** Un groupe d'étudiants de province vont passer une semaine à Paris. Où aller? Ils ne sont pas d'accord. Construisez des phrases avec les éléments donnés pour savoir ce que chacun souhaite faire. Employez le subjonctif dans les propositions subordonnées.

MODÈLE Paul/vouloir/on/aller/d'abord/aux Champs-Élysées
➔ Paul veut qu'on aille d'abord aux Champs-Élysées.

1. le professeur / exiger / nous / visiter tous les monuments de Paris

____

2. Barbara / souhaiter / nous / commencer / par la visite du Louvre

____

3. Martin / désirer / le groupe / faire / le tour de Paris en autobus

____

4. Monique / demander / on / voir / les Tuileries

____

5. Georges / recommander / nous / aller / à l'Arc de Triomphe

____

6. Gustave / suggérer / nous / monter / à Montmartre

____

7. Diane / ordonner / tout le monde / suivre l'itinéraire

____

8. Édouard / aimer mieux / on / faire une promenade à pied dans le Marais

____

9. Renée / vouloir / nous / prendre le déjeuner

____

10. Véronique / ne pas vouloir / nous / passer / toute la journée à discuter

____

Note culturelle

- **Les Champs-Élysées:** Grande et belle avenue qui va de l'Arc de Triomphe à la place de la Concorde. Cette avenue imposante est un grand centre commercial.
- **Le Louvre:** Un des plus célèbres musées d'art du monde. À son origine un palais royal, le Louvre est devenu musée pendant la Révolution. Sa collection comprend plus de 6 000 tableaux et plus de 150 000 pièces de l'antiquité égyptienne, grecque et romaine.
- **Les Tuileries:** Aujourd'hui un jardin public, c'était le site d'un palais construit pour Catherine de Médicis, incendié en 1871 pendant la Guerre civile de la Commune.
- **L'Arc de Triomphe:** La construction de cet arc monumental a été initiée sous les ordres de Napoléon. Il commémore les victoires militaires de l'empereur.
- **Montmartre:** Quartier charmant situé sur la butte Montmartre dans le nord de la ville de Paris. C'est ici qu'on a construit la fameuse église blanche du Sacré-Cœur qui domine le panorama de Paris. Montmartre était pendant longtemps le quartier des artistes et est un des endroits que les touristes ne manquent jamais de visiter.
- **Le Marais:** Ce quartier de la rive droite au nord de l'île de la Cité doit son nom aux inondations dues aux crues de la Seine. Pendant le dix-septième siècle c'était le quartier où habitait la noblesse dans de petits palais splendides appelés **hôtels.** De nos jours, plusieurs des vieux hôtels ont été restaurés pour devenir les résidences des cadres et des hommes d'affaires. La nuit, l'illumination des hôtels rend ce quartier un des plus beaux et des plus intéressants de Paris.

D. Nos souhaits et désirs. Joignez les éléments donnés en une seule phrase qui exprime le désir que les actions se réalisent. Employez le subjonctif dans la proposition subordonnée.

MODÈLE Tu fais le linge. (j'ai besoin)
➔ J'ai besoin que tu fasses le linge.

1. Tout est en règle. (je désire)

____

2. Les enfants ont peur. (je ne veux pas)

____

3. Cette famille vit mal. (nous ne voulons pas)

____

4. Il boit trop de vin. (ses parents empêcheront)

____

5. Il sait les réponses. (je recommande)

____

6. Ils conduisent prudemment. (je demande)

____

7. Elle rejoint son fiancé. (ses parents aiment mieux)

____

8. Elle sort avec Jean-Philippe. (ses parents ne permettent pas)

____

E. Une lettre. Rozianne, qui habite Québec, écrit à son amie Isabelle, Parisienne. Pour savoir ce que Rozianne écrit dans sa lettre, complétez-en le texte avec la forme correcte des verbes entre parenthèses. Choisissez entre le subjonctif et l'indicatif.

Ma chère Isabelle,

J'espère que tu (1. aller) ____________ bien. Mes parents et moi, nous (2. être) ____________ en bonne santé. J'ai reçu ta lettre hier et je suis vraiment contente que tu puisses venir me voir pendant les vacances. Je préfère que tu (3. venir) ____________ au mois de juillet. Mes parents demandent que tes parents t' (4. accompagner) ____________. Je recommande que vous (5. prendre) ____________ les billets d'avion aussitôt que possible. Je suggère aussi que vous (6. mettre) ____________ quelques pulls dans les valises. À Québec il fait souvent frais le soir, même en été. Je voudrais que nous (7. aller) ____________ tous aux Laurentides et que nous (8. visiter) ____________ ensemble la vieille ville. Mes parents et moi, nous désirons (9. passer) ____________ un mois merveilleux au Canada.

Amitiés,

Rozianne

Note culturelle

- C'est l'explorateur Jacques Cartier qui a découvert Terre-Neuve et qui a remonté le fleuve Saint-Laurent. Il prend possession du Canada pour la France en 1536. La colonisation française commence en 1605. La ville de Québec est fondée par Samuel de Champlain en 1608. Montréal est fondée en 1642.

- Le Québec s'appelle au début la Nouvelle-France, nom qu'elle gardera jusqu'à la défaite française de la guerre de Sept Ans en 1763 quand la France cède le Canada à l'Angleterre.

- Les Laurentides sont des montagnes célèbres pour leurs stations de ski et leurs jolis paysages.

- Aujourd'hui, le Canada est officiellement un pays bilingue. L'anglais et le français sont les deux langues officielles. Le quart de la population est francophone, concentrée au Québec et dans le Nouveau-Brunswick. De nos jours, un mouvement sécessionniste domine la politique au Québec. En 1995, un référendum sur l'indépendance du Québec a préservé l'unité du Canada, mais par très peu de voix.

F. À vous de vous exprimer sur l'avenir de votre école. Quels changements sont nécessaires pour améliorer votre école? Exprimez-les dans des termes de désirs ou souhaits. Utilisez le vocabulaire donné ou ajoutez d'autres idées qui reflètent la réalité de votre école. Exprimez ces changements souhaités comme des désirs à vous ou comme la volonté de vos amis.

MODÈLES Je veux (voudrais) qu'il y ait moins d'élèves dans chaque classe.
Les étudiants demandent qu'on améliore la qualité des sandwichs qu'on sert à la cantine.
Mes amis souhaitent qu'on offre des cours d'informatique.

Pour améliorer (*improve*) l'école

acheter des ordinateurs dotés de lecteurs de CD-ROM *to buy computers with CD-ROM drives*
aménager le terrain de sports *to fix up the playing field*
donner des bourses d'études à tous les étudiants *to give all students scholarships*
embaucher de nouveaux professeurs *to hire new teachers*
faciliter l'accès à la bibliothèque *to make it easier to use the library*
inaugurer un festival de cinéma *to start a film festival*
offrir des cours du soir *to offer evening classes*
renforcer le programme d'orientation *to strengthen the guidance program*
servir de bons desserts à la cantine *to serve good desserts in the cafeteria*
trouver des stages pour les étudiants *to find internships for students*

1. ______________________________
2. ______________________________
3. ______________________________
4. ______________________________
5. ______________________________
6. ______________________________
7. ______________________________
8. ______________________________
9. ______________________________
10. ______________________________

D *Uses of the subjunctive: emotion and opinion*

- The subjunctive is used following verbs and impersonal expressions that express emotion.

Fear

avoir peur que *to be afraid that*
craindre que *to fear that*

Surprise or curiosity

s'étonner que *to be surprised that*
cela m'étonne que *I'm surprised that*
il est étonnant que *it's surprising that*
il est bizarre/curieux/extraordinaire que *it's strange/strange/extraordinary that*

Happiness and sadness

être content(e)/heureux(-se)/triste que *to be happy/happy/sad that*
être ravi(e)/satisfait(e)/désolé(e) que *to be delighted/satisfied/sorry that*
regretter que *to be sorry that*
se réjouir que *to rejoice, be glad that*

Annoyance

cela m'ennuie/m'agace/m'énerve que *it annoys me that*
se plaindre que *to complain that*
se fâcher que *to get angry that, because*
être fâché(e)/furieux(-se) que *to be angry/furious that*
avoir honte que *to be ashamed that*
il est ennuyeux/agaçant/énervant que *it's annoying/irritating that*

—**Le chef est ravi que vous puissiez** l'aider.	***The boss is delighted that you can*** *help him.*
—**Je suis heureux qu'il ait** confiance en moi.	***I'm happy that he has confidence*** *in me.*
—**Je m'étonne que le travail ne soit pas** fini.	***I'm surprised that the work is not*** *finished.*
—**Cela m'ennuie qu'il** nous **fasse** attendre.	***I'm annoyed that he's keeping*** *us waiting.*

- The subjunctive is used after verbs and impersonal expressions that show that the action of the subordinate clause is an opinion, an evaluation, or a possibility.

Evaluation and opinion

accepter que *to accept that*
approuver que *to approve of someone's doing something*
désapprouver que *to disapprove of someone's doing something*
il convient que *it is suitable, advisable*
il importe que *it matters that, is important that*
peu importe que *it matters little that*
il suffit que *it is enough*
il vaut mieux que *it is better that*
il est logique/normal/naturel/juste que *it's logical/normal/natural/right that*
c'est une chance que *it's lucky that*
ce n'est pas la peine que *it's not worth it that*
il est rare que *it is not often that*

Possibility

il se peut que *it's possible that*
il est possible/impossible que *it's possible/impossible that*
il n'y a aucune chance que *there's no chance that*
il n'y a pas de danger que *there's no danger that*

G. C'est bien. On raconte à Marcelle tout ce qu'il y a de neuf. Dans chaque cas elle exprime sa satisfaction en disant qu'elle est contente de ce qui arrive. Écrivez ce que dit Marcelle en employant le subjonctif dans la proposition subordonnée.

MODÈLE —Pierre ne travaille pas aujourd'hui.
➔ —Je suis contente qu'il ne travaille pas aujourd'hui.

1. Marianne et Justine sont là.
____
2. Gérard vend sa bicyclette.
____
3. Mes parents partent en vacances.
____
4. Jean-Claude nous attend.
____
5. Le petit Charles ne désobéit jamais.
____
6. Christine et moi, nous dînons ensemble.
____
7. Toi et moi, nous complétons le programme cette année.
____
8. Frédéric connaît Odile.
____

H. En une seule phrase, s'il vous plaît. Changez l'ordre des deux phrases données pour en faire une seule. Faites les modifications nécessaires.

MODÈLES Il n'est pas encore là. C'est étonnant.
➔ Il est étonnant qu'il ne soit pas encore là.

Je maigris. Le médecin se réjouit.
➔ Le médecin se réjouit que je maigrisse.

1. Tu comprends tout. Je suis ravi.
____
2. Ils ne veulent pas nous aider. Nous sommes furieux.
____
3. Le prof ne nous reconnaît pas. Cela m'étonne.
____
4. Il y a eu un accident. J'ai peur.
____
5. Tu ne peux pas venir. Elle est désolée.
____

6. Elle met le foulard que je lui ai offert. Je suis content.

7. Philippe n'apprend pas beaucoup. Son professeur se plaint.

8. Ces enfants se battent tout le temps. Je suis fâché.

9. Un professeur perd son travail. C'est rare.

10. Vous me le dites. Cela suffit.

11. Il ne s'aperçoit pas du problème. Nous craignons.

12. Elle sait conduire un camion. C'est extraordinaire.

I. Vos réactions, s'il vous plaît! Voici une liste de faits et d'événements. Exprimez votre opinion ou votre réaction dans chaque cas. Commencez par un des verbes ou une des expressions de cette section.

MODÈLE La bibliothèque est fermée le dimanche.
→ Je désapprouve que/Cela m'ennuie que/Je suis fâché(e) que la bibliothèque soit fermée le dimanche.

1. On augmente les prix à la cantine.

2. Le latin et le grec sont obligatoires.

3. On ne peut pas passer le permis de conduire à quatorze ans.

4. On interdit l'emploi des gros mots (*vulgar words*) dans les chansons de rock.

5. On abolit la peine de mort.

6. Les professeurs font grève demain.

7. Mon ami Serge perd toujours ses affaires.

8. Le port de la cravate est obligatoire à l'école.

9. Le professeur d'anglais n'écrit jamais rien au tableau.

____

10. Nous lisons trois cents pages par semaine pour le cours d'histoire.

____

J. **Quel fouillis! Et voilà maman qui arrive!** Vous habitez un appartement avec trois camarades de chambre. Cette fin de semaine les parents viennent voir leurs enfants à l'université. Vous êtes contents de voir vos parents, mais l'état de l'appartement vous inquiète un peu. L'appartement est une vraie porcherie (*pigsty*)! Pour décrire la situation, joignez les verbes et les expressions entre parenthèses aux phrases.

MODÈLE Nos parents viennent nous rendre visite. (nous sommes contents)
→ Nous sommes contents que nos parents viennent nous rendre visite.

Pour une demeure propre

balayer le parquet *to sweep the floor*
la bibliothèque *bookcase*
cirer le parquet *to wax the floor*
épousseter les meubles (j'époussette) *to dust the furniture*
faire le ménage *to do the housework*
le fouillis *mess*
ranger *to put away*
récurer les casseroles *to scour the pots*
la toile d'araignée *spiderweb, cobweb*

1. Je vis dans le désordre. (ma mère n'acceptera pas)

____

2. Nous faisons le ménage. (il est essentiel)

____

3. Nous époussetons les meubles. (il faut que)

____

4. Bernard et toi, vous récurez les casseroles. (je suis content[e])

____

5. Toi et moi, nous balayons le parquet. (il convient que)

____

6. Nous cirons le parquet aussi. (il est possible)

____

7. Lise et Émile, vous rangez les livres dans les bibliothèques. (il vaut mieux)

____

8. Philomène enlève les toiles d'araignée. (je me réjouis)

____

K. **La flemme (*laziness*) de fin de cours.** C'est le mois de juin et tout le monde a la flemme, sauf vous. Vous essayez de remonter leur morale (*buck them up, get them going again*) en leur conseillant de travailler avec un peu de diligence. Employez le subjonctif dans l'expression de vos conseils.

Modèle Charles: Je ne veux pas assister au cours de chimie aujourd'hui. (il est important)
➔ Vous: Écoute, Charles. Il est important que tu y assistes.

1. Annette: Je n'étudie pas pour les examens. (il est bizarre)

 ____

2. Michel: Je n'ai aucune envie de travailler à la bibliothèque. (ça m'étonne)

 ____

3. Françoise: Je n'écris pas la dissertation de philosophie. (il vaut mieux que)

 ____

4. André: Je n'écoute pas les cassettes au laboratoire de langues. (il est utile)

 ____

5. Sylvie: Je ne prends plus de notes dans la classe d'histoire. (il est indispensable)

 ____

6. Albert: Je ne fais pas mes devoirs. (les profs seront fâchés)

 ____

7. Catherine: Je ne lis plus le livre de biologie. (je regrette)

 ____

8. Corine: Je m'endors dans la classe d'anglais. (je n'approuve pas)

 ____

9. Sébastien: Je fais des dessins dans mon cahier dans la classe de maths. (il n'est pas normal)

 ____

10. Bruno: Je perds mes cahiers. (il est agaçant)

 ____

E *Uses of the subjunctive: negation of fact and opinion*

- The subjunctive is used after verbs that negate the action or idea of the subordinate clause. Such verbs and impersonal expressions include:

nier *to deny*
douter *to doubt*
il est douteux que *it is doubtful that*
il est exclu que *it's out of the question that*

—**Je doute qu'il sache** le faire.	***I doubt that he knows how** to do it.*
—**Mais il n'est pas exclu qu'il puisse** nous aider.	***But it isn't out of the question that he can** help us.*

Note: The indicative is usually used after the *negative* of **nier** and **douter**, since when those verbs are used in the negative, they no longer negate facts: **Je ne doute pas qu'il sait le faire.**

- When the following verbs and expressions are negative, they are followed by the subjunctive. When they are affirmative, they are followed by the indicative.

il n'est pas certain que *it's not certain that*
il n'est pas sûr que *it's not sure that*
il n'est pas évident que *it's not evident that*
il n'est pas clair que *it's not clear that*
il n'est pas exact que *it's not correct, accurate that*
il n'est pas vrai que *it's not true that*
il est peu probable que *it's not probable that*
il ne paraît pas que *it doesn't seem that*
je ne suis pas sûr(e) que *I'm not sure that*
je ne dis pas que *I'm not saying that*
ça ne veut pas dire que *it doesn't mean that*
ce n'est pas que *it's not that*

—**Il n'est pas certain qu'il vienne.**	***It's not certain that he's coming.***
—**Ça ne veut pas dire qu'il ne veuille pas** nous voir.	***That doesn't mean that he doesn't want*** *to see us.*
—**Il n'est pas évident qu'elle sache** la réponse.	***It is not evident that she knows*** *the answer.*
—Moi, **je suis sûr qu'elle** la **sait.**	***I'm sure that she knows*** *it.*

- The verbs **penser, croire,** and **espérer** are followed by the indicative when affirmative, but by the subjunctive when negative or interrogative.

—**Je ne crois pas que cet étranger** te **comprenne.**	***I don't think that that foreigner understands*** *you.*
—**Penses-tu que je doive** tout répéter?	***Do you think that I ought to*** *repeat everything?*
—**Oui, je crois que c'est** nécessaire.	***Yes, I think it's*** *necessary.*

- The indicative may be used after the negative and interrogative of **penser** and **croire** instead of the subjunctive to convey that the speaker is certain about the action. Compare:

Je ne crois pas que tu as raison.	***I don't think you're right.*** *(I think you're wrong.)*
Je ne crois pas que tu aies raison.	***I don't think you're right.*** *(But I'm not sure.)*

L. Conversation. Pierrette et Joceline causent ensemble. Pierrette demande à son amie si elle sait ce que leurs amis vont faire. Joceline répond dans chaque cas qu'elle ne croit pas que leurs amis comptent faire tout ça. Reconstruisez leur conversation en employant le subjonctif dans la proposition subordonnée de la réponse de Joceline.

MODÈLE Stéphane/arriver aujourd'hui.
→ Pierrette: Tu sais si Stéphane arrivera aujourd'hui?
Joceline: Je ne crois pas qu'il arrive aujourd'hui.

1. notre professeur / finir la leçon

Pierrette: ______________________________

Joceline: ______________________________

2. Ghislaine / rompre avec son petit ami

Pierrette: ______________________________

Joceline: ______________________________

3. ton cousin / revenir cette semaine

Pierrette: ______________________________

Joceline: ______________________________

4. Nadine / servir de la pizza à la surboum

Pierrette: ______________________________

Joceline: ______________________________

5. Philippe / sortir avec Mireille

Pierrette: ______________________________

Joceline: ______________________________

6. Paul / pouvoir nous rejoindre

Pierrette: ______________________________

Joceline: ______________________________

7. Alice / être ici ce soir

Pierrette: ______________________________

Joceline: ______________________________

8. toi et moi / étudier assez

Pierrette: ______________________________

Joceline: ______________________________

9. Chloë / aller au concert

Pierrette: ______________________________

Joceline: ______________________________

10. Daniel / prendre un taxi

Pierrette: ______________________________

Joceline: ______________________________

M. **Exprimez vos doutes.** Utilisez les expressions données entre parenthèses pour exprimer vos doutes sur les faits suivants.

MODÈLE Nous avons un examen aujourd'hui. (je ne crois pas)
➔ Je ne crois pas que nous ayons un examen aujourd'hui.

1. Laurence réussit à tous ses examens. (il n'est pas clair)

____

2. Nous offrons des disques compacts à Renée. (il est douteux)

____

3. Tu suis un cours d'histoire. (il n'est pas exclu)

____

4. Il fait des progrès en anglais. (ça ne veut pas dire)

____

5. Lucette t'écrit. (il est peu probable)

____

6. Il nous connaît. (je ne suis pas sûr)

____

7. L'élève apprend tout ça. (je doute)

____

8. Elle descend faire les courses. (je ne crois pas)

____

9. Son père vit très mal. (il nie)

____

10. Ce pays produit des voitures. (il ne paraît pas)

____

N. Au sujet des amis. Deux étudiants parlent de leurs amis au lycée. Ils confirment et nient ce qu'on dit à leur sujet. Écrivez ce qu'ils disent en joignant les deux phrases données en une seule. Choisissez entre l'indicatif et le subjonctif dans les subordonnées.

MODÈLE Marcelle suit un cours de maths. (je crois)
➔ Je crois que Marcelle suit un cours de maths.

1. La voiture de Jean-François est toujours en panne. (je ne pense pas)

____

2. Gisèle compte abandonner le lycée. (il est évident)

____

3. Marc et Luc peuvent s'acheter un ordinateur. (je doute)

____

4. Michèle sort avec Hervé Duclos. (tout le monde sait)

____

5. Paul ne fait pas attention en classe. (son frère nie)

____

6. Chantal se plaint de tout. (il n'est pas exact)

____

7. Martin étudie beaucoup. (je suis sûr que)

____

8. Éliane va en France cette année. (il est peu probable)

____

F Uses of the subjunctive: special cases

- After expressions of fear, after **empêcher que,** and after the interrogative of **douter,** the word **ne** may be placed before the verb in the subjunctive. This **ne** does not make the verb negative, but rather makes the style more formal. This **ne** is omitted in informal speech and writing.

J'ai peur qu'il **ne** comprenne.	***I'm afraid** he understands.*
J'ai empêché qu'il **ne** sorte.	***I kept him from** going out.*
Doutez-vous que ce livre **ne** soit utile?	***Do you doubt that** this book is useful?*

- The subjunctive can be used to express an indirect command for third-person subjects. The English equivalent is *have* or *let him/her/them do something.*

—Suzanne a besoin de nous parler.	*Suzanne needs to speak to us.*
—**Qu'elle vienne** nous voir, alors.	***Let her come** see us then.*
—Monsieur, l'avocat est arrivé.	*Sir, the lawyer is here.*
—Je descends tout de suite. **Qu'il attende** dans mon bureau.	*I'm coming right down.* ***Have him wait*** *in my office.*
—Les étudiants ne comprennent pas vos conférences, monsieur.	*The students don't understand your lectures, sir.*
—**Qu'ils fassent** attention.	***Let them pay** attention.*

O. **Le style soutenu.** Refaites les phrases suivantes dans le style soutenu en ajoutant le **ne** explétif.

1. J'ai peur que vous preniez un rhume.

____

2. Elle craint que nous soyons en colère.

____

3. Doutez-vous qu'il soit d'accord?

____

4. Elle empêche que nous finissions notre travail.

____

P. **C'est aux autres de le faire!** Employez **que** suivi du subjonctif pour donner des ordres à une troisième personne. Remplacez les compléments directs et indirects par les pronoms convenables.

MODÈLE —Marc veut suivre le cours de philosophie.
→ —Qu'il le suive alors.

1. Marianne et Lisette veulent apprendre le japonais.

____

2. Serge veut rejoindre ses amis.

____

3. Simone doit faire son linge.

4. Alexandre doit prendre le train.

5. Les Durand veulent vendre leur voiture.

6. Monique peut nous rendre l'argent.

7. Christian veut traduire le poème.

8. Stéphane doit finir le travail.

Q. En français, s'il vous plaît! Traduisez ces phrases en français. Faites attention à l'emploi du subjonctif.

1. We want you (**tu**) to come.

2. Let him phone me if he wants to speak to me.

3. The mother allows the children to go down(stairs) alone.

4. I need you (**vous**) to help me.

5. I'm afraid the child has fever.

6. It's surprising that this country produces so many trucks.

7. It's improbable that the weather will be nice.

8. It's not true that she's a doctor. I'm sure that she's a lawyer.

R. Exercice oral. Impressions et réactions. Avec un(e) camarade, parlez de ce qui vous surprend à l'école, de ce qui vous rend heureux(-se) ou triste, de ce qui vous paraît bizarre, des changements que vous voudriez voir. Parlez aussi de vos craintes et doutes. Employez le subjonctif autant que possible.

CHAPTER 25 THE PAST SUBJUNCTIVE; LITERARY SUBJUNCTIVES*

A Forms and use of the past subjunctive

- The past subjunctive is composed of the subjunctive of the auxiliary verb (**avoir** or **être**) plus the past participle. The same rules of agreement apply as in the passé composé.

Verbs conjugated with **avoir**	Verbs conjugated with **être**
que j'**aie parlé, fini, perdu** que tu **aies parlé, fini, perdu** qu'il/qu'elle **ait parlé, fini, perdu**	que je **sois parti(e)** que tu **sois parti(e)** qu'il **soit parti** qu'elle **soit partie**
que nous **ayons parlé, fini, perdu** que vous **ayez parlé, fini, perdu** qu'ils/qu'elles **aient parlé, fini, perdu**	que nous **soyons parti(e)s** que vous **soyez parti(e)(s)** qu'ils **soient partis** qu'elles **soient parties**

- The past subjunctive is used to indicate that the action of the subordinate clause happened before the action of the main clause. Compare the following pairs of sentences:

Je suis désolé **que tu perdes.**	*I'm sorry **that you're losing.***
Je suis désolé **que tu aies perdu.**	*I'm sorry **that you lost.***
Tu crains **qu'elle ne** te **comprenne pas.**	*You fear that **she won't understand you.***
Tu crains **qu'elle ne** t'**ait pas compris.**	*You fear that **she didn't understand you.***
Il est content **que nous venions.**	*He's happy **that we're coming.***
Il est content **que nous soyons venus.**	*He's happy **that we've come.***

A. Les sentiments. Claudine est en train de vivre un moment difficile. Elle exprime ses sentiments dans cette situation. Écrivez ce qu'elle dit en formant une seule phrase avec les éléments donnés. Employez le passé du subjonctif dans les propositions subordonnées.

MODÈLE Mon petit ami Jacques est tombé malade. (je suis désolée)
→ Je suis désolée que mon petit ami Jacques soit tombé malade.

*For recognition only.

1. a. Il a pris une bronchite. (je crains)

   b. Il est allé voir le médecin. (je doute)

2. a. Ma sœur a reçu une mauvaise note en français. (j'ai peur)

   b. Elle a étudié pour l'examen. (je ne crois pas)

   c. Elle a eu des ennuis avec son petit ami. (je soupçonne)

   d. Elle ne nous a pas montré son examen. (je n'approuve pas)

   e. Sylvie ne nous en a pas parlé. (ma mère se plaint)

3. a. Mon père a perdu son emploi. (je suis étonnée)

   b. Il en a trouvé un autre. (il est possible)

   c. Il l'a déjà accepté. (il est peu probable)

4. a. Le prof d'histoire nous a demandé une dissertation de 15 pages. (je suis furieuse)

   b. Il ne nous en a pas demandé deux! (c'est une chance que)

B. Au passé! Refaites les échanges suivants en changeant le verbe de la proposition subordonnée au passé du subjonctif. Ensuite, traduisez vos nouvelles phrases en anglais.

Modèle —Je suis content que tu reviennes.
—Et moi, je suis contente que tu m'attendes.
➔ —Je suis content que tu sois revenue.
—Et moi, je suis contente que tu m'aies attendue.
I'm happy that you came back (that you've come back).
And I'm happy that you waited for me.

1. —Le prof est content que Jacquot réponde.
   —Ça ne veut pas dire qu'il comprenne.

   —

   —

2. —Je suis ravi qu'elle puisse venir.
—Mais il est agaçant que son mari ne vienne pas avec elle.

3. —Colette se réjouit que son chef ait confiance en elle.
—Il faut qu'elle soit très capable.

4. —Ma mère regrette que ma sœur ne mette pas son nouveau pull.
—Il est curieux que ce pull ne plaise pas à ta sœur.

5. —Je suis surpris qu'Irène ne m'attende pas.
—Ça ne veut pas dire qu'elle sorte.

C. Contrastes. Traduisez ces paires de phrases en français en faisant attention à l'emploi du présent et du passé du subjonctif.

1. a. I'm happy that they're leaving.

   b. I'm happy that they left.

2. a. It's not that she's going out.

   b. It's not that she went out.

3. a. I'm not sure that she's taking a course.

   b. I'm not sure that she took a course.

4. a. I don't think the boy is reading the book.

   ____

   b. I don't think the boy read the book.

   ____

5. a. It's improbable that they're on vacation.

   ____

   b. It's improbable that they were on vacation.

   ____

6. a. We're surprised that the children don't fight (**se battre**).

   ____

   b. We're surprised that the children didn't fight.

   ____

B *Forms and use of the imperfect subjunctive*

- The imperfect subjunctive is a literary form, reserved for formal writing. It is formed by adding the following endings to the stem of **-er** verbs: **-asse, -asses, -ât, -assions, -assiez, -assent.**
- For **-ir** and **-re** verbs and for irregular verbs, the endings of the imperfect subjunctive are added to the **passé simple** form minus the consonants of the ending. The circumflexes of the **nous** and **vous** forms are dropped. The imperfect subjunctive endings for this group of verbs is **-sse, -sses, -^t, -ssions, -ssiez, -ssent.**

parler	finir	vendre
que je **parlasse** que tu **parlasses** qu'il/qu'elle **parlât**	que je **finisse** que tu **finisses** qu'il/qu'elle **finît**	que je **vendisse** que tu **vendisses** qu'il/qu'elle **vendît**
que nous **parlassions** que vous **parlassiez** qu'ils/qu'elles **parlassent**	que nous **finissions** que vous **finissiez** qu'ils/qu'elles **finissent**	que nous **vendissions** que vous **vendissiez** qu'ils/qu'elles **vendissent**

Note: Verbs such as **commencer** and **manger** have their spelling changes in all persons of the imperfect subjunctive: **que je commençasse, que je mangeasse.**

- Study the imperfect subjunctive forms of **avoir, être, faire,** and **venir.**

avoir	être
que j'**eusse** que tu **eusses** qu'il/qu'elle **eût**	que je **fusse** que tu **fusses** qu'il/qu'elle **fût**
que nous **eussions** que vous **eussiez** qu'ils/qu'elles **eussent**	que nous **fussions** que vous **fussiez** qu'ils/qu'elles **fussent**

faire	venir
que je **fisse** que tu **fisses** qu'il/qu'elle **fît**	que je **vinsse** que tu **vinsses** qu'il/qu'elle **vînt**
que nous **fissions** que vous **fissiez** qu'ils/qu'elles **fissent**	que nous **vinssions** que vous **vinssiez** qu'ils/qu'elles **vinssent**

- In formal written French the imperfect subjunctive is used in a subordinate clause when the subjunctive is required and the main verb is in a past tense.

Everyday French	**Formal French**
Je veux **qu'il vienne**. Je voulais **qu'il vienne**.	Je veux **qu'il vienne**. Je voulais **qu'il vînt**.
Je ne crois pas **qu'il puisse** le faire. Je ne croyais pas **qu'il puisse** le faire.	Je ne crois pas **qu'il puisse** le faire. Je ne croyais pas **qu'il pût** le faire.
Il faut **qu'il réponde**. Il a fallu **qu'il réponde**.	Il faut **qu'il réponde**. Il a fallu **qu'il répondît**.

- An inverted third person singular imperfect subjunctive (especially of **être**) often means *even if*. This construction is commonly used for stylistic effect in newspaper writing.

Il ne pourrait pas agir seul, **fût-il** le président. — *He couldn't act alone, **even if he were** the president.*

Elle rêvait d'être à Paris, ne **fût-ce** que pour deux ou trois jours. — *She dreamed of being in Paris, **even if it were** only for two or three days.*

In everyday French the above sentences would be:

Il ne pourrait pas agir seul, **même s'il était** le président.

Elle rêvait d'être à Paris, **même si ce n'était que** pour deux ou trois jours.

D. Dans le style de tous les jours. Refaites ces phrases en français courant en éliminant l'imparfait du subjonctif.

MODÈLE Je n'ai pas voulu qu'il vous parlât.
➔ Je n'ai pas voulu qu'il vous parle.

1. Je tenais à ce qu'il finît son travail.

____

2. Il n'y a eu aucune chance qu'elle comprît.

____

3. J'avais peur que l'enfant ne tombât.

____

4. Il valait mieux que le chef lût le compte rendu.

____

5. Il fallait travailler tous les jours, fût-ce un jour de fête.

____

C Forms and use of the pluperfect subjunctive

- The pluperfect subjunctive consists of the imperfect subjunctive of the auxiliary verb (**avoir** or **être**) plus the past participle.

Verbs conjugated with **avoir**	Verbs conjugated with **être**
que j'**eusse parlé, fini, perdu** que tu **eusses parlé, fini, perdu** qu'il/qu'elle **eût parlé, fini, perdu**	que je **fusse parti(e)** que tu **fusses parti(e)** qu'il **fût parti** qu'elle **fût partie**
que nous **eussions parlé, fini, perdu** que vous **eussiez parlé, fini, perdu** qu'ils/qu'elles **eussent parlé, fini, perdu**	que nous **fussions parti(e)s** que vous **fussiez parti(e)(s)** qu'ils **fussent partis** qu'elles **fussent parties**

- The pluperfect subjunctive is used to indicate that the action of the subordinate clause happened before the action of the main clause when the verb of the main clause is in the past. Compare the following pairs of sentences in formal language.

J'étais heureux **qu'il fût** là. — *I was happy **that he was there**.*
J'étais heureux **qu'il eût été** là. — *I was happy **that he had been** there.*

On ne croyait pas **qu'il partît**. — *We didn't think **he was leaving**.*
On ne croyait pas **qu'il fût parti**. — *We didn't think **he had left**.*

Those same sentences in less formal French are:

J'étais heureux **qu'il soit** là.
J'étais heureux **qu'il ait été** là.

On ne croyait pas **qu'il parte**.
On ne croyait pas **qu'il soit parti**.

- The pluperfect subjunctive can also replace the pluperfect and the conditional perfect in both parts of a conditional sentence.

S'**il** me l'**eût dit, j'eusse compris**. — *If **he had told** me, **I would have understood**.*

S'**il fût venu, nous eussions parlé**. — *If **he had come, we would have talked**.*

Those same sentences in less formal French are:

S'**il** me l'**avait dit, j'aurais compris**.

S'**il était venu, nous aurions parlé**.

As in the case of the imperfect subjunctive, you need only recognize the forms of the pluperfect subjunctive.

E. À refaire en français moderne. Voici des phrases littéraires, d'un style très surveillé. Refaites-les dans la langue courante.

MODÈLES Je ne pensais pas qu'il fût revenu.
→ Je ne pensais pas qu'il soit revenue.

Si vous eussiez vécu en Chine pendant la guerre, vous eussiez beaucoup souffert.
→ Si vous aviez vécu en Chine pendant la guerre, vous auriez beaucoup souffert.

1. Si la France eût modernisé son armée, elle n'eût pas perdu la Deuxième Guerre mondiale.

____

2. Si cet écrivain ne fût pas mort à l'âge de 30 ans, il eût été un des grands romanciers de notre littérature.

____

3. Si les étrangers eussent parlé en français, nous eussions compris.

____

4. Si la ligne aérienne n'eût pas fait grève, ils fussent partis en vacances.

____

5. Si les soldats se fussent approchés de cette maison, ils eussent été tués.

____

CHAPTER 26

THE SUBJUNCTIVE (CONTINUED)

The subjunctive after certain conjunctions

- The subjunctive is used after the following conjunctions:

pour que *so that, in order that*
afin que *so that, in order that (formal)*
de façon que *so that, in order that*
bien que/quoique *although*
encore que *although (literary)*
sans que *without*
avant que *before*
jusqu'à ce que *until*
en attendant que *until*
de peur que/de crainte que *for fear that*
à moins que *unless*
pourvu que *provided that, as long as*
à condition que *on the condition that, provided that*
malgré que *in spite of the fact that*

—Partons **sans que personne ne s'en rende compte.**	*Let's leave* ***without anyone's realizing****.*
—Alors, parlons tout bas **pour qu'on ne nous entende pas**.	*Then let's speak very softly* ***so that people don't hear us.***
—Il faut continuer à travailler **bien qu'il fasse chaud.**	*It's necessary to continue working* ***although it's hot.***
—Je vais t'aider **pour que tu puisses** finir.	*I'll help you* ***so that you can*** *finish.*
—Allons-nous-en **avant que Paul revienne**.	*Let's go away* ***before Paul comes back****.*
—Je préfère rester **jusqu'à ce qu'il vienne**.	*I prefer to stay* ***until he comes****.*
—J'irai **pourvu que vous puissiez** m'accompagner.	*I'll go* ***as long as you can*** *accompany me.*
—D'accord. Je vais chercher mon parapluie **de peur qu'il pleuve**.	*OK. I'll go get my umbrella* ***for fear that it may rain.***

In formal style **ne** may precede the subjunctive after **avant que, de peur que, de crainte que,** and **à moins que.**

Allons-nous-en **avant que** Paul **ne** revienne.	*Let's go* ***before*** *Paul comes back.*
Je vais chercher mon parapluie **de peur qu'**il **ne** pleuve.	*I'm going to look for my umbrella* ***in case*** *it rains. (Literally:* ***for fear that*** *it will rain)*
Il viendra **à moins qu'**il **ne** soit malade.	*He'll come* ***unless*** *he's sick.*

- An infinitive construction replaces the subjunctive if the subject of both clauses is the same.

J'écris l'adresse **pour que tu ne l'oublies pas.**	*I'll write down the address* ***so that you won't forget it.***
J'écris l'adresse **pour ne pas l'oublier.**	*I'll write down the address* ***so that I won't forget it.***

Il mangera **avant que nous partions.**	*He'll eat **before we leave.***
Il mangera **avant de partir.**	*He'll eat **before he leaves.***

A. Jusqu'à quand? Un groupe de garçons attendent leurs petites amies, mais elles sont en retard. Ils parlent entre eux pour décider combien de temps ils vont attendre. Écrivez ce qu'ils disent en utilisant la conjonction **jusqu'à ce que.**

MODÈLE Marc: j'attendrai/Cybèle/arriver
→ Marc: J'attendrai jusqu'à ce que Cybèle arrive.

1. Paul: j'attendrai / Marie-Claire / m'appeler

____

2. Philippe: j'attendrai / Yvette / venir

____

3. Serge: j'attendrai / l'autobus / arriver pour me ramener

____

4. Luc: j'attendrai / Robert / revenir de la cabine téléphonique

____

5. Baudoin: j'attendrai / vous / s'en aller

____

6. Maurice: j'attendrai / nous / pouvoir vérifier où elles sont

____

7. Daniel: j'attendrai / nous / savoir quelque chose

____

8. Richard: j'attendrai / ma petite amie / apparaître

____

B. À ceci près (*with this exception*). Un groupe d'amis parlent de ce qu'ils feront, mais posent dans chaque cas une condition qui pourrait les en empêcher avec **à moins que.** Écrivez ce qu'ils disent.

MODÈLE Marc: J'irai au cinéma.
Lise: Mais si nous avons une composition à rédiger . . .
→ Marc: Oui. J'irai au cinéma à moins que nous ayons une composition à rédiger.

1. Renée: Hélène sortira avec Nicolas.
Marie: Mais si elle est occupée . . .
Renée: _______________

2. David: Jocelyne partira en Italie.
Alice: Mais si son père lui défend d'y aller . . .
David: _______________

3. Paul: Christophe t'expliquera la leçon.
Luc: Mais s'il ne fait pas attention en classe . . .
Paul: ______________________

4. Julie: Michel veut inviter tous ses amis chez lui.
Sara: Mais si ses parents reviennent . . .
Julie: ______________________

5. Papa: On peut aller chez les Laurentin.
Maman: Mais s'ils ont des choses à faire . . .
Papa: ______________________

6. Odile: Il faudra partir sans Jacqueline.
Diane: Mais si elle peut aller avec nous . . .
Odile: ______________________

7. Joseph: Nous pouvons faire un pique-nique demain.
André: Mais s'il fait mauvais . . .
Joseph: ______________________

C. Des événements qui nous empêchent de faire des choses. Lucille rappelle à ses amis toutes les choses qu'il faut faire. Mais dans chaque cas son amie Odile lui rappelle une possibilité qui les empêcherait de faire ces choses. Exprimez ces possibilités posées par les amis de Lucille avec **à moins que** suivi du passé du subjonctif.

MODÈLE Lucille: Nous devons aller voir Agnès. (mais si elle est partie . . .)
Odile: À moins qu'elle soit partie.

1. Lucille: Nous pouvons aller au cinéma. (mais si Gérard a vu le film . . .)
Odile: ______________________

2. Lucille: Il nous faut faire les courses. (mais si on a déjà fermé les magasins . . .)
Odile: ______________________

3. Lucille: Nous devons attendre Vincent. (mais s'il a oublié notre rendez-vous . . .)
Odile: ______________________

4. Lucille: Alain nous emmènera au stade. (mais si sa voiture est tombée en panne . . .)
Odile: ______________________

5. Lucille: On peut aller écouter des disques chez Henri. (mais s'il est allé à la bibliothèque . . .)
Odile: ______________________

6. Lucille: Christian peut nous prêter son livre d'histoire. (mais s'il l'a perdu . . .)
Odile: ______________________

7. Lucille: Je dois téléphoner à Lise. (mais si elle n'est pas encore rentrée . . .)
Odile: ______________________

D. **Pas si vite!** Jacquot veut sortir, voir ses amis, etc., mais sa mère pose des conditions. Écrivez ce que sa mère lui dit en formant des phrases avec **pourvu que.**

MODÈLE —Maman, je vais au cinéma avec Albert ce soir. (tu/finir tes devoirs avant)
➔ —Oui, pourvu que tu finisses tes devoirs avant.

1. Maman, je sors prendre un café avec Éloïse ce soir. (tu/prendre le dessert avec nous)

____

2. Maman, je vais à la surboum de Victor. (tu/être de retour avant minuit)

____

3. Maman, je veux aller voir le match de football dimanche. (ton frère/pouvoir t'accompagner)

____

4. Maman, je dois aller à la bibliothèque. (tu/mettre de l'ordre dans ta chambre)

____

5. Maman, Guy m'invite à passer l'après-midi chez lui. (tu/faire les courses avant)

____

6. Maman, je veux inviter Lise à prendre le goûter avec nous. (elle/ne pas venir avant 4 heures)

____

7. Maman, je peux prendre la voiture ce soir? (ton père/te permettre)

____

8. Maman, je peux dîner dans un restaurant de luxe? (nous/pouvoir aller avec toi)

____

E. **C'est pour ça.** Formez des phrases avec **pour que** qui expliquent le pourquoi des actions.

MODÈLE L'agent de police parle lentement. (l'étranger/le comprendre)
➔ L'agent de police parle lentement pour que l'étranger le comprenne.

François est souffrant.

1. Le médecin lui ordonne des antibiotiques. (il/se remettre [*recover*])

____

2. Sa mère a baissé les stores (*blinds*). (François/dormir)

____

3. Elle prépare une bonne soupe. (il/prendre quelque chose de chaud)

___

4. On lui donne trois couvertures (*blankets*). (il/ne pas avoir froid)

___

M. et Mme Durand essaient d'orienter un étudiant étranger qui habite chez eux.

5. Nous allons t'acheter un poste de télé. (tu/regarder des émissions en français)

___

6. On va te dessiner un petit plan du quartier. (tu/ne pas te perdre)

___

7. On te donne une carte avec notre numéro de téléphone. (tu/pouvoir nous appeler)

___

8. Nous allons inviter nos neveux et nos nièces. (tu/faire leur connaissance)

___

F. Courage! Vous encouragez votre ami à faire ce qu'il doit faire malgré les ennuis qui se présentent. Employez une proposition avec **bien que** pour lui dire qu'il faut surmonter les obstacles.

Modèle —Tu ne sors pas?
—Il pleut.
➔ —Tu dois sortir bien qu'il pleuve.

1. —Tu ne fais pas tes devoirs?
—Je suis fatigué.

___

2. —Tu ne descends pas faire les courses?
—Il fait mauvais.

___

3. —Tu ne lis pas le livre de chimie?
—Je n'en ai pas envie.

___

4. —Tu ne téléphones pas à Renée?
—Nous sommes brouillés (*mad at each other*).

___

5. —Tu ne vas pas au cours?
—Je ne me sens pas bien.

___

6. —Tu ne mets pas de cravate?
—J'ai chaud.

____

7. —Tu n'écris rien?
—Je ne sais pas la réponse.

____

8. —Tu ne finis pas ta rédaction?
—Il est tard.

____

G. Sans ça. Joignez chaque paire de phrases en une seule avec la conjonction **sans que** de façon à ce que la nouvelle phrase exprime la même idée.

MODÈLES Elle part. Je ne la vois pas.
➔ Elle part sans que je la voie.

Elle est partie. Je ne l'ai pas vue.
➔ Elle est partie sans que je l'aie vue.

1. Il entre doucement. On ne s'en aperçoit pas.

____

2. Cet étudiant copie. Le professeur ne s'en rend pas compte.

____

3. Marc a eu des ennuis avec la police. Ses parents ne sont pas au courant.

____

4. Il parle au téléphone. Je ne peux pas entendre ce qu'il dit.

____

5. Je te passerai un petit mot (*note*). Le prof ne me verra pas.

____

6. Il est parti. Nous ne le savions pas.

____

7. Il est rentré. Nous ne l'avons pas vu.

____

8. Elle s'est fâchée. Je ne lui ai rien dit.

____

H. On fait les courses. Un groupe d'amis sont en train de faire leurs courses. Décrivez leur activité en formant des phrases avec une proposition adverbiale. Employez les conjonctions indiquées.

MODÈLE j'irai à la boucherie/avant/vous/revenir/ de la charcuterie
→ J'irai à la boucherie avant que vous (ne) reveniez de la charcuterie.

Les boutiques/les commerçants

Les boutiques		*Les commerçants*
la bijouterie	*jewelry store*	**le bijoutier/la bijoutière**
la blanchisserie	*laundry*	**le blanchisseur/la blanchisseuse**
la boucherie	*butcher shop*	**le boucher/la bouchère**
la boutique du coiffeur	*barbershop*	**le coiffeur/la coiffeuse**
la boulangerie	*bakery*	**le boulanger/la boulangère**
la charcuterie	*delicatessen*	**le charcutier/la charcutière**
la crémerie	*dairy*	**le crémier/la crémière**
la droguerie	*drugstore*	
l'épicerie	*grocery*	**l'épicier/l'épicière**
le kiosque (à journaux)	*newsstand*	**le vendeur/la vendeuse de journaux**
la librairie	*bookstore*	**le/la libraire**
la pâtisserie	*pastry shop*	**le pâtissier/la pâtissière**
la pharmacie	*drugstore (pharmacy)*	**le pharmacien/la pharmacienne**
le salon de coiffure	*beauty salon*	**le coiffeur/la coiffeuse**
la station-service	*gas station*	**le/la pompiste, le mécanicien/la mécanicienne**
le pressing	*dry cleaners*	**le teinturier/la teinturière**

1. je ne passerai pas à la blanchisserie / jusqu'à / Louise / descendre au marché

   ____

2. Marc ira à la pâtisserie / pour / nous / prendre un bon dessert ce soir

   ____

3. Claire ira au kiosque du coin / pourvu / nous / l'accompagner

   ____

4. je vais vite au pressing / de peur / ils / fermer pour le déjeuner

   ____

5. nous attendrons Chantal à la station-service / jusqu'à / elle / faire le plein

   ____

6. Philippe attendra à la station-service / jusqu'à / le mécanicien / changer l'huile

   ____

7. nous regarderons l'étalage de la librairie / en attendant / Jean / sortir de chez le coiffeur

   ____

8. Odile veut passer à la droguerie / à moins / vous / être pressés pour rentrer

   ____

Note culturelle

- Bien que les Français fassent la plupart de leurs achats dans les grandes surfaces (supermarchés, hypermarchés), dans le centre des villes le système commercial traditionnel des petites boutiques spécialisées continue.

- Il y a des boulangeries où l'on ne fait que du pain, et des pâtisseries où l'on ne fait que des tartes et des gâteaux, mais il y a aussi beaucoup de boulangeries-pâtisseries où l'on vend tout ce qu'on trouve dans un *bakery* américain.

- Les Français font une distinction entre la pharmacie, où on va avec l'ordonnance du médecin, et la droguerie. Les pharmacies sont indiquées par une croix verte. La droguerie est la boutique où on achète les articles de toilette, mais pas les médicaments. Les Français emploient aussi le mot *drugstore,* mais il signifie une espèce de bazar élégant avec restaurant. Le Drugstore des Champs-Élysées est un rendez-vous favori des Parisiens.

- L'influence anglo-américaine se fait sentir même dans le petit commerce français. La boutique du teinturier s'appelle de nos jours «le pressing» et non «la teinturerie».

I. Vos idées. Complétez ces phrases selon vos idées, vos opinions et vos projets. Choisissez une des conjonctions proposées pour former votre phrase.

1. Le prof continuera à parler (sans que/jusqu'à ce que)
   ____
2. Je m'achèterai de nouveaux disques compacts (pourvu que/de façon que)
   ____
3. Je sortirai ce week-end (bien que/pour que)
   ____
4. Sophie nous attendra devant le lycée (jusqu'à ce que/malgré que)
   ____
5. Les étudiants doivent se tenir (*behave*) (de peur que/pour que)
   ____
6. Je retrouverai mes amis après les cours (à moins que/quoique)
   ____
7. Je finirai de rédiger cette composition (avant que/bien que)
   ____
8. Il faut prendre de l'essence (avant que/pour que)
   ____

J. En français, s'il vous plaît. Traduisez ces phrases en français.

1. I'll call them before I get to the airport.

____

2. We'll watch the soccer match until it begins to rain.

____

3. Mrs. Dulac set the table an hour before her friends arrived.

____

4. They stood in line in order to buy (**prendre**) tickets.

____

5. You (**vous**) didn't want to go to the department store without our going too.

____

6. Even though it's cold, we should take a walk.

____

7. I'll lend you (**tu**) the book unless you have already bought it.

____

8. You (**tu**) can go as long as your brother goes with you.

____

B *The subjunctive in relative clauses*

- The subjunctive is used in a relative clause if the antecedent in the main clause does not exist, is sought but not yet found, or is indefinite.

Il n'y a **personne qui** me **comprenne**.	*There's* ***no one who understands*** *me.*
Je ne vois **pas d'endroit où nous puissions** nous asseoir.	*I don't see* ***anyplace where we can*** *sit down.*
L'entreprise a besoin de **secrétaires qui sachent** trois langues.	*The firm needs* ***secretaries who know*** *three languages.*
Je cherche **une voiture qui fasse** du 150 à l'heure.	*I'm looking for* ***a car that does*** *150 kilometers per hour.*
Connaissez-vous **quelqu'un qui puisse** nous aider?	*Do you know* ***someone who can*** *help us?*

- If the antecedent in the main clause actually exists, the indicative is used in the relative clause.

J'ai besoin **des secrétaires qui savent** trois langues.	*I need* ***the secretaries who know*** *three languages.*
J'ai acheté **la voiture qui fait** du 150 à l'heure.	*I bought* ***the car that does*** *150 kilometers per hour.*
Voilà **quelqu'un qui peut** nous aider.	*There's* ***someone who can*** *help us.*

K. On cherche un logement. Jacquot cherche un appartement avec trois autres étudiants. Il décrit ce que chacun désire dans un logement. À partir des éléments donnés, formez des phrases qui expriment ce qu'il dit.

MODÈLE nous/chercher un appartement/avoir quatre chambres à coucher
→ Nous cherchons un appartement qui ait quatre chambres à coucher.

1. toi, tu / vouloir un appartement / avoir deux salles de bains
____

2. Mathieu / avoir besoin d'un appartement / être climatisé
____

3. Philippe et moi, nous / préférer un appartement / être près de la faculté
____

4. nous / vouloir un appartement / ne pas avoir besoin de beaucoup de rénovation
____

5. moi, je / chercher un appartement / avoir le confort moderne
____

6. Charles / désirer un appartement / se trouver dans un immeuble neuf
____

7. Mathieu et Philippe / chercher un appartement / être en face de l'arrêt d'autobus
____

8. nous / chercher un voisin / ne pas se plaindre des surboums
____

L. La femme idéale. Pour savoir ce que Stéphane raconte à son ami Édouard sur la femme idéale qu'il cherche, complétez les propositions relatives avec le subjonctif du verbe entre parenthèses.

1. (savoir) Je cherche une petite amie qui ____________ être une copine.
2. (pouvoir) Je veux trouver une fille avec qui je ____________ parler facilement.
3. (comprendre) J'ai besoin d'une fiancée qui me ____________.
4. (être) Je préférerais une petite amie qui ____________ très intelligente.
5. (avoir) Je veux une fille qui ____________ de l'humour.
6. (aimer) Je cherche une petite amie qui n'____________ que moi.
7. (dire) J'ai besoin d'une fille qui me ____________ toujours la vérité.
8. (faire) Je cherche une fille qui ____________ des études dans notre faculté.

Note culturelle

Pour chercher la femme idéale, vous pouvez aller au Louvre, un des plus grands musées d'art du monde. Vous y trouverez une sélection internationale: «La Gioconde» (*Mona Lisa*) de Léonard de Vinci, «La Dentellière» de Jan Vermeer et le portrait de la Marquise de Solana de l'artiste espagnol Francisco Goya.

La France est représentée par le tableau de Delacroix «La liberté guidant le peuple» et par les paysannes dépeintes dans «Les glaneuses» de Jean-François Millet.

M. Pas de candidates au poste! (*No candidates for the job!*) Édouard ne peut pas aider son ami Stéphane. Il n'a pas d'amies qui aient toutes les qualités requises pour être la petite amie de Stéphane. Complétez les phrases suivantes avec la forme correcte du verbe entre parenthèses pour savoir ce qu'Édouard dit à son ami.

1. (réussir) Je ne connais pas de fille qui ____________________ à te plaire.
2. (être) Il n'y a aucune fille qui ____________________ si merveilleuse.
3. (pouvoir) Tu ne vas pas trouver une fille qui ____________________ te comprendre.
4. (mentir) Il n'y a personne qui ne ____________________ jamais.
5. (avoir) Je ne connais pas de fille qui ____________________ toutes les qualités que tu cherches.
6. (vouloir) Il n'y a personne avec qui tu ____________________ sortir.

N. Au bureau. La compagnie où travaille Chantal cherche des employés. Complétez les phrases suivantes avec le subjonctif ou l'indicatif, selon le cas, pour savoir quels candidats doivent faire une demande d'emploi auprès de son bureau.

Le bureau moderne

l'interconnexion de réseau (fem.) *networking*
l'infographie (fem.) *computer graphics*
le représentant/la représentante de commerce *traveling salesperson*
le traitement de données *data processing*
le traitement de texte *word processing*

1. (savoir) Nous avons une représentante de commerce qui ____________________ l'espagnol.
2. (savoir) Nous cherchons quelqu'un qui ____________________ l'italien.
3. (connaître) Nous avons besoin d'un secrétaire qui ____________________ bien les programmes pour le traitement de texte.
4. (avoir) Il faut trouver quelqu'un qui ____________________ des connaissances d'infographie.

5. (pouvoir) Nous n'avons personne qui __________________ mettre à jour nos systèmes de traitement de données.
6. (être) Nous n'avons pas encore de collègue qui __________________ spécialisé dans l'interconnexion de réseau.
7. (avoir) Nous avons des employés qui __________________ une expérience internationale.
8. (être) Mais il n'y a personne qui __________________ capable d'ouvrir des bureaux en Asie.

C *The subjunctive after superlatives*

- The subjunctive is used in clauses after superlatives. These sentences usually express a subjective or personal opinion or evaluation.

—C'est l'entreprise **la plus dynamique que je connaisse**. *It's **the most dynamic** company **that I am acquainted with**.*
—Et ses produits sont **les plus solides qu'on puisse** trouver. *And its products are **the most solid ones that you can** find.*
—C'est **le meilleur** livre **que j'aie lu**. *It's **the best** book **that I have read**.*
—Et la dissertation **la plus difficile que** nous **ayons écrite**. *And **the hardest** term paper **that we have written**.*

- The subjunctive is also used after **seul, unique, dernier,** and **premier.**

Vous êtes la **seule** personne **qui puisse** comprendre. *You're the **only** person **who can** understand.*
C'est le **premier** livre **qui soit** utile. *It's the **first** book **that is** useful.*

O. Un peu d'enthousiasme! Joignez les deux phrases en une seule. Employez un superlatif (ou un de ces adjectifs: **seul, unique, dernier, premier**). Utilisez le subjonctif dans la proposition subordonnée.

MODÈLES Ce roman est facile. Nous le lisons.
➔ C'est le roman le plus facile que nous lisions.

Vous êtes la seule personne. Vous m'avez téléphoné.
➔ Vous êtes la seule personne qui m'ait téléphoné.

1. Cette fille est belle. Je la connais.

____

2. Ce cours est ennuyeux. Je le suis.

____

3. Ce compte rendu est intéressant. Marc l'écrit.

____

4. Ce village est joli. Vous le visitez.

____

5. Ce patient est le premier. Il vient au cabinet du dentiste.

____

6. Vous êtes la seule étudiante. Vous faites du chinois.

____

7. Cette employée est la dernière. Elle s'en va du bureau.

____

8. Ce repas est mauvais. On l'a servi à la cantine.

____

9. Ce restaurant est bon. Nous le fréquentons.

____

10. Ce tableau est beau. Tu l'as peint.

____

11. Ce loyer est élevé. Je l'ai payé.

____

12. Tu es le seul ami. Tu me comprends.

____

P. Et maintenant il s'agit de vous. Puisez dans (*draw on*) vos expériences personnelles pour parler de vos opinions et de vos impressions. Utilisez des superlatifs ou des adjectifs comme **seul, unique, dernier, premier.** Employez le subjonctif dans les propositions subordonnées s'il le faut.

MODÈLE le meilleur livre que vous ayez lu cette année
➔ *La Peste* de Camus est le meilleur livre que j'aie lu cette année.

1. le cours le plus intéressant que vous suiviez

____

2. l'émission (*TV show*) la plus amusante que vous regardiez

____

3. la première fois que vous êtes sorti(e) avec votre petit(e) ami(e)

____

4. l'affiche la plus jolie que vous ayez achetée

____

5. la personne la plus intéressante que vous connaissiez

____

6. le garçon le plus charmant ou la fille la plus charmante que vous connaissiez

____

7. le meilleur film que vous ayez vu cette année

____

8. l'excursion la plus amusante que vous ayez faite cette année

____

9. le vêtement le plus élégant que vous ayez acheté cette année

____

10. la dernière fois que vous êtes allé(e) à la plage

____

D *The subjunctive in certain types of indefinite clauses**

- French uses the following construction to express *however + adjective* or *no matter + adjective:*

  tout(e)
  quelque
  pour
  aussi
  si
  } + *adjective* + **que** + *subjunctive of* **être, paraître,** etc.

toute confiante que vous soyez	*however confident you may be*
pour petit qu'il paraisse	*as small as he may seem*
aussi fort que ce pays soit	*however strong this country is*
si peu que ce soit	*however little it may be*

- **Quel(le)(s)** + **que** + *subjunctive of* **être** + *noun* expresses the idea of *whatever.*

quels que soient les problèmes	*whatever the problems may be*
quelles que soient vos craintes	*whatever your fears may be*
quel que soit l'obstacle	*whatever the obstacle may be*

- **Qui que** and **quoi que** followed by the subjunctive mean *whoever* and *whatever,* respectively. **Où que** + subjunctive means *wherever.*

qui que vous soyez	*whoever you may be*
qui que ce soit	*whoever, anyone*
quoi que vous fassiez	*whatever you're doing*
quoi que ce soit	*anything*
où que tu ailles	*wherever you go*

Q. À traduire. Traduisez les phrases suivantes en anglais.

1. Qui qu'elle soit, elle n'a pas le droit d'entrer.

____

2. Si riches qu'ils soient devenus, ils ne peuvent oublier la pauvreté de leur jeunesse.

____

3. Tout doué que tu sois, il faut que tu études.

____

4. Il comptait nous offrir quoi que ce soit.

____

*For recognition only.

5. Je ne lui pardonnerai jamais, quoi qu'il dise.

____

6. Ce candidat accepte l'argent de qui que ce soit.

____

7. Quelle que soit la somme offerte, elle ne sera pas suffisante.

____

8. Où que tu ailles tu trouveras les mêmes difficultés.

____

R. On téléphone. Lisez l'annonce suivante en faisant attention aux propositions relatives. Ensuite, répondez aux questions.

Avec le réseau Itineris, vous n'êtes jamais très loin de vos proches collaborateurs.

itineris

Et vice versa ! Avec l'Option Europe, vous pouvez utiliser votre téléphone mobile dans 17 pays et surtout, vous passez les frontières sans changer de numéro. Quoi qu'il arrive et où que vous soyez on peut donc vous joindre à tout moment... et vice versa !

N° VERT 05 10 07 07

On va beaucoup plus loin avec Itineris.

1. Quel produit est-ce qu'on annonce ici?

2. Qu'est-ce que c'est que l'option Europe?

3. Quelles commodités sont offertes par l'Option Europe?

4. Expliquez le sens de la phrase «vous n'êtes jamais très loin de vos proches collaborateurs».

5. Quelle phrase écririez-vous pour préciser l'idée exprimée par «vice versa» dans l'annonce?

6. Est-ce qu'on peut téléphoner à France Telecom sans payer le coup de fil? Justifiez votre réponse.

7. Trouvez les équivalents français de *whatever may happen* et *wherever you may be* dans l'annonce et écrivez-les ci-dessous.

PART FIVE

Idiomatic Usage

CHAPTER 27 THE PASSIVE VOICE AND SUBSTITUTES FOR THE PASSIVE

A *The passive voice*

Verbs may be in either the active voice or the passive voice. In the active voice, the subject performs the action described by the verb. In the passive voice, the action described by the verb is done to the subject.

- The passive voice is formed with the verb **être** + the past participle. The past participle agrees in gender and number with the subject of the sentence. The person who performs the action of a verb (the agent) is introduced by **par.**

Active voice

Les étudiants **lisent** le livre.	*The students **read** the book.*
Le professeur **pose** des questions.	*The teacher **asks** some questions.*

Passive voice

Le livre **est lu par** les étudiants.	*The book **is read by** the students.*
Des questions **sont posées par** le professeur.	*Some questions **are asked by** the teacher.*

- The passive voice may appear in any tense.

Ces pièces **seront peintes par** mon frère.	*These rooms **will be painted by** my brother.*
La cuisine **devrait être modernisée**.	*The kitchen **ought to be modernized**.*

- The passive voice focuses on the person or thing performing the action.

Mes parents ont acheté cet appartement.	*My parents bought this apartment. (no emphasis)*
Cet appartement **a été acheté par mes parents.**	*This apartment **was bought by my parents.** (focus on **my parents**)*

- The passive voice may also focus on an action without identifying the performer of the action.

Cet immeuble **a été construit** en 1890.	*This apartment house **was built** in 1890.*

- After verbs expressing mental processes, such as feeling and thinking, the agent is often introduced by **de** rather than by **par.**

Ce professeur est respecté **de tous ses étudiants.**	*This teacher is respected **by all his students.***
La grand-mère est aimée **de ses petits-enfants.**	*The grandmother is loved **by her grandchildren.***

A. Au bureau. Refaites les phrases suivantes à la voix passive pour raconter ce qui se passe au bureau. Gardez le même temps verbal dans la phrase que vous formez.

MODÈLE La secrétaire ouvre le bureau à huit heures.
→ Le bureau est ouvert à huit heures par la secrétaire.

Les affaires

le chèque *check*
la demande d'emploi *job application*
l'échantillon (masc.) *sample*
expédier *to ship*
la facture *bill*
faire un versement sur le compte de *to make a deposit*
lancer un produit *to launch a product*
livrer des marchandises *to deliver goods*
la marchandise *merchandise, goods*
le marché *market*
passer une commande *to place an order*
présenter une demande d'emploi *to submit a job application*
signer *to sign*

1. La réceptionniste reçoit les clients.

____

2. Les employés passent des commandes.

____

3. La secrétaire a fait un versement sur le compte de l'entreprise.

____

4. Un camion a livré des marchandises.

____

5. Le bureau a expédié des échantillons.

____

6. Le patron a signé des chèques.

____

7. La secrétaire envoie des factures.

____

8. Un jeune homme a présenté une demande d'emploi.

____

9. L'entreprise va lancer un nouveau produit.

____

10. Des experts vont étudier le marché.

____

B. Le déménagement. Décrivez ce qui est arrivé pendant le déménagement des Martel en formant des phrases à la voix passive avec les éléments proposés. Ajoutez **par** pour indiquer l'agent.

MODÈLE les meubles/mettre dans le fourgon/les déménageurs
➔ Les meubles ont été mis dans le fourgon par les déménageurs.

Le déménagement

accrocher *to hang, hang up*
brancher *to plug in*
la caisse *crate*
le déménageur *mover*
le fauteuil *armchair*
le fourgon (de déménagement) *moving truck*
la machine à laver *washing machine*
la penderie *closet, walk-in closet*
le placard *cupboard*
le plombier *plumber*
ranger *to put away*
le sous-sol *basement*

1. les lits / monter / trois hommes

___

2. les tableaux / accrocher au mur / Pierre et sa sœur

___

3. la machine à laver / installer / un plombier

___

4. le fauteuil / placer en face de la télé / M. Martel

___

5. les vêtements / accrocher dans la penderie / Mme Martel

___

6. deux grosses caisses en bois / laisser dans le sous-sol / les déménageurs

___

7. la vaisselle / ranger dans les placards / Mme Martel

___

8. les lampes / brancher / M. Martel

___

C. Oui, c'est lui. Monique essaie de vérifier qui va faire les choses nécessaires pour l'organisation de la surboum. Olivier répond à l'affirmatif avec une phrase à la voix passive. Écrivez les réponses d'Olivier.

MODÈLE —C'est Charles qui va acheter le gâteau?
➔ —Oui, le gâteau va être acheté par Charles.

1. Ce sont Luc et Catherine qui vont préparer la quiche?

___

2. C'est Marie qui va inviter les amis du lycée?

___

3. C'est Bernard qui va apporter le cassettophone?

4. Ce sont Geneviève et Virginie qui vont mettre les couverts?

5. C'est Suzanne qui va acheter le chocolat?

6. C'est Antoine qui va faire le café?

7. C'est Anne et Danielle qui vont choisir les cassettes?

8. C'est Eugène qui va servir les amuse-gueules?

D. **La société idéale.** Édouard a une formule pour améliorer (*improve*) la société. Exprimez ses idées en formant des phrases à la voix passive avec le verbe **devoir.**

MODÈLE améliorer l'éducation
➔ L'éducation doit être améliorée.

1. protéger les enfants

2. respecter les personnes âgées

3. bien payer la police

4. honorer le drapeau

5. obéir à la loi

6. bien former les professionnels

7. subventionner (*subsidize*) les musées

8. moderniser les transports en commun (*public transportation*)

9. encourager les petites entreprises (*small business*)

10. embaucher (*hire*) les jeunes

B Substitutes for the passive voice

- The passive voice is used less in French than in English, and has a slightly formal or literary tone. It is often replaced by the active voice.

  Le conte **a été écrit par Louis.** ➔ **Louis a écrit** le conte.

- When a speaker wants to focus on the person who performed an action, the passive can be replaced by a sentence beginning with **c'est** or **ce sont.**

  Le conte a été écrit **par Louis.** ➔ **C'est Louis** qui a écrit le conte.

- When the performer of the action is not expressed, **on** may be used.

  La chambre **sera nettoyée.** ➔ **On nettoiera** la chambre.

  Ici le français **est parlé.** ➔ Ici **on parle** français.

- In many cases, but not all, a pronominal construction can be used instead of the passive when the performer of the action is not expressed.

  Cette revue **est** beaucoup **lue.** ➔ Cette revue **se lit** beaucoup.

  Ce mot **est** facilement **compris.** ➔ Ce mot **se comprend** facilement.

Additional examples:

Ça ne se fait pas.	*That's not done.*
Ça ne se dit plus.	*That's not said anymore.*
Ce produit ne se vend qu'en pharmacie.	*This product is only sold in pharmacies.*
Les œufs ne se mangent pas le matin en France.	*They don't eat eggs in the morning in France.*
Les portes se ferment à 6 heures.	*They close the doors at six o'clock.*

E. Comment se tenir à table en France. Les bonnes manières à table ne sont pas les mêmes en France que dans le monde anglo-saxon. Refaites ces indications avec **on** pour en faire une liste de conseils utiles au visiteur américain ou canadien.

MODÈLE offrir des fleurs (mais pas des chrysanthèmes) à Madame
➔ On offre des fleurs (mais pas des chrysanthèmes) à Madame.

1. ne pas pencher (*tilt*) l'assiette pour finir sa soupe

   ____

2. tenir toujours le couteau dans la main droite

   ____

3. tenir toujours la fourchette dans la main gauche

   ____

4. ne pas essuyer la sauce avec un morceau de pain

   ____

5. ne pas poser les coudes sur la table

   ____

6. poser les mains sur le bord de la table

____

7. ne pas couper le pain avec le couteau

____

8. casser son morceau de pain

____

9. répondre «Avec plaisir» pour accepter de reprendre (*have a second helping of*) un des plats

____

10. répondre «Merci» pour ne pas accepter de reprendre un des plats

____

Note culturelle

- Il faut remarquer les différences entre la façon française de se tenir à table et les coutumes américaines. N'oubliez pas que pour dire «non» quand on vous offre quelque chose à manger, on dit «Merci». Si vous voulez accepter, vous dites «Avec plaisir, s'il vous plaît».
- Le chrysanthème est la fleur de la mort en France et s'utilise aux enterrements. On ne l'offre donc pas à la famille qui vous invite à dîner.

F. Conseils de cuisine. Formulez ces conseils de cuisine de deux façons: avec **on** et avec la construction pronominale.

Modèle prendre un apéritif avant le repas
➔ a. On prend un apéritif avant le repas.
➔ b. Un apéritif se prend avant le repas.

1. offrir des amuse-gueules avec l'apéritif

   a. ____________________________________

   b. ____________________________________

2. couper un fromage en cubes pour servir avec l'apéritif

   a. ____________________________________

   b. ____________________________________

3. préparer une bonne soupe la veille (*the day before*)

   a. ____________________________________

   b. ____________________________________

4. déboucher le vin au moins une heure avant de le servir

   a. ____________________________________

   b. ____________________________________

5. préparer ce plat une heure avant le repas

a. ___

b. ___

6. servir cette viande froide

a. ___

b. ___

7. boire ce vin doux après le repas

a. ___

b. ___

8. servir des fruits comme dessert

a. ___

b. ___

G. Des renseignements utiles pour un ami étranger. Roger reçoit John, un ami américain, à Paris. Il le renseigne sur la France en employant la construction pronominale équivalente à la voix passive. Écrivez ce que Roger dit à son ami.

MODÈLE en France/les distances/calculer/en kilomètres
➔ En France les distances se calculent en kilomètres.

1. le base-ball / ne pas jouer / en France

___

2. les journaux américains / vendre / partout

___

3. les bouquinistes / trouver / le long de la Seine

___

4. les films américains / projeter / dans beaucoup de cinémas

___

5. les chansons américaines / entendre / à la radio

___

6. des festivals de théâtre / donner / en été

___

7. un marché volant / installer / deux fois par semaine dans ce quartier

___

8. les billets de métro / pouvoir acheter / en carnets de dix

___

Note culturelle

- Les bouquinistes vendent des livres d'occasion. À Paris le long de la Seine il y a des dizaines de bouquinistes dont les étalages sont de grosses boîtes en métal. Beaucoup de ces bouquinistes vendent aussi des cartes postales et des affiches qui attirent le regard du touriste. Le mot **bouquiniste** vient de **bouquin,** un mot familier pour **livre.**

- En été, et surtout en province, il y a des festivals de théâtre, de danse, de musique et de cinéma. Le visiteur peut se renseigner là-dessus dans les offices de tourisme.

- Les marchés volants sont des marchés mobiles qui s'installent dans un quartier urbain deux ou trois fois par semaine. Au marché on peut acheter des fruits et des légumes, des conserves et aussi des articles de ménage (*housewares*).

- Pour prendre le métro à Paris il faut acheter un billet. Il y a une réduction sur le tarif si on achète dix billets à la fois. Ces dix billets achetés ensemble s'appellent **un carnet.**

H. C'est à vous d'être le professeur de français! Exprimez les aspects suivants de la langue française à une classe d'anglophones. Employez la construction pronominale (**se** + verbe) dans chaque cas pour formuler les règles.

MODÈLE **exagérer**/écrire/avec un seul **g**
→ **Exagérer** s'écrit avec un seul **g.**

1. le verbe **monter** / conjuguer / avec **être** au passé composé

____

2. dans le mot **clef** / le **f** final / ne pas prononcer

____

3. le subjonctif / utiliser / après **jusqu'à ce que**

____

4. **les rebuts** (*trash*) est un mot / employer / au Canada

____

5. *a silent film* / traduire en français / par **un film muet**

____

6. les mots **amoral** et **immoral** / confondre / souvent

____

7. le sujet / placer / devant le verbe dans les déclarations

____

8. le vocabulaire technique / apprendre / sans difficulté

____

I. La grammaire en action. Lisez l'annonce suivante pour le EBS (*European Business School*) et répondez aux questions qui suivent.

Paris - Madrid - Londres - Munich- Milan - Dublin.

PARIS

Établissement d'enseignement supérieur technique privé de commerce et de gestion.

L'École est assez fière d'être reconnue par l'État,

mais plus encore d'être reconnue par les entreprises.

Quatre années d'études après bac.
Un an dans deux pays européens pour connaître leur langue, leur culture et leurs marchés. 13 mois de stages en entreprise en France et à l'étranger pour acquérir un savoir-faire.

La plus concrète des Grandes Écoles.

EBS - 27, bld Ney - 75018 PARIS - Tél : (1) 40 36 16 88 - Fax : (1) 40 36 40 20 - Minitel : 3614 EBS

Bon Angle

1. Combien de temps dure le programme de l'EBS?

 ___

2. Quand est-ce qu'on peut s'inscrire?

 ___

3. Comment est-ce que cette école de gestion (*business administration*) assure aux étudiants une formation internationale?

 ___

 ___

4. En quoi consiste la fierté de l'EBS?

 ___

 ___

CHAPTER 28

IMPORTANT IDIOMS AND PROVERBS

A Idioms with **avoir** and **être**

Expressions with **avoir** *(see also Chapter 2)*

Je t'ai eu! *I've tricked you! Gotcha!*
Ils m'ont eu! *I've been had!*
avoir lieu *to take place*
avoir qqn dans sa peau *to have someone under one's skin*
en avoir marre, en avoir assez, en avoir par-dessus la tête *to be fed up (colloquial)*
en avoir ras le bol, en avoir plein le dos *to be fed up (slang)*
en avoir pour son argent *to get one's money's worth*
avoir maille à partir avec qqn *to have a bone to pick with someone*
avoir le cafard *to have the blues, be depressed*
avoir du toupet *to have a lot of nerve*
avoir horreur de qqch *to detest something, loathe something*
avoir le cœur sur la main *to be generous*
avoir toujours le mot pour rire *to be a real joker, to have a good sense of humor*
n'avoir ni queue ni tête *to make no sense*
avoir bonne/mauvaise mine *to look good/bad (usually refers to health)*
avoir hâte de faire qqch *to be impatient, in a rush to do something*
avoir des complexes *to have hang-ups*
avoir le fou rire *to have the giggles, to laugh uncontrollably*
avoir la langue bien pendue *to be a good talker, have the gift of gab*
avoir du mal à faire qqch *to have difficulty doing something*
avoir le mal du pays *to be homesick*
avoir le mal de mer *to be seasick*
avoir de l'oreille *to have an ear for music*
en avoir pour cinq minutes *to take (someone) five minutes (to do something)*
J'ai le cœur qui bat. *My heart is beating (with excitement, nervousness).*
J'ai la tête qui tourne. *I'm dizzy.*
avoir six mètres de haut/long/large *to be six meters high/long/wide*
Qu'est-ce qu'il a? *What's wrong with him?*
Tu n'avais qu'à me demander. *All you had to do was ask me.*
Il n'a qu'à étudier un peu. *All he has to do is study a little.*
Il n'y a que toi pour faire ça! *Only you would do that! It takes you to do that!*
Il n'y a pas de quoi. *Don't mention it. You're welcome.*
Il doit y avoir une raison. *There must be a reason.*
Il y a un froid entre eux. *They're on bad terms. They're angry with each other.*
Ce gosse n'a pas froid aux yeux! *That kid is plucky, gutsy!*

Expressions with **être** *(see also Chapter 2)*

J'y suis! *I've got it! Now I understand!*
être au courant *to be informed, be up to date about a matter*
être en nage *to be in a sweat*
être sur la même longueur d'ondes *to be on the same wavelength*

être dans la lune *to be off in the clouds somewhere*
être sur le point de faire qqch *to be on the verge of doing something*
comme si de rien n'était *as if nothing had happened*
c'est à moi/toi/lui de . . . *it's up to me/you/him to . . .*
être des nôtres *to join us (for an activity)*
être de mèche avec *to be in cahoots with*
être reçu à un examen, au bac *to pass a test, the baccalaureate exam*
être de retour *to be back*
être de trop *to be in the way, out of place*
être en vue *to be the object of public attention, to be in the public eye*
Il y est pour beaucoup. *He's largely responsible.*
Je n'y suis pour rien. *I'm not at all at fault. I'm not to blame.*
Tout est à refaire. *Everything has to be redone.*
Il est + singular or plural noun *there is, there are (literary substitute for* ***il y a****)*
Il est des gens qui croient cela.
On en est là. *We've come to that.*
Où en sommes-nous? *Where are we up to?*
Nous sommes quittes. *We're even.*
J'en suis à ma dernière année au lycée. *I'm in my last year at school.*
J'en suis à me demander si . . . *I'm beginning to wonder if . . .*
J'en suis pour mes frais/pour ma peine! *I've gotten nothing for my money/ for my trouble!*

A. Comment le dire? Laquelle des deux possibilités exprime l'idée proposée?

1. Vous voulez dire à un ami que vous serez bientôt prêt.
   a. J'en ai pour cinq minutes.
   b. Tu n'as qu'à attendre.
2. C'est un enfant courageux.
   a. Ce gosse est en nage.
   b. Ce gosse n'a pas froid aux yeux.
3. Vous voulez dire que quelqu'un vous a trompé.
   a. J'en ai par-dessus la tête!
   b. On m'a eu!
4. Vous voulez dire que Marie est généreuse et franche.
   a. Elle a le cœur sur la main.
   b. Elle y est pour beaucoup.
5. Vous entrez tard dans la classe et vous voulez savoir à quelle page on lit. Vous demandez:
   a. Vous y êtes?
   b. Où en sommes-nous?
6. Vous voulez dire que vous ne savez rien au sujet de l'affaire dont on parle.
   a. Il doit y avoir une raison.
   b. Je ne suis pas au courant.
7. Vous voulez nier votre responsabilité. Vous dites:
   a. Je n'y suis pour rien.
   b. Tu as du toupet.
8. Vous voulez exprimer votre émotion. Vous dites:
   a. Je t'ai dans la peau.
   b. J'ai le cœur qui bat.

9. Le travail est tellement mal fait qu'il faut recommencer.
   a. Ça n'a ni queue ni tête.
   b. Tout est à refaire.
10. Vous voulez dire que vos efforts ont été inutiles. Vous dites:
   a. J'en suis pour ma peine.
   b. J'ai maille à partir avec toi.

B. **Qu'est-ce que ça veut dire?** Laquelle des deux possibilités définit l'expression donnée?

1. J'en suis à me demander si . . .
   a. Je voudrais vous demander si . . .
   b. Je commence à penser que . . .
2. Nous en sommes là.
   a. Nous voilà dans un état lamentable.
   b. Nos efforts ont produit l'effet souhaité.
3. Lui, il ne manque pas de toupet!
   a. Il est audacieux et arrogant.
   b. Il est gentil et généreux.
4. Jacqueline a toujours le mot pour rire.
   a. Elle rit beaucoup.
   b. Elle fait rire les autres.
5. Cet homme d'affaires n'a pas froid aux yeux.
   a. Il est trop prudent.
   b. Il n'a pas peur de prendre des risques.
6. J'ai la tête qui tourne.
   a. J'ai oublié.
   b. J'ai le vertige.
7. Cette histoire n'a ni queue ni tête.
   a. Elle est incohérente.
   b. Elle est difficile.
8. Il y a un froid entre eux.
   a. Ils sont fâchés.
   b. Ils ont froid.
9. Tu n'as qu'à me téléphoner.
   a. Tu ne m'as pas téléphoné.
   b. Il suffit de me téléphoner.
10. Comme si de rien n'était.
   a. Comme si nous n'avions rien à faire.
   b. Comme s'il n'y avait aucun problème.
11. La réunion a eu lieu hier.
   a. On s'est réunis hier.
   b. Il y avait de la place pour la réunion.
12. Il n'a pas bonne mine.
   a. Il n'a pas d'argent.
   b. Il a l'air malade.

B Idioms with **faire** (see also Chapter 2)

faire à sa tête *to act impulsively, to do whatever one wants*
faire acte de présence *to put in an appearance*
faire de la peine à qqn *to hurt someone's feelings*
faire de la photographie *to do photography as a hobby*
faire des bêtises *to get into mischief*
faire du bricolage *to do odd jobs, to putter around*
faire du sport, du ski, de la natation *to play sports, to ski, to swim*
faire du théâtre *to be an actor (professional); to do some acting (amateur)*
faire du violon, du piano *to study the violin, piano*
faire l'école buissonnière *to play hooky*
faire l'enfant, l'idiot *to act like a child, act the fool*
faire l'Europe *to travel to Europe, visit Europe*
faire la moue *to pout*
faire la queue *to stand in line*
faire le singe *to play the fool*
faire peau neuve *to turn over a new leaf*
faire preuve de *to show, display a quality or virtue*
faire savoir *to let someone know*
faire semblant de faire qqch *to pretend to*
faire ses bagages, ses valises *to pack*
faire ses quatre cents coups *to sow one's wild oats, to get into a lot of trouble*
faire son bac, son droit *to study for one's baccalaureate, one's law degree*
faire son marché *to go grocery shopping*
faire toute une histoire de qqch *to make a federal case out of something*
faire un beau gâchis de qqch *to make a real mess of something*
faire un clin d'œil à qqn *to wink at someone*
faire une croix dessus *to give up on something, kiss something goodbye*
faire un voyage, une promenade *to take a trip, a walk*
faire une drôle de tête *to make a strange, funny face*
faire une fugue *to run away from home*
faire une gaffe *to blunder, make a mistake (in conduct)*
Si cela ne vous fait rien. *If you don't mind.*
Ça me fait froid dans le dos. *That gives me the shivers.*
Ça ne me fait rien. *That's OK. That doesn't matter.*
Qu'est-ce que cela peut bien te faire? *What can that possibly matter to you?*
C'est bien fait pour toi! *It serves you right!*
Que faites-vous dans la vie?/Quel métier faites-vous? *What do you do for a living?*
Qu'est-ce que j'ai fait de mes gants? *What have I done with my gloves?*
Rien à faire. *No use insisting.*
Il n'y a rien à faire. *It's hopeless.*
L'accident a fait huit victimes. *Eight people were killed in the accident.*

Expressions with ***se faire***

se faire fort de + ***infinitive*** *to be confident, claim that one can do something*
se faire du mauvais sang *to worry*
se faire du souci/des soucis *to worry*
s'en faire *to worry*
se faire une raison *to resign oneself to something*
se faire tout(e) petit(e) *to make oneself inconspicuous, try not to be noticed*
se faire à qqch *to get used to something*
se faire des idées, des illusions *to be fooling oneself*

se faire une montagne de qqch *to exaggerate the importance of something*
se faire passer pour *to pass oneself off as*
se faire mal *to hurt oneself*

C. Même sens. Trouvez dans la deuxième colonne des synonymes pour chacune des expressions de la première.

_____ 1. faire une drôle de tête
_____ 2. faire son marché
_____ 3. se faire du mauvais sang
_____ 4. se faire une montagne de qqch
_____ 5. C'est bien fait pour toi!
_____ 6. se faire à qqch
_____ 7. Rien à faire.
_____ 8. se faire une raison

a. faire toute une histoire de qqch
b. s'habituer à qqch
c. acheter à manger
d. se résigner
e. s'inquiéter
f. faire une grimace
g. se couper
h. C'est bien mérité.
i. Ça ne vous regarde pas.
j. Inutile d'insister.

D. À compléter. Une expression avec **faire** décrit ce que cette personne fait dans chaque cas. Trouvez la bonne expression pour compléter chaque phrase.

1. Rachelle va en Turquie et en Israël. Elle fait ____________________.
2. Robert fait une tête de mécontentement. Il fait ____________________.
3. Samuel veut que personne ne le remarque. Il se fait ____________________.
4. Michèle se coupe au doigt. Elle se fait ____________________.
5. Charles étudie pour devenir avocat. Il fait ____________________.
6. Mon père cherche toujours quelque chose à réparer à la maison. Il fait ____________________.
7. Mon frère fait des actes dangereux. Il fait ____________________.
8. Chantal est sûre qu'elle va gagner à la loterie. C'est impossible. Elle se fait ____________________.

C *Idioms with **prendre** (see also Chapter 2)*

passer prendre qqn *to go pick someone up*
prendre à gauche/à droite *to turn left/right*
prendre au pied de la lettre *to take literally*
prendre au sérieux *to take seriously*
prendre des risques *to take chances*
prendre du poids *to gain weight*
prendre feu *to catch fire*
prendre fin *to come to an end*
prendre froid, prendre un rhume *to catch cold*

prendre garde *to be careful, watch out*
prendre goût à qqch *to take a liking to something, to begin to like something*
prendre l'air, prendre le frais *to get a breath of fresh air*
prendre qqn en grippe *to take a dislike to someone*
prendre qqn la main dans le sac *to catch someone red-handed*
prendre qqn par son point faible *to take advantage of someone's weak spot*
prendre rendez-vous avec *to make an appointment with*
prendre sa retraite *to retire (from one's career)*
prendre ses jambes à son cou *to run off, flee*
prendre son courage à deux mains *to get up one's courage*
être pris *to have previous engagements, be tied up*
être pris de vertige/remords/panique *to get dizzy/be stricken by remorse/ be panic-stricken*
un parti pris *prejudice, preconceived notion*
Pourriez-vous me prendre un journal? *Could you buy/get a newspaper for me?*
Je t'y prends! *I've got you! I've caught you!*
On m'a pris pour un Allemand. *I was taken for a German.*
Que je t'y prenne . . . ! Si je t'y prends encore! *Just let me catch you doing that (again)!*
Il a bien/mal pris la chose. *He took it well/badly.*
Qu'est-ce qui t'a pris? *What's gotten into you?*
On ne sait jamais par quel bout le prendre. *You never know how to take him.*

Expressions with ***se prendre***

s'en prendre à qqn *to attack someone, pick on someone*
s'y prendre *to go about doing something*
s'y prendre bien/mal *to do a good/bad job*
se faire prendre *to get caught*
Pour qui te prends-tu? *Who do you think you are?*
Ils se prennent pour des intellectuels. *They think they're intellectuals.*

E. De nouvelles phrases. Refaites les phrases suivantes avec une des expressions avec **prendre.**

1. Il s'est retiré des affaires.
____
2. Il s'attaque à ses critiques.
____
3. C'est un préjugé.
____
4. Fais attention!
____
5. Tu peux me procurer un journal?
____
6. Le petit garçon m'a compris littéralement.
____
7. Je me suis enrhumé(e).
____

8. L'enfant a grossi.

____

9. On a attrapé le voleur en train de fouiller dans les tiroirs.

____

10. J'ai été frappé(e) par un sentiment de panique.

____

11. Il ne sait pas faire ce travail.

____

12. Il sort respirer un peu dehors.

____

D *Idioms with* ***mettre***

mettre à jour *to bring up-to-date*
mettre qqn au courant *to inform someone, bring someone up-to-date*
mettre le feu à qqch *to set fire to something*
mettre qqn à la porte *to throw someone out; to fire someone*
mettre le couvert, mettre la table *to set the table*
mettre du soin à faire qqch *to take care in doing something*
mettre les bouts, mettre les voiles *to leave, scram (slang)*
mettre en cause *to call into question, to implicate*
mettre en contact *to put in touch*
mettre en garde contre *to warn someone against*
mettre qqch en lumière *to bring something to light, to bring something out in the open*
mettre en marche *to get something going, start up*
mettre en œuvre *to implement, make use of*
mettre qqn en quarantaine *to give someone the silent treatment*
mettre au point *to fine-tune, adjust, perfect*
mettre en relief *to emphasize*
mettre en service *to bring into service, put into operation*
mettre en train *to get something under way*
mettre en valeur *to develop (property)*
mettre fin à qqch *to put an end to something*
mettre sens dessus dessous *to turn things upside down*
mettre qqn sur la voie *to put someone on the right track*
J'ai mis une heure à le faire. *I took an hour to do it.*
J'en mettrais ma main au feu! *I'd swear to it!*
Mettons que . . . *Let's say that . . .*

Expressions with ***se mettre***

se mettre en quatre pour qqn *to go all out, make a superhuman effort for someone*
se mettre en colère *to get angry*
se mettre d'accord *to agree, come to an agreement*
se mettre à genoux *to kneel, get on one's knees*
se mettre au lit *to go to bed*
se mettre au travail *to get to work*
se mettre en route *to set out on a trip*
se mettre au français *to begin the study of French, get down to the business of studying French*

se mettre à faire qqch *to begin to do something*
se mettre à l'abri *to take shelter*
se mettre à table *to sit down to eat*
n'avoir rien à se mettre *to have nothing to wear*
Je ne savais plus où me mettre. *I didn't know where to hide (out of embarrassment, etc.)*
Le temps se met au beau. *It's clearing up.*

F. Savez-vous une expression avec *mettre*? Écrivez l'expression avec **mettre** qui est l'équivalent de chacune des locutions données.

1. congédier qqn

   ____

2. se coucher

   ____

3. s'agenouiller

   ____

4. brûler qqch

   ____

5. faire savoir

   ____

6. commencer à faire qqch

   ____

7. s'asseoir pour manger

   ____

8. partir

   ____

9. faire un grand effort pour qqn

   ____

10. mettre qqn à l'écart, ne pas lui parler

    ____

G. Comment est-ce qu'on pourrait dire ça? Choisissez une des expressions avec **mettre** de la liste suivante pour compléter ces phrases. Modifiez la forme de l'expression pour l'intégrer correctement s'il le faut.

Le temps se met au beau.	mettre sur la voie
mettre en relief	n'avoir rien à se mettre
mettre en service	se mettre à l'abri
mettre en valeur	se mettre aux maths
mettre les bouts	se mettre en colère

1. Il commence à pleuvoir. On va ______________________________ pour ne pas se mouiller.

2. Beaucoup de touristes viennent dans cette région et toi, tu as un terrain près du lac. Tu dois le ______________________.
3. Viens, ma belle. Il est tard. On doit y aller. Excuse-nous, Marguerite. Véronique et moi, on ______________________.
4. On a ______________________ un TGV entre Paris et Rennes.
5. L'examen de maths est dans un mois. La dernière fois tu n'as pas réussi. Il te faut ______________________ dès aujourd'hui.
6. Toutes mes robes sont vieilles et démodées. Je n'ai ______________________.
7. Il m'a donné de très bons conseils. Je dirais même qu'il m'a ______________________.
8. Je répète cette idée pour la ______________________.
9. Si tu arrives en retard encore une fois, le prof va ______________________.
10. Regardez! Il ne pleut plus et le soleil se montre. ______________________!

E Idioms with **voir**

voir trente-six chandelles *to see stars*
voir la vie en rose *to see life through rose-colored glasses*
se voir en cachette *to meet secretly*
n'y voir goutte *not to be able to see a thing (because of the dark, etc.)*
n'y voir que du feu *to be completely fooled, taken in*
en faire voir de dures/de toutes les couleurs/des vertes et des pas mûres *to give someone a hard time*
ne voir aucun mal à qqch *not to see any harm in something*
Fais voir! *Show me!*
faire voir trente-six chandelles à qqn *to knock the living daylights out of someone*
Vous voyez d'ici le tableau! *Just picture it!*
On aura tout vu! *That would be the limit. That would be too much.*
Cela n'a rien à voir avec . . . *That has nothing to do with . . .*
Je n'ai rien à voir dans cette affaire. *I have nothing to do with that. I'm not responsible for that.*
Je ne peux pas les voir (en peinture)! *I can't stand them!*
Ils ne peuvent pas se voir. *They can't stand each other.*
C'est quelque chose qui ne se voit pas tous les jours. *It's a rare thing.*
Je te vois venir! *I know what you're up to!*
Je l'ai vu de mes propres yeux. *I saw it with my own eyes.*
On verra bien! *We'll see!*
Je voudrais vous y voir! *I'd like to see how well you'd do (in that situation)!*
Voyons! *Come on, now!*
On n'en voit pas la fin. *The end is nowhere in sight.*
Je n'y vois pas d'inconvénient. *I don't see any problem. I have no objection.*
Essaie un peu pour voir! *Just you try it! (colloquial)*
C'est mal vu. *People don't like that, don't look favorably on that.*

H. Comment le dire? Laquelle des deux possibilités exprime l'idée proposée?

1. Tu n'oserais pas faire ça!
   a. Tu n'y vois aucun mal.
   b. Essaie un peu pour voir.
2. Tu ne ferais pas mieux que moi.
   a. Je te vois venir!
   b. Je voudrais vous y voir.
3. J'ai eu très, très mal.
   a. J'ai vu trente-six chandelles.
   b. Je n'y ai vu que du feu.
4. Je n'ai pas eu la vie facile.
   a. C'est quelque chose qui ne se voit pas tous les jours.
   b. J'en ai vu des vertes et des pas mûres.
5. Les gens n'aiment pas les choses comme ça.
   a. Ils se voient en cachette.
   b. C'est mal vu.
6. Ça c'est le comble.
   a. On aura tout vu!
   b. On verra bien!
7. Jean a été dupe.
   a. Il n'y voit que du feu.
   b. Il ne peut pas le voir.
8. Je me rends compte de vos intentions.
   a. Je l'ai vu de mes propres yeux.
   b. Je vous vois venir.

I. Les expressions avec *voir*. Utilisez une des expressions avec **voir** pour exprimer les idées suivantes.

1. Vous voulez que quelqu'un vous montre quelque chose. Vous dites:

   ____

2. Vous voulez dire que votre ami Pierre est toujours optimiste, confiant. Vous dites:

   ____

3. Vous voulez dire que l'obscurité vous empêche de distinguer quoi que ce soit. Vous dites:

   ____

4. Vous voulez menacer quelqu'un en lui disant que vous le battrez très fort. Vous dites:

   ____

5. Vous demandez à une amie d'imaginer une scène amusante. Vous dites:

   ____

6. Vous voulez dire que pour vous le plan ne présente pas de problèmes. Vous dites:

   ____

7. Vous voulez dire qu'à votre avis la situation va continuer pour longtemps. Vous dites:

____

8. Vous voulez dire que Marc et sa petite amie ne se rencontrent que secrètement. Vous dites:

____

9. Vous voulez dire que deux personnes ne se supportent pas. Vous dites:

____

10. Vous voulez dire que quelque chose n'arrive que très rarement. Vous dites:

____

F Idioms with **dire**

dire à qqn ses quatre vérités, dire à qqn son fait *to tell someone off*
dire que . . . *to think that*
dire ce qu'on a sur le cœur *to get something off one's chest*
dire des sottises *to talk nonsense*
dire toujours amen *to be a yes-man*
à vrai dire *to tell the truth*
à ce qu'il dit *according to him, according to what he says*
ou pour mieux dire *to put it another way*
c'est-à-dire *that is to say, in other words*
pour ainsi dire *so to speak*
comme on dit *so to speak*
on dirait que . . . *you'd think that . . .*
ne pas se le faire dire deux fois *not to have to be told twice*
autrement dit *in other words*
vouloir dire *to mean*
À qui le dites-vous (le dis-tu)? *You're telling me?*
C'est moi qui vous le dis. *Just take my word for it.*
C'est vous qui le dites. *That's what you say.*
Cela va sans dire. *It goes without saying.*
Ça te dit? *Does that appeal to you? Do you feel like doing that?*
Ça ne me dit rien. *That doesn't appeal to me at all. I don't feel like doing that.*
Ça ne me dit pas grand'chose. *I don't think much of that.*
Ça me dit quelque chose. *That rings a bell.*
C'est peu dire. *That's an understatement.*
C'est beaucoup dire. *That's saying a lot.*
C'est trop dire. *That's saying too much.*
C'est plus facile à dire qu'à faire. *That's easier said than done.*
Je ne dis pas non. *I won't say no.*
Je ne vous le fais pas dire! *I'm not putting words into your mouth.*
Il n'y a pas à dire. *There's no doubt about it.*
Je vous l'avais dit. *I told you so.*
Vous dites? *I beg your pardon.*
On se dirait en France. *You'd think you were in France.*

J. Qu'est-ce que cela veut dire? Trouvez dans la deuxième colonne des équivalents pour chacune des expressions avec **dire** de la première.

_____ 1. Ça te dit?
_____ 2. Ça me dit quelque chose.
_____ 3. Je ne dis pas non.
_____ 4. comme on dit
_____ 5. C'est beaucoup dire.
_____ 6. Vous dites?
_____ 7. C'est vous qui le dites.
_____ 8. Cela va sans dire.
_____ 9. Je vous l'avais dit.
_____ 10. Je ne me le fais pas dire deux fois.
_____ 11. autrement dit
_____ 12. Il n'y a pas à dire.

a. C'est évident.
b. C'est une façon de parler.
c. Je ne suis pas de votre avis.
d. Il n'y a pas de doute.
e. J'accepte.
f. Je crois que je m'en souviens.
g. en d'autres termes
h. Vous exagérez l'importance de l'affaire.
i. Je le fais avec empressement, sans attendre.
j. Je l'avais prévu.
k. Répétez, s'il vous plaît.
l. Tu en as envie?

G *Expressions with other common verbs*

Expressions with ***casser***

se casser la jambe/le bras *to break one's leg/arm*
se casser la figure *to fall flat on one's face*
se casser la tête *to rack one's brains*
Ça ne casse rien. *That's no great shakes.*
Tu me casses les pieds! *You're a pain in the neck! You're annoying me!*

Expressions with ***chercher***

chercher midi à 14 heures *to look for problems where there are none, to complicate things*
chercher querelle/noise à qqn *to pick a fight*
chercher des histoires à qqn *to try to make trouble for someone*
chercher la petite bête *to split hairs*
aller/venir chercher qqn *to go/come get someone, go/come pick someone up*

Expressions with ***demander***

se demander *to wonder*
On vous demande au téléphone. *You're wanted on the phone.*
Je ne demande qu'à vous voir. *All I ask for is to see you.*
Je ne demande pas mieux que rester ici. *I ask for nothing better than to stay here.*

Expressions with ***donner***

donner la chair de poule à qqn *to give someone gooseflesh*
donner du fil à retordre à qqn *to give someone a load of work, a lot of trouble*
donner le feu vert à *to give the go-ahead to*
donner le la *to set the tone*
donner l'exemple *to set an example*
donner rendez-vous à *to make an appointment with*
donner un coup de fil à qqn *to give someone a ring, call someone up*

donner un coup de main à qqn *to help someone out*
donner une fête *to throw a party*

Expressions with ***entrer***

entrer dans les mœurs *to become a way of life*
entrer en vigueur *to take effect (of laws, regulations, etc.)*
faire entrer qqch dans *to fit something into, make something fit into*
faire entrer qqn *to show someone in*
Entrez sans frapper. *Walk right in. Enter without knocking.*

Expressions with ***payer***

être payé pour le savoir *to have learned something the hard way, to know through bitter experience*
se payer la tête de qqn *to make fun of somone*
payer les pots cassés *to pay for the damage*
payer ses dettes, ses impôts *to pay one's debts, one's taxes*
les congés payés *paid vacation*
payer comptant *to pay cash*
Je te paie un café. *I invite you to have a cup of coffee.*

Expressions with ***perdre***

perdre connaissance *to lose consciousness, to black out*
perdre courage *to lose courage*
perdre le nord *to lose one's bearings*
perdre patience *to lose patience*
perdre du poids *to lose weight*
perdre qqn de vue *to lose sight of someone*
perdre son temps *to waste one's time*
perdre du terrain *to lose ground*
se perdre *to get lost*
Tu n'y perds rien! *It's no loss.*

Expressions with ***rouler***

rouler sur l'or *to be loaded, very rich*
Sur l'autoroute on roule à 90 à l'heure. *On the superhighway we go 90 kilometers an hour.*
se faire rouler *to get taken, to get swindled*
se rouler par terre de rire *to be rolling on the ground with laughter*
C'est à se rouler (par terre)! *It's a scream! It's a riot!*

Expressions with ***sonner***

Il est trois heures sonnées. *It's already past three.*
Minuit sonne. *The clock strikes midnight.*

Expressions with ***tenir***

tenir bon *to hold one's ground*
tenir compte de *to keep in mind, take into account*
tenir le coup *to hold out, to make it through, to weather the storm*
se tenir au courant de qqch *to keep informed about something*
se tenir les côtes *to split one's sides laughing*
Ce raisonnement ne tient pas debout. *That reasoning doesn't hold water.*
Tenez votre droite/gauche. *Keep to the right/left (driving).*
Qu'à cela ne tienne. *That's no problem.*

Expressions with ***tirer***

se tirer d'affaire *to manage, get along*
s'en tirer *to manage, get along*

s'en tirer à bon compte *to get off cheaply, easy*
tiré à quatre épingles *dressed to kill*
tiré par les cheveux *far-fetched*
tirer au sort *to draw lots*
tirer la langue *to stick out one's tongue*

K. Exprimez-vous comme il faut. Choisissez dans la liste ci-dessous l'expression convenable pour les situations proposées.

Tu me casses les pieds.	Il roule sur l'or.
Donne-moi un coup de main.	Tu me tiens au courant.
tient bon	cherchent la bagarre
Il a perdu le nord.	Ce raisonnement ne tient pas debout.
On va tirer au sort.	Il a payé ses dettes.
entrent dans les mœurs	Il cherche midi a 14 h.
Ils me donnent du fil à retordre.	On vous demande au téléphone.

1. Quand quelque chose manque de logique, on dit:

 ____

2. Quand une armée ne cède pas devant l'attaque de l'ennemi, on dit qu'elle

 ____

3. Quand quelqu'un vous ennuie avec ses questions et ses objections, vous lui dites:

 ____

4. Quand vous voulez appeler quelqu'un parce qu'il y a un coup de fil pour lui, vous dites:

 ____

5. Pour exprimer l'idée que quelqu'un est très, très riche, vous dites (d'une façon familière):

 ____

6. Vous êtes professeur. Pour dire que vos étudiants vous font travailler trop, vous dites:

 ____

7. Pour dire à quelqu'un que Charles a remboursé l'argent qu'il devait, vous dites:

 ____

8. Vous notez que Serge est désorienté. Vous dites:

 ____

9. Vous proposez une méthode impartielle pour choisir la personne qui va demander au prof de remettre l'examen à la semaine prochaine. Vous dites:

 ____

10. Vous voulez que votre ami vous aide. Vous lui dites:

 ____

L. Répondez. Choisissez la réponse ou la réaction correcte.

1. L'enfant a fait un geste de mépris?
   a. Oui, il a tiré la langue.
   b. Oui, il m'a donné la chair de poule.
2. Cette fille sert de modèle aux autres?
   a. Oui, elle donne l'exemple.
   b. Oui, elle se roule par terre.
3. La solution va être difficile à trouver.
   a. Oui, il faudra se casser la figure.
   b. Oui, il faudra se casser la tête.
4. Tu vas te faire avoir!
   a. Non, je ne me fais jamais rouler.
   b. Non, je ne me fais jamais entrer.
5. Est-ce que Jeanne a résisté jusqu'à la fin?
   a. Oui, elle a donné du fil à retordre.
   b. Oui, elle a tenu le coup.
6. Vous avez déjà commencé?
   a. Oui, on nous a donné le la.
   b. Oui, on nous a donné le feu vert.
7. Il a maigri?
   a. Oui, il a perdu du poids.
   b. Oui, il nous a perdu de vue.
8. On dit que ces idées sont moins importantes qu'avant.
   a. C'est vrai. Elles sont entrées en vigueur.
   b. C'est vrai. Elles ont perdu du terrain.
9. Il se moque de nous?
   a. Oui, il se paie notre tête.
   b. Oui, il cherche la petite bête.
10. Pourquoi est-ce que tu dis que je cherche midi à 14 heures?
    a. Parce que tu cherches des complications inutiles.
    b. Parce que tu paies les pots cassés.

H *Idioms from rural life: the farm, cats, dogs, and cabbages*

Rural images

aller comme un tablier (*apron*) **à une vache** *to look terrible on someone (item of clothing)*
avoir un bœuf sur la langue *to be hesitant to speak up*
la brebis galeuse *black sheep*
connu comme le loup blanc *well-known, easily recognized*
doux comme un agneau *gentle as a lamb*
entre chien et loup *at twilight*
être sur la paille *to be destitute*
faire l'âne pour avoir du son *to play dumb (with the idea of getting something)*
fauché comme les blés *flat broke*
ménager la chèvre et le chou *to sit on the fence, to not take sides*
mettre la charrue devant les bœufs *to put the cart before the horse*
mourir sur le fumier *to die in poverty, to die destitute*

têtu comme une mule *stubborn as a mule*
un nid de poule *a pothole*
C'est une pierre dans mon jardin. *It's an insult to me, a dig at me.*
Le champ est libre. *The coast is clear.*
On n'a pas gardé les cochons ensemble! *Why are you getting so familiar with me?*
Quand les poules auront des dents. *That'll be the day.*

Les chats

À bon chat, bon rat. *Tit for tat.*
Chat échaudé craint le feu. *He won't make the same mistake twice.*
ne pas réveiller le chat qui dort *to let sleeping dogs lie*
avoir un chat dans la gorge *to have a frog in one's throat*
Il n'y avait pas un chat! *There wasn't a soul!*
Je donne ma langue au chat. *I give up (trying to answer a riddle, etc.).*
acheter chat en poche *to buy a pig in a poke*
appeler un chat un chat *to call a spade a spade*
avoir d'autres chats à fouetter *to have other fish to fry*
s'entendre comme chien et chat *not to get along at all*

Les chiens

arriver comme un chien dans un jeu de quilles (*bowling*) *to turn up when least needed or wanted*
avoir du chien *to have style*
Ce n'est pas fait pour les chiens. *It's meant to be used.*
Chien méchant. *Beware of the dog. (sign)*
dormir en chien de fusil *to sleep all curled up*
Il fait un temps de chien. *The weather is terrible.*
être d'une humeur de chien *to be in a lousy mood*
malade comme un chien *sick as a dog*
s'entendre comme chien et chat *not to get along at all*
se donner un mal de chien *to work like a dog*
se regarder en chiens de faïence *to glare at each other*
traiter qqn comme un chien *to treat someone like a dog*

Les choux

C'est bête comme chou. *It's as easy as pie.*
ménager la chèvre et le chou *to play both ends against the middle*
C'est chou vert et vert chou. *It's six of one and half dozen of the other. It's all the same.*
être dans les choux *to be in difficulty, be out of the running, to have done badly on one's tests*
Ta chambre est très chou. *Your room is lovely.*
Cette enfant est très chou dans sa nouvelle jupe. *This little girl is adorable in her new skirt.*

M. Les expressions à l'œuvre. Utilisez une des expressions de cette section pour exprimer les idées suivantes.

1. Le patron a l'air très irrité aujourd'hui.

___

2. Tu fais toujours d'abord ce qui doit être fait ensuite.

___

3. Cette chaussée est pleine de trous.

4. Marc a raté ses examens.

5. C'est un type qui n'aime pas prendre parti.

6. Les rues étaient désertes.

7. On l'a fait pour être utilisé.

8. Ils se regardent avec beaucoup d'hostilité.

9. Il n'y a vraiment pas de différence.

10. Ce couple est toujours en train de disputer.

11. Il arrive toujours à un moment inopportun et il dérange tout le monde.

12. Il est trop prudent à cause de l'accident qu'il a eu.

13. C'est un homme trop décidé, incapable de changer d'avis.

14. Me voici absolument sans argent.

15. Pourquoi me tutoyez-vous?

16. Qu'est-ce que tu as? Tu as la voix enrouée (*hoarse*).

17. Il faut appeler les choses par leur nom.

18. Le professeur m'a traité très, très mal.

19. Lucie fait semblant de ne pas comprendre pour gagner quelque chose.

20. C'est très facile à faire.

Note culturelle

Il y a des expressions françaises qui sont difficiles à comprendre sans avoir des connaissances de la culture française.

- **une fenêtre à guillotine** *sash window:* La fenêtre française (la porte-fenêtre) typique s'ouvre au milieu, comme deux portes. La fenêtre américaine qui s'ouvre de haut en bas s'appelle **fenêtre à guillotine** parce qu'elle rappelle la machine à exécution française dont l'adoption en 1791 a été proposée par le docteur Joseph Guillotin.
- **traverser entre les clous** *to cross in the crosswalk:* En France la traversée des piétons dans les villes est marquée non pas par des lignes peintes sur la chaussée mais par deux lignes de clous enfoncés dans la rue.
- **être Gros-Jean comme devant** *to be back to square one, back where one started from:* Gros-Jean est une figure traditionnelle qui représente un homme simple et ignorant.
- **un violon d'Ingres** *a hobby:* Le fameux peintre français du dix-neuvième siècle, Jean Auguste Ingres, jouait du violon à ses heures libres.
- **se porter comme le Pont Neuf** *to be in the best of health, feel fit as a fiddle:* Le Pont Neuf est le plus vieux pont de Paris, un pont de pierre très solide, utilisable même aujourd'hui pour les piétons et les voitures.

I *Idioms relating to time, weather, the life-cycle, and eating*

Le passage du temps

La semaine des quatre jeudis. *Never in a month of Sundays.*
Tous les trente-six du mois. *Once in a blue moon.*
remettre qqch à la Saint-Glinglin *to postpone something forever, till the cows come home*
à la dernière minute *at the last minute, under the wire*
renvoyer aux calendes grecques *to put off till the cows come home*
en ce moment *at this time*
pour le moment *for the time being*
Il est grand temps. *It's high time.*
à ses heures *when one is free, when one feels like doing something*
à une heure avancée *late*
les heures d'affluence, de pointe *rush hour*
du jour au lendemain *overnight*

Le temps qu'il fait

Il pleut à seaux/Il pleut des cordes. *It's pouring. It's raining cats and dogs.*
parler de la pluie et du beau temps *to make small talk*
Je ne suis pas tombé(e) de la dernière pluie. *I wasn't born yesterday.*
Il fait lourd. *It's humid out.*
rapide comme l'éclair *fast as lightning*

La vie humaine

être né(e) coiffé(e) *to be born with a silver spoon in one's mouth*
en bas âge *little, young*

faire les quatre cents coups *to sow one's wild oats, have a wild youth*
avoir le coup de foudre *to fall head over heels in love with someone*
avoir quarante ans bien sonnés *to be well past forty*
friser la cinquantaine *to be pushing fifty*
Quel âge me donnez-vous? *How old do you think I am?*
d'un certain âge *middle-aged*
se faire vieux *to be getting on in years*
faire de vieux os *to live to a ripe old age*
Sa vie ne tient qu'à un fil. *His life hangs by a thread. He's deathly ill.*
mourir de sa belle mort *to die of old age*
casser sa pipe *to kick the bucket*
trouver la mort *to lose one's life*

À table

aimer la table *to like good food*
une bonne fourchette *a hearty eater*
avoir/vendre qqch pour une bouchée de pain *to get/sell something for a song*
casser la croûte *to have a bite*
avoir l'estomac dans les talons *to be famished*
manger à sa faim *to eat one's fill*
manger son pain blanc le premier *to eat one's cake first, to not save the best for last*
manger comme quatre *to eat like a horse, to eat for four*
marcher sur des œufs *to walk on eggs, to tread lightly*
mourir de faim *to be dying of hunger*
faire venir l'eau à la bouche à qqn *to make someone's mouth water*
avoir un appétit d'oiseau *to eat like a bird*
n'avoir rien à se mettre sous la dent *to have nothing to eat*
long comme une journée sans pain *endless*
avoir un bon fromage *to have a cushy job, a soft job*
entre la poire et le fromage *at the end of a meal*

N. Vous comprenez? Laquelle des deux possibilités est une réponse logique?

1. Pierre mange beaucoup.
   a. Oui, il a l'estomac dans les talons.
   b. Oui, c'est une bonne fourchette.
2. Le vieux monsieur Jospin a cassé sa pipe.
   a. Oui, je sais qu'il est mort.
   b. Oui, il faut le remettre à la Saint-Glinglin.
3. Tu es amoureux?
   a. Oui, c'était le coup de foudre.
   b. Oui, je suis né coiffé.
4. C'est un type qui connaît tout, n'est-ce pas?
   a. Oui, il a un bon fromage.
   b. Oui, il n'est pas tombé de la dernière pluie, lui.
5. Je crois qu'elle a presque quarante ans.
   a. Moi aussi, je crois qu'elle frise la quarantaine.
   b. Moi aussi, je crois qu'elle a quarante ans bien sonnés.
6. C'est un jeune homme trop prudent.
   a. Oui, il fait de vieux os.
   b. Oui, il marche sur des œufs.

7. Tu le vois très peu, n'est-ce pas?
   a. Tous les trente-six du mois.
   b. À la petite semaine.

8. Ce film est interminable.
   a. Oui, long comme une journée sans pain.
   b. Oui, rapide comme l'éclair.

9. Il m'ennuie. Il ne dit que des banalités, des choses sans importance.
   a. Je sais. Il fait ses quatre cents coups.
   b. Je sais. Il parle de la pluie et du beau temps.

10. Quel beau manteau! Il t'a coûté cher?
    a. Non, j'ai mangé mon pain blanc le premier.
    b. Non, je l'ai eu pour une bouchée de pain.

J *Other idioms*

Prepositions and prepositional phrases

à base de *composed of, made of*
à deux pas de *just a stone's throw from*
à part *aside from*
d'après *according to*
à raison de *at the rate of*
à titre de *in the capacity of*
au lieu de *instead of*
en dépit de *in spite of*
en qualité de *in one's capacity of*
en raison de *on account of*
y compris *including*

Conversational fillers, reactions, interjections, transition words

d'abord *first*
À d'autres! *What a ridiculous story!*
à mon avis *in my opinion*
à propos *by the way*
À quoi bon? *What's the good of it? What's the use?*
au fait *by the way*
au fond *actually, basically*
au reste, du reste *moreover*
avant tout *above all*
C'est dommage. *It's a shame, pity.*
Bien entendu! *Of course!*
C'est de la blague! *It's not serious! It's ridiculous!*
Bon débarras! *Good riddance!*
Ça alors! *Well I'll be darned!*
Ça va de soi. *It goes without saying.*
C'est entendu. *Agreed.*
dans l'ensemble *on the whole*
de toute façon *anyway*
en fait *as a matter of fact*
Et comment! *And how!*
Et pour cause! *And for good reason!*
Et après? *So what?*
Je m'en fiche! *I don't give a darn! (slang)*
Fiche-moi la paix! *Leave me alone!*

Mon œil! *My eye!*
Motus! *Keep it quiet! Don't breathe a word of it!*
par contre *on the other hand*
Pas question! *Nothing doing!*
Sans blague! *No kidding!*
selon le cas *as the case may be*
somme toute *all in all*
Ta gueule! *Shut up! (somewhat vulgar slang)*
Tant mieux! *Great! So much the better!*
Tant pis! *Too bad! Tough luck!*
Vous voulez rire. *You're joking.*

Expressions of time

à plusieurs reprises *several times*
à tour de rôle *in turn*
d'avance *in advance*
dans huit jours *in a week*
d'ici là *until then, in the meantime*
encore une fois *again*
une fois pour toutes *once and for all*
il y a belle lurette *it's been a long time, it happened a long time ago*
jusqu'ici *so far, thus far*
sous peu *shortly*
le temps de *just give me enough time to*
tour à tour *in turn*

Descriptions

à bout, à plat *exhausted*
à la page *in the know, up-to-date*
à la perfection *just right, perfectly done, to a T*
à perte de vue *as far as the eye can see*
à point *well-done (meat)*
à quatre pattes *on all fours*
à souhait *perfectly, to perfection, as well, as much as you could want*
au bout du monde *in the middle of nowhere*
au-dessous de tout *hopeless, disgracefully bad, incompetent*
bel et bien *altogether*
C'est du gâteau! *It's easy as pie. It's a piece of cake!*
C'est son pere tout craché. *He's the spitting image of his father.*
C'est le dernier cri. *It's the latest thing. It's the latest fashion.*
C'est tout un. *It's really the same thing.*
être collant *to be a real leech, to be hard to shake, hard to get rid of*
cousu d'or *filthy rich*
dans le vent *in the swing of things*
de mal en pis *from bad to worse*
en cachette *on the sly*
en douceur *gently, softly*
en bon/mauvais état *in good/bad condition*
en panne *out of order, broken*
en panne sèche *out of gas*
en un clin d'œil *in a jiffy, in a flash*
une femme de tête *a capable woman*
fort en anglais *good at English*
hors de soi *beside oneself*
de la peine perdue *wasted effort*

Expressions of manner and degree

à bout portant *point-blank*
à contrecœur *reluctantly*
à fond *thoroughly*
à moitié *halfway*
à mi-chemin *halfway*
à peine *hardly*
à peu près *almost, just about*
à tout prix *at all costs*
de bon gré *willingly*
peu s'en faut *almost, very nearly*
raison de plus pour *all the more reason to*

Other idioms

à la une *on the front page*
arriver à faire qqch *to manage to do something*
au besoin *if you need it, if need be*
au loin *in the distance*
Au secours! *Help!*
Ça fait mon affaire. *That's just what I wanted, what I was looking for.*
Ça m'arrange. *That suits me just fine.*
Ça revient à la même chose. *That amounts to the same thing.*
C'est bonnet blanc et blanc bonnet. *It's six of one and half a dozen of the other.*
un coup de tête *an impulse*
un coup monté *a setup*
coûte que coûte *at any cost, come what may*
se débrouiller *to get along, manage*
de loin *from far, from afar, far and away*
Défense de fumer! *No smoking.*
Défense d'entrer! *No admittance. Keep out.*
l'échapper belle *to have a narrow escape*
entre l'enclume et le marteau *between a rock and a hard place (the anvil and the hammer)*
et ainsi de suite *and so on*
En avant! *Let's move along! Let's go ahead! Let's get going!*
faire l'appel *to take attendance*
faute de mieux *for want of anything better (to do, etc.)*
ficher le camp *to scram, get out of here (slang)*
une mauvaise langue *a gossip, a viper (evil-tongued)*
Monsieur un Tel *Mr. So-and-so, Mr. What's-his-name*
On n'en est pas trop avancé. *A lot of good that did us.*
le petit coin *the bathroom, the john*
pile ou face *heads or tails*
un pot de vin *a bribe*
Pour l'amour de Dieu! *For God's sake!*
pour rire *as a joke, just for fun*
pour une fois *for a change*
sauf avis contraire *unless you hear something to the contrary*
sauf erreur *unless there is a mistake*

O. Traduction. Écrivez l'équivalent français de ces locutions anglaises.

1. on the other hand ______________________________
2. wasted effort ______________________________

3. as the case may be ______

4. in turn ______

5. Don't breathe a word of it! ______

6. to be hard to get rid of ______

7. And for good reason! ______

8. once and for all ______

9. a setup ______

10. thus far ______

11. a gossip ______

12. point blank ______

13. What's the use? ______

14. No kidding. ______

15. thoroughly ______

16. instead of ______

17. No admittance. ______

18. beside oneself ______

19. My eye! ______

20. broken, out of order ______

P. Synonymes. Trouvez dans la deuxième colonne des synonymes pour chacune des expressions de la première.

______	1. Vous voulez rire.	a. au reste
______	2. au fait	b. ne . . . guère
______	3. à tout prix	c. faute de mieux
______	4. en ce moment	d. filer
______	5. au besoin	e. C'est bonnet blanc et blanc bonnet.
______	6. Ça fait mon affaire.	f. malgré
______	7. à peine	g. maintenant
______	8. à bout	h. Tant mieux!
______	9. du reste	i. presque
______	10. en dépit de	j. à plat
______	11. en un clin d'œil	k. C'est dommage.
______	12. C'est tout un.	l. Tais-toi.
______	13. Ta gueule!	m. s'il le faut
______	14. ficher le camp	n. coûte que coûte
______	15. à titre de	o. Vous blaguez.
______	16. peu s'en faut	p. à propos
		q. en qualité de
		r. tout de suite
		s. entre l'enclume et le marteau
		t. Ça m'arrange.

K Proverbs

À bon vin, point d'enseigne. *The reputation of a good thing precedes it.*
Après la pluie, le beau temps. *Every cloud has a silver lining.*
Aux grands maux, les grands remèdes. *Big problems require big solutions.*
Les beaux esprits se rencontrent. *Great minds think alike.*
Les bons comptes font les bons amis. *Don't let money squabbles ruin a friendship.*
Charbonnier est maître chez soi. *Every man's home is his castle.*
Le chat parti, les souris dansent. *When the cat's away, the mice will play.*
Comme on fait son lit, on se couche. *As you make your bed, so you shall lie in it.*
Deux avis valent mieux qu'un. *Two heads are better than one.*
L'enfer est pavé de bonnes intentions. *The road to hell is paved with good intentions.*
C'est en forgeant qu'on devient forgeron. *Practice makes perfect.*
Des goûts et des couleurs il ne faut pas discuter. *There's no accounting for taste.*
La goutte d'eau qui fait déborder le vase. *The straw that breaks the camel's back.*
L'habit ne fait pas le moine. *Clothes don't make the man.*
Une hirondelle ne fait pas le printemps. *One swallow doesn't make a summer.*
Il faut battre le fer pendant qu'il est chaud. *Strike while the iron is hot.*
Il n'est pire eau que l'eau qui dort. *Still water runs deep.*
Il n'y a pas de fumée sans feu. *There's no smoke without a fire.*
Il y a loin de la coupe aux lèvres. *There's many a slip twixt the cup and the lip.*
Loin des yeux, loin du cœur. *Out of sight, out of mind.*
Ce n'est pas la mer à boire. *It's not very difficult to do.*
Mieux vaut tard que jamais. *Better late than never.*
Paris ne s'est pas fait en un jour. *Rome wasn't built in a day.*
Petit à petit, l'oiseau fait son nid. *Slow and steady wins the race.*
Pierre qui roule n'amasse pas mousse. *A rolling stone gathers no moss.*
Plus on est de fous, plus on rit. *The more the merrier.*
Point de nouvelles, bonnes nouvelles. *No news is good news.*
Qui se ressemble, s'assemble. *Birds of a feather flock together.*
Santé passe richesse. *Health is better than riches.*
Tel père, tel fils. *Like father, like son.*
Un(e) de perdu(e), dix de retrouvé(e)s. *There are plenty more like him/her out there.*
Vouloir, c'est pouvoir. *Where there's a will, there's a way.*

Q. Quel proverbe? Écrivez le proverbe que vous utiliseriez dans chaque cas.

1. You want to tell a friend that clothes are not as important as he or she thinks.

____

2. You try to warn a friend not to be too encouraged by one positive sign.

____

3. You want to console a friend who has just broken up with his girlfriend.

____

4. You want to say that every person can make the rules in his or her own house.

____

5. You and your friend come up with the same brilliant idea at the same time.

____

6. You want to advise a friend who can't settle down that he will have no future if he doesn't.

____

7. You encourage people to invite more friends to the party.

____

8. You want to warn a friend that she shouldn't overwork and ruin her health.

____

9. You want to say that great things take a long time to accomplish.

____

10. You warn a friend that something drastic may have to be done because the situation is so serious.

____

11. You claim that the children were mischievous because their parents weren't around.

____

12. You tell your friend to take advantage of the opportunities that have presented themselves or they may disappear.

____

Examination

Section I

A. Complétez les phrases suivantes avec la forme correcte du présent du verbe entre parenthèses.

1. Il ________________ (travailler) dans un magasin.
2. Nous ________________ (s'efforcer) d'étudier tous les jours.
3. Les élèves ne ________________ (jeter) pas de papier par terre.
4. J'________________ (emmener) ma copine au cinéma.
5. Jacqueline et moi, nous ________________ (manger) à la maison aujourd'hui.
6. Si tu as un problème, tu m'________________ (appeler).
7. Je vois que vous ________________ (réussir) à tous les examens.
8. Ils ________________ (vendre) leur voiture.
9. Lequel est-ce que vous ________________ (préférer)?
10. Le bébé ________________ (peser) cinq kilos maintenant.

B. Complétez les phrases suivantes avec la forme convenable du présent du verbe entre parenthèses.

1. Claude et Philippe ne ________________ (vouloir) pas étudier à la bibliothèque.
2. Je ne ________________ (savoir) pas faire la cuisine.
3. À quelle heure est-ce que vous ________________ (faire) les courses?
4. Tu ________________ (mettre) un pull tous les jours.
5. La petite fille ________________ (cueillir) des fleurs dans le jardin.
6. Ces fermiers ________________ (produire) du fromage.
7. Nous ________________ (recevoir) beaucoup de courier.
8. Le malade ne ________________ (reconnaître) pas ses parents.
9. Nous ________________ (souffrir) d'allergies.
10. Elle ________________ (suivre) des cours d'informatique.
11. Vous ________________ (apprendre) beaucoup de français.
12. Donne-moi quelque chose à boire. Je ________________ (mourir) de soif.
13. Je suis fatigué parce que je ne ________________ (dormir) pas assez.
14. Nous ________________ (dire) toujours ce que nous pensons.

C. Transformez les phrases suivantes en questions en employant l'inversion du sujet et du verbe.

1. Le médecin peut me voir maintenant.
2. Les ministres discutent de l'économie.
3. Mme Durocher compte vendre sa maison.
4. Vos tantes ne sortent pas en hiver.
5. Notre professeur n'arrive jamais en retard.

D. Refaites les phrases suivantes au passé composé.

1. Ils dînent en ville.
2. Nous ouvrons les fenêtres.
3. Elle descend faire les courses.
4. Hélène et Lise vont à l'école à bicyclette.
5. Vous réfléchissez beaucoup à l'avenir.
6. Beaucoup de soldats meurent pendant la guerre.
7. Les élèves n'interrompent jamais le professeur.
8. Elle promet de nous aider.
9. Les employés ont des ennuis avec le directeur.
10. Nous peignons notre maison.
11. Nous écrivons des lettres à nos amis.
12. Vous lisez l'article.

E. Complétez les phrases suivantes avec la forme correcte de l'imparfait ou du passé composé des verbes entre parenthèses.

1. Il ____________________ (faire) très beau quand Jacques et Christine ____________________ (sortir).
2. Quand il ____________________ (arriver) il ____________________ (être) 3 heures et demie.
3. Je ____________________ (manger) quand tu me (m')____________________ (téléphoner).
4. Quand tu nous ____________________ (voir), nous ____________________ (lire) le journal.

F. Écrivez la forme convenable du futur des verbes entre parenthèses.

1. Vous ____________________ (faire) un voyage.
2. Nous ____________________ (venir) plus tard.
3. Je crois que j'____________________ (avoir) froid.
4. Tu m'____________________ (envoyer) une carte postale, n'est-ce pas?
5. Elles ____________________ (être) en retard.

G. Écrivez la forme convenable du conditionnel des verbes entre parenthèses.

1. Nous ____________________ (vouloir) faire du latin.
2. Elles ____________________ (devoir) attendre un peu.
3. J'étais sûr qu'il ____________________ (pleuvoir).
4. Est-ce que tu ____________________ (pouvoir) le faire?
5. Si j'avais le temps, je ____________________ (courir) tous les jours.

H. Formez des phrases au plus-que-parfait avec les éléments donnés.

1. je / ne pas s'habiller / encore

   ____

2. il / prendre / son café

   ____

3. elles / arriver / en avance

   ____

4. les enfants / se coucher / déjà

   ____

5. nous / préparer / le repas

   ____

I. Complétez les phrases suivantes avec le futur antérieur des verbes entre parenthèses.

1. Je ne sais pas si j'__________ (finir).
2. Tout le monde __________ (partir) quand vous arrivez.
3. Nous viendrons après que les enfants __________ (s'endormir).
4. Vous écouterez les disques que nous __________ (choisir).

J. Complétez les phrases suivantes avec le plus-que-parfait ou le conditionnel antérieur. Ces phrases expriment toutes des conditions.

1. Si tu m'__________ (appeler), je __________ (venir).
2. Si Loïc et Paul __________ (se lever) de bonne heure, ils __________ (ne pas manquer) la conférence.
3. Si nous t'__________ (voir), nous t'__________ (donner) les notes de philo.
4. Philippe __________ (étudier) si vous lui __________ (dire) qu'il y avait un examen.

K. Complétez les phrases suivantes avec la préposition qui manque. Si la phrase est complète telle qu'elle est, marquez le blanc d'un X.

1. Les enfants se mettent __________ jouer.
2. La secrétaire a renoncé __________ son poste.
3. Je sais __________ préparer une tarte aux fraises.
4. Le bruit m'empêche __________ étudier.
5. Un petit effort suffit __________ le faire.
6. On ne m'a pas laissé __________ sortir.
7. Le professeur est prêt __________ nous aider.
8. Nous avons passé l'après-midi __________ visiter les musées.
9. Il faut faire __________ réparer la voiture.
10. J'étais surpris __________ la voir au bureau.
11. Ils nous ont conseillé __________ attendre un peu.
12. Marc a été très content __________ nous voir.

Section II

A. Écrivez les articles défini et indéfini qui conviennent aux substantifs.

	article défini	*article indefini*	
1.	____________	____________	siècle
2.	____________	____________	fenêtres
3.	____________	____________	ingénieur
4.	____________	____________	dictionnaire
5.	____________	____________	vitrine
6.	____________	____________	ordinateurs

B. Écrivez les mots suivants au pluriel.

1. un travail ____________
2. un idéal ____________
3. un clou ____________
4. un cours ____________
5. une voix ____________
6. un chou ____________

C. Écrivez les formes correctes des adjectifs de nationalité qui correspondent aux pays de la liste.

pays	*masc. sing.*	*fem. sing.*	*masc. pl.*	*fem. pl.*
1. la France	____________	____________	____________	____________
2. la Grèce	____________	____________	____________	____________
3. la Chine	____________	____________	____________	____________
4. le Canada	____________	____________	____________	____________

D. Complétez les phrases suivantes en écrivant la forme correcte de l'adjectif entre parenthèses.

1. Ils ont trouvé un ____________ (beau) appartement à Paris.
2. Je vais te faire écouter ma chanson ____________ (favori).
3. On a construit de ____________ (nouveau) immeubles dans le quartier.
4. Elle porte une jupe ____________ (blanc).
5. Je cherche des chaussures ____________ (marron).

E. Complétez les phrases suivantes en écrivant l'équivalent français des mots entre parenthèses.

1. Michèle a apporté sa cassette et Maurice a apporté ______________ (*his*).
2. J'ai deux revues. ______________ (*Which one*) voulez-vous lire?
3. Nous ne comprenons pas ______________ (*these*) articles.
4. Où est ______________ (*my*) assiette?
5. Nous allons écouter ______________ (*our*) disques et ______________ (*the ones*) d'Odile.
6. Les poèmes de Richard sont intéressants, mais ______________ (*ours*) sont ______________ (*better*).
7. —______________ (*Which*) chambre préférez-vous?

   —______________ (*The one*) qui est au troisième étage.

F. Complétez les phrases suivantes avec le(s) pronom(s) qui manque(nt).

1. On m'a dit qu'il y a un pressing dans cette rue, mais je ne __________ vois pas.
2. Voici les questions. Tu pourras __________ répondre?
3. Nous avons beaucoup de livres à lire. J'__________ ai déjà lu trois.
4. Je lui ai demandé les papiers, mais il ne __________ __________ a pas donnés.
5. Il y a du poulet dans le frigo. Tu peux __________ prendre si tu as faim.
6. Voici une photo de notre hôtel à Marseille. Vous vous __________ souvenez?
7. Barbara n'a plus sa bicyclette. On __________ __________ a volée.
8. Les enfants adorent le musée scientifique. Je vais __________ __________ emmener.
9. Je veux du lait. Si tu descends au marché, tu peux __________ __________ rapporter.
10. Philippe et Sylvie ne comprennent pas ces mots.

    Explique-__________-__________.

Section III

A. Complétez les phrases suivantes en écrivant l'équivalent français des mots ou des chiffres entre parenthèses

1. (80) ______________________________ étudiants
2. (300) ______________________________ habitants
3. (810) ______________________________ kilomètres
4. (12:30 P.M.) arriver à ______________________________
5. (April 10) La réunion est prévue pour ______________________________.

B. Écrivez l'adverbe qui correspond aux adjectifs suivants.

1. heureux ______________________
2. courant ______________________
3. confus ______________________
4. facile ______________________
5. intelligent ______________________

C. Complétez les phrases suivantes avec les prépositions qui manquent. N'oubliez pas les contractions **au, aux, du, des.**

1. Je vais au lycée ________ pied.
2. Un sandwich ________ saucisson, s'il vous plaît.
3. J'ai changé ________ avis.
4. Je ne savais pas qu'il était fâché, mais il m'a répondu ________ colère.
5. Les enfants adorent voyager ________ avion.
6. Nous avons passé les vacances ________ Haïti.
7. La salle à manger est longue ________ cinq mètres.
8. Tu peux me prêter de l'argent? Je suis ________ le sou.
9. Fais-moi confiance. Je te parle ________ ami.
10. Qui est ________ l'appareil?
11. Mon beau-frère travaille ________ Japon.
12. J'ai envie de faire un stage ________ Allemagne.

Section IV

A. Complétez les phrases suivantes avec le pronom relatif qui manque.

1. Je ne connais pas l'acteur ________ joue dans cette pièce.
2. Expliquez-moi ________ il s'agit.
3. C'est un cours ________ me donne beaucoup de mal.
4. Je vais t'emmener chez un médecin ________ je connais.
5. Nous ne comprenons pas très bien ________ vous voulez dire.
6. Il a réussi à trouver tout ________ manquait.
7. Voici l'ordinateur ________ je me sers pour rédiger.
8. C'est un client à ________ je téléphone tous les mois.
9. La table sur ________ je travaille est dans la cuisine.
10. C'est le problème à cause ________ il a renoncé à son poste.

B. Complétez les phrases suivantes avec la forme correcte du verbe entre parenthèses. Choisissez entre l'indicatif et le subjonctif.

1. Je veux qu'elle ____________________ (revenir) aujourd'hui.
2. Il n'est pas vrai que vous ____________________ (savoir) la réponse.
3. Ils devront prendre un taxi à moins que je (j')____________________ (aller) les chercher.
4. Il est évident que les problèmes ____________________ (être) graves.
5. Je cherche une maison qui ____________________ (être) près de la gare.
6. Nous insistons pour que tout le monde ____________________ (finir) son travail.
7. J'espère que vous ____________________ (pouvoir) venir.
8. Ta mère est contente que tu ____________________ (avoir) de bonnes notes en maths.
9. Il est peu probable qu'il ____________________ (s'en rendre) compte.
10. Je répète l'explication pour que tu le ____________________ (comprendre).

PART SIX

French and Francophone Culture

CHAPTER 29

THE FRENCH LANGUAGE

LES ORIGINES DE LA LANGUE FRANÇAISE

- La langue française représente la continuation ininterrompue du latin parlé de la Gaule, nom celtique de la France. Le latin fut implanté par les Romains en Gaule un peu avant le début de notre ère, après leur conquête de la Gaule documentée par Jules César dans son livre *La guerre des Gaules*. Le français, comme l'espagnol, le portuguais, l'italien et le roumain, fait partie de la famille de langues néolatines ou romanes, langues qui dérivent toutes du latin.
- Jules César ne conquiert pas un pays sans habitants. Sur la Côte méditerranéenne les Grecs ont une colonie à Massilia, aujourd'hui Marseille. L'arrière-pays est habité par les Gaulois, peuple celtique dont la présence date des invasions celtiques du septième siècle avant Jésus-Christ.
- Le latin parlé de l'Empire romain n'est pas la même chose que le latin classique littéraire. La langue parlée est pleine d'emprunts grecs, soit de niveau populaire tels que **gouverner, pierre, coup, place,** soit de niveau cultivé tels que **philosophie, idée**. D'origine grecque sont aussi de nombreux mots qui relèvent du domaine de la religion chrétienne: **évêque, église, prêtre, ange, diable**.
- La langue gauloise ne disparaît pas tout de suite. Les Romains n'avaient aucun programme d'assimilation culturelle et linguistique forcée, et la latinisation de la population de la Gaule était donc graduelle. Pendant une longue période de bilinguisme, le latin parlé de la Gaule s'enrichit d'emprunts celtiques. Ces emprunts se groupent dans plusieurs catégories: la production de la bière: **le tonneau** (*keg*), **brasser** (*to brew*); le foyer (*hearth*) celtique: **la suie** (*soot*), **la broche** (*spit to roast meat on*), **le berceau** (*cradle*); la maison celtique en bois (les Romains construisaient en pierre): **le charpentier, les copeaux** (*wood shavings*); le paysage: **la lande** (*moor*), **le chêne** (*oak tree*), **l'if** (*yew tree*), **la bruyère** (*heather*), **la boue** (*mud*). Celtique aussi était un système numérique basé sur vingt (au lieu de dix) dont le terme français **quatre-vingts** est peut-être le vestige le plus frappant.
- La Gaule est presque entièrement romanisée (c'est-à-dire, tout le monde parle latin) à la fin du cinquième siècle de notre ère, époque des invasions germaniques qui mèneront à la chute de l'Empire romain. La plupart du territoire français est maintenant gouverné par des peuples germaniques, les Francs et les Burgondes. La classe dominante est de langue germanique, mais les Francs étaient plus tolérants que les autres peuples germaniques (par exemple, les Wisigoths qui ont fondé un royaume en Espagne) et ils permettaient le mariage entre Francs et Latins. Ils ont adopté le latin comme langue de la religion et langue de l'administration. Les Francs ont laissé une empreinte très marquée sur le latin parlé de la Gaule, la langue qui allait devenir le français. Ils ont même donné leur nom au pays. **Frantia** (terre des Francs, d'où **France**) remplace **Gallia** (terre des Gaules) et la langue néolatine de la région parisienne s'appelle **le francien**. L'influence germanique sur le français est beaucoup plus marquée que l'influence germanique des Wisigoths sur l'espagnol ou celle des Ostrogoths et des Lombards sur l'italien.

- Les emprunts linguistiques pris aux Francs, comme ceux pris aux Gaulois, peuvent se classer par catégorie. Du domaine de l'agriculture et de l'élevage nous avons **le blé, le troupeau, la hanche, l'échine** (*backbone, spine*), **la houe** (*hoe*), **la hache** (*axe*), **le jardin, la haie** (*hedge*). Les mots **la salle, la halle, le banc, le fauteuil** relèvent du domaine du logement. Les Francs ont laissé plusieurs mots dans le domaine du vêtement: **la robe, l'écharpe.** De l'administration des Francs nous avons **le maréchal** (*marshal*), **le marquis, le baron**, et du domaine de la guerre, **la bannière, le gonfanon** (*battle flag*), **la flèche** (*arrow*).

LA FORMATION DU FRANÇAIS

- Les Serments de Strasbourg de 844 sont la première manifestation écrite du «français». Ce document trilingue, écrit en latin, en germanique et en «romain», reproduit un serment juré par Louis et Charles, les fils de Louis le Pieux. L'inclusion de cette traduction romaine montre que le peuple ne comprenait déjà plus le latin et qu'on avait déjà conscience de l'existence d'une langue romane différente du latin. Le texte de ce serment est donc un vestige des débuts de la langue française.
- Au moyen âge apparaissent les premiers monuments littéraires en français. Comme partout en Europe, la langue écrite montre peu d'uniformité et la fragmentation dialectale est partout évidente. Mais le prestige de Paris, siège de la cour royale des rois capétiens depuis 987, donne une importance spéciale au francien, la langue de l'Île de France. Vers la fin du douzième siècle, les gens cultivés font un effort pour parler et écrire en francien.
- La grande division linguistique du territoire français est celle qui sépare la langue d'oïl de la langue d'oc. Les mots **oïl** et **oc** sont les mots pour **oui** dans ces langues. C'est la langue d'oïl, parlée au nord de la Loire, qui devient le français. La langue d'oc devient le provençal, langue du midi de la France. Jusqu'au treizième siècle l'essor littéraire du Midi rivalise avec celui du Nord. Mais sous l'instigation du Pape Innocent III, une croisade est lancée contre les hérétiques albigeois du Midi. La couronne française se sert de cette guerre religieuse pour briser l'influence des nobles méridionaux et étendre l'influence et le pouvoir de la cour de Paris. Sous Philippe Auguste et Louis VIII la couronne française s'empare du Midi, et le provençal commence son déclin, déplacé peu à peu par le français. Aujourd'hui, malgré quelques efforts de renouveau de l'occitan (nom donné actuellement au provençal), le français est presque la seule langue qu'on emploie dans le Midi.
- Au cours des siècles, le français a subi d'autres influences étrangères. À l'époque de la Renaissance, l'influence italienne est notable. La montée de l'Espagne à la fin du quinzième siècle et la découverte de l'Amérique donnent à la France plusieurs mots espagnols. C'est l'espagnol qui transmet les noms des nouveaux produits américains (**tomate, chocolat, tabac**) au français et aux autres langues européennes. À partir du dix-neuvième siècle l'intérêt en Angleterre est en amont et le français emprunte des mots à la langue de son voisin d'outre-Manche. Au vingtième siècle c'est surtout l'anglais américain qui a fourni les emprunts les plus nombreux au français **(le look, le Walkman, cool, les stars du cinéma, le parking**, etc.).

LA LANGUE FRANÇAISE AUJOURD'HUI

- Aujourd'hui le français est une langue mondiale et un véhicule de culture très important. Langue officielle de la France et langue officielle en Belgique (avec le néerlandais), en Suisse (avec l'allemand, l'italien, et le romanche), au Luxembourg (avec l'allemand), le français est soit officiel, soit une langue de culture dans beaucoup de pays qui étaient des colonies françaises. Au Canada, le français et l'anglais sont les deux langues officielles, et le quart des Canadiens (entre 6 et 7 millions de personnes) sont francophones. Aux États-Unis le français subsiste à peine dans la Nouvelle-Angleterre, lieu d'immigration franco-canadienne au dix-neuvième siècle et en Louisiane, lieu de refuge des Acadiens, expulsés de l'Acadie (aujourd'hui le Nouveau-Brunswick et la Nouvelle-Écosse) afin de réduire l'influence de la France dans cette région cédée aux Anglais en 1713. Le mot **cajun** vient du mot français **acadien**.

- Aux Antilles, le français est la langue officielle des deux départements d'outre-mer qui s'y trouvent, la Guadeloupe et la Martinique, et en Haïti, où la plupart de la population parle créole, une langue créée par le contact entre le français et les langues africaines des esclaves amenés au Nouveau Monde. Le français est aussi la langue officielle en Guyane, sur la côte nord de l'Amérique du Sud.
- Dans le Pacifique les territoires français de Tahiti et de Nouvelle-Calédonie parlent français (la Polynésie française). Au Moyen-Orient le français reste une langue importante parmi les chrétiens du Liban et parmi les juifs émigrés en Israël de l'Afrique du Nord. En Asie le français est toujours une langue de prestige dans les pays de l'ancienne Indochine, bien que concurrencée de nos jours par l'anglais.
- L'extension la plus marquée de l'influence du français est en Afrique où il est officiel ou jouit d'un statut privilégié dans les anciennes colonies françaises et belges. Le français reste important, et dans beaucoup des pays suivants est officiel dans l'administration nationale et dans l'enseignement dans les pays du Maghreb: Algérie, Maroc, Tunisie et dans ces pays de l'Afrique au sud du Sahara: Bénin, Burkina Faso, Burundi, Cameroun, Comores (îles de l'océan Indien), Côte-d'Ivoire, Djibouti, Gabon, Guinée, Madagascar, Mali, Maurice (île de l'océan Indien), Mauritanie, Niger, Réunion (île de l'océan Indien), Rwanda, Sénégal, Seychelles, Tchad, Togo, Zaïre. On calcule que le français est la langue utilisée par plus de 125 000 000 de personnes dans le monde, soit comme langue maternelle, soit comme langue seconde. Les organisations internationales de la francophonie se réunissent pour favoriser la coopération culturelle et technique entre les pays francophones.
- Les pays francophones de l'Afrique ont produit en français une littérature de haute qualité, très variée et très intéressante. Si l'on y ajoute les auteurs européens, canadiens et antillais, on comprend que le français, comme l'anglais, est une langue littéraire internationale dans laquelle on trouve des œuvres qui décrivent les sociétés les plus variées, de celle des Esquimaux qui habitent le nord du Québec à celle des Malgaches de Madagascar.
- Cette importance internationale du français lui donne une place privilégiée aux Nations unies et dans d'autres organismes internationaux. Aux Nations unies on a accordé à deux langues, le français et l'anglais, le statut de «langues de travail». Tous les documents de l'organisation sont rédigés dans ces deux langues, et l'on s'attend à ce que tout employé des Nations unies sache parler au moins une d'elles.

EXAMEN

A. Mais c'est faux! Toutes ces constatations sur la langue française sont fausses. Corrigez-les selon l'article que vous venez de lire.

1. Le français est une langue dérivée du grec.

   ____

2. Le gaulois était la langue du midi de la France au moyen âge.

   ____

3. À l'époque de la Renaissance le français s'enrichit d'emprunts anglais.

___

4. Le français transmet les nouveaux mots américains à l'Europe.

___

5. Les Comores se trouvent dans l'océan Pacifique.

___

6. Le français ne jouit d'aucun statut spécial en Belgique.

___

7. Les envahisseurs germaniques n'ont laissé aucune empreinte sur le français.

___

8. Le français est la seule langue de travail aux Nations unies.

___

B. Laquelle des possibilités proposées identifie correctement l'élément donné?

_____ 1. blesser
- a. mot d'origine latine
- b. mot d'origine germanique

_____ 2. Frantia
- a. nom latin de la France
- b. nom de la France donné par les Francs

_____ 3. Guyane
- a. pays francophone sud-américain
- b. pays francophone asiatique

_____ 4. Marseille
- a. ville fondée par les Gaulois
- b. ville fondée par les Grecs

_____ 5. tomate
- a. emprunt à l'italien
- b. mot américain emprunté à l'espagnol

_____ 6. Burgondes
- a. peuple germanique installé en France
- b. région francophone de la Suisse

_____ 7. créole
- a. langue parlée en Haïti
- b. Canadiens expulsés par les Anglais

_____ 8. Bénin
- a. ancienne colonie belge
- b. pays francophone africain

C. Identifications. Reliez les mots dans la première colonne à leur description dans la deuxième colonne.

_____ 1. l'occitan

_____ 2. la Guadeloupe

_____ 3. la Polynésie

_____ 4. la Nouvelle-Écosse

_____ 5. Jules César

_____ 6. les Albigeois

_____ 7. la Réunion

_____ 8. le Maghreb

a. île francophone de l'océan Indien

b. ancienne colonie française du Pacifique

c. département d'outre-mer

d. hérétiques du moyen âge

e. nom donné aux pays de l'Afrique du Nord

f. général romain qui a conquis la Gaule

g. nom moderne du provençal

h. province canadienne, anciennement l'Acadie

i. mot germanique signifiant un vêtement

j. nom donné aux Belges de langue française

CHAPTER 30

HISTORY OF FRANCE

LA FRANCE PRÉHISTORIQUE

- La partie du continent européen que nous appelons aujourd'hui «France» est une des régions les plus riches en vestiges préhistoriques des **Cro-Magnon**, des hommes du paléolithique assez proches de l'homme moderne. Dans la vallée de la Dordogne, dans le sud-ouest de la France, on a trouvé des statues de femmes sculptées il y a 22 000 ans, sûrement un témoignage d'un ancien culte de fertilité. Les Cro-Magnon étaient aussi des artistes. On a trouvé de merveilleuses peintures rupestres dans les grottes de **Lascaux**, toutes représentant des animaux comme les taureaux, les bisons, les chevaux et les cerfs, dépeints peut-être pour assurer le succès des chasseurs. En 1994, dans la vallée de l'Ardèche à la Combe-d'Arc près du Rhône on a découvert encore une grotte avec des peintures rupestres spectaculaires. Aux animaux de toujours s'ajoutent l'ours et la renne, l'hyène et la panthère. Les artistes de cette grotte savaient représenter le mouvement, et à côté des peintures ils ont réalisé aussi des gravures. Cette grotte s'appelle **la grotte Chauvet**, nom du chercheur qui l'a découverte.
- Au paléolithique des Cro-Magnon succède **le néolithique**, époque révolutionnaire dans l'évolution humaine. L'agriculture et l'élevage font leur apparition et remplacent la chasse et la cueillette comme moyens de subsistence. C'est l'époque de la sédentarisation où les nomades se transforment en agriculteurs et s'organisent en villages. La poterie apparaît, le tissage aussi. Les bases de la civilisation ont été posées. On trouve en France beaucoup d'outils et de restes de poterie qui nous donnent une idée plus ou moins exacte de la vie de ces ancêtres lointains des Européens d'aujourd'hui.
- Les hommes apprennent à travailler le métal. On distingue en général trois âges différents: **l'âge du cuivre, l'âge du bronze** et **l'âge du fer**. Nos informations sur cette époque en France sont assez précises. Nous pouvons identifier les peuples qui habitent la France pendant l'âge du fer. Nous savons, par exemple, qu'au septième siècle avant Jésus-Christ **les Grecs** ont fondé un comptoir sur la Côte méditerranéenne. Le nom de cette colonie était **Massilia**, aujourd'hui Marseille. Au sixième siècle **les Celtes** ont envahi la France et l'ont transformée en un pays celtique. Ces Gaulois, surtout ceux de Provence, ont subi l'influence de la civilisation grecque de Massilia. Les Gaulois ont fondé de petites villes fortifiées comme Lugdunum (aujourd'hui Lyon) et la tribu celtique des Parisii s'est installée dans l'Île de la Cité. C'est du mot **Parisii** qu'on a tiré le nom de **Paris.**

LA CONQUÊTE ROMAINE

- En 125 avant J.-C. **les Romains** sont appelés par les Grecs de Massilia à les défendre contre les tribus du nord qui les menacent. Rome garde le territoire conquis et l'étend jusqu'à la Garonne, à l'ouest et jusqu'aux Pyrénées au sud. Cette conquête de la Provence donne aux Romains le moyen de joindre par terre l'Italie et l'Espagne. Ils fondent les villes d'Aix-en-Provence et Narbonne et construisent la voie Domitienne qui traverse la Provence et relie l'Italie et l'Espagne. La colonisation romaine de la Provence amène très vite la romanisation du pays. Déjà influencé par les Grecs de Marseille, le monde romain n'est pas étrange pour ces Gaulois du Midi. L'ordre imposé par les Romains facilite le développement économique de Provence, qui s'intègre à l'Empire.

- Au milieu du premier siècle avant J.-C. les Romains décident d'entreprendre la conquête de la Gaule indépendante. Cette Gaule non-romaine est rendue instable par les incessantes guerres entre tribus, faiblesse dont **Jules César**, nommé gouverneur de la Provence en 59 avant J.-C., saura profiter. Sous prétexte de défendre la Gaule d'une invasion germanique, César attaque la Gaule indépendante en 58 et soumet la Gaule entière en six ans. La bataille décisive est celle d'**Alésia** dans le département de Côte d'Or au nord-ouest de Dijon où le chef des Gaulois, **Vercingétorix**, se rend à Jules César (52 avant J.-C.).
- La victoire de Jules César donne à Rome tout le territoire français et la plupart de la Belgique. L'armée de César franchit la Manche pour passer en Angleterre dont la conquête commencera un siècle plus tard. **La Gaule** devient la province la plus riche de l'Empire. La stabilité imposée par les Romains favorise le développment d'un pays riche en ressources naturelles. La Gaule, fertile et bien arrosée par la pluie, exporte du blé, des fruits et de la laine. Les Romains introduisent la vigne, et les vins gaulois ont une réputation dans l'antiquité égale à celle des vins français de nos jours. Les Romains construisent des routes à travers la France entière; la Gaule est donc intégrée à l'Empire, et la romanisation va vite, sans que les Romains y contraignent la population. Le latin devient la langue de la Gaule et les écoles transforment les petits Gaulois en Romains. Un siècle après la conquête de César, il y a déjà des sénateurs gaulois à Rome.
- Ce monde romain subit deux transformations fondamentales dans les cinq siècles et demi qui mènent de la conquête à la chute de Rome. La première est la christianisation**. Le christianisme**, à ses origines une secte du judaïsme, commence à gagner des adeptes partout dans l'Empire. Après avoir longtemps persécuté les chrétiens, **l'empereur Constantin** se convertit au christianisme au début du quatrième siècle et décrète la tolération du christianisme. Le christianisme se répand en France. Vers la fin du quatrième siècle **saint Martin**, évêque de Tours, fonde les premiers monastères. En 391 le christianisme devient la religion d'état de l'Empire romain.

LES FRANCS

- La seconde transformation profonde de la Gaule romaine résulte des **invasions germaniques**. Celles-ci mènent peu à peu à la chute de l'Empire romain et à son remplacement en Europe par des états plus petits. Vers la fin du cinquième siècle **les Francs** établissent leur royaume en France. **Clovis** est le roi et la cour est à Paris, devenu capitale du royaume. En 506 **Clovis** se convertit au christianisme. Les Francs élargissent leur emprise sur l'ensemble du territoire français jusqu'à le dominer presque tout entier. Leur règne transforme profondément la France. Ils lui donnent son nom (**Frantia** remplace **Gallia** comme nom du pays) et créent un royaume qui préfigure par son extension et son unité la France moderne. Clovis et ses descendants constituent la dynastie **mérovingienne**, première des grandes familles royales de France.
- Il faut remarquer que les Germains, appelés Barbares par les Romains, ont deux fois sauvé l'Europe des invasions de l'extérieur. En 451 les **Huns** sous **Attila** s'avancent sur **Lutèce** (nom romain de Paris) et Orléans. **Sainte Geneviève** encourage les habitants de Paris à rester dans leur ville et à la défendre contre les envahisseurs. Les événements justifient sa foi. Les Huns ne s'approchent pas de Paris et Sainte Geneviève devient la patronne de France. **Aetius**, général des dernières légions romaines, avec l'aide de Germains alliés à Rome arrête la

poussée des Huns entre Châlons-sur-Marne et Troyes en Champagne. Cette **bataille des champs Catalauniques** écarte la menace des Huns sur la France. Trois siècles plus tard, les Arabes, après leur conquête de la péninsule Ibérique (Espagne et Portugal) font irruption en France et leur armée monte vers le nord. C'est **Charles Martel**, grand-père de Charlemagne, qui, à la tête de l'armée française, attend les musulmans près de Poitiers en 732. La bataille est dure, mais les troupes de Charles Martel sortent vainqueurs. Les Arabes battent la retraite vers les Pyrénées et se réfugient en Espagne. Ils ne menaceront plus la France.

- Le fils de Charles Martel, **Pépin le Bref**, est élu roi en 751. Avec lui commence la dynastie carolingienne. Pépin meurt en 767. Selon la coutume des Francs son héritage est partagé entre ses deux fils, **Charles le Grand (Charlemagne)** et Carloman. Ce système de succession partagée avait ses défauts, les ambitions des héritiers menant souvent à des guerres civiles. Mais Carloman meurt quatre ans plus tard, laissant Charlemagne seul à exercer le pouvoir à partir de 771.
- Charlemagne transforme le royaume des Francs en empire, prenant exemple sur Rome. Des victoires militaires dans l'Italie du nord et en Allemagne lui donnent de vastes territoires à administrer. Sa seule défaite était en Espagne. La retraite des Français par le col de Roncevaux dans les Pyrénées est le thème du grand poème épique français *La chanson de Roland*. En 800 le pape Léon III sacre Charlemagne «empereur de l'Empire romain d'Occident reconstitué». Charlemagne, bien que peu cultivé lui-même, comprend l'importance des études et favorise la reproduction des manuscrits latins. On appelle cet épanouissement des lettres classiques sous Charlemagne **la Renaissance carolingienne.**
- L'empire de Charlemagne dure peu. Charlemagne meurt en 814 et son fils **Louis le Pieux** lui succède. Louis le Pieux est un roi faible. À sa mort la guerre éclate entre ses fils. En 843 **le traité de Verdun** est signé, confirmant le partage de l'Empire. Cette époque est malheureuse pour d'autres raisons aussi. La faiblesse des descendants de Charlemagne laisse la France presque sans défense devant les invasions des **Normands** (hommes du Nord). Ces Vikings dévastent le pays et réussissent à en conquérir de vastes territoires. On réussit à les repousser de Paris et d'autres régions et on leur donne de la terre pour s'installer. Cette région porte encore leur nom: **la Normandie**. Le pouvoir royal s'affaiblit de plus en plus et la dynastie carolingienne disparaît avec la mort de Louis V en 987. La France arrive à un des grands tournants de son histoire.

LE MOYEN ÂGE

- **Hugues Capet** monte sur le trône en 987, fondant **la dynastie capétienne**. En 996, son fils, Robert le Pieux, devient roi. La France se remet peu à peu de la dévastation du dixième siècle. Une nouvelle stabilité rend possible le développement économique. On construit des églises partout dans le pays. La société est organisée selon les principes de la **féodalité**. Dans une époque où le moyen de transport le plus rapide est le cheval, le roi est loin de la plupart de ses sujets. Ceux-ci s'allient au seigneur le plus proche qui leur offre une défense en échange d'une partie de leurs récoltes. Parmi les nobles les plus puissants étaient les ducs de Normandie. Ces descendants des Normands étaient déjà tout à fait francisés. L'un d'eux, **Guillaume le Conquérant**, envahit l'Angleterre, la conquiert et implante l'état anglo-normand. Le français y est la langue de la cour pendant les quatre siècles qui suivent, et il transforme profondément l'anglais. Cette langue germanique se remplit d'emprunts français à un tel point que son vocabulaire mixte devient un des traits principaux qui distinguent l'anglais des autres langues germaniques.
- À la fin du onzième siècle le Pape Urbain II lance l'appel à **la croisade** pour libérer les Terres saintes de l'emprise des musulmans. La première croisade a deux aspects. Une croisade populaire de gens exaltés mais peu armés et mal

organisés part en 1096. Mal habillés et mal alimentés, ils se livrent au pillage et au massacre des Juifs. En 1097, les nobles français, chefs militaires, partent en tête de 30 000 hommes et prennent Jérusalem en 1099.

- Au siècle suivant la deuxième et la troisième croisades ont lieu. Au milieu du siècle **Aliénor d'Aquitaine** reçoit la permission de l'Église de divorcer d'avec son mari Louis VII. Elle épouse **Henri II**, duc de Normandie, qui deviendra roi d'Angleterre. Aliénor apporte au mariage ses possessions: tout le sud-ouest de la France, devenu maintenant territoire du roi d'Angleterre. C'est un exemple frappant de la façon dont à l'époque de la féodalité, les nobles pouvaient démembrer un royaume.
- En 1214 il y a une bataille décisive pour l'avenir de la France. **Philippe-Auguste** vainc les Anglais et leurs alliés à **Bouvines**, près de Lille. Bouvines marque la fin de la présence des Anglais au nord de la Loire. C'est aussi l'époque de la croisade contre **les Albigeois**. L'hérésie se répandait depuis longtemps dans le Midi et l'Église voulait l'extirper. La couronne a profité de cette occasion pour étendre son pouvoir aux dépens des nobles comme le comte de Toulouse. La victoire des Français sur les nobles du sud marque le début de la fin de la civilisation en langue provençale qui fleurissait dans le Midi.
- Le treizième siècle est surtout caractérisé par le règne de **Louis IX**, dit **Saint Louis**, qui commence son long règne en 1234. C'est un homme religieux qui règnera jusqu'en 1270. Sous Saint Louis on fonde la Sorbonne. Le roi même part à la septième croisade en 1248. Il repart à la huitième et dernière croisade en 1270 et meurt de la peste à Tunis. Louis IX laisse une France respectée et forte ainsi que le souvenir d'avoir été un roi juste et charitable. C'est Louis IX qui choisit les trois fleurs de lys comme symbole de la France.
- Vers la fin du siècle **Philippe IV (Philippe le Bel)** monte sur le trône français. Un conflit éclate avec la papauté. Le Pape Boniface VIII essaie d'affermir le principe de la supériorité de l'Église sur le pouvoir temporel. Philippe le Bel résiste. En 1305, à la mort de Boniface, Philippe annonce le transfert du Saint-Siège de Rome à **Avignon**. Cette démarche a donné au midi de la France un de ses monuments les plus imposants: **le palais des Papes** d'Avignon.
- Plusieurs années après la mort de Philippe le Bel en 1314 la France a des problèmes de succession. Le candidat écarté, Édouard III d'Angleterre, déclare la guerre. Les premiers conflits éclatent en 1336, et la guerre durera plus d'un siècle. C'est la guerre de Cent ans. Elle fera des ravages en France, aidée par **la peste noire** qui sévit dans le pays en 1348 et qui éliminera le tiers de la population française. Les Français subiront beaucoup de défaites. Le tournant est marqué par un événement extraordinaire—l'intervention d'une fille de dix-huit ans: **Jeanne d'Arc**. C'est elle qui encourage les habitants d'Orléans, ville assiégée par les Anglais, et le siège est levé. Trahie et vendue aux Anglais, elle est brûlée vive pour hérésie sur la place de Rouen en 1431. La guerre de Cent ans continue jusqu'en 1453, année de la bataille de Castillon en Guyenne, au sud-est de Bordeaux. Les Anglais sont chassés de l'ensemble du territoire français, sauf de la ville de Calais. Le moyen âge s'achève.

LA RENAISSANCE

- Le roi **Louis XI** essaie d'en finir avec la féodalité et réussit à triompher sur son ennemi, Charles le Téméraire, duc de Bourgogne. Il renforce l'organisation royale et a à sa disposition une armée permanente qu'aucun de ses rivaux ne peut maintenir. Cet affermissement définitif de la royauté vis-à-vis des nobles est un des jalons qui marquent la fin du moyen âge et la transition à la Renaissance.
- Vers la fin du quinzième siècle deux autres événements clés de la Renaissance aident à transformer la vie française. Le premier est l'invention de la presse typographique par Gutenberg. La diffusion des connaissances est maintenant

beaucoup plus facile et beaucoup plus rapide. Le premier atelier typographique est établi à Paris en 1470. C'est encore une rupture avec le moyen âge où on copiait les livres à la main. En 1492 Christophe Colomb rentre de son premier voyage au Nouveau Monde. Bien que l'explorateur ait été déçu de ne pas avoir trouvé l'or et les épices des Indes, sa découverte allait changer la vie du monde entier d'une façon profonde et irréversible.

- Quand **Charles VIII** fait campagne en Italie, il ne remporte aucune victoire, mais ses soldats remportent un magnifique butin qui montre aux Français le style somptueux de la Renaissance italienne. Cet intérêt ne fera que s'intensifier sous **François Ier** qui mène aussi quelques campagnes en Italie. On s'intéresse à l'art, à la littérature, à la musique italiens. Les Français aussi commencent à s'intéresser à l'antiquité classique, objet d'étude depuis longtemps déjà en Italie. Quand François Ier rentre en France il invite Léonard de Vinci à l'accompagner. D'autres grands artistes italiens le suivront. Ces artistes sont responsables du décor du château de **Fontainebleau** et de la magnifique résidence de chasse de **Chambord**, que François Ier fait édifier sur les bords de la Loire. François Ier impose l'emploi du français au lieu du latin pour les actes officiels et fonde le **Collège de France** pour encourager les recherches.
- La France participe à l'exploration de l'Amérique. **Jacques Cartier** découvre Terre-Neuve et le fleuve Saint-Laurent qu'il remonte jusqu'au site du Montréal moderne. Il prend possession du Canada au nom de François Ier en 1534. D'autres explorateurs français s'embarqueront pour l'Amérique au siècle suivant.
- Le seizième siècle est marqué par **les guerres de Religion**. Luther affiche ses 95 thèses sur la porte de la cathédrale de Wittemburg en 1517. Ce défi à l'Église déclenche **la Réforme protestante**. Jean Calvin prêche la nouvelle religion depuis Genève, en Suisse, où il est en exil. La Réforme fait de grands progrès en France, surtout dans la bourgeoisie et la noblesse. Cet essor du protestantisme fait trembler un peu les catholiques. On croit que les protestants, devenus très vite assez nombreux, doivent être empêchés de devenir trop puissants. On a peur aussi d'éventuelles alliances entre les protestants français et leurs coreligionnaires allemands, hollandais ou anglais. La persécution des protestants atteint son point culminant le 24 août 1572, à la Saint-Barthélemy quand 30 000 protestants sont massacrés en France. C'est le roi **Henri IV** qui mettra fin aux persécutions. Né protestant, il se convertit au catholicisme pour faciliter son accession au trône en 1589. À cette occasion il prononce un dicton fameux pour résumer les raisons de sa conversion religieuse: *Paris vaut bien une messe*. En 1598 il proclame **l'édit de Nantes** qui garantit la liberté de conscience et la liberté de pratiquer le protestantisme. Son règne restaure la monarchie absolue et crée des conditions favorables au développement économique.

LE GRAND SIÈCLE ET LE SIÈCLE DES LUMIÈRES

- Le dix-septième siècle commence sous le règne d'Henri IV, assassiné en 1610. **Louis XIII** succède à Henri IV et fait une innovation importante dans le gouvernement. Il nomme le cardinal **Richelieu** son ministre et lui donne le droit d'agir en son nom. Richelieu dirige des guerres à l'étranger et des guerres internes contre les protestants. En 1635 Richelieu fonde l'Académie française.
- À la mort de Louis XIII en 1643, son successeur**, Louis XIV**, n'a que quatre ans. La reine, Anne d'Autriche, devient régente et le cardinal **Mazarin** devient premier ministre. Comme Richelieu, il détient un pouvoir absolu. Mazarin meurt en 1661.
- **Louis XIV** décide maintenant de tout. C'est le prototype du monarque absolu. Il s'entoure de conseillers, choisissant des hommes qui sont habitués à servir l'État et dont le plus connu est **Colbert**. Colbert s'occupe de l'économie et des subventions à la vie culturelle. Pour augmenter les revenus de l'État il

développe l'industrie et fait construire des routes qui couvrent le pays pour faciliter le commerce. Louis XIV fait construire le magnifique château de **Versailles** où il installe sa cour. C'est une cour fabuleuse. La maison du roi comprend 10 000 personnes. Louis XIV se considère le représentant de Dieu sur la terre, le Roi-Soleil. Il gouverne d'une façon absolue. La littérature et l'art s'inspirent de l'antiquité—c'est l'époque du classicisme. Pour ce monarque absolu la tolérance religieuse ne représente qu'une menace sur son pouvoir. Il persécute les jansénistes, catholiques qui donnaient plus d'importance à la conscience de l'homme qu'aux injonctions de l'Église. En 1685 il révoque l'édit de Nantes. Deux cent mille protestants, craignant le pire, abandonnent le pays. Pour la France, c'est une perte. Ils s'en vont en Allemagne et en Hollande avec leurs connaissances, leurs capacités et leur argent. Louis XIV meurt en 1715 ne laissant pour lui succéder que son arrière-petit-fils, Louis XV, qui n'a que cinq ans et dont l'oncle, le duc d'Orléans, est nommé régent.

- Le règne personnel de **Louis XV** commence en 1743. Son règne est marqué par **la guerre de Sept ans** (1756–1763), un conflit européen avec des échos dans les colonies en Amérique et en Asie. Appelée dans l'histoire américaine *the French and Indian War*, la guerre finit mal pour la France, qui perd presque tout son premier empire colonial, y compris le Canada, la moitié est de la Louisiane et l'Inde. La France cède la partie occidentale de la Louisiane à l'Espagne, alliée avec la France pendant la guerre.
- L'exploration et la colonisation de l'Amérique continuent. Samuel de Champlain fonde la ville de Québec en 1608. Colbert, conseiller économique de Louis XIV, crée en 1664 la Compagnie des Indes, chargée de la mission de développer les colonies existantes et d'en établir de nouvelles. Marquette, un jésuite français en compagnie de Louis Joliet, un Français né à Québec, découvre le Mississippi en 1672. Bien que les Français ne soient plus une présence en Amérique du Nord, plusieurs noms de lieu portent témoignage du passage de leurs explorateurs et colonisations: New Orleans, Louisiana, Saint Louis, Joliet, Des Plaines, Lake Champlain, Montpellier, Detroit, etc. En 1682 Cavalier de la Salle s'empare de la Louisiane. Au cours du siècle les Français s'établissent aussi à la Guadeloupe et à la Martinique, deux îles des Antilles. Les Français commencent aussi la pénétration de l'Afrique et de l'Inde. En 1642 on fonde Fort-Dauphin à Madagascar. En 1659 on fonde Saint-Louis au Sénégal. En 1668 un comptoir français est établi près de Bombay.
- La vie intellectuelle fleurit en France pendant le dix-huitième siècle, la vie élégante aussi. Paris devient le centre artistique de l'Europe, connu pour ses salons, dirigés tous par des femmes cultivées. Les salons sont une institution aristocratique. On y cultive la conversation, l'expression élégante et l'analyse des sentiments, surtout celle des sentiments amoureux. Mais on discute aussi des idées philosophiques. Les écrits de **Montesquieu** et de **Voltaire** montrent les défauts de l'absolutisme et expliquent les vertus du régime constitutionnel des Anglais. Les idées anti-religieuses sont discutées aussi. L'encyclopédiste **Diderot** prêche la libre pensée. Sa grande œuvre, *l'Encyclopédie*, présente toutes les idées philosophiques de l'époque et nous donne une image authentique de ce siècle où la France et la langue française dominent la vie intellectuelle de l'Europe, le siècle des lumières.
- **Louis XVI** monte sur le trône en 1774. Pendant son règne la France intervient dans la guerre de l'Indépendance américaine. Au début, la France se limite à envoyer des armes et de l'argent. Quelques volontaires, comme La Fayette, vont en Amérique pour aider les troupes rebelles contre l'Angleterre. En 1778 la France reconnaît l'indépendance des colonies américaines et intervient activement dans la lutte. C'est une flotte française qui oblige les Anglais à lever le siège de Philadelphie. La capitulation de Yorktown, bataille décisive de la guerre de l'Indépendance, est réalisée avec le secours des troupes françaises qui encerclent

Yorktown par terre et par mer. Ce blocus de la principale armée anglaise en Amérique est un élément important de la victoire américaine. L'indépendance des États-Unis est reconnue par le traité de Versailles de 1783.

- Louis XVI est connu comme un monarque faible qui ne sait pas résister aux privilégiés qui s'opposent aux réformes fiscales. Les problèmes économiques deviennent graves. Le peuple s'émeute plus d'une fois à cause de la hausse des prix et à cause des impôts, toujours plus écrasants pour les pauvres parce que les nobles refusent de payer. Cette ignorance du mécanisme de la fiscalité conduit l'État à la banqueroute. Le roi est obligé de convoquer en juin de 1789 les **États généraux**, une assemblée composée des trois ordres de la nation: la noblesse, le clergé et le peuple (le tiers état). Traditionnellement les États généraux votent par ordre, c'est-à-dire, un vote pour la noblesse, un vote pour le clergé et un vote pour le peuple. Mais les représentants du peuple exigent le vote par personne, ce qui aurait donné la majorité au peuple. Le roi essaie de dissoudre l'assemblée. Le lendemain, le tiers état se réunit au Jeu de paume et se proclame Assemblée nationale. On prête le fameux serment du Jeu de paume de ne pas se séparer avant d'avoir donné à la France une constitution. La monarchie n'est plus absolue.

LA RÉVOLUTION

- Le 14 juillet le peuple de Paris prend la vieille prison de **la Bastille**, symbole de l'absolutisme de la monarchie et de son pouvoir arbitraire. **La Révolution française** a commencé. Le 14 juillet deviendra la fête nationale de la France. Les premières années de la Révolution sont les plus prometteuses. Le 26 août 1789, l'Assemblée nationale vote un document qui a eu une grande influence sur les siècles à venir. C'est la **Déclaration des droits de l'homme et du citoyen**. Parmi ses stipulations les plus remarquables pour l'époque:
  - Les hommes naissent et demeurent libres et égaux en droit.
  - Le principe de toute souveraineté réside essentiellement dans la Nation. Nul corps, nul individu ne peut exercer d'autorité qui n'en émane expressément.
  - La liberté consiste à pouvoir faire tout ce qui ne nuit pas à autrui.
  - La loi est l'expression de la volonté générale.
  - Nul ne doit être inquiété pour ses opinions, même religieuses.
  - La libre communication des pensées et des opinions est un des droits les plus précieux de l'homme; tout citoyen peut donc parler, écrire, imprimer librement.
- La Révolution provoque la fuite des nobles en Allemagne. En 1791, le roi Louis XVI s'enfuit aussi. Il est détenu à Varennes (Lorraine) et ramené à Paris. Du mois d'octobre 1791 au mois d'août 1792, la France est une monarchie constitutionnelle. Les souverains étrangers ne voient pas la Révolution française d'un bon œil, craignant que les mêmes revendications populaires puissent affaiblir leur pouvoir. L'empereur d'Autriche est le neveu de la reine, **Marie-Antoinette**, et il est hostile à la Révolution. Le roi et la reine attendent que ce neveu les délivre de la Révolution et restaure la monarchie absolue. Les Français se voient maintenant comme les opposants à toute tyrannie. Les Prussiens, alliés aux Autrichiens, avancent vers la Champagne, mais sont battus par les Français à **Valmy** le 20 septembre 1792. Le 25 septembre, la République est déclarée, Louis XVI est détrôné. Lui et Marie-Antoinette seront guillotinés l'année suivante.
- C'est maintenant la **Convention** qui gouverne la France, dominée par les Girondins, une faction modérée. Leur domination cèdera à celle des Montagnards, plus radicaux. C'est la Terreur. C'est une période terrible caractérisée par des arrestations arbitraires, de nombreuses exécutions et une répression brutale de la révolte royaliste en Vendée (ouest de la France). La figure

dominante est **Robespierre**. En juillet 1794 il y a un coup d'état contre Robespierre et un gouvernement plus modéré est instauré. Nous sommes maintenant sous **le Directoire**.

- L'époque révolutionnaire, malgré ses excès, a posé les bases de la France moderne. Parmi ses innovations:
  - Lègue à la France un gouvernement républicain: le peuple se gouverne sans roi.
  - Déclare que le but du gouvernement est d'assurer le bonheur de ses citoyens.
  - En 1792, un capitaine de l'armée française, Roger de l'Isle, compose *la Marseillaise,* l'hymne national français.
  - Le pays est divisé en départements et le vieux système de provinces est aboli.
  - Le drapeau tricolore est adopté.
  - Le système métrique est adopté.
  - On fonde le musée d'Histoire naturelle.
  - On fonde l'École normale supérieure.

NAPOLÉON

- Au mois de novembre 1799, le général **Napoléon Bonaparte** organise un coup d'état et se fait proclamer premier consul. Il prend à son compte tous les pouvoirs exécutifs et législatifs du Directoire. **Talleyrand**, ministre des relations extérieures, est de mèche avec Napoléon dans le coup d'état. Il reste à son poste. Le Directoire est remplacé par **le Consulat**.
- Le Consulat dure cinq ans. En 1804 le Sénat proclame **l'Empire**. Napoléon devient empereur à vie. La politique extérieure de Napoléon se base officiellement sur le désir d'étendre les libertés humaines de la Révolution française à l'Europe entière. Sous ce prétexte les armées françaises réussissent à soumettre presque tout le continent. Le déclin commence en 1812 avec l'invasion de la Russie. Les soldats de Napoléon ne sont pas préparés pour l'hiver russe et battent la retraite. Tout va de mal en pis jusqu'à la déroute définitive de **Waterloo** en 1815. La France est destituée de tous les territoires acquis par Napoléon et Napoléon est exilé à l'île de Sainte-Hélène dans l'Atlantique du sud.
- L'Empire de Napoléon a eu une influence profonde sur la France. Son administration centralisée dans laquelle tout rayonne de Paris reste le modèle de l'administration française de nos jours. Sous Napoléon on a codifié les lois françaises (**le code Napoléon**). L'Empire a vu l'achèvement de la construction de la route du Simplon à travers les Alpes et l'aménagement des ports de Cherbourg (France) et d'Anvers (Belgique). Pour les États-Unis il y a eu des conséquences importantes aussi. En 1803 Napoléon a vendu la Louisiane aux USA, acquisition qui a doublé le territoire du pays.

LE DIX-NEUVIÈME SIÈCLE

- À partir de 1815, c'est la restauration de la monarchie. **Louis XVIII** règne de 1815 à 1824. En 1824 c'est **Charles X** qui monte sur le trône. Les deux monarques ont eu beaucoup de difficultés à concilier cette monarchie restaurée avec la nouvelle mentalité des Français. Le dix-neuvième siècle est le siècle de **la bourgeoisie** qui demande la liberté d'opinion et la liberté d'action, surtout dans le domaine du commerce. En juillet 1830, une révolte éclate quand Charles X essaie de rétablir la censure en utilisant ses privilèges de souverain. L'insurrection dure trois jours et s'appelle «les Trois Glorieuses». Le roi abdique et s'enfuit en Angleterre.
- **Louis-Philippe,** duc d'Orléans, est nommé roi des Français. C'est une monarchie constitutionnelle qui garantit la liberté de la presse. Elle dure jusqu'en 1848 quand une révolution qui exige le suffrage universel éclate. Le roi abdique et

la seconde République est proclamée. L'insurrection française n'est pas sans parallèles dans le reste de l'Europe, où l'impatience populaire avec l'absolutisme éclate à Vienne, à Berlin, à Milan et en Tchécoslovaquie et en Pologne. **Louis-Napoléon**, neveu de l'ancien empereur, est élu président. Cette république sera de très courte durée.

- La première moitié du dix-neuvième siècle voit des progrès dans tous les domaines. La littérature, l'art et la musique s'épanouissent dans la France bourgeoise. On commence la construction des chemins de fer, ce qui représente une véritable révolution dans les transports. Depuis l'époque romaine, la vitesse des déplacements humains n'a pas changé: on se déplace soit à pied, soit à cheval. Le réseau ferroviaire se développe vite en France: en 1848 il y a déjà plus de 1 300 kilomètres de voies. L'industrie se développe aussi et avec elle une classe ouvrière pauvre et exploitée.
- La France commence à se refaire un empire colonial. En 1830, les Français prennent la ville d'Alger et la présence coloniale de la France au Maghreb commence. Dans le Pacifique, l'île de Tahiti est conquise. Mais c'est la deuxième moitié du dix-neuvième siècle qui verra une expansion coloniale sur tous les continents.
- En décembre 1851, Louis-Napoléon réalise un coup d´état. L'année suivante il est nommé empereur par un plébiscite universel et règnera sous le nom de Napoléon III. C'est **le second Empire**. C'est aussi le moment où la France devient une puissance industrielle. En 1870 il y a déjà 18 000 kilomètres de voies ferrées en France. Fernand de Lesseps organise la construction du canal de Suez. Un câble télégraphique est posé sous la Manche et relie la ville anglaise de Douvres à Calais. Les machines à vapeur font tourner les machines de l'industrie. La production du charbon et de l'acier augmente considérablement. Le baron Haussmann est nommé préfet de Paris. Il organise de grands travaux, comme la percée des Grands Boulevards, qui donneront à la ville son aspect moderne. Zénobe Gramme, inventeur belge, construit la première dynamo électrique, une invention qui va transformer l'industrie.
- L'expansion coloniale de la France progresse. Les Français arrivent en Nouvelle-Calédonie dans l'océan Pacifique et fondent Dakar au Sénégal en Afrique. En Asie, la France s'établit en Indochine: Viêt-nam, Cambodge, Laos. En Afrique l'Empire colonial français comprend le Congo (Brazzaville—le grand Congo est pris par les Belges), la Tunisie, le Soudan, Djibouti, les Comores, la Côte-d'Ivoire, la Guinée, le Dahomey (Bénin), Madagascar. Le profil du monde francophone d'aujourd'hui se dessine.
- En 1870, la France déclare la guerre à l'Allemagne pour empêcher que Bismarck réussisse à unifier le pays et à en faire un état trop puissant. Les Allemands envahissent la France et infligent aux Français une défaite désastreuse à Sedan dans le département des Ardennes, près de la frontière belge. L'empereur est fait prisonnier. Après sa libération, il se réfugie en Angleterre. La défaite dans la guerre Franco-Allemande est dure pour la France. Les Allemands annexent l'Alsace et la partie de la Lorraine où on parlait allemand (ces deux régions sont à l'origine germanophones). En 1871 le peuple de Paris se soulève et déclare **la Commune**, un gouvernement populaire d'orientation radicale. La suppression de la Commune est sanglante: plus de 20 000 morts.
- **La troisième République** est inaugurée. Elle va durer jusqu'à la Deuxième Guerre mondiale. Sous la troisième République la modernisation de la France se poursuit. Jules Ferry, Ministre de l'instruction publique, établit l'école primaire obligatoire et gratuite pour tous les enfants français. La ville de Paris s'agrandit et atteint deux millions d'habitants. Il y a un nouvel Opéra à Paris. Les Français envoient **la statue de la Liberté éclairant le monde** aux États-Unis comme cadeau pour le premier centenaire de la République américaine. En 1889, la France célèbre le centenaire de la Révolution française. On organise l'Exposition

universelle de Paris pour laquelle on construit la tour Eiffel. La bicyclette et l'automobile font leur apparition dans les rues des villes.

- Mais la société française n'est pas sans ses divisions. Elles se font noter **dans l'affaire Dreyfus**. En 1894, un capitaine de l'armée française, Alfred Dreyfus, est accusé d'avoir livré des secrets militaires aux Allemands. Dreyfus est dégradé et condamné à résider à l'île du Diable, près de la Guyane française, pour le reste de sa vie. Beaucoup soupçonnent que Dreyfus est innocent de trahison, mais coupable d'être juif. Il y a des manifestations antisémites à Paris. Le grand écrivain Émile Zola défend Dreyfus dans un fameux article publié dans le journal *l'Aurore* titré «J'accuse». Dreyfus est prouvé innocent et réhabilité (1906), mais les fissures ouvertes dans la société française dureront longtemps. Sous prétexte de défendre l'honneur de l'armée, l'extrême-droite intègre l'antisémitisme à son programme politique. Dans la France industrialisée il y a d'importants mouvements syndicalistes. Les socialistes sous **Jean Jaurès** sont une force politique importante.
- Les rivalités européennes comme, par exemple, celle de la France contre l'Allemagne au sujet de l'Alsace-Lorraine risquent de plonger l'Europe dans la guerre. En 1914, la Première Guerre mondiale commence. La France, l'Angleterre, la Russie, l'Italie et le Japon sont rangés contre l'Allemagne et l'Autriche. On croit que la guerre va être courte. Elle dure quatre ans et fait 9 000 000 de morts en Europe, dont 1 850 000 Français. Cette guerre voit aussi l'intervention des États-Unis. Le général Pershing débarque en France, où il commande les troupes américaines, en annonçant «La Fayette, nous voilà». Les Alliés gagnent la guerre. La France reprend l'Alsace-Lorraine et les colonies allemandes sont réparties entre les pays victorieux. Parmi les conséquences sociales de la Première Guerre mondiale en France on trouve l'augmentation de la main-d'œuvre féminine. Dans une France privée de ses hommes par la guerre, c'est aux femmes de les remplacer dans le monde du travail.

LE VINGTIÈME SIÈCLE

- Après les années vingt, assez prospères, le monde entier sombre dans la crise économique mondiale. En Allemagne, le chômage atteint le chiffre de 6 000 000 et l'inflation ravage le pays. Hitler prend le pouvoir en 1933. La démocratie allemande est écartée et un régime fasciste basé sur des idées raciales est mis en place. Les Juifs sont les premiers visés. La victoire électorale de Hitler et de son parti nazi encourage la droite antisémite française. La gauche française s'organise. Les communistes, les socialistes et les radicaux forment le **Front populaire**, qui prend le pouvoir aux élections de 1936 sous **Léon Blum**. Des mesures de réforme sont prises: on garantit deux semaines de congés payés aux ouvriers et on leur concède la semaine de travail de 40 heures. Mais le chômage augmente et la production baisse.
- La France des années trente ne comprend pas la menace allemande de Hitler. Pendant que les Allemands s'arment et développent leur force aérienne et des unités offensives de chars blindés (les Panzer), les Français comptent sur la **Ligne Maginot,** une ligne fortifiée sur la frontière de l'est. Le 1er septembre 1939, les Allemands envahissent la Pologne et **la Deuxième Guerre mondiale** commence. En mai 1940 la France est envahie. Le désordre règne dans le pays. Les routes sont bloquées par des colonnes de refugiés qui fuient devant l'armée allemande—c'est ce qu'on appelle l'exode de 40. En six semaines, c'est la défaite. La France signe l'armistice avec l'Allemagne et est divisée en deux zones. Le nord (y compris Paris) et l'ouest sont occupés par les Allemands. Le centre et le sud forment la zone libre, gouvernée par le maréchal Pétain et son régime collaborateur de Vichy. Tout procédé démocratique est aboli et des lois discriminatoires contre les Juifs sont instituées.

- **Le général de Gaulle**, passé en Angleterre, lance un appel à la résistance par radio au peuple français le 18 juin 1940. La plupart des colonies françaises se rallient au général. De Gaulle rassemble les troupes françaises restées à l'étranger. Elles le rejoignent et forment la force armée de la France libre. Elle participera à beaucoup d'opérations militaires à côté des Anglais et Américains.
- Sous l'occupation allemande, la vie est difficile en France. Le régime est brutal, et les conditions de vie s'empirent. Les vivres se font de moins en moins abondants et un système de rationnement est mis en place (les cartes d'alimentation). Pour les Juifs de France, c'est la catastrophe. Les lois antisémites de l'Allemagne sont imposées. Le port de l'étoile jaune est obligatoire. En 1942 les déportations vers Auschwitz et les autres camps de la mort commencent. Bien qu'il y ait eu des collaborateurs qui ont participé aux râfles des Juifs, beaucoup de Français ont essayé d'aider les Juifs en les cachant ou en les aidant à fuir. La France perd environ le tiers de ses Juifs (100 000 personnes dont 8 000 enfants) pendant la Guerre, mais deux tiers sont vivants à la libération, un pourcentage beaucoup plus élevé que dans la plupart des pays occupés par les nazis.
- En juin 1944 les Alliés débarquent en **Normandie** et la libération de l'Europe commence. La résistance devient de plus en plus active pour aider les Alliés et affaiblir les Allemands. Paris est libéré le 25 août et le général de Gaulle entre dans la ville. Pour l'Europe le bilan de la Deuxième Guerre mondiale est atroce: plus de 38 000 000 de morts. La France, comme le reste de l'Europe se reconstruit avec les crédits du **plan Marshall** américain. Des efforts d'unité européenne comme le marché commun sont inaugurés.
- En 1946, la quatrième République est proclamée. La structure même de cette quatrième République provoque une instabilité chronique. C'est un régime de partis, nombreux à l'époque. Puisqu'aucun d'eux n'arrive à la majorité, il faut toujours entrer en coalition avec d'autres partis pour prendre des décisions. Les alliances se font et se défont rapidement et les changements de gouvernement sont nombreux.
- La France doit faire face maintenant aux guerres d'indépendance de ses colonies. La guerre éclate en Indochine en 1946 et finit en 1954 avec la défaite française de Diên Biên Phu. Au Maghreb, le Maroc et la Tunisie deviennent indépendants, mais la France n'a aucune intention de renoncer à son emprise sur **l'Algérie** qu'elle considère une partie de la France. Mais en 1954, l'insurrection éclate. L'organisation motrice est le F. L.N., Front de libération nationale. Un million de Français vivent en Algérie et l'armée française défend leur droit d'y rester. La guerre d'Algérie affaiblit la quatrième République. Le général de Gaulle est rappelé au pouvoir en 1958 et il propose une nouvelle constitution qui établit un système présidentiel qui remédie aux plus graves défauts de la quatrième République. Devenu Président en 1959, de Gaulle se déclare favorable à l'auto-détermination pour l'Algérie, qui devient indépendante en 1962. Un million de «pieds-noirs», Français d'Algérie, abandonnent le pays pour la France.
- Le régime présidentiel initié par le général de Gaulle a donné à la France la stabilité politique dont elle manquait. Après le général de Gaulle, la France a eu quatre présidents: Georges Pompidou, Valéry Giscard d'Estaing, François Mitterrand et Jacques Chirac. Après la guerre d'Algérie, la France connaît la paix, sauf pendant quelques brefs intervalles. À l'intérieur elle a connu des vagues d'actes terroristes qui ont fait de nombreuses victimes innocentes. À l'extérieur, ses forces combattent avec ses alliés contre l'Irak pendant la guerre du Golfe et font partie de la force pour la paix en Bosnie.

EXAMEN

A. Quel siècle? Indiquez à côté de chaque événement le siècle au cours duquel il a eu lieu.

_____ 1. l'édit de Nantes

_____ 2. la conquête normande de l'Angleterre

_____ 3. la mort de Charlemagne

_____ 4. le Front populaire

_____ 5. la prise de la Bastille

_____ 6. la guerre de Sept ans

_____ 7. l'affaire Dreyfus

_____ 8. le règne de Saint Louis

B. Identification. Identifiez chaque personne, chose ou lieu en le reliant à sa description.

_____ 1. le Tchad

_____ 2. le plan Marshall

_____ 3. Alésia

_____ 4. Jules Ferry

_____ 5. Lascaux

_____ 6. Sainte Geneviève

_____ 7. Bouvines

_____ 8. Diderot

a. victoire décisive de Jules César sur les Gaulois

b. fondateur de l'école primaire obligatoire en France

c. auteur de *l'Encyclopédie*

d. patronne de la France

e. ancienne colonie française en Afrique

f. programme américain pour la reconstruction de l'Europe

g. grotte avec peintures rupestres

h. victoire de Philippe Auguste sur les Anglais

C. À compléter. Complétez ces phrases avec le(s) mot(s) qui manque(nt).

1. Les Grecs fondent le comptoir de Massilia pendant l'âge ____________________.
2. Les Romains construisent la voie Domitienne à travers ____________________ pour relier ____________________ et ____________________.
3. C'est ____________________ qui réalise la conquête de la Gaule.
4. ____________________, évêque de Tours, fonde les premiers monastères en France.
5. ____________________ est le premier roi mérovingien.
6. La retraite des Français par le col de Roncevaux est le thème de ____________________.
7. À partir de 987 la France est gouvernée par les rois ____________________.
8. Guillaume le Conquérant conquiert ____________________ en 1066.
9. La ville de Québec est fondée par ____________________.

10. Charles le Téméraire était le ________________.
11. Le traité de Versailles reconnaît ________________.
12. La phrase «Les hommes naissent et demeurent libres et égaux en droit» vient de ________________.
13. Robespierre est la figure dominante pendant ________________.
14. La période entre 1815 et 1830 s'appelle ________________.
15. La période entre 1851 et 1870 s'appelle ________________.
16. Fernand de Lesseps organise la construction du ________________.
17. Dans son article «J'accuse», le fameux écrivain ________________ défend le capitaine Dreyfus.
18. Le général ________________ commande les troupes américaines en France pendant la Première Guerre mondiale.
19. Pendant la Deuxième Guerre mondiale le maréchal ________________ est le chef du gouvernement de Vichy.
20. Le système présidentiel de la cinquième République était l'idée du ________________.

D. **Mais c'est faux!** Les phrases suivantes sont toutes fausses. Corrigez-les d'après ce que vous avez appris sur l'histoire de France.

1. Dans la grotte Chauvet on trouve des peintures de l'âge du cuivre.

   ____

2. Les Romains n'ont jamais réussi à romaniser la Gaule.

   ____

3. À la bataille des Champs Catalauniques, l'invasion des Arabes est arrêtée.

   ____

4. Le but des croisades était de convertir les musulmans.

   ____

5. On fonde la Sorbonne sous Louis XIV.

   ____

6. Philippe le Bel annonce le transfert du Saint-Siège de Rome à Jérusalem.

   ____

7. C'est Jean Calvin qui découvre le Saint-Laurent.

   ____

8. L'édit de Nantes garantit la semaine de travail de 40 heures.

   ____

9. En 1848 on proclame le second Empire.

   ____

10. Avec la bataille de Diên Biên Phu, la France prend l'Indochine.

    ____

CHAPTER 31

FRENCH LITERATURE

LE MOYEN ÂGE

- La caractéristique principale de la littérature médiévale en France est son oralité. C'est-à-dire que la littérature médiévale était destinée à être lue à haute voix ou récitée par un acteur professionnel appelé «jongleur». Le jongleur était un poète ambulant qui récitait des vers et qui jouait d'un instrument de musique aussi. Souvent, les amateurs de cette littérature ne savaient pas lire et la voie orale était essentielle pour faire connaître les œuvres littéraires à un public analphabète.
- Les genres littéraires reflétaient l'oralité de la littérature médiévale. Les **chansons de geste** (**geste** vient du mot latin **gesta,** *choses accomplies*) racontent les aventures héroïques de figures historiques ou mythiques. La plus connue est *La chanson de Roland,* poème épique qui raconte la retraite des troupes de Charlemagne d'Espagne. Roland, lieutenant de Charlemagne, est trahi par Ganelon. Roland et ses troupes d'arrière-garde sont massacrés par les Basques en traversant le col de Roncevaux dans les Pyrénées. Roland meurt en sonnant son cor, une image noble et héroïque devenue classique en France.
- D'autres genres oraux du moyen âge: **le fabliau**, des vers satiriques, souvent grossiers, et **le lai**, une poésie historique qui raconte une aventure. Poésie brève, on peut réciter le fabliau en une seule séance. **Marie de France** est peut-être l'auteur le plus connu de lais. *Le roman de Renart* est un célèbre fabliau.
- Parmi les genres destinés à être lus se trouvent **la poésie lyrique**, toujours amoureuse, dont le maître est **François Villon** (1431–1463?), et le roman. **Le roman** médiéval comprend des œuvres classiques telles que *Tristan et Iseult, Le roman de Perceval* de **Chrétien de Troyes** et *Le roman de la rose* de **Guillaume de Lorris** et **Jean de Meung**.

LA RENAISSANCE

- Le seizième siècle marque la Renaissance en France. La Renaissance se différencie du moyen âge par l'expansion de l'intérêt porté à l'antiquité classique. Le latin ecclésiastique fait place au latin des auteurs classiques dans l'usage des intellectuels. On commence aussi à étudier le grec classique. Les idées et les modèles artistiques et littéraires de l'antiquité prennent un grand essor. Le monde médiéval, centré sur la religion et l'église, commence à perdre du terrain face au monde moderne, où, comme dans l'antiquité, l'homme est la mesure de toute chose. C'est aussi l'époque du foisonnement des connaissances scientifiques. Pour encourager les intellectuels de l'époque, appelés **humanistes**, François Ier fonde le **Collège de France** en 1530. Le seizième siècle exploite aussi l'invention de l'imprimerie par Gutenberg, et le livre devient le moyen de diffusion du nouveau savoir.
- Parmi les auteurs du seizième siècle, celui qui a eu le plus d'influence sur la littérature française et mondiale est **François Rabelais** (1490–1553). Rabelais a écrit une série de cinq livres: *Gargantua, Pantagruel, Tiers Livre, Quart Livre* et *Cinquième Livre.* Les personnages principaux des romans sont Gargantua, son fils

Pantagruel et Panurge, le fidèle compagnon de Pantagruel. Rabelais peint un monde de joie et de plaisir où la bonne table est reine.

- En poésie, le mouvement de **la Pléiade** représente les courants intellectuels de la Renaissance. Portant le nom d'une constellation qui déjà dans la Grèce antique s'employait pour désigner un groupe de poètes, la Pléiade cherchait à donner à la France une poésie en langue française digne des modèles classiques où elle puisait son inspiration. **Pierre de Ronsard** et **Joachim du Bellay** sont les poètes les plus connus de cette école.
- **Michel Eyquem de Montaigne** fut le grand essayiste du seizième siècle. Son œuvre *Les essais* est un effort pour comprendre l'essence de l'être humain en étudiant ses propres réactions et ses observations de lui-même. Montaigne dépeint la difficulté à laquelle les hommes font face en essayant d'arriver à connaître la vérité.

L'ÂGE CLASSIQUE

- **L'âge classique** en France est lié au règne de **Louis XIV** (1660–1715), mais il se prépare même avant lui. Le dix-septième siècle est marqué par Richelieu, Louis XIII, Mazarin et Louis XIV, qui mènent à l'absolutisme royal et à l'effacement du pouvoir des nobles. Autour du pouvoir royal se développe une société aristocratique, caractérisée par un grand raffinement, des goûts précis et un vif intérêt porté à la vie culturelle. Les **salons** littéraires organisés par des femmes aristocratiques et cultivées comme la marquise de Rambouillet et Mademoiselle de Scudéry font circuler les idées. Les normes linguistiques et artistiques sont établies par l'Académie française et L'Académie royale de peinture et de musique. L'innovation dans les sciences est promue par l'Académie des sciences, fondée en 1666.
- Le dix-septième siècle est un siècle soucieux de doctrines et de normes. **Boileau**, dans son œuvre *L'art poétique*, établit des formules pour le théâtre dont la plus connue est **la règle des trois unités**: unité de lieu, unité de temps, unité d'action. Cette règle est d'inspiration classique et puise ses origines chez Aristote. **Malherbe** et **Vaugelas** posent les normes linguistiques qui ont pour but de donner à la langue française une unité qui reflète l'unité politique du royaume. Le souci de la clarté et de la beauté d'expression montre l'inspiration aristocratique de cette standardisation.
- Dans la philosophie, les deux grands noms du siècle sont **Descartes** et **Pascal. René Descartes** (1596–1650) crée une méthode philosophique axée sur la pensée et la raison humaine. Son systeme de pensée est fondé sur la déduction: on va du simple au complexe. L'importance que Descartes donne à l'activité mentale de l'homme se trouve résumée dans son dicton fameux *Cogito ergo sum*, en français, «Je pense, donc je suis». Parmi ses œuvres les plus importantes se trouvent *Discours de la méthode* et *Méditations métaphysiques*. **Blaise Pascal** (1623–1662) était mathématicien et physicien. Même sa jeunessse fut marquée par des prouesses scientifiques. À l'âge de seize ans il publie un *Essai sur les coniques;* à dix-huit ans il invente la machine à calculer. En 1654, suivant l'exemple de sa sœur devenue religieuse, il subit une espèce de conversion. Son œuvre *Pensées* est une méditation sur la condition humaine et une défense de la religion chrétienne et de la place centrale occupée par Dieu dans les actes des êtres humains.
- La littérature française du dix-septième siècle atteint son sommet dans le théâtre. Trois grands dramaturges laissent leur empreinte sur l'époque: **Corneille, Molière** et **Racine**. Dans les pièces de Corneille (1606–1684) nous voyons des thèmes espagnols (*Le Cid, Don Sanche d'Aragon*) et classiques (*Horace, Cinna*). Molière (1622–1673) est le grand dramaturge comique de la littérature française. Ses œuvres se lisent et se représentent avec le même plaisir aujourd'hui qu'au dix-septième siècle et ses situations mettent en relief les faiblesses humaines.

Ses personnages n'ont pas perdu leur actualité avec le passage des siècles. Parmi ses pièces les plus connues se trouvent *Les précieuses ridicules*, *L'école des femmes*, *Le misanthrope*, *Le bourgeois gentilhomme*, *Le malade imaginaire*, *Tartuffe* et *Dom Juan*. Le grand tragédien du dix-septième siècle est Racine (1639–1699). Racine analyse dans ses pièces telles que *Phèdre*, *Bérénice*, *Andromaque* et *Britannicus* le conflit entre la passion fatale affrontée à la morale ou aux normes de la société.

- Une autre grande figure du siècle classique est **Jean de la Fontaine** (1621–1695). Cet auteur de fables emploie une technique employée déjà dans l'antiquité: peindre la société humaine avec des personnages qui sont des animaux. Beaucoup de vers tirés de ses fables sont devenus des expressions courantes dans la langue française.

LE DIX-HUITIÈME SIÈCLE

- Le dix-huitième siècle s'appelle **le siècle des lumières**. Il commence par une continuation de l'époque classique. Les idées sont diffusées dans les salons, mais d'autres lieux de conversation se créent: les clubs et les cafés. C'est un siècle philosophique qui donne un grand essor aux raisonnements dans le domaine de la morale, de la politique, de la nature humaine. La confiance dans l'esprit humain donne lieu à un projet monumental: ***l'Encyclopédie.*** Le but de cette entreprise était de recueillir toutes les connaissances humaines dans une seule œuvre en divisant cette énorme tâche parmi des spécialistes divers. Le directeur de *l'Encyclopédie* était **Denis Diderot** (1713–1784).
- La pensée philosophique est représentée par **Montesquieu** (1689–1755), dont l'œuvre principale est *L'esprit des lois*. Ce livre a posé les bases des doctrines constitutionnelles et de la pensée politique libérale classique. Les idées de Montesquieu sur la séparation des pouvoirs comme défense de la liberté des citoyens a influencé les auteurs de la constitution américaine.
- **Voltaire** (1694–1778) représente l'homme du dix-huitième siècle. Sorti d'un milieu bourgeois, il devient le défenseur du citoyen contre le despotisme du gouvernement et contre celui du clergé. Doué d'un esprit critique mordant, il a critiqué toutes les institutions de la société de l'époque. Parmi ses œuvres les plus connues on trouve les contes *Candide* et *Zadig*, les poèmes philosophiques tels que *Poème sur le désastre de Lisbonne* (écrit à la suite du terrible tremblement de terre qui ravage la capitale portuguaise en 1755) et des livres d'histoire comme *Le siècle de Louis XIV*.
- L'œuvre de **Jean-Jacques Rousseau** (1712–1778) marque une transition entre le siècle des lumières et le romantisme qui deviendra le mouvement littéraire dominant au dix-neuvième siècle. Pour Rousseau, l'homme est bon de nature et quand il vit dans l'état de nature. C'est la société qui corrompt l'être humain et le rend mauvais. Il s'éloigne des autres écrivains de son époque qui cherchent à améliorer la société et à la rendre plus juste. Son œuvre *Confessions* est autobiographique. Dans *Émile* Rousseau présente ses idées sur la pédagogie. Dans son livre *Du contrat social* Rousseau résume ses idées sur les droits naturels de l'homme et pose l'idée que si l'individu cède quelques-uns de ses droits à l'état, l'état lui doit des bénéfices comme le bien-être et la liberté. Ces idées ont inspiré *la Déclaration des droits de l'homme*.

LE DIX-NEUVIÈME SIÈCLE

- Le début du dix-neuvième siècle est caractérisé par la montée du romantisme, une doctrine philosophique et littéraire élaborée par **Madame de Staël** (1766–1817). Son livre *De l'Allemagne* a présenté les idées principales du romantisme et a eu une immense influence. **Madame de Staël** préconisait une création littéraire contraire aux normes classiques. Avec le romantisme les sentiments prennent une grande importance dans la littérature. L'auteur le plus caractéristique du début du dix-neuvième siècle est **René de Chateaubriand** (1768–1848). Dans ses œuvres comme *René* et *Atala* il introduit les thèmes de la solitude et du «mal du siècle», l'inquiétude de sa génération secouée par des changements politiques et sociaux. Les thèmes d'aliénation, de déception et de révolte face à la société bourgeoise marqueront toute la littérature qui suivra.

- Deux grands romanciers romantiques sont **Victor Hugo** (1802–1885) (poète et dramaturge aussi) et **Stendhal** (1783–1842). Hugo est l'auteur de *Notre-Dame de Paris* et *Les misérables* parmi beaucoup d'autres œuvres. Stendhal est connu pour son roman *Le rouge et le noir* où il étudie le conflit entre le héros et la société, et la désillusion qui est si souvent le sort de l'individu. Une autre figure intéressante de la littérature romantique est **George Sand** (1804–1876), pseudonyme d'Aurore Dupin, une baronne qui s'habillait en homme. Elle a eu plusieurs liaisons, dont la plus connue est peut-être celle qui l'attachait au compositeur polonais Chopin. Cette femme de lettres française a écrit des romans d'inspiration sentimentale ou rustique.
- Le romantisme comme école littéraire avait ses ramifications. **Alphonse Daudet** (1840–1897), né à Nîmes dans le Midi, écrit des romans comme *Tartarin de Tarascon* et des collections de contes telles que *Lettres de mon moulin* qui reflètent les coutumes et l'ambiance de sa région. L'écrivain **Alexandre Dumas** (1802–1870) écrit des romans historiques qui ont été traduits en beaucoup de langues, ainsi des millions de personnes à travers le monde connaissent *Le comte de Monte-Cristo* et *Les trois mousquetaires*. Un autre romancier français de l'époque qui a fasciné des millions de lecteurs dans le monde entier est **Jules Verne** (1828–1905), créateur du roman scientifique d'anticipation. Le monde fantastique qu'il a créé a souvent anticipé les progrès scientifiques et techniques du vingtième siècle et ses romans tels que *Le voyage au centre de la terre, Le tour du monde en quatre-vingts jours, Vingt mille lieues sous les mers* et *Voyage dans la lune* ont servi d'inspiration à plusieurs films.
- Pendant le dix-neuvième siècle les sciences et la technologie connaissent un essor remarquable. Le modèle des sciences physiques où l'observation du concret et du réel joue un si grand rôle crée une réaction dans la littérature. Les écrivains réagissent contre l'idéalisme romantique et le culte de l'imagination. La deuxième moitié du dix-neuvième siècle est caractérisée par le réalisme, doctrine littéraire qui vise à la représentation de la réalité objective. Cette nouvelle école s'épanouit dans les romans. Le premier grand représentant du réalisme est **Honoré de Balzac** (1799–1850) dont les romans constituent un tableau de la société française de son époque. Champion de la description détaillée de la réalité même prosaïque, inventeur d'intrigues compliquées et de tout un monde de personnages, il étudie la société du dix-neuvième siècle où le pouvoir de l'argent prend la place des privilèges de naissance de la noblesse du siècle antérieur. Parmi ses romans il faut mentionner *Le père Goriot*, *Eugénie Grandet* et *La cousine Bette*.
- Le réalisme continue avec deux grands auteurs: **Gustave Flaubert** (1821–1880) et **Guy de Maupassant** (1850–1893). Le roman de Flaubert *Madame Bovary* est un chef-d'œuvre de description minutieuse, de souci de précision dans les détails. Flaubert est aussi l'auteur de *Salammbô, L'éducation sentimentale* et *Bouvard et Pécuchet*. Maupassant est connu surtout pour ses contes qui ont eu une influence énorme sur la littérature mondiale. Un écrivain très soucieux de décrire avec précision et de choisir le mot juste, Maupassant est un maître stylistique de la langue française.
- Le réalisme évolue et se transforme en naturalisme, école littéraire qui vise à utiliser les méthodes scientifiques dans la création artistique. Le naturalisme cherche à décrire la réalité dans tous ses détails, même dans ses aspects répugnants et vulgaires. **Les frères Goncourt**, **Edmond** (1822–1896) et **Jules**

(1830–1870), et **Jules Vallès** (1832–1885) sont des représentants de ce genre. Mais le plus important c'est **Émile Zola** (1840–1902). Dans ses romans il donne beaucoup d'importance aux conditions sociales et aux conditions matérielles, voyant en elles l'origine des passions humaines. Il peint un grand tableau de son époque, surtout des milieux défavorisés et des conflits entre les classes sociales créés par la révolution industrielle. Parmi ses nombreux romans il faut mentionner *Germinal, La bête humaine, L'assommoir* et *Le ventre de Paris*. L'engagement social de Zola se voit dans son intervention dans l'affaire Dreyfus où il prit le parti du capitaine juif accusé de trahison sans justification.

- Les écoles littéraires transforment aussi la poésie française. **Gérard de Nerval** (1808–1855) est un poète romantique qui préfère le monde du rêve à la réalité et le passé au présent. Il écrit *Les chimères* et *Les illuminés*, parmi d'autres livres de poésie. Parmi les autres poètes romantiques il faut mentionner **Victor Hugo**, **Alphonse de Lamartine** (1790–1869) et **Alfred de Vigny** (1797–1863). **Charles Baudelaire** (1821–1867) continue la tradition du romantisme, mais y ajoute son pessimisme et sa vision subjective et mystique du monde. On retrouve dans ses œuvres comme *Les fleurs du mal* une sensibilité assez proche de celle de notre siècle. C'est un poète symboliste. **Paul Verlaine** (1844–1896) écrit une poésie imprécise, peu contrainte par les formes traditionnelles, influencée par les lignes floues de l'art impressionniste de son époque. **Arthur Rimbaud** (1854–1891) crée une poésie moins personnelle que celle de l'époque romantique. Pour lui, la poésie est un mariage du mot et du sens, et il exprime parfois son mépris de la poésie traditionnelle. Un artiste révolutionnaire, conscient de renverser les conventions du passé, Rimbaud annonce le vingtième siècle. **Lautréamont** (1846–1870) et **Stéphane Mallarmé** (1842–1898) sont deux poètes importants de cette époque où le romantisme s'achève, le symbolisme est en vogue et le vingtième siècle se fait déjà voir dans le crépuscule du dix-neuvième.
- Le dix-neuvième siècle voit naître un nouveau type d'écrivain: l'historien moderne. **Jules Michelet** (1798–1874) en est un bon exemple. Il était chef de la section historique aux Archives nationales et professeur au Collège de France. Pour lui, les recherches historiques et l'enseignement lui donnaient l'occasion de diffuser ses idées anticléricales et libérales. Il mit l'histoire au service de la nation et de ses causes politiques de prédilection. Un grand écrivain, habile styliste, il a écrit une œuvre monumentale intitulée *Histoire de France*.

LE VINGTIÈME SIÈCLE

- Notre siècle, théâtre de tant de bouleversements profonds, a vu naître beaucoup de mouvements littéraires et intellectuels. Le début du vingtième siècle jusqu'à la Première Guerre mondiale continue à peu près le siècle antérieur, mais le dix-neuvième siècle en France a fini sur le déchirement de l'affaire Dreyfus. Dans la première décennie du vingtième siècle **Jules Romains** (1885–1972) publie un roman, *Les copains*, et en 1923 une pièce de théâtre très connue, *Knock*. Romains était un adepte de l'**unanimisme**, un mouvement littéraire qui essayait de représenter les sentiments des groupes humains, comme par exemple ceux d'une classe sociale, comme si tous les membres du groupe partageaient des traits psychologiques.
- **André Gide** (1869–1951) étudie dans ses romans le conflit entre l'intelligence et les instincts. Né dans la bourgeoisie protestante, il examine aussi la répression des passions exigée par la foi religieuse. Il écrit, parmi d'autres romans, *L'immoraliste, La porte étroite, La symphonie pastorale, Les caves du Vatican* et *Les faux-monnayeurs*. **Jean Giono** (1895–1970), né à Manosque en Provence, situe ses romans dans le Midi. Il a écrit *Un de Beaumugnes, Regain* et *Le hussard sur le toit*. Les thèmes ruraux sont en évidence dans son œuvre. **Marcel Proust** (1871–1922) a laissé un grand ensemble de romans intitulés *À la recherche du temps perdu* où il analyse

l'importance de la mémoire et des souvenirs dans la psychologie humaine. Proust a une grande influence sur les écrivains qui le suivent.

- **Le surréalisme**, un mouvement né après la Première Guerre mondiale, est une révolte contre les conventions artistiques, sociales et morales. Le poète **Guillaume Apollinaire** (1880–1918) a eu une grande influence sur le surréalisme et **André Breton** (1896–1966) définit les normes de cette école. Parmi ses autres adeptes se trouvent les poètes **Paul Éluard** (1895–1952) et **Jacques Prévert** (1900–1977). Le romancier **Raymond Queneau** (1903–1976), auteur de *Zazie dans le métro,* se comptait aussi à une certaine époque parmi les surréalistes.
- **L'existentialisme** est un courant intellectuel qui a eu beaucoup d'influence en France et à l'étranger. Ses idées dérivent du philosophe danois Kierkegaard (dix-neuvième siècle), mais le mouvement littéraire dérivant de sa philosophie a connu son plus grand essor après la Deuxième Guerre mondiale. Le choc des années tragiques d'une guerre qui a dévasté l'Europe ont sensibilisé la jeunesse intellectuelle à l'idée que l'existence humaine est absurde. L'angoisse créée par ce sentiment de l'absurde effraie l'être humain et le pousse à l'action. C'est l'action et surtout l'engagement politique qui nous aident à échapper à la notion de l'absurde. Pour beaucoup d'écrivains existentialistes, l'engagement politique aboutissait à l'appui du communisme soviétique ou chinois. Certains des plus grands, comme **Jean-Paul Sartre,** défendaient le barbarisme totalitaire de Staline, voyant dans le capitalisme et surtout dans le capitalisme américain un système ennemi de l'humanité. Les principaux auteurs français existentialistes sont **Albert Camus** (1913–1960), auteur de *L'étranger* et *La peste*; **Jean-Paul Sartre** (1905–1980), auteur de *La nausée, Les jeux sont faits* et *Les chemins de la liberté*; **Simone de Beauvoir** (1908–1986), féministe, auteur d'essais (*Le deuxième sexe*) et du roman *Les Mandarins*.
- Plusieurs courants littéraires s'unissent dans **le nouveau roman**. Une attention au détail et à la description minutieuse typiques du naturalisme se joignent au souci de reproduire le rêve du surréalisme. Dans les romans de cette école il n'y a ni déroulement chronologique ni psychologie ni héros. Toute la pensée de l'auteur se saisit à travers la description de choses externes. Parmi les écrivains les plus connus de cette école on trouve **Michel Butor**, né en 1926 (*La modification*), **Alain Robbe-Grillet**, né en 1922 (*La jalousie*), **Nathalie Sarraute**, née en 1902 (*Portrait d'un inconnu*), **Jean-Marie Le Clézio**, né en 1943 (*Le procès-verbal*) et **Marguerite Duras** (1914–1996) (*Le marin de Gibraltar, L'amant*). D'autres auteurs dont les œuvres pourraient se classer sous cette catégorie sont **Claude Simon**, né en 1913, **Claude Mauriac**, né en 1914, et **Patrick Modiano**, né en 1947.
- **Le théâtre du vingtième siècle** est très varié. Vers la fin du dix-neuvième siècle, en 1897, **Edmond Rostand** (1868–1918) présente sa pièce la plus célèbre, *Cyrano de Bergerac*. Ses autres pièces, comme *L'aiglon* et *Chantecler,* sont du vingtième siècle. **Paul Claudel** (1868–1955), dramaturge catholique, a écrit la plupart de ses œuvres théâtrales au vingtième siècle (*Partage de midi, L'annonce faite à Marie, L'otage* et *Le soulier de satin*). **Jean Giraudoux** (1882–1944) a écrit *La guerre de Troie n'aura pas lieu, Ondine* et *La folle de Chaillot*, parmi d'autres pièces. Il met en scène un univers fantastique, unissant parfois les thèmes classiques avec les préoccupations modernes. **Jean Anouilh** (1910–1987) a écrit des pièces fantastiques et satiriques comme *Le bal des voleurs* et *Le rendez-vous de Senlis* et des pièces pessimistes comme *Antigone* et *Le voyageur sans bagages*. **Henri de Montherlant** (1895–1972) écrit des pièces qui ont un fond moral comme *Les bestiaires, Les célibataires* et *Les jeunes filles.* Le **théâtre de l'absurde** fait partie de la littérature de dérision qui dénonce l'absurdité et le ridicule de la vie et plusieurs de ses dramaturges ont acquis une renommée internationale. **Eugène Ionesco** (1912–1994) est l'auteur de *La cantatrice chauve, Les chaises* et *Rhinocéros*. **Samuel Beckett** (1906–1989) est surtout connu pour ses pièces *En attendant Godot* et *Fin de partie.* Les existentialistes ont aussi écrit des pièces de théâtre. Sartre a écrit *Les*

mains sales, Huis clos, Le Diable et le Bon Dieu. Camus est l'auteur de *Le malentendu* et de *Caligula*.

- Parmi les poètes du vingtième siècle il faut mentionner **Paul Valéry** (1871–1945) qui continue le courant symboliste de Mallarmé, **Saint-Jean Perse** (1887–1975) qui examine dans ses vers les rapports entre l'être humain et la nature et **Paul Éluard** (1895–1952), surréaliste, puis engagé politique dans la Résistance anti-nazie. L'engagement politique se voit aussi dans l'œuvre poétique de **Louis Aragon** (1897–1982) qui, lui aussi, a débuté dans le surréalisme, mais les événements politiques des années 30 et 40 le détournent vers le communisme.
- Il y a d'autres noms importants dans la littérature française du vingtième siècle. **Roger Martin du Gard** (1881–1958) décrit la crise entre la foi et la science dans son roman *Jean Barois* et peint un tableau magistral des conflits sociaux dans *Les Thibault*, un roman en plusieurs tomes. **Colette** (1873–1954) peint la psychologie féminine dans ses romans tels que *La vagabonde* et *Gigi*. **Marguerite Yourcenar** (1903–1987), auteur des romans *Le coup de grâce, Mémoires d'Hadrien* et *L'œuvre au noir*, était la première femme élue à l'Académie française. **Antoine de Saint-Exupéry** (1900–44), pilote et écrivain, a écrit, entre autres, *Vol de nuit* et *Le petit prince*. **Françoise Sagan**, née en 1935, a écrit des romans comme *Un certain sourire, Aimez-vous Brahms?* et *Bonjour tristesse* qui ont connu un succès international. **André Malraux** (1901–1976) est un écrivain engagé. Il a participé à la guerre d'Espagne du côté des républicains. Les thèmes politiques sont importants dans ses romans *La condition humaine* et *L'espoir*. **Henri Troyat**, un Russe réfugié du communisme, a écrit toute une série de romans sur la Révolution russe comme *Tant que la terre durera, Le sac et la cendre, Étrangers sur la Terre* et *Les semailles et les moissons*.
- Il y a aussi des écrivains très connus en France qui ne font pas de belles-lettres mais qui écrivent sur des thèmes littéraires, historiques ou sociaux. **Roland Barthes** (1915–1980) est un structuraliste qui écrit sur des thèmes anthropologiques et linguistiques. **Claude Lévi-Strauss**, né en 1908, est un autre structuraliste qui a une grande importance dans l'anthropologie moderne. **Raymond Aron** (1905–1983) écrit sur l'économie et la politique. Opposé à Jean-Paul Sartre, il a reconnu et exposé l'horreur du totalitarisme communiste. **Jean-François Revel**, né en 1924, suit le même courant politique qu'Aron. Il admire la démocratie et respecte les réussites des États-Unis. **Hélène Carrère d'Encausse**, née en 1929, a analysé les conflits ethniques en Union Soviétique et le rôle que ces conflits ont joué dans la chute de l'URSS.
- Un genre très apprécié dans la littérature française est le roman policier. Son représentant le plus connu est **Georges Simenon** (1903–1989), un Belge de langue française, auteur de plus de 200 romans policiers, beaucoup d'entre eux reliés par la présence de son personnage le plus connu, le commissaire de police Maigret. On trouve des antécédents du roman policier moderne au dix-neuvième siècle avec **Gaston Leroux** (1868–1927) qui a écrit *Le mystère de la chambre jaune* et *Le parfum de la dame en noir*. Parmi les autres auteurs de romans policiers en langue française il faut citer **Pierre Boileau** (1906–1989) et **Thomas Narcejac** (né en 1908) qui écrivent ensemble, **Alain Demouzon** (né en 1945) et **Michel Lebrun** (né en 1930).

LA LITTÉRATURE FRANCOPHONE

- L'expansion du français comme langue officielle ou comme langue de culture à travers le monde dans les anciennes colonies de France et de Belgique a produit une vaste littérature internationale en français. Nous ne pouvons citer ici que quelques noms importants de cette littérature francophone. Dans beaucoup de ces pays, la littérature nationale est écrite en français.

- **Le Canada français** a produit une littérature en langue française qui est très variée et de haute qualité. Les romanciers **Gabrielle Roy** (1909–1983) et **Yves Thériault** (1915–1983) ont peint des tableaux merveilleux de la vie canadienne. Gabrielle Roy, née dans le Manitoba, a décrit la vie sur la vaste plaine canadienne dans *Ces enfants de ma vie* et *Rue Deschambault*. Yves Thériault décrit la vie des Esquimaux canadiens (les Inuit) dans son roman *Agaguk*. D'autres romanciers importants sont **Roch Carrière** (né en 1937), **Jacques Ferron** (1921–1985), **Anne Hébert** (née en 1916), **Roger Lemelin** (né en 1919) et **Michel Tremblay** (né en 1943). Parmi les poètes et les poètes-chanteurs il faut citer **Jacques Brault** (né en 1933), **Alain Grandbois** (1900–1975) et **Gilles Vigneault** (né en 1928). Le théâtre canadien a été enrichi par des dramaturges importants tels que **Marcel Dubé** (né en 1930), **Michel Garneau** (1925–1971) et **Gratien Gelinas** (né en 1909). Les romanciers Roch Carrière et Michel Tremblay ont aussi fait du théâtre.
- Les écrivains francophones d'**Afrique noire** sont très nombreux. Le poète sénégalais **Léopold Senghor** (né en 1906) analyse l'idée de négritude dans ses poèmes. Il a été aussi président de son pays. Le romancier sénégalais **Ousmane Sembène** (né en 1923), d'orientation marxiste, écrit *Le docker noir* et *O pays mon beau peuple*. Le roman *L'enfant noir* de l'écrivain guinéen **Camara Laye** est connu dans le monde anglophone aussi. Né en Côte-d'Ivoire en 1916 **Bernard Dadié** est l'auteur d'une œuvre riche et variée. Il a écrit onze pièces de théâtre (*Les villes, Assémien Déhylé, Roi du Sanwi, Béatrice du Congo, Îles de tempête, Les voix dans le vent*), le roman *Un nègre à Paris*, plusieurs recueils de contes et de poésie, des chroniques et des livres de pensées. **Mongo Beti**, né en 1932 au Cameroun, est un romancier important: *Ville cruelle, Le pauvre Christ de Bomba* et *Main basse sur le Cameroun*. Un autre Camérounais, **Ferdinand Oyono** (né en 1929), écrit des romans qui étudient la confrontation entre colonisateur et colonisé (*Une vie de Boy, Le vieux nègre et la médaille, Chemin d'Europe*). Au Bénin (le Dahomey de l'époque coloniale) la poésie a pris un grand essor avec l'œuvre de poètes tels que **Paulin Joachim** (né en 1931) et **Émile Ologoudou** (né en 1935). À Madagascar, une femme de lettres, **Michèle Rakotoson** (née en 1948) est connue pour ses nouvelles psychologiques telles que *Dadabé*.
- Aux Antilles il y a une littérature francophone très intéressante. À Haïti, le premier roman (*Stella* d'**Émile Bergeaud**) apparaît en 1859 et décrit la guerre d'indépendance. Le romancier **Jacques Roumain** (1907–1944) écrit *La montagne ensorcelée* et *Gouverneurs de la rosée*. Important aussi est le poète et dramaturge **Félix Morisseau-Leroy**, né en 1912. À la Martinique nous avons le poète et dramaturge **Aimé Césaire** (né en 1913), le poète et essayiste **Edouard Glissant** (né en 1928) et l'excellent romancier et conteur **Joseph Zobel** (né en 1915) auteur de *La rue Cases-nègres* (porté au cinéma) et du *Soleil partagé*. À la Guadeloupe, **Maryse Condé** (née en 1937) a publié des études littéraires, des essais, des pièces de théâtre et des romans comme *Ségou*. La Guadeloupe compte aussi parmi ses créateurs littéraires **Simone Schwarz-Bart** (née en 1938), romancière, et **Henri Corbin** (né en 1935), poète et dramaturge.
- On écrit aussi en français dans les trois pays du **Maghreb** et au **Liban**. Le romancier marocain **Tahar ben Jelloun** (né en 1944) a reçu le prix Goncourt pour son roman *L'enfant de sable*. L'Algérien **Kateb Yacine** (1929–1989) est un auteur prolifique. Il a écrit des recueils de poésie tels que *Soliloques*, des romans (*Nedjma*) et des pièces de théâtre (*Le cadavre encerclé, Mohammed, prends ta valise, L'homme aux sandales de caoutchouc*). Le Juif tunisien **Albert Memmi** a analysé les effets psychologiques du colonialisme dans son essai *Portrait du colonisé* et la vie et la situation des Juifs en Tunisie dans son roman autobiographique *La statue de sel*. Parmi les écrivains libanais d'expression française on pense tout de suite au romancier **Amin Maalouf** (né en 1949), auteur de romans historiques tels que *Léon l'Africain*.

EXAMEN

A. Reliez les auteurs de la première colonne à leurs œuvres de la deuxième colonne.

_____	1. Montesquieu	a. *Discours de la méthode*
_____	2. Rabelais	b. *Le mystère de la chambre jaune*
_____	3. Descartes	c. *Les Mandarins*
_____	4. Stendhal	d. *La peste*
_____	5. Corneille	e. *Gargantua*
_____	6. Molière	f. *Le roman de Perceval*
_____	7. Maalouf	g. *Horace*
_____	8. Gaston Leroux	h. *Huis clos*
_____	9. Chrétien de Troyes	i. *L'amant*
_____	10. Marguerite Duras	j. *L'école des femmes*
_____	11. Jean-Paul Sartre	k. *Le rouge et le noir*
_____	12. Albert Camus	l. *Léon l'Africain*
		m. *L'esprit des lois*
		n. *Vol de nuit*

B. Indiquez moyennant la clé suivante le genre littéraire des œuvres suivantes: R *roman*, T *pièce de théâtre*, P *poésie*, E *essai(s)*, H *livre d'histoire*, C *recueil de contes*. Écrivez le nom de l'auteur de chaque œuvre dans la colonne de droite.

_____	1. *Phèdre*	____________________
_____	2. *Portrait du colonisé*	____________________
_____	3. *Lettres de mon moulin*	____________________
_____	4. *Mémoires d'Hadrien*	____________________
_____	5. *Le siècle de Louis XIV*	____________________
_____	6. *L'enfant noir*	____________________
_____	7. *Notre-Dame de Paris*	____________________
_____	8. *Les fleurs du mal*	____________________
_____	9. *Un certain sourire*	____________________
_____	10. *Les chimères*	____________________
_____	11. *L'étranger*	____________________
_____	12. *Don Sanche d'Aragon*	____________________

C. Identification. Identifiez les auteurs et œuvres suivants en choisissant la description correcte.

1. *Un de Beaumugnes*
   a. roman de Jean Giono
   b. conte d'Alphonse Daudet
2. *Chanson de Roland*
   a. poème canadien contemporain
   b. chanson de geste médiévale
3. La Pléiade
   a. groupe de philosophes du siècle de Louis XIV
   b. groupe de poètes de la Renaissance
4. *Germinal*
   a. roman naturaliste d'Émile Zola
   b. poème symboliste de Stéphane Mallarmé
5. Roland Barthes
   a. poète du dix-neuvième siècle
   b. anthropologue de l'école structuraliste
6. George Sand
   a. femme de lettres qui s'habillait en homme
   b. romancier canadien du dix-neuvième siècle
7. Boileau
   a. établit les règles pour le théâtre classique
   b. fonde une nouvelle école poétique
8. Madame de Staël
   a. initiatrice du romantisme
   b. chef de salon à Versailles
9. Michel Butor
   a. dramaturge contemporain
   b. auteur de *La modification*
10. Alphonse de Lamartine et Alfred de Vigny
    a. poètes romantiques
    b. écrivains de romans policiers
11. *L'enfant de sable*
    a. roman marocain
    b. pièce de théâtre du dix-neuvième siècle
12. Gabrielle Roy
    a. essayiste française
    b. romancière canadienne
13. François Villon
    a. poète du moyen âge
    b. mathématicien de la Renaissance
14. Pierre de Ronsard et Joachim du Bellay
    a. poètes de la Pléiade
    b. romanciers réalistes

15. *Rue Cases-nègres*
   a. roman africain
   b. roman antillais

16. *La vagabonde* et *Gigi*
   a. romans de Colette
   b. personnages de Françoise Sagan

D. À compléter. Complétez les phrases suivantes avec les informations qui manquent.

1. *Dadabé* est le titre d'une œuvre de ____________________.
2. ____________________ est un poète sénégalais.
3. Selon les existentialistes, le sentiment de l'absurdité de l'existence humaine mène à ____________________.
4. Le roman *Agaguk* décrit la vie des ____________________.
5. Le poète ambulant du moyen âge s'appelait le ____________________.
6. Michel Eyquem de Montaigne est le grand ____________________ du seizième siècle.
7. La règle des trois unités impose l'unité de temps, de ____________________ et d'____________________.
8. Jules Michelet est ____________________.
9. Alphonse Daudet et Jean Giono situent l'action de leurs romans dans ____________________.
10. ____________________ est le créateur du roman scientifique d'anticipation.
11. Marie de France est l'auteur de ____________________, poèmes médiévaux.
12. *Le père Goriot* et *Eugénie Grandet* sont des romans de ____________________.
13. Le roman le plus connu de Flaubert s'appelle ____________________.
14. Guy de Maupassant est connu pour ses ____________________.
15. *La statue de sel* est un roman autobiographique de l'écrivain tunisien ____________________.

E. Thème et œuvres. Choisissez dans la deuxième colonne le thème de chaque œuvre de la première colonne.

_____ 1. *La chanson de Roland*

_____ 2. les romans de Rabelais

_____ 3. *Les essais* de Montaigne

_____ 4. *Discours de la méthode*

_____ 5. *Les pensées* de Pascal

_____ 6. *L'esprit des lois* de Montesquieu

_____ 7. *Du contrat social* de Rousseau

_____ 8. *René* de Chateaubriand

_____ 9. *Le rouge et le noir*

_____ 10. *Jean Barois*

_____ 11. *Le sac et la cendre*

_____ 12. *Rue Deschambault*

a. la vie dans le Manitoba

b. arriver à la vérité par l'observation de soi-même

c. bases des doctrines constitutionnelles et de la pensée politique libérale classique

d. retraite des troupes de Charlemagne

e. roman qui étudie le conflit entre le héros et la société

f. étude sur les droits naturels de l'homme

g. l'aliénation et le «mal du siècle»

h. l'importance de la pensée et de la raison humaine

i. la Révolution russe

j. le conflit entre la foi et la science

k. le plaisir de la bonne table

l. méditation sur la condition humaine et défense de la religion chrétienne

CHAPTER 32 FRENCH ART, MUSIC, SCIENCE, AND TECHNOLOGY

L'ART EN FRANCE: PEINTURE

- **Le seizième siècle** est celui de la **Renaissance** en France. François Ier invite des artistes italiens à décorer le château de Fontainebleau. Ces Italiens ont influencé des artistes français tels que **Goujon** et les **Cousin** (père et fils) qui incorporaient à leurs œuvres les thèmes classiques déjà utilisés en Italie. **Le dix-septième siècle** a vu la montée du classicisme. Le peintre le plus important de l'époque est **Nicolas Poussin** (1594–1665). Son goût pour le classique se joignait à son intérêt pour la nature. Poussin eut une grande influence sur ses contemporains et sur les artistes du siècle suivant. Parmi ses œuvres: *Ruth et Booz, Les bergers d'Arcadie, L'enlèvement des Sabines*. D'autres peintres de ce siècle, comme les frères **Le Nain,** ont peint avec un grand réalisme. Le peintre **Charles Lebrun** (1619–1690) dirigea la décoration du palais de Versailles.
- **Le dix-huitième siècle** voit une grande floraison de la peinture française. **Antoine Watteau** (1684–1721) fut un peintre académicien et un grand maître dans l'emploi des couleurs. Ses œuvres reflètent la société raffinée au milieu de laquelle il vivait et peignait. **François Boucher** (1703–1770) rappelle Watteau dans son raffinement aristocratique et dans ses dons de dessinateur. Les tableaux de **Jean-Baptiste Chardin** (1699–1779) sont des scènes de genre, c'est-à-dire tirées de la vie quotidienne. Chardin est connu aussi pour ses natures mortes qui, malgré le manque de sujets humains, transmettent une intensité remarquable. **Jean-Honoré Fragonard** (1732–1806) unit dans ses portraits l'ardeur et la grâce (*Fête à Saint-Cloud*). Le peintre **Pierre Paul Prud'hon** (1758–1823) marqua la transition du classicisme au romantisme du dix-neuvième siècle (*Tête de Vierge*).
- **Le dix-neuvième siècle** fut marqué par une succession rapide de mouvements artistiques, souvent contemporains les uns des autres. Au début du siècle il y a eu un renouveau d'intérêt porté aux normes de la peinture classique. Les peintres les plus importants de cette école néoclassique furent **Louis David** (1748–1825) et son élève **Jean Auguste Dominique Ingres** (1780–1867). Louis David fut le peintre de Napoléon et montra une grande créativité dans la représentation de scènes classiques ou historiques. Ingres est connu surtout pour ses portraits. Les œuvres des deux peintres sont remarquables pour la précision du dessin et de l'observation. Un autre élève de Louis David, **François Gérard** (1770–1837), fut un portraitiste célèbre sous la Restauration.
- La nouvelle tendance artistique du dix-neuvième siècle est **le Romantisme**. Cette réaction contre la raison et les normes académiques du néoclassicisme de Louis David produit un art qui donnait libre cours aux sentiments de l'artiste, et qui préférait la subjectivité au rationalisme. **Théodore Géricault** (1791–1824) se considère le premier des romantiques. Son tableau *Le radeau de la Méduse* représente les marins survivants au naufrage et montre la faim, la terreur et la folie de ces infortunés qui flottaient sur un radeau qu'ils avaient eux-mêmes façonné. La violence du sujet et le commentaire social ont scandalisé les critiques. **Eugène Delacroix** (1798–1863) fut le chef de l'école romantique. Lui aussi peignait des scènes de massacres comme les *Scènes des massacres de Scio* où il employait la peinture pour éveiller l'attention de ceux qui regardaient son œuvre

à la lutte des Grecs pour leur indépendance. Son tableau célèbre *Liberté guidant le peuple* dépeint la Révolution de 1830. Le Romantisme admettait les thèmes nationalistes et politiques dans la création artistique. Le contact avec l'Orient et l'Afrique du Nord poussa les artistes à représenter des scènes exotiques. Delacroix a peint *Les femmes d'Alger dans leur appartement*. Le renouveau d'intérêt du romantisme pour le moyen âge a ses retentissements dans la peinture, comme dans le tableau de Delacroix *Entrée des croisés à Constantinople*.

- La réaction contre la peinture romantique ne s'est pas fait attendre. Les courants réalistes qui transformèrent la littérature se faisaient sentir dans l'art. **Honoré Daumier** (1808–1879) est célèbre par ses caricatures qui s'inspirèrent de la réalité politique et sociale de son époque. Il a peint les pauvres gens, thème inacceptable aux académiciens. **Gustave Courbet** (1819–1877) se considère le chef de l'école réaliste. Il essayait de peindre la vie de tous les jours, d'observer et de représenter le monde matériel. *Un enterrement à Ornans* est un bon exemple de ce réalisme. Parfois il s'égarait du monde matériel comme dans son tableau *L'atelier du peintre: allégorie réelle* où la représentation de l'observé est enrichie par des éléments autobiographiques. **Jean-François Millet** (1814–1875) peignait des scènes rurales, dont les plus fameuses sont *Les glaneuses* et *L'angélus*. Cet intérêt pour la vie des paysans lui a valu le mépris des critiques de son époque.
- En 1872 **Claude Monet** (1840–1926) a exposé son tableau *Impression, soleil levant*. Du nom de ce tableau on a créé le mot ***impressionnisme*** pour désigner ce nouveau mouvement artistique qui fait de la lumière l'élément essentiel de la peinture. Monet peignait souvent la même scène (comme la cathédrale de Rouen) à de différents moments de la journée pour étudier les changements produits par la lumière. D'autres impressionnistes importants sont **Édouard Manet** (1832–1883) (*Le déjeuner sur l'herbe, Olympia, Un bar aux Folies-Bergère*); **Camille Pissarro** (1830–1903), connu pour ses paysages délicats (*Le potager*) et ses représentations de paysans (*Jeune fille à la baguette*); **Auguste Renoir** (1841–1919), peintre de la gaîté et maître de la représentation de la forme féminine (*Le moulin de la Galette, La balançoire, Les baigneuses, Gabrielle à la Rose*) et **Edgar Degas** (1834–1917) qui exprimait le mouvement dans ses peintures de danseuses, de courses de chevaux et de scènes quotidiennes (*Les danseuses bleues, Les repasseuses au travail*). Deux peintres femmes sont importantes dans l'impressionnisme: **Berthe Morisot** (1841–1895), belle-sœur de Manet (*Eugène Manet et sa fille*), et **Mary Cassatt** (1845–1926), une Américaine qui habitait Paris. Conseillée par Degas, elle fréquentait tous les impressionnistes et se distinguait dans la représentation des enfants.
- L'impressionnisme provoqua des réactions. Un autre grand peintre des lieux de plaisir est **Henri de Toulouse-Lautrec** (1864–1901), auteur de *La goulue au Moulin-Rouge*. On peut dire que Toulouse-Lautrec est le père de l'affiche moderne. **Paul Cézanne** (1839–1906) essaie d'approfondir l'impressionnisme en déformant parfois les figures, en cherchant une troisième dimension et en centrant ses efforts sur la composition. Parmi ses tableaux les plus connus on peut citer *La montagne Sainte-Victoire* (montagne de Provence peinte et repeinte par lui à plusieurs reprises) et *Les joueurs de cartes*. **Georges Seurat** (1859–1891) continua la ligne de pensée des impressionnistes. Au lieu de mélanger les couleurs sur la palette et d'en déposer des taches sur les toiles, Seurat posait de petites touches de couleur sur la toile. Cette technique s'appelle **le divisionnisme** (parce que le peintre divisait la toile en parties pour poser les touches) ou **le pointillisme**. Parmi ses œuvres: *Un dimanche d'été à la Grande Jatte, Les poseuses, Le cirque, Le chahut*.
- Le peintre néerlandais **Vincent Van Gogh** (1853–1890) est étroitement lié aux impressionnistes français. L'œuvre de Van Gogh s'éloigne un peu des impressionnistes par la vivacité des couleurs et l'intensité des sentiments d'un homme tourmenté par des problèmes d'ordre psychologique. Les lignes courbes, les formes arrondies et l'intensité émotive préfigurent l'expressionnisme. Parmi ses œuvres: *La chaise et la pipe, La nuit étoilée, Café de nuit à Arles*.

- Plusieurs peintres importants sont issus de l'impressionnisme. **Paul Gauguin** (1848–1903) s'installa en Océanie, région qui lui a servi d'inspiration dans beaucoup de ses tableaux aux noms polynésiens comme *Vairumati, Mahana no Atua, Nave Nave Moe*. Son art est caractérisé par la hardiesse des couleurs. Gauguin a influencé les peintres dont les innovations agressives leur ont valu le nom de «**fauves**», c'est-à-dire, «bêtes sauvages». Pour les fauves, les couleurs devaient exprimer non pas le monde réel mais les émotions de l'artiste. Parmi les fauves les plus importants nous trouvons **Henri Matisse** (1869–1954) (*La Japonaise au bord de l'eau, La fenêtre bleue, Intérieur, Le bocal de poissons rouges, Odalisque à la culotte rouge*) et **Raoul Dufy** (1877–1953) (*Les affiches à Trouville*) qui a souvent peint des scènes de la côte normande. D'autres fauves importants sont **Henri Manguin** (1874–1949)**, Maurice de Vlaminck** (1876–1958) et **André Derain** (1880–1954).
- **Le cubisme** succède au fauvisme. L'exaltation de la couleur des fauves est remplacée par la réduction des images en formes, de vrais cubes qui forçaient celui qui regardait le tableau à comprendre le sujet par un effort intellectuel. On est loin du rapport émotif recherché par les fauves. Parmi les représentants principaux du cubisme en France nous pouvons mentionner l'Espagnol **Pablo Picasso** (1881–1973) qui vécut la plupart de sa vie en France (*Les demoiselles d'Avignon, La femme qui pleure, Portrait de D.H. Kahnweiler, Trois musiciens*); **Georges Braque** (1882–1963), auteur des tableaux *Le violon, Broc et violon, Nature morte ovale, Violon et cruche, Atelier*; **Albert Gleizes** (1881–1953); **Fernand Léger** (1881–1955) et **Ossip Zadkine** (1890–1967).
- **Le surréalisme** a laissé son empreinte dans la peinture comme dans la littérature. Le paysage du rêve est représenté par le peintre belge **René Magritte** (1898–1967) (*Le conquérant*), **Yves Tanguy** (1900–1955) (*Jours de lenteur, Le soleil dans son écrin*) et **André Masson** (1896–1987) (*Le mangeur de pommes*).
- Les peintres français importants du **vingtième siècle** sont nombreux. Parmi les plus connus on trouve **Georges Rouault** (1871–1958), expressionniste et réaliste social; **Pierre Soulages**, né en 1919, peintre abstrait et **Maurice Utrillo** (1883–1955), connu pour ses représentations des scènes parisiennes, surtout des rues de Montmartre. Entre les deux guerres mondiales un groupe international de peintres se réunit à Paris pour s'associer aux peintres français. Parmi eux on trouve **Amedeo Modigliani, Marc Chagall, Chaïm Soutine, Foujita Tsuguharu** et **Constantin Brancusi**.

L'ART EN FRANCE: SCULPTURE

- La sculpture française a produit beaucoup de chefs-d'œuvre. Au **dix-septième siècle** l'architecte et sculpteur **Pierre Puget** (1620–1694) a sculpté des œuvres religieuses et classiques, comme *Les Atlantes* et *Milon de Crotone*. Il a exécuté cette dernière statue pour Versailles. **François Girardon** (1628–1715) fut le modèle du classicisme de Versailles. Pour le parc du château il a exécuté *Le bain des nymphes* et *Le tombeau du Cardenal Richelieu* à la Sorbonne. Au **dix-huitième siècle** nous avons **Jean-Baptiste Pigalle** (1714–1785); **Claude Michel**, dit **Clodion** (1738–1814); et **Jean Antoine Houdon** (1741–1828), auteur non seulement de statues classiques comme ses collègues mais de bustes des hommes célèbres de son époque, y compris d'Américains: Rousseau, Voltaire, Diderot, Thomas Jefferson, John Paul Jones, Robert Fulton et Benjamin Franklin.
- Au **dix-neuvième siècle** la sculpture romantique refléta les mêmes tendances monumentales et nationales que la peinture. **François Rude** (1784–1855) exécuta le haut-relief *Départ des volontaires de 1792*, dit *La Marseillaise*, de l'arc de triomphe de Paris. **Jean-Pierre Cortot** (1787–1843) est l'auteur d'un autre haut-relief de l'arc de triomphe, *L'apothéose de Napoléon*. À l'époque du réalisme, **Jean-Baptiste Carpeaux** (1827–1875) a sculpté pour la décoration de l'Opéra de Paris. Cette époque était aussi celle de l'œuvre du sculpteur français le plus connu, **Auguste**

Rodin (1840–1917), considéré un des plus grands sculpteurs du monde. Bien représentées aux États-Unis dans le musée Rodin de Philadelphie, ses œuvres les plus célèbres comprennent *Le penseur, Le baiser, Les bourgeois de Calais, Les portes de l'enfer, Fugit Amor*. Rodin fut suivi par **Aristide Maillol** (1861–1944), sculpteur de la forme féminine. Au **vingtième siècle** on pense tout de suite à **Jacques Lipschitz** (1891–1973), représentant du cubisme.

L'ART EN FRANCE: ARCHITECTURE

- **Au moyen âge** l'art français était surtout un art religieux. **L'art gothique** représente la cime de la création artistique du moyen âge. L'art gothique s'épanouit surtout dans l'architecture, et les cathédrales françaises devinrent le modèle pour celles des autres pays. La première cathédrale entièrement gothique est la cathédrale Saint-Étienne à Sens, au sud-est de Paris, dont on a commencé la construction vers 1130. Au siècle suivant l'art gothique est modifié par le **style rayonnant** qui a produit la très belle Sainte-Chapelle à Paris et la magnifique cathédrale d'Amiens, en Picardie. D'autres cathédrales gothiques de grande renommée sont Notre-Dame de Paris et Notre-Dame de Chartres.
- Pays de monuments, de châteaux, d'hôtels et de palais, la France ne manque pas d'architectes. **Salomon de Brosse** (1571–1626) a construit le palais du Luxembourg à Paris. **Louis Le Vau** (1612–1670) a construit plusieurs résidences élégantes à Paris et a influencé le plan du palais de Versailles. **Claude Perrault** (1613–1688) était l'architecte de la façade et de la colonnade du Louvre. **André Le Nôtre** (1613–1700) était le créateur du jardin sculpté à la française et dessinateur des jardins de Versailles. **Jules Hardouin-Mansart** (1646–1708) était un des architectes principaux de Versailles. On lui doit aussi la place Vendôme à Paris et le Grand Trianon à Versailles. Avec le peintre **Charles Lebrun** (1619–1690), responsable de la décoration, Hardouin-Mansart a exécuté la magnifique Galerie des Glaces à Versailles.
- Au **dix-neuvième siècle** l'architecture et l'urbanisme ont pris un nouvel essor, d'abord avec Napoléon et ensuite avec le progrès technologique. **Pierre-Alexandre Vignon** (1762–1820) exécuta l'église néoclassique de la Madeleine à Paris. Le Paris de Napoléon exigea des monuments triomphaux. **Charles Percier** (1764–1838) et **Pierre F. L. Fontaine** (1762–1853) étaient les architectes de l'arc de triomphe du Carrousel. **Jean Chalgrin** (1739–1811) était l'auteur des plans de l'arc de triomphe de l'Étoile. Le baron **Georges Haussmann** (1809–1891) a planifié la modernisation de Paris sous Louis-Napoléon, y compris le tracé de plusieurs boulevards et l'emplacement des gares. **Gustave Eiffel** (1832–1923), ingénieur, a édifié la tour Eiffel à l'occasion de l'Exposition universelle de 1889 et a donné à Paris un de ses symboles les plus célèbres. Au **vingtième siècle** on pense à **Charles-Édouard Jeanneret-Gris**, dit **Le Corbusier** (1887–1965), architecte et théoricien de l'architecture moderne.

LA MUSIQUE FRANÇAISE

- La musique française a une très longue tradition. Déjà au **dixième siècle, Odon, l'abbé de Cluny** (879–942) a inventé le premier système de notation musicale en Europe. Sa façon de représenter les notes a créé la possibilité de chanter n'importe quelle composition en lisant sa notation. C'est lui qui a désigné par les lettres de A à G les tons de la gamme musicale. Au **moyen âge**, la musique dite gothique se développe en Île-de-France. Cette musique polyphonique utilisait plusieurs voix qui se complémentaient et convenait aux vastes espaces des cathédrales gothiques. Le maître de cette école polyphonique fut le compositeur **Pérotin le Grand** (1160?–1220?), qui travaillait à la fin du douzième siècle et au début du treizième.

- C'est au **dix-septième siècle** à la cour de Louis XIV que la musique a fait de grands progrès. C'est ici qu'on forma le premier orchestre à cordes d'Europe (Les vingt-quatre violons) et qu'on développa le genre complexe de divertissement musical appelé **le ballet de cour**. Le compositeur le plus connu de l'époque était **Jean-Baptiste Lully** (1632–1687), Italien de naissance mais de formation française. Lully est le créateur de l'opéra français et le fondateur de l'Académie royale de musique. Ses opéras (*Alceste, Armide*) étaient des tragédies, mais il a composé de la musique pour les comédies de Molière aussi. **François Couperin**, dit **le Grand** (1668–1733), a composé pour le clavecin, instrument dont il était un très grand maître. Un autre claveciniste, **Jean-Philippe Rameau** (1683–1764), s'est distingué avec son *Traité de l'harmonie* où il a établi les normes de la science de l'harmonie.
- Au **dix-huitième siècle André Modeste Grétry** (1741–1813) a composé des opéras-comiques et **Jean-François Le Sueur** (1760–1837) a composé des opéras et de la musique religieuse. Mais c'est surtout au **dix-neuvième siècle** que la musique française a atteint une renommée universelle. Le compositeur romantique **Hector Berlioz** (1803–1869) a écrit *La damnation de Faust*, *La symphonie fantastique* et *La grande messe des morts*, parmi d'autres œuvres. Il a introduit une grande complexité orchestrale et chorale dans ses compositions. Par exemple, dans son *Requiem* il faut 500 voix et quatre orchestres de cuivres. **Jacques-François Halévy** (1799–1862) était professeur de musique au Conservatoire et auteur d'opéras, dont *La Juive*. Gounod et Bizet étaient ses élèves. **Charles Gounod** (1818–1893) est l'auteur d'opéras comme *Faust* et *Roméo et Juliette*. **César Franck** (1822–1890), né en Belgique, était organiste. Il est l'auteur de chorales, d'une symphonie et de musique de chambre. Il est connu pour la richesse de ses mélodies. **Camille Saint-Saëns** (1835–1921) était pianiste et organiste. Il est l'auteur d'une énorme production musicale qui comprend de la musique de chambre, des concertos, une symphonie, des poèmes symphoniques comme *La danse macabre* et *Le carnaval des animaux*. Son œuvre la plus célèbre est son opéra *Samson et Dalila*. **Georges Bizet** (1838–1875) est l'auteur de plusieurs opéras dont *Carmen* est un des plus appréciés du monde. **Jules Massenet** (1842–1912) a écrit des opéras (*Hérodiade, Manon, Thaïs, Le jongleur de Notre-Dame*). **Gabriel Fauré** (1845–1924), créateur de mélodies exquises, est l'auteur de musique de chambre, de pièces pour piano et des opéras *Pénélope* et *Prométhée*. Il faut aussi mentionner **Jacques Offenbach** (1819–1880), auteur des *Contes d'Hoffmann*, un opéra fantastique, et **Léo Delibes** (1836–1891), auteur d'opéras-comiques comme *Lakmé* et de ballets comme *Coppélia*.
- Deux grands noms dominent la musique de la fin du dix-neuvième siècle et du début du vingtième: **Claude Debussy** (1862–1918) et **Maurice Ravel** (1875–1937). Debussy a renouvelé l'art musical et a transformé l'opéra. Il a cherché à apporter à la musique les idées des symbolistes, et une de ses œuvres est *Pelléas et Mélisande*, une version musicale de la pièce de Maurice Maeterlinck. Il a aussi écrit de la musique pour le poème de Mallarmé *L'après-midi d'un faune*. Parmi ses autres œuvres il faut mentionner *Préludes, Études pour piano, La mer* et un ballet, *Jeux*. Ravel est connu pour son orchestration et ses mélodies. Parmi ses œuvres les plus appréciées il faut mentionner *La valse, Boléro, Daphnis et Chloé* et son *Concerto pour la main gauche*. **Paul Dukas** (1865–1935), associé de Debussy, a écrit pour l'orchestre. Son œuvre la plus connue est *L'apprenti sorcier*. Au cours du vingtième siècle la musique devient de moins en moins traditionnelle. Le *groupe des Six* essaie de trouver une expression différente de celle de Debussy et de Ravel. Ces six compositeurs sont **Georges Auric** (1899–1983), **Louis Durey** (1888–1979), **Arthur Honegger** (1892–1955), **Darius Milhaud** (1892–1974), **Francis Poulenc** (1899–1963) et **Germaine Tailleferre** (1892–1983). Célèbres aussi au vingtième siècle sont **Olivier Messiaen** (1908–1992), un grand innovateur, et **Jacques Ibert** (1892–1962), auteur d'un concerto pour flûte.

- Parmi les artistes français dans le monde de la musique il faut mentionner **Pierre Monteux** (1875–1964) qui a fait une carrière historique comme chef d'orchestre. Il dirigea l'Orchestre Symphonique de Boston entre 1919 et 1924 et était le fondateur et chef de l'Orchestre Symphonique de Paris. À l'âge de 86 ans il a été nommé chef de l'Orchestre Symphonique de Londres. **Charles Munch** (1891–1968) a aussi dirigé l'Orchestre Symphonique de Boston entre 1949 et 1962. La première femme qui ait dirigé l'Orchestre Philharmonique de New York était la Française **Nadia Boulanger** (1887–1979). Elle était aussi pianiste et compositrice. **Jean-Pierre Rampal** (né en 1922) est un flûtiste français de renommée internationale. La célèbre soprano **Lily Pons** (1898–1976) a fait son début au Metropolitan Opera House de New York en 1931. Les **sœurs Labèque, Katia** (née en 1950) et **Marielle** (née en 1952) sont deux pianistes qui travaillent ensemble et exécutent souvent des duos sur un ou deux pianos. **Pierre Boulez** (né en 1925) est compositeur et chef d'orchestre.

LES SCIENCES ET LA TECHNOLOGIE

- Au **seizième siècle**, à l'époque de la Renaissance, le médecin **Ambroise Paré** (1510–1590) fait des découvertes importantes en chirurgie, surtout dans le traitement des amputations. **Pierre Franco** (1500–1561) est considéré le père de la chirurgie plastique et publie en 1556 une étude qui s'appelle *La chirurgie*.
- Au **dix-septième siècle**, avec l'encouragement et le soutien de la cour, les sciences se développent rapidement. Sous la rubrique de littérature nous avons mentionné les contributions philosophiques de **René Descartes** (1596–1650) et **Blaise Pascal** (1623–1662). Ces deux hommes ont aussi eu une influence fondamentale sur les mathématiques et les sciences. Descartes a créé plusieurs aspects de la géométrie et a raffiné l'algèbre. Sa contribution au raisonnement scientifique a aidé à créer la science moderne en éliminant les confusions de la scolastique médiévale. Avec le mathématicien **Pierre de Fermat** (1601–1665) il créa la géométrie analytique. Fermat collabora aussi avec Pascal dans la théorie des probabilités. Pascal inventa la machine à calculer et travailla dans plusieurs domaines scientifiques. Dans le domaine de la médecine **Jean Pecquet** (1622–1674) découvre la circulation du système lymphatique. **L'abbé Edme Mariotte** (1620–1684), physicien, étudia les rapports entre le volume et la pression des gaz.
- Au **dix-huitième siècle** il y a eu des progrès dans plusieurs domaines. À la fin du siècle on introduit **le système métrique** en France, dont le mètre, l'unité de longueur, est fixé à un 10 millionième de la distance entre le pôle et l'équateur. Ce système de mesures est officiel dans presque tous les pays du monde. La famille Jussieu produit plusieurs botanistes importants: **Antoine Jussieu** (1686–1758) et son neveu, **Antoine Laurent Jussieu** (1748–1836), connu pour sa classification des plantes. Le physicien et naturaliste **René Antoine Ferchault de Réaumur** (1683–1757) étudia la structure des métaux et aussi la vie et les mœurs des insectes. Le physicien et astronome **Pierre Simon Laplace** (1749–1827) étudia le mouvement des corps célestes et élabora une théorie sur l'origine du système solaire. **Charles de Coulomb** (1736–1806), physicien, fit des découvertes importantes en électrostatique et en magnétisme. Le naturaliste **Georges Louis Leclerc Buffon** (1707–1788) organise le jardin des Plantes à Paris et, avec la collaboration du naturaliste **Louis Daubenton** (1716–1800), écrit une *Histoire naturelle* en 44 volumes. **Gaspard Monge, Comte de Peluse** (1746–1818), fut un mathématicien important dans le domaine de la géométrie et participa à la fondation de l'École polytechnique. **Jean-Baptiste Lamarck** (1744–1829), naturaliste, a publié des œuvres sur le transformisme des animaux. C'est un précurseur important de Darwin. À **Georges Cuvier** (1769–1832) nous devons deux sciences importantes: l'anatomie comparée et la paléontologie. L'homme de science le plus remarquable du dix-huitième siècle est peut-être **Antoine Laurent de Lavoisier** (1743–1794). Chimiste et physicien, il fut le père de la chimie

moderne. Il créa la nomenclature chimique et il analysa aussi la composition de l'air et de l'eau. Nous lui devons la découverte du rôle de l'oxygène dans la respiration et des recherches importantes sur la combustion. Lavoisier fut guillotiné sous la Terreur.

- Au **dix-neuvième siècle** il y a une explosion de recherches scientifiques et de découvertes importantes. **André Ampère** (1775–1836) élabora la théorie de l'électromagnétisme. À cause de ses contributions on emploie le nom «ampère» pour désigner l'unité de mesure d'intensité d'un courant électrique. Il travailla avec le physicien et astronome **François Arago** (1786–1853), l'homme qui a découvert que l'électricité pouvait aimanter le fer.
- **Médecine et sciences naturelles**
  René Laennec (1781–1826) inventa le stéthoscope. **Louis Braille** (1809–1852), aveugle dès l'âge de trois ans, créa l'alphabet des aveugles qui permet la lecture tactile qui porte son nom. Braille utilisa 63 combinaisons de points en relief pour former les symboles nécessaires pour la lecture et les mathématiques. **Paul Broca** (1824–1880) étudia le cerveau et ses fonctions et le langage humain. L'homme de sciences dont l'œuvre a marqué tout le dix-neuvième siècle est **Louis Pasteur** (1822–1895). Ses recherches sur les microbes et la démonstration de l'effet antibiotique ont rendu possible la production de vaccins (lui-même a réalisé le vaccin contre la rage) et aussi une méthode pour tuer les micro-organismes dangereux dans les liquides: la pasteurisation. Son disciple **Émile Roux** (1853–1933) a réalisé des travaux importants sur les toxines et a découvert un traitement de la diphtérie.
- **Physique et chimie**
  Louis Joseph Gay-Lussac (1778–1850) découvrit la loi de la dilatation des gaz. Le **comte Hilaire Bernigaud de Chardonnet** (1839–1924) créa l'industrie des étoffes artificielles avec l'invention de la rayonne. **Marcellin Berthelot** (1827–1907) est le créateur de la thermochimie et réalisa des travaux importants dans le domaine de la chimie organique. **Pierre Curie** (1859–1906) et sa femme **Marie** née Sklodowska (1867–1934) découvrirent le radium. Ce couple a reçu le Prix Nobel de physique en 1903 et Marie Curie a eu le Prix Nobel de chimie en 1911. **Léon Foucault** (1819–1868) inventa le gyroscope et démontra le mouvement de rotation de la terre avec le pendule. **Henri Becquerel** (1852–1908) découvrit la radioactivité, ce qui lui a valu le Prix Nobel de physique (avec les Curie) en 1903.
- **Mathématiques et astronomie**
  Urbain Le Verrier (1811–1877), spécialiste en mécanique céleste, fit les calculs nécessaires pour la découverte de la planète Neptune en 1846.
- **Génie et inventions**
  Émile Levassor (1843–1897) fut un des inventeurs du moteur et créa l'industrie des moteurs automobiles en France. Avec **René Panhard** (1841–1908) il fonda une entreprise qui construisit la première automobile avec un moteur à essence. **Jacques Daguerre** (1787–1851) et **Nicéphore Niepce** (1765–1833) inventèrent la photographie.
- Le **vingtième siècle** a vu une grande expansion de l'activité scientifique.
- **Médecine et sciences naturelles**
  Le chirurgien et physiologiste **Alexis Carrel** (1873–1944) a fait des découvertes importantes sur la culture des tissus. On lui a décerné le Prix Nobel en 1912. **Jacques Monod** (1910–1976), **François Jacob** (né en 1920) et **André Lwoff** (né en 1902) ont reçu le Prix Nobel de médecine et de physiologie en 1965 pour leurs travaux de biochimie et de génétique. D'autres Prix Nobel de médecine ont été décernés aux chercheurs français suivants:
  1907 **Alphonse Laveran** (1845–1922) pour ses recherches sur le paludisme.
  1913 **Charles Richet** (1850–1935) a découvert l'anaphylaxie, c'est-à-dire la sensibilisation d'un corps moyennant l'injection d'une substance. L'anaphylaxie est synonyme d'allergie et le contraire de l'immunité.

1928 **Charles Nicolle** (1866–1936) pour ses recherches sur le typhus.
1980 **Jean Dausset** (né en 1916) pour ses recherches sur les leucocytes, importants pour la transplantation des organes.

- **Physique**
  On a décerné plusieurs Prix Nobel de physique à des Français:
  1908 **Gabriel Lippmann** (1845–1921) pour un procédé de photographie en couleurs.
  1926 **Jean Perrin** (1870–1942) pour l'identification des rayons cathodiques.
  1929 **Louis-Victor, prince puis duc de Broglie** (1892–1987), comme créateur de la mécanique ondulatoire.
  1966 **Alfred Kastler** (1902–1984) pour l'invention du «pompage optique» utilisé dans les lasers.
  1970 **Louis Néel** (né en 1904) pour la découverte de nouveaux types de magnétisme.
  1991 **Pierre-Gilles de Gennes** (né en 1932) pour son travail dans le domaine du magnétisme et de la superconductivité.
  1992 **Georges Charpak** (né en 1924) pour son invention de détecteurs de particules.
- **Chimie**
  Plusieurs Français ont reçu le Prix Nobel de chimie:
  1906 **Henri Moissan** (1852–1907) pour l'isolement du fluor et du silicium.
  1911 **Marie Curie** (voir ci-dessus).
  1912 **Victor Grignard** (1871–1935) pour la découverte des composés organométalliques du magnésium et **Paul Sabatier** (1854–1941) pour ses recherches sur les propriétés du nickel et les hydrocarbures synthétiques.
  1935 **Frédéric Joliot-Curie** (1900–1958) et **Irène Joliot-Curie** (1897–1956) pour leurs recherches sur la radioactivité artificielle. Irène Joliot-Curie était la fille de Pierre et Marie Curie.
  1987 **Jean-Marie Lehn** (né en 1939) pour son travail sur les molécules artificielles.
- **Mathématiques et économie**
  Deux Prix Nobel à noter:
  1983 **Gérard Debreu** (Américain d'origine française né en 1921) pour son travail dans l'économétrie, c'est-à-dire sur l'emploi des statistiques en économie.
  1988 **Maurice Allais** (né en 1911) pour sa contribution au développement de l'économie mathématique et à la théorie de la monnaie et le crédit et pour ses recherches sur l'équilibre économique.

LE CINÉMA

- La France est un des grands pays cinématographiques et a toujours eu une industrie du film importante. Le gouvernement français subventionne le cinéma français à travers le Centre national de cinématographie (CNC), organisme sous l'autorité du Ministère de la culture et de la communication.
  Parmi les plus grands directeurs français et leurs chefs-d'œuvre nous avons:
  Claude Berri (né en 1934): *Tchao, Pantin* (1983), *Jean de Florette* et *Manon des sources* (1986)
  Claude Chabrol (né en 1930): *La femme infidèle* (1970), *Que la bête meure* (1970), *Madame Bovary* (1991)
  Henri-Georges Clouzot (1907–1977): *Le salaire de la peur* (1953), *Les diaboliques* (1954)
  Jean Cocteau (1889–1963): *La belle et la bête* (1946), *Les parents terribles* (1948)
  Constantin Costa-Gavras (né en 1933): *Compartiment tueurs* (1965), *Z* (1968), *État de siège* (1973)
  Jacques Demy (1931–1990): *Les parapluies de Cherbourg* (1964)

Jean-Luc Godard (né en 1930): *À bout de souffle* (1960), *Une femme mariée* (1964), *Masculin féminin* (1967)
Claude Lanzmann (né en 1925): *Shoah* (1985)
Claude Lelouch (né en 1937): *Un homme et une femme* (1967)
Louis Malle (1932–1995): *Zazie dans le métro* (1959), *Viva Maria* (1965), *Le souffle au cœur* (1971), *Lacombe, Lucien* (1974), *Au revoir, les enfants* (1987)
Jean-Pierre Melville (1917–1973): *Les enfants terribles* (1950)
Édouard Molinaro (né en 1928): *La cage aux folles* (1978)
Jean Renoir (1894–1979): *La grande illusion* (1937), *La bête humaine* (1938)
Alain Resnais (né en 1922): *Nuit et brouillard* (1956), *Hiroshima mon amour* (1958), *L'année dernière à Marienbad* (1961), *La guerre est finie* (1966)
Éric Rohmer (né en 1920): *Ma nuit chez Maud* (1969), *Le genou de Claire* (1970)
Jacques Tati (1907–1982): *Les vacances de M. Hulot* (1953)
François Truffaut (1932–1984): *Les 400 coups* (1959), *Tirez sur le pianiste* (1961); *Jules et Jim* (1961), *Fahrenheit 451* (1966), *L'argent de poche* (1977), *Le dernier métro* (1980), *La femme d'à côté* (1981)
Roger Vadim (né en 1928): *Et Dieu créa la femme* (1956), *Les liaisons dangereuses* (1959), *Le repos du guerrier* (1962), *Château en Suède* (1963)

EXAMEN

A. Reliez les artistes de la première colonne avec leurs œuvres de la deuxième colonne.

_____	1. Claude Monet	a. *Le radeau de la Méduse*
_____	2. Jean-Honoré Fragonard	b. *Déjeuner sur l'herbe*
_____	3. Pierre Paul Prud'hon	c. *Les glaneuses*
_____	4. Édouard Manet	d. *Fête à Saint-Cloud*
_____	5. Théodore Géricault	e. *Impression, soleil levant*
_____	6. Eugène Delacroix	f. *La fenêtre bleue*
_____	7. Jean-François Millet	g. *La liberté guidant le peuple*
_____	8. Henri Matisse	h. *Les bergers d'Arcadie*
_____	9. Edgar Degas	i. *Les repasseuses au travail*
_____	10. Nicolas Poussin	j. *Tête de Vierge*

B. Indiquez la profession de chacune de ces personnes célèbres selon la clé suivante: P, peintre; S, sculpteur; A, architecte; C, compositeur.

_____ 1. Olivier Messiaen
_____ 2. Charles Percier
_____ 3. Jean Antoine Houdon
_____ 4. Hector Berlioz
_____ 5. Raoul Dufy
_____ 6. Pierre-Alexandre Vignon
_____ 7. Pérotin le Grand
_____ 8. Honoré Daumier
_____ 9. François Rude
_____ 10. Camille Pissarro
_____ 11. Jules Hardouin-Mansart
_____ 12. Albert Gleizes
_____ 13. Georges Seurat
_____ 14. Jules Massenet
_____ 15. Antoine Watteau

C. Identifiez le siècle ou le mouvement de chacun des artistes suivants.

1. Jean Auguste Ingres
   a. XVIe
   b. XIXe
2. Paul Gauguin
   a. impressionnisme
   b. romantisme
3. François Poulenc
   a. XXe
   b. XVIIIe
4. Gustave Courbet
   a. surréalisme
   b. réalisme
5. Georges Braque
   a. cubisme
   b. fauvisme
6. Jean-Baptiste Lully
   a. XVIIe
   b. XXe
7. Jacques Offenbach
   a. XVIe
   b. XIXe
8. Pierre Puget
   a. XIXe
   b. XXe

D. Écrivez le nom du compositeur ou de l'artiste à côté du nom de l'œuvre dont il est auteur.

1. *Carmen* ________________
2. *Les demoiselles d'Avignon* ________________
3. *La mer* ________________
4. *Les bourgeois de Calais* ________________
5. *Traité de l'harmonie* ________________
6. *Faust* ________________
7. *Daphnis et Chloé* ________________
8. *Eugène Manet et sa fille* ________________
9. *La montagne Sante-Victoire* ________________
10. *Le moulin de la Galette* ________________

E. Le monde de la musique. Complétez chacune des phrases suivantes avec un des noms de la liste ci-dessous.

Jacques-François Halévy
Nadia Boulanger
Paul Dukas
Katia Labèque
Pierre Monteux
Jean-Pierre Rampal
Lily Pons
Charles Munch

1. ________________ a été chef de l'Orchestre Symphonique de Londres et fondateur de l'Orchestre Symphonique de Paris.
2. Le compositeur de l'opéra *La Juive* s'appelle ________________.
3. La soprano ________________ a fait son début au Metropolitan Opera House en 1931.
4. ________________ est le compositeur de *L'apprenti sorcier.*
5. ________________ est un flûtiste célèbre.

6. Le premier chef d'orchestre femme au New York Philharmonic était

   ____________________________.

7. ____________________________ est une pianiste qui travaille avec sa sœur.

8. Le Français qui a dirigé l'Orchestre Symphonique de Boston de 1949 à 1962 s'appelle ____________________________.

F. Reliez les hommes de science de la première colonne avec leurs découvertes ou leurs inventions.

_____	1. Louis Pasteur	a.	le radium
_____	2. Antoine Laurent de Lavoisier	b.	le mouvement de rotation de la terre
_____	3. Léon Foucault	c.	la théorie de l'électromagnétisme
_____	4. Pierre et Marie Curie	d.	la photographie
_____	5. Blaise Pascal	e.	la nomenclature chimique
_____	6. Louis Braille	f.	la machine à calculer
_____	7. René Descartes	g.	les vaccins
_____	8. André Ampère	h.	l'anatomie comparée et la paléontologie
_____	9. Louis Daguerre	i.	la géométrie analytique
_____	10. Georges Cuvier	j.	l'alphabet des aveugles

G. Indiquez le directeur des films suivants.

1. *La grande illusion*
   a. Jean Renoir
   b. Jacques Demy
2. *Le dernier métro*
   a. François Truffaut
   b. Jean Cocteau
3. *Les vacances de M. Hulot*
   a. Jean-Pierre Melville
   b. Jacques Tati
4. *La guerre est finie*
   a. Alain Resnais
   b. Claude Chabrol
5. *Jean de Florette*
   a. Roger Vadim
   b. Claude Berri
6. *Au revoir, les enfants*
   a. Louis Malle
   b. Jean-Luc Godard
7. *La cage aux folles*
   a. Henri-Georges Clouzot
   b. Édouard Molinaro
8. *Ma nuit chez Maud*
   a. Constantin Costa-Gavras
   b. Éric Rohmer
9. *Shoah*
   a. Claude Berri
   b. Claude Lanzmann
10. *Que la bête meure*
    a. Claude Chabrol
    b. Jacques Tati

Verb Charts

Auxiliary Verbs

avoir *to have*	
indicative mood	
PRESENT	ai, as, a, avons, avez, ont
IMPERFECT	avais, avais, avait, avions, aviez, avaient
PASSÉ COMPOSÉ	ai eu, as eu, a eu, avons eu, avez eu, ont eu
PLUPERFECT	avais eu, avais eu, avait eu, avions eu, aviez eu, avaient eu
FUTURE	aurai, auras, aura, aurons, aurez, auront
CONDITIONAL	aurais, aurais, aurait, aurions, auriez, auraient
PASSÉ SIMPLE	eus, eus, eut, eûmes, eûtes, eurent
FUTURE PERFECT	aurai eu, auras eu, aura eu, aurons eu, aurez eu, auront eu
CONDITIONAL PERFECT	aurais eu, aurais eu, aurait eu, aurions eu, auriez eu, auraient eu
subjunctive mood	
PRESENT	aie, aies, ait, ayons, ayez, aient
PAST	aie eu, aies eu, ait eu, ayons eu, ayez eu, aient eu
IMPERFECT	eusse, eusses, eût, eussions, eussiez, eussent
imperative mood	
	aie (*but:* aies-en), ayons, ayez
present participle	
	ayant

être *to be*	
indicative mood	
PRESENT	suis, es, est, sommes, êtes, sont
IMPERFECT	étais, étais, était, étions, étiez, étaient
FUTURE	serai, seras, sera, serons, serez, seront
CONDITIONAL	serais, serais, serait, serions, seriez, seraient
PASSÉ COMPOSÉ	ai été, as été, a été, avons été, avez été, ont été
PASSÉ SIMPLE	fus, fus, fut, fûmes, fûtes, furent
PLUPERFECT	avais été, avais été, avait été, avions été, aviez été, avaient été
FUTURE PERFECT	aurai été, auras été, aura été, aurons été, aurez été, auront été
CONDITIONAL PERFECT	aurais été, aurais été, aurait été, aurions été, auriez été, auraient été
subjunctive mood	
PRESENT	sois, sois, soit, soyons, soyez, soient
PAST	aie été, aies été, ait été, ayons été, ayez été, aient été
IMPERFECT	fusse, fusses, fût, fussions, fussiez, fussent
imperative mood	sois, soyons, soyez
present participle	étant

Regular Verbs

-er Verbs

parler *to speak*	
indicative mood	
PRESENT	parle, parles, parle, parlons, parlez, parlent
IMPERFECT	parlais, parlais, parlait, parlions, parliez, parlaient
FUTURE	parlerai, parleras, parlera, parlerons, parlerez, parleront
CONDITIONAL	parlerais, parlerais, parlerait, parlerions, parleriez, parleraient
PASSÉ COMPOSÉ	ai parlé, as parlé, a parlé, avons parlé, avez parlé, ont parlé
PASSÉ SIMPLE	parlai, parlas, parla, parlâmes, parlâtes, parlèrent
PLUPERFECT	avais parlé, avais parlé, avait parlé, avions parlé, aviez parlé, avaient parlé
FUTURE PERFECT	aurai parlé, auras parlé, aura parlé, aurons parlé, aurez parlé, auront parlé
CONDITIONAL PERFECT	aurais parlé, aurais parlé, aurait parlé, aurions parlé, auriez parlé, auraient parlé
subjunctive mood	
PRESENT	parle, parles, parle, parlions, parliez, parlent
PAST	aie parlé, aies parlé, ait parlé, ayons parlé, ayez parlé, aient parlé
IMPERFECT	parlasse, parlasses, parlât, parlassions, parlassiez, parlassent
imperative mood	parle (*but:* parles-en), parlons, parlez
present participle	parlant

Compound tenses of **arriver,** a verb conjugated with **être:**

arriver *to arrive*	
indicative mood	
PASSÉ COMPOSÉ	suis arrivé(e), es arrivé(e), est arrivé(e), sommes arrivé(e)s, êtes arrivé(e)(s), sont arrivé(e)s
PLUPERFECT	étais arrivé(e), étais arrivé(e), était arrivé(e), étions arrivé(e)s, étiez arrivé(e)(s), étaient arrivé(e)s
FUTURE PERFECT	serai arrivé(e), seras arrivé(e), sera arrivé(e), serons arrivé(e)s, serez arrivé(e)(s), seront arrivé(e)s
CONDITIONAL PERFECT	serais arrivé(e), serais arrivé(e), serait arrivé(e), serions arrivé(e)s, seriez arrivé(e)(s), seraient arrivé(e)s
subjunctive mood	
PAST	sois arrivé(e), sois arrivé(e), soit arrivé(e), soyons arrivé(e)s, soyez arrivé(e)(s), soient arrivé(e)s

-ir Verbs

finir *to finish*	
indicative mood	
PRESENT	finis, finis, finit, finissons, finissez, finissent
IMPERFECT	finissais, finissais, finissait, finissions, finissiez, finissaient
FUTURE	finirai, finiras, finira, finirons, finirez, finiront
CONDITIONAL	finirais, finirais, finirait, finirions, finiriez, finiraient
PASSÉ COMPOSÉ	ai fini, as fini, a fini, avons fini, avez fini, ont fini
PASSÉ SIMPLE	finis, finis, finit, finîmes, finîtes, finirent
PLUPERFECT	avais fini, avais fini, avait fini, avions fini, aviez fini, avaient fini
FUTURE PERFECT	aurai fini, auras fini, aura fini, aurons fini, aurez fini, auront fini
CONDITIONAL PERFECT	aurais fini, aurais fini, aurait fini, aurions fini, auriez fini, auraient fini
subjunctive mood	
PRESENT	finisse, finisses, finisse, finissions, finissiez, finissent
PAST	aie fini, aies fini, ait fini, ayons fini, ayez fini, aient fini
IMPERFECT	finisse, finisses, finît, finissions, finissiez, finissent
imperative mood	finis, finissons, finissez
present participle	finissant

-re Verbs

vendre *to sell*	
indicative mood	
PRESENT	vends, vends, vend, vendons, vendez, vendent
IMPERFECT	vendais, vendais, vendait, vendions, vendiez, vendaient
FUTURE	vendrai, vendras, vendra, vendrons, vendrez, vendront
CONDITIONAL	vendrais, vendrais, vendrait, vendrions, vendriez, vendraient
PASSÉ COMPOSÉ	ai vendu, as vendu, a vendu, avons vendu, avez vendu, ont vendu
PASSÉ SIMPLE	vendis, vendis, vendit, vendîmes, vendîtes, vendirent
PLUPERFECT	avais vendu, avais vendu, avait vendu, avions vendu, aviez vendu, avaient vendu
FUTURE PERFECT	aurai vendu, auras vendu, aura vendu, aurons vendu, aurez vendu, auront vendu
CONDITIONAL PERFECT	aurais vendu, aurais vendu, aurait vendu, aurions vendu, auriez vendu, auraient vendu
subjunctive mood	
PRESENT	vende, vendes, vende, vendions, vendiez, vendent
PAST	aie vendu, aies vendu, ait vendu, ayons vendu, ayez vendu, aient vendu
IMPERFECT	vendisse, vendisses, vendît, vendissions, vendissiez, vendissent
imperative mood	vends, vendons, vendez
present participle	vendant

Verbs with Spelling Changes

1. Verbs whose stems end in **c,** such as **commencer,** add a cedilla under the **c** (**ç**) before the letters **a** and **o:**

commencer *to begin*	
PRESENT	commence, commences, commence, commen**ç**ons, commencez, commencent
IMPERFECT	commen**ç**ais, commen**ç**ais, commen**ç**ait, commencions, commenciez, commen**ç**aient
PASSÉ SIMPLE	commen**ç**ai, commen**ç**as, commen**ç**a, commen**ç**âmes, commen**ç**âtes, commencèrent
PRESENT PARTICIPLE	commen**ç**ant

2. Verbs whose stems end in **g,** such as **manger,** add an **e** after the **g** before the letters **a** and **o:**

manger *to eat*	
PRESENT	mange, manges, mange, mang**e**ons, mangez, mangent
IMPERFECT	mang**e**ais, mang**e**ais, mang**e**ait, mangions, mangiez, mang**e**aient
PASSÉ SIMPLE	mang**e**ai, mang**e**as, mang**e**a, mang**e**âmes, mang**e**âtes, mangèrent
PRESENT PARTICIPLE	mang**e**ant

3. Verbs whose stems end in **y,** such as **nettoyer,** change the **y** to **i** before a silent **e:**

nettoyer *to clean*	
PRESENT	netto**i**e, netto**i**es, netto**i**e, nettoyons, nettoyez, netto**i**ent
PRESENT SUBJUNCTIVE	netto**i**e, netto**i**es, netto**i**e, nettoyions, nettoyiez, netto**i**ent
FUTURE	netto**i**erai, netto**i**eras, netto**i**era, netto**i**erons, netto**i**erez, netto**i**eront
CONDITIONAL	netto**i**erais, netto**i**erais, netto**i**erait, netto**i**erions, netto**i**eriez, netto**i**eraient
IMPERATIVE	netto**i**e, nettoyons, nettoyez

Note: Verbs ending in **-ayer** may either change **y** to **i** before a silent e or keep the **y** in all forms: **je paie** or **je paye.** Verbs in **-oyer** and **-uyer** must change **y** to **i** before a silent **e.**

4. In **-er** verbs that have mute **e** as their stem vowel (**acheter, appeler, jeter, mener,** etc.), the mute **e** is pronounced **è** in those forms where the ending has a mute **e.** In the present tense, this means all singular forms and the third person plural. This change in sound may be spelled in one of two ways.

   a. Verbs such as **lever** change the **e** to **è** to show the change in pronunciation.

lever *to raise*	
PRESENT	lève, lèves, lève, levons, levez, lèvent
PRESENT SUBJUNCTIVE	lève, lèves, lève, levions, leviez, lèvent
FUTURE	lèverai, lèveras, lèvera, lèverons, lèverez, lèveront
CONDITIONAL	lèverais, lèverais, lèverait, lèverions, lèveriez, lèveraient
IMPERATIVE	lève, levons, levez

   b. Verbs like **appeler** and **jeter** double the consonant after the mute **e** to show the sound change of mute **e** to **è.**

appeler *to call*	
PRESENT	appelle, appelles, appelle, appelons, appelez, appellent
PRESENT SUBJUNCTIVE	appelle, appelles, appelle, appelions, appeliez, appellent
FUTURE	appellerai, appelleras, appellera, appellerons, appellerez, appelleront
CONDITIONAL	appellerais, appellerais, appellerait, appellerions, appelleriez, appelleraient
IMPERATIVE	appelle, appelons, appelez

jeter *to throw*	
PRESENT	jette, jettes, jette, jetons, jetez, jettent
PRESENT SUBJUNCTIVE	jette, jettes, jette, jetions, jetiez, jettent
FUTURE	jetterai, jetteras, jettera, jetterons, jetterez, jetteront
CONDITIONAL	jetterais, jetterais, jetterait, jetterions, jetteriez, jetteraient
IMPERATIVE	jette, jetons, jetez

c. First conjugation verbs such as **espérer,** which have **é** as the stem vowel, change **é** to **è** when the ending has a mute **e.** However, unlike verbs like **lever,** verbs like **espérer** keep the acute accent in the future and conditional.

espérer *to hope*	
PRESENT	esp**è**re, esp**è**res, esp**è**re, espérons, espérez, esp**è**rent
PRESENT SUBJUNCTIVE	esp**è**re, esp**è**res, esp**è**re, espérions, espériez, esp**è**rent
FUTURE	espérerai, espéreras, espérera, espérerons, espérerez, espéreront
CONDITIONAL	espérerais, espérerais, espérerait, espérerions, espéreriez, espéreraient
IMPERATIVE	esp**è**re, espérons, espérez

Irregular Verbs

For the conjugation of the following irregular verbs, consult the listing under the infinitive indicated in parentheses.

accueillir to welcome *(like **cueillir**)*
admettre to admit *(like **mettre**)*
apercevoir to perceive *(like **recevoir**)*
apparaître to appear *(like **connaître**)*
appartenir to belong *(like **tenir**)*
apprendre to learn *(like **prendre**)*
atteindre to reach, attain *(like **peindre**)*
combattre to fight, combat *(like **battre**)*
comprendre to understand *(like **prendre**)*
construire to build *(like **conduire**)*
contenir to contain *(like **tenir**)*
contredire to contradict *(like **dire**, but: **vous contredisez** [pres.])*
couvrir to cover *(like **ouvrir**)*
décevoir to disappoint *(like **recevoir**)*
découvrir to discover *(like **ouvrir**)*
décrire to describe *(like **écrire**)*
défaire to undo *(like **faire**)*
détruire to destroy *(like **conduire**)*
devenir to become *(like **venir**)*
disparaître to disappear *(like **connaître**)*
dormir to sleep *(like **partir**)*
éteindre to put out, extinguish *(like **peindre**)*
interdire to forbid *(like **dire**, but: **vous interdisez** [pres.])*
maintenir to maintain *(like **tenir**)*
mentir to lie *(like **partir**)*
obtenir to get, obtain *(like **tenir**)*
offrir to offer *(like **ouvrir**)*
paraître to seem, appear *(like **connaître**)*
permettre to permit *(like **mettre**)*
plaindre to pity *(like **craindre**)*

poursuivre to pursue, continue *(like **suivre**)*
prévoir to foresee *(like **voir**)*
produire to produce *(like **conduire**)*
promettre to promise *(like **mettre**)*
reconnaître to recognize *(like **connaître**)*
réduire to reduce *(like **conduire**)*
refaire to redo *(like **faire**)*
remettre to delay, postpone *(like **mettre**)*
reprendre to take again, begin again *(like **prendre**)*
retenir to retain *(like **tenir**)*
revenir to come back *(like **venir**)*
revoir to see again *(like **voir**)*
sentir to feel *(like **partir**)*
servir to serve *(like **partir**)*
sortir to go out *(like **partir**)*
souffrir to suffer *(like **ouvrir**)*
sourire to smile *(like **rire**)*
soutenir to sustain, support *(like **tenir**)*
se souvenir to remember *(like **venir**)*
surprendre to surprise *(like **prendre**)*
se taire to keep quiet *(like **plaire**)*
traduire to translate *(like **conduire**)*

aller *to go, be going (to)*	
PRESENT	vais, vas, va/allons, allez, vont
IMPERFECT	allais, allais, allait/allions, alliez, allaient
PASSÉ COMPOSÉ	suis allé(e), etc.
FUTURE	irai, iras, ira/irons, irez, iront
CONDITIONAL	irais, irais, irait/irions, iriez, iraient
PASSÉ SIMPLE	allai, allas, alla/allâmes, allâtes, allèrent
PRESENT SUBJUNCTIVE	aille, ailles, aille/allions, alliez, aillent
IMPERATIVE	va, allons, allez
PRESENT PARTICIPLE	allant

s'asseoir *to sit down*	
PRESENT	m'assieds, t'assieds, s'assied/nous asseyons, vous asseyez, s'asseyent (m'assois, t'assois, s'assoit/nous assoyons, vous assoyez, s'assoient)
IMPERFECT	m'asseyais, t'asseyais, s'asseyait/nous asseyions, vous asseyiez, s'asseyaient (m'assoyais, t'assoyais, s'assoyait/nous assoyions, vous assoyiez, s'assoyaient)
PASSÉ COMPOSÉ	me suis assis(e), etc.
FUTURE	m'assiérai, t'assiéras, s'assiéra/nous assiérons, vous assiérez, s'assiéront (m'assoirai, t'assoiras, s'assoira/nous assoirons, vous assoirez, s'assoiront)
CONDITIONAL	m'assiérais, t'assiérais, s'assiérait/nous assiérions, vous assiériez, s'assiéraient (m'assoirais, t'assoirais, s'assoirait/nous assoirions, vous assoiriez, s'assoiraient)
PASSÉ SIMPLE	m'assis, t'assis, s'assit/nous assîmes, vous assîtes, s'assirent
PRESENT SUBJUNCTIVE	m'asseye, t'asseyes, s'asseye/nous asseyions, vous asseyiez, s'asseyent (m'assoie, t'assoies, s'assoie/nous assoyions, vous assoyiez, s'assoient)
IMPERATIVE	assieds-toi, asseyons-nous, asseyez-vous (assois-toi, assoyons-nous, assoyez-vous
PRESENT PARTICIPLE	s'asseyant (s'assoyant)

battre *to beat, strike, hit*	
PRESENT	bats, bats, bat/battons, battez, battent
IMPERFECT	battais, battais, battait/battions, battiez, battaient
PASSÉ COMPOSÉ	ai battu, etc.
FUTURE	battrai, battras, battra/battrons, battrez, battront
CONDITIONAL	battrais, battrais, battrait/battrions, battriez, battraient
PASSÉ SIMPLE	battis, battis, battit/battîmes, battîtes, battirent
PRESENT SUBJUNCTIVE	batte, battes, batte/battions, battiez, battent
IMPERATIVE	bats, battons, battez
PRESENT PARTICIPLE	battant

boire *to drink*	
PRESENT	bois, bois, boit/buvons, buvez, boivent
IMPERFECT	buvais, buvais, buvait/buvions, buviez, buvaient
PASSÉ COMPOSÉ	ai bu, etc.
FUTURE	boirai, boiras, boira/boirons, boirez, boiront
PASSÉ SIMPLE	bus, bus, but/bûmes, bûtes, burent
PRESENT SUBJUNCTIVE	boive, boives, boive/buvions, buviez, boivent
IMPERATIVE	bois, buvons, buvez
PRESENT PARTICIPLE	buvant

conduire *to drive*	
PRESENT	conduis, conduis, conduit/conduisons, conduisez, conduisent
IMPERFECT	conduisais, conduisais, conduisait/conduisions, conduisiez, conduisaient
PASSÉ COMPOSÉ	ai conduit, etc.
FUTURE	conduirai, conduiras, conduira/conduirons, conduirez, conduiront
CONDITIONAL	conduirais, conduirais, conduirait/conduirions, conduiriez, conduiraient
PASSÉ SIMPLE	conduisis, conduisis, conduisit/conduisîmes, conduisîtes, conduisirent
PRESENT SUBJUNCTIVE	conduise, conduises, conduise/conduisions, conduisiez, conduisent
IMPERATIVE	conduis, conduisons, conduisez
PRESENT PARTICIPLE	conduisant

connaître *to know (a person, place, etc.)*	
PRESENT	connais, connais, connaît/connaissons, connaissez, connaissent
IMPERFECT	connaissais, connaissais, connaissait/connaissions, connaissiez, connaissaient
PASSÉ COMPOSÉ	ai connu, etc.
FUTURE	connaîtrai, connaîtras, connaîtra/connaîtrons, connaîtrez, connaîtront
CONDITIONAL	connaîtrais, connaîtrais, connaîtrait/connaîtrions, connaîtriez, connaîtraient
PASSÉ SIMPLE	connus, connus, connut/connûmes, connûtes, connurent
PRESENT SUBJUNCTIVE	connaisse, connaisses, connaisse/connaissions, connaissiez, connaissent
IMPERATIVE	connais, connaissons, connaissez
PRESENT PARTICIPLE	connaissant

courir *to run*	
PRESENT	cours, cours, court/courons, courez, courent
IMPERFECT	courais, courais, courait/courions, couriez, couraient
PASSÉ COMPOSÉ	ai couru, etc.
FUTURE	courrai, courras, courra/courrons, courrez, courront
CONDITIONAL	courrais, courrais, courrait/courrions, courriez, courraient
PASSÉ SIMPLE	courus, courus, courut/courûmes, courûtes, coururent
PRESENT SUBJUNCTIVE	coure, coures, coure/courions, couriez, courent
IMPERATIVE	cours, courons, courez
PRESENT PARTICIPLE	courant

craindre *to fear*	
PRESENT	crains, crains, craint/craignons, craignez, craignent
IMPERFECT	craignais, craignais, craignait/craignions, craigniez, craignaient
PASSÉ COMPOSÉ	ai craint, etc.
FUTURE	craindrai, craindras, craindra/craindrons, craindrez, craindront
CONDITIONAL	craindrais, craindrais, craindrait/craindrions, craindriez, craindraient
PASSÉ SIMPLE	craignis, craignis, craignit/craignîmes, craignîtes, craignirent
PRESENT SUBJUNCTIVE	craigne, craignes, craigne/craignions, craigniez, craignent
IMPERATIVE	crains, craignons, craignez
PRESENT PARTICIPLE	craignant

croire *to believe, think*	
PRESENT	crois, crois, croit/croyons, croyez, croient
IMPERFECT	croyais, croyais, croyait/croyions, croyiez, croyaient
PASSÉ COMPOSÉ	ai cru, etc.
FUTURE	croirai, croiras, croira/croirons, croirez, croiront
CONDITIONAL	croirais, croirais, croirait/croirions, croiriez, croiraient
PASSÉ SIMPLE	crus, crus, crut/crûmes, crûtes, crurent
PRESENT SUBJUNCTIVE	croie, croies, croie/croyions, croyiez, croient
IMPERATIVE	crois, croyons, croyez
PRESENT PARTICIPLE	croyant

cueillir *to gather, pick (flowers)*	
PRESENT	cueille, cueilles, cueille/cueillons, cueillez, cueillent
IMPERFECT	cueillais, cueillais, cueillait/cueillions, cueilliez, cueillaient
PASSÉ COMPOSÉ	ai cueilli, etc.
FUTURE	cueillerai, cueilleras, cueillera/cueillerons, cueillerez, cueilleront
CONDITIONAL	cueillerais, cueillerais, cueillerait/cueillerions, cueilleriez, cueilleraient
PASSÉ SIMPLE	cueillis, cueillis, cueillit/cueillîmes, cueillîtes, cueillirent
PRESENT SUBJUNCTIVE	cueille, cueilles, cueille/cueillions, cueilliez, cueillent
IMPERATIVE	cueille, cueillons, cueillez
PRESENT PARTICIPLE	cueillant

devoir *to owe; must, should, ought to*	
PRESENT	dois, dois, doit/devons, devez, doivent
IMPERFECT	devais, devais, devait/devions, deviez, devaient
PASSÉ COMPOSÉ	ai dû, etc.
FUTURE	devrai, devras, devra/devrons, devrez, devront
CONDITIONAL	devrais, devrais, devrait/devrions, devriez, devraient
PASSÉ SIMPLE	dus, dus, dut/dûmes, dûtes, durent
PRESENT SUBJUNCTIVE	doive, doives, doive/devions, deviez, doivent
IMPERATIVE	dois, devons, devez
PRESENT PARTICIPLE	devant

dire *to say, tell*	
PRESENT	dis, dis, dit/disons, dites, disent
IMPERFECT	disais, disais, disait/disions, disiez, disaient
PASSÉ COMPOSÉ	ai dit, etc.
FUTURE	dirai, diras, dira/dirons, direz, diront
CONDITIONAL	dirais, dirais, dirait/dirions, diriez, diraient
PASSÉ SIMPLE	dis, dis, dit/dîmes, dîtes, dirent
PRESENT SUBJUNCTIVE	dise, dises, dise/disions, disiez, disent
IMPERATIVE	dis, disons, dites
PRESENT PARTICIPLE	disant

écrire *to write*	
PRESENT	écris, écris, écrit/écrivons, écrivez, écrivent
IMPERFECT	écrivais, écrivais, écrivait/écrivions, écriviez, écrivaient
PASSÉ COMPOSÉ	ai écrit, etc.
FUTURE	écrirai, écriras, écrira/écrirons, écrirez, écriront
CONDITIONAL	écrirais, écrirais, écrirait/écririons, écririez, écriraient
PASSÉ SIMPLE	écrivis, écrivis, écrivit/écrivîmes, écrivîtes, écrivirent
PRESENT SUBJUNCTIVE	écrive, écrives, écrive/écrivions, écriviez, écrivent
IMPERATIVE	écris, écrivons, écrivez
PRESENT PARTICIPLE	écrivant

envoyer *to send*

PRESENT	envoie, envoies, envoie/envoyons, envoyez, envoient
IMPERFECT	envoyais, envoyais, envoyait/envoyions, envoyiez, envoyaient
PASSÉ COMPOSÉ	ai envoyé, etc.
FUTURE	enverrai, enverras, enverra/enverrons, enverrez, enverront
CONDITIONAL	enverrais, enverrais, enverrait/enverrions, enverriez, enverraient
PASSÉ SIMPLE	envoyai, envoyas, envoya/envoyâmes, envoyâtes, envoyèrent
PRESENT SUBJUNCTIVE	envoie, envoies, envoie/envoyions, envoyiez, envoient
IMPERATIVE	envoie, envoyons, envoyez
PRESENT PARTICIPLE	envoyant

faire *to do, make*

PRESENT	fais, fais, fait/faisons, faites, font
IMPERFECT	faisais, faisais, faisait/faisions, faisiez, faisaient
PASSÉ COMPOSÉ	ai fait, etc.
FUTURE	ferai, feras, fera/ferons, ferez, feront
CONDITIONAL	ferais, ferais, ferait/ferions, feriez, feraient
PASSÉ SIMPLE	fis, fis, fit/fîmes, fîtes, firent
PRESENT SUBJUNCTIVE	fasse, fasses, fasse/fassions, fassiez, fassent
IMPERATIVE	fais, faisons, faites
PRESENT PARTICIPLE	faisant

falloir *to be necessary*

PRESENT	il faut
IMPERFECT	il fallait
PASSÉ COMPOSÉ	il a fallu
FUTURE	il faudra
CONDITIONAL	il faudrait
PASSÉ SIMPLE	il fallut
PRESENT SUBJUNCTIVE	il faille

joindre *to join*

PRESENT	joins, joins, joint/joignons, joignez, joignent
IMPERFECT	joignais, joignais, joignait/joignions, joigniez, joignent
PASSÉ COMPOSÉ	ai joint, etc.
FUTURE	joindrai, joindras, joindra/joindrons, joindrez, joindront
CONDITIONAL	joindrais, joindrais, joindrait/joindrions, joindriez, joindraient
PASSÉ SIMPLE	joignis, joignis, joignit/joignîmes, joignîtes, joignirent
PRESENT SUBJUNCTIVE	joigne, joignes, joigne/joignions, joigniez, joignent
IMPERATIVE	joins, joignons, joignez
PRESENT PARTICIPLE	joignant

lire *to read*

PRESENT	lis, lis, lit/lisons, lisez, lisent
IMPERFECT	lisais, lisais, lisait/lisions, lisiez, lisaient
PASSÉ COMPOSÉ	ai lu, etc.
FUTURE	lirai, liras, lira/lirons, lirez, liront
CONDITIONAL	lirais, lirais, lirait/lirions, liriez, liraient
PASSÉ SIMPLE	lus, lus, lut/lûmes, lûtes, lurent
PRESENT SUBJUNCTIVE	lise, lises, lise/lisions, lisiez, lisent
IMPERATIVE	lis, lisons, lisez
PRESENT PARTICIPLE	lisant

mettre *to put*

PRESENT	mets, mets, met/mettons, mettez, mettent
IMPERFECT	mettais, mettais, mettait/mettions, mettiez, mettaient
PASSÉ COMPOSÉ	ai mis, etc.
FUTURE	mettrai, mettras, mettra/mettrons, mettrez, mettront
CONDITIONAL	mettrais, mettrais, mettrait/mettrions, mettriez, mettraient
PASSÉ SIMPLE	mis, mis, mit/mîmes, mîtes, mirent
PRESENT SUBJUNCTIVE	mette, mettes, mette/mettions, mettiez, mettent
IMPERATIVE	mets, mettons, mettez
PRESENT PARTICIPLE	mettant

mourir *to die*	
PRESENT	meurs, meurs, meurt/mourons, mourez, meurent
IMPERFECT	mourais, mourais, mourait/mourions, mouriez, mouraient
PASSÉ COMPOSÉ	suis mort(e), etc.
FUTURE	mourrai, mourras, mourra/mourrons, mourrez, mourront
CONDITIONAL	mourrais, mourrais, mourrait/mourrions, mourriez, mourraient
PASSÉ SIMPLE	mourus, mourus, mourut/mourûmes, mourûtes, moururent
PRESENT SUBJUNCTIVE	meure, meures, meure/mourions, mouriez, meurent
IMPERATIVE	meurs, mourons, mourez
PRESENT PARTICIPLE	mourant

naître *to be born*	
PRESENT	nais, nais, naît/naissons, naissez, naissent
IMPERFECT	naissais, naissais, naissait/naissions, naissiez, naissaient
PASSÉ COMPOSÉ	suis né(e), etc.
FUTURE	naîtrai, naîtras, naîtra/naîtrons, naîtrez, naîtront
CONDITIONAL	naîtrais, naîtrais, naîtrait/naîtrions, naîtriez, naîtraient
PASSÉ SIMPLE	naquis, naquis, naquit/naquîmes, naquîtes, naquirent
PRESENT SUBJUNCTIVE	naisse, naisses, naisse/naissions, naissiez, naissent
IMPERATIVE	nais, naissons, naissez
PRESENT PARTICIPLE	naissant

ouvrir *to open*	
PRESENT	ouvre, ouvres, ouvre/ouvrons, ouvrez, ouvrent
IMPERFECT	ouvrais, ouvrais, ouvrait/ouvrions, ouvriez, ouvraient
PASSÉ COMPOSÉ	ai ouvert, etc.
FUTURE	ouvrirai, ouvriras, ouvrira/ouvrirons, ouvrirez, ouvriront
CONDITIONAL	ouvrirais, ouvrirais, ouvrirait/ouvririons, ouvririez, ouvriraient
PASSÉ SIMPLE	ouvris, ouvris, ouvrit/ouvrîmes, ouvrîtes, ouvrirent
PRESENT SUBJUNCTIVE	ouvre, ouvres, ouvre/ouvrions, ouvriez, ouvrent
IMPERATIVE	ouvre, ouvrons, ouvrez
PRESENT PARTICIPLE	ouvrant

partir *to leave*

PRESENT	pars, pars, part/partons, partez, partent
IMPERFECT	partais, partais, partait/partions, partiez, partaient
PASSÉ COMPOSÉ	suis parti(e), etc.
FUTURE	partirai, partiras, partira/partirons, partirez, partiront
CONDITIONAL	partirais, partirais, partirait/partirions, partiriez, partiraient
PASSÉ SIMPLE	partis, partis, partit/partîmes, partîtes, partirent
PRESENT SUBJUNCTIVE	parte, partes, parte/partions, partiez, partent
IMPERATIVE	pars, partons, partez
PRESENT PARTICIPLE	partant

peindre *to paint*

PRESENT	peins, peins, peint/peignons, peignez, peignent
IMPERFECT	peignais, peignais, peignait/peignions, peigniez, peignaient
PASSÉ COMPOSÉ	ai peint, etc.
FUTURE	peindrai, peindras, peindra/peindrons, peindrez, peindront
CONDITIONAL	peindrais, peindrais, peindrait/peindrions, peindriez, peindraient
PASSÉ SIMPLE	peignis, peignis, peignit/peignîmes, peignîtes, peignirent
PRESENT SUBJUNCTIVE	peigne, peignes, peigne/peignions, peigniez, peignent
IMPERATIVE	peins, peignons, peignez
PRESENT PARTICIPLE	peignant

plaire *to please*

PRESENT	plais, plais, plaît/plaisons, plaisez, plaisent
IMPERFECT	plaisais, plaisais, plaisait/plaisions, plaisiez, plaisaient
PASSÉ COMPOSÉ	ai plu, etc.
FUTURE	plairai, plairas, plaira/plairons, plairez, plairont
CONDITIONAL	plairais, plairais, plairait/plairions, plairiez, plairaient
PASSÉ SIMPLE	plus, plus, plut/plûmes, plûtes, plurent
PRESENT SUBJUNCTIVE	plaise, plaises, plaise/plaisions, plaisiez, plaisent
IMPERATIVE	plais, plaisons, plaisez
PRESENT PARTICIPLE	plaisant

pleuvoir *to rain*

PRESENT	il pleut
IMPERFECT	il pleuvait
PASSÉ COMPOSÉ	il a plu
FUTURE	il pleuvra
CONDITIONAL	il pleuvrait
PASSÉ SIMPLE	il plut
PRESENT SUBJUNCTIVE	il pleuve
PRESENT PARTICIPLE	pleuvant

pouvoir *can, to be able to*

PRESENT	peux, peux, peut/pouvons, pouvez, peuvent
IMPERFECT	pouvais, pouvais, pouvait/pouvions, pouviez, pouvaient
PASSÉ COMPOSÉ	ai pu, etc.
FUTURE	pourrai, pourras, pourra/pourrons, pourrez, pourront
CONDITIONAL	pourrais, pourrais, pourrait/pourrions, pourriez, pourraient
PASSÉ SIMPLE	pus, pus, put/pûmes, pûtes, purent
PRESENT SUBJUNCTIVE	puisse, puisses, puisse/puissions, puissiez, puissent
IMPERATIVE	*not used*
PRESENT PARTICIPLE	pouvant

prendre *to take*

PRESENT	prends, prends, prend/prenons, prenez, prennent
IMPERFECT	prenais, prenais, prenait/prenions, preniez, prenaient
PASSÉ COMPOSÉ	ai pris, etc.
FUTURE	prendrai, prendras, prendra/prendrons, prendrez, prendront
CONDITIONAL	prendrais, prendrais, prendrait/prendrions, prendriez, prendraient
PASSÉ SIMPLE	pris, pris, prit/prîmes, prîtes, prirent
PRESENT SUBJUNCTIVE	prenne, prennes, prenne/prenions, preniez, prennent
IMPERATIVE	prends, prenons, prenez
PRESENT PARTICIPLE	prenant

recevoir *to receive*

PRESENT	reçois, reçois, reçoit/recevons, recevez, reçoivent
IMPERFECT	recevais, recevais, recevait/recevions, receviez, recevaient
PASSÉ COMPOSÉ	ai reçu, etc.
FUTURE	recevrai, recevras, recevra/recevrons, recevrez, recevront
CONDITIONAL	recevrais, recevrais, recevrait/recevrions, recevriez, recevraient
PASSÉ SIMPLE	reçus, reçus, reçut/reçûmes, reçûtes, reçurent
PRESENT SUBJUNCTIVE	reçoive, reçoives, reçoive/recevions, receviez, reçoivent
IMPERATIVE	reçois, recevons, recevez
PRESENT PARTICIPLE	recevant

rire *to laugh*

PRESENT	ris, ris, rit/rions, riez, rient
IMPERFECT	riais, riais, riait/riions, riiez, riaient
PASSÉ COMPOSÉ	ai ri, etc.
FUTURE	rirai, riras, rira/rirons, rirez, riront
CONDITIONAL	rirais, rirais, rirait/ririons, ririez, riraient
PASSÉ SIMPLE	ris, ris, rit/rîmes, rîtes, rirent
PRESENT SUBJUNCTIVE	rie, ries, rie/riions, riiez, rient
IMPERATIVE	ris, rions, riez
PRESENT PARTICIPLE	riant

savoir *to know*

PRESENT	sais, sais, sait/savons, savez, savent
IMPERFECT	savais, savais, savait/savions, saviez, savaient
PASSÉ COMPOSÉ	ai su, etc.
FUTURE	saurai, sauras, saura/saurons, saurez, sauront
CONDITIONAL	saurais, saurais, saurait/saurions, sauriez, sauraient
PASSÉ SIMPLE	sus, sus, sut/sûmes, sûtes, surent
PRESENT SUBJUNCTIVE	sache, saches, sache/sachions, sachiez, sachent
IMPERATIVE	sache, sachons, sachez
PRESENT PARTICIPLE	sachant

suivre *to follow*

PRESENT	suis, suis, suit/suivons, suivez, suivent
IMPERFECT	suivais, suivais, suivait/suivions, suiviez, suivaient
PASSÉ COMPOSÉ	ai suivi, etc.
FUTURE	suivrai, suivras, suivra/suivrons, suivrez, suivront
CONDITIONAL	suivrais, suivrais, suivrait/suivrions, suivriez, suivraient
PASSÉ SIMPLE	suivis, suivis, suivit/suivîmes, suivîtes, suivirent
PRESENT SUBJUNCTIVE	suive, suives, suive/suivions, suiviez, suivent
IMPERATIVE	suis, suivons, suivez
PRESENT PARTICIPLE	suivant

tenir *to hold*

PRESENT	tiens, tiens, tient/tenons, tenez, tiennent
IMPERFECT	tenais, tenais, tenait/tenions, teniez, tenaient
PASSÉ COMPOSÉ	ai tenu, etc.
FUTURE	tiendrai, tiendras, tiendra/tiendrons, tiendrez, tiendront
CONDITIONAL	tiendrais, tiendrais, tiendrait/tiendrions, tiendriez, tiendraient
PASSÉ SIMPLE	tins, tins, tint/tînmes, tîntes, tinrent
PRESENT SUBJUNCTIVE	tienne, tiennes, tienne/tenions, teniez, tiennent
IMPERATIVE	tiens, tenons, tenez
PRESENT PARTICIPLE	tenant

valoir *to be worth*

PRESENT	vaux, vaux, vaut/valons, valez, valent
IMPERFECT	valais, valais, valait/valions, valiez, valaient
PASSÉ COMPOSÉ	ai valu, etc.
FUTURE	vaudrai, vaudras, vaudra/vaudrons, vaudrez, vaudront
CONDITIONAL	vaudrais, vaudrais, vaudrait/vaudrions, vaudriez, vaudraient
PASSÉ SIMPLE	valus, valus, valut/valûmes, valûtes, valurent
PRESENT SUBJUNCTIVE	vaille, vailles, vaille/valions, valiez, vaillent
IMPERATIVE	vaux, valons, valez
PRESENT PARTICIPLE	valant

venir *to come*

PRESENT	viens, viens, vient/venons, venez, viennent
IMPERFECT	venais, venais, venait/venions, veniez, venaient
PASSÉ COMPOSÉ	suis venu(e), etc.
FUTURE	viendrai, viendras, viendra/viendrons, viendrez, viendront
CONDITIONAL	viendrais, viendrais, viendrait/viendrions, viendriez, viendraient
PASSÉ SIMPLE	vins, vins, vint/vînmes, vîntes, vinrent
PRESENT SUBJUNCTIVE	vienne, viennes, vienne/venions, veniez, viennent
IMPERATIVE	viens, venons, venez
PRESENT PARTICIPLE	venant

vivre *to live*

PRESENT	vis, vis, vit/vivons, vivez, vivent
IMPERFECT	vivais, vivais, vivait/vivions, viviez, vivaient
PASSÉ COMPOSÉ	ai vécu, etc.
FUTURE	vivrai, vivras, vivra/vivrons, vivrez, vivront
CONDITIONAL	vivrais, vivrais, vivrait/vivrions, vivriez, vivraient
PASSÉ SIMPLE	vécus, vécus, vécut/vécûmes, vécûtes, vécurent
PRESENT SUBJUNCTIVE	vive, vives, vive/vivions, viviez, vivent
IMPERATIVE	vis, vivons, vivez
PRESENT PARTICIPLE	vivant

voir *to see*

PRESENT	vois, vois, voit/voyons, voyez, voient
IMPERFECT	voyais, voyais, voyait/voyions, voyiez, voyaient
PASSÉ COMPOSÉ	ai vu, etc.
FUTURE	verrai, verras, verra/verrons, verrez, verront
CONDITIONAL	verrais, verrais, verrait/verrions, verriez, verraient
PASSÉ SIMPLE	vis, vis, vit/vîmes, vîtes, virent
PRESENT SUBJUNCTIVE	voie, voies, voie/voyions, voyiez, voient
IMPERATIVE	vois, voyons, voyez
PRESENT PARTICIPLE	voyant

vouloir *to want*	
PRESENT	veux, veux, veut/voulons, voulez, veulent
IMPERFECT	voulais, voulais, voulait/voulions, vouliez, voulaient
PASSÉ COMPOSÉ	ai voulu, etc.
FUTURE	voudrai, voudras, voudra/voudrons, voudrez, voudront
CONDITIONAL	voudrais, voudrais, voudrait/voudrions, voudriez, voudraient
PASSÉ SIMPLE	voulus, voulus, voulut/voulûmes, voulûtes, voulurent
PRESENT SUBJUNCTIVE	veuille, veuilles, veuille/voulions, vouliez, veuillent
IMPERATIVE	veuille, veuillons, veuillez
PRESENT PARTICIPLE	voulant

French-English Vocabulary List

This vocabulary list contains all words used in the exercises. It also contains the vocabulary of the cultural chapters, except for obvious cognates. It does not contain basic vocabulary covered in first-year French, nor does it include the words introduced in the **La grammaire en action** sections. Numbers and regular adverbs have been omitted to save space. Also omitted from this list are idioms and proverbs introduced in Chapter 28. Verbs marked *irreg.* should be looked up in the verb charts. Conjugation reminders are given for verbs with spelling changes. An entry such as **nager (g > ge/a, o)** should be read as "**g** changes to **ge** before **a** and **o.**"

à to, at
à bout de souffle breathless
à cause de because of
à cheval on horseback
à condition que on the condition that, provided that
à côté next door, nearby; aside
à côté de next to
à deux pas de right near
à genoux on one's knees
à juste titre rightfully
à l'endroit right side out (of clothing)
à l'envers inside out (of clothing)
à l'époque at the time, at that time
à l'époque où nous sommes in this day and age
à l'heure on time
à l'instant a moment ago
à la fois at the same time, at once
à la hâte hastily, in a rush
à la hauteur equal to the task
à la longue in the long run
à la page up-to-date
à la perfection perfectly, just right
à la suite de following
à la une on the front page
à merveille wonderfully
à moins que unless
à moitié halfway
à moitié ivre half-drunk
à part besides
à partir de maintenant from now on
à peine hardly
à peu près approximately
à pied on foot
à plusieurs reprises several times
à prix d'or at a very high price
à point well-done (meat)
à rebours backwards
à regret regretfully
à ses heures (perdues) in one's free time
à souhait to perfection
à temps in time
à titre confidentiel off the record
à titre de père as a father
à tort wrongfully
à tour de rôle in turn
à tout moment all the time
à tout prix at all costs
à travers through
abattre *(like **battre**)* to cut down (a tree)
abdiquer to abdicate
l' **aboiement** *(masc.)* bark (of a dog)
abolir to abolish
aboutir à to end up at, wind up as
aboyer (y > i/e) to bark
l' **abri** *(masc.)* shelter
abriter to house
l' **absence** *(fem.)* absence, time away
l' **absolutisme** *(masc.)* absolute rule
s' **abstenir de** to refrain from
abstrait abstract
abuser de to take (unfair) advantage of
accabler de to overwhelm with
l' **accent** *(masc.)* accent
accepter to accept; **accepter de** to agree to
l' **accès** *(masc.)* access
l' **accessoire** *(masc.)* accessory
l' **accident** *(masc.)* accident
accompagner to accompany
accomplir to accomplish
l' **accord** *(masc.)* agreement; **être d'accord** to agree
accorder to grant, award
accoudé leaning on one's elbows
s' **accouder** to lean on one's elbows
accrocher to hang, hang up
accroupi crouching
s' **accroupir** to crouch
accueillant cozy
accueillir *(like **cueillir**)* to welcome
accuser qqn de to accuse someone of
s' **acharner à** to try desperately to
acheter (qqch à qqn) to buy (something from someone)
achever (de) to finish
l' **acier** *(masc.)* steel
acquérir *(irreg.)* to acquire
l' **acronyme** *(masc.)* acronym
l' **acte** *(masc.)* act; deed
l' **acteur** *(masc.)* actor
actif(-ve) active
l' **action** *(fem.)* action
l' **activité** *(fem.)* activity
l' **actrice** *(fem.)* actress
l' **actualité** *(fem.)* news, current events
actuel(le) present, present-day
actuellement at present
l' **addition** *(fem.)* bill, check (restaurant)
l' **adepte** *(masc. & fem.)* highly skilled person, expert
administratif(-ve) administrative
s' **adonner à** to devote oneself to
adorer to adore, love
s' **adosser à/contre** to lean with one's back against
s' **adresser à** to address, speak to, be aimed at
aérien(ne) air *(adj.)*

l' **aéronautique** *(fem.)* aeronautics
l' **aéroport** *(masc.)* airport
l' **aérospatiale** *(fem.)* aerospace industry
affaiblir to weaken
s' **affaiblir** to weaken, grow weak
l' **affaire** *(fem.)* business; matter
les **affaires** *(fem. pl.)* business; things, personal effects
affecter de to pretend to
affermir to make firm, strengthen
l' **affermissement** *(masc.)* strengthening
l' **affiche** *(fem.)* poster
afficher to post
affirmer to assert
affreux(-se) horrible
affronté à confronting
afin que so that, in order that (formal)
africain African
agaçant annoying
agacer to annoy
l' **agence** *(fem.)* agency; **agence de voyages** travel agency
l' **agenda** *(masc.)* appointment book
agenouillé kneeling
s' **agenouiller** to kneel
l' **agent** *(masc.)* agent
l' **agglomération urbaine** *(fem.)* metropolitan area
agir to act; to work (of medication): **il s'agit de** it's about, it's a question of
agité agitated, unsettled
agiter to shake
l' **agneau** *(masc.)* lamb
agrandir to enlarge
agréable pleasant
agricole agricultural
l' **agriculture** *(fem.)* agriculture
agro-alimentaire agricultural, pertaining to food production
aider to help; **s'aider** to help each other
l' **ail** *(masc.)* garlic
ailleurs elsewhere, somewhere else; **être ailleurs** to not be paying attention
aimable kind
aimanter to magnetize
aimer to like, love; **aimer mieux** to prefer; **aimer quelqu'un à la folie** to be mad about someone
l' **aîné(e)** the older child
ainsi thus
l' **air** *(masc.)* air, manner
ajouter to add
albigeois pertaining to the southern French city of Albi
les **alentours** *(masc. pl.)* surroundings, outskirts
l' **algèbre** *(fem.)* algebra
alimentaire pertaining to food
alimenter to feed
l' **allée** *(fem.)* going
aller *(irreg.)* to go
aller à bicyclette, à pied to go by bike, on foot
aller bien à qqn to look nice on someone
aller pieds nus to go barefoot
s' **en aller** to go away
l' **allié** *(masc.)* ally; **les Alliés** the Allies
s' **allier à** to ally oneself with
allumer to light, turn on
l' **allusion** *(fem.)* reference; **faire allusion à** to refer to
alors then
l' **alphabet** *(masc.)* alphabet
alpin Alpine
l' **ambassade** *(fem.)* embassy
l' **ambassadeur** *(masc.)* ambassador
l' **ambiance** *(fem.)* atmosphere
ambitieux(-se) ambitious
ambulant wandering
améliorer to improve
l' **aménagement** *(masc.)* fixing up
aménager (**g** > **ge/a, o**) to fix up, convert (a room, etc.)
l' **amende** *(fem.)* fine, penalty
amener (**e** > **è/e**) to bring (someone); bring about
amer(-ère) bitter
américain American
l' **amertume** *(fem.)* bitterness
l' **amitié** *(fem.)* friendship
l' **amour** *(masc.)* love; **les amours** *(fem.)* love, love-making, passions
l' **amphithéâtre** *(masc.)* amphitheater
amuser to amuse; **s'amuser** to have a good time
les **amuse-gueules** *(m. pl.)* hors-d'œuvres
l' **an** *(masc.)* year
analphabète illiterate
l' **anatomie comparée** *(fem.)* comparative anatomy
l' **ancêtre** *(masc. & fem.)* ancestor
ancien(ne) ancient; former
l' **angoisse** *(fem.)* anguish
l' **animal** *(masc.)* animal
l' **animateur(-trice)** camp counselor
s' **animer** to feel more lively
l' **année** *(fem.)* year
l' **anniversaire** *(masc.)* birthday, anniversary
l' **annonce** *(fem.)* ad
annoncer (**c** > **ç/a, o**) to announce
l' **annuaire** *(masc.)* telephone book
l' **anorak** *(masc.)* ski jacket
l' **anse** *(fem.)* handle
antérieur previous
l' **anticipation** *(fem):* **d'anticipation** science fiction
antique ancient
l' **antiquité** *(fem.)* antiquity, ancient times, ancient world
août August
apercevoir *(like **recevoir**)* to notice; **s'apercevoir de** to notice, become aware of
l' **aperçu** *(masc.)* summary, overview
apparaître *(like **connaître**)* to appear
l' **appareil acoustique** *(masc.)* hearing aid
l' **appareil-photo** *(masc.)* camera
les **apparences** *(fem. pl.)* appearances
l' **apparition** *(fem.)* appearance
l' **appartement** *(masc.)* apartment

appartenir (à) to belong (to)
l' **appel** *(masc.)* appeal, call
applaudir to applaud
s' **appliquer à** to apply oneself to
apporter to bring
apprécier to appreciate (value, rate highly)
apprendre (à) to learn (how to)
s' **apprêter à** to get ready to
s' **approcher de** to approach
approfondir to go deeply into
approuver to approve
l' **appui** *(masc.)* support
appuyer (**y** > **i/e**) to support; **s'appuyer sur/à** to lean on, support oneself on
après after, afterward
après-demain the day after tomorrow
apte à capable of
l' **aqueduc** *(masc.)* aqueduct
arabe Arab, Arabic
arabiser to arabize
l' **arbre** *(masc.)* tree
l' **arc** *(masc.)* arch
l' **architecte** *(masc. & fem.)* architect
l' **architecture** *(fem.)* architecture
l' **arène** *(fem.)* arena
l' **argent** *(masc.)* money
l' **armement** *(masc.)* weapon
l' **armistice** *(masc.)* armistice
arracher (qqch à qqn) to snatch (something from someone)
arranger (**g** > **ge/a, o**) to arrange
l' **arrêt** *(masc.)* stop (bus, etc.)
s' **arrêter (de)** to stop
l' **arrière-garde** *(fem.)* rear guard (military)
l' **arrivée** *(fem.)* arrival
arriver to arrive; **arriver à** to manage to
arrondir to round, round out
l' **arrondissement** *(masc.)* administrative division of Paris
arroser to water
l' **art** *(masc.)* art
l' **article** *(masc.)* article
l' **artiste** *(masc. & fem.)* artist
artistique artistic
l' **ascenseur** *(masc.)* elevator
les **asperges** *(fem. pl.)* asparagus
l' **aspirine** *(fem.)* aspirin
s' **asseoir** *(irreg.)* to sit down
assez de enough
assidu assiduous, diligent
assiéger to besiege
l' **assiette** *(fem.)* plate
s' **assimiler** to assimilate
assis sitting
assister à to attend
l' **associé(e)** associate
l' **assommoir** *(masc.)* slaughterhouse
assurer to insure, assure
l' **astronome** *(masc. & fem.)* astronomer
l' **atelier** *(masc.)* workshop, studio
atroce atrocious, horrible
attacher to attach, link
atteindre *(like **craindre**)* to reach, attain
attendre to wait for; **s'attendre à** to expect to
l' **attente** *(fem.)* wait
attentif(-ve) attentive
l' **attention** *(fem.)* attention; **faire attention à** to pay attention to, watch out for
attirer to attract
l' **attitude** *(fem.)* attitude
les **attractions** *(fem. pl.)* entertainment
attraper un rhume to catch a cold
au bout de at the end of (space)
au cours de during, during the course of
au sujet de about
au-dessous de below
au-dessus de above
l' **auberge** *(fem.)* inn
aucun(e) no, not any
audiovisuel(le) audiovisual
l' **augmentation** *(fem.)* raise
augmenter to increase
aujourd'hui today
auparavant previously, beforehand
aussi also; as
aussitôt immediately; **aussitôt que** as soon as
autant (de) as much, as many
l' **autel** *(masc.)* altar
l' **auteur** *(masc.)* author
l' **autobus** *(masc.)* bus
l' **autocar** *(masc.)* intercity bus, coach
l' **autodétermination** *(fem.)* self-determination
l' **automne** *(masc.)* fall, autumn
l' **automobile** *(fem.)* automobile
autoriser qqn à to authorize someone to
l' **autorité** *(fem.)* authority
autour de around
autrefois formerly, in the past
autrui someone else
auvergnat pertaining to the region of Auvergne
avancé advanced; to be fast (of a watch)
avancer (**c** > **ç/a, o**) to advance: **s'avancer sur** to move on, advance on
avant (que) before
avant-hier the day before yesterday
l' **avantage** *(masc.)* advantage
l' **avenir** *(masc.)* future
l' **aventure** *(fem.)* adventure
l' **avenue** *(fem.)* avenue
avertir to warn
aveugle blind
l' **aviateur(-trice)** aviator
l' **avion** *(masc.)* airplane
s' **aviser de** to dare to, take it into one's head to
l' **avocat(e)** lawyer
avoir *(irreg.)* to have
avoir à to have to
avoir beau faire qqch to do something in vain
avoir besoin de to need
avoir de la chance to be lucky

avoir envie de to feel like
avoir faim, soif, sommeil, chaud, froid to be hungry, thirsty, sleepy, warm, cold
avoir honte de qqch, de qqn to be ashamed of something, someone
avoir l'air + *adjective* to look
avoir l'air de + *noun* to look like a
avoir l'intention de to intend to
avoir lieu to take place
avoir mal à la tête, aux yeux, à l'estomac to have a headache, pain in the eyes, a stomach ache
avoir mal au cœur to be sick to one's stomach
avoir peur de to be afraid of
avoir raison (de) to be right (to)
avoir tort (de) to be wrong (to)
avril April
axé sur revolving around, based on

le **bac, baccalauréat** secondary-school diploma
les **bagages** *(masc. pl.)* luggage
la **baguette** stick; thin loaf of French bread
se **baigner** to go swimming
la **baigneuse** female bather
le **bail** lease
le **baiser** kiss
baisser to decline, decrease
le **bal** dance
la **balançoire** swing
balayer (**y** > **i/e**) to sweep
le **balcon** balcony
le **ballet** ballet
banal banal
le **banc** bench
la **bande magnétique** recording tape
les **bandes dessinées** *(fem. pl.)* comics
la **banque** bank
la **banqueroute** bankruptcy
le **banquier (la banquière)** banker
le **barbarisme** barbarity
les **bas** *(masc. pl.)* stockings
bas(se) low; **parler (tout) bas** to speak (very) softly
la **base** base; **base de données** database
le **basket** basketball
le **bateau** boat
le **bâtiment** building
bâtir to build
battre *(irreg.)* to beat, hit
bavard talkative
bavarder to chat
beau (bel, belle) beautiful
le **beau-fils** son-in-law; stepson
le **beau-frère** brother-in-law
le **beau-père** father-in-law; stepfather
beaucoup de much, many
la **beauté** beauty
les **beaux-arts** *(masc. pl.)* fine arts
les **beaux-parents** *(masc. pl.)* in-laws
belge Belgian
la **belle-fille** daughter-in-law; stepdaughter
la **belle-mère** mother-in-law; stepmother
la **belle-sœur** sister-in-law
le **bénéfice** benefit
le **berceau** cradle
la **bête** beast
bête stupid, silly
la **bêtise** foolishness, stupidity
le **beurre** butter
la **bibliothèque** library; bookcase
la **bicyclette** bicycle
bien de a lot of
bien que although
le **bien-être** welfare
bientôt soon
la **bière** beer
le **bifteck** steak
le **bijou** jewel
le **bilan** balance sheet
le **bilinguisme** bilingualism
le **billet** ticket
la **biochimie** biochemistry
le **bison** bison, buffalo
le **bistrot** café-restaurant
bizarre strange, peculiar
le **blagueur (la blagueuse)** kidder, joker
blanc (blanche) white
le **blanc** blank, blank space
le **blé** wheat
blesser to wound
le **blocus** blockade
se **blottir contre** to huddle, snuggle, nestle against
le **blouson** windbreaker
le **blue-jean** jeans
le **bocal** jar
le **bœuf** beef
la **boisson** drink
la **boîte** box
le **bol** bowl
bon(ne) good **sentir bon** to smell good; **tenir bon** to hold fast, stand firm
bon marché cheap *(invariable)*
les **bonbons** *(masc. pl.)* candy
le **bonheur** happiness
la **bonne** maid
le **bonnet** cap, wool hat
le **bord** edge; **au bord de la mer** at the seashore
bordé de lined with
se **borner à** to limit oneself to
les **bottes** *(fem. pl.)* boots
le **boucher (la bouchère)** butcher
la **boucherie** butcher shop
la **boue** mud
la **bouillabaisse** seafood stew
la **boulangerie** bakery
le **boulevard** boulevard
le **bouleversement** upset
le **boulot** job *(colloq.)*
le **bouquin** book *(colloq.)*
le **bourgeois (la bourgeoise)** bourgeois

la **bourse (d'études)** scholarship (monetary award)

la **bouteille** bottle

la **boutique** shop, store

brancher to plug in

le **bras** arm

brave decent; brave

bref(-ève) brief, short

breton(ne) Breton

le **brevet** patent, license

le **bricolage** puttering around

bricoler to fix things, tinker, putter

brièvement briefly

la **brillance** brilliance

la **brioche** light, slightly sweet bread

la **brique** brick

briser to break, shatter

broncher to flinch

se **brosser les cheveux, les dents** to brush one's hair, one's teeth

brouillé mad at each other

broyer (y > i/e) to grind, make into powder

la **bru** daughter-in-law

bruiner to drizzle

le **bruit** noise

brûler to burn; **brûler de** to be burning to, dying to

brun dark-haired

la **brute** brute

le **bureau** office; desk

le **buste** bust

le **but** goal

le **butin** booty

la **butte** mound, small hill

le **cabinet** doctor's office

la **cacahuète** peanut

cacher (qqch à qqn) to hide (something from someone); **se cacher** to hide *(intrans.)*

le **cadeau** gift

le **cadet (la cadette)** the younger child

le **cadre** professional person

le **cafard** cockroach; **avoir le cafard** to be down in the dumps, have the blues; **donner le cafard** to get (someone) down, to give (someone) the blues

le **café** coffee; café

le **cahier** notebook

la **caisse** crate

le **calcul** calculation

la **calculatrice** calculator

calculer to calculate, figure

la **calculette** calculator

le **calendrier** calendar

le **calme** calm

se **calmer** to calm down

le **camarade (la camarade)** friend, buddy, classmate

le **cambriolage** burglary

la **caméra** movie camera

le **camion** truck

le **camp de concentration** concentration camp

la **campagne** country(side)

camper to go camping

le **campeur (la campeuse)** camper

le **camping** camping

canadien(ne) Canadian

le **canal** canal

le **canard** duck

le **candidat (la candidate)** candidate

la **canne** cane; **canne à sucre** sugar cane

la **cantine** school lunchroom

capable de likely to

le **capitaine** captain

la **capitale** capital city

le **caractère** character

caractériser to characterize

caractéristique characteristic

la **caractéristique** characteristic

le **caravaning** traveling by trailer or motor home

la **cargaison** shipment

le **carnaval** carnival

le **carnet** notebook; **carnet de chèques** checkbook

la **carotte** carrot

carré square

le **carreau** window pane

le **carrefour** crossroads, intersection

la **carte** map

la **carte de crédit** credit card

la **carte postale** postcard

le **cas** case

casser to break

la **casserole** pot

la **cassette** cassette

la **catastrophe** catastrophe

la **cathédrale** cathedral

cathodique cathode *(adj.)*

catholique Catholic

céder (é > è/e) to yield

célèbre famous

celtique Celtic

la **censure** censorship

la **centaine** about a hundred

la **centrale** power station

le **centre** center, downtown

le **centre communautaire** community center

le **centre diététique** health-food store

centrer to concentrate

les **céréales** *(fem. pl.)* cereal

la **cérémonie** ceremony

le **cerf** deer

la **cerise** cherry

certain certain, sure; **d'un certain âge** middle-aged

le **cerveau** brain

cesser (de) to stop

chacun(e) each one, each person; **chacun pour soi** every man for himself; **tout un chacun** every Tom, Dick, and Harry

le **chahut** ruckus

la **chaîne** channel, TV station; **chaîne stéréo** stereo system
la **chaleur** heat
la **chambre (à coucher)** bedroom
le **champ** field
le **champagne** champagne
le **champignon** mushroom
le **champion (la championne)** champion
la **chance** luck
le **changement** change
changer (g > **ge/a, o**) to change; **changer d'idée** to change one's mind
la **chanson** song
chanter to sing
le **chanteur (la chanteuse)** singer
le **chantier** construction site
le **chapeau** hat
le **chapitre** chapter
le **char blindé** tank
la **charcuterie** delicatessen
se **charger de** to take care of, be in charge of
charitable charitable
la **charité** charity
charmant charming
la **chasse** hunting
le **chasseur** hunter; bellhop
le **chat** cat
le **château** castle
chaud warm, hot
la **chaussette** sock
la **chaussure** shoe; **chaussure de sport** sneaker
le **chef** boss
le **chef-d'œuvre** masterpiece
le **chef d'orchestre** conductor, orchestra leader
le **chef-lieu** capital of a French *département*
la **cheminée** fireplace
la **chemise** shirt
le **chemisier** blouse
le **chêne** oak tree
le **chèque** check
cher(-ère) dear; expensive; **acheter/vendre cher** to buy/sell at a high price; **coûter cher** to cost a lot; **payer cher** to pay a high price for
chercher to look for; **chercher à** to try to
le **chercheur (la chercheuse)** researcher
le **cheval** horse
la **chèvre** goat
chic stylish
le **chien (la chienne)** dog
le **chiffre** figure, number
la **chimie** chemistry
chimique chemical
chinois(e) Chinese
la **chirurgie** surgery
le **choc** shock
le **chocolat** chocolate
choisir (de) to choose (to)
le **chômage** unemployment
choral choral, pertaining to the chorus or singing
le **chou** cabbage
la **choucroute** sauerkraut
la **chute** fall
le **ciel** sky, heaven
la **cime** peak
le **ciment** cement
le **cimetière** cemetery
le **cinéma** movies
la **circonstance** circumstance
le **circuit** circuit, wiring
circuler to get around, move around, move along
cirer to polish, wax
le **cirque** circus
les **ciseaux** *(masc. pl.)* scissors
la **cité** housing project
citer to quote, mention
le **citoyen (la citoyenne)** citizen
le **citron** lemon; **citron pressé** lemonade
civil civil
la **civilisation** civilization
clair light (of colors)
la **clarinette** clarinet
la **clarté** clarity
classer to classify; **se classer** to be ranked
classique classic
le **clavecin** harpsichord
le **claveciniste** harpsichord player
le **clavier** keyboard
la **clé** key; **fermer la porte à clé** to lock the door
le **clergé** clergy
le **client (la cliente)** customer
le **climat** climate
la **climatisation** air conditioning
climatiser to air condition
la **cloche** bell
la **clôture** fence
le **clou** nail
le **club** club (organization)
le **cochon** pig
codifier to codify
le **cœur** heart; **savoir/apprendre par cœur** to know/learn by heart
le **coiffeur (la coiffeuse)** hairdresser, barber
le **coin** corner; **au coin** at the corner
le **col** mountain pass
la **colère** anger; **être en colère** to be angry
collaborateur(-trice) collaborationist
le **collant** body stocking; tights
la **collecte** collection of money
la **collection** collection
le **collège** French equivalent of middle school
le **collègue (la collègue)** colleague
le **collier** necklace
la **colonie** colony; **colonie de vacances** summer camp
la **colonisation** colonization
la **colonnade** colonnade
le **combat** fight
le **combattant** fighter, soldier
combattre *(like **battre**)* to fight, combat
combien de how much? how many?

commander à qqn de to order someone to
comme il faut properly
commémorer to commemorate
le commencement beginning
commencer (c > ç/a, o) (à) to begin (to); commencer par faire qqch to begin by doing something
le commentaire comment, commentary
le commerçant (la commerçante) storekeeper
commercial commercial, business *(adj.)*
le commis clerk (in a store)
le commissaire de police police captain
commode convenient
la communauté community
la Commune Paris Commune
communément commonly
le communisme communism
la compagnie company
le compartiment compartment (on a train)
se complaire à to take pleasure in
se complémenter to complement each other
complet(-ète) complete
compléter (é > è/e) to complete
le compliment compliment
compliqué complicated
le composé compound
le compositeur (la compositrice) composer
comprendre to understand; to include; comprendre à demi-mot to be able to take a hint
le comprimé tablet; comprimé d'aspirine aspirin tablet
compris included; y compris including
le compte rendu report
compter to count; to plan to do something; compter sur qqn to rely on someone
le comptoir trading post
le comte count
la comtesse countess
concentrer to concentrate; se concentrer sur to concentrate on
la conception conception, conceiving
le concert concert
concilier to reconcile, adjust, conciliate
la concision concision
concret(-ète) concrete
concurrencer (c > ç/a, o) to compete with, challenge
condamner to condemn
le condiment spice
le conditionnel conditional mood
conduire *(like construire)* to drive; se conduire to behave
la conférence lecture
la confiance confidence
confier to confide; se confier à qqn to confide in someone
confirmer to confirm
la confiture jam
le conflit conflict
le confluent confluence, meeting point of rivers
confondre to confuse
le confort moderne modern conveniences
confusément confusedly
le congé leave, vacation
congédier to fire
la conique cone (geometry)
la connaissance acquaintance; knowledge; faire la connaissance de to make the acquaintance of
les connaissances *(fem. pl.)* knowledge
connaître *(irreg.)* to know; faire connaître to familiarize, acquaint
connu famous
la conquête conquest
se consacrer à to devote oneself to
conscient (de) conscious (of)
le conseil piece of advice
le conseiller (la conseillère) adviser
conseiller à qqn de to advise someone to
consentir à to consent to
conserver to preserve
la consistence consistency
consommer 10 litres aux 100 (kilomètres) to get 100 kilometers to every 10 liters of gasoline
constamment constantly
la consternation dismay
construire *(like conduire)* to build
le contact contact; au contact de in touch with
contacter to contact
le conte short story
contemporain contemporary
contenir *(like tenir)* to contain
content (de) happy (to)
le continent continent
continental continental, on the mainland/continent
continuer (à) to continue
contraindre (qqn à faire qqch) *(like craindre)* to compel (someone to do something)
contraint constrained
contraster to contrast
le contrat contract
contre against
convaincre *(like vaincre)* to convince
convenable suitable, appropriate, fitting
convenir (à) to be suitable (for)
le copain (la copine) friend, pal
la copie copy, written exercise
le coq rooster
coquet(te) flirtatious
le cor horn (musical instrument)
la corbeille basket
la corde string (music)
le corps céleste heavenly body
la correction spanking
corriger (g > ge/a, o) to correct
cosmopolite cosmopolitan, international
le costume man's suit
la côte coast
la côtelette cutlet, chop

le **coton** cotton
couché lying down
se **coucher** to lie down, go to bed; **coucher, dormir à la belle étoile** to sleep outdoors
le **coup de main** helping hand
le **coup de téléphone** phone call
le **coup de tonnerre** thunderclap
coupable guilty
couper to cut; **se couper les cheveux** to cut one's hair; **se couper au doigt** to cut one's finger
la **cour** court
le **courage** courage
couramment fluently
le **courant** current; **être au courant** to be informed, be in the know
courant running; current
courbe curved, wavy
la **couronne** crown
couronner to crown
le **cours** course; **donner libre cours à** to give free rein to
la **course** race; **course aux taureaux** bullfight
court short; **tout court** for short; simply; **s'arrêter court** to stop short; **couper court à qqch** to cut something short; **se trouver court** to be at a loss
le **couscous** couscous (North African grain dish)
le **cousin (la cousine)** cousin
le **couteau** knife; **couteau de poche** pocket knife
la **coutume** custom
le **couturier (la couturière)** clothes designer
le **couvert** place setting
couvert de covered with
la **couverture** blanket
couvrir *(irreg.)* to cover
craindre *(irreg.)* to fear
la **cravate** necktie
le **crayon** pencil
créer to create
la **crème** cream; **crème caramel** caramelized custard
crémeux(-se) creamy
le **crépuscule** twilight
crevassé cracked (ground)
le **cri** shout, scream
crier to shout
le **crime** crime
la **crise** crisis
le **cristal** crystal
critique critical
le **critique** critic
la **critique** criticism, review
critiquer to criticize
croire to believe; **croire à cette histoire** to believe this story; **croire en Dieu** to believe in God
la **croisade** crusade
croiser to run across, happen into; **se croiser** to run into each other
le **croissant** croissant, crescent-shaped roll
la **croyance** belief
la **cruche** pitcher, jug
les **crudités** *(fem. pl.)* raw vegetables, salads
la **crue** flood
la **cueillette** gathering
cueillir *(irreg.)* to gather, pick (flowers)
cuire *(like **construire**)* to cook (be cooking)
la **cuisine** kitchen; cooking
cuisiner to cook
la **cuisinière** stove
cuit cooked; **bien cuit** well done
les **cuivres** *(masc. pl.)* brass (music)
la **culotte** knickers, panties
le **culte** cult, worship
cultivé well-educated, cultured
la **culture** culture
culturel(le) cultural
curieux(-se) curious; strange; **curieux de** curious to
le **cycle** cycle
le **cyclisme** cycling

d'abord at first
d'ailleurs besides
le **dancing** dance hall
dangereux(-se) dangerous
dans in
la **danse** dance
danser to dance
le **danseur (la danseuse)** dancer
la **date** date
dater de to date from
davantage more
de bon matin early in the morning
de bonne heure early
de ce côté on this side
de crainte que for fear that
de luxe luxury *(adj.)*
de nos jours in our day
de peur que for fear that
De rien. You're welcome.
débarrasser to clear out; **se débarrasser de** to get rid of
le **débat** debate
débattre *(like **battre**)* to debate
le **débouché** job opportunity
debout up; awake; standing
débrancher to unplug
le **début** beginning
décédé deceased
décembre December
la **décennie** decade
la **déception** disappointment
décerner to award
décevoir *(like **recevoir**)* to disappoint
le **déchirement** rift
déchirer to tear
décidé à resolved, determined to
décider (de) to decide (to); **se décider à** to make up one's mind to
la **décision** decision; decisiveness

déclarer to declare
déclencher to unleash
le **déclin** decline
se **décoller** to peel off
déconseiller (à qqn de faire qqch) to advise (someone not to do something)
décourager (qqn de faire qqch) (**g** > **ge/a, o**) to discourage (someone from doing something)
la **découverte** discovery
découvrir *(like **ouvrir**)* to discover
décréter *(like **espérer**)* to decree
décrocher to unhook
dedans inside
la **déesse** goddess
défaire *(like **faire**)* to undo
la **défaite** defeat
le **défaut** defect, fault
défavorisé underprivileged
défendre (à qqn de faire qqch) to forbid (someone to do something)
la **défense** defense
le **défenseur** defender
la **déférence** deference
le **défi** challenge
le **défilé** parade; **le défilé de mode** fashion show
définir to define
déformer to deform
dégrader to demote, deprive of one's rank
se **déguiser (en)** to disguise oneself (as)
dehors outside
déjà already, ever
déjeuner to have lunch
le **délégué (la déléguée) de classe** student council representative
délicat delicate
délicieux(-se) delicious
demain tomorrow
la **demande** request; **demande d'emploi** job application
demander (à qqn de faire qqch) to ask (someone to do something); **demander qqch** to ask for something
se **demander** to wonder
la **démarche** step, measure
démarrer to start (motor)
démembrer to dismember, take apart
déménager (**g** > **ge/a, o**) to move (change residence)
le **déménageur** mover
se **démettre de** to resign from
la **demeure** dwelling
la **demi-douzaine** half dozen
le **demi-frère** stepbrother
la **demi-heure** half hour
la **demi-sœur** stepsister
démissionner (de) to resign (from)
démographique demographic
dense dense
déplaisant unpleasant
la **dépanneuse** tow truck
le **départ** departure
dépasser to pass, go beyond
se **dépêcher (de)** to hurry (to)
dépeindre *(like **peindre**)* to depict
dépendre de qqch to depend on
dépens: aux dépens de at the expense of
dépenser to spend (money)
déplacer (**c** > **ç/a, o**) to displace; **se déplacer** to move, travel
déplaire à qqn *(like **plaire**)* to displease someone
déporter to deport
déposer to put down, lay down; to drop (someone) off
depuis since, for
déranger (**g** > **ge/a, o**) to bother
dernier(-ère) last
dernièrement lately
le **déroulement** development, unfolding
la **déroute** defeat
derrière behind
dès le début from the beginning
dès le lendemain starting the day after
dès le matin from the morning on
dès maintenant starting now
dès mon enfance ever since I was a child
dès mon retour as soon as I get back
dès que as soon as
désagréable unpleasant
désapprouver to disapprove
le **désastre** disaster
descendre to go down(stairs); to stay at a hotel; to bring down
le **désert** desert
se **déshabiller** to get undressed
le **désir** desire
désirer to desire, want, wish
désireux(-se) de desirous of
désobéir (à) to disobey
désolé terribly sorry
le **désordre** disorder, mess
désormais from now on
le **despotisme** despotism
le **dessert** dessert
le **dessin** drawing
le **dessinateur (la dessinatrice)** drafter; designer
dessiner to draw
dessous below
dessus above
destiné à meant to
le **détail** detail
détaillé detailed
le **détecteur** detector
se **détendre** to relax
détenir to arrest, detain
déterminé à determined to
détester to hate
détourner to divert, distract
détrôner to unseat, dethrone
détruire *(like **construire**)* to destroy
devant in front of

dévaster to devastate
développer to develop
devenir *(like **venir**)* to become
devoir *(irreg.)* ought, must; to owe
les **devoirs** *(masc. pl.)* homework
le **diable** devil
le **dialecte** dialect
le **dictionnaire** dictionary
le **dicton** saying
le **dieu** god
la **différence** difference
se **différencier de** to be differentiated from
la **difficulté** difficulty
diffuser to spread
la **diffusion** circulation, spreading
digestif(-ve) digestive
digne de worthy of
la **dilatation** expansion
la **diligence** diligence
diligent diligent
dimanche Sunday
le **dindon** turkey
le **dîner** dinner
dîner to have dinner
le **diplôme** diploma
dire to say, tell
le **directeur (la directrice)** director
diriger (g > ge/a, o) to direct; **se diriger vers** to head toward
discret(-ète) discreet
discriminatoire discriminatory
disjoint disjunctive
disparaître *(like **connaître**)* to disappear
la **disposition** disposal
disposé à willing to
la **dispute** argument
se **disputer (avec)** to quarrel (with)
le **disque** record; disc; **disque compact** compact disc; **disque dur** hard drive
la **disquette** diskette
dissoudre to dissolve
dissuader (qqn de faire qqch) to dissuade (someone from doing something)
se **distinguer** to distinguish oneself
dit called
divers different
le **divertissement** divertimento (music); distraction, entertainment
diviser to divide
divorcer (c > ç/a, o) to divorce
la **dizaine** about ten
le **docteur** doctor, physician
la **doctrine** doctrine
la **documentation** literature, instructions (for a product)
documenter to document, record
le **dolmen** stone monument in Brittany
le **domaine** domain, field, area
le **domicile** residence
dominant dominant
dominer to dominate
le **don** gift
les **données** *(fem. pl.)* data
donner to give
donner le vertige à to make dizzy
donner rendez-vous à to make an appointment to, make a date with
donner un prix to give a prize
se **donner rendez-vous** to make arrangements to see each other
se **donner la peine de faire** to take the trouble to do
dormir *(irreg.)* to sleep
le **dos** back
doté de equipped with
la **douceur** sweetness, gentleness
doué de blessed with, having
le **doute** doubt; **sans doute** no doubt; **dans le doute** when in doubt
douter (de qqch) to doubt (something); **se douter (de)** to suspect
douteux(-se) doubtful
doux (douce) sweet; mild, gentle
la **douzaine** dozen
le **dramaturge** dramatist, playwright
le **drapeau** flag
dresser la tente to set up the tent
le **droit** law (discipline); right
droit: aller tout droit to go straight ahead; **se tenir droit** to sit straight
la **droite** right; **à droite** to the right
drôle funny
drôlement very *(colloq.)*
du coup as a result
du reste moreover
le **duo** duet
dur d'oreille hard of hearing
la **durée** duration
durer to last

l' **eau** *(fem.)* water; **eau minérale** mineral water; **eau de cologne** cologne
éblouissant dazzling
écarter to remove, put aside
l' **échange** *(masc.)* exchange
l' **échantillon** *(masc.)* sample
s' **échapper de** to run away from, escape from
l' **écharpe** *(fem.)* scarf, muffler
l' **échec** *(masc.)* failure
l' **éclair** *(masc.)* lightning
éclater to burst, to break out
l' **école** *(fem.)* school
l' **économie** *(fem.)* economy; **faire des économies** to save money
économique economic
économiser to save, be thrifty
écouter to listen to
l' **écran couleur** *(masc.)* color screen
écrasant crushing
écrire to write; **écrire au crayon** to write in pencil

l' **écrivain** *(masc.)* writer
édifier to build
l' **édit** *(masc.)* edict
éducatif(-ve) educational
l' **éducation civique** *(fem.)* civics
l' **effacement** *(masc.)* wiping out, elimination
effacer (**c** > **ç/a, o**) to erase
s' **efforcer de** (**c** > **ç/a, o**) to strive, try hard to
l' **effort** *(masc.)* effort
effrayer (**y** > **i/e**) to frighten
égal equal; **ne pas avoir d'égal** to have no equal, no parallel
l' **égalité** *(fem.)* equality
s' **égarer de** to stray from
l' **église** *(fem.)* church
égyptien(ne) Egyptian
élaborer to prepare, work up
élargir to broaden, widen
les **élections** *(fem. pl.)* election
l' **électricité** *(fem.)* electricity
l' **électrostatique** *(fem.)* electrostatics
l' **élevage** *(masc.)* raising of animals, cultivation
l' **élévation** *(fem.)* altitude
élevé high
élever to raise
l' **élève** *(masc. & fem.)* pupil
élire *(like **lire**)* to elect
éloigné distant from
s' **éloigner (de)** to move away (from)
émanciper to emancipate
émaner to emanate, derive from
s' **embarquer** to set out (by boat)
embaucher to hire
embêter to annoy *(colloq.)*; **s'embêter** to be/get bored
l' **embouteillage** *(masc.)* traffic jam
embrasser to kiss; **Je t'embrasse** Love (at end of letter)
s' **émerveiller de qqch** to marvel at something
s' **émeuter** to riot
l' **émigration** *(fem.)* emigration
émigrer to emigrate
l' **émission** *(fem.)* broadcast, TV show
emmener (**e** > **è/e**) to take (someone somewhere)
émotif(-ve) emotional
l' **émotion** *(fem.)* emotion
émouvant exciting
s' **emparer de** to seize
empêcher qqn de to prevent someone from; **s'empêcher de** to refrain from
l' **empereur** *(masc.)* emperor
l' **empire** *(masc.)* empire
s' **empirer** to get worse
l' **emplacement** *(masc.)* placement; location
l' **emploi** *(masc.)* job
employer (**y** > **i/e**) to use
emporter to carry/take away, carry off
l' **empreinte** *(fem.)* mark, trace
l' **empressement** *(masc.)* haste
s' **empresser de** to hurry, rush to
l' **emprise** *(fem.)* hold, grip
l' **emprunt** *(masc.)* borrowing
emprunter (qqch à qqn) to borrow (something from someone)
ému moved, touched
en arrière in back, backward
en attendant que until
en avance early
en avant in front, ahead, forward
en bas down, downstairs
en danger in danger
en désordre in a mess
en différé recorded (TV, radio broadcast)
en direct live (TV, radio broadcast)
en face (de) across (from), opposite
en fait in fact
en haut up, upstairs
en pagaille in a mess
en plus besides, in addition, moreover
en retard late
en semaine during the week
en tout cas in any case
encercler to encircle
enchanté delighted to
enclin à inclined, prone to
encombré (de) blocked (by), congested (with), cluttered (with)
encore still; **encore que** although *(literary)*; **encore une fois** again
encourager (qqn à) (**g** > **ge/a, o**) to encourage (someone to)
endimanché dressed in one's Sunday best
s' **endormir** to fall asleep
l' **endroit** *(masc.)* place
l' **énergie** *(fem.)* energy
énervant annoying
énerver to annoy; **s'énerver** to get nervous, upset
l' **enfance** *(fem.)* childhood
l' **enfant** *(masc. & fem.)* child
l' **enfer** *(masc.)* hell
enfin at last, finally
s' **enfuir** to flee
engagé committed
l' **engagement** *(masc.)* commitment
engager (**g** > **ge/a, o**) to hire; **engager qqn à** to urge someone to
l' **enlacement** *(masc.)* linking
enlever (**e** > **è/e**) to take off, remove
ennuyer (**y** > **i/e**) to bore; **s' ennuyer** to be/get bored
l' **enquête criminelle** *(fem.)* criminal investigation
s' **enrhumer** to catch cold
enrichir to enrich
l' **enseignant (l'enseignante)** teacher, instructor
l' **enseigne** *(fem.)* sign
l' **enseignement** *(masc.)* teaching, education
enseigner to teach
ensemble together
l' **ensemble** *(masc.)* collection
ensuite next, following that

l' **entassement** *(masc.)* pile-up, crowding
entendre to hear; **s'entendre bien/mal avec** to get along/not get along with; **entendre dire** to hear
l' **enterrement** *(masc.)* burial, funeral
s' **enthousiasmer** to get enthusiastic
s' **enticher de qqn** to fall for someone
entier(-ère) entire
entouré de surrounded by
s' **entourer de qqch** to surround oneself with, be surrounded by something
s' **entraider** to help each other
s' **entraîner à** to train to, to practice
entre between, among; **entre nous** just between us
l' **entrée** *(fem.)* entrance
entreprendre *(like **prendre**)* to undertake
l' **entreprise** *(fem.)* business, firm; undertaking
entrer to enter, come/go in; to enter (data)
envahir to invade
l' **envahisseur** *(masc.)* invader
l' **enveloppe** *(fem.)* envelope
envers toward *(figurative)*
environ approximately
s' **envoler** to fly away
envoyer (y > i/e) to send
épais (épaisse) thick
s' **épanouir** to flourish
l' **épanouissement** *(masc.)* flowering, expansion, flourishing
l' **épaule** *(fem.)* shoulder
épeler (l > ll/e) to spell
l' **épice** *(fem.)* spice
l' **épicerie** *(fem.)* grocery
l' **épicier (l'épicière)** grocer
l' **épine** *(fem.)* thorn
l' **époque** *(fem.)* epoch, era; **à l'époque** at the time
épouser to marry
épousseter (t > tt/e) to dust
épuisé exhausted
l' **équateur** *(masc.)* equator
l' **équilibre** *(masc.)* balance, equilibrium
l' **équipe** *(fem.)* team
s' **équiper** to equip oneself
éreinté exhausted
l' **érosion** *(fem.)* erosion
erroné mistaken
escalader to climb over
l' **escalier** *(masc.)* staircase; **l'escalier roulant** escalator
l' **espace vert** *(masc.)* green space, park
espagnol Spanish
l' **espèce** *(fem.)* kind, sort
espérer (é > è/e) to hope
l' **espoir** *(masc.)* hope
l' **esprit** *(masc.)* mind
l' **essai** *(masc.)* essay
essayer (y > i/e) to try, try on; **essayer de** to try to
l' **essayiste** *(masc. & fem.)* essayist
l' **essence** *(fem.)* gasoline; essence
essentiel(le) essential
l' **essor** *(masc.)* rapid development
essuyer (y > i/e) to wipe
l' **est** *(masc.)* east
l' **estuaire** *(masc.)* estuary
établir to establish
l' **établissement** *(masc.)* school; establishment
l' **étage** *(masc.)* floor, story
l' **étagère** *(fem.)* bookcase
étaler to spread out, stagger
l' **étang** *(masc.)* pond
étant donné given
l' **étape** *(fem.)* stage, step
l' **état** state; **d'état** state *(adj.)*
l' **été** *(masc.)* summer
éteindre *(like **craindre**)* to put out, extinguish
étendre to extend, stretch out; **étendre le linge sur le fil** to hang the clothes on a line
l' **éternité** *(fem.)* eternity; forever
éternuer to sneeze
l' **étoffe** *(fem.)* cloth
étonnant surprising
s' **étonner (de)** to be surprised (at)
étrange strange
étranger(-ère) foreign; **à l'étranger** abroad
l' **être** *(masc.)* being
être *(irreg.)* to be
être à to belong to
être à l'étroit to be cramped for space
être à l'étude to be under study
être à l'heure to be on time
être à la page to be up-to-date
être au régime to be on a diet
être bien to be nice looking; be comfortable
être d'accord avec to be in agreement with
être de bonne/mauvaise humeur to be in a good/bad mood
être de retour to be back
être en avance to be early
être en colère to be angry
être en forme to be in shape
être en retard to be late
être en train de faire qqch to be busy doing something
être en vacances to be on vacation
être payé au mois to be paid by the month
être sur le point de faire qqch to be about to do something
l' **étrenne** *(fem.)* New Year's gift
étroit narrow
étroitement closely
l' **étude** *(fem.)* study
l' **étudiant (l'étudiante)** student
étudier to study
européen(ne) European
l' **événement** *(masc.)* event
éventuel(le) possible
éviter de to avoid
évolué highly developed
évoluer to evolve
évoquer to evoke, recall
l' **exactitude** *(fem.)* punctuality, exactness

exalter to exalt, fill with enthusiasm
exceller à to excel in
l' **excès** *(masc.)* excess
exclu excluded, out of the question
s' **excuser de** to apologize for
exécuter to execute, carry out, achieve
l' **exemple** *(masc.)* example
s' **exercer à (c > ç/a, o)** to practice
l' **exercice** *(masc.)* exercise
exigeant demanding
exiger to demand
l' **exil** *(masc.)* exile
l' **exode** *(masc.)* Exodus
expédier to ship
l' **expérience** *(fem.)* experiment
expliquer to explain
exploiter to exploit; make use of
l' **explorateur (l'exploratrice)** explorer
exporter to export
l' **exposé** *(masc.)* report
l' **exposition** *(fem.)* exhibit; **exposition universelle** *(fem.)* world's fair
exprès on purpose
exprimer to express
exquis exquisite
l' **extérieur** *(masc.)* outside
extirper to extirpate, uproot
extraordinaire extraordinary

la **fable** fable
fabriquer to manufacture
fabuleux(-se) fabulous, terrific
la **fac** school, university department *(slang)*
face à opposite, across from
face: faire face à to face
se **fâcher** to get angry
facile easy
faciliter to make easier, more convenient; facilitate
la **façon** way
façonner to fashion, craft, make
le **facteur** mail carrier
la **facture** bill
la **faculté** school or division of the university
faible weak
la **faiblesse** weakness
faire *(irreg.)* to make; to do
faire 10 kilomètres to travel, cover 10 kilometers
se **faire accompagner de qqn** to get someone to go with you
faire allusion à qqch to refer to something
faire attendre qqn to keep someone waiting
se **faire avoir** to be fooled, taken in
faire boire un enfant to give a child something to drink
faire bouillir de l'eau to boil water
faire chanter qqn to blackmail someone
se **faire comprendre** to make oneself understood
se **faire couper les cheveux** to get one's hair cut
faire cuire qqch to cook something
faire des projets to make plans
faire du 70 à l'heure to do 70 kilometers an hour
faire du bricolage to do odd jobs, putter around
faire du sport, du jogging, du vélo to play sports, to jog, to bike ride
faire écouter un disque à to play a record for
se **faire engueuler** to get scolded, yelled at *(slang)*
se **faire entendre** to be heard
faire entrer/sortir qqn to show someone in/out
faire faire le tour du propriétaire à qqn to show someone around one's house
faire faire les devoirs aux enfants to help the children with their homework
se **faire faire une robe** to have a dress made
se **faire gronder** to get scolded, yelled at
faire la cuisine to do the cooking
faire la grasse matinée to sleep in, sleep late
faire la vaisselle to do the dishes
faire le jardin to do the gardening
faire le linge, faire la lessive to do the laundry
faire le lit to make the bed
faire le ménage to do the housework
faire le plein to fill up with gas
faire le(s) lit(s) to make the bed(s)
faire les carreaux to wash the windows
faire les courses to do the shopping, marketing
faire les valises to pack
se **faire mal (au pied)** to hurt oneself (one's foot)
faire manger un malade to feed a sick person
faire mijoter une soupe to simmer soup
faire monter qqn to invite someone up
se **faire nettoyer les dents par le dentiste** to get one's teeth cleaned by the dentist
se **faire noter** to be seen
se **faire opérer** to get operated on
se **faire payer** to get paid
faire pousser (l'herbe) to make the (grass) grow, to grow (grass)
se **faire prendre** to get caught (of a criminal, etc.)
se **faire prier** to be begged, coaxed
faire remarquer to point out; **se faire remarquer** to get noticed, to call attention to oneself
se **faire renverser par une voiture** to get run over by a car
se **faire renvoyer** to get fired
faire rôtir un poulet to roast a chicken
faire sa toilette to wash up and get dressed (especially in the morning)
faire sauter des tranches d'oignon to sauté onion slices
faire savoir to inform, let know
faire semblant de to pretend to
faire signe (à qqn de faire qqch) to signal (someone to do something)
se **faire soigner** to see a doctor, get medical treatment
faire suivre le courrier to forward the mail
faire traverser la rue à un vieillard to help an old man across the street

se **faire tuer** to get oneself killed
faire un versement sur le compte de to make a deposit to the account of
faire un voyage to take a trip
faire une promenade à pied/en voiture to go for a walk/ride
faire venir le médecin to send for the doctor
faire visiter la ville à qqn to show someone around the city
faire voir to show
faire: Tu me fais suer! You're a real pain in the neck!
faire: bien faire de to be right in doing something, do the wise thing by doing something
faire: Il fait 30 degrés. It's thirty degrees.
faire: Il fait beau/mauvais. The weather's good/bad.
faire: Il fait chaud/froid. It's hot/cold (outside).
faire: Il fait du soleil/vent. It's sunny/windy.
faire: Il fait jour/nuit. It's daytime/dark.
faire: Il fait un sale temps. The weather is lousy.
faire: Quel temps fait-il? What's the weather?
faire: Quelle température fait-il? What's the temperature?
le **fait** fact
fait à la main made by hand
falloir *(irreg.)*: **il faut** it is necessary
se **familiariser avec** to familiarize oneself with
la **farine** flour
le **fascisme** fascism
fatal fatal
la **fatigue** fatigue
se **fatiguer** to get tired
la **fausse monnaie** counterfeit money
la **faute** mistake
le **fauteuil** armchair
le **faux numéro** wrong number
faux: chanter/jouer faux to sing/play out of tune; **sonner faux** to sound false, have a hollow ring
favori(te) favorite
favoriser to favor
fédéré federated
féliciter qqn d'avoir fait qqch to congratulate someone for having done something
la **femme** woman; **femme d'affaires** businesswoman; **femme de lettres** female literary figure
la **fenêtre** window
la **féodalité** feudalism
le **fer** iron
la **ferme** farm
fermer to close
ferroviaire railway *(adj.)*
le **festival** festival
la **fête** celebration, party, holiday
la **fête des Rois** Three Kings' Day (January 6)
fêter to celebrate
le **feu** fire
feuilleter (**t** > **tt/e**) to leaf through
le **feutre** felt-tipped pen
la **fève** bean
février February
se **fiancer (avec)** to get engaged (to)
fictif(-ve) fictional
le **fidèle** adherent of a religion
fier(-ère) proud
se **fier à** to trust
la **filière** channel; path; course of study
la **fille** daughter; girl
le **film** film; **film d'horreur** horror film
le **fils** son
la **fin** end; **fin de cours** end of the school year; **fin de semaine** weekend
final final
les **finances** *(fem. pl.)* finances
financier(-ère) financial
finir (de faire qqch) to finish (doing something); **finir par faire qqch** to wind up doing something
fiscal fiscal, pertaining to taxation
la **fiscalité** tax system
la **fissure** crack, fissure, split
fixer to fix, set
flâner to stroll
se **flatter de** to claim to (be able to)
flatteur(-se) flattering
la **flemme** laziness *(slang)*
la **fleur** flower; **fleur de lys (lis)** fleur de lis, lily flower
fleurir to flower; put flowers on (graves)
le **fleuve** river
la **floraison** flowering
flou imprecise, vague
le **fluor** fluoride
la **flûte** flute
la **foi** faith
la **fois** time, occasion, occurrence
le **foisonnement** proliferation
la **folie** madness
foncé dark (colors)
fondamental fundamental
fonder to found
fondre to melt
le **football** soccer
la **force** strength
forcer qqn à to force someone to
la **forêt** forest
la **forme: être en pleine forme** to be in good physical shape
formidable terrific
la **formule** formula
fort strong; **Mon cœur battait fort.** My heart was pounding; **respirer bien fort** to take a deep breath; **parler/crier fort** to speak/yell, cry out loudly; **sentir fort** to have a strong smell
la **forteresse** fortress
fortifier to fortify
fou (fol, folle) crazy
fouiller to ransack, search
le **fouillis** mess

le **foulard** scarf, kerchief
la **foule** crowd
se **fouler la cheville** to sprain one's ankle
le **fourgon (de déménagement)** moving truck
fourmiller de to swarm with
fournir (de) to supply (with)
le **fournisseur (la fournisseuse)** supplier
frais (fraîche) fresh, cool
les **frais** *(masc. pl.)* expenses, cost
franc (franche) frank
franchir to cross
francophone French-speaking
frappant striking
frapper to strike, hit; knock (door)
fréquenter to frequent
le **frère (aîné/cadet)** (older/younger) brother
le **frigo** refrigerator
froid cold
le **fromage** cheese
la **frontière** border
le **fruit** fruit; **fruits de mer** *(masc. pl.)* seafood
la **fuite** flight, escape
fumé smoked
fumer to smoke
furieux(-se) furious
la **fusée** rocket
le **futur** future tense

le **gâchis** mess
gagnant winning
gagner to earn, win
la **gaieté** gaiety, cheer
la **galette** cracker
la **gamme** range, line; scale (music)
le **garage** garage
garantir to guarantee
le **garçon** boy
la **garde** guard; **être en garde** to be on guard
garder to keep; to care for (a child); **se garder de** to be wary of
la **gare** railway station
garer to park
gastrique gastric
le **gâteau** cake
la **gauche** left; **à gauche** to the left
gaulois Gallic, pertaining to the Celtic inhabitants of pre-Roman France
le **gaz** gas
geler (e > **é/e**) to freeze
le **gendre** son-in-law
général general
le **général** general
généreux(-se) generous
la **générosité** generosity
génial clever
le **génie** engineering
le **genou** knee
le **genre** genre, type of literature
les **gens** people
gentil(le) nice, kind, friendly
la **gentillesse** kindness
gentiment nicely, kindly
la **géographie** geography
la **géologie** geology
géologique geological
la **glace** mirror; ice cream
le **gobelet** paper cup
le **goulu (la goulue)** glutton
le **goût** taste
le **goûter** afternoon snack
le **gouvernement** government
gouverner to govern
grand big
la **grand-mère** grandmother
le **grand-père** grandfather
la **grande école** elite university (in France)
les **grands magasins** *(masc. pl.)* department stores
les **grands titres** *(masc. pl.)* headlines
gras(-se) fat, fatty; **en caractères gras** in boldface
la **gratitude** gratitude
le **gratte-ciel** skyscraper
grave serious
la **gravure** engraving
grec (grecque) Greek
grêler to hail
grelotter to shiver
le **grenier** attic
la **grève** strike (labor); **faire grève** to go on strike
grièvement seriously, gravely
griller to toast
grimper to climb; **grimper aux arbres** to climb trees
gris grey
gronder to scold
gros(-se) big, fat; **risquer gros** to risk a great deal; **gagner/perdre gros** to win/lose heavily
grossier(-ère) coarse, vulgar
la **grossièreté** coarseness
grossir to get fat
la **grotte** cave
le **groupe** group
guère: ne . . . guère hardly
guérir to cure, make better
la **guerre** war
le **guerrier** warrior
le **guide** guide
le **guignol** French puppet theater
les **guillemets** *(masc. pl.)* quotation marks
la **guitare** guitar

habile à skillful at
habiller to dress; **s'habiller** to get dressed
l' **habitant (l'habitante)** inhabitant
habiter to live (reside)
l' **habitude** *(fem.)* habit
s' **habituer à** to get used to, accustomed to
la **haine** hatred

la **hardiesse** boldness
le **haricot** bean; **haricots verts** green beans
la **hâte** haste
la **hausse** raise, rise
le **haut-relief** high relief
haut: lire tout haut to read aloud; **mettre la radio plus haut** to turn the radio up louder; **les gens haut placés** highly placed people
la **hauteur** height
l' **hebdomadaire** *(masc.)* weekly publication
l' **hérésie** *(fem.)* heresy
l' **héritage** *(masc.)* heritage, inheritance
l' **héritier (l'héritière)** heir
le **héros** hero
hésiter (à) to hesitate (to)
l' **heure** *(fem.)* hour, clock time; **de bonne heure** early
heureux(-se) de happy to
hier yesterday
l' **histoire** *(fem.)* history, story
l' **historien (l'historienne)** historian
historique historical
l' **hiver** *(masc.)* winter
l' **homme** *(masc.)* man; **homme d'affaires** businessman
honnête honest
l' **honnêteté** *(fem.)* honesty
la **honte** shame; **avoir honte** to be ashamed
l' **hôpital** *(masc.)* hospital
l' **horaire** *(masc.)* schedule
l' **horreur** *(fem.)* horror
les **hors-d'œuvre** *(masc. pl.)* hors d'œuvres
l' **hôtel** *(masc.)* hotel
humain human
humide damp, humid
le **hurlement** howling, wailing
hurler to scream, shriek, howl
l' **hydrocarbure** *(masc.)* hydrocarbon
hydroélectrique hydroelectric
l' **hyène** *(fem.)* hyena
hypocrite hypocritical
hypothétique hypothetical
l' **hymne** *(masc.)* anthem

ici here
l' **idéal** *(masc.)* ideal
l' **idée** *(fem.)* idea
idiot stupid, idiotic
l' **idiotie** *(fem.)* stupidity
l' **île** *(fem.)* island
illuminer to light up
l' **imagination** *(fem.)* imagination
l' **immeuble** *(masc.)* apartment house
l' **immigré (l'immigrée)** immigrant
immobilier(-ère) real estate *(adj.)*
l' **impatience** *(fem.)* impatience
s' **impatienter** to get impatient
l' **imperméable** *(masc.)* raincoat
implanter to implant, to impose
l' **importance** *(fem.)* importance; **donner de l'importance à** to consider something important
imposant impressive
l' **impôt** *(masc.)* tax
l' **imprimante** *(fem.)* printer (computer)
imprimer to print
l' **imprimerie** *(fem.)* printing press, print shop
l' **imprudence** *(fem.)* carelessness
inaugurer to start, initiate, inaugurate
incendier to set on fire
incessant ceaseless
l' **incident** *(masc.)* incident
incomplet(-ète) incomplete
incrédule incredulous
l' **indépendance** *(fem.)* independence
l' **indifférence** *(fem.)* indifference
l' **indignation** *(fem.)* indignation
s' **indigner de qqch** to get indignant about something
indiscret(-ète) indiscreet
indispensable indispensable
l' **individu** *(masc.)* individual
l' **industrie** *(fem.)* industry
industriel(le) industrial
l' **infirmier (l'infirmière)** nurse
l' **influence** *(fem.)* influence
l' **infographie** *(fem.)* computer graphics
les **informations** *(fem. pl.)* news
l' **informatique** *(fem.)* computer science
l' **infortuné (l'infortunée)** unfortunate person
l' **ingénieur** *(masc.)* engineer
ininterrompu uninterrupted
initier to begin
l' **injonction** *(fem.)* injunction, command
l' **innovateur (l'innovatrice)** innovator
l' **innovation** *(fem.)* innovation
l' **inondation** *(fem.)* flood
inquiet(-ète) restless, upset, nervous
s' **inquiéter** to worry; **s' inquiéter (de)** to be worried (about)
l' **inquiétude** *(fem.)* restlessness, nervousness
insister sur to insist on
l' **inspecteur (l'inspectrice)** inspector
s' **inspirer de** to draw inspiration from
installer to install; **s' installer** to move in, settle in
instituer to institute
l' **instituteur (l'institutrice)** elementary school teacher
l' **instruction publique** *(fem.)* public education
l' **instrument** *(masc.)* instrument
insuffisant insufficient
insultant insulting
s' **intégrer** to become part of
intellectuel(le) intellectual
intensif(-ve) intensive
l' **interconnexion de réseau** *(fem.)* networking
interdire à qqn de *(irreg.)* to forbid someone to
interdit forbidden
s' **intéresser à** to be interested in

l' **intérêt** *(masc.)* interest

interne internal

l' **interprète** *(masc. & fem.)* interpreter

interrompre to interrupt

l' **intervalle** *(masc.)* interval

l' **intervention** *(fem.)* intervention

introduire *(like **construire**)* to introduce

l' **inverse** *(masc.)* opposite

l' **inversion** *(fem.)* inversion

l' **invité (l'invitée)** guest

inviter to invite

l' **irruption: faire irruption** to burst in

islamiser to convert (someone) to Islam; **s'islamiser** to become converted to Islam

l' **isolement** *(masc.)* isolation

italien(ne) Italian

l' **itinéraire** *(masc.)* itinerary

jadis formerly

le **jalon** step, milestone

la **jalousie** jealousy

jaloux(-se) jealous

jamais never; **à jamais** forever; **à tout jamais** forever and ever; **Il n'en manque jamais une!** He's always blundering. He always puts his foot in it.

Jamais de la vie! Not on your life!

Jamais deux sans trois. Misfortunes always come in three's.

la **jambe** leg

le **jambon** ham

janvier January

le **jardin** garden; **jardin potager** vegetable garden; **jardin zoologique** zoo

jaune yellow

je ne sais combien I'm not sure how much/many

je ne sais comment somehow

je ne sais où somewhere or other

je ne sais pourquoi for some reason or other

je ne sais quand sometime or other

je ne sais quel + *noun* some + (*noun*) or other

je ne sais qui someone or other

je ne sais quoi something or other

se **jeter (t > tt/e)** to empty (of a river)

le **jeu** game

jeudi Thursday

jeune young

la **jeune fille** girl

les **jeunes gens** *(masc. pl.)* young people, young men

la **jeunesse** youth

joindre *(irreg.)* to join

joli pretty

le **jongleur** medieval actor or reader of poetry

jouer to play

jouer aux cartes/aux échecs/au football to play cards/chess/soccer

jouer de *(+ name of instrument)* to play (an instrument)

le **jouet** toy

le **joueur (la joueuse)** player

jouir de qqch to enjoy, be in possession of, have something for one's use

le **jour** day; **de nos jours** nowadays

le **journal (les journaux)** newspaper

le **journaliste (la journaliste)** journalist

la **journée** day, period of a day

le **judaïsme** Judaism

le **juge** judge

le **jugement** judgment, court case

juif(-ve) Jewish

juillet July

juin June

les **jumelles** *(fem. pl.)* binoculars

la **jupe** skirt

jurer (de) to swear (to)

le **jus** juice; **jus de fruits** fruit juice

jusqu'à ce que until

juste fair; **chanter/jouer juste** to sing/play in key; **raisonner juste** to reason soundly

kaki *(invar.)* khaki

le **kilo** kilogram

le **klaxon** car horn

klaxonner to honk the horn

là there; **là-bas** over there; **là-dedans** in there; **là-dessous** underneath there; **là-dessus** on top of it, on it; **là-haut** up there

le **laboratoire** laboratory

le **lac** lake

le **lai** medieval genre of poetry

la **laïcité** secularism

la **laine** wool

laisser to let, leave behind

le **lait** milk

la **lampe de poche** flashlight

lancer (c > ç/a, o) to launch; **lancer un produit** to launch a product

la **langue** language

large wide

le **lave-vaisselle** dishwasher

laver to wash; **se laver** to wash up; **se laver la tête, les mains, la figure** to wash one's hair, one's hands, one's face

la **leçon** lesson

le **lecteur (la lectrice)** reader; **lecteur de CD-ROM** CD-ROM drive

la **lecture** reading

léger(-ère) light (weight)

léguer *(like **espérer**)* to bequeath

le **légume** vegetable

le **lendemain** the day after

lent à slow in

la **lenteur** slowness

les **lettres** *(fem. pl.)* literature

le **leucocyte** white blood cell

levant rising

lever (e > è/e) to pick up, raise; **se lever** to get up
se **lézarder** to crack (wall)
la **liaison** love affair
libérer to liberate
la **liberté** liberty, freedom; **liberté de conscience** freedom of conscience
la **librairie** bookstore
libre (de) free (to)
la **libre pensée** freethinking
lier to bind, link
le **lieu** place
la **lieue** league (measure of distance)
la **ligne** line; **ligne aérienne** airline
lilas *(invar.)* lilac-colored
se **limer les ongles** to cut/file one's nails
la **limonade** lemon-flavored soda, soft drink
le **linge** linen, laundry
le **lion (la lionne)** lion
lire à haute voix to read aloud
le **lit** bed
littéraire literary
la **littérature** literature
la **livraison** delivery
la **livre** pound
le **livre** book
livrer to deliver; **se livrer à** to resort to
la **locution** phrase
le **logement** lodging, housing
loger (g > ge/a, o) to house, put someone up
le **logiciel** software package; **logiciel de traitement de texte** word processing software package
logique logical
la **loi** law
loin (de) far (from)
long(ue) long; **être long à** to take a long time to
longer (g > ge/a, o) to walk along, go along
longtemps for a long time
la **longueur** length
lorsque when
la **loterie** lottery
louer (qqch à qqn) to rent (something from someone)
la **lumière** light
lundi Monday
la **lune** moon
les **lunettes** *(fem. pl.)* eyeglasses
la **lutte** struggle, fight
lutter to struggle, fight
le **luxe** luxury
luxueux(-se) luxurious
le **lycée** French secondary school
lymphatique lymph, lymphatic

mâcher to chew
la **machine à calculer** adding machine
la **machine à laver** washing machine
le **magasin** store
le **magazine** magazine
le **Maghreb** North Africa
le **magnétoscope** VCR
magnifique magnificent
mai May
maigrir to lose weight
le **maillot de bain** bathing suit
la **main-d'œuvre** labor
main: faire main basse sur to make off with
maintenant now
maintenir to maintain, support (financially)
le **maire** mayor
la **maison** house; **maison de la culture** arts center
le **maître** master
maîtriser to master, control
majorer de to increase by
mal badly; **mal écrit** incorrectly spelled or written
le **mal** sickness, disease; evil; pain; difficulty; **avoir du mal à** to have difficulty doing something; **se faire mal** to hurt oneself
la **maladie** illness, disease
malgré que in spite of the fact that
le **malheur** unhappiness, misfortune
malheureux(-se) unfortunate
la **Manche** English Channel
la **manche** sleeve
manger (g > ge/a, o) to eat; **manger à belles dents** to eat with appetite, with gusto
la **manière** way, manner
la **manifestation** demonstration (political)
le **manque** lack, absence
manquer to miss (train, appointment); **manquer de** to fail to; lack, be short of
le **manteau** coat
le **manuel** schoolbook, textbook
se **maquiller** to put on makeup
le **marais** swamp
le **marchand (la marchande)** merchant
la **marchandise** merchandise, goods
le **marché** market
marcher to walk; to work (appliance); **marcher comme sur des roulettes** to go like clockwork
mardi Tuesday
la **mariée** bride
se **marier (avec)** to get married (to)
le **marin** sailor
maritime maritime, pertaining to the sea
marocain Moroccan
la **marque** brand
marquer to mark, signal
marron *(invar.)* brown
mars March
masqué wearing a mask, masked
massacrer to massacre
le **massif** high plain
le **match** game (sports, competitive)
le **match nul** tie game
le **mathématicien (la mathématicienne)** mathematician
les **maths** *(fem. pl.)* math
la **matière** school subject

matinal early riser
mauvais bad; **sentir mauvais** to smell bad
la **mécanique céleste** celestial mechanics
la **mécanique ondulatoire** wave mechanics
méchant wicked, mean, nasty
la **mèche: être de mèche avec** to be in cahoots with *(fam.)*
mécontent de unhappy to
le **médecin** doctor
la **médecine** medicine (field of study)
la **médiathèque** resource center, technology center
le **médicament** medicine (remedy)
méditerranéen Mediterranean
se **méfier de** to be wary of, distrustful of
la **mégarde: par mégarde** inadvertently
meilleur better *(adj.)*
mélanger to mix
se **mêler de qqch** to meddle with, interfere with something
la **mélodie** melody
le **membre** member
même even; *(adj.)* same, very
la **menace** threat
menacer (c > ç/a, o) to threaten
le **ménage** household; housework
mener (e > è/e) to lead
le **menhir** stone monument in Brittany
le **mensonge** lie
la **mentalité** mindset
le **menteur (la menteuse)** liar
menteur(-se) lying
mentir *(irreg.)* to serve
le **mépris** scorn
la **mer** sea
mercredi Wednesday
la **mère** mother
le **merghez** North African sausage
mériter de to deserve to
la **merveille** wonder
merveilleux(-se) wonderful
la **mésaventure** misadventure
le **message** message
la **messagerie électronique** electronic bulletin board
la **messe** mass (Catholic church service)
la **mesure** measure
le **métal** metal
la **métallurgie** steel industry
la **méthode** method
le **métro** subway
la **métropole** metropolis
mettre *(irreg.)* to put
se **mettre à** to begin to
se **mettre à faire qqch** to begin to do something
mettre de l'ordre to straighten up
se **mettre en colère** to get angry
se **mettre en panique** to fly into a panic
se **mettre en route** to get going
mettre fin à to put an end to
le **meuble** piece of furniture; **les meubles** furniture
le **miaulement** meowing
miauler to meow
le **micro-ordinateur** microcomputer
le **microbe** germ
le **Midi** south of France
le **mien (la mienne, les miens, les miennes)** mine
mieux better *(adv.)*
mignon(ne) cute
le **milieu** background, environment
militaire military
millénaire thousands of years old
le **millet** millet
le **millier** about a thousand
mince thin
mincir to get thin
la **mine** mine
le **ministère** government ministry or department
le **ministre** minister (government)
le **miracle** miracle
le **miroir** mirror
le **misanthrope** misanthrope, someone who hates people
mixte mixed
la **mobylette** moped
moche unattractive, homely
la **mode** fashion; **la mode féminine** women's fashion
le **modèle** model
modéré moderate
moderniser to modernize
les **mœurs** *(fem. pl.)* morals, customs, habits
moins less
la **moitié** half
la **molécule** molecule
le **monarque** monarch
le **monastère** monastery
le **monde** world; **tout le monde** everyone; **du monde** people
mondial world *(adj.)*
le **moniteur** monitor
la **monnaie** currency
le **monstre** monster
montagnard of the mountains
la **montagne** mountain
montagneux(-se) mountainous
la **montée** rise
monter to go up(stairs); to bring up
la **montre** (wrist)watch
montrer to show
le **monument** monument
se **moquer de** to make fun of
la **moquette** wall-to-wall carpeting
la **morale** morale, morality; **remonter la morale à qqn** to buck someone up
le **morceau** piece
mordant biting, sarcastic
mordre to bite
la **mort** death
le **mot** word
moteur (motrice) driving *(adj.)*

la **moto(cyclette)** motorcycle

mou (mol, molle) soft

le **mouchoir** handkerchief

se **mouiller** to get wet

le **moulin** mill

mourir *(irreg.)* to die; **mourir d'ennui** to be bored to death; **mourir de faim** to starve, be very hungry; **mourir de soif** to be very thirsty

le **mouton** sheep

le **mouvement** movement

le **moyen** means

moyen(ne) average

le **moyen âge** Middle Ages

moyennant by means of

la **moyenne** average

muet(te) mute

municipal municipal

la **muraille** wall (around a town)

le **musée** museum

le **musicien (la musicienne)** musician

la **musique** music

la **musique de chambre** chamber music

le **musulman (la musulmane)** Moslem

n'importe combien any amount; no matter how much, how many

n'importe comment anyhow

n'importe lequel, laquelle, lesquels, lesquelles whichever one(s), any one(s)

n'importe où anywhere

n'importe quand at any time

n'importe quel + *noun* any + *noun*

n'importe qui anyone

n'importe quoi anything

la **nage** swimming; **être en nage** to be all sweated up

nager (g > ge/a, o) to swim

le **nageur (la nageuse)** swimmer

naïf(-ve) naive

la **naissance** birth

naître *(irreg.)* to be born

la **nappe** tablecloth

natal native

la **natation** swimming

la **nation** nation

le **naturaliste (la naturaliste)** naturalist

la **nature morte** still life

naturel(le) natural

le **naufrage** shipwreck

naval naval

navigable navigable

la **navigation** navigation, sailing

nécessaire necessary

négliger de to neglect to

la **négritude** negritude, black racial consciousness

la **neigée** snowfall

neiger to snow; **il neige** it's snowing

néolatin deriving from Latin

le **néolithique** Neolithic, New Stone Age

nerveux(-se) nervous

nettoyer (**y** > **i/e**) to clean

neuf(-ve) new

le **neveu** nephew

le **nez** nose

ne . . . que only

ni: Cela ne me fait ni chaud ni froid. It's all the same to me. I don't feel strongly about it.

ni: Cette histoire n'a ni queue ni tête. This story doesn't make any sense at all.

la **nièce** niece

nier to deny

le **niveau** level

la **noblesse** nobility

Noël Christmas

noisette *(invar.)* light brown

le **nom** name

le **nombre ordinal** ordinal number

nombreux(-se) numerous; **famille nombreuse** family with many children

non compris not including

non plus neither

le **nord** north

nord-africain North African

le **nord-ouest** northwest

normal normal

la **norme** norm

la **note** bill; grade (school)

le **nôtre (la nôtre, les nôtres)** ours

la **nourriture** food

nouveau (nouvel, nouvelle) new

la **nouvelle** piece of news

la **Nouvelle-Écosse** Nova Scotia

novembre November

noyer (**y** > **i/e**) to drown; **se noyer** to drown

nucléaire nuclear

nuire à to harm

la **nuit** night

nul(le) no one; nothing; no one; poor (in a subject or field)

nulle part nowhere; **nulle part ailleurs** nowhere else

la **nullité** nonentity

le **numéro** number; issue (periodical); **numéro (de téléphone)** (phone) number

obéir (à) to obey

obéissant obedient

l' **objet** *(masc.)* object

obligatoire mandatory

obliger qqn à to oblige someone to

obscurément obscurely

l' **observateur (l'observatrice)** observer

l' **observé** *(masc.)* that which is observed

s' **obstiner à** to persist stubbornly in

obtenir *(like* ***tenir****)* to get, obtain

occupé busy

s' **occuper de** to take care of

octobre October

l' **œil** *(masc.)* eye (*pl.* **les yeux**); **de mes propres yeux** with my own eyes; **ne pas fermer l'œil de la nuit** not to sleep a wink all night
l' **œuf** *(masc.)* egg
l' **œuvre** *(fem.)* work (of art, literature, etc.)
s' **offenser (de)** to get offended (at)
officiel(le) official
l' **offre** *(fem.)* offer
offrir *(irreg.)* to offer; give (as a gift)
l' **oignon** *(masc.)* onion
l' **omelette** *(fem.)* omelet
omettre (de) *(like **mettre**)* to omit, neglect (to)
l' **oncle** *(masc.)* uncle
l' **opposant (l'opposante)** opponent
l' **or** *(masc.)* gold
l' **orage** *(masc.)* storm
l' **oralité** *(fem.)* oral nature
l' **orange** *(fem.)* orange (fruit)
orange *(invar.)* orange
orchestral orchestral, pertaining to the orchestra
l' **orchestre** *(masc.)* orchestra; **orchestre de cuivres** brass band
ordinaire ordinary, dull
l' **ordinateur** *(masc.)* computer
l' **ordonnance** *(fem.)* prescription
ordonner to prescribe; **ordonner (à qqn de faire qqch)** to order (someone to do something)
l' **ordre** *(masc.)* order
les **ordures** *(fem. pl.)* garbage
l' **organe** *(masc.)* organ (body)
organiser to organize
l' **organisme** *(masc.)* organization
oriental oriental
l' **orientation** *(fem.)* guidance
l' **origine** *(fem.)* origin
oser faire qqch to dare to do something
oublier (de) to forget (to)
l' **ouest** *(masc.)* west
l' **ours (l'ourse)** bear
l' **outil** *(masc.)* tool
outre-Manche across the English Channel
outre-mer overseas
l' **ouverture** *(fem.)* opening
l' **ouvrier (l'ouvrière)** worker
ouvrir *(irreg.)* to open; turn on (appliance)

la **pagaïe** (*also* **pagaille**) disorder, mess
la **page** page
païen(ne) pagan
le **pain** bread
paisible peaceful, calm
la **paix** peace
le **palais** palace
le **paléolithique** Paleolithic, Old Stone Age
la **paléontologie** paleontology
le **paludisme** malaria
la **panne**: **en panne** out of order, broken; **panne d'électricité** power failure
le **panorama** view, panorama
le **pansement** bandage; dressing
le **pantalon** pants
la **panthère** panther
les **pantoufles** *(fem. pl.)* slippers
la **papauté** papacy
le **papier** paper; **papier (peint)** wallpaper; **papier à lettres** stationery
Pâques *(fem. pl.)* Easter
le **paquet** package
par by
par conséquent consequently
par écrit in writing
par ici/là this way/that way
par intervalles intermittently
par la poste by mail
par mégarde inadvertently
par souci d'exactitude for the sake of accuracy
par terre on the ground
par un temps pareil in weather like this
paraître *(like **connaître**)* to seem, appear
parcourir *(like **courir**)* to cover, travel
pardonner à qqn to forgive someone
pareil(le) similar
la **paresse** laziness
paresseux(-se) lazy
parfait perfect
parfois sometimes
le **parfum** perfume
parisien(ne) Parisian
parler to speak; **parler à tort et à travers** to talk nonsense, say any old thing
parmi among
le **parquet** wooden floor
le **partage** sharing, division
partager (**g** > **ge/a, o**) to share
le **parti** (political) party
participer à qqch to participate in
la **partie** part; **faire partie de** to be a part of
partir *(irreg.)* to leave
partout everywhere; **partout ailleurs** everywhere else
parvenir à to manage to, succeed in
le **pas** step
le **passage** passing
passant busy (of a street, etc.)
le **passé** past
le **passeport** passport
passer to pass; spend (time); **se passer** to happen; **se passer de** to do without
passer l'aspirateur to run the vacuum cleaner
passer le permis de conduire take one's driving test
passer prendre qqn to go by to pick someone up
passer son temps à to spend one's time doing
passer une commande to place an order
passionnant thrilling, exciting
se **passionner (pour)** to get excited (about)
la **pastille** tablet, pill
la **patience** patience
le **patin** skate

le **patron (la patronne)** boss
la **patronne** patron saint
pauvre poor
la **pauvreté** poverty
payant that charges admission
payer (y > i/e) to pay; **payer qqch** to pay for something
le **pays** country, nation
le **paysage** landscape, scenery
la **peau** skin
la **pêche** peach; fishing
la **pédagogie** pedagogy, education
se **peigner** to comb one's hair
peindre *(irreg.)* to paint
la **peine** trouble, bother; **ce n'est pas la peine** it's not worthwhile; **peine de mort** death penalty
le **peintre** painter
la **peinture** painting
peler (e > è/e) to peel
le **pèlerinage** pilgrimage
penché leaning, bending
se **pencher** to lean, bend
la **penderie** closet, walk-in closet
pendre to hang
le **pendule** pendulum
pénétrer (é > è/e) to penetrate
la **péniche** barge
la **pensée** thought
penser to think; **penser à** to think of; **penser de qqch** to have an opinion about something; **penser faire qqch** to intend to do something
le **penseur** thinker
pensif(-ve) pensive
la **percée** opening, breakthrough
perdre to lose; **perdre son temps** to waste one's time; **se perdre** to get lost
le **père** father
permettre (à qqn de faire qqch) *(like* ***mettre****)* to allow (someone to do something)
le **permis (de conduire)** driver's license
les **persécutions** persecutions
persistant persistent
le **personnage** character (literary)
personne no one, nobody
la **personne** person
persuader qqn de to persuade someone to
peser (e > è/e) to weigh
la **peste** plague
la **pétanque** traditional game resembling bowling
petit small
le **petit ami** boyfriend
le **petit déjeuner** breakfast
le **petit rouge** glass of red wine
le **petit-fils** grandson
la **petite amie** girlfriend
la **petite-fille** granddaughter
les **petits pois** *(masc. pl.)* peas
le **pétrin** fix, jam
pétrochimique petrochemical
le **pétrole** oil
peu little, few; not very; **peu à peu** little by little; **peu de** few, little, not much
le **peuple** people, nation
peupler to populate, people
le **peuplier** poplar tree
la **peur** fear
pharmaceutique pharmaceutical
le **pharmacien (la pharmacienne)** pharmacist
la **philo** philosophy *(school slang)*
le **philosophe (la philosophe)** philosopher
la **photo(graphie)** photo(graph)
photographier to photograph
le **physicien (la physicienne)** physicist
la **physique** physics
le **piano** piano
le **pic** peak
la **pièce** room (house); play (theater); coin; **pièce de théâtre** play (theater)
le **pied** foot; **à pied** on foot
la **pierre** stone
pieux(-se) pious
pile sharp, on the dot (time)
le **pillage** pillage, robbery
la **pillule** pill
le **pilote (la pilote)** pilot
la **piqûre** injection
pire worse *(adj.)*; **le pire** the worst
pis worse *(adv.)*
la **piscine** swimming pool
la **piste** clue
le **placard** cupboard
place: faire place à to give way to
le **placement** placement; investment
placer (c > ç/a, o) to place; invest
la **plage** beach
plaindre *(like* ***craindre****)* to pity; **se plaindre (de)** to complain (about)
la **plaine** plain
plaire (à qqn) *(irreg.)* to please (someone)
le **plaisir** pleasure
le **plan** plan; street map; **sur le plan de** in the area, field of
le **plancher** floor
planter to plant
le **plat** dish
plat flat
le **plateau** plain
plein (de) full (of)
pleurer to cry
pleureur(-se) weepy
pleuvoir *(irreg.)* to rain; **il pleut** it's raining
plier la tente to fold up the tent
le **plombier** plumber
plonger (g > ge/a, o) to dive, plunge
la **pluie** rain
la **plupart de** most of
le **pluriel** plural
plus (de) more; **ne . . . plus** no more, not anymore
plutôt rather
pluvieux(-se) rainy

le **pneu** tire; **pneu crevé** flat tire
la **poêle** frying pan
le **poème** poem
la **poésie** poetry
le **poète** poet
le **point** point, dot
la **pointe** point, forefront
la **poire** pear
le **poisson** fish; **poisson d'avril** April fool
la **poitrine** chest
le **pôle** pole
poli polite
policier(-ère) police, detective *(adj.)*
la **politesse** politeness
la **politique** policy; politics
politique political
la **pomme** apple
la **pomme de terre** potato
populaire popular, of the people, working-class
la **population** population
le **porc** pork
la **porcelaine** china
le **port** port; wearing
la **porte** door
le **porte-parole** spokesperson
la **portée** scope, repercussion
le **portefeuille** wallet
porter to carry, bear; wear; **se porter candidat** to run for office
le **portrait** portrait
le **portraitiste** portrait painter
poser to set down, lay down; **poser une question** to ask a question
posséder (**é > è/e**) to possess
la **possession** possession
la **poste** mail, postal service
le **poste** job; radio or TV set
poster to mail
le **potager** vegetable garden
la **poterie** pottery
la **poubelle** trash can, wastebasket
le **poulet** chicken
la **poupée** doll
pour que so that, in order that
le **pourboire** tip (restaurant)
le **pourcentage** percentage
les **pourparlers** *(masc. pl.)* talks, discussions
poursuivre *(like* ***suivre****)* to pursue, continue
pourvu que provided that, as long as
pousser to grow; to push; **pousser qqn à faire qqch** to talk someone into doing something
pouvoir to be able; **il se peut que** it's possible that
le **pouvoir** power
pratiquant observant, religious
pratique practical
pratiquer to practice
le **pré** meadow
précédemment previously
prêcher to preach
précis precise
précisément precisely
préconiser to favor, advocate
le **précurseur** precursor
la **prédilection** preference; **de prédilection** favorite
prédire to predict
préférer (**é > è/e**) to prefer
le **préjugé** prejudice
premier(-ère) first
prendre to take; to have (with names of meals and with food and drink)
prendre de l'essence to get (buy) gasoline
prendre du poids to put on weight
prendre froid, prendre un rhume to catch cold
prendre part à qqch to take part in, collaborate in
prendre place to have a seat
prendre plaisir à to take pleasure in
prendre un bain, une douche to take a bath, shower
prendre: être pris de panique to be overcome by panic
se **préoccuper** to worry
le **préparatif** preparation
préparé à prepared to
préparer to prepare; **se préparer à** to get ready to
près de near
présenter to present; **présenter une demande d'emploi** to submit a job application
préserver to preserve
la **présidence** presidency
le **président (la présidente)** president
présidentiel(le) presidential
presque almost
pressé in a hurry
la **presse** press
la **presse typographique** printing press
se **presser de** to hurry, rush to
le **pressing** dry cleaner's
la **pression** pressure
prestigieux(-se) prestigious
prêt (à) ready (to)
le **prêt-à-porter** ready-to-wear clothing
prétendre to claim
prêter to lend; **prêter serment** to swear an oath
le **prétexte** pretext, excuse
le **prêtre** priest
prévu scheduled
prier qqn de to beg someone to
primaire primary, elementary
le **prince** prince
la **princesse** princess
le **printemps** spring
la **priorité** priority
la **prise** taking, capture
privé de deprived of
se **priver de** to deprive oneself of
privilégié privileged
le **problème** problem
le **procédé** process, procedure
prochain next
proche close, near

le **producteur (la productrice)** producer
la **production** production
produire *(like construire)* to produce
le **produit** product
le **professeur** teacher
professionnel(le) professional, vocational
le **profil** profile
profiter de to take advantage of
profond deep
la **programmation** programming
le **programme d'action** plan of action
le **programme d'études** curriculum
le **programmeur (la programmeuse)** programmer
le **progrès** progress
le **projet** project, plan
projeter (t > tt/e) to project
la **promenade** walk; ride
promener to take for a walk; **se promener** to go for a walk
le **promeneur (la promeneuse)** stroller, walker
la **promesse** promise
prometteur(-se) promising
promettre *(like mettre)* to promise
promouvoir to promote
promu promoted
prononcer (c > ç/a, o) to pronounce
proposer (à qqn de faire qqch) to suggest (to someone to do something)
se **proposer de** to set out, mean, intend to
la **proposition** clause
propre clean; one's own
le **propriétaire (la propriétaire)** owner
prospère prosperous
le **protectorat** protectorate
protéger (**g > ge/a, o; é > è** *as in* **espérer**) to protect
protestant Protestant
la **prouesse** prowess
la **province** province
prudemment carefully
la **prudence** caution
public (publique) public
publier to publish
puiser to fish for, fish out; take from (literary passage)
la **puissance** power
puissant powerful
le **pull(-over)** sweater
le **pupitre** student's school desk
le **pyjama** pajamas

le **quai** platform (train station)
qualifié qualified, skilled
la **qualité** quality
quand when
quant à as for
le **quart** fourth, quarter
le **quartier** neighborhood
québécois from Quebec
quelconque any; any old; ordinary
quelque: et quelques a little past (clock time)
quelqu'un someone, somebody
quelque chose something
quelque part somewhere
quelque peu a bit, a little
quelquefois sometimes
quelques-un(e)s some
la **querelle** quarrel, argument
la **quiche** quiche
quitte à even if it means
quoi que ce soit anything
quoique although
quotidien(ne) daily
le **quotidien** daily newspaper

le **rabais** price reduction, sale price
racheter (e > è/e) to buy back, redeem
raconter to tell, narrate
le **radeau** raft
le **raffinement** refinement
raffiner to refine
la **raffinerie** refinery
la **rafle** roundup
la **rage** rabies
rager to fume, be fuming (with anger)
le **rail** rail
la **raison** reason
le **raisonnement** reasoning
se **rallier à** to rally to
ramasser to pick up
ramener (e > è/e) to bring (someone) back
ramper to creep
la **randonnée** hike
le **rang** rank
ranger (g > ge/a, o) to put away; **se ranger** to unite, side with
râper to grate
rapide fast
rappeler (l > ll/e) to call back; **se rappeler** to recall, remember
le **rapport** relationship; report
rapporter to bring back, report
le **rapprochement** reconciliation
la **raquette** racket (for tennis, etc.)
rarement rarely, seldom
se **raser** to shave
rassembler to gather
rassurer to reassure
le **rationnement** rationing
le **ravage: faire des ravages** to ravage, devastate
ravager (g > ge/a, o) to ravage
ravi (de) delighted (to)
ravoir to get back
rayer (y > i/e) to cross out
le **rayon** section of a store, department; ray
la **rayonne** rayon
rayonner to shine forth
la **réaction** reaction

réagir to react
la réalité reality
le rebelle rebel
récemment recently
la réception reception
recevoir (irreg.) to receive
le réchaud hot plate
les recherches (fem. pl.) research
le récit story, recounting
le récital recital
la récolte harvest
recommander to recommend
récompenser to reward
reconnaître (like connaître) to recognize
recueillir (like cueillir) to gather
récurer to scour
le recyclage recycling
la rédaction writing; drafting, drawing up
rédiger (g > ge/a, o) to draft, write
redouter de to dread
réduire (like construire) to reduce
réel(le) real
refaire to redo
le référendum referendum
réfléchir (à) to think (about), reflect (on)
le reflet reflection
refléter (like espérer) to reflect
la réflexion reflection, thought
le réfugié (la réfugiée) refugee
refuser (de) to refuse (to)
regarder to look at
le régime diet; regime, system of government
la région region
régional regional
la règle rule, ruler; être en règle to be in order
régler la note (like espérer) to pay the bill, settle the account
le règne reign
régner (like espérer) to reign
regorger de (g > ge/a, o) to be bursting with
regretter to be sorry
regrouper to group together
réhabiliter to rehabilitate
la reine queen
rejeter (t > tt/e) to reject
rejoindre (like craindre) to rejoin
se réjouir to rejoice
la relâche respite, rest
relatif(-ve) relative (adj.)
relevé spicy
relever (e > è/e) to bring out (flavor); to spice up; pick up; derive from
le relief contours of the land; relief (art); en relief raised; mettre en relief to emphasize, make stand out
relier to link, connect, tie together
religieux(-se) religious
remarquer to notice
remédier à to fix, remedy
remercier to thank
remettre (like mettre) to postpone; se remettre de to recover from
remonter à to go back to, be traced back to
le remplacement replacement
remplacer (c > ç/a, o) to replace
remplir to fill; se remplir de to become filled with
la renaissance Renaissance
rencontrer to meet (by chance); se rencontrer to meet, run into each other
rendre to give back
renforcer (c > ç/a, o) to strengthen
la renne reindeer
la renommée renown
renoncer à (c > ç/a, o) to resign, quit
le renouveau renewal
renouveler (l > ll/e) to renew
renseigner to inform; se renseigner sur to get information about
rentrer to return, go back; to bring inside
renverser to knock over, overturn, upset
renvoyer (y > i/e) to send back, dismiss
répandre to spread; se répandre to spread
répartir to divide
repartir (like partir) to go away again
le repas meal
la repasseuse (female) ironer
repeindre (like peindre) to repaint
se repentir de to regret
répéter (like espérer) to repeat
le répondeur answering machine
répondre à to answer
la réponse answer
le repos rest
se reposer to rest
repousser to push back
reprendre to start again
le représentant (la représentante) representative; représentant de commerce traveling salesperson
la reprise resumption, repeat; à plusieurs reprises several times
reprocher à qqn de to reproach someone for
la république republic
la réputation reputation
le réseau network
se résigner à to resign oneself to
résolu à resolved to
résoudre to solve; résoudre de to resolve to; se résoudre à to resolve to
respecter to respect
la respiration breathing
responsable de responsible for
ressembler à to look like; se ressembler to look alike
la ressource resource
le restaurant restaurant
restaurer to restore
restituer to return, give back to an owner
résumer to summarize
retapisser to repaper

retarder to be slow (of a watch)
retenir *(like **tenir**)* to retain, hold back
le **retentissement** stir, repercussion
retourner to return, come back, go back
la **retraite** retreat; **battre la retraite** to beat a retreat
retrouver to meet (by appointment)
la **réunion** meeting
se **réunir** to get together
réussir (à) to succeed (in)
la **réussite** success
le **rêve** dream
réveiller to wake up; **se réveiller** to wake up
le **réveillon** midnight dinner
révéler *(like **espérer**)* to reveal
le **revendeur (la revendeuse)** dealer
la **revendication** demand
revenir *(like **venir**)* to return
rêver to dream
réviser to review
la **révolte** rebellion, revolt
la **révolution** revolution
révoquer to revoke
la **revue** magazine
le **rez-de-chaussée** ground floor
le **rhume** cold (illness)
riche rich
la **richesse** richness
le **rien** trifle; **un rien de** a dash of, hint of; **un rien du tout** a nothing, an insignificant person; **en un rien de temps** in no time at all
rien nothing; **rien moins que** + *adj.* really *(adj.)*; **rien que cinq minutes** just five minutes
rien: Ça ne fait rien. It doesn't matter. That's OK. (Answer to *Pardon.*)
rien: Comme si de rien n'était. As if nothing had happened.
rien: n'avoir rien à voir avec to have nothing to do with
rien: pour rien for no particular reason
rien: pour rien au monde not for anything in the world
rien: rien qu'à le voir just by looking at him
rien: Si cela ne vous fait rien. If you don't mind.
rire (de) to laugh (at)
le **rire** laughter
risquer de to risk, run the risk of
le **rival (la rivale)** rival
rivaliser avec to rival
la **rive** river bank
le **riz** rice
la **robe** dress
le **roi** king
le **rôle** role; **jouer un rôle** to play a role
romain Roman; Romanesque
roman deriving from the Romans; Romanesque
le **roman** novel
le **romancier (la romancière)** novelist
romaniser to Romanize, Latinize
le **romantisme** romanticism
rompre (avec) to break off (with)
le **rosbif** roast beef
la **rose** rose
le **rosier** rosebush
rouge red; **voir rouge** to see red, be furious; **le poisson rouge** goldfish
rougir (de) to blush (at), be ashamed of
roumain Romanian
roussir to redden
routier(-ère) pertaining to roads
rouvrir *(like **ouvrir**)* to reopen
roux(-sse) red-headed
le **royaume** kingdom
la **rubrique** heading
rude rough
la **rue** street; **rue piétonne** street closed to traffic
la **ruine** ruin
rupestre cave *(adj.)*
la **rupture** break
russe Russian

le **sac** bag; **sac à dos** backpack; **sac à main** handbag; **sac de couchage** sleeping bag
sacrer to crown
sage well-behaved
le **saint (la sainte)** saint
la **Saint-Sylvestre** New Year's Eve
la **Sainte Vierge** Holy Virgin Mary
la **salade** lettuce; salad; **salade niçoise** mixed Mediterranean salad
le **salaire** salary
sale dirty; awful
salir to dirty; **se salir** to get dirty
la **salle à manger** dining room
la **salle de concert** concert hall
la **salle de permanence** study hall
le **salon** living room; salon
saluer to greet
samedi Saturday
les **sandales** *(fem. pl.)* sandals
sanglant bloody
le **sanglot** sob
sangloter to sob
sans que without
les **sans-emploi** *(masc. pl.)* the unemployed
le **sans-gêne** inconsiderate person
la **santé** health
le **sapin** fir tree
satisfait de satisfied to
la **saucisse** sausage
le **saucisson** sausage, salami
le **saumon** salmon
saumon *(invar.)* salmon-colored
sauvage wild
la **saveur** flavor
le **savoir** knowledge
savoir faire qqch to know how to
le **scandale** scandal
scandaliser to scandalize
le **scepticisme** scepticism

scolaire pertaining to school
la **scolarité** schooling
la **scolastique** scholasticism (medieval philosophy)
sculpter to sculpt
le **sculpteur** sculptor
la **séance** showing (film)
sec (sèche) dry; **parler/répondre sec** to speak/answer curtly
sécessionniste secessionist, separatist
sécher *(like **espérer**)* to dry; **se sécher les cheveux** to dry one's hair; **sécher un cours** to cut class
secouer to shake
secret(-ète) secretive
le **secret** secret
le **secrétaire (la secrétaire)** secretary
le **secteur** sector
la **sécurité personnelle** personal safety
la **sédentarisation** settling process; abandonment of nomadic life
le **séjour** living room; stay
la **semaine des quatre jeudis** a month of Sundays
semaine: en semaine during the week
semer (**e** > **è/e**) to sow
la **semoule** semolina
le **sénateur** senator
le **sens** meaning, sense
sensationnel(le) great, terrific
la **sensibilisation** sensitizing
sensibiliser to sensitize
la **sensibilité** sensitivity
le **sentiment** feeling
sentir *(irreg.)* to feel; **se sentir** to feel
séparer to separate
septembre September
sérieux(-se) serious
le **serment** oath
la **serviette** napkin; towel; briefcase
servir *(irreg.)* to serve; **servir à qqn** to be useful to someone; **se servir de** to use
le **seuil** threshold
sévir to rage, be rampant
le **shopping** shopping
le **siècle** century
le **siège** headquarters, main office (of an organization); siege; **lever le siège** to lift the siege
le **sien (la sienne, les siens, les siennes)** his, hers, its; **faire des siennes** to be up to one's old tricks
signaler to notify, inform, point out
signer to sign
signifier to signify, mean
simple simple; ordinary
sincère sincere
le **sirop** syrup; **sirop pour la toux** cough syrup
le **site** site, location
la **situation** situation
situer to locate; **se situer** to be located
le **skieur (la skieuse)** skier
le **slogan** slogan
le **socialisme** socialism
la **société** society
la **sœur (aînée/cadette)** (older/younger) sister
le **sofa** couch, sofa
la **soie** silk
soigné formal (style)
se **soigner** to take care of oneself
soigneux(-se) careful
le **soir** evening
la **soirée** evening
le **solde** sale item, reduced item; **en solde** on sale
le **soleil** sun
la **solitude** loneliness
sombrer to sink, wallow
le **sommet** summit, pinnacle
somptueux(-se) sumptuous
songer à to be thinking of
sonner to ring, ring the doorbell; to sound
la **sonnette** doorbell
le **sort** fate
la **sorte** kind, sort
sorti de coming from
la **sortie** date (going out with someone); exit
sortir *(irreg.)* to go, come out; to bring, take out
sot(te) foolish
la **sottise** nonsense
le **sou** cent (old coin); **être sans le sou** to be broke
le **souci** care, concern
se **soucier de** to worry, be concerned about
soucieux(-se) de concerned with
souffrir *(irreg.)* to suffer
le **souhait** wish, desire
souhaiter que to wish
le **soulèvement** uprising, rebellion
soumettre *(like **mettre**)* to subjugate
soupçonner to suspect
la **soupe** soup
soupirer to sigh
la **source** source; **prendre sa source** to have its source (of a river)
sourire to smile
la **souris** mouse
sous under; **sous la tente** in the tent
le **sous-sol** basement
soutenir *(like **tenir**)* to support, hold up
le **soutien** support
le **souvenir** memory, remembrance; souvenir
se **souvenir de** to remember
souvent often
le **souverain (la souveraine)** sovereign
la **souveraineté** sovereignty
spatial space *(adj.)*
spécial special
la **spécialisation** specialty; major, main field of study
le **spectacle** show
spectaculaire spectacular
splendide splendid
le **sport** sport
sportif(-ve) athletic; pertaining to sport
le **stade** stadium
la **station de ski** ski resort

la **station-service** gas station
la **station thermale** hot springs resort
le **statut** status, statute
le **store** venetian blind
la **stratégie** strategy
le **stylo** pen
subir to undergo
suburbain suburban
la **subvention** subsidy
subventionner to subsidize
succéder à *(like* ***espérer****)* to succeed, follow
le **succès** success
la **succursale** branch (of a store)
le **sucre** sugar
le **sud** south
suffire to be enough; **il suffit** it's enough/ sufficient, it suffices; **il suffit de** all you have to do is
suggérer à qqn de (**é** > **è**/**e**) to suggest to someone to
se **suicider** to commit suicide
le **Suisse (la Suisse)** Swiss person
la **suite** aftermath; continuation
suite: à la suite de following
suivant following
suivre *(irreg.)* to follow
suivre l'actualité to keep up with the news
suivre un cours to take a course
suivre un régime to be on a diet
le **sujet** subject
superbe superb, great
la **superficie** surface, area
supérieur higher
le **supermarché** supermarket
supporter to bear, stand
sur on; about; close to, approximately
la **(sur)boum** party
sûr (de) sure (to)
sur le moment at first
sur les 3 heures at about three o'clock
sur une période de deux ans over a period of two years
sur: un jour sur deux every other day
la **surface** surface
surprenant surprising
surprendre *(like* ***prendre****)* to surprise
surpris de surprised at, by
la **surprise** surprise
survivre to survive
sympathique pleasant, nice
syndicaliste union *(adj.)*
le **syntagme** phrase

la **table: bonne table** good eating, good food
le **tableau** picture, painting
la **tache** spot, dot
la **tâche** task
tâcher de to try to
le **tact** tact
tactile pertaining to the sense of touch
la **taille** size
le **tailleur** suit (woman's)
se **taire** *(like* ***plaire****)* to keep quiet
le **talent** talent
tant (de) so much, many
la **tante** aunt
se **tapir** to lurk, hide, crouch
le **tapis** carpet
tard late
tarder à to delay (doing something)
le **taureau** bull
technique technical
la **technologie** technology
le **tee-shirt** T-shirt
tel(le)(s) que such as
le **télécopieur** fax machine
le **télégramme** telegram
téléphoner (à qqn) to telephone (someone)
la **télévision, la télé** television, TV
le **témoignage** testimony, proof
le **témoin** witness
la **température** temperature
la **tempête** storm
le **temple** temple
temporel(le) temporal, earthly
le **temps** time, weather; **de temps en temps** from time to time
la **tendance** tendency
tendre à to tend to
tenir à *(irreg.)* to insist on
la **tente** tent
tenter de to try to
la **terminale** last year of studies at a *lycée*
le **terrain** terrain; **perdre du terrain** to lose ground
le **terrain de camping** campsite, campground
le **terrain de sports** playing field
la **terrasse** outside seating of a café; terrace
la **Terre-Neuve** Newfoundland
la **terreur** terror
terrible terrible; great, tremendous
le **territoire** territory
la **tête** head; **en tête de** at the head of
le **texte** text
le **thé** tea
le **théâtre** theater
le **thème** subject, topic, theme
le **théoricien (la théoricienne)** theoretician
thermal thermal, pertaining to hot springs
la **thermochimie** thermochemistry
le **thon** tuna
le **tien (la tienne, les tiens, les tiennes)** yours
le **tiers** third
le **timbre** postage stamp
timide shy
le **tirage** drawing (lottery); circulation (press)
tirer to draw, pull, take
le **tissage** weaving
tisser to weave
le **tissu** tissue (body); cloth

la **toile** canvas
la **toile d'araignée** spiderweb, cobweb
les **toilettes** *(fem. pl.)* bathroom
la **tolérance** tolerance
la **tombe** grave
le **tombeau** tomb
tomber to fall; **tomber amoureux(-se) de** to fall in love with; **tomber malade** to get sick
le **ton** tone
tonner to thunder
la **tonnerre** thunder
la **toponymie** place names
tordre to twist
tôt early
totalitaire totalitarian
touchant touching
la **touche** touch; small amount
toujours always
la **tour** tower
le **tour** tour, trip
le **tourisme** tourism
touristique tourist *(adj.)*
tourmenter to torment
le **tournant** turning point
la **tournée** tour (performers)
tourner autour de to revolve around
tous les deux both
tous les trois mois every three months
la **Toussaint** All Saints' Day
tousser to cough
tout à l'heure a short while ago; very soon
tout au plus at the very most
tout de suite immediately
tout le monde everyone
la **toux** cough
la **toxine** toxin
tracasser to worry, vex
le **tracé** layout, route
traditionnel(le) traditional
traduire *(like **construire**)* to translate
la **tragédie** tragedy
trahir to betray
la **trahison** treason
traîner to be lying around
le **trait** characteristic
le **traité** treaty; treatise
le **traitement** treatment; processing; **traitement de données** data processing; **traitement de texte** word processing
traiter to deal with, write about
la **tranche** slice
la **tranquillité** calm, tranquillity
la **transformation** transformation
transformer to transform
se **transformer en** to become, change into
le **transformisme** transformism, evolution
transmettre *(like **mettre**)* to transmit
la **transplantation** transplant
le **transport** transportation
le **travail** work
travailler to work
le **travailleur (la travailleuse)** worker
travailleur(-se) hard-working
les **travaux** *(masc. pl.)* repairs, roadwork
traverser to cross
le **tremblement de terre** earthquake
trembler to shake, tremble
la **trentaine** about thirty
la **trêve** truce; **trêve de** enough, stop your . . .
la **tribu** tribe
le **tribunal** court
tricolore three-colored (refers to French flag)
triomphal triumphal
triompher to triumph
triste sad
la **tristesse** sadness
tromper to deceive; **se tromper** to make a mistake
trompeur(-se) deceptive
le **trône** throne
trop de too much, too many; **de trop** in the way
le **trottoir** sidewalk
le **trou** hole
le **trouble-fête** party pooper
les **troupes** *(fem. pl.)* troops
trouver to find; **se trouver** to be located
la **turbine** turbine
turc (turque) Turkish
tutoyer (y > i/e) to use the *tu* form to address someone
le **tuyau** pipe
le **type** type, kind, sort; guy *(slang)*

uni close (relationship)
l' **union** *(fem.)* union
l' **unité** *(fem.)* unity; **unité de disque** disk drive
l' **univers** *(masc.)* universe
universitaire university *(adj.)*
urbain urban, city
l' **urbanisme** *(masc.)* city planning
urgent urgent
l' **usage** *(masc.)* use
l' **usine** *(fem.)* factory
utile useful
utiliser to use, utilize

les **vacances** *(fem. pl.)* vacation
le **vacancier (la vacancière)** vacationer
le **vaccin** vaccine
la **vache** cow
vachement very *(slang)*
vaincre *(irreg.)* to conquer
le **vainqueur** victor
la **vaisselle** dishes
la **valise** suitcase
la **vallée** valley
valoir *(irreg.)* to be worth; **valoir qqch à qqn** to earn somebody something
la **valse** waltz

la **vantardise** boasting
se **vanter de** to boast of
varié varied
la **variété** variety
la **vedette** movie star
le **véhicule** vehicle
la **veille** the evening before
veiller à to see to, attend to
le **vélo** bike
le **vendeur (la vendeuse)** salesperson
vendre to sell; **vendre au kilo, au mètre** to sell by the kilogram, meter
vendredi Friday
venir *(irreg.)* to come; **venir de** to have just done something
la **venue** coming
le **verglas** ice on the road
vérifier to check
la **vérité** truth
le **verre** glass
vers toward
le **vers** verse
vert green *(adj.)*
le **vertige** dizziness
vertigineux(-se) dizzy
la **veste** jacket, sports jacket
le **vêtement** article of clothing
le **veuf (la veuve)** widow
la **viande** meat
la **victime** victim
vide empty
la **vie** life
vieux (vieil, vieille) old
vif(-ve) lively
la **vigne** vine
le **vignoble** vineyard
le **village** village
le **vin** wine
la **vingtaine** about twenty
violent violent
violet(te) purple, violet
viser à to aim at, aim to
la **visite** visit; **rendre visite à** to visit someone
le **visiteur (la visiteuse)** visitor
la **vitamine** vitamin
vite quickly, fast
la **vitesse** speed
viticole wine producing
le **vitrail** stained-glass window
la **vitrine** store window
la **vivacité** liveliness, brightness
vivre *(irreg.)* to live; **vivre de qqch** to live off something
les **vivres** *(masc. pl.)* foodstuffs
le **vocabulaire** vocabulary
la **voie** way, road, track; **voie ferrée** railroad track
la **voile** sail
le **voile** veil
voir to see; **voir trente-six chandelles** to see stars
le **voisin (la voisine)** neighbor
la **voiture** car
la **voix** voice; vote
le **vol** theft; **vol à main armée** armed robbery
voler qqch à qqn to steal something from someone
la **volonté** will
volontiers gladly
le **vôtre (la vôtre, les vôtres)** yours
vouloir *(irreg.)* to want
vouvoyer (y > i/e) to use the *vous* form to address someone
le **voyage** trip
voyager (g > ge/a, o) to travel
voyant showy, gaudy
vrai real, true
la **vue** sight; **bien en vue** prominent

le **yaourt** yogurt

le **zéro** zero; **zéro de conduite** failing grade in conduct

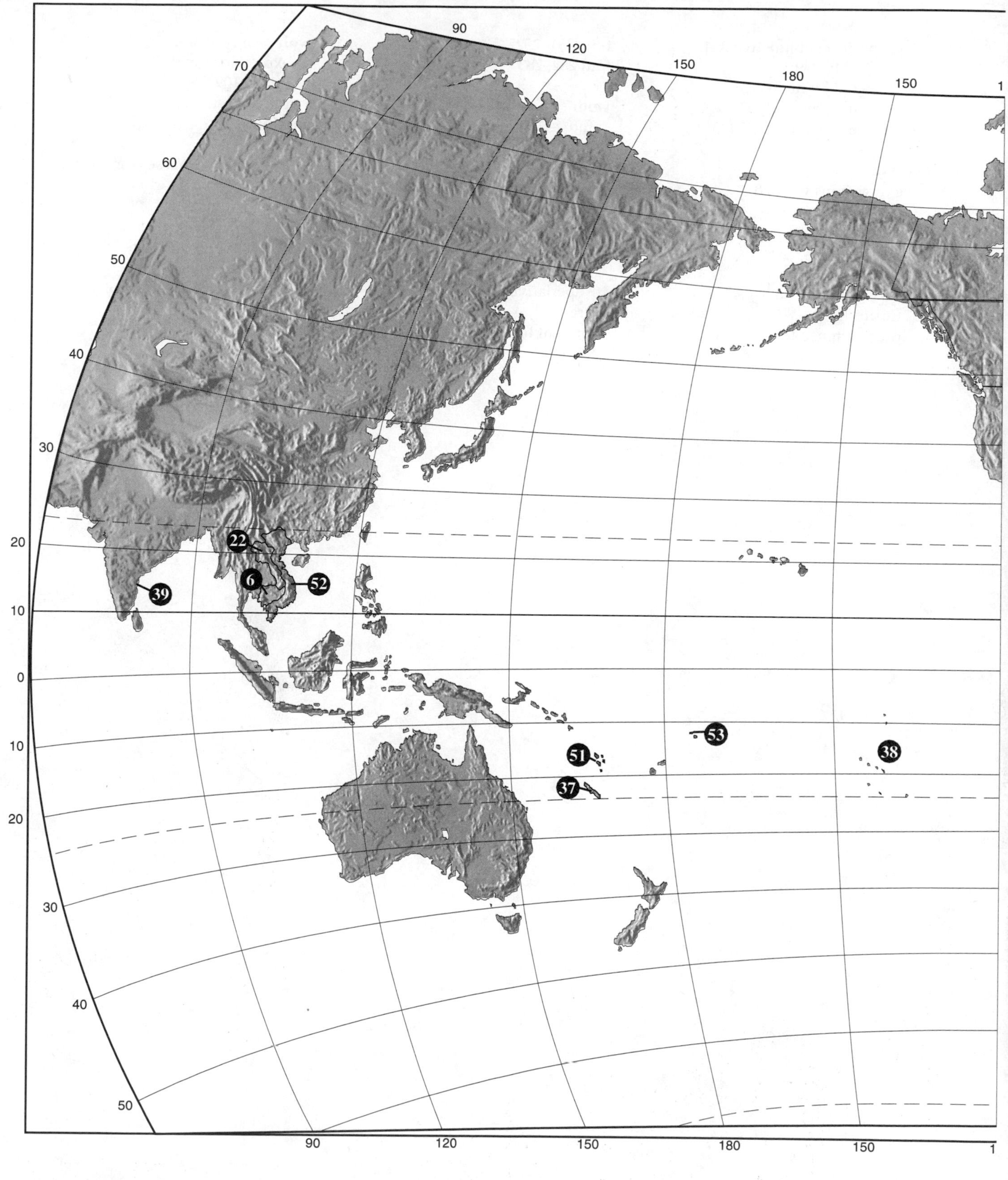

Le Monde francophone

1. Algérie
2. Belgique
3. Bénin
4. Burkina Faso
5. Burundi
6. Cambodge
7. Cameroun
8. Canada
9. République Centrafricaine
10. Comores
11. Congo
12. Côte-d'Ivoire
13. Dominique
14. Djibouti
15. Égypte
16. France
17. Gabon
18. Guadeloupe
19. Guyane française
20. Guinée
21. Haïti
22. Laos
23. Liban
24. Louisiane
25. Luxembourg
26. Madagascar
27. Mali

INDEX

show *(verb)* montrer
sick malade
sister la sœur
sitting assis
sleep *(verb)* dormir
sleep in faire la grasse matinée
slowly lentement
snow *(noun)* la neige
so many tant de
soccer le football
someone quelqu'un
somewhere quelque part
song la chanson
soup la soupe
speak parler
spend (time) passer
spring le printemps
stairs l'escalier *(masc.)*
stand in line faire la queue
station la gare
steal from voler à
store le magasin
street la rue
strive s'efforcer de
student l'étudiant (l'étudiante)
study étudier
suffer souffrir
suit le costume
supporting oneself appuyé
sure sûr
surprising surprenant, étonnant

take prendre
take a course suivre un cours
take a walk faire une promenade
take a trip faire un voyage
tape la cassette
taste *(verb)* essayer
tea le thé
teach enseigner
teacher le professeur
television la télévision, la télé
test l'examen *(masc.)*
therefore donc
think about penser à
time le temps; l'heure *(fem.)*
tire le pneu
today aujourd'hui
tomorrow demain
too (also) aussi
toward vers
town la ville; **in town** en ville
track la piste
train le train
tricks: be up to one's old tricks faire des siennes
trip le voyage
trouble: take the trouble to se donner la peine de
truck le camion
true vrai
trust se fier à
try to essayer de, tenter de, chercher à, tâcher de
turn; to be someone's turn être à qqn

under sous
understand comprendre
unpleasant antipathique
until jusqu'à
upstairs en haut
use employer

vacation les vacances *(fem. pl.)*; **on vacation** en vacances
vegetable le légume
voice la voix
vote la voix

waiter le garçon, le serveur
walk la promenade
wall le mur
want vouloir
war la guerre
wary: be wary of se méfier de
waste perdre
watch la montre
weather le temps; **the weather is nice** il fait beau
Wednesday mercredi
week la semaine
when quand
wife la femme
wind le vent
window la fenêtre
wine le vin
wonder *(verb)* se demander
word le mot
work *(verb)* travailler; *(noun)* le travail
worry s'inquiéter de, se soucier de

year l'an *(masc.)*, l'année *(fem.)*
yell at gronder, engueuler
yesterday hier

long long(ue)
look at regarder
look for chercher
lost: get lost se perdre
lurking tapi
lying down couché

make faire
man l'homme *(masc.)*
many beaucoup (de)
March mars
marketplace le marché
match le match
math les mathématiques *(fem. pl.)*, les maths
mediocre quelconque
member le membre
meter le mètre
mill le moulin
mind: to make up one's mind se décider à
money l'argent *(masc.)*
morning le matin
most of la plupart de
mother la mère
mountain la montagne
movies le cinéma

name le nom
near près de
need avoir besoin de
neighborhood le quartier
neither, not . . . either ni . . . non plus
neither . . . nor . . . ni . . . ni . . .
nestling blotti
never ne . . . jamais
new neuf(-ve)
newspaper le journal (les journaux)
next prochain
nice sympathique

old vieux (vieil, vieille)
old man le vieillard
on time à l'heure
once une fois
only ne . . . que, seulement
operate (on) opérer
other autre
over there là-bas
overwhelmed with accablé de
own (one's own) propre

package le paquet
paint *(verb)* peindre
painter le peintre
pajamas le pyjama
park le parc
participate in participer à
pastry la pâtisserie
pastry cook le pâtissier (la pâtissière)
people les gens
phone téléphoner
pick up prendre
picture le tableau
plan le projet, le plan
plan to compter
play *(verb)* jouer
pollution la pollution
pound la livre
powerful puissant
prefer préférer
produce produire
promise *(verb)* promettre

question la question
quickly vite

rain: it rains il pleut; **to rain** pleuvoir
read lire
realize se rendre compte de
recognize reconnaître
record: off the record à titre confidentiel
red rouge
refrain from s'empêcher de
remember se souvenir de
remorse le remords
repeat répéter
responsible responsable
restaurant le restaurant
resting on one's elbows accoudé
right (corrrect) bon(ne)
right away tout de suite
risk *(verb)* risquer de
role le rôle; **play a role** jouer un rôle
roof le toit
run over renverser

sadness la tristesse
Saturday samedi
say dire; **be said** se dire
school *(adj.)* scolaire; *(noun)* l'école *(fem.)*
seat la place
secret le secret
see voir
see to veiller à
seldom rarement
sell vendre
send for faire venir
serious sérieux(-se)
serve servir
set out se mettre en route
set the table mettre la table
sharp pile; **six o'clock sharp** six heures pile
shopping: do the shopping faire le marché
short court

door la porte
downstairs en bas; **go downstairs** descendre
during pendant

early riser matinal
early: be early être en avance
eat manger
ecology l'écologie
encourage encourager
end la fin
English anglais
enough assez (de)
every tous/toutes les
everyone tout le monde
everywhere partout
explain expliquer

family la famille
fear la peur
fed up: be fed up with avoir assez de, en avoir marre de
feel like avoir envie de
fever la fièvre
film le film
find trouver
finger le doigt
finish finir, achever, terminer
fire *(verb)* renvoyer
floor (story) l'étage *(masc.)*
for *(with time expressions)* depuis
forget oublier
formerly auparavant
free libre
French français
Friday vendredi
friend l'ami (l'amie)
friendly gentil(le)
frightening effrayant

generosity la générosité
get recevoir; avoir
get to arriver à
get up se lever
girl la (jeune) fille
give donner
go aller
go away s'en aller
go back rentrer
go by passer
go downstairs descendre
go in entrer
go out sortir
go up monter
go: to be going to aller + *infinitive*
good bon(ne)
good in calé en
grade *(school)* la note
gram le gramme
green vert

hair les cheveux *(masc. pl.)*
half la moitié
hanging pendu
happy heureux(-se); content
hard (difficult) difficile
harmful: to be harmful faire mal
hate la haine
have avoir; *(food or drink)* prendre
health la santé
heart: put one's heart into it mettre du sien
help *(verb)* aider
here ici
history l'histoire *(fem.)*
homework les devoirs *(masc. pl.)*
hotel l'hôtel *(masc.)*
hour l'heure *(fem.)*
house la maison
how much combien

ice cream la glace
idea l'idée *(fem.)*
identity l'identité *(fem.)*
important important
improbable peu probable
in spite of malgré
incessant sans cesse; incessant
inform faire savoir
intelligent intelligent
intend avoir l'intention de
interested: be interested in s'intéresser à
invitation l'invitation *(fem.)*

join: to join us être des nôtres
joy la joie
just: to have just done something venir de + *infinitive*

know savoir; connaître
know how to savoir + *infinitive*

lady la dame
lawyer l'avocat(e)
leaning adossé
leaning on penché sur
learn apprendre
leave partir *(intrans.)*; quitter *(trans.)*
lend prêter
letter la lettre
listen to écouter
literature la littérature
little petit
live habiter; vivre

This list contains words and expressions necessary to do the translation exercises. Idioms and expressions are sometimes omitted if they are listed in the chapter where the English-to-French exercise occurs.

able: be able pouvoir
abroad à l'étranger
accept accepter
according to selon, d'après
across à travers
across the way en face
afraid: be afraid avoir peur
after après
against contre
airport l'aéroport *(masc.)*
allow permettre
alone seul(e)(s)
aloud à haute voix
already déjà
angry fâché
animal l'animal, les animaux *(masc.)*
answer *(verb)* répondre à, *(noun)* la réponse
anymore ne . . . plus
anytime n'importe quand
anywhere n'importe où
anywhere (nowhere) nulle part
apologize s'excuser
apple la pomme
arm le bras
arrive arriver
as for quant à
as long as pourvu que
ask demander; **ask a question** poser une question
at present actuellement
attention l'attention *(fem.)*; **pay attention** faire attention
average la moyenne

baby le bébé
backpack le sac à dos
bad mauvais
bakery la boulangerie
beach la plage
because of à cause de
before avant
begin commencer à
bench le banc
blond blond(e)
book le livre
boring ennuyeux(-se)
bother déranger
bread le pain
bring apporter
brother le frère
bus le bus
business les affaires *(fem. pl.)*
business trip le voyage d'affaires
busy occupé
buy acheter; **buy tickets** prendre les billets

café le café
cake le gâteau (les gâteaux)
calculator la calculatrice
call appeler; téléphoner à; **be called** s'appeler
can (be able) pouvoir
cane la canne
car la voiture
care le soin
cat le chat
chair la chaise
child l'enfant *(masc. & fem.)*
chocolate le chocolat
cigarette la cigarette
city la ville
class la classe; **in class** en classe
client le client (la cliente)
coffee le café
cold: it's cold il fait froid
come venir
come back revenir
come downstairs descendre
come in entrer
compact disc le disque compact
composition la composition
computer l'ordinateur *(masc.)*
contact *(verb)* contacter
counter le comptoir
courage le courage
courageous courageux(-se)
course le cours
cousin le cousin (la cousine)
covered with couvert de
criticize critiquer
croissant le croissant
cross *(verb)* transverser
crouching accroupi
cut couper; **cut oneself** se couper

danger le danger
date la date
day la journée, le jour
department store le grand magasin
detective le détective
difficulty la difficulté
dinner *(verb)* dîner; *(noun)* le dîner
do faire
doctor le médecin
dog le chien (la chienne)
doll la poupée

English-French Vocabulary List